IF FOUND, please notify and arrange return to owner. The own[illegible] the Certified Management Accountant Examination.

Name of CMA Candidate ______________________

Address ______________________

City, State, Zip ______________________

Telephone (   ) ______________________

Additional Gleim *CMA Review* books, software, and other accounting study materials are available directly from

Gleim Publications, Inc.
P.O. Box 12848
University Station
Gainesville, Florida 32604
(800) 87-GLEIM • (352) 375-0772
FAX: (352) 375-6940
Internet: www.gleim.com

This is *CMA Review, Volume I, Problems and Solutions*, 7th ed., available for $27.95. Also available is the companion book:

CMA Review, Volume II, Outlines and Study Guides, 7th ed. $27.95

Also available for CMA candidates is Gleim's *CMA Test Prep* software (see pages 756 and 757). This exhaustive compendium of multiple-choice questions offers a unique, interactive study environment. CFM candidates will find *CFM Review* ($22.95) and *CFM Test Prep* ($35.00) invaluable aids in their preparation for the new CFM (Certified in Financial Management) designation offered by the IMA.

We also have a series of objective question and explanation books ($16.95 each) to supplement your CMA Review. Each book contains 1,200-2,400 questions and explanations:

- *Auditing & Systems*
- *Business Law/Legal Studies*
- *Federal Tax*
- *Financial Accounting*
- *Managerial Accounting*

Other review manuals available are

CIA Review, Volume I, Outlines and Study Guides, 6th ed. 25.95
CIA Review, Volume II, Problems and Solutions, 6th ed. 25.95
CIA Review, 1996 Updating Edition 18.95

CPA Review: A System for Success (free with the purchase of any *CPA Review* book)
CPA Review: Auditing 24.50
CPA Review: Business Law 24.50
CPA Review: TAX-MAN-GOV 24.50
CPA Review: Financial 24.50

Order forms for these and all of our other publications are provided at the back of this book.

All mail orders must be prepaid. Shipping and handling charges will be added to telephone orders, and to library and company orders which may be on account. Add applicable sales tax to shipments within Florida. All payments must be in U.S. funds and payable on a U.S. bank. Please write or call for prices and availability of all foreign country shipments. Books will usually be shipped the day after your order is received. Allow 10 days for delivery in the United States. Please contact us if you do not receive your shipment within 2 weeks.

Gleim Publications, Inc. guarantees the immediate refund of all resalable texts purchased directly from Gleim Publications, Inc. if they are returned within 30 days. Shipping and handling charges are nonrefundable. Returns of books purchased from bookstores and other resellers should be made to the respective bookstore or reseller.

REVIEWERS AND CONTRIBUTORS

Grady M. Irwin, J.D., University of Florida Holland Law Center, has taught in the University of Florida College of Business. Mr. Irwin provided many answer explanations and extensive editorial assistance throughout.

Karen Louviere, B.A., University of Florida, provided production assistance throughout the project.

Travis Moore, B.A., University of Florida, is our production coordinator. Mr. Moore coordinated and supervised the production staff, prepared the page layout for the entire edition, and reviewed the final manuscript.

Nancy Raughley, B.A., Tift College, is our editor. Ms. Raughley reviewed the entire manuscript and assisted in all phases of production.

A PERSONAL THANKS

This manual would not have been possible without the extraordinary effort and dedication of Jim Collis, Terry Hall, Gail Luparello, Diana K. Nagy, and Rhonda L. Powell, who typed the entire manuscript and all revisions as well as prepared the camera-ready pages.

The authors appreciate the proofreading and production assistance of Adam Cohen, Chad Houghton, Mark Moore, Carrie Newman, Larry Pfeffer, and Anthony Snowball.

The authors also appreciate the critical reading assistance of Bettina Fernandez, Heather O'Brien, Bradley Smerage, and Marc Wilson.

Finally, we appreciate the encouragement and tolerance of our families throughout the project.

SEVENTH EDITION

CMA REVIEW

Volume I
OUTLINES and STUDY GUIDES

by Irvin N. Gleim, Ph.D., CPA, CIA, CMA

and

Dale L. Flesher, Ph.D., CPA, CIA, CMA

ABOUT THE AUTHORS

Irvin N. Gleim is Professor Emeritus in the Fisher School of Accounting at the University of Florida and is a member of the American Accounting Association, Academy of Legal Studies in Business, American Institute of Certified Public Accountants, Association of Government Accountants, Florida Institute of Certified Public Accountants, Institute of Internal Auditors, and the Institute of Management Accountants. He has had articles published in the *Journal of Accountancy, The Accounting Review,* and *The American Business Law Journal* and is author/coauthor of numerous accounting and aviation books and CPE courses.

Dale L. Flesher is the Arthur Andersen Alumni Professor in the School of Accountancy at the University of Mississippi and has written over 150 articles for business and professional journals, including *Management Accounting, Journal of Accountancy,* and *The Accounting Review,* as well as numerous books. He is a member of the Institute of Management Accountants, American Institute of Certified Public Accountants, Institute of Internal Auditors, American Accounting Association, and American Taxation Association. He is currently the editor of *The Accounting Historians' Journal* and a trustee and past president of the Academy of Accounting Historians.

Gleim Publications, Inc.
P.O. Box 12848
University Station
Gainesville, Florida 32604
(352) 375-0772
(800) 87-GLEIM
FAX: (352) 375-6940
Internet: www.gleim.com

Library of Congress Catalog Card No. 95-081932

ISBN 0-917537-85-8 (Volume I)
ISBN 0-917537-86-6 (Volume II)
ISBN 0-917537-84-X (set)

Second Printing: September, 1996

Visit our Internet site (www.gleim.com/updates.html) for the latest information and updates on all of our products.

ACKNOWLEDGMENTS

The authors are indebted to the Institute of Certified Management Accountants for permission to use problem materials from past CMA examinations. Questions and unofficial answers from the Certified Management Accountant Examinations, copyright © 1972, 1973, 1974, 1975, 1976, 1977, 1978, 1979, 1980, 1981, 1982, 1983, 1984, 1985, 1986, 1987, 1988, 1989, 1990, 1991, 1992, 1993, 1994, and 1995 by the Institute of Certified Management Accountants, are reprinted and/or adapted with permission.

PREFACE FOR CMA CANDIDATES

The purpose of this manual is to help YOU prepare YOURSELF to pass the CMA examination. The overriding consideration is an inexpensive, effective, and easy-to-use study program. This manual

1. Explains how to optimize your grade by analyzing how the CMA exam is constructed and graded.
2. Illustrates **individual question answering techniques** to enable you to prepare complete and well-presented answers to satisfy the exam graders.
3. Suggests **exam-taking techniques** to help you maximize your exam score.
4. Defines topics tested on each of the four sections of the exam.
5. Outlines all of the subject matter tested on the CMA exam in 33 easy-to-complete study units.

This is the Seventh Edition of *CMA Review*. It reflects CMA exams through the December 1995 examination, and relevant authoritative pronouncements through December 31, 1995.

Now is the time to take and pass the CMA exam. The examination has been administered annually since 1972. The number of CMA candidates has increased from 410 in 1972 to a combined total of over 8,000 for both 1995 examinations. The pass rate for each section of the exam averages about 40%, which is about 33% greater than the CPA exam pass rate. This higher (more favorable) pass rate is consistent with the more mature CMA candidate (average age 30+) and the professional development nature of the CMA program.

To maximize the efficiency of your review program, begin by **studying** (not reading) Chapters 1 through 4 in Volume I. They are very short, but very important. They have been carefully organized and written to provide you with important information to assist you in successfully completing the CMA and other professional certification examinations.

The outline format and spacing in Volume I and the question and answer formats in Volume II are designed to facilitate learning and readability. Our ***CMA Test Prep*** software is designed to help you learn in an interactive environment. It provides thousands of additional questions for you to study. Even though this two-volume manual constitutes a complete self-study program for the CMA exam, CMA candidates should consider enrolling in a formal review program. Local colleges and universities as well as IMA chapters throughout the country have coordinated CMA review programs in the past and will probably continue to do so.

Thank you for your interest in our materials. We deeply appreciate the thousands of letters and suggestions received from CIA, CMA, and CPA candidates during the last 21 years. Please send your suggestions, comments, and corrections concerning this manual. The last page of each volume has been designed to help you note corrections and suggestions throughout your study process. Please tear it out and mail it to us with your comments.

Good Luck on the Exam,

Irvin N. Gleim
Dale L. Flesher

September 1996

PREFACE FOR ACCOUNTING PRACTITIONERS

The first purpose of this study manual is to help you become knowledgeable about the topics covered on the CMA exam. The second purpose is to engage you in an MBA-type self-study program. The CMA exam differs significantly from the CPA exam. Part 1 and much of Part 4 are not tested on the CPA exam but are crucial to most economic activity. Parts 2 and 3 of the CMA exam cover topics germane to the CPA exam but from a user's point of view rather than the preparer's point of view adopted by the CPA exam. Volume I contains outlines of the material and Volume II contains questions, answer explanations, and answers from past CMA exams. The third purpose is to provide CPE credit for your self-assessment and review/update study effort.

Our approach to CPE is both interactive and intense. In Volume I, you will encounter concepts that you can relate to your daily work experience soon after you study them. You should be continually challenged to answer each question in Volume II correctly. As you work through these study books and take the open-book CPE final exams, you may find you need to refer to the outlines in Volume I or a current textbook.

We ask for any supplemental comments, reactions, suggestions, etc., that you may have as you complete our CPE program. The last page of each volume has been designed to help you note corrections and suggestions throughout your study process. Please attach it to the Course Evaluation (handwritten notes are fine).

To maximize the efficiency of your review program, begin by **studying** (not reading) Chapters 1 through 4 in Volume I. They have been carefully organized and written to provide you with important information.

You should be sure to read carefully "Introduction: How to Use This CPE Program" in the accompanying CPE book.

Thank you for your interest, and we look forward to hearing from you.

Best Wishes in Your CPE Endeavors,

Irvin N. Gleim
Dale L. Flesher

September 1996

TABLE OF CONTENTS

GLEIM *CMA REVIEW* SEVENTH EDITION STUDY UNIT LISTING

We have arranged the subject matter tested on the examination into 33 subtopics or study units. The review outlines (Volume I) and prior CMA exam questions and answers (Volume II) are organized as follows:

Part 1: ECONOMICS, FINANCE, AND MANAGEMENT
- Study Unit 1: Microeconomics
- Study Unit 2: Macroeconomics
- Study Unit 3: International Economics
- Study Unit 4: Institutional Environment of Business
- Study Unit 5: Working Capital Finance
- Study Unit 6: Capital Structure Finance
- Study Unit 7: Organization Theory
- Study Unit 8: Motivation and the Directing Process
- Study Unit 9: Communication
- Study Unit 10: Ethics and the Management Accountant*

Part 2: FINANCIAL ACCOUNTING AND REPORTING**
- Study Unit 11: Financial Accounting: Development of Theory and Practice
- Study Unit 12: Financial Statement Presentation
- Study Unit 13: Special Financial Reporting Problems
- Study Unit 14: SEC Reporting Requirements
- Study Unit 15: Ratio and Accounts Analysis
- Study Unit 16: Internal Control
- Study Unit 17: External Auditing
- Study Unit 18: Income Taxes***

Part 3: MANAGEMENT REPORTING, ANALYSIS, AND BEHAVIORAL ISSUES
- Study Unit 19: Process and Job Order Costing
- Study Unit 20: Variable and Absorption Costing
- Study Unit 21: Planning
- Study Unit 22: Budgeting
- Study Unit 23: The Controlling Process
- Study Unit 24: Standard Costs and Variance Analysis
- Study Unit 25: Responsibility Accounting

Part 4: DECISION ANALYSIS AND INFORMATION SYSTEMS
- Study Unit 26: Incremental Costing
- Study Unit 27: Cost-Volume-Profit Analysis
- Study Unit 28: Capital Budgeting
- Study Unit 29: Decision Making under Uncertainty
- Study Unit 30: Inventory Models
- Study Unit 31: Quantitative Methods
- Study Unit 32: Information Systems
- Study Unit 33: Internal and Operational Auditing

*May be tested on all four parts. See Study Unit 10.
**Not required if you have passed the CPA exam.
***May be tested on Parts 1, 2, and 4. See Study Unit 18.

These study units differ somewhat from the subtopic titles used by the ICMA in its outlines of the contents of each part of the CMA exam. The ICMA content specification outlines are presented in the introductions of Chapters 5 through 8 as part of the explanation of the material tested. The selection of study units in *CMA Review* is based on the types and number of questions that have appeared on past CMA exams as well as the extensiveness of exam coverage.

CMA Review, Volume II, Problems and Solutions, contains representative questions from recent CMA exams, including a commentary on how to answer essay questions and how to solve computational problems, as well as the ICMA's unofficial answers. Also, it provides discussions of correct answers and explanations of incorrect ones adjacent to the multiple-choice questions.

LEVEL OF PERFORMANCE REQUIRED

All parts of the exam appear to be tested at the skill level of a final examination for the appropriate course at a good school of business. See page 24 for a discussion of the course content covered by each part of the exam. You can easily evaluate and compare the difficulty of each part of the CMA exam as you work the questions and problems in Volume II.

CURRENT STATUS OF THE CMA EXAM

The last significant change in the CMA program took effect in 1990. The current status is

1. The CMA exam has **four 4-hour parts**.
2. **Federal income taxes** are tested in Parts 1, 2, and 4.
   a. Part 1 will test taxes as they affect decision analysis regarding whether to issue debt or equity. Examples are the deductibility of payments for use of capital and the after-tax cost of capital.
   b. Part 2 will test the financial reporting requirements for income taxes, including the proper treatment of deferred income taxes. Part 2 will cover accounting for net operating losses and other special issues affecting deferred income taxes.
   c. Part 4 will test the tax code provisions that affect investment decisions. Included are topics such as operating income subject to income taxes, gains and losses subject to taxes, and tax credits.
3. **Ethics**. Questions raising ethical issues may appear on any two or more parts of the examination. These issues will be addressed within the context of specific subject areas. Ethics content will not be less than the equivalent of one 30-minute question or more than two 30-minute questions.
4. **Internal auditing** is tested in Part 4.
5. The examination will continue to include **optional questions** (i.e., you may be presented with three questions and required to answer only two). However, they will be subject to the content specification outline constraints. Because each major topic will be tested on each examination in accordance with its designated percentage range, optional and required questions will most likely cover the same major topics.
6. **Content specification outlines**. The ICMA has developed content specification outlines and has committed to follow them on each examination. Thus, each examination will cover the major topics specified on the facing page; e.g., microeconomics will constitute 10%-15% of Part 1 on each examination. Moreover, questions may combine two or even three topics. For example, a question might be considered 30% microeconomics and 70% working capital management.

CHAPTER ONE
THE CMA PROGRAM: AN OVERVIEW

INTRODUCTION

CMA is the acronym for Certified Management Accountant. CMA, CIA (Certified Internal Auditor), and CPA (Certified Public Accountant) are the three most recognized professional designations within the accounting profession in the United States.

The CMA examination is administered in 100 locations in the U.S. as well as in San Juan, Puerto Rico; Amman, Jordan; Amsterdam; Bahrain; Cairo; Dhahran, Saudi Arabia; Hong Kong; London; Taipei; and Zurich. The CMA exam has been administered by the Institute of Certified Management Accountants (ICMA) since 1972. The exam consists of four 4-hour parts that are given on the second or third Wednesday and Thursday of June and December. It is similar to the CIA and CPA exams, with the most notable difference being that a score of 70% per part constitutes a passing grade rather than the 75% for the CIA and CPA examinations.

This is Volume I, Outlines and Study Guides, which contains four introductory chapters and four chapters of outlines that cover the material tested on the four parts of the CMA exam. Chapter 1 includes exam content, pass rates, administration, sponsorship, organization, and other background information. Chapters 2, 3, and 4 are also very important. We urge you to read them carefully because they provide important suggestions on how to improve dramatically your study and test taking procedures.

Chapter 2: CMA Exam: Preparation, Administration, and Grading
Chapter 3: Preparing to Pass the CMA Exam
Chapter 4: Writing the CMA Exam

Practitioners using this book to earn CPE credit should also refer to the INTRODUCTION in their CPE final exam booklet.

Volume II, Problems and Solutions, contains four chapters, one for each of the four parts of the CMA exam. Volume II presents the following:

1. Multiple-choice questions
2. Explanations of each question, including why each incorrect response is incorrect
3. Essay questions and computational problems
4. Authors' comments on the essay questions and computational problems
5. The ICMA's unofficial answers to the essay questions and computational problems

OBJECTIVES AND CONTENT OF THE EXAMINATION

The primary purpose of the CMA examination program is "to establish an objective measure of an individual's knowledge and competence in the field of management accounting." Three other objectives set forth by the ICMA are to

1. "Establish management accounting as a recognized profession by identifying the role of the management accountant and financial manager, the underlying body of knowledge, and a course of study by which such knowledge is acquired"
2. "Encourage higher educational standards in the management accounting field"
3. "Encourage continued professional development by management accountants"

The exam tests the candidates' knowledge and ability with respect to the current state of the art in the field of management accounting. Below are the four parts of the exam with the exam schedule:

1. Economics, Finance, and Management	Day One	8:00 - 12:00	4 hours
2. Financial Accounting and Reporting	Day One	1:30 - 5:30	4 hours
3. Management Reporting, Analysis, and Behavioral Issues	Day Two	8:00 - 12:00	4 hours
4. Decision Analysis and Information Systems	Day Two	1:30 - 5:30	4 hours
			16 hours

Part 1: Economics, Finance, and Management

A. Microeconomics--10%-15%
B. Macroeconomics and International Economics--10%-15%
C. Institutional Environment of Business--10%-15%
D. Working Capital Management--10%-15%
E. Long-term Finance and Capital Structure--10%-15%
F. Organization and Management Theory--20%-30%
G. Communication--10%-15%

Part 2: Financial Accounting and Reporting

A. Financial Statements--30%-40%
B. Reporting Requirements--30%-40%
C. Analysis of Accounts and Statements--15%-20%
D. External Auditing--10%-15%

Part 3: Management Reporting, Analysis, and Behavioral Issues

A. Cost Measurement--20%-30%
B. Planning--20%-30%
C. Control and Performance Evaluation--20%-30%
D. Behavioral Issues--20%-30%

Part 4: Decision Analysis and Information Systems

A. Decision Theory and Operational Decision Analysis--20%-30%
B. Investment Decision Analysis--20%-30%
C. Quantitative Methods for Decision Analysis--10%-15%
D. Information Systems--20%-30%
E. Internal Auditing--10%-15%

7. **CPAs** (those who have previously passed the CPA examination) are exempt from Part 2. Individuals must apply to the ICMA for the exemption and provide the ICMA with written verification of CPA exam passage (CPA licensure is not required).
8. **Full-time professors**. Full-time faculty members are permitted to take the examination once at no charge. The fee for any parts that must be retaken is 50% of the normal fee. To qualify, a faculty member must submit a letter on school stationery affirming his/her full-time status. Faculty should sit for the CMA examination because a professor's status as a CMA encourages students to enter the program.
9. **Full-time doctoral students** who plan to pursue a teaching career are treated as faculty members for purposes of qualifying for the free examination.

THE INSTITUTE OF MANAGEMENT ACCOUNTANTS (IMA)

Conceived as an educational organization to develop the individual management accountant professionally and to provide business management with the most advanced techniques and procedures, the IMA was founded as the National Association of Accountants in 1919 with 37 charter members. It grew rapidly, with 2,000 applications for membership in the first year, and today it is the largest management accounting association in the world, with over 84,000 members and 325 chapters in the U.S. and abroad.

The IMA has made major contributions to business management through its continuing education program, with courses and seminars conducted in numerous locations across the country; the monthly magazine *Management Accounting*; other literature, including research reports, monographs, and books; a technical inquiry service; a library; the annual international conference; and frequent meetings at chapter levels.

IMA members are men and women from every professional and industrial group involved or interested in some phase of accounting. Membership in the IMA is open to all persons interested in advancing their knowledge of accounting. It is required for CMA candidates and CMAs.

IMA Dues in the USA and Canada

1. **Regular**: 1 year, $130; 2 years, $250; 3 years, $360
2. **Associate**: $43.00 (2nd year, $87.00); must apply within 2 years of completing full-time studies; automatic transfer to regular dues at end of second year
3. **Academic member**: $65.00; must be a full-time faculty member
4. **Student**: $26.00; not less than 6 equivalent hours per semester

Membership application forms may be obtained by writing the Institute of Management Accountants, 10 Paragon Drive, Montvale, NJ 07645-1759, or calling (201) 573-6300 or (800) 638-4427. A sample of the two-page form appears on pages 7 and 8.

As stated in its constitution, the IMA's broad objectives are to

1. Develop through research, discussion, and exchange of information a better understanding of the sources, types, purposes, and uses of accounting and related data as applied to all types of economic endeavor; and to make this information available to members and others
2. Assist in and encourage, with respect to the role of accounting, the implementation and development of the socioeconomic structure
3. Stimulate worldwide acquaintance and fellowship among members
4. Unite, through membership in the association, persons interested in accounting
5. Provide opportunities for members to increase their knowledge of accounting practices and methods and to increase their individual capabilities
6. Promote the profession of management accounting by providing for the recognition of educational attainment and professional competence of management accountants

The major emphasis is on education, as evidenced by the following IMA activities:

1. Chapter technical meetings
2. Publications
3. Technical research service
4. Continuing education program
5. Self-study program
6. New York library
7. Regional conferences
8. Annual international conference

INSTITUTE of MANAGEMENT ACCOUNTANTS
CERTIFIED MANAGEMENT ACCOUNTANT PROGRAM

MEMBERSHIP APPLICATION

10 PARAGON DRIVE, MONTVALE, N. J. 07645-1760 • 201-573-9000 • 1-800-638-4427 • FAX 201-573-0559

FOR OFFICE USE ONLY

PAYMT. BY CK.	AMOUNT
☐ PERSONAL	
☐ COMPANY	

PERSONAL INFORMATION: *(Print Clearly or Type)* Use Black or Blue Ink
Mr. ☐ Ms. ☐ Miss ☐ Mrs. ☐ Dr. ☐ Male ☐ Female ☐ Social Security Number - - Send IMA Mail To ☐ Home ☐ Business Telephone Preference ☐ Home ☐ Business

Professional Designations Earned ☐ CPA ☐ CFA ☐ CIA Other: ______

First Name | Middle Name | Last Name | Suffix

Home Street Address | Date of Birth / /

City | State | Zip Code (9 Digit) | First Name or Nickname for IMA Badges (Optional)

Part Time/School Address Street | City | State | Zip Code (9 Digit) | Telephone Number at Part Time Address ( )

Spouse's First Name | Middle Name | Last Name | Nickname for IMA Badges (Optional) | Spouse's Professional Designation

COMPANY NAME: *(Print Clearly or Type)* | Home Telephone Number ( ) | SIC Code (See Reverse Side)

Street Address (include suite, room and/or mail stop) | Business Telephone ( ) Extension | Job Title Code (See Reverse Side)

City | State | Zip Code (9 Digit) | Fax Number ( ) | Responsibility Code (See Reverse Side)

Company Size (Check One)
☐ Under $50 Million
☐ $50 - $500 Million
☐ $501 Million - $5 Billion
☐ Over $5 Billion

CHAPTER AFFILIATION: *(Name of Chapter/Student Chapter - Your Choice)* Chapter Number

Member-At-Large ☐ Check here if no chapter affiliation desired

EDUCATION HISTORY:
(Begin with current or last school attended)

	MAJOR(S)	DATE(S) ATTENDED OR EXPECTED GRADUATION DATE	DEGREE(S) OR EXPECTED DEGREE

ADMISSION CRITERIA FOR MEMBERSHIP: INSTITUTE OF MANAGEMENT ACCOUNTANTS, INC. *I affirm that I meet the criteria for membership (on reverse side) which I have circled. Please circle only one.* b: 1, 2, 3, 4, 5, 6

CPA Certificate Number | State | Year

CMA® Certified Management Accountant Program — Check Here ☐ to receive information about IMA's prestigious certification program

Have you ever been convicted of a felony? ☐ No ☐ Yes (See Reverse Side)

Are you required to report CPE hours annually? ☐ No ☐ Yes

MEMBERSHIP - FILL IN AS APPROPRIATE - *ALL PAYMENTS MUST BE IN U.S. DOLLARS*

DUES ☐ REGULAR: U.S.A. AND CANADA ☐ 1Yr. $130 ☐ 2Yr. $250 ☐ 3Yr. $360 $

☐ INTERNATIONAL MEMBER-AT-LARGE: You must reside outside the U.S.A. and CANADA $130

☐ ACADEMIC: U.S.A. AND CANADA — Must be a full-time faculty member $ 65

☐ ASSOCIATE: U.S.A. AND CANADA — Must apply within 2 years of completing full-time studies — 1st Year $ 43, 2nd Year $ 87

☐ STUDENT: U.S.A. AND CANADA — Not less than 6 equivalent hours per semester $ 26

OPTIONAL SERVICES IMA Membership Required
☐ Controllers Council $ 75
☐ Cost Management Group $ 75
☐ Research Publication Service $ 50

REGISTRATION / REINSTATEMENT FEE NOTE: Regular, Academic & International Members ONLY $ 15.00

TOTAL $

☐ I am enclosing a check payable to : INSTITUTE OF MANAGEMENT ACCOUNTANTS, INC.
☐ Charge my credit card: ☐ VISA ☐ MASTERCARD ☐ AMEX

CREDIT CARD NUMBER ➡ EXPIRATION DATE ➡

I affirm the statements on this application are correct and agree to abide by the Standards of Ethical Conduct for Management Accountants.

SIGNATURE X DATE / /

Sponsor's Name (if applicable), or Signature of Professor or Registrar (for student) | Sponsor's Member No. (if applicable)

INSTITUTE OF MANAGEMENT ACCOUNTANTS, INC.

Admission Criteria for Membership - All persons residing within the United States, its possessions, or Canada, and who are otherwise qualified for membership under the Bylaws, are eligible for membership as Regular Members, Associate Members or Student Members as defined in Article II, Section 2 of the Bylaws, provided they meet the following minimum criteria:

(b) (1) Have a full four-year college degree, or
(2) Have a two-year college degree with a minimum of 15 semester hours in accounting plus four years of experience in a management accounting position at the time of admission, or
(3) Hold a CPA certificate, or an international certificate comparable to a CPA or CMA certificate, or
(4) Have six years of experience in management accounting, or
(5) Agree to complete 18 Continuing Professional Education (CPE) hours in IMA-approved programs (local or national) in each of the five consecutive years from the date of admission. A member not fulfilling the commitment will automatically be dropped from membership, or
(6) Be a college student carrying a minimum of six undergraduate or graduate hours (or equivalent) per semester within a school, college or university in the United States.

NOTE: Prior felony conviction - This application, with a brief explanation of circumstances, should be sent directly to the Executive Director of IMA at the address on the reverse side of this form in an envelope marked "Confidential".

STANDARD INDUSTRY CLASSIFICATIONS (SIC)

AGRICULTURE, FORESTRY, FISHERIES
01 AGRICULTURAL PRODUCTION
07 AGRICULTURAL SVCS / HUNTING / TRAPPING
08 FORESTRY
09 FISHERIES

MINING
10 METAL MINING
11 ANTHRACITE MINING
12 BITUMINOUS COAL / LIGNITE MINING
13 CRUDE OIL / LIGNITE MINING
14 MINING / QUARRY NONMETALLICS

CONTRACT CONSTRUCTION
15 BLDG. CONSTRUCTION - GENERAL CONTRACTORS
16 CONSTRUCTION - OTHER
17 CONSTRUCTION - SPECIAL TRADE CONTRACTORS

MANUFACTURING
19 ORDINANCE / ACCESSORIES
20 FOOD / KINDRED PRODUCTS
21 TOBACCO MANUFACTURERS
22 TEXTILE MILL PRODUCTS
23 APPAREL / FINISHED FABRICS
24 LUMBER / WOOD PRODUCTS

MANUFACTURING CONTINUED
25 FURNITURE / FIXTURES
26 PAPER / ALLIED PRODUCTS
27 PRINTING / PUBLISHING
28 CHEMICALS / ALLIED PRODUCTS
29 OIL REFINING / RELATED INDUSTRIES
30 RUBBER / MISC. PLASTICS PRODUCTS
31 LEATHER PRODUCTS
32 STONE, CLAY, GLASS / CONCRETE PRODUCTS
33 PRIMARY METAL INDUSTRIES
34 FABRICATED METAL PRODUCTS
35 MACHINERY, NONELECTRICAL
36 ELECTRICAL MACHINERY
37 TRANSPORTATION
38 PROFESSIONAL , SCIENTIFIC, CONTROL INSTRUMENTS
39 MISC. MANUFACTURING INDUSTRIES

TRANSPORTATION, COMMUNICATION & UTILITY SERVICES
40 RAILROAD TRANSPORTATION
41 LOCAL AND SUBURBAN TRANSPORTATION
42 MOTOR FREIGHT / WAREHOUSING
44 WATER TRANSPORTATION
46 PIPE LINE TRANSPORTATION
47 TRANSPORTATION SERVICES
48 COMMUNICATION
49 ELECTRIC, GAS / SANITARY SERVICES

WHOLESALE & RETAIL TRADE
50 WHOLESALE TRADE
52 BUILDING / HARDWARE / FARM EQUIP DEALERS
53 RETAIL TRADE - GENERAL
54 FOOD STORES
55 AUTO DEALERS / SERVICE STATIONS
56 APPAREL / ACCESSORY STORES
57 FURNITURE / FURNISHINGS / STORES
58 EATING / DRINKING PLACES
59 MISC. RETAIL STORES

FINANCE, INSURANCE & REAL ESTATE
60 BANKING
61 CREDIT AGENCIES NOT BANKS
62 SECURITY / COMMODITY BROKERS, AND SERVICES
63 INSURANCE CARRIERS
64 INSURANCE AGENTS, BROKERS
65 REAL ESTATE
66 COMBINATIONS OF REAL ESTATE, INSURANCE, LOANS LAW OFFICES
67 HOLDING, INVESTMENT COMPANIES

SERVICES
70 HOTELS / ROOMING HOUSES / CAMPS, ETC.
72 PERSONAL SERVICES
73 MISC. BUSINESS SERVICES
75 AUTO REPAIR, AUTO SERVICES / GARAGES
76 MOTION PICTURES
79 AMUSEMENT / RECREATION SERVICES
80 MEDICAL / HEALTH SERVICES
81 LEGAL SERVICES
82 EDUCATIONAL SERVICES
84 MUSEUM / ART GALLERIES / GARDENS
86 NONPROFIT MEMBERSHIP ORGANIZATIONS
88 PRIVATE HOUSEHOLDS
89 PUBLIC ACCOUNTING

GOVERNMENT
91 FEDERAL GOVERNMENT
92 STATE GOVERNMENT
93 LOCAL GOVERNMENT
94 INTERNATIONAL GOVERNMENT

JOB TITLE
01 OWNER
03 CHAIRMAN OF THE BOARD
05 CHIEF EXECUTIVE OFFICER
06 CHIEF FINANCIAL OFFICER
07 PRESIDENT
09 GROUP PRESIDENT
11 CORPORATE SECRETARY
13 CORPORATE TREASURER
15 EXECUTIVE VICE PRESIDENT
17 SENIOR VICE PRESIDENT
19 VICE PRESIDENT
21 ASSISTANT VICE PRESIDENT
23 GROUP VICE PRESIDENT
25 DIVISIONAL VICE PRESIDENT
27 CORPORATE CONTROLLER
29 ASST. CORPORATE CONTROLLER
31 DIVISIONAL CONTROLLER
33 PLANT CONTROLLER
35 DIRECTOR
37 GENERAL MANAGER
39 MANAGER
41 GENERAL SUPERVISOR
43 SUPERVISOR
45 CHIEF ACCOUNTANT
47 ACCOUNTANT
49 ECONOMIST
51 ANALYST
53 SYSTEMS ANALYST
55 PROGRAMMER
57 ADMINISTRATOR
59 AUDITOR
61 BOOKKEEPER
63 ACCOUNTING CLERK
65 DEAN
67 PROFESSOR
69 ASSOCIATE PROFESSOR
71 ASSISTANT PROFESSOR
73 INSTRUCTOR
75 CONSULTANT
77 PRINCIPAL
79 PARTNER
99 OTHER

RESPONSIBILITY AREA
01 GENERAL MANAGEMENT
05 CORPORATE MANAGEMENT
10 PUBLIC ACCOUNTING
15 GENERAL ACCOUNTING
20 PERSONNEL ACCOUNTING
25 COST ACCOUNTING
30 GOVERNMENTAL ACCOUNTING
35 FINANCE
40 RISK MANAGEMENT
45 BUDGET AND PLANNING
50 TAXATION
55 INTERNAL AUDITING
60 EDUCATION
65 INFORMATION SYSTEMS
70 STUDENT
75 RETIRED
80 OTHER

***Management Accounting* subscription rates per year:**

- Members $20.00 (included in dues, nondeductible)
- Student members: $13.00 (included in dues, nondeductible)
- Nonmembers: $130.00
- Nonprofit Libraries: $65.00

126-40M- CMA KIT 5/95

THE INSTITUTE OF CERTIFIED MANAGEMENT ACCOUNTANTS (ICMA)

The ICMA is located at the IMA headquarters in Montvale, New Jersey. The only function of the ICMA is to offer and administer the CMA designation. The staff consists of the managing director, the director of examinations, and three associates (all of whom are professional accountants), plus support personnel. The ICMA occupies about 4,000 square feet of office space in the IMA headquarters. This office is where the examinations are prepared and graded, and all records are kept.

In 1989, the IMA approved recommendations of its Long Range Strategy Implementation Committee. This action represents a major commitment to increasing the number of CMAs and improving their professional standing. The goal is 80,000 CMAs by the year 2000 (the current number exceeds 16,000). The following resolution was adopted (NAA has been changed to IMA):

Resolved:

That IMA should maximize the number of CMA holders and the perceived value of the CMA certificate by enacting the recommendations of the Long Range Strategy Committee as follows:

- *Grant current CMA certificate holders full IMA membership.*
- *For qualified IMA members the fee is waived to join the ICMA.*
- *Grant CMA candidates full IMA membership.*
- *Continuing accreditation for CMA certificate holders requires continuing education fulfillment and maintenance of IMA member in good standing status.*
- *Institute IMA sponsored course material which would help IMA members to sit for the CMA examination and maintain CMA continuing education accreditation.*
- *Direct the immediate merger of IMA and ICMA staffs except for the development and administration of the CMA exam and annual continuing education renewal requirement. The responsibilities of the ICMA Board of Regents would be limited to the development and administration of the CMA exam and administration of the annual continuing education renewal requirement.*
- *Use the ICMA 501(c)6 subsidiary as an aggressive lobbying force to pursue state or federal sanction of the CMA designation.*

REQUIREMENTS TO ATTAIN THE CMA DESIGNATION

The Certified Management Accountant designation is granted only by the ICMA. Candidates must complete four steps to become a CMA:

1. File an application for admission with the ICMA and register for the CMA examination
2. Pass all four parts of the CMA examination within a 3-year period
3. Meet the CMA experience requirement
4. Comply with the Standards of Ethical Conduct for Management Accountants

Once the certificate is earned, the CMA is a member of the Institute of Certified Management Accountants and must comply with the program's continuing education requirement and maintain IMA membership in good standing. The certificate of a CMA delinquent in these requirements will be subject to recall by the ICMA.

ADMISSION TO THE CMA PROGRAM

Candidates seeking admission to the CMA program must

1. Hold a baccalaureate degree, in any area, from an accredited college or university. Students may apply when they attain senior standing and will be permitted to take the examination pending receipt of a degree. Degrees from foreign institutions must be evaluated by an independent agency approved by the ICMA.
    a. Hold a CPA certificate or a professional qualification comparable to the CMA or CPA issued in a foreign country
2. Be a member of the Institute of Management Accountants or submit an IMA application when applying to the ICMA
3. Be employed or expect to be employed in a position that meets the experience requirement
4. Submit the names of two character references. They will be confirmed on a random basis.
5. Be of good moral character
6. Abide by the Standards of Ethical Conduct for Management Accountants

CMA WORK EXPERIENCE REQUIRED

Two continuous years of professional experience in management accounting are required any time prior to, or within 7 years of, passing the examination.

1. Professional experience shall be defined as full-time continuous experience at a level where judgments are regularly made that employ the principles of management accounting, e.g.,
    a. Financial analysis
    b. Budget preparation
    c. Management information systems analysis
    d. Management accounting in government, finance, or industry
    e. Auditing in government, finance, or industry
    f. Management consulting
    g. Audit work in public accounting (3 years required)
    h. Research, teaching, or consulting related to management accounting (for teaching, a significant portion must be above the principles level)
2. Employment in functions that require the occasional application of management accounting principles but are not essentially management accounting oriented will not satisfy the requirement, e.g.,
    a. Computer operations
    b. Sales and marketing
    c. Manufacturing
    d. Engineering
    e. Personnel
    f. Employment in trainee, clerical, or nontechnical positions

If you have any questions about the acceptability of your work experience or baccalaureate degree, please write or call the ICMA. Include a complete description of your situation. You will receive a response from the ICMA as soon as your request is evaluated.

Institute of Certified Management Accountants
10 Paragon Drive
Montvale, NJ 07645-1759
(201) 573-6300

ICMA BOARD OF REGENTS AND STAFF

The ICMA Board of Regents is a special committee of the IMA established to direct the CMA program for management accountants through the ICMA.

The Board of Regents consists of nine regents, one of whom is designated as chair by the president of the IMA. The regents are appointed by the president of the IMA to serve 3-year terms. Membership on the Board of Regents rotates, with one-third of the regents being appointed each year. The following are regents for 1995-96:

Mr. Ned Ballengee, CMA
Financial Controller
Deloitte Touche Tohmatsu
ILA Group Ltd.
Washington, D.C.

Mr. Robert L. Barber, CMA
Director of Managed Care
Mercy Health Services, Inc.
Charlotte, North Carolina

Ms. Cheryl S. Billings, CMA, CPA
Corporate Controller
Silicon Valley Research
Mountain View, California

Mr. Billy B. Bowers, CMA, CPA
Owner
Billy Bowers CPA
Albuquerque, New Mexico

Dr. James W. Brackner, CMA, CPA
Professor
Utah State University
Logan, Utah

Mr. William L. Brower, Jr., CMA
Vice President, Finance
McNeil Consumer Products Co.
Fort Washington, Pennsylvania

Ms. Joan M. Burnett, CMA
Manager, Financial Accounting
Monsanto Company
St. Louis, Missouri

Mr. James R. Davis, CMA
Director of Finance
Diamond Power Specialty Co.
Lancaster, Ohio

Dr. Jack C. Gray, CMA
Professor
Michigan State University
E. Lansing, Michigan

Mr. James C. Horsch, CMA*
Director of Business Planning
Electric Strategic Business Unit
Consumers Power Company
Jackson, Michigan

Ms. Imogene A. Posey, CMA, CPA
Associate Professor
The University of Tennessee
Knoxville, Tennessee

Dr. Carl S. Smith, CMA, CPA
Associate Professor
University of Hartford
West Hartford, Connecticut

Mr. Gregory J. Stratis, CMA, CPA
National Director of
Entrepreneurial Consulting
Ernst & Young
Cleveland, Ohio

Ms. Terri D. Zinkiewicz, CMA
Director, Finance & Business
TRW Electronic Systems &
Technology Group
Redondo Beach, California

* Chair

The regents usually meet four times a year for 1 or 2 days. The Board is divided into the following committees:

1. The Promotion and Publicity Committee consults with the staff on how to promote and market the CMA designation. Three regents serve on this committee.
2. The Credentials Committee reviews the admission standards for the CMA program. Two regents serve on this committee.
3. The Continuing Education Committee sets continuing education standards for CMAs and advises the staff on implementation of the CPE monitoring process. Two regents serve on this committee.

4. The Examination Policy Committee is concerned with the overall content, grading, and administration of the CMA exams. Three regents serve on this committee.
5. An Examination Review Committee consisting of two regents and two outside CMAs exists for each of the four parts of the exam. The committee reviews the content specification and grading basis of each specific exam.

The senior director of the ICMA (currently Ms. Priscilla Payne), the director of examinations (currently Ms. Terri Funk), and the ICMA staff are located at the ICMA office in Montvale, NJ. They undertake all of the day-to-day work with respect to the CMA program:

1. Administration of receipt of applications, reviewing the qualifications of applicants for the CMA examinations, and notifying applicants of acceptance into the program
2. Preparation of the CMA examination
3. Handling arrangements for meetings, examination facilities, examination officials, and consultants under the direction of the Board of Regents
4. Arranging for printing and distribution of the examination
5. Hiring and supervision of the examination graders
6. Notifying all applicants of the results of the examination
7. Preparing CMA certificates for successful candidates
8. Maintaining complete and accurate files and records relating to all applications, certifications, exam results, continuing education status of active CMAs, etc.
9. Keeping the Board of Regents and the IMA informed about the fiscal condition of the program

HOW TO (1) APPLY AND (2) REGISTER FOR THE CMA EXAM

First, you are required to **apply** both for membership in the IMA (see sample application form on pages 7 and 8) and for admission into the CMA program (see sample application form on pages 13 and 14). Thus, two applications are required if you are not already an IMA member. Apply to join the IMA and to enter the CMA exam program **today** -- it only takes a few minutes. Application to the CMA program requires education, employment, and reference data. The educational experience requirements are discussed on page 10. You must provide two references: one from your employer and the second from someone other than a family member or fellow employee. Character reference forms are sent by the ICMA with your application forms. An official transcript providing proof of graduation is also required. There is no application fee other than that for IMA membership. Your application must be filed by March 1 for the June exam or September 1 for the December exam. Once a person has become a candidate, there is no participant's fee other than IMA membership dues.

INSTITUTE OF CERTIFIED MANAGEMENT ACCOUNTANTS
10 Paragon Drive • Montvale, New Jersey 07645-1759
201-573-9000 • 1-800-638-4427 • FAX 201-573-8438
Endorsed by the Institute of Management Accountants

APPLICATION FOR ADMISSION to the CERTIFIED MANAGEMENT ACCOUNTANT PROGRAM

TYPE OR PRINT

PERSONAL

☐ Mr. ☐ Ms. ☐ Mrs. ☐ Miss ☐ Dr. Social Security Number ☐ Male ☐ Female Birth Date Mo. Day Yr.

NAME

Last Name First Middle Initial Suffix

HOME ADDRESS AND PHONE ☐ **I wish my mail sent to my home address**

Address Phone

Address

City State Zip Code

BUSINESS ADDRESS AND PHONE ☐ **I wish my mail sent to my business address**

Firm Name Phone

Address Extension

Address

City State Zip Code

Are you a member of the Institute of Management Accountants? Yes ☐ No ☐ If yes, please provide:

IMA Membership No. IMA Chapter Name ______

* **If no , please note: IMA membership is required for acceptance into the CMA Program. You must complete and return the IMA Application. This application must include the appropriate dues payment.**

EDUCATIONAL QUALIFICATIONS

A. College or University

	COLLEGE OR UNIVERSITY	DEGREE	DATE RECEIVED/EXPECTED
Undergraduate	______	______	______
Graduate	______	______	______

Name on transcript if different than above ______

B. Candidates with CPA License State ______ Year ______ License No. ______

Check the appropriate box(es) and make arrangements for supporting documents to be forwarded to the ICMA.

☐ **College Graduate.** Submit official transcript showing university degree conferred and official university seal or arrange for university to send proof of degree directly to the ICMA. If you have more than one degree, submit only one transcript. Candidates with foreign degrees must have their degree evaluated by an independent agency. Contact the ICMA for details.

☐ **CPA.** Arrange to have proof of license sent directly from your State Board of Accountancy to the ICMA.

☐ **CPA Waiver for Part 2.** Arrange to have proof of CPA examination completion sent directly from your State Board of Accountancy to the ICMA. Enclose $60 waiver fee with this application or use space on reverse side to charge this fee to your credit card.

☐ **Applying as Student.** Be sure to provide, in the Character Reference Section on the reverse side of this form, the name of a professor who can verify student status. Upon graduation, be sure to arrange for an official copy of your transcript to be sent to the ICMA.

☐ **Applying as Faculty.** In addition to confirming your educational qualification, be sure to provide a letter on school stationery affirming full-time teaching status.

Please Complete Both Sides

CHARACTER REFERENCES

The names, addresses, and telephone numbers of two character references must be supplied - one, your current employer, or current professor if you are a student; the other, a person neither employed by your firm nor a member of your family. The ICMA may contact the references as appropriate.

EMPLOYER OR PROFESSOR: (circle one)	PERSONAL:
Name:	Name:
Title:	Title:
Address:	Address:
Phone No.	Phone No.

Have you ever been convicted of a felony? Yes ☐ No ☐ If yes, please explain in accompanying letter.

CMA EXPERIENCE REQUIREMENT

Accounting experience is required before the CMA designation is awarded. The experience listed below will be used by the ICMA to identify candidates whose experience may not meet the requirements, making them ineligible for the CMA. For students and others who do not have accounting experience, but who expect to be employed in the accounting field, please check the following space:

☐ Not currently employed in the accounting field but expect to be in the future.

DATES (Month and Year)	EMPLOYER, JOB TITLE, DUTIES & RESPONSIBILITIES
Start Date: End Date:	Employer: Title: Duties:
Start Date: End Date:	Employer: Title: Duties:

I agree to comply with the Standards of Ethical Conduct for Management Accountants. I declare and affirm that the statements made in the foregoing application, including accompanying statements and transcripts, are true, complete, and correct. I authorize the investigation of all statements contained in this application.

* SIGNATURE OF APPLICANT DATE

* Original signature required; do not fax this form.

NOTE: A separate Examination Registration Form is required

How did you obtain your CMA application?

☐ **Employer** ☐ **School** ☐ **Chapter** ☐ **Requested from IMA** ☐ **Other**

Charge my

☐ Visa ☐ MasterCard ☐ AMEX

For $60 Part 2 Waiver Fee

Card No.

Expiration Date

Signature

Please Complete Both Sides

Second, it is necessary to **register** each time you wish to sit for the exam. The exam registration form (see page 16) is very simple (it takes about 2 minutes to complete). The registration fee for each part of the exam is $60. But graduating seniors and full-time graduate students are charged a one-time special rate of $30 per part. Full-time faculty are permitted to take the exam one time at no cost and thereafter pay $30 per part.

Each time you sit for the exam, you may take any number of parts, and the parts may be taken in any order. The exam registration for a new applicant is due on March 1 for the June exam and September 1 for the December exam. Examination registrations must be returned by April 1 and October 1 for continuing candidates; the ICMA mails a registration form for continuing candidates in the CMA program in February or August for the upcoming exam. A photo must accompany your application.

If you have successfully completed the CPA exam, the ICMA will grant credit to you for Part 2, Financial Accounting and Reporting, of the CMA exam. To receive credit, arrange to have confirmation that you passed the CPA exam sent directly from your state board of accountancy to the ICMA. A $60 one-time waiver fee should accompany your application for admission to the CMA Program.

Approximately 3 weeks prior to the exam, candidates will receive authorization to take the parts selected and the address of the exam location. An identification number will be assigned ensuring each candidate confidentiality in grading.

Finally, remember that you have six consecutive exams in which to pass all four parts. You are not required to sit each time an exam is given, but the six-consecutive-exam period is not extended if you do not register for one or more sittings. If you do not pass all four parts in the six-exam period, you may continue in the program, but you lose credit for any parts passed on the first exam of the six-exam period; i.e., you continue to receive credit for parts passed on the previous five exams of any six-consecutive-exam period.

A sample of the first page of the CMA registration form available to candidates from the ICMA appears on page 16. There are other required pages such as character reference forms. Order a registration booklet and IMA membership application form from the ICMA at (800) 638-4427.

SCHEDULE OF DATES

Application -- by March 1 for June exam; September 1 for December exam

Registration -- by March 1 for June exam (April 1 for continuing candidates);
September 1 for December exam (October 1 for continuing candidates)

Future exam dates:

1996 -- June 12, 13
December 11,12

1997 -- June 11,12
December 10, 11

1998 -- June 10, 11
December 9,10

BATCH NUMBER	PAYMENT BY CHECK # ________ ☐ PERSONAL ☐ COMPANY	AMOUNT	OFFICE USE ONLY

INSTITUTE OF CERTIFIED MANAGEMENT ACCOUNTANTS
10 Paragon Drive • Montvale, New Jersey 07645-1759
201-573-9000 • 1-800-638-4427 • FAX 201-573-8438

Endorsed by the Institute of Management Accountants

TYPE OR PRINT

CMA EXAMINATION REGISTRATION FORM

☐ Mr. ☐ Ms. ☐ Mrs. ☐ Miss ☐ Dr. Social Security Number ___-__-____

NAME

Last Name ________ First ________ Middle Initial ___ Suffix ___

MAILING ADDRESS

Address ________

Address ________

City ________ State ___ Zip Code ________

Daytime Phone Number (Include area code) ________ Please specify ☐ Home ☐ Business

The separate Application for Admission to the CMA Program and an application to the IMA must accompany this CMA Examination Registration Form unless they have been previously submitted. These forms should be filed by March 1 for the June examination and September 1 for the December examination.

The ICMA will make every effort to process forms received after the above dates; however, examination seating cannot be guaranteed.

Please complete the following information:

I wish to take the examination at the following site ________ (select from sites on reverse side) ________ (site number)

I wish to take the parts checked at the examination scheduled for ________ (month - year)

Please place a check mark in the blank spaces below for the part(s) you wish to take this time.

PART 1	**PART 2**	**PART 3**	**PART 4**	**TOTAL PARTS**	____
Economics, Finance, and Management	Financial Accounting and Reporting	Management Reporting, Analysis, and Behavioral Issues	Decision Analysis and Information Systems	x $60 Fee	____
				Add $25 International Site Fee (if applicable)	____
____	____	____	____	Less Student/ Faculty Discount (if eligible)	____
				AMOUNT DUE	____

☐ I am enclosing a check payable to the Institute of Certified Management Accountants

☐ Charge my ☐ Visa ☐ MasterCard ☐ AMEX card number ________ expiration date ________

Signature ________

See Important Refund Information on Reverse Side

FEES SUBJECT TO CHANGE

ICMA REFUND POLICY

The following schedule will be used based on the postmark date on your letter of withdrawal:

Postmark Date June Exam	Postmark Date December Exam	Refund or Credit
On or before April 1	On or before October 1	100% refund or 100% credit available for either of the next two scheduled exams less a $25 processing fee.
April 2 to June 1	October 2 to December 1	50% credit available for either of the next two scheduled exams. Candidate forfeits remaining 50%. No refund available.
After June 1	After December 1	50% credit available for the next scheduled exam, no refund. Candidate forfeits remaining 50%.
Students and faculty withdrawing after April 1	Students and faculty withdrawing after October 1	No refund or credit.

SPECIAL STUDENT EXAMINATION FEE

Seniors and full-time graduate students may take the examination at a one-time fee of $30 per part (versus the normal $60). The procedure is to apply and register at the same time. This procedure requires completion and submittal of the following:

1. Name of someone who confirms your student status
2. The standard ICMA application form
3. A completed examination registration form
4. A check for $26 (IMA membership) plus $30 per part for the number of parts to be taken

The examination fee will be forfeited if no part is taken at the first scheduled examination after registration. A Student Performance Award is presented to the student applicant with the highest grades who passes all four parts on the first sitting.

EXAM LOCATIONS

The CMA exam is administered in major cities throughout the United States where sufficient applications warrant holding the test. Candidates may choose the location they wish to attend and state it on their applications. The 1995-1996 examinations are scheduled for the following cities, located throughout the United States:

AK Anchorage
Fairbanks
AL Birmingham
Mobile
AR Conway
AZ Phoenix
CA Chico
Fresno
Los Angeles
Orange County
Sacramento
San Diego
San Francisco
CO Denver
CT Hartford
DC Washington
DE Newark
FL Jacksonville
Miami
Orlando
Tampa
GA Atlanta
Columbus
HI Honolulu
IA Cedar Falls
ID Boise
IL Chicago
DeKalb
Peoria
IN Columbus
Indianapolis
Jasper
KS Wichita
KY Lexington
Louisville
LA New Orleans
Shreveport

MA Boston
MD Baltimore
ME Bangor
Portland
MI Detroit
Flint
Grand Rapids
Marquette
MN Minneapolis
Moorhead
MO Kansas City
Springfield
St. Louis
MS Mississippi State
MT Missoula
NC Charlotte
Raleigh
Winston-Salem
(High Point)
NE Omaha
NJ New Brunswick Area
NM Albuquerque
NV Las Vegas
Reno
NY Albany
Alfred
Buffalo
New York City
Rochester
Westchester County
OH Cincinnati
Cleveland
Columbus
Dayton
Toledo
OK Oklahoma City
Tulsa

OR Portland
PA Bethlehem
Erie
Lancaster
Philadelphia
Pittsburgh
SC Columbia
TN Knoxville
Memphis
Nashville
TX Austin
Houston
Odessa
Plano/Dallas
San Antonio
UT Logan
Salt Lake City
VA Alexandria
Norfolk
Richmond
WA Seattle
Spokane
Tri-Cities Area
WI Green Bay
Milwaukee
Stevens Point
PUERTO RICO
San Juan
INTERNATIONAL
Amman, Jordan
Amsterdam
Bahrain
Cairo
Dhahran, Saudi Arabia
Hong Kong
London
Taipei
Zurich

GRADE NOTIFICATION

A sample excerpt of the grade notification form that will be sent to you approximately March 15 for the December exam (or approximately September 15 for the June exam) is illustrated below. After each examination, you will receive a numerical score for each part for which you sat and your status on each of the four parts of the exam, i.e., (1) date passed, (2) not taken, or (3) not completed.

Examination papers submitted by the candidates become the property of the ICMA. They will not be returned to the candidates and will be destroyed 1 year after the exam.

Candidates may receive a Detail of Scores for any part(s) that they failed to pass on the CMA examination. The Detail of Scores is a comparison of maximum score available and score earned by question. There is a flat fee of $25.00 to receive the Detail of Scores for all failed parts of the examination. The request must include the candidate's Social Security number and IMA membership number and be accompanied by the $25.00 fee for this service. The fee also includes the latest question and answer booklet. We recommend this service very highly.

Sample Excerpt of an ICMA Grade Notification Form

CMA EXAMINATION RESULTS AND RESULTING STATUS

Mr. James R. Jones	166/40/0439
Street Address	4655
Anytown USA 00000-0000	800335

The scores you earned on the most recent CMA examination and your progress toward completing the examination requirements are reported below. The date an examination part was completed and the date on which credit for the part expires is indicated in the status portion of the report. Please read the bottom of this form for an explanation of the three-year period for completing the requirements of the CMA examination.

June 1995 Examination Results		Status after the June 1995 Examination		
Part	Score	Part	Date Passed	Date Credit Will Expire
1	73	1	6/95	12/97
2	NOT TAKEN	2	CPA	CREDIT
3	75	3	6/95	12/97
4	NOT TAKEN	4	NOT COMPLETED	--

CMA EXAM PASS RATES

The average pass rate on parts taken is currently about 40%, which is about 33% higher than the pass rate on the CPA exam and somewhat less than that for the CIA exam, which has an average pass rate of about 45%. The next table lists the number of candidates sitting and the pass rate for each part of the exam since December 1992. The table also shows the number of candidates successfully completing each exam and the totals to date.

PASS RATES ON THE CMA EXAMINATION

	Dec. 1992	June 1993	Dec. 1993	June 1994	Dec. 1994	June 1995
Part 1 • Economics, Finance, and Management	37%	38%	44%	38%	39%	37%
Part 2 • Financial Accounting and Reporting	31%	42%	36%	38%	36%	36%
Part 3 • Management Reporting, Analysis, and Behavioral Issues	34%	39%	44%	41%	41%	45%
Part 4 • Decision Analysis and Information Systems	40%	37%	38%	45%	44%	46%
Weighted average for entire examination	36%	39%	41%	41%	40%	42%
All parts passed in one sitting	13%	13%	13%	13%	13%	16%
Number of candidates sitting	3,746	3,982	3,897	4,038	4,221	4,327
Completed examination by taking parts omitted or failed in earlier years	45%	50%	48%	45%	42%	54%
Number of candidates completing examination	703	815	775	883	749	753
Total number of successful candidates since inception of the program	13,768	14,583	15,358	16,241	16,990	17,743

Certificates issued through July 31, 1995: 16,253

CMA CANDIDATE DEMOGRAPHIC DATA

The next table is also compiled by the ICMA to provide information on CMA candidates. The typical candidate has been out of school 6 years, works in industry, and is over 30 years old. The age of CMA candidates will probably decrease in the future as more undergraduates and recent graduates take the exam. This exam, like the CIA and CPA exams, emphasizes textbook information. The best time to take the exam is as soon as possible after graduation (and in conjunction with the CIA and CPA exams).

	JUNE 1992	DEC. 1992	JUNE 1993	DEC. 1993	JUNE 1994	DEC. 1994	JUNE 1995
Number of candidates sitting for exam	3,718	3,746	3,982	3,897	4,038	4,221	4,327
Attempted all parts	574	458	567	493	475	452	491
Attempted to complete all parts	1,288	1,272	1,354	1,820	1,905	2,025	1,751
Average age	33	33	34	34	35	34	35

MAINTAINING YOUR CMA DESIGNATION

Membership in the IMA is required to maintain your CMA certificate. The general membership fee is $120. There is no additional participant fee.

Continuing professional education is required of CMAs to maintain their proficiency in the field of management accounting. Every 3 years, 90 hours of CPE must be completed, which is about 4 days per year. Qualifying topics include management accounting, corporate taxation, mathematics and statistics, computer science, systems analysis, economics, finance, management skills, production, marketing, business law, insurance, and behavioral science.

Credit for hours of study will be given for participation in programs sponsored by businesses, educational institutions, or professional and trade associations at either the national or local level. Programs conducted by an individual's employer must provide for an instructor or course leader. There must be formal instructional training material. On-the-job training does not qualify. An affidavit from the employer is required to attest to the hours of instruction. The programs may be seminars, workshops, technical meetings, or college courses under the direction of an instructor. The method of instruction may include lecture, discussion, case studies, and teaching aids such as training films and cassettes.

Credit for hours of study may be given for technical articles published in business, professional, or trade journals, and for major technical talks given for the first time before business, professional, or trade organizations. The specific hours of credit in each case will be determined by the Institute. Credit also can be earned by examination. The ICMA will select a part of the June CMA examination to be completed with a passing score on a take-home, open-book basis within 3 months after the examination is given to CMA candidates. Call the ICMA at (800) 638-4427, extension 182 for more information.

OVERVIEW OF ACCOUNTING CERTIFICATION PROGRAMS

The CPA exam is the grandfather of all the professional accounting examinations. It has its origins in the 1896 public accounting legislation of New York. In 1916, the American Institute of CPAs (AICPA) began to prepare and grade a uniform CPA exam. It is currently used to measure the technical competence of those applying to be licensed as CPAs in all 50 states, Guam, Puerto Rico, the Virgin Islands, and the District of Columbia. Approximately 140,000 candidates sit for the two CPA exams each year.

The CIA and CMA examinations are newcomers compared with the CPA exam. The first CMA exam was administered in 1972 and the first CIA exam in 1974. Why were these certification programs begun? Generally, the requirements of the CPA designation instituted by the boards of accountancy, especially the necessity for public accounting experience, led to development of the CIA and CMA programs.

Certification is important to professional accountants because it provides

1. Participation in a recognized professional group
2. An improved professional training program arising out of the certification program
3. Recognition among peers for attaining the professional designation
4. An extra credential for the employment market/career ladder
5. The personal satisfaction of attaining a recognized degree of competency

These reasons hold particularly true in the accounting field because of the wide recognition given to the CPA designation. Accountants (and even accounting students) are frequently asked if they are CPAs when people learn they are accountants. Thus, there is considerable pressure for accountants to become certified.

A new development is multiple certification, which is important for the same reasons as initial certification. Accounting students and recent graduates should look ahead and obtain multiple certification. The CIA, CMA, and CPA examination summary on the next page provides an overview of these three accounting examinations. Note the growth rate of the number of candidates sitting for each exam.

Certification programs are also advantageous to professional organizations because they

1. Become an integral part of the organization's professional development program
2. Help attract members
3. Retain interest of members, i.e., reduce membership dropout
4. Provide for a higher level of visibility and acceptability of the profession
5. Provide greater recognition to the professional organization
6. Produce substantial revenues for the professional organization

How difficult is the CMA examination? Difficulty is relative, and the CMA exam should probably be compared with the CPA exam. The CMA exam tests more material, i.e., has broader coverage, but requires a lower score to pass (70% on the CMA exam versus 75% on the CPA exam). The 40% pass rate, which is 33% higher than that of the CPA exam, is encouraging.

Moreover, the CMA exam will appear much easier than the CPA exam to most candidates because they have already prepared for and/or taken the CPA exam. Also recall that those who have passed the CPA exam are not required to take Part 2. CMA exam topics beyond the scope of the CPA exam include

Microeconomics
Macroeconomics
Managerial finance (working capital and capital structure)
International economics, e.g., foreign exchange markets, balance of payments, etc.
SEC accounting requirements
Management (organizational and behavioral theory)
Internal auditing

For candidates who have already prepared or are preparing for the CPA exam, successful completion of the CMA exam will only require concentrated review of the above topics.

CIA, CMA, CPA EXAMINATION SUMMARY

	CIA	CMA	CPA
Sponsoring Organization	Institute of Internal Auditors 249 Maitland Avenue Altamonte Springs, FL 32701 (407) 830-7600	Institute of Certified Management Accountants 10 Paragon Drive Montvale, NJ 07645-1759 (201) 573-6300 (800) 638-4427	American Institute of Certified Public Accountants Harborside Financial Center 201 Plaza III Jersey City, NJ 07311-3881 (201) 938-3419
Passing Score	75%	70%	75%
Average Pass Rate by Exam Part	45%	40%	33%
Cost	$300*	$240*	$35-200**
Year Examination Was First Administered	1974	1972	1916
Major Exam Sections and Length	I. Internal Audit Process (3½ hours)	1. Economics, Finance, and Management (4 hours)	1. Business Law & Professional Responsibilities (3 hours)
	II. Internal Audit Skills (3½ hours)	2. Financial Accounting and Reporting (4 hours)	2. Auditing (4½ hours)
	III. Management Control and Information Tech. (3½ hours)	3. Management Reporting, Analysis, and Behavioral Issues (4 hours)	3. Accounting & Reporting -- Taxation, Managerial, & Governmental and Not-for-Profit Organizations (3½ hours)
	VI. The Audit Environment (3½ hours)	4. Decision Analysis and Information Systems (4 hours)	4. Financial Accounting & Reporting -- Business Enterprises (4½ hours)
Length of Exam	14 hours	16 hours	15½ hours
When Administered	2 weeks after CPA Wed, Thur	2nd week of June, Dec Wed, Thur	1st week of May, Nov Wed, Thur
Candidates Sitting for Exam:	Total number of candidates sitting for two examinations; many are repeaters.		
1990	4,363	4,839	143,572
1991	4,597	6,404	140,042
1992	4,961	7,464	136,541
1993	5,103	7,879	140,100
1994	4,557	8,259	131,000
1995***	2,254	4,327	60,000

* *50% student discount. CMA requires IMA membership.*
** *Varies by state.*
*** *Approximate numbers for the May/June exams only*

Other professional accounting-related designations include: CBA (Certified Bank Auditor), CDP (Certificate in Data Processing), CFA (Chartered Financial Analyst), CFE (Certified Fraud Examiner), CISA (Certified Information Systems Auditor), Enrolled Agent (one enrolled to practice before the IRS).

CMA EXAMINATION COURSE COVERAGE

The CMA exam coverage is broadest on the accounting-related parts (2 and 3) and narrowest on those parts less related to accounting (1 and 4). To further assist you in becoming familiar with the CMA exam and understanding the knowledge required for each of the four parts, the following grouping of typical undergraduate business courses related to each part of the exam is provided.

Part 1 -- Economics, Finance, and Management
- Microeconomics
- Macroeconomics
- Managerial Finance
- Organizational Behavior

Part 2 -- Financial Accounting and Reporting
- Financial through Advanced Accounting
- Auditing
- Taxes (Corporate Tax only)
- FASB, AICPA, and SEC Pronouncements

Part 3 -- Management Reporting, Analysis, and Behavioral Issues
- Managerial Accounting through Second Course

Part 4 -- Decision Analysis and Information Systems
- Quantitative Methods
- Managerial Accounting through Second Course
- Statistics
- Systems and Computers
- Internal Auditing

AUTHORITATIVE PRONOUNCEMENTS ON THE CMA EXAM

The ICMA has prepared a list of suggested readings reproduced on pages 25 through 27. The ICMA also indicates that the examination's scope includes the following public pronouncements by accounting organizations and governmental agencies. The pronouncements most likely to be tested are outlined in this text.

Pronouncements of the Financial Accounting Standards Board, High Ridge Park, Stamford, CT (Part 2), 203/329-8401

Opinions of the Accounting Principles Board (APB), American Institute of Certified Public Accountants, New York, NY (Part 2), 1-800-334-6961

Pronouncements of the Governmental Accounting Standards Board (GASB), Norwalk, CT, 203/847-0700

Standards issued by the Cost Accounting Standards Board, Washington, D.C., (Part 4)

Financial Reporting Releases issued by the Securities and Exchange Commission, Washington, D.C., (Part 2)

Accounting and Auditing Enforcement Releases issued by the Securities and Exchange Commission, Washington, D.C., (Part 2)

Statements on Management Accounting by the Management Accounting Practices Committee, Institute of Management Accountants, Montvale, NJ (all four parts)

Professional Internal Auditing Standards, The Institute of Internal Auditors, Altamonte Springs, FL (Part 4), 407/830-7600

REFERENCE MATERIALS

Articles from current professional periodicals such as *Management Accounting, Financial Executive, Journal of Accountancy, Business Week,* and *Wall Street Journal*

Research and other publications of accounting organizations including:

Institute of Management Accountants
American Institute of Certified Public Accountants
Financial Executive Institute
The Institute of Internal Auditors

The texts you will need to acquire (and use) to prepare for the CMA exam will depend on many factors, including

1. Your innate ability
2. The length of time since you left school
3. The thoroughness of your undergraduate education
4. Your familiarity with internal auditing through relevant experience

See the sideheading, Other Textbooks, on page 28 for further text recommendations.

ICMA SUGGESTED READING LIST

The ICMA suggested reading list that follows is reproduced to give you an overview of the scope of each part. It constitutes the reading list as of December 1995. We provide it for your information only.

PART 1 -- ECONOMICS, FINANCE, AND MANAGEMENT

Economics

An introductory economics book, such as:

Lipsey, Richard G., Steiner, Peter O., and Purvis, Douglas D., *Economics*, 10th edition, Harper & Row, New York, NY, 1993, or

McConnell, Campbell R., *Economics: Principles, Problems and Policies*, 12th edition, McGraw-Hill Book Co., New York, NY, 1993.

An international economics book, such as:

Root, Franklin R., *International Trade and Investment*, 7th edition, South-Western Publishing Co., Cincinnati, OH, 1994.

Government and Business

Frederick, William C., Post, James E. and Davis, Keith, *Business and Society: Corporate Strategy, Public Policy, Ethics*, 7th edition, McGraw-Hill Book Co., New York, N.Y., 1992.

Greer, Douglas F., *Business, Government, Society*, 3rd edition, Macmillan Publishing Company, New York, N.Y., 1992.

Business Finance

Van Horne, James C. and Wachowicz, John M., Jr., *Fundamentals of Financial Management*, 9th edition, Prentice-Hall, Inc., Englewood Cliffs, N.J., 1995.

Weston, J. Fred and Copeland Thomas, E., *Managerial Finance*, 9th edition, The Dryden Press, Chicago, IL, 1992.

Organization and Management Theory and Communication

Books that cover organization and management theory, such as:

Griffin, Ricky W., *Management*, 4th edition, Houghton Mifflin Company, Boston, MA, 1993.

Tosi, Henry L., Rizzo, John R., and Carroll, Stephen J., *Managing Organizational Behavior*, 2nd edition, Ballinger Publishing, Cambridge, MA, 1990.

PART 2 -- FINANCIAL ACCOUNTING AND REPORTING

Financial Statements and Reporting Requirements

An intermediate accounting book, such as:

Kieso, Donald E. and Weygandt, Jerry J., *Intermediate Accounting*, 8th edition, John Wiley & Sons, Inc., New York, NY, 1995, or

Nikolai, Loren A. and Bazley, John D., *Intermediate Accounting*, 6th edition, PWS-Kent Publishing Company, Boston, MA, 1994.

An advanced accounting book that covers the principles of consolidations and related topics, such as:

Larsen, E. John, *Modern Advanced Accounting*, 6th edition, McGraw-Hill Book Co., New York, NY, 1994.

Also:

Skousen, K. Fred, *An Introduction to the SEC*, 5th edition, South-Western Publishing Co., Cincinnati, OH, 1991.

Analysis of Accounts and Statements

See intermediate and advanced accounting books listed above, i.e., Kieso and Weygandt, and Nikolai and Bazley.

Also:

Gibson, Charles H., *Financial Statement Analysis*, 6th edition, South-Western Publishing Co., Cincinnati, OH, 1995.

External Auditing

A general book, such as:

Kell, Walter G. and Boynton, William C., *Modern Auditing*, 5th edition, John Wiley & Sons, New York, NY, 1992, or

Robertson, Jack C., *Auditing*, 7th edition, BPI/Irwin, Homewood, IL, 1993.

PART 3 -- MANAGEMENT REPORTING, ANALYSIS, AND BEHAVIORAL ISSUES

Management Reporting and Analysis

A managerial cost accounting book, such as:

Horngren, Charles, Foster, George, and Datar, Srikant, *Cost Accounting: A Managerial Emphasis,* 8th edition, Prentice-Hall, Inc., Englewood Cliffs, NJ, 1994.

Rayburn, Letricia Gayle, *Principles of Cost Accounting: Managerial Applications*, 5th edition, Richard D. Irwin, Inc., Homewood, IL, 1993.

Wolk, Harry I., Gerber, Quentin N., and Porter, Gary A., *Management Accounting: Planning and Control*, PWS-Kent Publishing Company, Boston, MA, 1988.

Also:

Welsch, Glenn, Hilton, Ronald W., and Gordon, Paul N., *Budgeting: Profit Planning and Control*, 5th edition, Prentice-Hall, Inc., Englewood Cliffs, NJ, 1988.

Behavioral Issues

See appropriate material on cost, budgeting, and responsibility centers in the managerial accounting books, i.e., Horngren and Foster, Rayburn, and Welsch.

PART 4 -- DECISION ANALYSIS AND INFORMATION SYSTEMS

Decision Analysis and Quantitative Methods

A managerial cost accounting book, such as:

Horngren, Charles, Foster, George, and Datar, Srikant, *Cost Accounting: A Managerial Emphasis,* 8th edition, Prentice-Hall, Inc., Englewood Cliffs, NJ, 1994.

Rayburn, Letricia Gayle, *Principles of Cost Accounting: Managerial Applications*, 5th edition, Richard D. Irwin, Inc., Homewood, IL, 1993.

A finance book that covers capital budgeting, such as:

VanHorne, James C., *Financial Management and Policy*, 10th edition, Prentice-Hall, Inc., Englewood Cliffs, NJ, 1995 (chapters on capital investment analysis).

Weston, J. Fred and Copeland, Thomas E., *Managerial Finance*, update of 9th edition, The Dryden Press, Chicago, IL, 1992 (chapters on capital investment analysis).

A tax reference, such as:

Sommerfield, Ray M., *Federal Taxes and Management Decisions*, current edition, Richard D. Irwin, Inc., Homewood, IL.

Also:

Bierman, Harold Jr., Bonini, Charles P., and Hauseman, Warren H., *Quantitative Analysis for Business Decisions*, 8th edition, Richard D. Irwin, Inc., Homewood, IL, 1991.

Information Systems

A business data processing book, such as:

Kroenke, David M. and Hatch, Richard, *Business Computer Systems*, 5th edition, Mitchell Publishing, Inc., Santa Cruz, CA, 1993, or

O'Brien, James A., *Introduction to Information Systems*, 7th edition, Irwin Professional Publishers, Barr Ridge, IL, 1993.

Also:

Cushing, Barry E. and Romney, Marshall B., *Accounting Information Systems*, 6th edition, Addison-Wesley Publishing Company, Reading, MA, 1994.

Moscove, Stephen A. and Simkin, Mark G., *Accounting Information Systems: Concepts and Practice for Effective Decision Making*, 4th edition, John Wiley & Sons, Inc., New York, NY, 1990.

Internal Auditing

An internal auditing book, such as:

Brink, Victor and Witt, Herbert, *Modern Internal Auditing: Appraising Operations and Controls*, 4th edition, John Wiley & Sons, New York, NY, 1982, or

Sawyer, Lawrence, *Internal Auditing*, Institute of Internal Auditors, Inc., Altamonte Springs, FL, 1988.

ICMA QUESTION AND UNOFFICIAL ANSWER BOOKLETS

After each exam, the ICMA publishes a question and answer booklet that is offered for sale. An order form is reproduced on page 29. Volume II of *CMA Review* does not present all of the questions from prior exams but contains most of the multiple-choice questions from the June 1993 through December 1995 exams, as well as many earlier questions selected to provide additional coverage of important topics. In addition, many recent essay questions and computational problems are included. You may wish to order question and answer booklets directly from the ICMA.

The ICMA answers are termed unofficial because the ICMA does not have authority to set authoritative management accounting or other standards. Also, there may be several acceptable answers to a particular question or problem, and only one is presented in the ICMA booklets.

NOTE: Beginning in 1997, the CMA exam will be undisclosed.

IMA PUBLICATIONS

The IMA offers several dozen pamphlets, books, and other publications. Educational, quantity, and library discounts are available. There is a 10% discount for IMA members. Call or write for the list of publications:

Institute of Management Accountants
Special Order Department
10 Paragon Drive
Montvale, NJ 07645-1759
(201) 573-9000
(800) 638-4427

OTHER TEXTBOOKS

Many fine textbooks are not listed in the preceding pages. You may be the best judge of which books to use. Is your text adequate to explain topics in the outlines with which you have trouble? If not, visit a large college bookstore and evaluate the possibilities.

Also available is the Gleim Series of objective question and answer explanation books:

Auditing & Systems
Business Law/Legal Studies
Federal Tax
Financial Accounting
Managerial Accounting

An order form is also provided for these books at the back of this book. They are unique in that they provide complete coverage of each area in an orderly progression of objective questions. Answer explanations are presented to the immediate right of each question.

INSTITUTE OF CERTIFIED MANAGEMENT ACCOUNTANTS
10 Paragon Drive • Montvale, New Jersey 07645-1759
201-573-9000 • 1-800-638-4427 • FAX 201-573-0559
Endorsed by the Institute of Management Accountants

ORDER FORM
CMA EXAMINATION QUESTIONS & UNOFFICIAL ANSWERS

CMA Reading List ________ NC
Detailed Examination Content Outline ________ NC
CMA Review Course/Review Materials List ________ NC
Transition Table relating prior examination questions to current examination structure ________ NC

Individual books include multiple choice and the essay and problem questions.

Dec. 1989	______	@ $6.00	______	June 1993	______	@ $6.00	______
June 1990	______	@ $6.00	______	Dec. 1993	______	@ $6.00	______
Dec. 1990	______	@ $6.00	______	June 1994	______	@ $6.00	______
June 1991	______	@ $6.00	______	Dec. 1994	______	@ $6.00	______
Dec. 1991	______	@ $6.00	______	June 1995 (Available 9/95)	______	@ $6.00	______
June 1992	______	@ $6.00	______	Dec. 1995 (Available 3/96)	______	@ $6.00	______
Dec. 1992	______	@ $6.00	______				

SUBTOTAL ________

20% discount available to IMA members who furnish their account number, and on orders accompanied by an IMA application. ________

(IMA Account Number ________________) **SUBTOTAL** ________

New Jersey Residents add 6 % sales tax ________

Shipping and handling charges (see rates below) ________

TOTAL DUE (U.S. Funds Only) ________

ALL ORDERS MUST BE PREPAID OR CHARGED TO A MAJOR CREDIT CARD.

Send remittance and this order form to address shown above, or to order books by phone, call toll-free 1-800-638-4427 or 201-573-9000

SHIPPING & HANDLING RATES: All orders within the continental United States are normally sent by United Parcel Service (UPS). Allow up to 2 weeks for delivery. Please note: **UPS will not deliver to a P. O. box.** Overnight via UPS Overnight or 2nd Day Delivery (Blue Label) via UPS is available **at your expense.** If rush service is desired, please have your UPS shipper ID number available; otherwise IMA will bill you for shipping and handling charges **(available only on orders over $25.00).**

Minimum shipping & handling charge per shipment is $3.50 for 1-3 items; $5.50 for 4-10 items; $10.50 for 11-20 items; and $15.50 for 21 or more items. Add $3.50 to total order for 2nd Day UPS Blue Label. All orders shipped outside the U.S. will be charged 35% of the amount of the order.

Important: When ordering by phone, please specify any rush shipping requirements.

Please Print Clearly:

Name ______________________________

Address (Do not use P.O. number) ______________________________

Address ______________ Phone ( ) ______________

City ______________ State ______________ Zip Code ______________

Enclosed is ☐ Check
☐ Money Order

Charge my ☐ Visa
☐ MasterCard
☐ AMEX

(Credit Card minimum $10.00)

Card No. ______________

Expiration Date ____|____|____

Signature ______________

Faculty members of colleges and universities, nonprofit libraries, and college and retail bookstores are entitled to a 40% educational discount on **prepaid orders**. Educational discounts and IMA member discounts may not be combined.

ALL SALES ARE FINAL. NO COPIES MAY BE RETURNED FOR CREDIT.
All Prices Shown Effective July 1, 1995. Prices Subject to Change Without Notice.

ORDERING TEXTUAL MATERIAL

Write directly to the publishers using the addresses given below if you cannot obtain the desired texts from your local bookstore. You should begin with Gleim's *CMA Review* and *CMA Test Prep* software. If you need additional reference material, you may attempt to borrow books from colleagues, professors, etc., or from a local university library.

Gleim Publications, Inc.
P.O. Box 12848 University Station
Gainesville, FL 32604

Addison-Wesley Publishing Company
Reading, MA 01867

Basic Books, Inc.
Harper & Row Publishers
10 East 53rd Street
New York, NY 10022

Business Publications, Inc.
1700 Alma, Suite 390
Plano, TX 75075

The Dryden Press
One Salt Creek Lane
Hinsdale, IL 60521-2902

Harcourt Brace Jovanovich
1250 Sixth Avenue
San Diego, CA 92101

Harper & Row
10 East 53rd Street
New York, NY 10022

Holt, Rinehart, Winston
383 Madison Avenue
New York, NY 10017

Houghton Mifflin Company
One Beacon Street
Boston, MA 02108

Institute of Internal Auditors, Inc.
249 Maitland Avenue
Altamonte Springs, FL 32701

Richard D. Irwin, Inc.
1818 Ridge Road
Homewood, IL 60430

Kent Publishing Company
20 Park Plaza
Boston, MA 02116

McGraw-Hill Book Company
1221 Avenue of the Americas
New York, NY 10020

Mitchell Publishing, Inc.
915 River Street
Santa Cruz, CA 95060

Prentice-Hall, Inc.
Englewood Cliffs, NJ 07632

Reston Publishing Company
11480 Sunset Hills Road
Reston, VA 22090

South-Western Publishing Company
5101 Madison Road
Cincinnati, OH 45227

West Publishing Company
P.O. Box 55165
St. Paul, MN 55101

John Wiley & Sons, Inc.
605 Third Avenue
New York, NY 10016

CHAPTER TWO
CMA EXAM: PREPARATION, ADMINISTRATION, AND GRADING

INTRODUCTION

The purpose of this chapter is to explain thoroughly the procedures of the Institute of Certified Management Accountants (ICMA) in preparing, administering, and grading the exam. Knowledge of these procedures instills confidence in the examination process. Understanding the entire examination process will help you to maximize your score.

The ICMA grading process is discussed first because of its importance and interest to CMA candidates. Knowledge of grading procedures is important to CMA candidates, whose objective is to score the maximum points possible in order to pass the exam. Also, knowledge of the grading process reduces candidate anxiety, which permits concentration on the subject matter tested. It is also important that candidates have confidence in the fairness of the grading procedures. Preparation and administration of the exam are discussed at the end of the chapter.

GRADING THE CMA EXAM

The CMA examinations are returned to Montvale, NJ by the proctors via express mail to guarantee the safety and security of the papers. The week following the examination, the exams are received and checked in against the entry cards that were collected by the proctors and mailed back to the ICMA separately from the exam booklets. Additionally, the exam papers are checked against the examination summary sheets (see page 68 in Chapter 4 for discussion) that were completed by every candidate to assure that all papers have been properly received by the ICMA. Individual candidate numbers are checked on each page of every candidate's exam. The highest priority is given to assuring that no candidate papers are misplaced or lost.

MULTIPLE-CHOICE QUESTIONS

As the papers are checked in, the multiple-choice answer sheets are separated from the rest of the candidate's papers (after the candidate's number on the answer sheet has been verified). The multiple-choice answer sheets are machine graded by an optical scanner, and an item analysis is prepared for each question. An item analysis is a listing of how frequently each answer was chosen by candidates. Each part is analyzed for question reliability.

The examination staff studies the item analysis to determine if any questions need review. For example, if 90% of the candidates selected an answer for a given question different from the answer that was supposed to be correct, there may have been either an error in grading or an unforeseen problem with the question. Errors in grading are easily corrected. If there is a problem, however, the question may be thrown out or credit may be given for more than one answer. Such an outcome is not disclosed because the ICMA suggested solution indicates that only the best answer is correct. Only on rare occasions are two answers found to be equally correct, in which case they are both accepted and listed in the unofficial answers.

The candidate's grade on multiple-choice questions is determined by the number of right answers; i.e., an incorrect answer is counted as a blank answer. The multiple-choice questions are normally graded on a linear basis. However, the total points earned may be adjusted if the analysis described above indicates that the questions were unusually difficult.

SCORING INDIVIDUAL QUESTIONS

The points awarded to the questions on each examination are proportional to the ICMA suggested times that appear on the cover of each exam booklet. The amounts may vary to make the total points equal to 100. Recall that each section of the CMA examination is 4 hours long (240 minutes). On recent exams, 60 minutes has been allocated to multiple-choice questions, and the remaining 3 hours of each exam session has mostly consisted of 30-minute essay questions and/or computational problems. Each 30-minute essay question/computational problem answered was allocated about 12% to 13% of the available points.

ESSAY QUESTION/COMPUTATIONAL PROBLEMS

As the papers containing answers to the essay questions and computational problems are checked in, they are gathered into control groups of approximately 30 papers. Each candidate's paper (for each part of the exam) averages 12 to 20 pages. A grading guide is attached to each candidate's paper. The grading guide, which is a grading instruction sheet as well as a grade record for the grading process, gives the grading concepts, maximum points, special grading instructions, and space for recording the results of grading. Special grading instructions, including maximum points per part, are discussed in the paragraphs numbered 1, 2, and 3 below. A hypothetical grading guide appears on page 38 as an illustration only. It assumes an exam with only a 60-minute section of multiple-choice questions, one 30-minute essay question, and one 30-minute computational problem. Remember that the actual examination parts are each 240 minutes long.

1. The first step is to allocate points to individual questions. Next, points must be allocated to parts of questions [part (a), part (b), etc.]. The allocation is based on the length and difficulty of the question parts. Consideration is given to the level of candidates' answers. This allocation may be changed during the sample gradings to make the result more equitable.
2. In special cases, the ICMA permits giving credit in one part for answers in other parts of the question (which is called cross grading). You should, of course, avoid the need for such generosity by answering each part of each question separately and thoroughly.
3. Certain elements of the desired answer may be weighted more or less heavily, e.g., receive 2 points or ½ point rather than 1 point, if they are more or less important. Frequently, all such elements within one part of a question receive equal points. The basis for point determination is usually the number of satisfactory answer elements and the number of points allocated to that particular part of a question.

Even though preliminary answers are prepared by the ICMA staff, sample grading is undertaken prior to the production grading. Each essay question/computational problem is graded by one or two persons, each of whom specializes in a single question and grades the papers later in the production stage.

During the first week of January and July, an ICMA staff member and the reviewers review the grading with each grader of an essay question/computational problem. After any revisions of grading guides, procedures, etc., production grading is begun. Production grading lasts from 3 to 4 weeks.

Graders are primarily CMAs who are college and university professors, management accountants from industry, or practicing accountants from public accounting. The graders are highly experienced because grader turnover at the ICMA is low. Each grader is thoroughly conversant with the question and answer (s)he is responsible for grading as a result of participating in development of the grading basis as described above. Additionally, each grader carefully reviews both the question and the grading basis at the beginning of each grading session with the reviewers and other graders.

SAMPLE ESSAY QUESTION GRADING ILLUSTRATION

The question below and the grading thereof constitute an illustration of the ICMA grading process for essay questions. The answer is termed unofficial because there are usually several acceptable approaches and/or formats. Also, the ICMA does not have the authority to promulgate accounting policies, principles, definitions, procedures, etc. The ICMA makes the following statement:

> *The answers are not official answers to the CMA examination questions. However, the answers have been prepared by experts in the fields covered by the examination. As such, they represent well-considered responses by qualified professionals to the issues raised in the examination.*

Question No. 2

CLK Co. is a manufacturer of electrical components. The company maintains a significant inventory of a broad range of finished goods because it has built its business upon prompt shipments of any stock item.

The company manufactured all items it sold until recently, when it discontinued the manufacturing of five items. The items were dropped from the manufacturing process because the unit costs computed by the company's full cost system did not provide a sufficient margin to cover shipping and selling costs. The five items are now purchased from other manufacturers at a price that allows CLK to make a very small profit after shipping and selling costs. CLK keeps these items in its product line in order to offer a complete line of electrical components.

The president is disappointed at recent profitability performance. He thought that switching from manufacturing to purchasing the five items would improve profit performance. However, the reverse has occurred. All other factors affecting profits -- sales volume, sales prices, and incurred selling and manufacturing costs -- were as expected, so the profit problem can be traced to this decision. The president has asked the controller's department to re-evaluate the financial effects of the decision.

The task was assigned to a recently hired assistant controller. She has reviewed the data used to reach the decision to purchase rather than manufacture. Her conclusion is that the company should have continued to manufacture the item. In her opinion the incorrect decision was made because full (absorption) cost data rather than direct (variable cost) data were used to make the decision.

Required:

a. Explain what features of direct (variable) costing as compared to full (absorption) costing make it possible for the assistant controller's conclusion to be correct.

b. For internal measurement purposes, compare the income, return on investment, and inventory values under full (absorption) costing and direct (variable) costing for periods in which inventory quantities are

1. Rising.
2. Declining.
3. Stable.

c. What advantages are said to accrue to decision making if direct (variable) costing is used?

ICMA Unofficial Answer

a. Full (absorption) costing assigns both variable and fixed manufacturing costs to the units produced. With direct (variable) costing, only the variable manufacturing costs are assigned to the units produced, and the fixed manufacturing costs are treated as period costs.

When CLK Co. decided to purchase rather than manufacture the five items, it compared the outside purchase price with the full cost to manufacture the items. The full cost included an allocated portion of the fixed manufacturing costs. The total fixed costs would not be affected by this decision and would continue to be incurred even though the five items were discontinued. In decisions of this type dealing with marginal production (and sales), only those costs that are relevant should be considered. They are more likely to be the variable costs. Hence, the direct cost approach would have been the more useful costing approach because it emphasizes the variable costs which are the relevant costs to be compared with the outside purchase price.

b. A portion of the fixed manufacturing costs in addition to the variable manufacturing costs are inventoried under the full (absorption) costing method while only variable manufacturing costs are inventoried under the direct (variable) costing method. Consequently, the inventory values are always higher in full (absorption) costing regardless of whether the physical quantities of inventory are rising, falling, or stable. The effects of net income and return on investment are explained as follows:

1. **Inventory quantities are rising.**

Under absorption costing a portion of the fixed manufacturing costs would be inventoried and identified with the inventory build-up during the period. This would result in lower cost of goods sold and a higher net income than under direct costing. Under direct costing the fixed costs would flow through to the income statement, resulting in the lower net income figure. The ROI comparison is not as easily made. Without specific data one cannot determine which method's ROI will be higher during a period in which inventory quantities rise.

The absorption costing income will be higher but its investment base also will be higher. The investment base will be higher by the amount of the inventoried fixed costs, including the fixed costs associated with the current increase in inventory quantity. If the amount of the difference in incomes is large relative to the income amount and the amount of fixed costs added to the inventory is small relative to the investment, the absorption costing ROI is likely to be higher than the direct costing ROI. If the income difference is small relative to the income and the effect on the investment base is also small, the absorption costing ROI will be lower than the direct costing ROI.

2. **Inventory quantities are declining.**

Absorption costing would release fixed costs previously inventoried as inventories decline, thus resulting in higher cost of goods sold for the period and lower net income than under direct costing. Under direct costing only current period fixed costs would be charged against income, resulting in the higher net income. The higher net income divided by the lower investment base (because direct cost inventories do not include assigned fixed costs) will result in a higher ROI for direct costing than for absorption costing.

3. **Inventory quantities are stable.**

When inventory quantities are stable, net income is the same for both methods. The ROI will be higher under direct costing.

c. The emphasis of direct (variable) costing is on cost behavior and the identification of costs that vary as activity levels change. Managers tend to think in direct costing terms, e.g., as activity increases costs increase. Managers focus upon the relevant costs in decision making which means they are interested in the change in contribution margin and the change in total fixed costs. Direct costing is useful for decision making because the relevant costs are more easily identifiable -- i.e., the variable costs are separated from the fixed and the changes in fixed costs are highlighted.

The grading guide is simply a brief summary of the suggested solution, with points assigned to the questions, parts, and answer elements. The points assigned to questions are proportional to the suggested times on the front of each examination booklet. Refer to the hypothetical grading guide on page 38, and note the credit given for each item listed in the ICMA unofficial answer. The number of points assigned to parts of each question is determined by the length and difficulty of each part. In Question No. 2, parts (a), (b), and (c) are allocated 4, 9, and 2 points, respectively. Also, all nine answers are required in part (b), whereas four of five answers are required in part (a), and two of three answers are required in part (c).

Usually, each answer element is worth only 1 point. Additional points are assigned when there are too few available elements relative to the number of points assigned to a particular question or question part. Finally, the time allocated to this question is 30 minutes, which certainly is adequate to prepare a very suitable answer.

SAMPLE COMPUTATIONAL PROBLEM GRADING ILLUSTRATION

An actual question from the CMA exam and its ICMA unofficial answer are reproduced below to illustrate the ICMA grading process for computational problems. The points assigned to the parts of the question are the same as those presented on the hypothetical grade sheet, not those used for the actual exam. The objective here is only to illustrate the grading process for computational problems.

Question No. 3

The Jason Plant of Cast Corporation has been in operation for 15 months. Jason employs a standard cost system for its manufacturing operations. The first 6 months' performance was affected by the usual problems associated with a new operation. Since that time the operations have been running smoothly. Unfortunately, however, the plant has not been able to produce profits on a consistent basis. As the production requirements to meet sales demand have increased, the profit performance has deteriorated.

The plant production manager commented at a staff meeting which the plant general manager, the corporate controller, and the corporate budget director attended that the changing production requirements make it more difficult to control manufacturing expenses. He further noted that the budget for the plant included in the company's annual profit plan was not useful for judging the plant's performance because of the changes in the operating levels. The meeting resulted in a decision to prepare a report which would compare the plant's actual manufacturing expense performance with a budget of manufacturing expense based on actual direct labor hours in the plant.

The plant production manager and the plant accountant studied the cost patterns for recent months and volume and cost data from other Cast plants. Then they prepared the following flexible budget schedule for a month with 200,000 planned production hours which at standard would result in 50,000 units of output. The corporate controller reviewed and approved the flexible budget.

	Amount	Per Direct Labor Hour
Manufacturing expenses		
Variable		
Indirect labor	$160,000	$ .80
Supplies	26,000	.13
Power	14,000	.07
		$1.00
Fixed		
Supervisory labor	64,000	
Heat and light	15,000	
Property taxes	5,000	
	$284,000	

The manufacturing expense reports prepared for the first 3 months after the flexible budget program was approved pleased the plant production manager. They showed that manufacturing expenses were in line with the flexible budget allowance. This was also reflected by the report prepared for November, which is presented below, when 50,500 units were manufactured. However, the plant was still not producing an adequate profit because the variances from standard costs were quite large.

Jason Plant
Manufacturing Expenses
November 1989
220,000 Actual Direct Labor Production Hours

	Actual Costs	Allowed Costs	(Over) Under Budget
Variable			
Indirect labor	$177,000	$176,000	$(1,000)
Supplies	27,400	28,600	1,200
Power	16,000	15,400	(600)
Fixed			
Supervisory labor	65,000	64,000	(1,000)
Heat and light	15,500	15,000	(500)
Property taxes	5,000	5,000	0
	$305,900	$304,000	$(1,900)

Required:

a. Explain the advantages of flexible budgeting over fixed budgeting for cost control purposes.

b. Calculate the excess amount over standard spent on manufacturing expense items during November 1989. Analyze this excess amount into those variances due to

1. Efficiency.
2. Spending.

c. Explain what the management of Jason Plant should do to reduce the

1. Efficiency variance.
2. Spending variance.

ICMA Unofficial Answer

a. Advantages of flexible budgeting over fixed budgeting for cost control purposes include the following:

- Budgeted costs are often separated into their fixed and variable components.
- The flexible budget serves as a useful planning tool because estimates for costs at many different possible activity levels can easily be made.
- Emphasis on controllability of costs is improved because the budgeted level of costs for the actual level of activity can be easily determined.
- Variations from budget, and their analysis as to cause, can be determined quickly and easily, which means that corrective action can be taken on a timely basis to control excessive costs.

b.1., b.2.

	(1) Actual Cost	(2) Budget at Actual Hours Worked (220,000 DLH)	(3) Budget at Standard Hours Allowed (202,000 DLH)	(1)-(3) Total Variance (Over) Under	(1)-(2) Spending Variance	(2)-(3) Efficiency Variance
Variable:						
Indirect labor	$177,000	$176,000	$161,600	$(15,400)	$(1,000)	$(14,400)
Supplies	27,400	28,600	26,260	(1,140)	1,200	(2,340)
Power	16,000	15,400	14,140	(1,860)	(600)	(1,260)
Fixed:						
Supervisory labor	65,000	64,000	64,000	(1,000)	(1,000)	--
Heat and light	15,500	15,000	15,000	(500)	(500)	--
Property taxes	5,000	5,000	5,000	0	--	--
Totals	$305,900	$304,000	$286,000	$(19,900)	$(1,900)	$(18,000)

c.1. The efficiency variance is associated exclusively with the activity measure for variable manufacturing expense. Variable manufacturing expenses vary with and are applied on the basis of direct labor hours. Consequently, the efficiency variance is tied to the excess direct labor hours (18,000 DLH) required to complete the monthly output. The management of Jason Plant should take steps to control the direct labor activity better, which will reduce the efficiency variance.

c.2. The spending variances are not significantly out of line, as shown below.

	Amount (Over) Under	Percent (Over) Under
Variable manufacturing	$ (400)	(0.2%)
Fixed manufacturing	(1,500)	(1.8%)
Total	$(1,900)	(0.6%)

Consequently, there may not be much Jason Plant management wants or needs to do to reduce the spending variances. If the variances were significant, then attention should be paid to the cost control procedure relative to the specific manufacturing expense items.

Hypothetical CMA Exam Grading Guide
Part 3 June 19XX

Ques. No.				Max. Points	Grading Points 1st	2nd	3rd
1.	30 multiple-choice questions (.833 point per correct answer)			25			
2a.	Max 4			15			
	Both FC & VC versus only VC	1 ___					
	Compared purchase cost to full cost	1 ___					
	Fixed costs unaffected by decision	1 ___					
	Consider only relevant costs	1 ___					
	Only variable costs are relevant	1 ___					
b.1	DC inventory less	1 ___					
	DC income lower	1 ___					
	DC ROI higher or lower	1 ___					
b.2	DC inventory less	1 ___					
	DC income higher	1 ___					
	DC ROI higher	1 ___					
b.3	DC inventory less	1 ___					
	DC income the same	1 ___					
	DC ROI higher	1 ___					
c.	Max 2						
	Cost/activity change	1 ___					
	Easily identifiable	1 ___					
	Contribution margin, FC change	1 ___					
3a.	Max 3			15			
	Separate FC & VC	1 ___					
	Useful planning tool	1 ___					
	Facilitate control	1 ___					
	Timely variation analysis	1 ___					
b.1	Max 4						
	Indirect labor	1 ___	(14,400)				
	Supplies	1 ___	(2,340)				
	Power	1 ___	(1,260)				
	Supervisory	1 ___	-0-				
	Heat & light	1 ___	-0-				
	Property tax	1 ___	-0-				
b.2	Max 5						
	Indirect labor	1 ___	$(1,000)				
	Supplies	1 ___	1,200				
	Power	1 ___	(600)				
	Supervisory	1 ___	(1,000)				
	Heat & light	1 ___	(500)				
	Property tax	1 ___	-0-				
c.1	Efficiency based on activity level	1 ___					
	Reduce direct labor	1 ___					
c.2	Variance not significant	1 ___					

Compare the content of the ICMA unofficial solution and the problem requirements with the grading guide on page 38. The bulk of the problem consists of computations required in part (b), which results in allocation of 9 of the 15 points. The requirements in part (c) are very specific, and all three responses are required for full credit. Part (a) is an open-ended question, and only four answer elements are required. Other elements would be accepted even though they are not listed on the grading guide. The maximum point limits on parts b.1 and b.2 permit a math error on one or two of the calculations without penalty. The rationale is, if you compute four or five of the variances correctly, you understand the material.

This typical CMA computation problem requires explanation of flexible budgeting and how to apply it in the context of the problem. This requirement reflects a significant difference between CMA and CPA computational problems. CMA problems usually include explanation requirements because, in the authors' opinion, the CMA exam is less preparer-oriented and more user-oriented than the CPA exam.

THE THREE GRADINGS

The first grading of the CMA exam is done by production graders who specialize in a single question and grade that question for all candidates on a particular exam (about 4,500 on each 1995 exam). The control batches of 25 exams each pass from grader to grader for each question. Then, reviewers regrade selected examination papers as a quality control and consistency check. During the first grading session, about 10% of the papers receive a review grading. If the grading of a particular question is unusually difficult, the percentage of papers reviewed is increased.

After the multiple-choice questions have been optically scanned, the score is placed on the candidate's grading guide. The points on each grading guide are totaled to determine candidate grades after the first grading. Papers with grades from 66 to 69 are subject to a second grading for score adjustment to either 65 or 70. Exams may be graded a third time for candidates who have passed three of the four parts of the overall exam or who are going to lose credit for sections previously passed (because of the six-consecutive-exam rule).

On the second and third gradings, the entire paper is graded as a unit. These gradings are undertaken by reviewers who are experienced graders or by the ICMA technical staff. The second and third gradings view the entire examination in perspective, whereas the first grading and the quality control review are directed toward individual questions.

POINTERS FOR CMA CANDIDATES

Knowledge of the grading process should give you confidence about the CMA exam. The grading process is fair, impartial, and designed to give you and other candidates the benefit of the doubt. Knowledge of the grading process permits you to provide the answers desired by the ICMA.

After studying the following pointers and reading the next section, CMA Examination Preparation, go on to Chapter 3.

1. Make a time budget for questions based on the recommended times on the cover of your exam booklet.
2. Do the same for parts within a question based on the relative length and difficulty of the parts.
3. Complete the requirements to each part of each question.
   a. Do not rely on a strong answer to part (a) to cover deficiencies on part (b).
4. Answer all required questions, even the ones you are unsure of.
   a. But remember that you will receive credit only for the maximum points allocated to the requirement even if you list more than the number required.
   b. Do **not** answer extra optional questions.
      1) If one of two is required, do only one.
      2) If you do both, only the first will be graded.
5. Organize your answers in strict accordance with each question's instructions.
6. Use clear, concise, complete sentences to explain each essay answer element.
7. Computations should be presented in an orderly fashion on attached and consecutively numbered answer sheets.
   a. Cross-reference clearly when necessary.
8. For multiple-choice questions, explanations will not be considered by the graders.
9. Start the answer to each question on a new page.
10. Number your answer sheets consecutively for each part of the exam.

CMA EXAMINATION PREPARATION

The CMA examination is prepared by the ICMA examination staff under the direction of the ICMA Board of Regents. The question specifications (a list of topics to be examined) for a particular examination is usually approved by the regents a year and a half in advance. The regents are divided into four examination review committees, each concentrating on one part of the exam. During the course of four or five Board of Regents meetings each year (and much work in between), the examination evolves from the question specifications to the final printed examinations that are sent to the exam proctors at the beginning of June and December.

ICMA EXAMINATION QUESTION SUBMITTAL PROGRAM

The ICMA has developed a program to solicit questions for the CMA examination. Unfortunately the response has not been great. As a result, the Institute has had to rely heavily on ICMA staff and outside consultants for questions. A description of the Institute's submission program is reproduced below to give you an overview of the ICMA examination preparation process.

If you are interested in submitting questions, you should contact the ICMA. The address is 10 Paragon Drive, Montvale, New Jersey, 07645-1759. The ICMA's exam division telephone number is (201) 573-9000, extension 153.

GUIDELINES FOR THE SUBMISSION OF QUESTIONS FOR THE CERTIFICATE IN MANAGEMENT ACCOUNTING EXAMINATION

Nature of the CMA Examination

The Certificate in Management Accounting Examination is designed to measure attainment of knowledge important to the management accountant. It tests the attainment of this knowledge and its application to the situations in which management accountants are likely to find themselves. The subject matter on the examination is broad in areas such as economics, organization and behavior, finance and quantitative methods, and deep in areas of accounting for control and decision making. The nature of the examination is such that questions are needed from many sources to properly cover the subject matter and situations pertinent to management accounting. Your interest in this program is appreciated; your contributed questions will be helpful to the program.

Honorarium for Questions Used

The Institute of Certified Management Accountants pays an honorarium for submitted questions used on the examination. The amount paid depends upon the type of questions submitted, the length of examination time it represents, and the amount of revision necessary to make it suitable for a national examination. The schedule of fees is illustrative of the amounts that will be paid for submitted questions, needing a minimum of revision, that are used on the examination. Lower amounts will be paid if substantial revision is necessary.

1. *Multiple-choice questions -- $20 per item. Questions submitted should cover a single area of the subject matter. Not fewer than 11 or 12 items on the same subject matter should be submitted as a package.*

2. *Problems, discussion questions, and combination problem/discussion questions -- $150 for a major question (1/2 to 3/4 hour in proposed examination time); $100 for shorter questions.*

The Topic Coverage of the Examination

Questions are sought for each of the 4 examination parts:

1. *Economics, Finance, and Management*
2. *Financial Accounting and Reporting*
3. *Management Reporting, Analysis, and Behavioral Issues*
4. *Decision Analysis and Information Systems*

The examination is intended to provide evidence of exposure to, and proficiency in, various areas of financial practice.

More detail on the examination content will be found in the CMA Program Announcement and from the reading list prepared by the Institute. They are available from the Institute on request.

Nature of the Questions Submitted

The questions submitted should recognize that candidates will be answering the questions out of the context in which the preparer conceived of or observed the situation represented in the question. The statement of the question situation and facts should provide the candidate with an adequate sense of the circumstances to permit a well-reasoned answer. All questions should be designed to have an answer which will contain a limited number of relevant issues rather than one which would encourage a vague and long-winded discussion of related but unimportant issues.

The best questions are those which test the candidate's ability to handle more than one of the following items:

a. *Identify a problem situation*
b. *Choose an appropriate solution technique*
c. *Support the choice of the solution technique from among the suitable alternatives*
d. *Apply the relevant facts to the solution technique*
e. *Specify the course of action indicated by the solution*
f. *Identify the limitations of the solution technique, the data used with the technique, and the answers given by the technique*
g. *Explain the results to a non-sophisticated third party, including the limitations*

Questions and problems submitted can appropriately contain irrelevant information, but the amount of such information should be controlled so as not to unnecessarily obscure the situation being presented.

Numerical data presented in a problem should be selected so as to minimize cumbersome arithmetic calculations. Examinees have a limited amount of time to spend on each question, and it should not be wasted on long and cumbersome calculations. If the problem requires a set of related calculations to reach a final conclusion, the development of the answer requirements for the problem should be designed to minimize the effect of follow-through errors (i.e., an arithmetic or conceptual error in the first calculation causes incorrect answers from subsequent calculations even though there are no further arithmetic or conceptual errors).

The estimated length of the examination time required of a candidate to complete the problem will be a factor in selecting problems and questions. As a general rule, combined problem/discussion questions should not exceed 60 minutes in length. Such questions requiring 30-45 minutes of examination time are most desirable. Discussion questions should normally require approximately 30 minutes of examination.

Efficient and equitable grading requires that the questions have gradable answers, that is, answers which must be limited to fairly specific concepts, issues, and facts. The nature of facts and situation in the question will help, but of equal importance are the specific instructions given the candidate. Instructions containing two or more requirements to be answered will help the candidate organize the answer, will assure the likelihood that the candidates will respond to issues desired, and will result in a more gradable answer.

Specific Format Requirements for Questions Submitted

1. *Questions should be typed, double-spaced on plain, white paper*
2. *The contributor's name, address, and submission date should appear on each page*
3. *Suggested answers should be submitted along with the questions*
4. *Supply references to appropriate source material in which the answer is supported. (The references need not be restricted to those books appearing on the ICMA reading list and can include current periodicals.)*
5. *Submit one copy to:*

   Examination Department
   Institute of Certified Management Accountants
   10 Paragon Drive
   Montvale, New Jersey 07645-1759

POINTERS FOR CMA CANDIDATES

Understanding how the CMA exam is prepared helps candidates to know what to expect. Volume II contains over 1,000 recent CMA questions with answers and analyses. It provides a basis for anticipating question format and content.

CMA EXAMINATION ADMINISTRATION

The CMA examination is administered on a Wednesday and Thursday in mid-June and mid-December. University classrooms and hotel ballrooms are frequently used. CMA exam proctors appointed by the ICMA conduct the examination. Both ICMA Instructions to Candidates and Instructions to CMA Exam Proctors are reproduced on pages 46 through 48. Page 44 contains samples of the authorization card, entry card, and site location card that will be sent to you by the ICMA.

You should have an entry card for each section of the examination for which you plan to sit. If you do not have one for each part, or if any are incorrect, call the ICMA, which will make arrangements for you to be admitted without an entry card.

ICMA INSTRUCTIONS TO CANDIDATES

The ICMA Instructions to Candidates and a sample of the ICMA's authorization materials are reproduced on the following pages for your information. They will probably not change much, if any. The purpose of reproducing them here is to give you further insight into actual exam procedures.

INSTITUTE OF CERTIFIED MANAGEMENT ACCOUNTANTS
10 PARAGON DRIVE, MONTVALE, NJ 07645-1759 (800) 638-4427

CMA EXAMINATION AUTHORIZATION CARD

THIS AUTHORIZATION CARD CONTAINS YOUR CANDIDATE ID NUMBER TO EACH REGISTERED EXAMINATION PART. THIS CARD AND AN APPROPRIATE SIGNED PHOTO ID PROVIDES ENTRY TO THE EXAMINATION. TAKE THE APPROPRIATE EXAMINATION ENTRY CARD TO EACH PART. THE SITE LOCATION CARD THAT ALSO IS ENCLOSED GIVES THE ADDRESS FOR THE SITE YOU SELECTED. REVIEW THE ENCLOSED MATERIALS INCLUDING THE INSTRUCTIONS TO CANDIDATES.

Candidate Name and Address — JUNE 1996 EXAMINATION

CANDIDATE I.D. NO. 961XXXXX

SOC. SEC. NO. nnn-nn-nnnn

JUNE 1996 CMA EXAMINATION SITE LOCATION CARD

TESTING SITE 0110 BIRMINGHAM

BUILDING: ROOM 315, SCHOOL OF BUSINESS WING
BUSINESS-ENGINEERING COMPLEX
UNIVERSITY OF ALABAMA AT BIRMINGHAM

ADDRESS: 1150 10TH AVENUE SOUTH
BIRMINGHAM, ALABAMA

PARKING: FREE ON-STREET PARKING AVAILABLE ON 10TH AVENUE SOUTH ADJACENT TO THE SCHOOL OF BUSINESS. LOT 15F IS ALSO AVAILABLE FOR USE.

CMA EXAMINATION ENTRY CARD

PART 1 ECONOMICS, FINANCE, AND MANAGEMENT

WEDNESDAY, JUNE 12, 1996 1:30 P.M. TO 5:30 P.M.

TESTING CENTER 0110-BIRMINGHAM

CANDIDATE I.D. NO. 961XXXXX 9610011000-90 1-5
SOC. SEC. NO. nnn-nn-nnnn

9610011000-961XXXXX 15

Candidate Name — THIS CARD MUST BE SIGNED IN THE PRESENCE OF THE EXAMINATION PROCTOR.

SIGNATURE ______________________________

CERTIFIED MANAGEMENT ACCOUNTANT EXAMINATION
INSTRUCTIONS TO CANDIDATES

Please read the following instructions carefully and take them with you to the examination.

A. **General instructions:**

1. Please review the AUTHORIZATION CARD, ENTRY CARD(S) and SITE LOCATION CARD to be sure that you are registered for the correct parts at the correct site.
2. Plan to arrive at the examination room at least 30 minutes before the examination so that the examination can begin promptly.
3. You are required to present a photo identification with signature for examination admission. Approved IDs are a passport, driver's license, military ID, credit card with photo, or company ID. Student IDs are not acceptable. You will not be permitted into the examination without proper photo identification.
4. In addition to the photo ID, take your AUTHORIZATION CARD and the ENTRY CARD for each part to the examination. You will be required to show the AUTHORIZATION CARD before being admitted to the examination. Retain the AUTHORIZATION CARD because your Candidate ID Number is printed on the card. The appropriate ENTRY CARD will be collected before each examination part begins. The ENTRY CARD must be signed in the proctor's presence when entering the examination room. **Do not fold** the ENTRY CARDS.
5. When you have completed the examination, turn in your solutions and the examination booklet. Candidates are **NOT PERMITTED TO TAKE THEIR EXAMINATION BOOKLETS OR SOLUTION PAPER OUT OF THE ROOM**. Those candidates who want their examination booklets must bring a self-addressed and stamped (55¢) 9" x 12" envelope. This is your responsibility; **do not** expect the proctor to provide envelopes or postage. At the end of the examination period, the examination booklet **will be inserted by the candidate** into the envelope, **which must remain unsealed,** and given to the site proctor. (Candidates at locations outside the United States will be required to use adequate local postage.) A separate envelope is required for each part. The site administrator will mail these envelopes at the end of the entire examination period.
6. The people at the site location are NOT involved in the grading of the examination. Do not contact them for information about your performance. Examination results will be mailed from the ICMA on **March 8, 1996**. To ensure receipt, any address change must be at the ICMA by February 15. Scores will not be released by phone or fax.

B. **Items needed at the examination:**

1. Your photo ID, AUTHORIZATION CARD, and the examination ENTRY CARD(S) for each part of the examination you are taking.
2. A sufficient supply of soft-lead (No. 2) pencils, an eraser, and a small ruler.
3. A calculator is permitted. However, **the only calculators allowed in the examination room must meet the following policy guidelines:** The calculator **(a)** must be a battery or solar-powered electronic type calculator, **(b)** must not exceed six functions -- addition, subtraction, multiplication, division, square root, and percent, **(c)** cannot be programmable, **(d)** cannot use any type of tape, and **(e)** must erase memory when turned off. Although calculators may be used, supporting calculations must be presented to receive credit for numerical answers.

C. **Items that will NOT be permitted at the examination:**

1. Books, notes, or other written material.
2. Scratch paper.
3. Flowcharting template.
4. Calculators that **do not** comply with the policy guidelines in topic B.3 above.

D. **Conditions under which the examination will be given:**

1. Do not begin writing until the proctor gives you instructions to start. The proctor will announce when 30, 15, and 5 minutes remain. Be sure to transcribe your multiple-choice answers on the appropriate form as no extra time will be allowed to transcribe your responses at the end of the examination period. **At the end of the examination, cease writing and turn in your solutions promptly upon request by the proctor.** The proctor has been instructed to identify papers not turned in promptly.
2. The proctor will **not** answer any questions about the content of the examination.
3. Smoking, food, and snacks are **not** permitted in the examination room. Beverages are permitted.

E. **Preparation of answers:**

1. All answers are to be placed on the solution paper provided at the examination. You should remove the staple from the package of solution paper (the paper was stapled for ease in collating). If you need additional paper, the proctor has an extra supply.

2. *Place your Candidate I.D. Number that is printed on your AUTHORIZATION CARD in the appropriate space of each sheet of solution paper. Do **not** put your name on the solution paper.*
3. *Enter the part number and question number in the appropriate space on each sheet of solution paper.*
4. *For Question Number 1, which consists of multiple-choice items, please be sure to follow the special instructions in the examination booklet and on the special multiple-choice answer sheet. Supporting calculations are not necessary for multiple-choice items. No credit will be given for multiple-choice responses unless you record them on the multiple-choice form provided.*
5. *Answers should be written on only one side of the solution paper.* ***Start each question on a new page.*** *Supporting calculations should be clearly referenced to your answers.*
6. *At the completion of each examination part, arrange the solution paper in numerical order by question (solution for Question Number 1 on top followed by Question Number 2, etc.). If there are any special answer sheets or solution paper, be sure to include them in order with the rest of your answers. The answers to the multiple-choice questions must be marked on the special multiple-choice answer sheet. This is the solution sheet for Question Number 1 and should be the first sheet (page 1) of your solutions. Number all pages of your solutions in consecutive order with Question Number 2 beginning with solution page 2, etc. Place the Examination Summary Sheet, indicating the questions worked and omitted, on top of your solution papers. Fasten all papers with the paper clip provided by the proctor and submit the entire package of solutions to the proctor.*
7. *If you do not stay for the entire time period of the examination part and do not submit a complete set of solution papers, please be sure to complete and submit the Examination Summary Sheet provided in the examination booklet.*

PLEASE FOLLOW THE ABOVE INSTRUCTIONS IN ORDER THAT THE EXAMINATION CAN PROCEED IN AN ORDERLY AND PROFESSIONAL MANNER.

ICMA INSTRUCTIONS TO CMA EXAM PROCTORS

The following instructions to exam proctors describe procedures used to administer the examination. Read the instructions, noting any procedures that may affect you.

INSTRUCTIONS FOR PROCTORING AND ADMINISTERING THE CERTIFIED MANAGEMENT ACCOUNTANT EXAMINATION

Examination Facilities:
The site administrator has arranged for facilities prior to the examination and ensured that the room(s) provide adequate temperature control, lighting, and ventilation. There should be sufficient space so that each candidate has at least seven square feet of table space with four feet of space between candidates. Alert the site administrator if conditions do not meet these requirements on examination day.

General Information:
Special accommodations for candidates with physical or health conditions are allowed with prior approval from the ICMA. Such situations will have been coordinated with the site administrator prior to the examination.

Proctors must arrive at the examination room(s), prepared with all appropriate materials, ***at least 30 minutes*** *before the examination is scheduled to begin in order to complete the administrative procedures in a timely manner. Candidates are instructed to arrive at the examination site at least 30 minutes prior to the start of the examination.*

The site administrator will provide you with the examination booklets, solution paper, related supplies, a roster of all candidates scheduled to take the examination, and a ***Confirmation of Examination Attendance and Solution Submission*** *form.*

The candidates should be seated about the room(s) to provide adequate working space and to preserve examination integrity. A proctor should be in the room(s) at all times. At least one proctor should be assigned per 25-35 candidates.

Smoking, food, and snacks are ***not*** *permitted in the room(s). Soft drinks, coffee, and water are permitted.*

Candidates should not bring books or supplies into the examination room(s) with the exception of pencils, pens, and rulers. An area for storage of any candidate reference materials should be designated as candidates are not permitted to use any reference materials during the examination. Try to have a pencil sharpener available during the examination.

Small battery or solar powered electronic calculators restricted to a maximum of six functions -- addition, subtraction, multiplication, division, square root, and percent -- are allowed. The calculator must be nonprogrammable, must not use any type of tape, and memory must erase when the calculator is turned off. Candidates ***will not*** *be allowed to use calculators that do not comply with these restrictions.*

*Candidates may leave the room to smoke or go to the restroom, but may **only** leave the room one at a time. At large examination sites, where it is impractical to limit candidates leaving the room to one at a time, the proctors should use their best judgment. Candidates must **not** take materials out of the examination room(s).*

Representatives of the ICMA will visit several of the examination sites to observe the facilities and administration of the examination. These representatives will have a letter of introduction from the ICMA.

Unauthorized individuals are not allowed to enter the examination room(s) during the two-day examination period. Furthermore, if these individuals come to the vicinity of the examination room(s), they should be requested to leave the vicinity so as not to disturb the administration of the examination.

Emergencies/Questions:
In case of emergencies or questions during the administration of the examination, contact the ICMA toll-free in the U.S. at 1-800-638-4427, extension 304; a staff person will be available from 8:00 a.m. to 6:00 p.m. Eastern Time, on all scheduled examination dates.

Examination Entry Card Collection/Photo IDs:
*Prior to the start of the examination, each candidate must **present to the proctor an authorization card and examination entry card** for each examination part taken. In the proctor's presence have the candidate sign the signature line on the entry card and collect it upon entrance to the examination room. The candidate keeps the authorization card as it contains the Candidate ID Number.*

***Candidates' photo IDs, with signatures, are required for entry into the examination room.** Candidates who do not bring photo IDs will **not** be allowed to sit for the examination even if they have entry cards. Acceptable photo IDs are drivers licenses, passports, company ID cards, military IDs and credit cards with photos. Student IDs are **not** acceptable.*

Unusual Examination Entry Card Situations:

- *The site administrator will be notified by phone of any new candidates who will have hand-written tickets rather than the computer-produced entry cards. They should be added to the roster of registered candidates if their names and ID numbers do not appear on it.*
- *Candidates without examination authorization cards and/or entry cards who are on the roster may be admitted if they have called the ICMA **and** obtained their ID numbers which appear on the roster. You should **not** provide candidates with their ID numbers.*
- *Candidates without entry cards who are not on the roster should **not** be admitted without obtaining prior approval from the ICMA.*

*For **each part**, candidates who do not have computer-produced entry cards, should sign a 3" x 5" index card which includes their full name (printed), address, Candidate ID Number, social security number, part number, and site number. The candidates must show a proper photo ID.*

Examination Distribution and Commencement:
Begin and end the examination at the designated times. Candidates should begin the examination promptly at 8:00 a.m. and 1:30 p.m. for the morning and afternoon sessions, respectively. The solution papers should be collected promptly at 12:00 noon and 5:30 p.m. for the morning and afternoon sessions, respectively. In order to accomplish this, please follow the three steps below.

(1) A package of solution paper should be distributed to each candidate at least fifteen minutes before the official starting time. After all papers have been distributed, instruct candidates to remove the staple and write their Candidate ID Number and part number on the solution sheets.

(2) Five minutes before the examination booklets are distributed, read the following announcement to the candidates.

*"Do not ask me any questions about the interpretation of the examination questions because I am not permitted to answer them. Smoking, food, and snacks are **not** permitted in the examination room. You may leave the room to smoke or go to the restroom; however, you may not take any material out of the examination room."*

"Allocate your time carefully. You have four hours. I will announce when 30, 15, and 5 minutes remain. At the end of the examination cease writing and turn in your solutions promptly upon request."

*"Only the Candidate ID Number, found on your authorization card, should be placed on the solution sheets. **Do not** put your name on the solution sheets. **No names are to be used.** Be sure to code your Candidate ID Number and the examination part number accurately on the multiple choice answer sheet."*

*"Answers should be written on only **one side** of the solution paper. Supporting calculations should be clearly referenced to your answers. All answers and supporting calculations are to be placed on solution paper provided at the examination. If insufficient paper is provided with the examination, I **have additional paper**."*

*"At the completion of the examination, arrange the solution paper **in accordance with the instructions on the Examination Summary Sheet** found in the examination booklet, and clip them together with the Summary Sheet on top. Give the entire package of solutions to me. If you are uncertain about arranging your solutions, **ask me**. Note: The multiple choice answer sheet is solution page 1. Only your Candidate ID Number, **not** your name, should be filled in on the Summary Sheet. I will furnish you with paper clips before the examination is over."*

*"You **cannot** take the examination booklet or solution paper out of the room. If you insert the examination booklet into an adequately stamped ($.55), self-addressed, **unsealed** envelope (9"x12") for **each** part at the end of each examination and give it to me, these envelopes will be mailed after the entire examination period is over.*

***Note**: Candidates at **international (non-U.S.) sites** will be required to use adequate local postage."*

*(3) Distribute the examination booklets promptly in order for the examination to commence at 8:00 a.m. and 1:30 p.m., respectively, so the candidates will have the full examination period to work on the examination. The back of the examination booklets may have printed examination questions; therefore, the examination booklets must be distributed **FACE UP ONLY**.*

***Proctor Duties**:*

Proctors must be in the examination room(s) throughout the examination period. Proctors must be alert to candidate behavior and observe the activities in the examination room(s). The most effective way to accomplish this is by walking around the room during the course of the examination. In larger rooms, discussion between proctors should be kept to a minimum so as not to distract the candidates.

Extra solution paper was provided in the shipment of supplies. Have it available when it is requested by the candidate.

Proctors must be objective and should not interpret examination questions for candidates.

On the roster of registered candidates, put a slash through the examination part number of each candidate who took the designated part to distinguish between those who did and did not take each examination part. This process can be completed once the examination has been started. Total the number of candidates taking the examination on the roster. This roster is to be returned to the ICMA. No copies of this roster should be retained locally.

Distribute paper clips (included in the supply shipment) before the candidates submit their papers. Instruct them to put their solutions in numerical order by question and clip their papers together.

Announce to candidates when 30, 15, and 5 minutes remain for each section.

***Suspected Cheating**:*

The ICMA does not anticipate incidents which will compromise the integrity of the examination; however, proctors must be alert to the possibilities, particularly of (1) impersonations, (2) crib notes, and (3) copying from another candidate's paper. If a proctor notices a candidate whose behavior is indicative of cheating, the proctor should walk to and stand beside the candidate briefly in order to better observe the candidate's actions and to provide a subtle warning that his/her behavior is suspicious. If possible, a second proctor should be asked to observe the candidate's actions. If the behavior continues, the proctor should verify the Candidate's ID Number by checking the entry card. The proctor must write a full report of the incident to the ICMA, including the candidate's name and Candidate ID Number, and the Candidate ID Numbers of others in the immediate area (those who may have observed the behavior or whose papers may have been copied). It is important that the proctor does not confront the candidate or disrupt the room during the examination.

***Examination Collection**:*

At the end of the examination period, the proctors should promptly collect all examination solutions.

*As covered in the instructions read to candidates, candidates are **not permitted to take the examination booklet or solution paper out of the room**. Adequately stamped, **unsealed** envelopes provided to you by candidates **should be turned over to the site administrator who will then mail these envelopes after the entire examination period is over**.*

*An **Examination Summary Sheet** should be completed by each candidate and clipped to the top of his/her solution package. The Candidate ID Number, **not** the candidate's name, should be filled in on the Examination Summary Sheet. If a candidate decides not to submit a solution, have him/her check the "omitted" column beside the unanswered question(s).*

*Be sure to count the number of solution packages returned at the end of the session. The number of candidates and solution packages should agree. To confirm the number of persons who attended each part of the CMA Examination and how many solutions per part you are returning, please complete the **Confirmation of Examination Attendance and Solution Submission** form provided to you by the site administrator.*

*After the reconciliation of the solution packages to the number of candidates is completed, the proctors should turn over to the site administrator the entry cards, roster of registered candidates, solution packages, the completed **Confirmation of Examination Attendance and Solution Submission** forms, and the envelopes provided by candidates for mailing of examination booklets.*

Thank you for your assistance and support of the CMA Program.

POINTERS FOR CMA CANDIDATES

The ICMA instructions give you a very clear picture of how the CMA exam is administered. Also see Chapter 4, Writing the CMA Exam, for discussion of how to plan and execute your examination.

CHAPTER THREE
PREPARING TO PASS THE CMA EXAM

INTRODUCTION

Success on the CMA examination, like most other endeavors, is largely dependent on how well you prepare. This chapter is designed to help **you** develop a preparation program (a control system) that will suit **your** study style and preparation needs.

HOW MANY PARTS TO TAKE

Unlike the CPA exam, you are not required to take the whole exam, or all of your remaining parts, at once. You may take one or more parts each time you sit for the CMA exam. However, you lose credit for any parts passed prior to a 3-year (six-consecutive-exam) period that includes the current exam.

Our recommendation to you is to take and pass all four parts (three if you have passed the CPA exam) the first time. Some candidates, however, will not be able to follow this approach for a variety of reasons. Parts 2 and 3 are the most accounting-related parts. Part 1 is the most unrelated to accounting. Thus, most candidates planning to sit for only two parts on the initial exam will choose Parts 2 and 3 because of their similarity and familiarity. As an alternative, you may choose Parts 3 and 4 if you do not have to take Part 2.

Part 1: Economics, Finance, and Management
Part 2: Financial Accounting and Reporting
Part 3: Management Reporting, Analysis, and Behavioral Issues
Part 4: Decision Analysis and Information Systems

Parts 2 and 3 cover most of the accounting topics included in a typical undergraduate accounting program. Part 1 covers the material found in management, microeconomics, macroeconomics, and corporate finance courses. Part 4 covers internal auditing, computer systems, quantitative methods, and statistics courses.

PRELIMINARY SELF-ASSESSMENT AND STUDY CONTROL

	Preliminary Evaluation (circle one)	Study Control (enter date completed) Outline	Questions
ECONOMICS, FINANCE, AND MANAGEMENT (Part 1)			
SU 1: Microeconomics	A B C D E	____	____
SU 2: Macroeconomics	A B C D E	____	____
SU 3: International Economics	A B C D E	____	____
SU 4: Institutional Environment of Business	A B C D E	____	____
SU 5: Working Capital Finance	A B C D E	____	____
SU 6: Capital Structure Finance	A B C D E	____	____
SU 7: Organization Theory	A B C D E	____	____
SU 8: Motivation and the Directing Process	A B C D E	____	____
SU 9: Communication	A B C D E	____	____
SU 10: Ethics and the Management Accountant	A B C D E	____	____
FINANCIAL ACCOUNTING AND REPORTING (Part 2)			
SU 11: Fin. Atg: Dev. of Theory & Practice	A B C D E	____	____
SU 12: Financial Statement Presentation	A B C D E	____	____
SU 13: Special Financial Reporting Problems	A B C D E	____	____
SU 14: SEC Reporting Requirements	A B C D E	____	____
SU 15: Ratio and Accounts Analysis	A B C D E	____	____
SU 16: Internal Control	A B C D E	____	____
SU 17: External Auditing	A B C D E	____	____
SU 18: Income Taxes	A B C D E	____	____
MANAGEMENT REPORTING, ANALYSIS, AND BEHAVIORAL ISSUES (Part 3)			
SU 19: Process and Job Order Costing	A B C D E	____	____
SU 20: Variable and Absorption Costing	A B C D E	____	____
SU 21: Planning	A B C D E	____	____
SU 22: Budgeting	A B C D E	____	____
SU 23: The Controlling Process	A B C D E	____	____
SU 24: Standard Costs & Variance Analysis	A B C D E	____	____
SU 25: Responsibility Accounting	A B C D E	____	____
DECISION ANALYSIS AND INFORMATION SYSTEMS (Part 4)			
SU 26: Incremental Costing	A B C D E	____	____
SU 27: Cost-Volume-Profit Analysis	A B C D E	____	____
SU 28: Capital Budgeting	A B C D E	____	____
SU 29: Decision Making under Uncertainty	A B C D E	____	____
SU 30: Inventory Models	A B C D E	____	____
SU 31: Quantitative Methods	A B C D E	____	____
SU 32: Information Systems	A B C D E	____	____
SU 33: Internal and Operational Auditing	A B C D E	____	____

THE PREPARATION PROCESS

In order to complete the CMA examination successfully, you need to undertake the following steps:

1. Understand the exam, including coverage, content, format, administration, and grading. See Chapters 1 and 2 in particular.
2. Learn and understand the subject matter tested. See Chapters 5 through 8 in this volume for outlines of the knowledge tested, and Chapters 1 through 4 in Volume II for recent CMA exam questions with complete explanations.
3. Practice answering recent CMA exam questions to perfect your exam answering technique. See Volume II, Problems and Solutions.
4. Plan exam execution. See Chapter 4, Writing the CMA Exam, in this volume.
5. Most importantly, **control** your preparation program to help **you** pass the exam. Study and restudy this chapter as an aid to developing a control system.

SELF-ASSESSMENT AND PLANNING YOUR PREPARATION

Planning is essential to a successful preparation program. After studying Chapters 1 and 2 to obtain a good understanding of the exam, its preparation, administration, and grading, you should undertake a preliminary self-assessment to enable you to plan your preparation.

On the previous page is a self-assessment and study control chart that lists the 33 study units tested on the CMA exam. Turn to each study unit in Volume II and

1. Answer only three to five multiple-choice questions.
2. Look over all of the remaining multiple-choice and essay questions.
3. Turn to the self-assessment chart on the previous page and rate your knowledge of the topic (circle the grade you feel represents your knowledge).
4. Spend about 5 minutes per study unit. Because there are 33 study units, you can get a good overview of the exam as well as an evaluation of your skill levels in about 3 to 4 hours.

You may wish to expand this process as you begin studying each study unit. Pretesting establishes the depth and extent of your required study.

As suggested above, you may decide to answer every fifth, tenth, etc., multiple-choice question in Volume II as a pretest before studying Volume I. The purpose is twofold: to gain an awareness of the standards to which you will be held and to measure your current knowledge level. Study the requirements of one or more essay questions/practice problems as well.

After you have completed your assessment on a study unit-by-study unit basis, you will have an overall CMA exam perspective. Based on this self-assessment and your knowledge of how the exam is graded (discussed in Chapter 2), you should understand the standards to which you will be held.

Now you can study individual study units. First, review the point allocation to various topics in each part of the CMA exam. The ICMA has committed to allocate **topical coverage on each CMA exam according to the content specification outlines** (see Chapter 1).

Before studying each study unit in Volume I page-by-page, make a mental outline of the study unit and attempt to understand or at least anticipate its contents based on your prior study and experience. Then study each study unit outline thoroughly so you can explain the concepts to the grader.

As you complete a study unit in Volume I, answer all the multiple-choice questions in Volume II, and at least one essay question/computational problem. Study the explanation of each multiple-choice question that you answered incorrectly or had difficulty answering.

Each study unit in Volume II has the following organization:

1. Multiple-choice questions
2. Explanation of the multiple-choice answers
3. Essay questions/computational problems
4. A one-paragraph commentary on each essay answer and a solution guide for the computational problems
5. ICMA suggested solutions

STUDY PLAN, TIME BUDGET, AND CALENDAR

Plan a study schedule such that you can complete one study unit at a time (there are 33). Set up a weekly study schedule (page 54) and adhere to it. Begin by budgeting 2 to 3 hours per study unit [1-2 hours studying the outline; 1-2 minutes each on all the multiple-choice questions; and at least one complete preparation of an essay question or computational problem (15-20 min.)]. This process leaves 15 minutes to grade yourself and to read the answer explanations for those questions you missed. In addition, use the self-assessment information from page 50 to decide which study units require more study time. You should also spend about 4 hours on the first four chapters, and about 1 hour as an introduction to each section of the exam (i.e., studying the introductions to Chapters 5 through 8). Then allow yourself 4 hours for general review.

Total preparation time required varies with the background, aptitude, and test-taking ability of each candidate. For persons who have recently prepared for the CPA exam, 40 to 80 hours will probably be sufficient (those who have passed the CPA exam are exempt from Part 2). Others will require additional time. If 4 hours are spent on Chapters 1 through 4, 1 hour each for the introductions of Chapters 5 through 8, 3 hours on each of the 33 study units, with a final 4-hour review, a TOTAL of 111 hours will be invested. Many candidates will spend additional hours studying textbooks and all the essay questions/computational problems, especially for unfamiliar topics.

Chapters 1 through 4	4
Introduction to Chapters 5 through 8	4
33 study units at 3 hours each	99
General review	4
Total Hours	111

As you progress through your study program, you will be able to adjust your time to suit your own needs. Work backward from the exam dates on the calendars on pages 55 and 56 to determine when to begin your preparation. If you start at the beginning of April or October, you will have to complete only three or four study units per week.

If you are studying Volumes I and II for CPE credit, your preparation will be considerably more structured and extensive. Study time will increase to about 200 hours.

Each week you should evaluate your progress and review your preparation plans for the time remaining prior to the exam. The Weeks-to-Go Schedule on page 54 and June 1996 and December 1996 CMA Calendars on pages 55 and 56 will assist you. Review your commitments, e.g., out-of-town assignments, personal responsibilities, etc., and note them on the appropriate CMA calendar. This precaution will assist you in keeping to your schedule.

ADDITIONAL SUGGESTIONS

1. **Answer CMA questions in Gleim books and software**. It is essential that you answer all of the multiple-choice questions in each study unit of Volume II. Also, you should prepare **complete** solutions to at least one essay question/computational problem in each study unit. Remember, the emphasis in your undergraduate accounting courses was on solutions to problems rather than essay questions. Thus, you need to practice your essay question answering technique.
2. **Study review outlines**. The outline volume is designed for review, not initial study. If your background is weak in a certain area, you may have to consult a basic textbook for further discussion. Then return to the outline for systematic review.
3. **Gather study materials**. Begin with *CMA Review* and your old undergraduate textbooks. Most candidates will find *CMA Review* sufficient. Use ***CMA Test Prep*** to further your multiple-choice question study. You may only need to borrow a book or visit a library to look up a few topics for further study.
4. **Locate a place to study**. A study area should permit you to work undisturbed.
5. **When to study.** This is clearly a personal preference item and is frequently dictated by personal and professional responsibilities and commitments. Take breaks. Alternate between ***CMA Test prep*** software and your Gleim books.
6. **Determine how much knowledge is enough**. You should not attempt to be perfect. A minimum passing score on each part is sufficient. Attaining complete mastery of one part or topic may cause you to underprepare for another part or topic. Most candidates will find mastering the material in this manual to be more than adequate preparation for the CMA exam. Do not forget to develop your question answering techniques and control systems **before** the exam.
7. **Study Chapters 1 through 4 before moving on to Chapters 5 through 8**. Understanding how the examination is prepared, administered, and graded is essential to developing confidence and maximizing your score. Developing your own preparation program will likewise foster success. Chapter 4 discusses the tactics employed (in addition to the specific question answering techniques described in Chapter 3) and logistical concerns relevant to the actual taking of the exam.

WEEKS-TO-GO SCHEDULE

Weeks Remaining	Study Units Scheduled	Comments
12		
11		
10		
9		
8		
7		
6		
5		
4		
3		
2		
1		
0		

JUNE 1996 CMA CALENDAR

Weeks to Exam	Sun	Mon	Tues	Wed	Thurs	Fri	Sat
FEB 17	11	12	13	14	15	16	17
16	18	19	20	21	22	23	24
MAR 15	25	26	27	28	29	1	2
14	3	4	5	6	7	8	9
13	10	11	12	13	14	15	16
12	17	18	19	20	21	22	23
11	24	25	26	27	28	29	30
APR 10	31	1	2	3	4	5	6
9	7	8	9	10	11	12	13
8	14	15	16	17	18	19	20
7	21	22	23	24	25	26	27
MAY 6	28	29	30	1	2	3	4
5	5	6	7	8	9	10	11
4	12	13	14	15	16	17	18
3	19	20	21	22	23	24	25
JUN 2	26	27	28	29	30	31	1
1	2	3	4	5	6	7	8
0	9	10	11	12 EXAM	13 EXAM	14	15

DECEMBER 1996 CMA CALENDAR

Weeks to Exam	Sun	Mon	Tues	Wed	Thurs	Fri	Sat
AUG 17	11	12	13	14	15	16	17
16	18	19	20	21	22	23	24
15	25	26	27	28	29	30	31
SEP 14	1	2	3	4	5	6	7
13	8	9	10	11	12	13	14
12	15	16	17	18	19	20	21
11	22	23	24	25	26	27	28
OCT 10	29	30	1	2	3	4	5
9	6	7	8	9	10	11	12
8	13	14	15	16	17	18	19
7	20	21	22	23	24	25	26
NOV 6	27	28	29	30	31	1	2
5	3	4	5	6	7	8	9
4	10	11	12	13	14	15	16
3	17	18	19	20	21	22	23
2	24	25	26	27	28	29	30
DEC 1	1	2	3	4	5	6	7
0	8	9	10	11 EXAM	12 EXAM	13	14

CONTROL

You have to be in control to be successful during exam preparation and execution. Perhaps more importantly, control can also contribute greatly to your personal and other professional goals.

What is control? Control is a process whereby you

1. Develop expectations, standards, budgets, and plans.
2. Undertake activity, production, study, and learning.
3. Measure the activity, production, output, and knowledge.
4. Compare actual activity with what was expected or budgeted.
5. Modify the activity, behavior, or production to better achieve the expected or desired outcome.
6. Revise expectations and standards in light of actual experience.
7. Continue the process.

The objective is to improve performance as well as be confident that the best possible results are achieved. Most accountants follow this process in relation to standard costs; i.e., they establish cost standards and compute cost variances.

Every day you rely on control systems implicitly. For example, when you prepare for work or school in the morning, you use a control system. You have expectations about your appearance, personal hygiene, and the time required to meet your standards. Implicitly you monitor your progress and make adjustments as appropriate.

The point is that either you have and enforce standards or you do not, or you are somewhere in between. In all of your endeavors, you do or do not exercise control, implicitly or explicitly. However, the results of most activities will improve with explicit control. This is particularly true of certification examinations.

1. Practice your question answering techniques (and develop control) as you prepare question solutions during your study program.
2. Develop an explicit control system over your study program (restudy this chapter).
3. Study Chapter 4 as a basis for planning a control system for examination execution to help you pass the CMA exam.
4. Think about using more explicit control systems over any and all of your endeavors.

ESSAY QUESTION ANSWERING TECHNIQUE

To institute **control** over your essay question answers, we suggest the following steps:

1. **Question overview**. Scan the question to get an overview of the topic covered. Do not pay too much attention to the details of the question.
2. **Understand the requirements**. This includes a mental outline of the grader's expected answer. Then picture how your answer should look. Make sure it conforms to the question requirements. There may be several requirements within a question. When answering the question, make sure you do not miss any of them. For example, if the requirement is to "list and explain," include the explanation!
3. **Mentally prepare a "to do" list.** Before you begin, you need to know what, where, when, and how in order to be in control.
4. **Focus your knowledge on the question.** Review core concepts, principles, rules, and exceptions that apply to the topic of the question and its requirements. Do this review prior to reading the question in more detail to avoid having your knowledge of the subject confused by the details of fact patterns.
5. **Read the entire question slowly and carefully**. Pause after each factual statement, and evaluate its significance to the requirements. Make notes in the margin. Circle, highlight, and underline words as appropriate.
6. **Write an abbreviation** for each gradable concept that can be developed in your answer.
7. **Reorganize your gradable concepts** for consistency with the question requirements. Reread the requirements to assure you are providing what the grader expects. Do not rewrite the concepts, but organize them with alphanumeric labels, e.g., 1, 2, 3, 3a, 3b, or A1, A2, A3, etc.
8. **Write your answer** using short, clear, uncomplicated sentences and paragraphs. Label your paragraphs so they are consistent with the labels used in the examination. Never write your answer in outline form. Write on every other line or leave 1/4 of the page blank at the bottom for any additional discussions or insertions when editing your answer. If you are asked to give examples or list advantages of . . . , always give more than required if you can (i.e., if asked to give 3 examples, give 5). This will increase the chance that you have given what the examiners want.
9. **Read the requirements again** to make sure that your answer is consistent with the requirements and that you have not missed any possible gradable concepts for each of the requirements. You should maximize the number of gradable concepts for each requirement in each question. Focusing your effort on only a few parts you know well will not allow you to obtain extra points. There is a limited number of points for each part. Thus, you cannot compensate for points lost on other parts of the question.
10. **Edit and reread** to assure a well-presented answer. Remember, your writing skill will also be graded.

Many CMA candidates struggle with essay questions, sometimes more than they do with computational questions. It's just like swimming: You have to get in the water and do it! As in learning to swim, practice helps! It's a sink or swim issue.

You should be very aggressive and dive into essay questions. Use the above technique to develop the habit of completing typical CMA essay questions including a first draft answer (on every other line) in 15 minutes. Do **not** develop a habit of starting essay questions and not finishing them.

Steps 1 through 5 on the previous page should take 1 to 2 minutes. Reading and analyzing the question, including writing down abbreviations of gradable concepts, could take 5 to 10 minutes. Organizing your concepts and writing your answer could take another 5 to 10 minutes. Your final edit will take a few more minutes.

COMPUTATIONAL QUESTION ANSWERING TECHNIQUE

In computational problems, you should compute partial answers as you study the question. Label and organize what you will use as backup for your final answer. For example, in an "earnings per share" problem, you might determine the average number of shares outstanding, the effect of outstanding options and warrants on both earnings and average shares outstanding, the effect of preferred dividends on net income, and so on. Also, whenever a business transaction is described, you should write down the journal entry to record it. Making T-accounts and journal entries may help you recall some concepts.

The suggested steps for the computational question answering technique are listed below. These steps are very similar to those for essay questions. Only steps 6 and 7 below differ from the essay question answering technique:

1. **Gain an overview of the question.**
2. **Understand the requirements.**
3. **Mentally prepare a "to do" list.**
4. **Focus your knowledge on the question.**
5. **Read the question slowly and carefully.**
6. **Compute partial answers.**
7. **Visualize and organize your answer.**
8. **Write your answer.**
9. **Read the requirements again.**
10. **Edit and reread.**

Recall that when studying essay questions you wrote down gradable concepts as you thought of them (step 6) and reorganized the concepts before you drafted your answer (step 7). In place of these two steps when studying through quantitative questions, you should prepare partial solutions.

MULTIPLE-CHOICE QUESTION ANSWERING TECHNIQUE

Multiple-choice questions are conceptual or computational. When computational, adapt the computational problem answering technique discussed above in conjunction with the following steps.

1. **Budget your time.**

   We make this point with emphasis. Just as you should fill up your gas tank prior to reaching empty, you should finish your exam before time expires.

   a. Calculate the time allowed for each multiple-choice question after you have allocated exam time to the other overall questions on the exam; e.g., if one overall question consists of 20 multiple-choice questions and is allocated 40 minutes on your exam, you should spend a little under 2 minutes per multiple-choice question (always budget extra time for transferring answers to answer sheets, interruptions, etc.).

   b. Before beginning a series of multiple-choice questions, write the starting time on the exam near the first multiple-choice question.

   c. As you work through the multiple-choice questions, check your time; e.g., assuming the above time allocation of 40 minutes for 20 questions, if you have worked five multiple-choice questions in 9 minutes, you are fine, but if you have spent 11 minutes on five questions, you need to speed up.

2. **Answer the questions in chronological order.**

   a. Do **not** agonize over any one question. Stay within your time budget.
   b. Mark any unanswered questions with a big **?** and return to them later if time allows.

3. **For each question**

   a. **Cover up the answer choices** with your hand or a piece of scratch paper. Do not allow the answer choices to affect your reading of the question.

      1) For example, if four answer choices are presented, three of them are incorrect. They are called **distractors** for a very good reason.

   b. **Read the question** stem carefully (the part of the question that precedes the answer choices) to determine the precise requirement.

      1) You may wish to underline or circle key language or data in the stem.

      2) Focusing on what is required enables you to ignore extraneous information and to proceed directly to determining the correct answer.

         a) Be especially careful to note when the requirement is an **exception**; e.g., "None of the following items is deductible in calculating taxable income **except**:"

   c. **Determine the correct answer** before looking at the answer choices.

      1) By adhering to the steps above, you know what is required and which are the relevant facts.

d. **Read the answer choices** with close attention.

1) Even if answer (a) appears to be the correct choice, do **not** skip the remaining answer choices. Answer (b), (c), or (d) may even be better.

2) Treat each choice as a true-false question. Consider marking a T or F next to each answer choice as you analyze it.

e. **Select the best answer**. Circle the most likely or best answer choice on the test paper. If you are uncertain, you must decide whether to guess.

1) Most examinations do not penalize guessing because the score is determined by the number of correct responses. In this situation, you should answer every question.

2) When a subtraction from the total of correct answers **is** made for incorrectly answered questions (and no subtraction for unanswered questions), guessing is penalized. Thus, you must decide whether the payoff outweighs the risk of guessing.

4. After you have answered all the questions, **transfer your answers to the answer sheet** (see sample answer sheet on page 62).

a. Do this step after completing all multiple-choice questions.

b. Make sure you are within your time budget so that you will be able to perform this vital step in an unhurried manner.

c. Do not wait to transfer answers until the very end of the exam session when you may run out of time.

d. Double-check that you have transferred the answers correctly; e.g., recheck every fifth or tenth answer from your test paper to your answer sheet.

CHAPTER RECAP

This chapter has suggested control systems for your exam preparation and for answering individual questions/problems. Establish and maintain control! Modify your implicit and explicit control systems as appropriate.

Go on to Chapter 4, Writing the CMA Exam, to help you develop control over your examination execution. PASS THE EXAM!

SCANTRON® FORM NO. 2409-ICMA

ENTER CANDIDATE I.D. NUMBER

50	0	0	0	0
55	1	1	1	1
60	2	2	2	2
65	3	3	3	3
70	4	4	4	4
75	5	5	5	5
80	6	6	6	6
85	7	7	7	7
90	8	8	8	8
95	9	9	9	9

1 2 3 4 ENTER EXAMINATION PART NUMBER

KEY

1 a b c d e
2 a b c d e
3 a b c d e
4 a b c d e
5 a b c d e
6 a b c d e
7 a b c d e
8 a b c d e
9 a b c d e
10 a b c d e
11 a b c d e
12 a b c d e
13 a b c d e
14 a b c d e
15 a b c d e
16 a b c d e
17 a b c d e
18 a b c d e
19 a b c d e
20 a b c d e
21 a b c d e
22 a b c d e
23 a b c d e
24 a b c d e
25 a b c d e
26 a b c d e
27 a b c d e
28 a b c d e
29 a b c d e
30 a b c d e
31 a b c d e
32 a b c d e
33 a b c d e
34 a b c d e
35 a b c d e
36 a b c d e
37 a b c d e
38 a b c d e
39 a b c d e
40 a b c d e
41 a b c d e
42 a b c d e
43 a b c d e
44 a b c d e
45 a b c d e

← FEED THIS DIRECTION

1592-C C1010-5 4 3 2 1

CERTIFIED MANAGEMENT ACCOUNTANT EXAMINATION

SOLUTION PAGE NO. 1

INSTRUCTIONS

THIS ANSWER SHEET IS A STANDARD FORM THAT IS USED FOR THE MULTIPLE CHOICE ITEMS ON THE CMA EXAMINATION. PLEASE COMPLETE THE FORM AS INDICATED BELOW. BE SURE TO BLACKEN THE APPROPRIATE SPACES WITH A SOFT LEAD (#2) PENCIL. MAKE YOUR MARKS HEAVY AND BLACK. ERASE COMPLETELY ANY MARKS IN SPACES YOU WISH TO CHANGE AND DO NOT MAKE ANY STRAY MARKS ON THE FORM.

1. CODE YOUR CANDIDATE I.D. NUMBER IN THE FIVE BOXES AT THE TOP OF THE COLUMN BY WRITING THE FIRST TWO DIGITS IN THE LEFTHAND BOX AND THE LAST FOUR DIGITS IN THE NEXT FOUR BOXES. THEN BLACKEN THE APPROPRIATE SPACE UNDER EACH BOX FOR THE DIGITS WHICH APPEAR IN THE BOX. PLEASE BE ACCURATE IN ENTERING YOUR CANDIDATE I.D. NUMBER BECAUSE IT IS USED FOR COMPUTER SCORING.

   EXAMPLE:

50	9	1	0	9
■	0	0	■	0
55	1	■	1	1
60	2	2	2	2
65	3	3	3	3
70	4	4	4	4
75	5	5	5	5
80	6	6	6	6
85	7	7	7	7
90	8	8	8	8
95	■	9	9	■

2. ENTER IN THE BOX ON THE PART NUMBER LINE THE EXAMINATION PART NUMBER TO WHICH THIS ANSWER SHEET APPLIES (1, 2, 3, OR 4) AND BLACKEN THE APPROPRIATE SPACE TO THE LEFT OF THE BOX.

3. THIS STANDARD FORM MAY CONTAIN MORE NUMBERED ANSWER LINES THAN ITEMS ON THE EXAMINATION. PLEASE BE SURE THAT YOU USE THE NUMBERED ANSWER LINE ON THIS FORM WHICH CORRESPONDS TO THE NUMBER OF THE MULTIPLE CHOICE ITEM IN THE EXAMINATION BOOKLET.

IMPORTANT REMINDER

- USE SOFT LEAD (#2) PENCIL
- BLACKEN APPROPRIATE SPACES COMPLETELY
- MAKE NO STRAY MARKS
- ERASE COMPLETELY TO CHANGE AN ANSWER
- EXAMPLE 101: a b ■ d e

CHAPTER FOUR
WRITING THE CMA EXAM

This chapter suggests procedures that constitute a control system to help **you** maximize **your** exam score. As in preparing for the exam and answering questions, you must be in control. Do not go to the site unprepared and without a plan for taking the exam.

CMA EXAMINATION CHECKLIST

1. **Apply** for membership in the IMA and for admission to the CMA program by March 1 for the June exam or September 1 for the December exam (see Chapter 1, page 12).
2. **Register** to take the desired parts of the exam using the examination registration form (see page 16 and send it with your application to the ICMA. For subsequent exams (if you do not pass all four parts the first time), the ICMA will send forms automatically. The ICMA wants candidates to register by March 1 for the June exam and September 1 for the December exam (April 1 and October 1, respectively, for continuing candidates).
   a. As soon as your examination location is confirmed by the ICMA (approximately 3 weeks prior to the examination date), make travel and lodging reservations.
3. Acquire your study materials (see Chapter 1). Rely on *CMA Review* until you determine that you need to locate, borrow, or purchase additional materials.
4. Plan your preparation process (see Chapter 3).
5. Find suitable study sites.
6. Prepare for success!
7. If necessary, periodically review, reassess, and revise your study plan.
8. Recognize that orderly, controlled preparation builds confidence, reduces anxiety, and produces success!
9. PASS THE EXAMINATION (study this chapter)!

LOGISTICAL AND HEALTH CONCERNS

As soon as the ICMA notifies you of the location of the examination, find suitable quarters at a hotel within walking distance of both the site and restaurants, if possible. Try to avoid being dependent on a car, parking spaces, etc., during the exam.

Most CMA examination sites are on university campuses. Begin by calling the student union to inquire about accommodations. Call the university's general number and ask for room reservations at the student union. If rooms are not available at the student union, ask for the office in charge of meetings, which should be able to recommend a convenient motel.

Even if the exam is being given within driving distance of your home, stay by yourself at a hotel on Tuesday and Wednesday evenings to be assured of avoiding distractions. The hotel should be soundproof and have a comfortable bed and desk suitable for study. If possible, stay at a hotel with recreational facilities you normally use, e.g., a swimming pool.

Plan to arrive at your hotel early enough Tuesday evening to be able to visit the examination site (remember, starting time is 8:00 a.m. Wednesday).

On Tuesday and Wednesday evenings, confine your study to a brief review of the major points covered in the next day's exam sessions. Concentrate on the sideheadings and key terms in *CMA Review*. For most CMA candidates, the best advice is to relax the evening before and get a good night's rest. Sleep disturbance is less likely if you follow your normal routines. However, individual tastes vary, and you should do what you know has led to exam success in the past.

Proper exercise, diet, and rest during and in the weeks before the exam are very important. High energy levels, reduced tension, and an improved attitude are among the benefits. A good aerobic fitness program, a nutritious and well-balanced diet, and a regular sleep pattern will promote your long-term emotional and physical well-being as well as contribute significantly to a favorable exam result. Of course, the use of health-undermining substances should be avoided.

EXAM PSYCHOLOGY

Plan ahead and systematically prepare. Then go to the exam and give it your best: neither you nor anyone else can expect more. Having undertaken a systematic preparation program, you will do fine.

Maintain a positive attitude and do not become depressed if you encounter difficulties either before or during the exam. An optimist will usually do better than an equally well-prepared pessimist. Remember, you have reason to be optimistic because you will be competing with many less qualified persons who have not prepared as well as you have.

CALCULATORS

Calculators **are** permitted on the CMA exam. You should be thoroughly experienced in the operations of your calculator. Make sure it has fresh batteries just prior to the examination. Consider bringing a backup calculator with you. Nonconforming calculators will be disallowed.

1. Only simple six-function calculators are permitted (i.e., addition, subtraction, multiplication, division, square root, percent).
2. Calculator instruction books are **not** permitted.
3. The calculator must be small, quiet, and battery- or solar-powered so it will not be distracting to other candidates.
4. The calculator may have a memory. However, the memory must be temporary and erase when the memory is cleared or the calculator is turned off.
5. The calculator must not use any type of tape.
6. The calculator must be nonprogrammable.
7. Appropriate supporting computations and other details must be presented as part of your answers. Credit will not be awarded for numerical answers unless supporting calculations are presented.
8. The CMA examination will continue to be constructed on the basis that a calculator is not necessary for solving the problems within the estimated time.

When you encounter a question requiring calculations, present them in the text of your answers, neatly labeled. If an essay question or computational problem requires extensive calculation, use a separate answer sheet, clearly referenced to your answers, but fill in the heading as you would all other answer sheets. Label the sheet and the calculations, and number the sheet consecutively with the other answer sheets. On the CMA exam, you receive most of the credit if you have set the problem up correctly, even if you make a computational error.

PENCILS, PENS, AND OTHER MATERIALS

The ICMA recommends No. 2 lead pencils to prepare your solutions. Currently, most candidates use pencils to prepare all of their answers. The only requirement is that answers be written neatly. Thus, you must plan ahead for the type of pen or pencil that you will use for essay answers. You should be comfortable with what you choose. The output should be neat and appealing to the grader. Remember that you will be writing for several hours during each part of the exam -- four times! Thus, you must have an adequate supply of pencils (for the multiple-choice questions) and pens (if you decide to use pens for the essays). Always take extra pens and pencils.

You will be given 8½ x 14-inch lined paper and four-column accounting paper on which to prepare your answers. The lined paper has two and one-half lines to the inch. All answer sheets have the following heading:

	Candidate I.D. No. _____
CERTIFIED MANAGEMENT ACCOUNTANT EXAMINATION	Examination Part No. _____
	Question No. _____
	Solution Page No. _____

You should also have a suitable eraser and a short ruler (to draw lines). A timepiece is **absolutely essential**. You may be able to bring a thermos so you can have a quick cup of tea, coffee, etc. (even if you have to step out of the exam room). Alternatively, there may be vending machines near the examination room. The instructions to candidates make no mention as to whether food and drink are allowed. You must abide by the rules and regulations of the organization providing the exam facilities. Many good test-takers prefer not to eat or drink during an exam. The time constraint is relatively tight and spilling coffee on the exam papers is not conducive to success!

EXAMINATION TACTICS

1. Remember to bring your authorization and entry cards and a valid photo ID to the exam site. The photo ID requirement initiated with the December 1993 exam will be **strictly** enforced.
2. Arrive at the site in time to have a margin of safety. Get checked in and select a seat. One advantage of being early is that you will have your choice of seats. If you have a "lucky" seat, sit in it!
3. Dressing for exam success means emphasizing comfort, not appearance. Be prepared to adjust for changes in temperature, e.g., to remove a sweater or put on a coat.
4. Do not bring notes, this text, other books, etc., to the exam. You will only make yourself nervous and confused by trying to cram the last 5 minutes before the exam. Books are not allowed in the exam room, anyway. You should, however, bring an adequate supply of authorized items, e.g., pencils, pens, erasers, a timepiece, a ruler, and an appropriate calculator.
5. Use a clear plastic storage bag to carry your exam supplies. They come in small, sandwich size, and larger sizes. The larger size is more appropriate to handle pencils, erasers, calculators, a 6-inch straight edge, breath mints, chewing gum, candy bars, etc.
6. A supply of answer paper will be placed on the desks prior to your arrival or given to you as you enter the room. You should complete the candidate information section in the upper right-hand corner on about 15 sheets. This will save you time during the examination. Write nothing else on the answer sheets until the examination begins.
7. After the exam begins, you may wish to jot down all relevant mnemonics on an official answer sheet before you do anything to confuse yourself or forget them. Do **not** write the mnemonics down before the exam starts.

8. Read the exam instructions carefully. The cover of Part 1, as well as the remainder of the December 1995 exam booklet, is reproduced on pages 71 through 80. The instructions for the other parts of the December 1995 exam were identical, and covers of future exam booklets should be similar, if not the same.

9. Before you begin working on individual questions, take the time to gain an overview of the exam. The number of questions and estimated times are listed on the front cover. Verify that about 1½ or 2 minutes have been allocated to each multiple-choice question.

   a. Skim over the multiple-choice questions to gain an overview. When you work through them later, you will have the feeling of having seen them before. Simply beginning with the first question and working straight through the exam is unwise. Even confident test-takers may suffer a mental block at the start of the exam. It is far better to familiarize yourself with the entire exam before attempting individual solutions. Once you have gotten in the flow of the exam, your nervousness will dissipate and you will be better able to concentrate.

   b. Next, read the **requirements** of each essay question/computational problem. Without having studied the question, write down major points that initially come to mind. The purpose is to become acquainted with each question and get it started. If you spend 1 minute on each essay question, you will have all of them started plus an inventory of the exam in only 10-12 minutes.

10. Establish a time budget based on the suggested times stated in the exam booklet. If you use up the allocated time for one question, move on to another. Your score will be optimized if you provide at least a partial answer to every question. Exceeding the time budget on early questions may cause you to omit a later question. The worst possible tactic is to omit a question. Point maximization, not perfection of answers, is the appropriate goal.

11. Before selecting an alternate question or problem, study the requirements of each alternative question and begin jotting down major points. Frequently, questions that appear unsolvable at first glance are actually the easiest.

12. The next step is to determine the sequence in which questions will be answered. This decision is a matter of personal preference and should have been anticipated during your pre-examination preparations. Some candidates may prefer the simplicity of answering questions in the order in which they appear. Others may believe that answering essay questions first is the point-maximizing approach.

13. After determining the sequence in which questions will be answered, work them in that order, taking special care to read each question with care. Make a special effort to focus on the requirements because extraneous elements are often found in the facts presented in questions. For this reason, our answer explanations in Volume II highlight the requirements for multiple-choice and essay questions and computational problems.

14. Be neat. You cannot receive credit for illegible answers.

15. Be organized.

   a. For essay questions, follow your English teacher's advice! Outline your main points before drafting the essay itself. Make certain that your essay is appropriately divided into paragraphs and that your ideas are presented in a logical manner. Thus, conclusions should be supported by reasons, including authoritative references. A clear, concise, and well-written essay will earn more points than a wordy, ungrammatical, and disorganized effort with the same technical content. Your exam preparation should include considerable practice in essay question analysis and composition.

b. For computational problems, the key is to provide supporting schedules, calculations, etc., in a neat, well-organized, and clearly labeled manner. If the grader can easily trace the processes by which you derived an answer, the effects of arithmetic errors will be minimized.

c. For multiple-choice questions, you must also adopt a logical and systematic procedure that you have practiced beforehand. Some candidates, for example, may prefer a process-of-elimination method, but others may choose to anticipate the answer before reading the choices.

Candidate I.D. No. ______________

CERTIFIED MANAGEMENT ACCOUNTANT EXAMINATION
DECEMBER 1995

Examination Summary Sheet
Part 1

Attach this sheet on the front of your solutions with the paper clip that has been supplied. Check the appropriate boxes below and **be sure that you have submitted solution page(s) for each question that you checked as having been worked.** Enter Examination Part Number 4, your Candidate I.D. Number, and Question Number where indicated on each solution page. Number all solution pages for this examination part in consecutive order on the line provided on each solution page. NOTE: The multiple-choice answer sheet for Question Number 1 is solution page one (1).

Question No.	Worked	Omitted
1		
2		
3		
4		
5		
6		
7		
8		

16. Complete your Examination Summary Sheet, which simply indicates the problems you answered. The format of the summary sheet is presented on the opposite page.
    a. The form provides a column for omitted questions. You should **not** omit any required questions, however. Only optional questions beyond the number required should be omitted.
    b. Note the instruction to place the summary sheet on top of your numbered answer sheets. The multiple-choice answer sheet is page 1.
17. As the instructions on the cover of each exam booklet indicate, each answer should begin on a separate page. At the conclusion of the exam (5 minutes before the end of the exam), you should carefully clean up your work:
    a. Put your exam papers in order.
    b. The answers to questions should be in numerical order.
    c. The sheets for each answer should be in order.
    d. The multiple-choice answer sheet is page 1 and is so numbered.
    e. Number all of the other answer sheets consecutively.
    f. On each sheet also indicate the total number of sheets submitted, e.g., "1 of 18," "2 of 18," etc., if 18 answer sheets are being submitted.
    g. Use the paper clips provided by the proctors to clip your answers together covered by the Examination Summary Sheet.
    h. Plan to have the entire process completed when the time limit is up.
18. Recap. The previous 17 points suggest a plan/control system for writing the CMA examination. Restudy them, personalize them, and make notes on **what you plan to do to write your CMA exam.** Obtain a copy of a CMA booklet and practice your exam writing technique. Pages 71 through 80 contain a reproduction of Part 1 of the December 1995 exam with the correct answers noted for the multiple-choice questions. Remember PRACTICE MAKES PERFECT.

TIME ALLOCATION ON REVISED CMA EXAM

On recent exams, the norm has been 30 multiple-choice questions in 60 minutes followed by six 30-minute questions/problems for a total of 240 minutes.

OPTIONAL QUESTIONS

The ICMA has affirmed its intention to present optional questions, but they probably will not be used as consistently as in the past. A major reason for their use was to provide broad exam coverage. But now coverage is controlled by the content specification outlines (see next page).

The typical optional question will probably be on the same major topic as one of the mandatory questions to ensure compliance with the content specification outlines. Also, two rather than the traditional three choices are likely to be provided. This reduction is intended to diminish the incremental preparation and grading costs of optional questions.

IMPLICATIONS OF NEW ICMA CONTENT SPECIFICATION OUTLINES

The ICMA has specified the following topical coverage for each examination:

Part 1: Economics, Finance, and Management

A. Microeconomics -- 10%-15%
B. Macroeconomics and International Economics -- 10%-15%
C. Institutional Environment of Business -- 10%-15%
D. Working Capital Management -- 10%-15%
E. Long-term Finance and Capital Structure -- 10%-15%
F. Organization and Management Theory -- 20%-30%
G. Communication -- 10%-15%

Part 2: Financial Accounting and Reporting

A. Financial Statements -- 30%-40%
B. Reporting Requirements -- 30%-40%
C. Analysis of Accounts and Statements -- 15%-20%
D. External Auditing -- 10%-15%

Part 3: Management Reporting, Analysis, and Behavioral Issues

A. Cost Measurement -- 20%-30%
B. Planning -- 20%-30%
C. Control and Performance Evaluation -- 20%-30%
D. Behavioral Issues -- 20%-30%

Part 4: Decision Analysis and Information Systems

A. Decision Theory and Operational Decision Analysis -- 20%-30%
B. Investment Decision Analysis -- 20%-30%
C. Quantitative Methods for Decision Analysis -- 10%-15%
D. Information Systems -- 20%-30%
E. Internal Auditing -- 10%-15%

Each part totals 80% to 120% if the minimum and maximum percentages are added, except Part 2 (85% to 115%). In a 4-hour session, each 30 minutes is about 12.5% of the effort for that part. Hence, the expected 30 multiple-choice questions (1 hour) should represent about 25% of that session's total points. You can also expect at least one essay question (or about 15 multiple-choice) on each major topic in the listing presented above.

Blended questions, those testing two or possibly more major topics, are expected to cover 15% to 20% of the content of the examination. For some subjects, one 30-minute essay may provide too little coverage of a topic (12.5%), but two may be excessive (25%). Alternatively, the multiple-choice questions may, and probably will, test more than one topic.

Note: Gleim Publications does not attempt to allocate pages or number of questions according to the ICMA content specification outlines. We select and design our outlines and sample CMA questions to help candidates pass the CMA exam, not to conform to the above listing.

The Certified Management Accountant Examination is given by the Institute of Certified Management Accountants, 10 Paragon Drive, Montvale, New Jersey 07645-1759. The CMA Program is endorsed by the Institute of Management Accountants.

EXAMINATION FOR PART 1
ECONOMICS, FINANCE, AND MANAGEMENT

Thursday, December 7, 1995; 8:00 a.m. to 12:00 noon

	Estimated Time	Point Values
Section A (All Questions Are Required)		
Number 1	60 minutes	25 points
Number 2	30 minutes	13 points
Number 3	30 minutes	12 points
Number 4	30 minutes	12 points
Number 5	30 minutes	12 points
Number 6	30 minutes	13 points
Section B (Answer Only One of the Two Questions)		
Number 7 or Number 8	30 minutes	13 points
	240 minutes	100 points

INSTRUCTIONS TO CANDIDATES

1. Place your Candidate I.D. Number at the top of each solution page you submit. Begin the answer to each question on a new sheet of paper. Arrange your answers in the numerical order of the questions, and then number all solution pages in order. The multiple choice answer sheet provided for Question Number 1 is to be considered solution page one (1). Indicate the questions worked and omitted on the Examination Summary Sheet provided, and place it on top of your solution pages.
2. Record your answers to Question Number 1 on the multiple choice answer sheet provided. Because these objective items are machine graded, comments and calculations in support of your answers will not be considered.
3. Answers to numerical and discussion questions should be well organized and well written. Illegible writing and lack of clear exposition will influence the evaluation by the examiners.
4. Appropriate schedules and calculations in support of numerical answers must be presented and referenced clearly to your answers. Credit will not be awarded for numerical answers for which there are no supporting calculations.

THE EVALUATION OF YOUR ANSWERS WILL BE ADVERSELY AFFECTED IF YOU DO NOT FOLLOW THESE INSTRUCTIONS.

Part 1 - CMA Examination - 12/95

SECTION A
All questions are required.

QUESTION NUMBER 1
25 points - Estimated time 60 minutes
(A required question)

INSTRUCTIONS: Use the multiple choice answer sheet provided to record your answers to this question. Be sure to enter your Candidate I.D. Number and Examination Part Number 1 on the multiple choice answer sheet. Select the **BEST** answer for each of the items below, and then record your answer on the multiple choice answer sheet by blackening the appropriate answer space with a soft lead (#2) pencil. Mark **ONLY ONE ANSWER** for each item. Your grade will be determined from your total of correct answers.

Sample Item:

101. The return paid for the use of borrowed capital is referred to as
   a. cash dividends.
   b. stock dividends.
   c. interest.
   d. principal payment.
   e. capital distribution.

Answer Sheet:

101. a. ::::::: b. ::::::: c. ████ d. ::::::: e. :::::::

Answer the Following Items:

1. The Stewart Co. uses the Economic Order Quantity (EOQ) model for inventory management. A decrease in which one of the following variables would increase the EOQ?
   a. Annual sales.
   b. Cost per order.
   c. Safety stock level.
   d. Carrying costs.
   e. Quantity demanded.

2. The working capital financing policy that subjects the firm to the **greatest** risk of being unable to meet the firm's maturing obligations is the policy that finances
   a. fluctuating current assets with long-term debt.
   b. permanent current assets with long-term debt.
   c. permanent current assets with short-term debt.
   d. fluctuating current assets with short-term debt.
   e. all current assets with long-term debt.

3. Average daily cash outflows are $3 million for Evans Inc. A new cash management system can add two days to the disbursement schedule. Assuming Evans earns 10 percent on excess funds, how much should the firm be willing to pay per year for this cash management system?
   a. $6,000,000.
   b. $3,000,000.
   c. $1,500,000.
   d. $600,000.
   e. $150,000.

4. The average collection period for a firm measures the number of days
   a. after a typical credit sale is made until the firm receives the payment.
   b. it takes a typical check to "clear" through the banking system.
   c. beyond the end of the credit period before a typical customer payment is received.
   d. before a typical account becomes delinquent.
   e. in the inventory cycle.

5. When the Economic Order Quantity (EOQ) model is used for a firm which manufactures its inventory, ordering costs consist primarily of
   a. insurance and taxes.
   b. obsolescence and deterioration.
   c. storage and handling.
   d. production set-up.
   e. cost of funds.

6. Jackson Distributors sells to retail stores on credit terms of 2/10, net 30. Daily sales average 150 units at a price of $300 each. Assuming that all sales are on credit and 60 percent of customers take the discount and pay on Day 10 while the rest of the customers pay on Day 30, the amount of Jackson's accounts receivable is
   a. $1,350,000.
   b. $990,000.
   c. $900,000.
   d. $810,000.
   e. $450,000.

7. Which one of the following statements concerning cash discounts is **correct**?
   a. The cost of not taking a 2/10, net 30 cash discount is usually less than the prime rate.
   b. With trade terms of 2/15, net 60, if the discount is not taken, the buyer receives 45 days of free credit.
   c. The cost of not taking the discount is higher for terms of 2/10, net 60 than for 2/10, net 30.
   d. If a firm purchases $1,000 of goods on terms of 1/10, net 30 and pays within the discount period, the amount paid would be $900.
   e. The cost of not taking a cash discount is generally higher than the cost of a bank loan.

Part 1 - Economics, Finance, and Management - 12/95

8. Shown below is a forecast of sales for Cooper Inc. for the first four months of 1996 (all amounts are in thousands of dollars).

	1996			
	January	February	March	April
Cash sales	$ 15	$ 24	$18	$14
Sales on credit	100	120	90	70

On average, 50 percent of credit sales are paid for in the month of sale, 30 percent in the month following the sale, and the remainder is paid two months after the month of sale. Assuming there are no bad debts, the expected cash inflow for Cooper in March is
   a. $138,000.
   b. $122,000.
   c. $119,000.
   d. $108,000.
   e. $99,000.

9. Which one of the following financial instruments generally provides the largest source of short-term credit for small firms?
   a. Installment loans.
   b. Commercial paper.
   c. Trade credit.
   d. Mortgage bonds.
   e. Bankers' acceptances.

10. The Dixon Corporation has an outstanding one-year bank loan of $300,000 at a stated interest rate of 8 percent. In addition, Dixon is required to maintain a 20 percent compensating balance in its checking account. Assuming the company would normally maintain a zero balance in its checking account, the effective interest rate on the loan is
   a. 6.4 percent.
   b. 8.0 percent.
   c. 9.6 percent.
   d. 10.0 percent.
   e. 28.0 percent.

11. Elan Corporation is considering borrowing $100,000 from a bank for one year at a stated interest rate of 9 percent. What is the effective interest rate to Elan if this borrowing is in the form of a discounted note?
   a. 8.10 percent.
   b. 9.00 percent.
   c. 9.81 percent.
   d. 9.89 percent.
   e. 10.00 percent.

12. When managing cash and short-term investments, a corporate treasurer is primarily concerned with
   a. maximizing rate of return.
   b. minimizing taxes.
   c. investing in Treasury bonds since they have no default risk.
   d. investing in common stock due to the dividend exclusion for federal income tax purposes.
   e. liquidity and safety.

13. Edwards Manufacturing Corporation uses the standard Economic Order Quantity (EOQ) model. If the EOQ for Product A is 200 units and Edwards maintains a 50-unit safety stock for the item, what is the **average** inventory of Product A?
   a. 250 units.
   b. 150 units.
   c. 125 units.
   d. 100 units.
   e. 50 units.

14. Foster Inc. is considering implementing a lock-box collection system at a cost of $80,000 per year. Annual sales are $90 million, and the lock-box system will reduce collection time by 3 days. If Foster can invest funds at 8 percent, should it use the lock-box system? Assume a 360-day year.
   a. Yes, producing savings of $140,000 per year.
   b. Yes, producing savings of $60,000 per year.
   c. No, producing a loss of $20,000 per year.
   d. No, producing a loss of $60,000 per year.
   e. No, producing a loss of $140,000 per year.

15. Which one of the following provide a spontaneous source of financing for a firm?
   a. Accounts payable.
   b. Mortgage bonds.
   c. Accounts receivable.
   d. Debentures.
   e. Preferred stock.

16. A firm's target or optimal capital structure is consistent with which one of the following?
   a. Maximum earnings per share.
   b. Minimum cost of debt.
   c. Minimum risk.
   d. Minimum cost of equity.
   e. Minimum weighted average cost of capital.

Part 1 - CMA Examination - 12/95

The Following Data Apply to Items 17-19.

Number of Workers	Total Product Units	Average Selling Price
10	20	$50.00
11	25	49.00
12	28	47.50

17. The marginal physical product when one worker is added to a team of 10 workers is
    a. 1 unit.
    b. 8 units.
    c. 5 units.
    d. 2 units.
    e. 25 units.

18. The marginal revenue per unit when one worker is added to a team of 11 workers is
    a. $35.00.
    b. $225.00.
    c. $105.00.
    d. $42.00.
    e. $47.50.

19. The marginal revenue product when one worker is added to a team of 11 workers is
    a. $42.00.
    b. $225.00.
    c. $105.00.
    d. $2,940.00.
    e. $47.50.

20. With respect to federal antitrust laws, regulated industries are
    a. completely exempt.
    b. covered as determined by statute and the courts.
    c. covered as determined by the Department of Justice.
    d. covered to the same extent as any other industry.
    e. covered as determined by the applicable regulatory agency.

21. Social regulation is often criticized by industry as inefficient. Firms perceive this inefficiency to be a result of
    a. the failure to consider the marginal benefits relative to the marginal costs.
    b. lenient enforcement policies.
    c. concern for the quality of life but not the quality of products.
    d. the use of the internal revenue tax code instead of strict compliance penalties.
    e. the use of flexible rather than rigid standards by government officials.

22. Which one of the following transactions would be considered a violation of the Robinson-Patman Act?
    a. The sale of goods of like quality at different prices to two different wholesalers, both of whom are located outside the United States.
    b. The sale of goods of like quality within the United States at different prices based on cost differences related to the method of delivery.
    c. The sale of goods of like quality within the United States at different prices to two different wholesalers; all parties are located within the same state.
    d. The sale of goods of like quality within the United States but across state lines at different prices to two different wholesalers in the same geographic area.
    e. The sale of goods of different quality and insignificantly different quantities to two or more wholesalers at different prices.

23. Which one of the following examples of corporate behavior would **most** clearly represent a violation of the Sherman Act?
    a. A retailer offers quantity discounts to large institutional buyers.
    b. The members of a labor union meet and agree not to work for a specific firm unless the starting wage is at least $10 per hour.
    c. Two firms that are in different, unrelated industries merge.
    d. A frozen yogurt producer advertises falsely that its product has "almost no fat."
    e. Two firms in the same industry agree in a telephone conversation to submit identical bids on a government contract.

24. The Clayton Act, as amended, prohibits all of the following **except**
    a. tying contracts that require a customer who is buying one product to buy a related but perhaps unwanted product.
    b. price discrimination by sellers.
    c. interlocking directorates in large competing organizations.
    d. unfair and deceptive business practices, such as misleading advertising.
    e. companies from merging if competition is substantially lessened.

25. The acquisition of a retail shoe store by a shoe manufacturer is an example of
    a. vertical integration.
    b. a conglomerate.
    c. market extension.
    d. product extension.
    e. horizontal integration.

Part 1 - Economics, Finance, and Management - 12/95

26. Blue sky laws are
    a. federal laws that make it unlawful to use deceptive practices in the sale of securities.
    b. federal laws that limit the amount of air pollution in a specific geographic area.
    c. state laws that regulate the sale of securities.
    d. state laws that regulate the environment.
    e. state laws that prohibit the sale of alcohol on Sunday.

27. Which one of the following federal acts requires unions to retain financial records and submit financial reports to federal authorities?
    a. Taft-Hartley Act of 1947.
    b. Wagner Act of 1935.
    c. Securities and Exchange Act of 1934.
    d. Landrum-Griffin Act of 1959.
    e. Norris-LaGuardia Act of 1932.

28. Which one of the following is **not** exempted from federal antitrust regulation?
    a. Labor unions.
    b. Intrastate commerce.
    c. Patents and copyrights.
    d. Telecommunications companies.
    e. Professional baseball.

29. Listed below are five federal agencies.
    I. Food and Drug Administration.
    II. National Highway Traffic Safety Administration.
    III. Consumer Product Safety Commission.
    IV. Occupational Safety and Health Administration.
    V. Environmental Protection Agency.

Which of the above agencies are considered social agencies?
    a. I, II, and IV only.
    b. I and II only.
    c. I, II, and III only.
    d. II, III, and IV only.
    e. all of the agencies.

30. The two major functions of the Federal Trade Commission are
    a. antitrust actions and the regulation of foreign trade.
    b. import quality inspections and anti-dumping measures.
    c. antitrust actions and consumer protection.
    d. price discrimination and unfair trade practices.
    e. import quota regulation and consumer advocacy.

QUESTION NUMBER 2
13 points - Estimated time 30 minutes
(A required question)

The Biller Co., a manufacturer of kitchen cabinets, has grown rapidly over the last five years and has expanded its operations from a local to a national organization. Much of the company's success is the result of cost advantages due to a management style that requires constant reviews of operations to insure that the company operates at peak efficiency.

Melanie Hay, president, has recently eliminated several tiers of management to change from a hierarchical to a flatter organization. Also, Hay has reorganized Biller into several self-managed project teams.

REQUIRED:

A. Discuss the likely effects that Biller Co.'s change to a flatter organizational structure **and** the implementation of self-managed project teams will have on
1. management planning and control.
2. the roles of managers, including interpersonal, informational, and decision making roles.
3. human resources, including recruitment and training.

B. Explain the likely effect that Biller Co.'s change to a flatter organizational structure coupled with the implementation of self-managed project teams will have on employee morale. Give at least three reasons for this effect.

Part 1 - CMA Examination - 12/95

QUESTION NUMBER 3
12 points - Estimated time 30 minutes
(A required question)

Digital Network Incorporated (DNI) is a relatively new orporation in the high-growth area of computer network ardware and software. The company has been profitable or the past three years. Up to now, the policy of the oard of Directors has been to reinvest all profits and not ay dividends on its 10,000 outstanding shares of comon stock. However, the Board plans to reconsider this olicy and has asked the chief financial officer of the ompany, Nancy Brown, to prepare a report analyzing lternative policies. This report is to discuss the factors nat should be considered when determining a dividend olicy, and quantify the financial impact of various diviend policies on the value of the firm.

EQUIRED:

A. Discuss at least four factors that the Board of irectors at Digital Network Incorporated should consid- as it develops a dividend policy.

B. According to the dividend model assumptions of odigliani and Miller (MM), the effect that dividends have the value of a firm primarily depends on whether or ot the company and/or shareholders are subject to xes.

Assume Digital Network Incorporated (DNI) earned 100,000 net income before dividends and is subject to corporate income tax rate of 40 percent. Assume furer that all of DNI's stock is held by individuals subject an individual income tax rate of 30 percent, the maxum capital gains tax rate is 20 percent, and DNI has a vidend payout of $5.00 per share.

Using the MM model, discuss and calculate the posble effects a dividend payment could have on the shareolders' valuation of DNI, assuming a business environent

1. without taxes.
2. with both corporate and individual taxation.

C. In a business environment without taxes, disss the effect on the shareholders' valuation of the firm Digital Network Incorporated chooses to pay dividends ther than invest in capital projects that exceed the areholders' required rate of return.

QUESTION NUMBER 4
12 Points - Estimated time 30 minutes
(A required question)

Frontier Development Inc. develops and markets a wide variety of products. The operational side of the firm is structured by project. A project encompasses the entire life cycle of a product, beginning with research and development, through production and actual sale. Currently, the firm has 37 projects in varying stages of development or in production. A manager is assigned to a project after presenting a proposal for it to the firm's management committee. Members of the management committee include the chief operating officer, chief financial officer, human resources director, chief engineer, chief logistics director, purchasing director, legal counsel, and two individuals from outside the firm.

Frontier has been very successful, and a number of the projects have resulted in new and highly successful products. However, there have been a number of projects that have failed. Mark Janowski, Frontier's founder and chairman, has become increasingly concerned about the time it takes to identify a failing project. Janowski is concerned that there is a waste of resources, and attributes this problem to the lack of an effective budgeting and monitoring program.

Janowski recognizes that it is difficult to budget and monitor progress on new projects without an historical track record. Historically, the budgeting and performance measurements for projects have been limited to an accumulation of direct costs and a single company-wide overhead rate. The management committee reviews these figures on a quarterly basis and decides whether or not to continue the projects. Harry Crown, budget director, has announced his retirement and will be replaced with an experienced budget director, Selena MacElroy. After familiarizing herself with the company and the projects, she has recommended to Janowski that the company adopt a management by objectives (MBO) program.

REQUIRED:

A. In general,

1. define and describe the basic characteristics of a management by objectives (MBO) program.
2. give at least three advantages to an organization that adopts an MBO program.
3. give at least three disadvantages to an organization that adopts an MBO program.

B. Describe the obstacles Frontier Development Inc. may encounter when implementing an MBO program.

C. Determine whether or not an MBO program will assist Frontier Development Inc. in its operations. Give at least two reasons for your conclusion.

Part 1 - Economics, Finance, and Management - 12/95

QUESTION NUMBER 5
12 points - Estimated time 30 minutes
(A required question)

As defined by economists, cost equals the value of inputs used by a firm to produce its output. To achieve and maintain success in the marketplace, a firm needs to thoroughly understand its costs to develop effective pricing strategies. Relevant and reliable cost information is critical to capital investment decisions and the allocation of corporate resources. A firm should analyze its cost structure over the long run as well as the short run in order to plan for future success in the marketplace.

REQUIRED:

A. What distinguishes a firm's cost structure in th short run from its cost structure in the long run?

B. Define the following economic terms.
1. Law of diminishing returns.
2. Economies of scale.
3. Opportunity costs.
4. Normal profit.

C. The graph below represents a firm's long-ru average cost curve (LRAC).
1. Describe, in general, what the LRAC show about a firm.
2. Referring to the specific graph below, describ what each of the following segments represents
   1. AB.
   2. BC.
   3. CD.

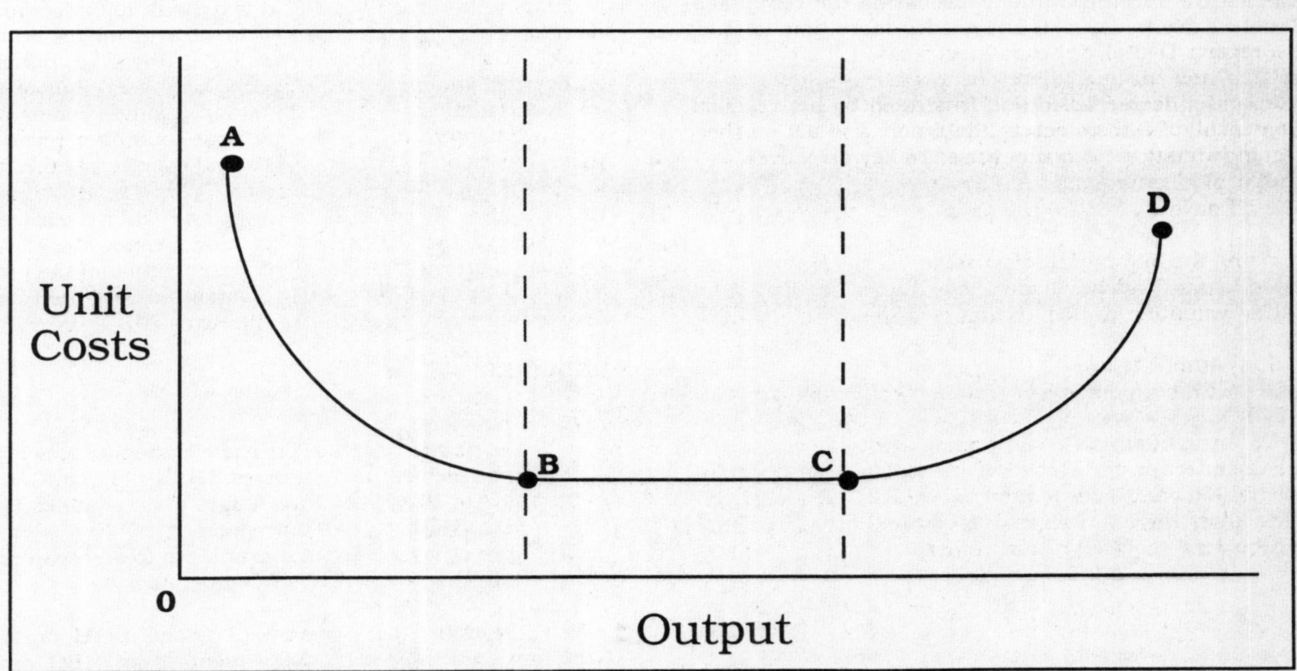

Part 1 - CMA Examination - 12/95

QUESTION NUMBER 6
13 points - Estimated time 30 minutes
(A required question)

Burt Russell is an internal auditor with the newly-formed Internal Audit Department of Scotch Insurance Company, a large multi-line insurance company located in New England and doing business in all fifty states. Russell has recently completed an operational audit of the Claims Department, which is managed by Christine Smith, a vice president with the company for over twenty years.

During the course of the audit, Russell discovered several major inefficiencies and has drafted a report suggesting improvements. Before presenting his findings to the Audit Committee of the Board of Directors, Russell wanted to review the report with Smith. Rather than sending a copy of the report to Smith, Russell decided to make a formal presentation of the findings and recommendations to Smith and her staff.

After several unsuccessful attempts to schedule a meeting, Russell suspected that Smith was trying to avoid him. When they finally did meet, Smith came alone and fifteen minutes late. During the meeting, she often seemed distracted and interrupted Russell several times to criticize his presentation and contradict his findings. She left the meeting without discussing the recommendations, only to say that she needed more time to study the report.

Russell is perplexed and frustrated by her reaction. Convincing Smith to accept the report and act on these recommendations is one of Russell's key objectives.

REQUIRED:

A. Effective communication is defined as the process of transmitting information in a way so that the message received is as equivalent as possible to the intended message. In general, identify

1. at least four barriers to effective communication.
2. at least four techniques used in effective communication.

B. Relating to the specific situation at Scotch Insurance Company, discuss at least two barriers to effective communication between Burt Russell and Christine Smith. Include in your discussion, recommendations to Russell that would help him more effectively communicate his message to Smith and convince her to accept the report and act on the recommendations.

Part 1 - Economics, Finance, and Management - 12/95

SECTION B
Answer one question from Questions 7 and 8.
If both questions are ansered, only the first one will be graded.

QUESTION NUMBER 7
13 points - Estimated time 30 minutes
(An alternate with Question 8)

U.S. companies that compete in the global market are affected by the fluctuations of the U.S. dollar as it appreciates or depreciates in value relative to other currencies in the world market. Although international factors and other currency fluctuations affect the value of the dollar, this value can also be controlled by the actions taken by the Board of Governors of the Federal Reserve System, the U.S. central bank. The functions performed by the Federal Reserve System are: (1) controller of the U.S. money supply; (2) regulator of money markets; (3) banker to commercial member banks; and (4) bank for the U.S. government.

REQUIRED:

A. Describe the basic structure of the Federal Reserve System.

B. 1. Identify and describe the tools that the Board of Governors uses to control the money supply.
2. Explain how the Board can use the tools described in Requirement B. 1. to tighten the money supply.
3. Explain why the Board would want to create an economy with a "tight" money supply, and explain how this might affect the value of the U. S. dollar.

C. When the value of the U.S. dollar depreciates relative to other currencies, identify at least two impacts on a U.S. company that is competing globally.

Part 1 - CMA Examination - 12/95

UESTION NUMBER 8
13 points - Estimated time 30 minutes
(An alternate with Question 7)

The graph below represents the fluctuations or ycles through which our economy constantly moves. 'he long-term growth trend line for the level of business ctivity shows a stable upward direction, but it is often nterrupted by either unemployment, inflation, or both. 'hese interruptions will undoubtedly recur with irregular ut inevitable frequency in the future. Many economists elieve, however, that the economy could grow at a teady and moderate rate indefinitely without producing igher inflation or unemployment through the use of fisal policy.

In order to implement fiscal policy effectively, forecasting tools are necessary to help recognize the impending turns in the business cycle. One tool that economists use to forecast the future direction of economic activity is the composite index of leading indicators. By alerting policymakers to possible shifts in the business cycle, these leading indicators reduce the "recognition lag" associated with the implementation of fiscal policy.

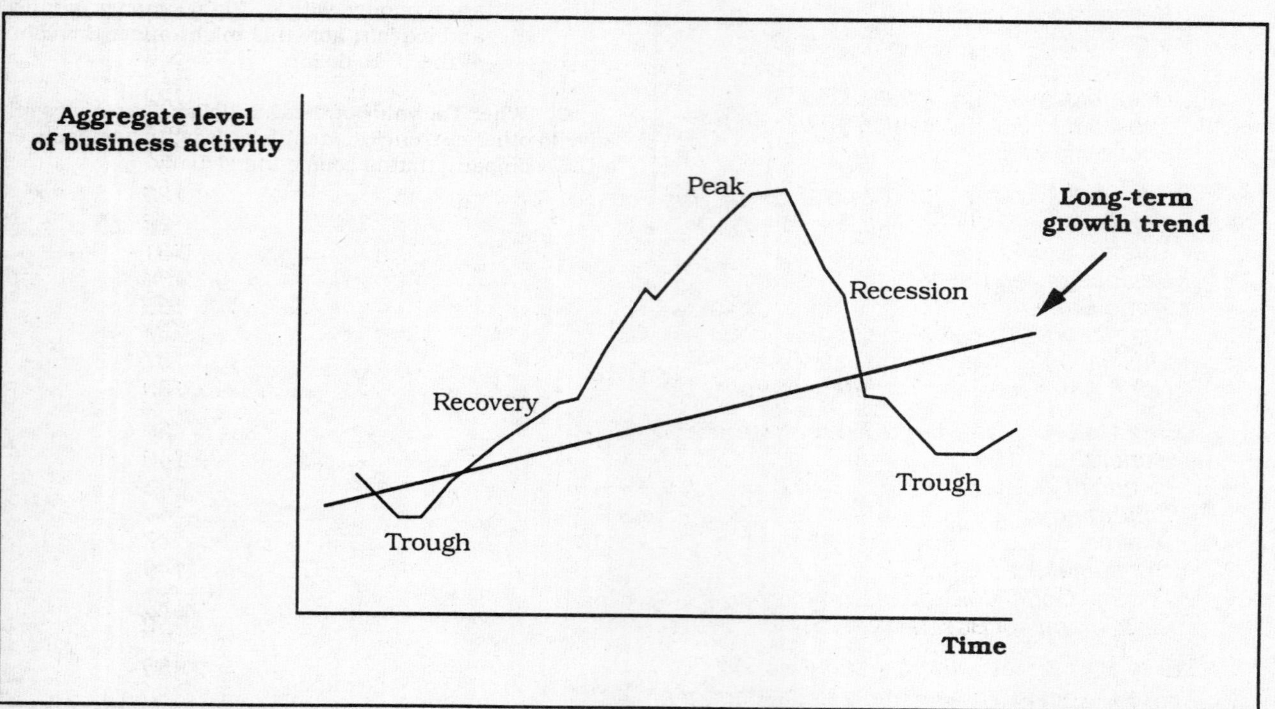

EQUIRED:

A. 1. Define fiscal policy.
2. Describe the tools used to implement fiscal policy.

B. Explain how fiscal policy could mitigate inflation d unemployment.

C. 1. Identify and explain the characteristic(s) that would qualify an economic variable to be used as a leading indicator.
2. By selecting **only two** of the three leading indicators given below, explain how each of the selected indicators might assist management in projecting business activity.
- Initial claims for unemployment insurance.
- New orders for consumer goods.
- Contracts and orders for new plant and equipment.

CHAPTER FIVE
EXAM PART 1
ECONOMICS, FINANCE, AND MANAGEMENT

This chapter covers Part 1: Economics, Finance, and Management. It consists of 10 study units numbered 1 through 10.

Study Unit 1: Microeconomics
Study Unit 2: Macroeconomics
Study Unit 3: International Economics
Study Unit 4: Institutional Environment of Business
Study Unit 5: Working Capital Finance
Study Unit 6: Capital Structure Finance
Study Unit 7: Organization Theory
Study Unit 8: Motivation and the Directing Process
Study Unit 9: Communication
Study Unit 10: Ethics and the Management Accountant

The ICMA Content Description of Part 1 follows:

A. ***Microeconomics (10% - 15%)***
Factors affecting the individual firm including demand, supply, and elasticity and their interaction; consumption of goods; production factors and their cost; market structures and pricing; various economic markets including the demand for resources, the labor market, and the capital market.

B. ***Macroeconomics and International Economics (10% - 15%)***
National income accounting, aggregate demand and supply, business cycles, fiscal and monetary policies, and other macroeconomic issues such as inflation, unemployment, and economic growth. International economics including trade policies, foreign exchange markets, and the role of U.S. business in the world economy.

C. ***Institutional Environment of Business (10% - 15%)***
Legal environment of business including the legal forms of business and the structure of government regulation; the impact on business of external forces including employee protection, antitrust policies, social legislation, and non-governmental groups such as consumer and environmental organizations, and financial institutions.

D. ***Working Capital Management (10% - 15%)***
Evaluating optimum levels of current assets and current liabilities and balancing profitability and risk; policies for the management of cash, marketable securities, accounts receivable, and inventories; short-term credit for financing current assets.

E. ***Long-Term Finance and Capital Structure (10% - 15%)***
Factors influencing the optimum capital structure including types of risk and leverage; objectives and policies of long-term financing; cost of capital; types of long-term financing instruments; dividend policies.

F. ***Organization and Management Theory (20% - 30%)***
Evolution of theory and practice; decision making in the organizational environment; planning concepts and practices; structure of organizations and their social and cultural environment; effective organization of jobs and groups. Roles and skills of managers; staffing and managing human resources; management theory and leadership styles; motivational theories and methods to influence behavior.

G. ***Communication (10% - 15%)***
Communication models; formal and informal organizational communication; deterrents to effective communication; managing communication and information content.

The ICMA has published a content specification outline for Part 1 that expands the above Content Description for Part 1.

A. ***Microeconomics (10% - 15%)***

1. *Factors affecting the individual firm*

    a. *Theory of demand*
    b. *Theory of supply*

c. Interaction of demand and supply to determine prices
d. The laws of demand and supply
e. Elasticity of demand and supply
f. Government intervention in market operations

2. Consumption of goods

a. Marginal utility theory
b. Indifference curve analysis

3. Production factors and cost functions

a. Economic costs
b. Economic profits
c. Production costs in the short run
d. Production costs in the long run
e. Economies and diseconomies of scale

4. Market structures and pricing

a. Pure competition
b. Monopoly
c. Monopolistic competition
d. Oligopoly
e. Effects of boycotts and cartels on prices and output

5. The economy as a system of markets

a. Production and demand for economic resources
b. The labor market
c. The capital market

B. **Macroeconomics and International Economics (10% - 15%)**

1. National income accounting (Gross National Product)

a. Expenditure approach
b. Income approach
c. Interpreting national income
d. Omissions from measured national income

2. National income and aggregate demand

a. Desired expenditure
b. Equilibrium national income
c. Shifts in the aggregate expenditure function
d. The multiplier effect
e. Inflation considerations

3. National income and aggregate supply

a. Aggregate supply in the short run
b. Aggregate supply in the long run

4. Business cycles

a. Nature and history of business cycles
b. Terminology used to explain business fluctuations
c. Reason for fluctuations
d. The accelerator effect
e. Theories of business cycles

5. Fiscal policy

a. Theory of fiscal policy
b. Tools of fiscal policy
c. Taxation policies

6. Money and monetary policy

a. Nature of money
b. The commercial banking system and the creation and destruction of deposits

c. Definition of the money supply and supply of and demand for money
d. Relation between money and national income
e. The central banking system and its actions to influence the money supply
f. The Federal Reserve Board and its actions to influence the money supply
g. Instruments and objectives of monetary policy

7. Issues and controversies in macroeconomics

a. Inflation
b. Employment and unemployment
c. Economic growth
d. Economic philosophies

8. International economics

a. Advantages of trade in international markets
b. Free trade and protectionism
c. Barriers in international trade
d. Nature and theory of foreign exchange
e. Role of U.S. business in the world economy

C. **Institutional Environment of Business (10% - 15%)**

1. Legal environment of business

a. Legal forms of business
b. Structure of government regulation

2. Impact on business of government intervention

a. Employee, employer, and union relations
b. Antitrust policies
c. Social legislation and government agencies

3. Non-governmental intervention

a. Consumer groups
b. Environmental groups
c. Financial institutions

D. **Working Capital Management (10% - 15%)**

1. Nature of working capital policy and management

a. Optimum level of current assets and current liabilities
b. Balancing profitability and risk
c. Types of risk

2. Cash management

a. Factors influencing the levels of cash
b. Reasons for holding cash
c. Synchronizing cash inflows and outflows
d. Methods to speed cash collections
e. Using the float
f. Compensating balances
g. Overdraft systems

3. Marketable securities

a. Factors influencing the level of marketable securities
b. Reasons for holding marketable securities
c. Strategies for holding marketable securities
d. Risk and return factors influencing the selection of marketable securities
e. Types of marketable securities

4. Accounts receivable management

a. Factors influencing the level of accounts receivable
b. Reasons for carrying accounts receivable
c. Variables and decisions regarding credit policy
d. Credit instruments

5. *Inventory management*
   a. *Factors influencing the level of inventory*
   b. *Reasons for inventory*
   c. *Costs of inventory*

6. *Short-term credit for financing current assets*
   a. *Alternative strategies for financial working capital*
   b. *Advantages and disadvantages of short-term credit*
   c. *Types of short-term credit*
   d. *Secured short-term credit*
   e. *Minimizing the cost of short-term credit*

E. ***Long-Term Finance and Capital Structure (10% - 15%)***

1. *Factors influencing the optimum capital structure*
   a. *Risk and the organization's attitude toward risk*
   b. *Operating and financial leverage*
   c. *Sales stability*
   d. *Growth rate*
   e. *Profitability*
   f. *Asset structure*
   g. *Control position of owners and management*
   h. *Management attitude and ability*
   i. *Lender and rating attitude*
   j. *Competitive position in the industry*

2. *Objectives and policies of long-term financing*
   a. *Amount and mixture of permanent assets*
   b. *Methods of financing permanent assets*
   c. *Policies to counteract risk*
   d. *Policies used to acquire/takeover firms*
   e. *Defenses to takeovers*

3. *The cost of capital*
   a. *Logic of weighted average cost of capital*
   b. *Cost of individual capital components*
   c. *Calculating the cost of capital*
   d. *Marginal cost of capital*
   e. *Models used in determining cost of capital*

4. *Types and nature of long-term financing*
   a. *Bonds*
   b. *Intermediate term loans*
   c. *Term loans*
   d. *Lease financing*
   e. *Common stock*
   f. *Preferred stock*
   g. *Convertible securities*
   h. *Stock warrants and rights*
   i. *Stock options*
   j. *Employee stock ownership plans (ESOPs)*

5. *Dividend policy*
   a. *Theory of dividend policy*
   b. *Factors which influence dividend policy*
   c. *Dividend payment procedures*
   d. *Stock repurchases*
   e. *Stock dividends and stock splits*
   f. *Automatic dividend reinvestment plans (ADRP)*

In conjunction with the long-term financing and capital structure topic, the income tax code provisions that affect financing decisions

-- Deductibility of payments for use of capital
-- After-tax cost of capital

F. *Organization and Management Theory (20% - 30%)*

1. *Evolution of theory and practice*
   a. *Classical approach to management*
   b. *Behavioral approach to management*
   c. *Changing management concepts*
2. *Decision making in the organizational environment*
   a. *Nature and process of decision making*
   b. *Techniques in group decision making*
3. *Management planning concepts and practices*
   a. *Goals and objectives*
   b. *Strategic planning*
   c. *Tactical and operational planning*
4. *Structural evolution in organizations*
   a. *Departmentalization*
   b. *Line and staff authority*
   c. *Centralization versus decentralization*
   d. *Matrix management*
5. *Social and cultural characteristics of effective organizations*
   a. *Sources of power*
   b. *Informal power and influence*
   c. *Delegation of authority*
6. *Effective organization of jobs and groups*
   a. *Nature of jobs*
   b. *Job design*
   c. *Groups and group processes*
7. *Roles and skills of managers*
   a. *Interpersonal roles*
   b. *Informational roles*
   c. *Decisional roles*
   d. *Technical and conceptual skills*
   e. *Role of management accountant in management and managing*
8. *Staffing and managing human resources*
   a. *Planning*
   b. *Recruitment*
   c. *Selection and orientation*
   d. *Training and development*
   e. *Compensation and benefits management*
   f. *Employee performance evaluation*
   g. *Transfers and terminations*
9. *Leadership theory and styles*
   a. *Theories of leadership*
   b. *Styles*
10. *Motivational theories and methods*
    a. *Content theories to motivation*
    b. *Process theories to motivation*
    c. *Reinforcement theory-organization behavior modification*
    d. *Other theories on motivation*

G. ***Communication (10% - 15%)***

1. *Communication models*
2. *Communication process*

   a. *Encoding*
   b. *Channel or media selection*
   c. *Decoding*
   d. *Feedback*

3. *Organizational communications*

   a. *Formal channels of communication*
   b. *Informal channels of communication*
   c. *Communication networks*

4. *Deterrents to effective communication*

   a. *Semantics*
   b. *Confusion*
   c. *Noise*
   d. *Listening*
   e. *Screening*
   f. *Bias*
   g. *Stereotyping*

5. *Managing communication and information content*

   a. *Elimination of deterrents to communication*
   b. *Understanding other persons' viewpoints*
   c. *Use of communication skills*

The topics and subject areas above may include ethical considerations in economics, finance and management of concern to management accountants.

Statement on Management Accounting No. 1C, Standards of Ethical Conduct for Management Accountants

-- *Competence*
-- *Confidentiality*
-- *Integrity*
-- *Objectivity*

Corporate social responsibility

The ICMA lists seven topics (A-G) and we have 10 study units. Our additional study units include an ethics study unit, a separate international economics study unit, and two study units to cover the topic of organization and management theory.

Ethics will be covered on at least two parts of each examination and will have between 30 and 60 total minutes of coverage (out of the 16 hours of testing), i.e., 3% to 6% of the total exam.

Macroeconomics and international economics are presented as a single topic by the ICMA, but we present them as separate study units.

We have chosen to divide coverage of organization and management theory into two study units:

Study Unit 7: Organization Theory
Study Unit 8: Motivation and the Directing Process

Much of this management material is covered in Part 3 in Study Units 21, 22, and 23.

The ICMA specifies that 20% to 30% of Part 3 will cover behavioral issues, but we do not present a separate study unit on this subject because it is integrated into various other major topics. Questions on behavioral issues are included with the related topics in Study Units 7, 8, 21, 22, and 23.

STUDY UNIT 1
MICROECONOMICS

INTRODUCTION

Microeconomics is the study of the individual economic units in the economy. The focus is on the consumer (as buyer of finished goods and seller of labor, entrepreneurial services, and capital) and the firm (as seller of finished goods and buyer of labor, entrepreneurial services, and capital). Microeconomics also includes the operation of markets.

Microeconomics covers 10%-15% of Part 1. The level of expertise required is that obtained from a rigorous introductory economics course.

OVERVIEW OF ECONOMICS

A. Economics is the social science addressing the allocation of scarce resources among competing or alternative ends.

1. Individuals face an economic problem when deciding how to spend limited income to maximize satisfaction.
2. The economy faces an economic problem in deciding how to allocate fixed resources (land, labor, capital, and entrepreneurial ability) to achieve maximum social welfare.

B. Economics is based on

1. The unlimited nature of human wants
2. Scarcity of resources or means to satisfy wants, i.e., the law of scarcity

C. Every economic system (capitalistic, socialistic, etc.) must answer the following questions:

1. What goods and services should be produced?
2. How much of these goods and services should be produced?
3. How should these goods and services be produced?
4. For whom should these goods and services be produced?

D. **Characteristics of Three Fundamental Economic Systems**

1. Capitalistic economies. Each economic unit (consumers, firms, resource owners) is free to pursue its own interests (sovereignty). There is private ownership of resources and firms, and freedom of choice. The what, how much, how, and for whom questions are primarily solved by a system of free markets, each with its own pricing mechanism.
2. Democratic socialist economies. Some government intervention to alter the allocation of resources is held to be beneficial. There is a mixture of private and public enterprise and decision making. The solutions to the four questions on the previous page result from government planning and regulation as well as the market system.
3. Communist economies. The state is deemed to be the best judge of the choices to be made, and industry is primarily publicly owned. The four economic questions are solved by government planning. Individual decision making plays only a small role.

E. **Macroeconomics Distinguished from Microeconomics**

1. **Macroeconomics** -- the study of economic aggregates and an overview of the economy, including levels of national income, employment, and prices and the effects of monetary and fiscal policies. Macroeconomics is covered in the next study unit.
2. **Microeconomics** -- the study of the individual economic units in the economy. Again, focus is on the consumer (as buyer of finished goods and seller of labor, entrepreneurial services, and capital) and the firm (as seller of finished goods and buyer of labor, entrepreneurial services, and capital).

DEMAND -- THE BUYER'S SIDE OF THE MARKET

A. Demand is the quantity of a good or service that consumers are willing and able to purchase at various prices during a period of time. Thus, demand is a schedule of amounts that will be purchased at various prices.

B. **The Law of Demand**. The price of a product and the quantity demanded are inversely (negatively) related; i.e., the lower the price, the higher the quantity demanded.

1. **Substitution effect**. With a price decrease, new buyers will enter the market. The good will be cheaper relative to other goods and is substituted for them.
2. **Income effect**. Individuals buy more when prices are lower.

C. The determinants of demand are variables that affect the amount of a product purchased.

1. Consumer income
   a. **Normal goods** -- commodities for which demand is positively (directly) related to income, e.g., steak, clothes, leisure time
   b. **Inferior goods** -- commodities for which demand is negatively (inversely) related to income, e.g., potatoes, bread
2. Consumer taste and preference
3. Prices of closely related goods (cross-elasticity of demand).
   a. **Substitutes**. If products A and B are substitutes, a price increase in A will generate an increase in the demand for B. For example, when beef prices rise, the demand for chicken increases.
   b. **Complements**. If products A and B are complements, a price increase in A will generate a decrease in the demand for B. For example, if the price of bread increases, the demand for jelly decreases.
4. Price expectations. Do consumers expect prices to rise or fall?

D. The demand schedule is a relationship between the prices of a commodity (on the vertical axis) and the quantity demanded at the various prices (horizontal axis), holding other determinants of the quantity demanded constant.

1. A movement along an existing demand curve occurs when the price is changed.
2. **Demand curve shift**. A change in quantity demanded must be distinguished from a shift in the demand curve itself. The latter occurs when one of the determinants changes. The graph illustrates an increase in demand; i.e., the demand curve shifts from D to D_1.

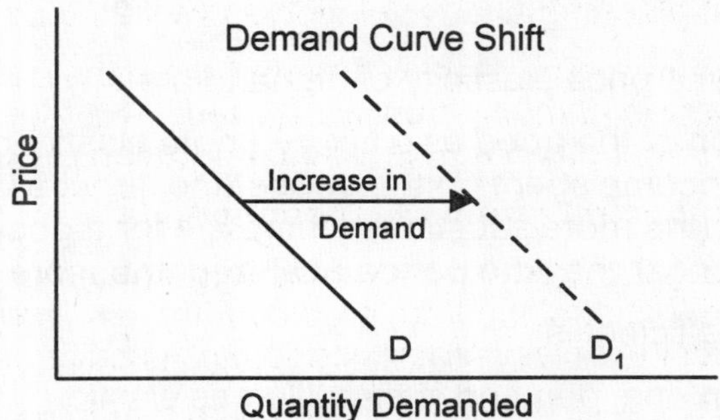

E. Such an increase in demand for commodity A (a shift in the demand schedule outward or to the right) can be caused by

1. A favorable change in the tastes and preferences of consumers toward commodity A (e.g., resulting from a successful advertising campaign)
2. An increase in consumer income, if A is a normal good
3. A decrease in consumer income, if A is an inferior good
4. An increase in the price of commodity Y, if Y is a substitute for A
5. A decrease in the price of commodity X, if X is a complement for A
6. The expectation of future price increases
7. The end of a group boycott

F. A decrease in demand for commodity A (a shift in the demand schedule inward or to the left) can be caused by the opposite of the factors listed in E. above.

ELASTICITY

A. **Price elasticity of demand** (E_d) is the percentage change in quantity demanded divided by the percentage change in price.

1. $$E_d = \frac{\textit{Percentage change in quantity demanded}}{\textit{Percentage change in price}}$$

2. It measures responsiveness of a change in quantity demanded to a change in the price of a product. For a demand schedule obeying the Law of Demand (downward sloping) the elasticity coefficient (E) is negative, but when interpreting E_d, the absolute value is ordinarily used.

3. But the numerator and denominator are computed as the change over the average, which results in the same percentage regardless of whether there is an increase or a decrease.

$$\frac{\% \Delta Q}{\% \Delta P} = \frac{(Q_1 - Q_2) \div \frac{(Q_1 + Q_2)}{2}}{(P_1 - P_2) \div \frac{(P_1 + P_2)}{2}}$$

4. Factors affecting the price elasticity of demand are
   a. Classification of the good as a luxury (more elastic) or a necessity
   b. Percent of income spent on the goods (the larger the %, the more elastic)
   c. Substitutes (the more substitutes there are for a good, the more elastic)
   d. Time (the longer the time period analyzed, the more elastic)
5. If the elasticity coefficient is
   a. Greater than one, demand is classified as elastic.
   b. Less than one, demand is classified as inelastic.
   c. Equal to one, demand is classified as having unitary elasticity.
6. In other words, if demand is elastic, it will change considerably relative to the size of a price change.
7. The relationship between price changes and total revenue (TR) changes is TR = price x quantity. It is summarized in the following table:

	E > 1	E < 1	E = 1
Price up	TR down	TR up	TR same
Price down	TR up	TR down	TR same

   a. EXAMPLE: Roxy's Bar sells 100 pitchers of beer a night at $2 each. One night Roxy decides to run a sale on beer and only charges $1 per pitcher. At that price, she sells 300 pitchers. The coefficient of elasticity, as determined by the formula, is

$$\frac{\textit{Percentage change in quantity demanded}}{\textit{Percentage change in price}} = \frac{1}{2/3} = \frac{3}{2} = 1.5$$

   because

$$\frac{\textit{300 pitchers} - \textit{100 pitchers}}{\textit{200 pitchers}} = 1 \qquad \frac{\$2 - \$1}{\$1.50} = \frac{2}{3}$$

   Since the coefficient is 1.5, demand at that point is said to be elastic. So, if the price is lowered to $1, total revenue will increase.

8. The concept of price elasticity is of considerable practical concern to the management accountant because a knowledge of the elasticity of the price of a particular product tells the accountant whether a price increase or decrease is required to increase total revenue.
9. Increases in sales and excise taxes, etc., are most easily passed on to the buyer when demand is inelastic.

B. **Price elasticity of supply** (E_s) is the responsiveness of a change in the quantity supplied to a percentage change in the price of the commodity.

1. $$E_s = \frac{\text{Percentage change in quantity supplied}}{\text{Percentage change in price}}$$

2. Factors that affect supply elasticity include
   a. Cost and feasibility of storage
      1) EXAMPLE: A high cost of storage results in low elasticity because, as the price of carrying a good increases, the tendency to hold that good decreases.
   b. Characteristics of the production process
      1) EXAMPLE: The supply elasticity of a joint product may be affected by the demand for the other joint products.
   c. Time
      1) EXAMPLE: Production of goods, i.e., the ability to supply them, becomes more elastic with time.

C. **Cross-elasticity of demand** measures the percentage change of one commodity demanded with a given percentage change in price of another commodity.

1. The cross-elasticity coefficient (E_{xy}) is found by using the following equation:

$$E_{xy} = \frac{\%\Delta Q_x}{\%\Delta P_y} = \frac{\text{Percentage change in Quantity demanded of good X}}{\text{Percentage change in Price of good Y}}$$

2. If the coefficient is
   a. Positive, the two commodities are substitutes (refer to the example below).
   b. Negative, the two commodities are complements.
   c. Zero, they are unrelated.

3. EXAMPLE: The price of orange soda goes up 20%, and the demand for root beer increases 10%. Therefore, orange soda and root beer are substitutes.

$$E_{xy} = \frac{10\%}{20\%} > 0$$

4. Cross-elasticity of demand can be used to define a market and determine appropriate marketing strategy. In addition, the information can be used to determine what and how much to produce.

D. **Income elasticity of demand** measures percentage change in quantity demanded for a given percentage change in income. The income elasticity (E_I) is found using the following equation:

$$E_I = \frac{\%\Delta Q}{\%\Delta I} = \frac{\text{Percentage change in Quantity demanded}}{\text{Percentage change in Income}}$$

1. If the coefficient is
   a. Greater than zero, the good is considered a normal good. This means that if income rises, consumption of the good rises.
   b. Less than zero, the good is considered an inferior good. This means that if income rises, consumption of the good decreases.

2. EXAMPLE: Income goes up 20%, and the demand for diamonds goes up 15%. Diamonds are normal goods; i.e., as people earn more, they purchase more diamonds.

$$E_I = \frac{15\%}{20\%} > 0$$

SUPPLY -- THE SELLER'S SIDE OF THE MARKET

A. **Supply** is the amounts of a good or service that producers are willing and able to offer to the market at various prices during a specified period of time.

B. **The Law of Supply**. The price of the product and the quantity supplied are positively related.

C. The determinants of supply are the variables that affect the amount supplied.

1. Production prices
2. Technology
3. Prices of other goods
4. Price expectations
5. Taxes and subsidies

D. The supply schedule is a relationship between the price of a good (on the vertical axis) and the quantity supplied to the market (horizontal axis) at each price, holding other determinants of the quantity supplied constant. A change in the price of a commodity is represented as a movement along the supply schedule.

1. **Supply curve shift.** A change in the quantity supplied must be distinguished from a shift in the supply curve itself. The latter is caused by a change in one of the determinants. The graph illustrates an increase in supply, which shifts the line from S to S_1.

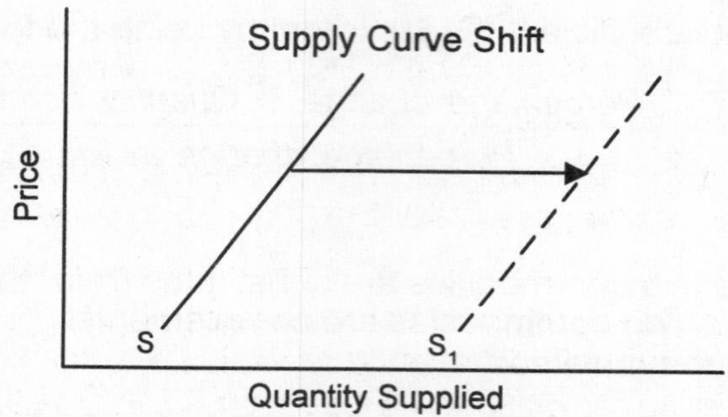

E. An increase in supply for commodity A (a shift in the supply schedule to the right) can be caused by changes in the determinants.

1. A decrease in a factor of the production price
2. An improvement in technology
3. A decrease in the demand for another commodity (B), inducing firms to divert resources from the production of B to A
4. The expectation of future price decreases
5. A decrease in taxation of a good or an increase in subsidization

F. A decrease in supply can be caused by the opposite of the above determinants.

G. **Market supply** is the sum of the individual supply curves of all sellers in the market.

H. **Economic Rent**. If any input is paid a higher amount than it would receive from the next highest bidder of that input, economic rent is said to be earned. When economic rent is earned, an input is being paid more for its services than is necessary to keep the input employed in production. For example, a $5,000,000-a-year baseball player is earning economic rent of $4,950,000 if the player could earn only $50,000 per year in another occupation.

1. But if the supply of a resource is fixed (e.g., land), the entire price paid is deemed to be a surplus (economic rent) because a change in price will not affect total supply (the productive potential of the economy).

THE MARKET

A. The market is the interaction of buyers and sellers of a commodity brought into contact with one another to engage in purchases and sales of economic goods.

B. **Equilibrium** between price and output is the point at which the demand and supply curves intersect. The graph illustrates the concept of market equilibrium, i.e., the intersection of a supply and demand curve.

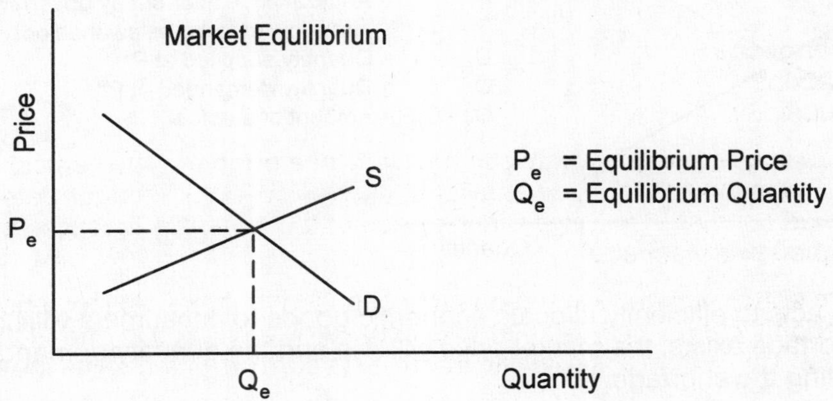

C. At the point of intersection of the supply and demand curves, anyone wishing to purchase the good at the market price can do so. The market forces of supply and demand thus create an automatic, efficient rationing system.

D. **Price fixing** is the setting of mandatory or artificial prices. It often interferes with the free operation of the market. Attempts to alter the output and price can have an effect on equilibrium.

1. **Price ceiling**. Price is established below the equilibrium price, causing shortages to develop (e.g., rent control). The usual result is nonprice competition among buyers (waiting lines are one form), which allocates the quantity that is supplied.

   a. The graph below depicts a shortage resulting from an artificially low price.

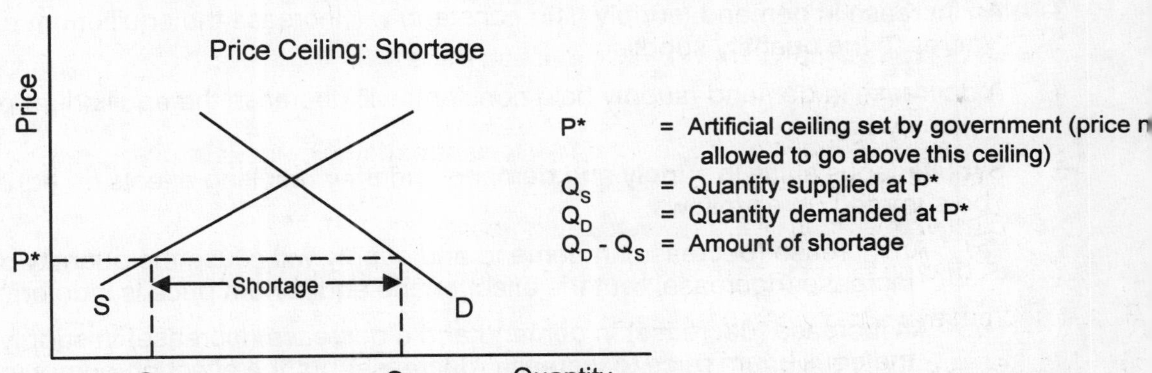

2. **Price floor**. Price is set above the equilibrium price, causing surpluses to develop (e.g., many agricultural products).

   a. The graph below illustrates a surplus because of an artificially high price.

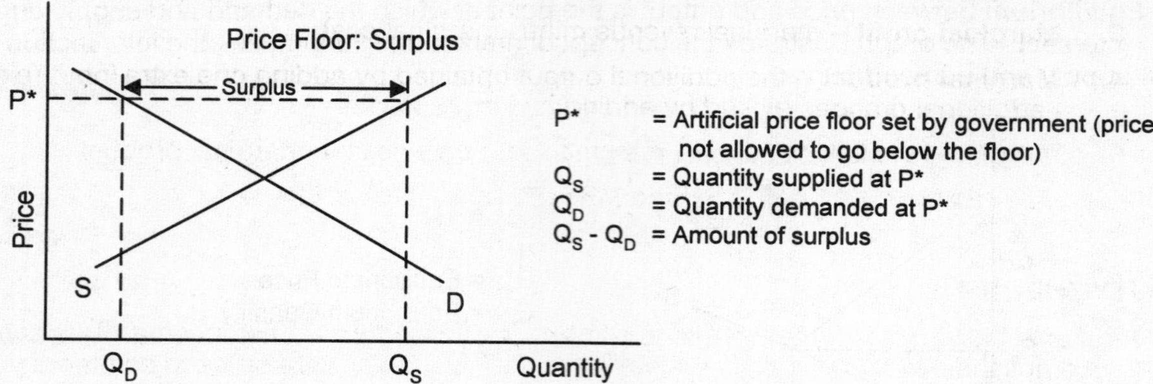

E. The pricing system acts to efficiently allocate economic goods to consumers willing to pay for them. When a shortage exists, the market price will rise and the quantity demanded will decrease, eliminating the shortage.

F. Attempts to circumvent the market often interfere with market forces, causing too many resources to go into one sector of the economy and too few into others.

   1. EXAMPLE: Under rent control, prices (to the renter) are set below their true equilibrium level. Because of this policy, fewer apartment owners are likely or willing to maintain (or increase) their stock of real estate, resulting in under-investment in the housing sector.

G. **The Impact on Equilibrium of Shifts in the Supply and Demand Schedules**

   1. An increase in supply (demand held constant) will decrease the equilibrium price and increase the quantity supplied.
   2. A decrease in supply (demand held constant) will increase the equilibrium price and decrease the quantity supplied.
   3. An increase in demand (supply held constant) will increase the equilibrium price and increase the quantity supplied.
   4. A decrease in demand (supply held constant) will decrease the equilibrium price and the quantity produced.
   5. Simultaneous shifts in supply and demand and their resulting effects on equilibrium can be summed up as follows:

      a. An increase (decrease) in demand and supply will cause the quantity of output to increase (decrease), but the effect on the equilibrium price is indeterminable.

      b. An increase (decrease) in demand and a decrease (increase) in supply will cause the equilibrium price to increase (decrease) but the effect on output is indeterminable.

H. **Externalities** (spillovers) can affect the allocation of resources. For example, if an automobile manufacturer pollutes Lake Michigan and does not clean it up, this results in lower costs (than if they used pollution equipment or other purification methods) and a cheaper car to the public. Because the cars are relatively cheaper, more people buy them, encouraging still more pollution. The result is too many cars produced at low cost and too much pollution.

I. Economic decisions are based on marginal analyses of output, revenue, profit, etc.

1. **Marginal revenue** -- the additional revenue obtained by increasing output by one unit
2. **Marginal cost** -- the addition to total cost as a result of increasing production by one unit
3. **Marginal profit** -- marginal revenue minus marginal cost
4. **Marginal product** -- the additional output obtained by adding one extra input (e.g., additional oranges picked by adding one more worker)
5. **Marginal revenue product** -- marginal revenue times the marginal product
    a. EXAMPLE: If MR is $1 and MP is 10 units, MRP is $10.

UTILITY THEORY

A. A rational individual's objective is to maximize total utility from his/her income. This can be accomplished when the utility obtained from the last dollar spent on each commodity purchased is the same.

B. Utility maximization can be expressed mathematically as

$$\frac{\textit{Marginal utility of A}}{\textit{Price of A}} = \frac{\textit{Marginal utility of B}}{\textit{Price of B}}$$

C. When the above formula holds, an individual has consumed in an optimal fashion. Given a certain or fixed amount of income, a higher level of utility could not have been achieved.

D. There are two ways to measure utility:

1. **Cardinal** -- numerically assign values of utils received from any good. A "util" is any arbitrary unit of worth.
2. **Ordinal** -- establish a ranking among goods, without assigning specific units of worth

E. **Principle of Diminishing Marginal Utility**. Equal increments of additional consumption of a good result in less than equal (smaller) additions of utility to the consumer. Thus, when a person is thirsty, the first glass of water tastes great, the second less so, and the third even less.

F. **Indifference curves** are all combinations of commodities X and Y (e.g., wine and cheese) that give equal utility to a consumer. The farther the indifference curve is from the origin, the higher the level of utility.

1. Indifference curves are nonlinear because of the principle of diminishing marginal utility. If consumers obtained equal amounts of utility from equal amounts consumed, irrespective of the ratio of X to Y, the indifference curves would be straight lines.
2. Characteristics of indifference curves
    a. Cannot intersect
    b. Are negatively sloped
    c. Are convex to the origin

3. The graph below depicts indifference curves (continuums of indifference points for bundles of goods).

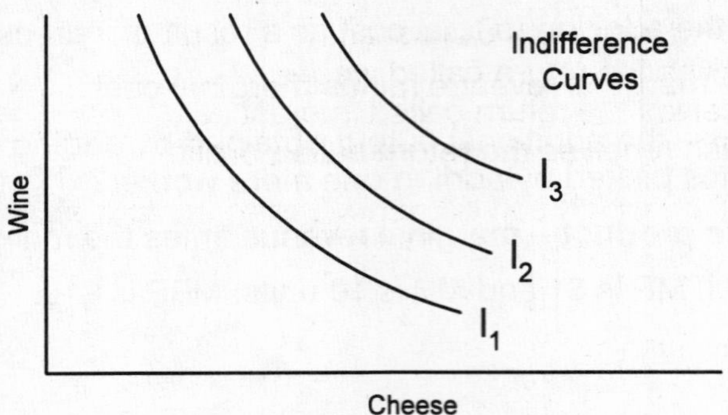

G. **Budget constraint lines** are all combinations of two commodities an individual can purchase with a given income and given prices of the two commodities.

1. The budget constraint is a straight line because its slope is constant.

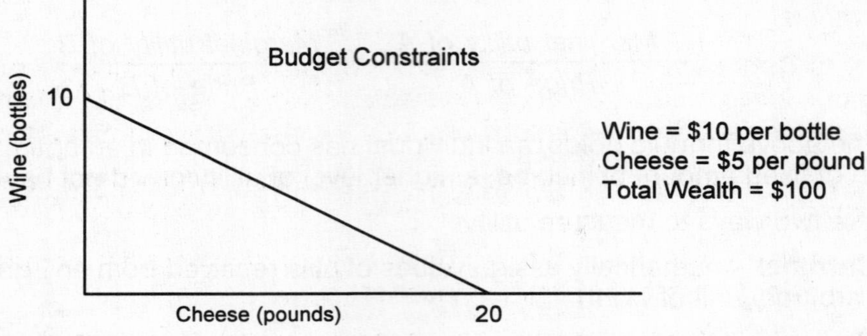

2. Properties of budget constraints include the following:
   a. A change in income causes a parallel shift in the budget constraint.
   b. A change in the price of one or both goods causes a change in slope of the budget constraint.
   c. If the relative prices of both goods change proportionately, a parallel shift in the budget line occurs.

H. Utility is maximized when the budget line is tangent to the highest possible indifference curve. At that point, the individual is getting the highest level of utility possible, given a fixed income.

1. In the following diagram, utility is maximized at point E, where the budget constraint line is tangent to the indifference curve.

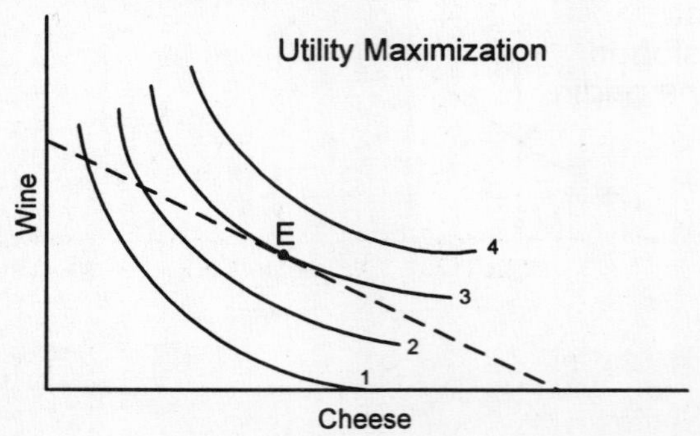

PRODUCTION AND COSTS IN THE SHORT RUN

A. Factors of production (inputs) are often classified as follows:

1. Land, which receives the return called rent
2. Labor, which receives the return called wages
3. Capital, which receives the return called interest
4. Management, which receives the return called profit

B. Other factors of production, which can be derived from the four above, include

1. Governmental services
2. Capital goods
3. Entrepreneurial services
4. R & D

C. The distinction in microeconomics between the short run and the long run is

1. The short run is a time period so brief that a firm has insufficient time to vary the amount of all inputs. Thus, the quantity of one or more inputs is fixed.
2. The long run is a time period long enough for all inputs, including plant capacity, to be varied.

D. **The Law of Diminishing Returns.** If increasing amounts of variable input are applied to a fixed input, there is some point beyond which additional units of the variable input will contribute less and less to the total product (i.e., marginal product will decline).

1. The law of diminishing returns governs the optional (profit-maximizing) use of variable inputs.
   a. An input is used up to the point at which the marginal increase in revenue from that input is equal to its marginal cost.
   b. The marginal revenue from an input is equal to its marginal physical product times the marginal revenue gained from the sale of an additional unit of output. This value is the marginal revenue product (MRP).
   c. The marginal resource cost (MRC) of an input is equal to its market price (e.g., the wage rate for labor).
   d. An enterprise will profit from using additional resources up to the point at which MRP equals MRC.
2. The following is a graph of returns to an input:

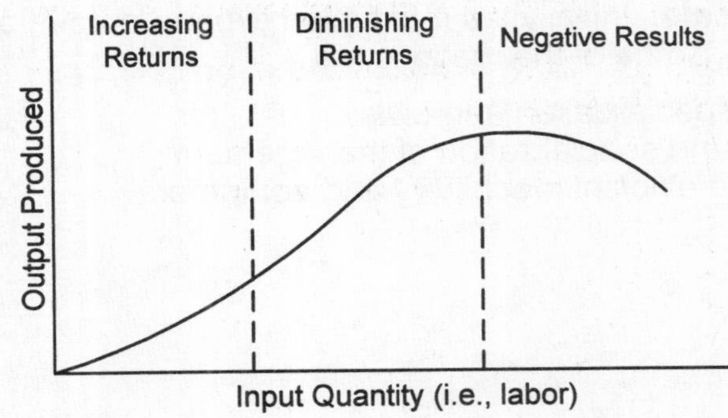

E. **Classification of Costs**

1. **Fixed costs** -- costs that do not change with the level of output
2. **Variable costs** -- costs that vary with output
3. **Total cost** -- the sum of fixed and variable costs
4. **Average fixed costs** -- total fixed costs divided by output
5. **Average variable costs** -- total variable costs divided by output
6. **Average costs** -- total costs divided by output
7. **Explicit (historical) costs** -- (as determined by accountants) the actual expenditures made in producing a product
8. **Implicit costs** -- the amounts that would have been received if self-owned resources had been used outside the firm's business. Thus, the lease payments forgone by not renting the firm's building to others is an implicit cost. The return necessary to keep resources employed in a given enterprise (normal profit) is also an implicit cost.
9. **Opportunity (alternative) costs** -- costs of any activity or product that must be forgone to perform the chosen activity or produce the chosen product
10. **Normal profit** -- cost of keeping entrepreneurial skills in the organization
11. **Economic cost** -- the income the firm must provide to a supplier to attract a resource away from an alternative use.
    a. Total revenue minus all economic costs equals economic profit (pure profit).

PRODUCTION AND COSTS IN THE LONG RUN

A. Since all inputs are variable in the long run, the relationship between input and output is dictated by the degree of returns to scale.

1. **Increasing returns to scale** -- if all inputs are changed by the same factor (k), but output changes by more than (k) (e.g., if all inputs are doubled and output more than doubles)
2. **Decreasing returns to scale** -- if all inputs are changed by the same factor (k), but output changes by less than (k)
3. **Constant returns to scale** -- if all inputs are changed by the same factor (k) and output also changes by the same factor (k)

B. The long-run average-cost curve is U-shaped because of economies and diseconomies of scale.

1. **Economies of scale.** Initially, as most firms expand output, average costs of production tend to decline. Some of the reasons are
    a. Increased specialization and division of labor
    b. Better use and specialization of management
    c. Use of more efficient machinery and equipment

2. **Diseconomies of scale.** Eventually, as most firms continue to expand output, the marginal cost of production tends to increase. The most frequent reason given for diseconomies of scale is the difficulty of managing a large-scale enterprise.

3. The following graph illustrates a long-run average-cost curve:

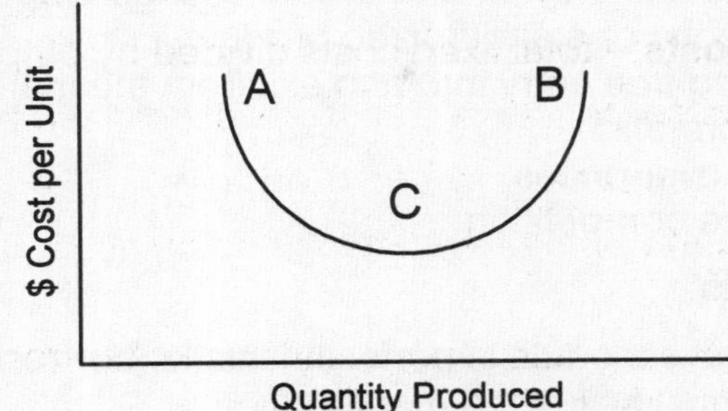

   a. A represents increasing returns to scale (or decreasing marginal cost).
   b. B represents decreasing returns to scale (or increasing marginal cost).
   c. C represents constant returns to scale (or constant marginal cost).

C. **Relationships of Marginal Cost and Average Cost**

1. When average cost is rising, marginal cost is above it.
2. When average cost is falling, marginal cost is below it.
3. Average cost = marginal cost whenever average cost is at a minimum or a maximum.
4. The following graph shows these relationships:

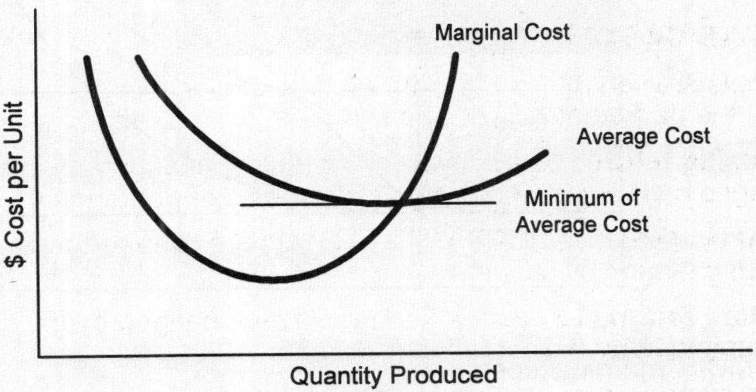

D. Technological changes result in higher costs and lower profits in older plants.

1. Technological efficiency is impaired when the ratio of the physical output of a given technology and the maximum output that is possible declines.

MARKET STRUCTURE AND PERFORMANCE

A. Pure (Perfect) Competition

1. Assumptions
   a. Large number of buyers and sellers acting independently
   b. Homogeneous or standardized product
   c. Firms having free entry into and exit from the market
   d. Perfect information
   e. No control over prices
   f. No nonprice competition
2. Short-run analysis
   a. The demand schedule is perfectly elastic (horizontal) because the firm is a price taker. It must sell at the market price.
   b. For profit maximization, the firm equates price and marginal cost. If price is less than average variable cost, the firm should shut down (to minimize losses).
   c. Competitors are in long-run equilibrium when price equals minimum average cost.
3. The following graph shows a competitive firm in the short run:

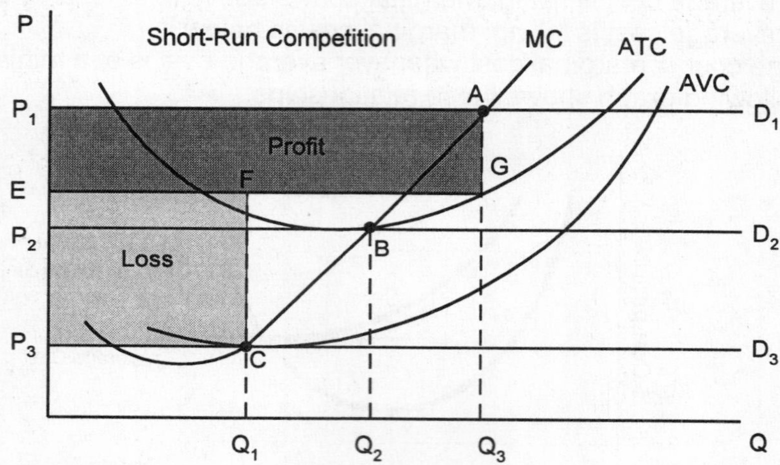

   a. MC = marginal cost
   b. ATC = average total cost
   c. AVC = average variable cost
   d. D = demand
   e. P_1 P_2 P_3 represent alternative prices.
      D_1 D_2 D_3 represent resulting demand.
      Q_1 Q_2 Q_3 represent related quantities produced.
   f. Point A represents maximum profit given price P_1.
   g. Point B represents the breakeven point where fixed and variable costs are covered.
   h. Q_2 is the long-run equilibrium quantity.
   i. C is the point below which the firm must close down because it will not recover its variable costs.

4. Long-run analysis

   a. On the graph on page 102, the firm is making an economic profit [(MC – ATC) per unit x Q_3, that is, the area P_1AGE] given demand at D_1 and price at P_1. In the long run, because profits are available, more firms will enter, eventually driving the price down to P_2, where no economic profits occur. If the demand is at D_3, the firm is taking a loss [(ATC – MC) per unit x Q_1, that is, the area P_3EFC], which will lead to firms dropping out of the industry, eventually causing price to rise to P_2 again.

   b. The standard theory assumes that all firms are equally efficient. This means that the minimum point on the average cost curve is the same for all firms. Consequently, when entry causes price to equal the minimum of the average cost, no firms are earning profits. However, if there are more efficient producers with lower average cost curves, these will earn economic profits in the long run.

   c. Because price equals marginal cost, allocation of resources is optimal.

   d. Firms produce the ideal output, the output at which average cost is lowest.

   e. Price is lower and output greater than in any other market structure.

   f. The following graph shows a competitive firm in long-run equilibrium. Because price equals minimum average cost at the optimal output, no profit is earned.

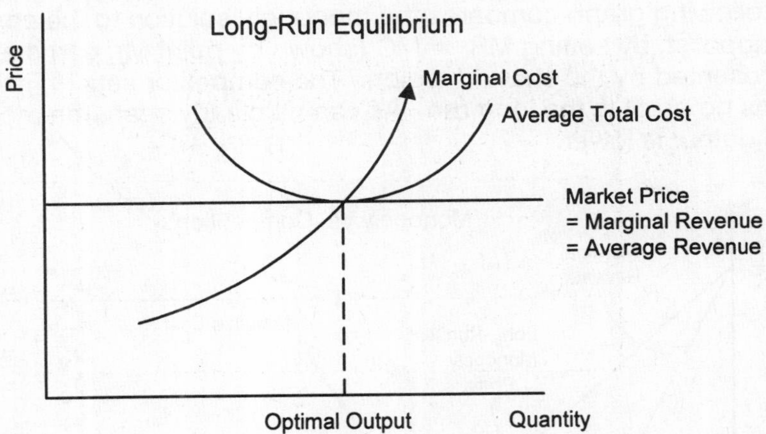

B. **Pure Monopoly**

1. Assumptions

   a. Single firm
   b. Unique product with no close substitutes
   c. Blocked entry of other firms
   d. Significant price control
   e. Goodwill advertising

2. Short-run analysis

   a. The demand schedule is negatively sloped.

   b. Marginal revenue lies below demand and is negatively sloped.

   c. For profit maximization, the firm equates marginal revenue with marginal cost unless price is less than average variable cost (the shutdown case).

3. Profit maximization for a monopolist
   a. MC = marginal cost
   b. AC = average cost
   c. MR = marginal revenue
   d. D = demand
   e. Point A (MR = MC) represents the maximum profit point. The shaded area represents the profit.
   f. Point B is the selling price and Q* is the quantity supplied.

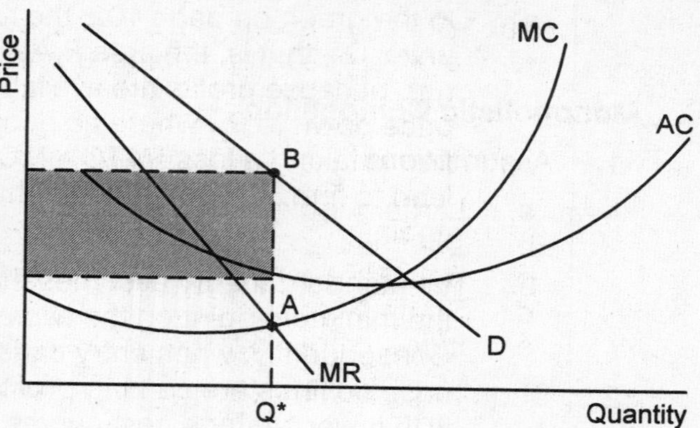

4. Long-run analysis
   a. Blocked entry allows the monopolist to earn a profit.
   b. Price exceeds marginal cost. There is an under-allocation of resources.
   c. Firm produces less than the ideal output.
   d. Price is higher and output lower than with pure competition.
5. EXAMPLE: Industry: public utilities
6. The following graph compares the monopoly solution to the competitive solution. The monopolist, by setting MR = MC (shown by point M), earns a profit in the long run represented by the shaded region. The competitor sets P = MC (shown at point C) and earns no profit in the long run. As can be clearly seen, the monopolist's price is higher and output is lower.

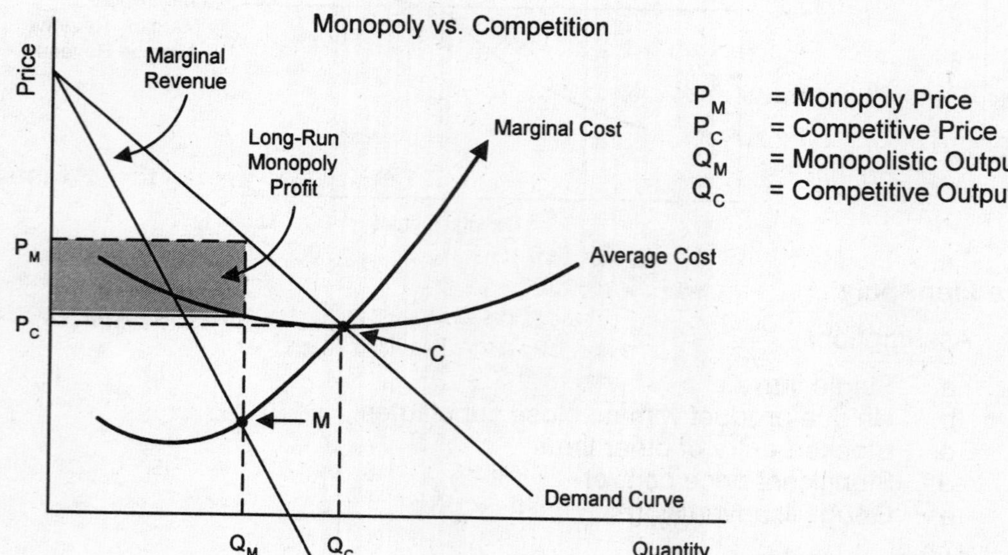

7. A **natural monopoly** exists when economic or technical conditions permit only one efficient supplier. It arises when economies of scale are very great; i.e., very large operations are needed to achieve low unit costs and prices. Thus, the unit cost (long-term average cost) of meeting demand is minimized when the industry has one firm.

C. **Monopolistic Competition**

1. Assumptions

   a. Large number of firms
   b. Differentiated products
   c. Relatively easy entry into market
   d. Some price control
   e. Large amounts of nonprice competition (advertising, brands, etc.)

2. Short-run analysis

   a. Demand schedule is negatively sloped.

   b. Marginal revenue lies below demand and is also negatively sloped.

   c. For profit maximization, the firm equates marginal revenue and marginal cost, unless price is less than average variable cost (the shut-down case).

3. Long-run analysis

   a. Firms tend to earn normal profit.

   b. Price exceeds marginal cost, and there is an under-allocation of resources.

   c. Firms produce less than the ideal output, and the industry is populated by too many firms that are too small. These conditions are often referred to as the waste of monopolistic competition.

   d. Foreign competition, when lightly restricted, restrains negative monopolistic behavior.

   e. Price is higher and output less than in pure competition.

4. EXAMPLE: Industries: computers, toothpaste

D. **Oligopoly**

1. Assumptions. The oligopoly model is much less specific than the previous three market structures, but the following are common assumptions:

   a. Few firms. The decisions of rivals do not go unnoticed.
   b. Products can be differentiated (autos) or standardized (steel).
   c. Prices tend to be rigid because of the interdependence among firms.
   d. Entry is difficult because of barriers, which can be

      1) Natural, e.g., an absolute cost advantage
      2) Created, e.g., ongoing advertising

2. The short-run and long-run analyses are indeterminate because of the effect of each company on the other companies.

3. The price rigidity normally found in oligopolistic markets can be explained in part by the **kinked demand curve** theory. Because competitors respond to price changes by one of the firms in an oligopolistic industry, the demand curve for an oligopolist tends to be kinked.

   a. If other firms do not match a price decrease by an oligopolist, it will capture more of the market. If other firms match the price decrease, less of the market will be captured.

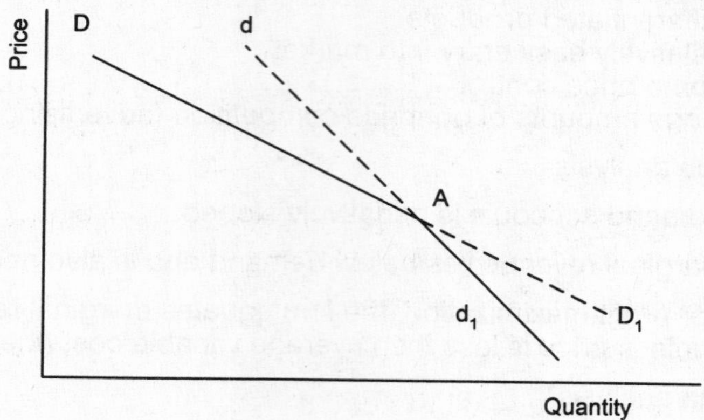

If: DD_1 is the firm's demand curve when competitors do not respond to changes in the current price (A)

dd_1 is the firm's demand curve when competitors match any price changes

Dd_1 is the firm's demand curve when competitors do not respond to increases in the current price but do respond to price decreases

4. **Price leadership** is typical in oligopolistic industries. Under price leadership, price changes are announced first by a major firm in the industry. Once the industry leader has spoken, everyone else in the industry matches the price charged by the leader.
5. A **cartel** arises when a group of oligopolistic firms join together for price-fixing purposes. This practice is illegal except in international markets. For example, the international diamond cartel DeBeers has successfully maintained the market price of diamonds for many years by incorporating into the cartel almost all major diamond-producing sources.
6. Oligopolistic industries include automobiles and steel.

GOVERNMENT'S ROLE IN MAINTAINING MARKET STRUCTURE AND PERFORMANCE

A. The two evils of monopoly power are

1. Higher price for the product (compared to perfect competition)
2. Lower quantity produced (compared to perfect competition)

B. Monopoly power decreases as the number of firms increases. Therefore, antitrust policy seeks to limit monopoly power and promote competition.

C. The following laws form the basis of public control in the United States:

1. **Sherman Act** (1890)
   a. Prohibits restraint of trade and monopolies in interstate and foreign trade, e.g., price fixing, boycotts, dividing markets, restrictions on resale, etc.
2. **Clayton Act** (1914)
   a. Prohibits the acquisition of stock of competitors (merger) if the result might be a tendency to lessen competition
   b. Prohibits price discrimination
   c. Keeps directors of one company from sitting on the board of a competitor
3. **Federal Trade Commission Act** (1914)
   a. Established FTC as an independent agency
   b. Prosecutes unfair competition and false or misleading advertising
4. **Robinson-Patman Act** (1936)
   a. Prohibits special discounts to large purchasers unless based on cost differences
5. **Celler-Kefauver Anti-Merger Act** (1950)
   a. Prohibits any corporation from acquiring the assets of another if the effect is to reduce competition
6. Also see the discussion of antitrust regulation in Study Unit 4, Institutional Environment of Business.

D. The effect of the size of a business on competition is a much-debated topic. Arguments for and against big business include the following:

1. For big business
   a. A larger scale operation is necessary for innovation (e.g., a large company can afford more research and development).
   b. Economies of scale
2. Against big business
   a. Inequitable flow of wealth to firms with market power
   b. Expansion of output restrictions
   c. Lack of incentive for innovation by a large company that may be able to afford it

E. One major way firms become large is through mergers. The three types are

1. **Vertical mergers** -- union of two companies, one of which supplies inputs (e.g., raw materials) for the other
2. **Horizontal mergers** -- union of two companies that engage in the same or similar activities
3. **Conglomerate mergers** -- union of two unrelated companies

F. Two approaches to formulating and implementing antitrust policy are

1. Performance
   a. Market performance
   b. Rate of technological growth
   c. Efficiency and profit
2. Industry market structure
   a. Number and size of competitors
   b. Distribution of buyers and sellers
   c. Ease of entry
   d. Product differentiation

G. **Concentration ratio** is the percentage of an industry's output produced by its four largest firms. Statistical studies often rely on the concentration ratio as a measure of monopoly market power in an industry.

H. **Taxes**

1. License fee -- a lump-sum tax that must be paid if a firm is to operate
   a. **Short-run effect**. The tax raises average cost but does not change marginal cost. Thus, the firm's output decision remains unchanged.
   b. **Long-run effect**. In a competitive industry, firms are not making profits after the tax. Some firms leave the industry. The industry price is higher, and total industry output is lower.
2. Profits tax. This tax does not change the firm's revenue or cost functions. This implies that the output to maximize pretax profits also maximizes after-tax profits. Hence, a firm's optimal output is unchanged.
3. Per unit tax. This tax, e.g., sales, excise, and value-added taxes, creates a difference between demand price (what consumers are willing to pay) and the price a firm receives. The effect is to decrease marginal revenue. The firm's response is to lower the quantity produced by moving down the marginal cost curve.

I. Governmental action is sometimes anticompetitive. Examples are

1. Patent, copyright, trademark, and trade name protection
2. Price supports, such as for certain agricultural commodities, or price ceilings, e.g., on utility rates
3. Licensing of television and radio stations
4. Tariffs, import quotas, and other restrictions on foreign producers' access to domestic markets
5. Costs driven up by governmental regulation
6. Larger, more established companies benefiting by governmental spending

STUDY UNIT 2
MACROECONOMICS

INTRODUCTION

Macroeconomics is the study of economic aggregates and an overview of the economy. It includes levels of national income, employment, and prices. Macroeconomics and international economics cover 10% to 15% of Part 1. We present international economics in the next study unit, which begins on page 129. The presentation is on the level of a rigorous introductory economics course.

NATIONAL INCOME ACCOUNTING

A. National income accounting is used to measure the output and performance of a nation's economy.

1. **Gross domestic product** (GDP), which replaces GNP (gross national product) as the principal measure of national economic performance, is the total market value of all fina goods and services produced within the boundaries of the U.S. during some specified period of time, usually a year.
2. The differences between GNP and GDP are
   a. The market value of goods and services produced by U.S. resources abroad is included in the calculation of GNP, but not GDP.
   b. Production by foreign-owned resources in the U.S. is included in the calculation of GDP, but not GNP.
3. There are two equivalent approaches to the measurement of GDP.
   a. **Income and cost approach.** GDP is the sum of
      1) Wages
      2) Interest
      3) Rent
      4) Profits
      5) Depreciation
      6) Indirect business taxes
   b. **Expenditure approach.** GDP is the sum of
      1) Consumption
      2) Investment
      3) Government expenditures
      4) Net exports

4. To avoid double counting in the computation of GDP, the value added to each good or service at each stage of production over the period must be summed.
   a. Alternatively, the total market value of all final goods and services may be added.
5. GDP is not an ideal measure of economic well-being. Some reservations are
   a. GDP is a monetary measure; therefore, comparing GDP over a period of time requires adjustment for price changes, inflation, etc.
   b. Increases in GDP often involve environmental damage such as noise, congestion, or pollution.
   c. GDP is not adjusted for changes in the population (which changes the per capita income).
   d. Changes in the value of leisure time are not considered.
   e. Some nonmarket transactions are excluded, e.g., the value of homemakers' work.
   f. Military expenditures are included at cost, not incremental total value.
6. Other national income concepts
   a. **Net domestic product** (NDP) = GDP - depreciation
   b. **National income** (NI) = NDP + U.S. net income earned abroad - indirect business taxes (e.g., sales taxes)
   c. **Personal income** (PI) = NI - corporate income taxes and undistributed profits - Social Security contributions + transfer payments (public and private)
   d. **Disposable income** = PI - personal income taxes
7. Disposable income is divided between
   a. Consumption and interest payments
   b. Savings
8. Real per capita output is GDP divided by population, adjusted for inflation. It is used as a measure of the standard of living.

CLASSICAL ECONOMICS

A. According to classical theory, the economy is capable of generating and maintaining full employment over the long run without government intervention because of price and wage flexibility.

B. **Adjustment Mechanisms**
   1. **Say's Law**: Supply creates its own demand.
   2. Flexible interest rates provide equality of savings and investments.
   3. Flexible prices allow self-correcting of surpluses or shortages in product or labor markets.

C. **Demand for Money**
   1. **The equation of exchange**, the fundamental, classical equation, is an identity that serves as a framework for analyzing the impact of money on the level of national income (aggregate demand). It is usually stated as

$$MV = GDP$$
or
$$MV = PQ$$

If: M = Money stock (supply)
V = Velocity (defined on page 111)
GDP = Gross domestic product
P = Aggregate price index
Q = Aggregate output index

2. **The income velocity of money** (V) reflects the average turnover rate of the money stock in the transactions that constitute our national income. The velocity of money can be defined as the ratio of gross domestic product to the money supply.

3. A major classical proposition is that an increase in money will lead to an increase in aggregate demand (as opposed to Keynes, who argued that an increase in M will be completely offset by a decrease in V, leaving PQ unchanged). A classical economist would use either of the following arguments:

   a. V may be unstable, but the money supply is an important aspect of aggregate demand (thus an increase in M is not offset by a decrease in V).

   b. V is quite stable. Therefore, a change in the money supply has a powerful effect on aggregate demand.

D. Unemployment does not exist in the classical model because if people (or capital) are unemployed, downward pressure is placed on wage rates until all of the people who want to work at prevailing wage rates are working.

E. Classical economics has no well-defined position on fiscal policy and its effectiveness as a stimulant to aggregate demand. Some classical views on this subject are

1. An increase in government spending would have little effect on demand (if it were financed by debt) because it would draw from the same pool as the private (business) sector.

2. High government spending will have an effect on demand when it is financed by printing money (which in itself stimulates demand).

3. An increase in government spending will lead to an increase in velocity, resulting in an increase in aggregate demand.

KEYNESIAN ECONOMICS

In 1936, John Maynard Keynes published his theory maintaining that the economy could be in equilibrium at less than full employment. These new ideas gained acceptance because of the failure of classical economics during the Great Depression.

A. **Three General Assumptions of Keynesian Economics**

1. The difference between savings plans and investment plans is fundamental to an understanding of changes in the level of income.

   a. Keynesian analysis emphasizes that saving and investing are undertaken by different people with different motivations.

2. Price flexibility cannot be relied upon to provide full employment because prices tend to be sticky downward; i.e., they are not lowered easily.

3. Equilibrium income does not necessarily provide full employment.

B. **Consumption and Saving**

1. The major determinant is income.
2. Propensities to consume and save (Δ means the change in.)
   a. *Average propensity to consume* = *Consumption* ÷ *Income*
   b. *Average propensity to save* = *Savings* ÷ *Income*
   c. *Marginal propensity to consume* = *Δ Consumption* ÷ *Δ Income*
   d. *Marginal propensity to save* = *Δ Savings* ÷ *Δ Income*
3. Nonincome determinants
   a. Price expectations (includes expectations about availability, future prices, future incomes). Consumer expectations about price increases, or the lack of future availability, cause an increase in current purchases to avoid higher prices or to guarantee access to the good.
   b. Interest rates. As interest rates increase, the incentive to save is increased (which leads to reduced consumption).
   c. Quantity of liquid assets. If people have larger stocks of assets, they tend to spend more money at every level of disposable income.
   d. Credit. If consumers are deeply in debt, they are likely to reduce their rate of growth in consumption.
   e. Attitudes. If individuals believe that saving money is virtuous, aggregate consumption is lower than if the feeling is "consume for today."
   f. Consumer stock of durable goods. With a high stock of durables, consumers can cease purchasing durable goods but still consume a high level (depleting the stock). Since there is no cash flow associated with the use of durables, spending decreases at all levels of disposable income.
4. The savings rate in the U.S. is relatively low compared with that in Japan and other countries.
   a. The low savings rate causes a scarcity of equity capital for U.S. businesses.
   b. U.S. productivity is reduced because companies cannot invest in modern capital equipment and new and cheaper sources of energy. Improvements and replacements are curtailed.
   c. U.S. companies are placed at a competitive disadvantage in international markets.
   d. The U.S. tax law often has a negative influence on the savings rate of U.S. households because interest, dividends, and capital gains are taxed at progressive rates.
   e. Other reasons for the low savings rate in the U.S. include fears of continuing inflation (which impairs the purchasing power in the future of money saved today), the wide availability of consumer credit, and programs such as Medicare, Social Security, and unemployment insurance, which may reduce the incentive to save for retirement or contingencies.

C. Investment

1. The major determinant of investment is its profitability as expected by the business sector. Profitability is affected by the following variables:
   a. Rate of growth of technology. Because new products and innovations are often profitable, firms will invest more when the technological growth rate is high.
   b. Interest rates. As real interest rates increase, marginal investments are not undertaken, thus lowering total business investment.
      1) Real interest rate -- the nominal rate minus the inflation premium (See G.6. on page 117.)
   c. Stock of capital goods. The higher the stock, the lower the demand for new capital goods (until the stock is depleted).
   d. Government actions. Changes in tax rates, depreciation allowances, and government spending can change the expected profitability of a given investment.
   e. Acquisition and maintenance costs. The higher the purchase price and life-long operating costs of a capital good, the lower the expected profitability on the investment.
2. Components of investment
   a. Plant and equipment expenditures
      1) The capital consumption allowance (depreciation) is a negative component of investment.
   b. Residential construction expenditures
   c. Inventories
3. Autonomous investment -- investment expenditures made by businesses that are independent of the level of national income and that are undertaken for their expected profitability. The level of autonomous investment will be constant regardless of an expansion or a recession of economic activity.
4. Induced investment -- investment made as a result of increased economic activity
5. Investment tends to be the most volatile component of private spending. For that reason, it is given central importance in income determination theory. Reasons for this volatility are
   a. Capital durability. Because a piece of equipment can be either repaired or scrapped, the timing option (when to purchase new capital) is usually open. Only when expectations about future business conditions are bright will new durables be purchased (only then would new debt be wise).
   b. State of technology. Major breakthroughs in technology are fairly rare and irregular. However, when a breakthrough does occur, large amounts of investment are undertaken, increasing the volatility of investment expenditures.
   c. Expectations. Changing expectations can radically alter expected profits from investment.
   d. **Acceleration principle**. Fluctuations in sales tend to produce larger fluctuations in inventory and capital equipment investments.

D. A model can be devised for **income determination in a closed economy**, i.e., one without a government and money market.

1. Equilibrium income occurs when aggregate savings equals aggregate investment.
2. Alternatively, equilibrium income occurs when aggregate demand (consumption plus investment) equals aggregate supply (production).
3. The following graph illustrates equilibrium income using these two approaches.
   a. First, equilibrium income occurs when aggregate savings equals aggregate investment in graph (a).
   b. Alternatively, equilibrium occurs when aggregate demand (C+I) intersects the aggregate supply function (45° line) in graph (b).

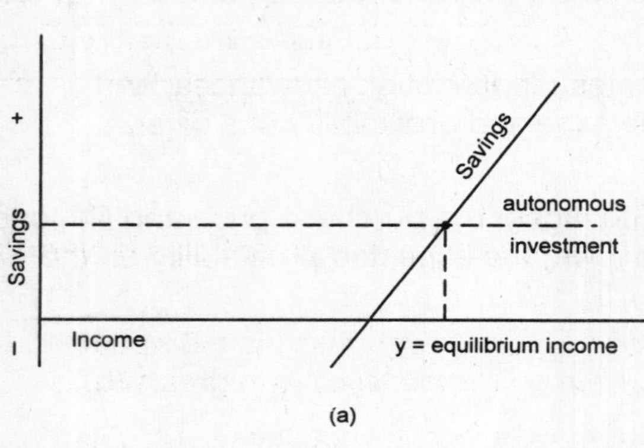

(a)

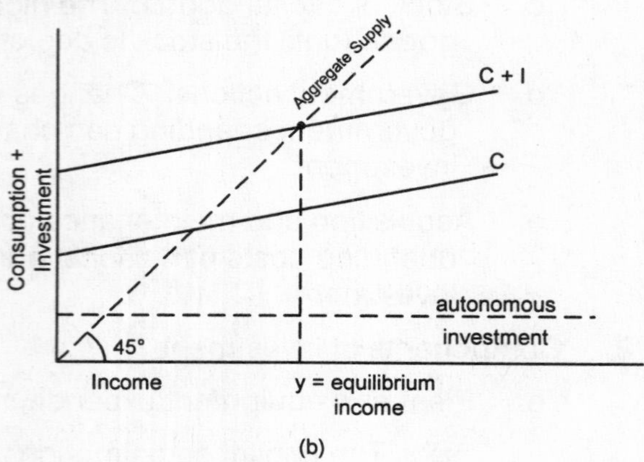

(b)

E. **The Multiplier**

1. An increase in autonomous investment, consumption, or government spending will result in a multiplied increase in national income. This multiplier phenomenon occurs because the same income is spent several times (how many times depends on the marginal propensity to consume).
2. **The marginal propensity to consume** (MPC) -- the percentage of **additional** income that is consumed
3. **The marginal propensity to save** (MPS) -- the percentage of **additional** income that is saved
   a. $MPC + MPS = 1$ (Income can be either spent or saved.)
      $MPS = 1 - MPC$
4. The formula for the multiplier is $1/MPS$ or $1/1 - MPC$.
   a. EXAMPLE: Assume the MPC = .8, and a company decides to invest an additional $10 this year. The effect on national income (NI) can be computed as follows:

      The company spends the $10, and some other entity receives it as income. Because the MPC is .8, that entity (on the average) will spend $8 (and save $2). The $8 just spent becomes income for yet another individual (or firm), who also spends 80% of the $8, or $6.40, which is received as income by still another person, etc. When the whole set of transactions is complete, the series sums to $10 + $8 + $6.40 + $5.12 + $4.10 . . . = $50.

      Alternatively, the change in equilibrium income from an increase in investment is

$$\frac{1}{1 - MPC} \times \Delta\ Spending = \frac{1}{1 - .8} \times \$10 = \$50, \textit{ the change in NI}$$

5. To determine the change in national income caused by a change in spending, determine the multiplier coefficient and then multiply it by the change in spending.
   a. The change in spending may be negative or positive.

F. A model can be devised for income determination in a closed economy that includes government spending. The graphs illustrate equilibrium income in this model.

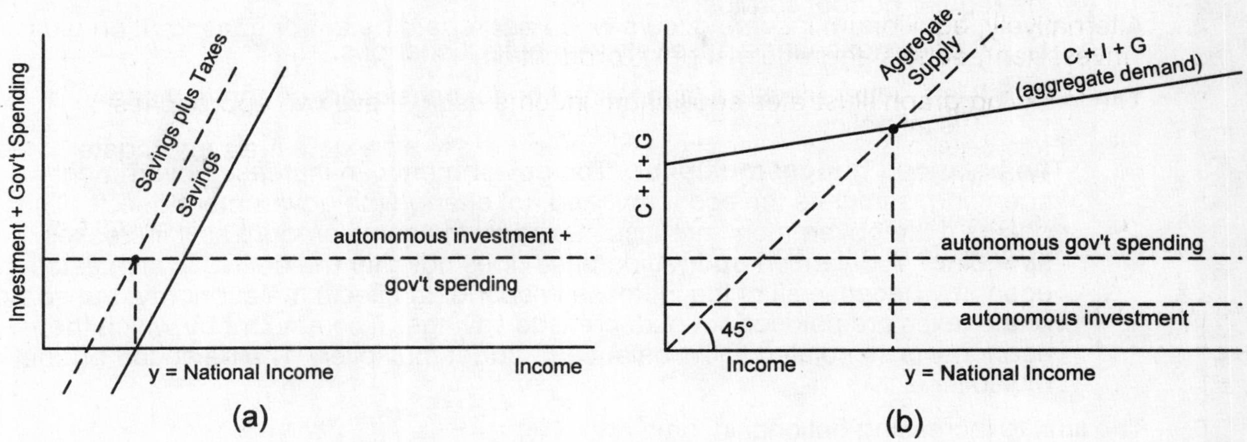

1. Equilibrium income occurs when savings plus taxes equals investment plus government expenditures in graph (a).
2. Alternatively, equilibrium income occurs when aggregate demand (consumption + investment + government expenditures) equals aggregate supply in graph (b).
3. Changes in aggregate demand will change national income because
   a. An increase in autonomous consumption, investment, or government spending will increase aggregate demand, subsequently increasing national income (by a multiplied amount as determined by the increase in spending times the multiplier).
   b. Decreases in autonomous spending will decrease national income.
4. The model can be further modified for the effects of net exports. Positive net exports increase aggregate demand compared with that in a closed economy. Negative net exports have the opposite effect.
5. Some additional relationships
   a. **The tax multiplier**. Changes in taxes do not affect the economy through the standard multiplier. Because changes in taxes affect the economy through changes in consumption, the tax multiplier is

$$\frac{-\,MPC}{1\,-\,MPC}$$

   Accordingly, the Δ national income $= \dfrac{-\,MPC}{1\,-\,MPC} \times \Delta\ taxes$

      1) The reason this differs from the regular multiplier, 1÷(1−MPC), is that the regular multiplier is applied directly to changes in spending. Changes in taxes are not changes in spending, but cause them.

   b. **The government budget surplus (deficit)** -- the excess of government tax collections over government transfers and purchases. It can either be positive (a surplus) or negative (a deficit).

c. **The full employment budget surplus** -- the excess of government tax collections over government transfers and purchases that would occur if the economy were at full employment. It has the following characteristics that make it preferable to the regular budget surplus:

   1) It does not change passively with output changes.
   2) It is a better measure of the direction (expansionary or contractionary) of fiscal policy.

d. **The balanced budget multiplier.** The government can increase government spending, stimulate the economy, and not change the government deficit. This occurs if the government increases taxes by the same amount as it increases spending. A balanced budget increase does not alter the deficit. It stimulates the economy because all of the increase in spending affects the economy, but some of the taxes are paid for out of decreased savings. The amount by which the economy is stimulated is the balanced budget multiplier. The balanced budget multiplier is 1.

6. The limit to increasing national income in the short run is determined by the amount of resources (land, labor, and capital) and can be depicted graphically. The production possibility frontier (PPF) depicts all possible combinations of output (assuming a two-good world) that a society can have, all other things held constant.

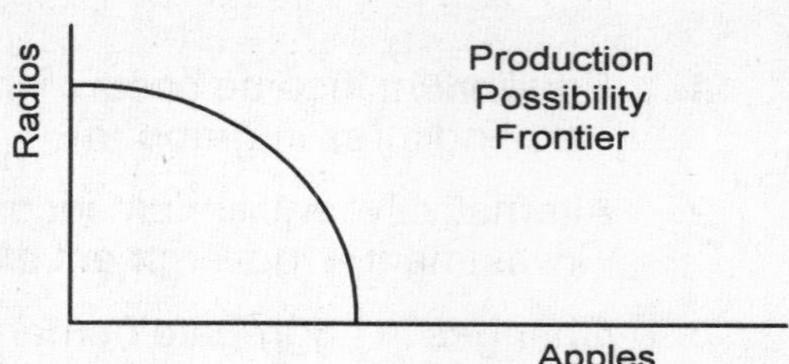

7. Assuming the society is on the outer boundary (which implies full employment and optimal use of resources for a given state of technology), the only way to have more apples is to give up some radios (or vice versa). In the long run, the frontier can be shifted (out or in). Factors causing such a shift include

   a. Increases in land, labor, or capital
   b. Technological advancements

      1) With an outward shift, society can now have both more apples **and** more radios.

8. By definition, if society is producing on the boundary of the PPF, all resources are in use and no additional output can be produced in the short run. Hence, even with an increase in aggregate demand, the production capability may not exist to supply the quantity demanded. If supply cannot be increased, consumers will bid up the prices of existing goods, creating an erosion of the price level.

9. The next graph illustrates the concept of an **inflationary gap** (AB), and the increase (BC) in its size caused by an increase in aggregate demand. Additional consumption, investment, or government spending would increase the size of the inflationary gap (resulting in a higher price level). In the diagram, the 45° line reflects the points in this model at which output equals demand. The intersection of the aggregate demand line and the 45° line is the equilibrium income level.

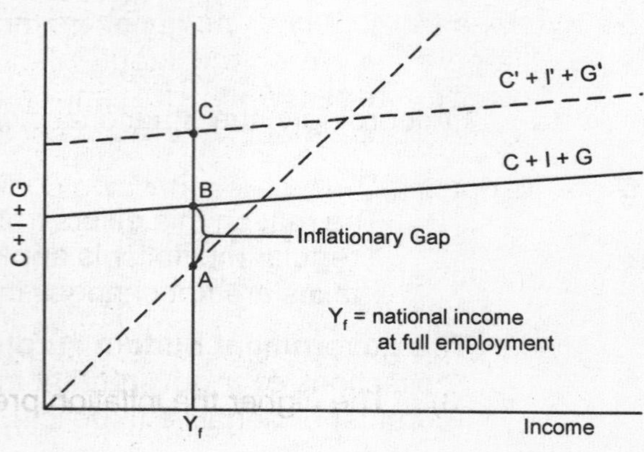

G. In Keynesian analysis, the supply and demand for money determine the interest rate.

1. Supply of money is determined by the monetary authorities (Federal Reserve Board).
2. Demand for money is determined by liquidity preference, which depends on the following reasons for holding money:
   a. Transactions motive -- day-to-day business transactions
   b. Precautionary motive -- in case money is needed for other purposes (e.g., to take advantage of a bargain price on a car)
   c. Speculative motive -- in expectation of interest rate increases, which will cause bond prices to go down
3. The supply of money (fixed in the short run) and the liquidity preference function (demand for money) give money market equilibrium and determine the equilibrium interest rate (price of money), I_e.
4. The liquidity preference schedule below, which incorporates the above reasons for holding cash, is the demand curve for money.

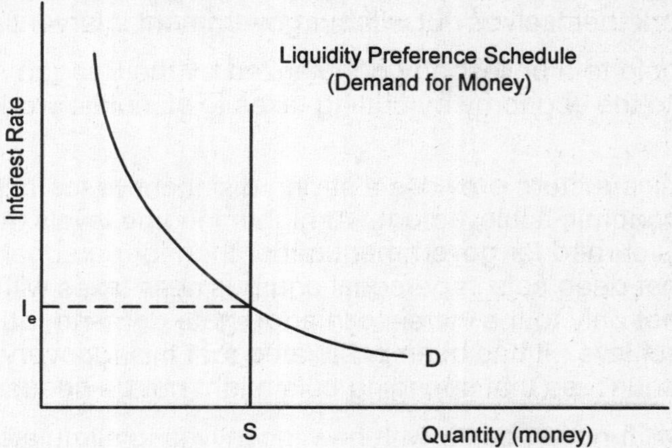

   a. The function slopes downward because, at higher interest rates, people hold less cash.
   b. The intersection of the money supply (fixed by the monetary authorities) and demand (liquidity preference) is the equilibrium interest rate depicted by the graph.
   c. This schedule assumes income as fixed.
5. Varying the supply of money alters the interest rate, affecting investment in society. For example, increasing the supply of money moves one down and to the right along the liquidity preference schedule shown above. This decreases the interest rate and increases the amount of investment in the economy.
6. The nominal interest rate has two components.
   a. Real rate (historically 2% to 4% average)
   b. Inflation premium
      1) The size of the premium is a function of the expected inflation rate.
      2) The higher the expected inflation rate, the higher the inflation premium.
      3) The higher the inflation premium, the higher the nominal interest rate.

MONETARISTS, SUPPLY-SIDERS, AND OTHERS

A. Critics believe that the Keynesian emphasis on spending and taxation (fiscal policy) overlooked the powerful effect that money supply and credit have on the economy. **Monetarists** believe that a steady, restrained growth of the money supply is more influential than budget policy on economic performance, inflation, and unemployment.

1. In the long run, inflation is caused by increases in the money supply. Excessive monetary growth will result in excessive inflation. Thus, inflation can be controlled only by maintaining a firm grip on the growth of the nation's money supply.
2. According to the monetarists, fiscal policy (federal taxes and spending) should not be used to counteract the turns of a business cycle.
3. Monetarists believe that government attempts to eliminate fluctuations in the economy have made them worse, not better. The monetarists' argument is that, by the time an economic disturbance is perceived and a policy is formulated and implemented to correct it, it is too late. The effects of the policy will not be felt until the economy has begun to recover from the disturbance. Thus, such policy serves to magnify rather than to dampen fluctuations in the economy. Accordingly, monetarists favor letting small fluctuations work themselves out without government intervention.

B. **Supply-siders** (who hold to a philosophy popularized by the Reagan Administration) favor restoring incentives to the economy by cutting taxes to stimulate work, savings, and investment.

1. A progressive tax structure provides a strong disincentive for increasing effort and subsequent economic achievement. At higher income levels, more and more of every dollar gained is earned for government rather than for personal use. Hence, supply-siders argue that deep cuts in personal and business taxes will produce a strong recovery due not only to the increase in aggregate demand, but also to the increased motivation to achieve. It has been postulated that this recovery would offset tax losses with rising revenues, so that spending cuts might not be needed.
2. The economy will function better with new incentives to stimulate investment and production than with federal programs to redistribute wealth from rich to poor.

C. **Neo-Keynesians** represent a middle ground between Keynesians and monetarists. They continue to have confidence in the ability of aggregate demand policies (changes in government purchases, taxes, etc.) to influence economic activities. In addition, they accept that excessive monetary growth will lead inevitably to higher inflation. They believe, however, that at some levels of unemployment, money supply growth will lead primarily to increases in output and not just higher inflation. This theory is supported by an increasing number of moderate monetarists.

MONEY AND THE ECONOMY

A. Money functions as a

1. Medium of exchange
2. Standard of value
3. Store of value

B. **Definitions of Money**

1. **Narrow money** (M_1) **stock** includes
   a. Coins and currency
   b. Checking deposits
2. The Federal Reserve's targets for monetary growth emphasize M_2, which includes
   a. Coins and currency
   b. Checking deposits
   c. Nonchecking savings
   d. Small (less than $100,000) time deposits
3. M_1 and M_2 are the most common measures of money and are reported weekly in the *Wall Street Journal*.
4. A still broader definition (M_3) includes M_2 plus large ($100,000 or more) time deposits.
5. All assets have some degree of liquidity. One group of assets is referred to as **near money**. Short-term government securities are examples of near money, as are time deposits and nonchecking savings deposits.
   a. Financial assets are debt instruments, whereas real assets are productive items.

C. **Supply of Money -- Banks and Deposit Creation**

1. Commercial banks are businesses that must balance profits and liquidity.
2. A bank must have on reserve a certain percentage of its total deposits. These fractional reserve requirements are required by law in order to
   a. Insure that money will be on hand to carry out transactions
   b. Control the total supply of money
3. **Money multiplier**
   a. If a bank's actual reserves exceed the reserves required by law, it has excess reserves with which it can (and will, if it is a profit-maximizing bank) extend loans.
   b. An individual bank creates money equal to its excess reserves when it lends the excess reserves rather than investing in securities.
   c. For the banking system as a whole, assuming no leakage (i.e., assuming that all the money in the economy is in the bank), money creation is measured by a multiple of excess reserves, as follows:

   $$D = 1/r$$

   If: D = the money multiplier
   r = the legal reserve requirement

   d. EXAMPLE: Assume the banking system's excess reserves increase by $100 and we want to determine how much the money supply is increased. Using the above formula (and assuming the reserve requirement is 20%), we get the following increase in the money supply:

   $D = 1/.2 = 5$ The money supply is multiplied by 5.
   $5 \times \$100 = \$500$

4. The interest rate is expressed as a percentage.
   a. A basis point is 1/100 of 1%.

D. Monetary Policy

1. The **Federal Reserve Board (the Fed)** controls the money supply independently of the federal government. Any policy designed by the Fed to affect the money supply, and thus the economy, is known as monetary policy. Control of the growth of the money supply by the Fed is viewed as essential to control the availability of credit, spending, and inflation. One reason is that the money supply must grow at the same rate as the economy in order for the economy to be completely healthy.

2. Structure of the Fed

   a. The Board of governors has seven members appointed by the President and confirmed by the Senate.

      1) They serve fourteen-year terms, and their appointments are staggered.

      2) The board of governors is responsible for administering monetary policy and running the banking system.

      3) The chair and vice-chair are appointed for 4-year terms by the President and confirmed by the Senate.

   b. The Federal Reserve System is divided into twelve geographical districts.

   c. The federal open-market committee buys and sells bonds on the open market (changing the money supply).

3. The functions of the Federal Reserve include

   a. Control of the money supply
   b. Check collection
   c. Serving as the fiscal agent of the U.S. government
   d. Supervision of the entire banking system
   e. Holding deposits (reserves) for member institutions

      1) As a result, a federal funds market has developed for the lending member banks' reserves to other member banks.

         a) Thus, if one bank has excess reserves, it can earn additional interest by lending to another member bank that needs additional reserves.

         b) Federal funds loans are usually made for 1 day at a time.

         c) The federal funds rate is the rate paid on these overnight loans.

4. The Fed controls the money supply by using monetary policy tools.

   a. Major tools

      1) **Open-market operations.** Purchase and sale of government securities is the primary mechanism of monetary control.

         a) Fed purchases are expansionary; they increase bank reserves and the money supply.

         b) Fed sales are contractional. Paying money into the Federal Reserve takes the money out of circulation, reduces bank reserves, and contracts the money supply.

2) **Reserves**. The legal reserve requirement is the percentage of deposits that must be kept on hand.
   a) Lowering the percentage is expansionary (allowing banks to put more of their excess reserves into circulation through loans).
   b) Raising the percentage is contractional.
   c) This tool is not frequently used because it has very powerful effects on the economy.
3) **Changing the discount rate**. This rate is the interest rate at which member banks may borrow from the Fed.
   a) Lowering the rate encourages borrowing and increases the money supply.
   b) Raising the rate discourages borrowing, increases saving, and decreases the money supply.

b. Minor tools
   1) Moral suasion. "Jawbone control" entails merely asking banks to hold down rates.
   2) Margin requirements. The margin is the percentage of the purchase price of securities that cannot be borrowed. It determines the down payment requirements on stock purchases.
   3) Selective credit controls. For example, the Fed may require a certain percentage of down payment on durable good purchases.

5. The Federal Reserve cannot stabilize interest rates and at the same time control growth in reserves and the money supply because there is an inverse relationship between (1) interest rates and bank reserves and (2) interest rates and the money supply. Thus, the Federal Reserve has adopted the pragmatic policy of sometimes targeting interest rates and sometimes targeting the money supply.
   a. If the Fed wants to stabilize interest rates, more reserves must be supplied (which in turn can increase the money supply).
   b. EXAMPLE: If the reserve requirement is increased (giving banks lower free reserves to lend to borrowers), banks will not be able to supply all borrowers who want loans. Interest rates will be driven up to equalize the supply and demand for loans.

UNEMPLOYMENT AND INFLATION

A. **Unemployment**

1. **Full employment**

    a. Theoretical definition: Full employment exists when all individuals willing to work at prevailing market wages are employed at tasks appropriate for their skills.

    b. Policy definition: Full employment exists when the unemployment rate is approximately 5% to 7%. Normal workings of the market will result in about a 6% level of unemployment because of job turnover.

2. Types of unemployment

    a. **Frictional unemployment** is the amount of unemployment caused by the normal workings of the labor market. Thus, it is approximately 4% at "full" employment according to the policy definition. This definition acknowledges that there will be some unemployment at any given time as workers change jobs or are temporarily laid off.

    b. **Structural unemployment** exists when aggregate demand is sufficient to provide full employment, but the distribution of the demand does not correspond precisely to the composition of the labor force; e.g., some NASA engineers were unemployed at the end of the race to the moon.

    c. **Cyclical unemployment** is caused by insufficient aggregate demand. During economic downturns, there will be unemployment due to lack of demand.

3. Costs of unemployment

    a. Economic cost can be measured in terms of the forgone output, i.e., the gap between potential GDP under full employment and actual GDP.

    b. Noneconomic costs of unemployment, such as the individual and social degradation implicit in the loss of meaningful employment and income, are equally important.

B. **Inflation**

1. Inflation is an increase in the general level of prices. The general price level is negatively related to the purchasing power of money. There are several theories on the causes of inflation.

    a. **Cost-push**. Inflation is generated by increased production costs, which are passed on to consumers in the form of higher prices. Labor unions are often considered the source of these increased costs.

        1) More recently, labor unions have become relatively less powerful because of expansion of service industries relative to basic manufacturing.

        2) Relatedly, blue-collar membership has declined on a relative basis.

    b. **Demand-pull**. Inflation is generated by excess aggregate demand for goods and services.

        1) This problem is possible with fiscal policy spending, i.e., creating excessive demand.

        2) Conversely, increasing taxes decreases consumer spending and lessens inflationary pressures.

2. Measuring inflation

   a. **The consumer price index (CPI)** measures inflation by a monthly pricing of items on a typical household shopping list.

   b. **The wholesale price index (WPI)** measures increases in prices at the wholesale level. It is often accepted as a proxy for future inflation.

   c. **GDP deflator** includes every item produced in the economy at the price at which it entered the GDP account.

3. Costs of inflation

   a. The rate is difficult to predict.
   b. Usury laws may prevent borrowing if interest rates are too high.
   c. Negotiating long-term contracts may be difficult.
   d. The efficiency of business relationships is reduced.
   e. Breach of existing contracts is encouraged.

4. Redistributive effects of inflation

   a. Inflation hurts creditors, fixed-income groups, and savers.

      1) But inflation benefits debtors because they pay back their debts in less valuable dollars.

   b. Inflation is an arbitrary redistribution of income that does not reflect the operations of the free market or the government's attempt to alter income distribution.

C. **Inflation versus Unemployment Trade-off**

1. Economic theory has historically treated inflation and unemployment as mutually exclusive agents.

2. Fluctuations in aggregate demand reveal an inverse relationship between inflation and unemployment. The underlying reason for this trade-off is that the aggregate supply curve is upward sloping (i.e., more goods will be produced only at a higher price).

3. Modern macroeconomic theory suggests there is little or no relationship between inflation and unemployment. In the long run, unemployment will be near the natural rate (5% – 7%) regardless of the inflation rate. The downward-sloping Phillips curve that postulates an inverse relationship between inflation and unemployment is true only in the short run, although this short run may last 2 or 3 years.

4. **Phillips curve** -- an attempt to quantify the trade-off between inflation and unemployment. It is an empirical relationship showing the trade-offs between the rate of inflation and the rate of unemployment.

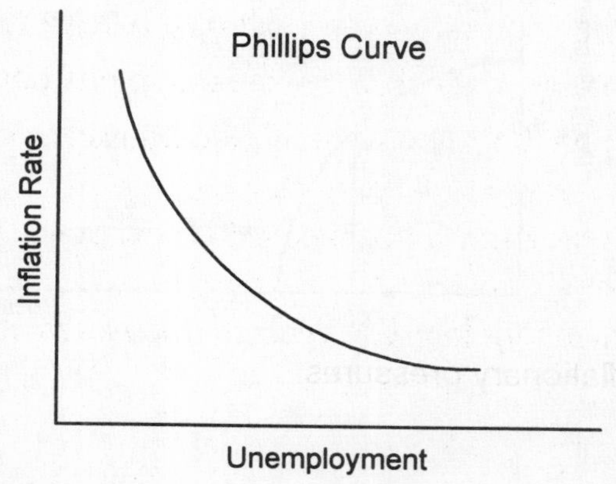

THE ROLE OF GOVERNMENT IN AN ECONOMIC SYSTEM

A. **Fiscal policy.** Government expenditures and taxation are aimed at certain socially acceptable goals (level of income, unemployment, distribution of income, etc.).

B. With the Full Employment Act of 1946, the Federal Government assumed responsibility for full employment, price stability, and economic growth.

C. Thus, government can justify entering a market in which market forces will not allocate resources efficiently.

D. Dividing consumption goods into two categories facilitates analysis of government's role in the market place.

   1. **Public goods** are characterized by

      a. Indivisibility of services (e.g., a public park)
      b. Difficulty of excluding individuals from the benefits (e.g., national defense)

   2. **Private goods**

      a. One individual's consumption of a private good excludes another from consuming that particular good (e.g., only one person can consume a strawberry milkshake, but everyone benefits from national defense).

   3. The relationship of government spending to private consumption and savings can be expressed graphically as shown below. The curvilinear line represents the maximum production level for the economy.

E. The market may not allocate resources efficiently with respect to public goods. Because a public good such as defense cannot be excluded from certain individuals, people often receive the benefit without paying for it. This is known as the "free rider" effect. Refer to the graph below.

   1. At point A, total societal consumption consists of Y amount of public goods and X amount of private goods. Because point A lies on the frontier, resources are being used efficiently.
   2. A society at point B has unemployment and inefficient use of its resources.
   3. The combination of public and private consumption represented by point C cannot be obtained in the short run. It lies beyond the frontier, which, by definition, is set at the maximum production level in the short run.

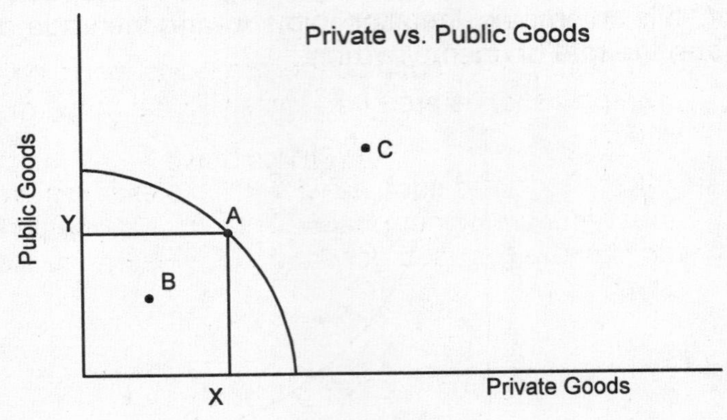

F. Government finances its expenditures by

1. **Taxation**

a. Two principles of taxation

1) Benefits received. Individuals should pay tax based on the benefits received from the services (e.g., paying for the use of a public park or swimming pool).

2) Ability to pay. Consumers should pay taxes based on their ability to pay them (e.g., taxes on income and wealth).

b. Three classifications of taxes reflecting ability-to-pay principles

1) **Progressive**. With a higher income, individuals pay a higher percentage of their income in taxes (e.g., income tax).

2) **Proportional**. At all levels of income, the percentage paid in taxes is constant (e.g., sales tax).

3) **Regressive**. As income increases, the percentage paid in taxes decreases (e.g., payroll or excise taxes).

a) EXAMPLE: An excise tax is regressive because its burden falls disproportionately on lower-income persons. As personal income increases, the percentage of income paid declines since an excise tax is a flat amount per quantity of the good or service purchased.

c. Taxes also may be classified as either direct or indirect.

1) **Direct taxes** are imposed upon the taxpayer and paid directly to the government, e.g., the personal income tax.

2) **Indirect taxes** are levied against others and thus only indirectly on the individual taxpayer, e.g., sales and Social Security taxes paid by employers.

d. **Incidence of taxation** -- the parties who actually bear a particular tax. For example, the person who actually bears the burden of an indirect tax may not be the same one who pays the tax to the government.

1) The incidence of taxation becomes important when a government wants to change the tax structure. Because taxation is a form of fiscal policy, the government needs to know who will actually bear the incidence of taxation, not just who will pay the tax.

2) EXAMPLE: Taxes such as the corporate income tax and corporate property and excise taxes are often shifted to the consumer in the form of higher prices.

3) EXAMPLE: Taxes such as windfall profits taxes are not shifted to the consumer via higher prices. This type of one-time-only tax levied on part of the output produced does not increase the equilibrium price of the taxed good.

e. In recent years, some authorities have supported a tax based on consumption -- a **value-added tax**.

1) Many major industrial nations have already adopted a value-added tax.

2) The tax is levied on the value added to goods by each business unit in the production and distribution chain.

a) The amount of value added is measured by the difference between a firm's sales and its purchases.

b) Each firm in the chain collects the tax on its sales, takes a credit for taxes paid on purchases, and remits the difference to the government.

c) The consumer ultimately bears the incidence of the tax through higher prices.

3) A value-added tax encourages consumer saving because taxes are paid on consumption only, not on savings.

a) Because the value-added tax is based on consumption, people in the lower income groups would spend a greater proportion of their income on taxes.

b) The value-added tax is thus regressive.

4) Only those businesses that make a profit have to pay income taxes. Under the value-added tax, however, all businesses have to pay taxes, regardless of income.

2. Debt -- an alternative means of financing

a. Individuals lend to the government on a voluntary basis, whereas taxation is mandatory.

b. Debt spreads the cost over time, allowing future generations to share in the payment of public goods.

1) In contrast, taxation is immediate payment for the goods.

c. **The crowding-out effect**. When the government sells bonds to finance its expenditures, it competes with corporations that are trying to sell their own shares or bonds, thereby dividing a limited market, increasing interest rates, and reducing corporate borrowing and investment.

d. **The crowding-in effect**. In times of slack economic conditions, additional government spending will increase national income (by shifting aggregate demand), which will encourage investment.

G. **Other Government Activities**

1. The activity in which government has increased the most since 1929 is that of welfare expenditures. These **transfer payments** include Medicare, Social Security, welfare, unemployment compensation, and food stamps.
2. Through taxation, the government can alter society's distribution of income, which can be depicted by the Lorenz curve. The Lorenz curve below illustrates the inequality of income distribution. The more bowed out (convex to the X-axis) the curve, the more unequal the distribution of wealth in a country.

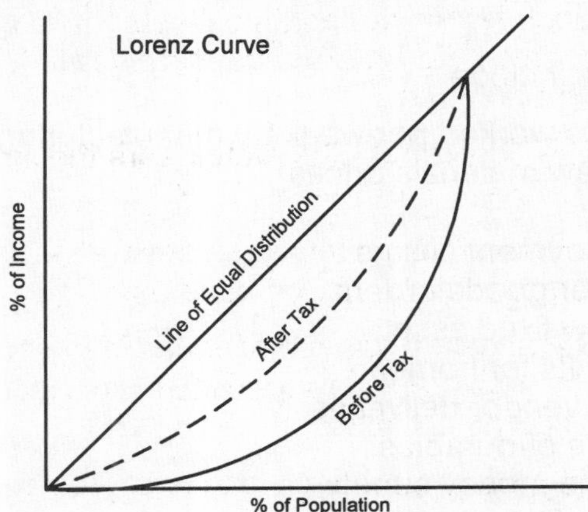

   a. If all individuals had equal incomes, the Lorenz curve would lie on the 45° line. The actual income distribution may approximate the before-tax line.
   b. With progressive taxation, however, the government can shift the curve closer to equal distribution of income (as shown by the broken line).

3. **Automatic stabilizers** -- elements in the economy that support aggregate demand when it would otherwise be weak (e.g., during a recession) and hold down aggregate demand when it would otherwise be increasing (e.g., during an expansionary period). They reduce the economy's sensitivity to shifts in demand.
   a. Examples of automatic stabilizers
      1) Income taxes
      2) Unemployment insurance
      3) Corporate profits tax
      4) Agricultural price supports
   b. Income tax rates are indexed to inflation so that tax liabilities will not increase solely because of inflation. The enactment of indexation, however, has eliminated an automatic stabilizer. Thus, even though individual taxpayers have more after-tax income with indexation, inflation may get worse as a result.

ECONOMIC INDICATORS

A. The study of **business cycles** focuses on the periodic upswings and downturns in the economy.

1. A business cycle has four stages: trough, recovery, peak, and recession.
2. A **trough** is marked by low levels of economic activity and underuse of resources.
3. **Recovery** is marked by increasing economic activity.
4. The **peak** is that period when economic activity is booming.
5. **Recession** means economic activities and employment levels contract.
   a. During the recessionary phase of a business cycle, economic activities and employment levels contract, and there is underuse of a society's resources.

B. Economists use a variety of economic indicators to forecast turns in the business cycle.

1. Economic indicators are variables that in the past have had a high correlation with aggregate economic activity.

2. Indicators may lead, lag, or coincide with economic activity.

   a. A leading indicator is one that changes before the stage in the business cycle changes.

   b. A lagging indicator is one that changes after the business cycle itself has changed direction.

3. **Leading indicators** include

   a. Average hours worked per week by manufacturing workers
   b. Changes in raw materials prices
   c. Stock prices
   d. Initial unemployment claims
   e. New consumer goods orders
   f. Orders for new fixed assets
   g. Building permits for homes
   h. Timeliness of vendor deliveries
   i. Unfilled orders of durables
   j. Changes in the money supply
   k. Consumer confidence

4. **Lagging indicators** include

   a. Average duration of employment in weeks
   b. Unit labor costs in the private business sector
   c. Average prime rate charged by banks

C. Investment expenditure is a focal point used by economists to explain why business cycles occur.

1. The **accelerator theory** gives a model for volatility of investment and the subsequent effects on national income.

   a. The accelerator theory states that capital investment is related to the rate of change in national income.

   b. It assumes a particular level of capital equipment needed to produce a given level of output.

2. Given an economy producing at capacity and a subsequent increase in product demand, an increase in capital investment is required to meet the increased demand. The demand for capital goods then creates an additional increase in demand, which in turn requires an additional investment in capital goods. In this fashion, the process of investing to meet demand continues to accelerate.

3. Once an upswing is under way, it builds momentum and continues for a period of time.

STUDY UNIT 3
INTERNATIONAL ECONOMICS

INTRODUCTION

International economics as covered on Part 1 of the CMA exam is both macro (e.g., principles of international supply and demand, foreign currency, etc.) and, to a lesser extent, micro (e.g., the effects of trade restrictions on individual companies). In the ICMA's content specification outlines, international economics is a subject area under the major topic of macroeconomics and international economics. These combined topics account for 10% to 15% of Part 1. As you can see from this short outline, the level tested is quite basic.

COMPARATIVE AND ABSOLUTE ADVANTAGE

A. When nations specialize in what they produce most efficiently and then exchange with others, more is produced and consumed than if each nation tries to be self-sufficient. We know that specialization of labor is beneficial for individuals; the same principle applies to nations.

B. Countries vary greatly in their efficiency in producing certain goods because of the immobility of resources. This difference can be largely attributed to differences from country to country in the following five factors:

1. Climatic and geographical conditions
2. Human capacities
3. Supply and type of capital accumulation
4. Proportions of resources
5. Political and social climates

C. Given the above differences, it is clear that countries can mutually benefit from trade. The greatest advantage from trade will be obtained if each nation specializes in producing what it can produce most efficiently.

D. This principle of **comparative advantage** can be explained with the help of the following chart:

Comparative Costs of Production

	U.S.	Japan
Food (1 bushel)	1	2
Cars	1.5	1

If the countries consume only the above two goods, is there an advantage to specializing? Yes, there will be an increase in total output if the U.S. uses its resources to grow food and Japan uses its resources to produce cars (given a fixed amount of inputs).

1. Total output will be maximized when each nation specializes in the products in which it has the greatest comparative advantage or the least comparative disadvantage.
2. EXAMPLE: Assume that the costs in the chart on the previous page are solely for labor and that labor is the only input required for the production of food and cars. Thus, for 100,000 units of labor input, the U.S. economy can produce either 100,000 bushels of food or 66,667 cars. If the labor input is divided equally, however, the U.S. economy can produce 50,000 bushels of food and 33,333 cars. At the same time, if the Japanese economy divides its efforts equally, input of 100,000 units of labor can produce 25,000 bushels of food and 50,000 cars. In the absence of world trade, the two economies together can produce 75,000 bushels of food (50,000 + 25,000) and 83,333 cars (33,333 + 50,000). But if each country concentrates on the product in which it has a comparative advantage, the total production will be 100,000 bushels of food (all produced in the U.S.) and 100,000 cars (all produced in Japan).
3. Comparative advantage is different from absolute advantage. In the above example, the U.S. has an **absolute** advantage with respect to food production because the price of food is lower in the U.S. than in Japan. Japan has an absolute advantage in car production. Along with its absolute advantage, the U.S. has a **comparative** advantage in food production because its opportunity cost for food production (cars forgone) is lower than Japan's. Similarly, Japan's opportunity cost for car production (food forgone) is lower. Hence, Japan has a comparative advantage in car production.
    a. **Comparative advantage** compares costs within a single country. No matter what the costs may be elsewhere, the U.S. will always have a comparative advantage in the production of food rather than cars. Similarly, Japan has a comparative advantage in the production of cars as opposed to food.
    b. **Absolute advantage** compares the costs of inputs between countries. Thus, a given country might have an absolute advantage with respect to every product compared with a specific other country.
    c. In the above example, Japan would continue to have a comparative advantage with respect to cars even if its costs were 1.6. In that case, the U.S. would have an absolute advantage (1.5 is less than 1.6).
4. A nation will export goods in which it has a comparative advantage and import goods in which it has a comparative disadvantage.
    a. Developing countries exporting primarily raw materials are dependent on vibrant economies in developed (importing) countries.
5. If a country has only two factors of production (labor and capital) and a relative abundance of capital, it will tend to export capital-intensive goods and import labor-intensive goods. Thus, factors of production and the varying efficiency in producing goods determine which products a country will export and import.
    a. Capital-intensive goods are those requiring a high level of investment, e.g., oil refining.
    b. Labor-intensive goods are those requiring a high level of labor, e.g., manufacture of fashion clothes.
6. For nations to receive the full advantages of international specialization and exchange, free trade must be allowed among all countries.

FOREIGN EXCHANGE

A. For international trade to take place, the two currencies involved must be easily converted at some prevailing exchange rate. The **exchange rate** is the price of one country's currency in terms of another country's currency.

1. Currency appreciates when it can buy more units of another currency.
2. Currency depreciates when it can purchase fewer units of another currency.
3. In other words, depreciation in country A's currency is an appreciation of the currency of country B.

B. Exchange rates are determined in three ways.

1. Equilibrium exchange rates in floating markets are determined by the supply of and demand for the currencies.

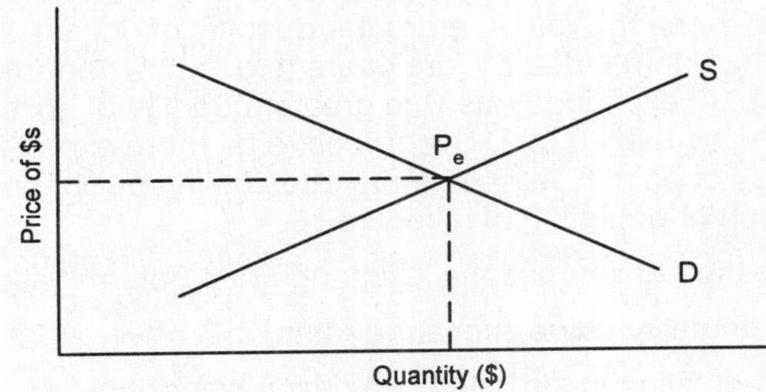

The equilibrium rate of P_e will prevail in the market. No surplus (or deficit) occurs at P_e.

   a. Demand for currencies comes from
      1) Importing goods and services
      2) Investor global trading
         a) EXAMPLE: An American buys a French stock or bond.
      3) International corporate activity
   b. Supply of currencies comes from reversing these transactions (e.g., a French citizen buys an IBM computer or Exxon stock).

2. Fixed exchange rates are set by some outside force (e.g., the government).
   a. An exchange rate set too high creates a deficit balance of payments. This deficit must be financed by drawing down foreign reserves or by borrowing from the central banks of the foreign countries. This is short-term because at some time the country will run out of foreign reserves.
      1) A major reason for a country's devaluation is to improve its balance of payments.

b. An exchange rate set too low creates a surplus balance of payments. In this case, surplus reserves build up. At some time, the country will not want any greater reserve balances and will have to raise the value of its currency.

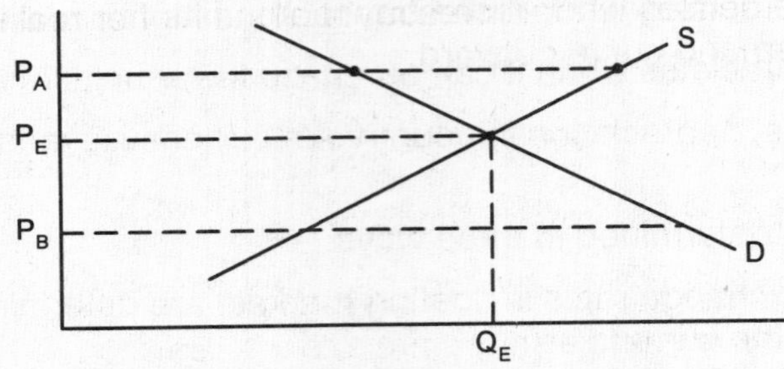

c. Assuming the vertical axis is measured in foreign currency units per dollar and the horizontal axis in dollars, at exchange rate A, a greater quantity of dollars is supplied by U.S. sources than demanded by foreigners (e.g., more imports into the U.S. and fewer exports). At exchange rate B, a greater quantity of dollars is demanded by foreigners than supplied by U.S. sources (e.g., more exports from the U.S. than imports). Only at point E will exchange rates be in equilibrium; i.e., there will be no accumulation or depletion of reserves.

3. A **managed float** is the current method of international exchange rate determination.

   a. Supply and demand forces primarily guide exchange rates.

   b. During periods of extreme fluctuation in the value of a nation's currency, intervention by governments and/or central banks may occur to maintain fairly stable exchange rates.

C. Floating exchange rates may fluctuate differently in the long, medium, and short term.

1. Long-term exchange rates are dictated by purchasing-power parity.

   a. In the long run, real prices should be the same (net of government taxes or trade barriers and transportation costs) for all goods in all countries, i.e., **purchasing-power parity**. Exchange rates will adjust until purchasing-power parity is achieved.

2. Medium-term exchange rates are dictated by the economic activity in a country.

   a. When the U.S. is in a recession, spending on imports (as well as domestic goods) will decrease.

   b. This reduced spending on imports shifts the supply curve for dollars to the left, causing the equilibrium value of the dollar to increase (assuming the demand for dollars is constant); that is, at any given exchange rate, the supply to foreigners is less.

   c. If more goods are exported because of an increased preference for U.S. goods, the demand curve for dollars shifts to the right, causing upward pressure on the value of the dollar.

   d. An increase in imports or a decrease in exports will have effects opposite to those described above.

3. Short-term exchange rates are dictated by interest rates.
   a. Big corporations and banks invest their large reserves of cash where the real interest rate is highest.
   b. A rise in the real interest rate will lead to an appreciation of that currency because it will be demanded for investment at the higher real interest rate, thereby shifting the demand curve outward.
   c. The reverse holds true for a fall in real interest rates because that currency will be sold as investors move their money out of the country.

D. **Interaction in Foreign Exchange Markets**

1. **Spot rate** -- exchange rate paid for delivery of currency on the spot (today)
2. **Forward exchange rate** -- future price of the currency
   a. If the forward rate is greater than the spot rate, the currency is selling at a premium; speculators expect the currency to appreciate.
   b. If the spot rate is greater than the forward rate, it is selling at a discount; speculators expect the currency to depreciate.
3. The discount or premium is related to the difference between the nominal interest rates paid by foreign and domestic banks (differences in interest rates are largely related to differences in expected inflation).
   a. When the foreign nominal interest rate is lower than the domestic nominal rate, the forward foreign currency sells at a premium.
      1) If this were not true, investors would borrow at the lower interest rate, invest at the higher rate, and buy a forward contract for the principal and interest.
   b. If the foreign nominal rate exceeds the domestic nominal rate, the forward foreign currency sells at a discount.
4. A foreign currency will depreciate relative to the dollar at a rate equivalent to the amount by which its inflation rate exceeds the dollar's inflation rate (everything else constant).
   a. EXAMPLE: If the inflation rate in UK is 12% and the inflation rate in the U.S. is 10%, the dollar should appreciate by 2%.
5. Borrowing in a country with the lowest nominal rate is not always best (but it is always best when the **real** rate is lowest).
   a. The foreign currency exchange rates equalize inflation rates.

E. **Avoidance of Risk in Foreign Exchange Markets**

1. Hedging by purchasing or selling forward exchange contracts
   a. Buy foreign exchange futures contracts to cover liabilities denominated in a foreign currency.
   b. Sell foreign exchange futures contracts to cover receivables denominated in a foreign currency.
   c. Any gain or loss on the foreign receivables or payables because of changes in exchange rates is offset by the loss or gain on the foreign exchange contract.
2. Minimizing receivables and liabilities denominated in foreign currencies

3. Maintaining balance between receivables and payables denominated in a foreign currency
    a. Large multinational corporations have established multinational netting centers as special departments to attempt to achieve balance between foreign receivables and payables.
        1) They also enter into foreign exchange futures contracts when necessary to achieve balance.

F. **Analysis of Foreign Investments**
1. Relevant cash flows are the dividends and possible future sales price of the investment paid to the investor.
2. Cost of capital in foreign projects is higher because of the increased
    a. Exchange risk -- changing exchange rates
    b. Sovereignty risk -- possibility of nationalization (or other restrictions), with net losses to the parent company
3. Foreign operations are more difficult to manage and control than domestic operations.

G. Foreign investments are funded by
1. Parent company resources
2. Common stock sale in the foreign country
3. Bond sales in the foreign country
4. Borrowing in world financial markets

BALANCE OF PAYMENTS

A. The balance of payments includes all international payments made by one nation to another, including those for imports, exports, investments, unilateral transfers, and capital movements. The principal accounts are the **current account** and the **capital account**.
1. The current account records
    a. Exports (credits) and imports (debits) of goods
        1) The **balance of trade** is the difference between total exports and total imports of goods.
    b. Exports (credits) and imports (debits) of services
        1) The **balance on goods and services** is the difference between total exports and total imports of goods and services.
    c. Interest and dividends received on investments abroad (credits) and interest and dividends paid on foreign investments in the U.S. (debits)
    d. Net unilateral transfers, e.g., foreign aid, pension payments, and remittance to relatives (credits or debits depending on whether the flow is into or out of the U.S., respectively)
    e. The balance on the current account
2. The capital account records capital flows resulting from the purchase and sale of fixed or financial assets.
    a. Inflows of foreign capital (credits) are effectively exports of stocks and bonds and therefore result in inflows of foreign exchange.
    b. Outflows of capital (debits) use up supplies of foreign exchange.
    c. A capital account surplus therefore indicates that inflows exceeded outflows.

3. The balance of payments deficit or surplus is the net of the current and capital account balances.
4. The references to debits and credits treat the balance of payments account as if it were a revenue or expense account. In other words, a debit is similar to an expense in that it is unfavorable for the country's balance of payments position.
   a. EXAMPLE: A debit (such as an import) is undesirable because it contributes to an unfavorable balance of payments. The U.S. has an unfavorable balance of payments when payments by the U.S. to foreign countries exceed the payments made from foreign countries to the U.S. It is also unfavorable because foreign currency reserves held by the U.S. must be given up to correct the imbalance.
   b. A credit in the balance of payments account is desirable (exports, for instance) because foreigners will be paying more to the U.S. than the U.S. is paying out. Thus, the foreign currency reserves available to the U.S. increase.
5. In addition to decreasing the reserves of foreign currencies held by the U.S., an unfavorable balance of payments can also affect the domestic economy.
   a. EXAMPLE: An excess of imports can cause an unfavorable balance of payments. At the same time, consumers may not be buying domestic products, which may result in domestic layoffs and production cutbacks. These in turn will mean less investment opportunity domestically, and investors will begin sending their investment dollars overseas. The flow of capital overseas compounds the balance of payments problem because investing in a foreign country is essentially the same as importing a product (i.e., the investor is importing foreign stocks and bonds).
   b. Steps to correct an unfavorable balance of payments
      1) Establish import quotas.
         a) One country's unfavorable balance of payments may be caused by another nation's import quotas. For example, if the U.S. has a continuing unfavorable balance of payments with Japan, it might be possible to encourage Japan to remove the trade barriers set up to keep U.S. electronics products out. The removal of Japan's trade restrictions would help the U.S. balance of payments (but might result in an unfavorable balance of payments for Japan).
      2) Provide export incentives.
         a) EXAMPLE: The tax law provisions for Domestic International Sales Corporations (DISCs) and Foreign Sales Corporations (FSCs) permit exporters to postpone or avoid income taxes on export-related income as long as that income is reinvested in export-related assets.
      3) Develop substitutes for products currently being imported.
         a) EXAMPLE: The U.S. has tried to develop substitutes or local sources for imported oil. Products such as gasohol and solar energy have grown in popularity as the government has emphasized the patriotic aspects of these new products; i.e., they contribute to a favorable balance of payments.
6. A balance of payments deficit (imbalance) must be equalized by shipments of goods or reductions in reserves.
   a. Gifts and grants are also used.

7. In the 1980s, the U.S. became the nation with the largest foreign debt. The reasons include the following:
   a. Federal budget deficits financed by foreigners
   b. Growth in the economy that attracted foreign investors
   c. High real interest rates
   d. A strengthened dollar in the early 1980s that encouraged imports
   e. The shift from a manufacturing to a service economy
   f. A decrease in exports of agricultural goods
8. The following are the actual or potential effects of the U.S.'s position as a debtor:
   a. An increase in the percentage of the GDP used for debt service
   b. Reduced reserves leading to a devalued dollar, inflation, and increased exports
   c. A decline in net imports and improvement in the trade balance
   d. Increased savings as a result of economic uncertainty
   e. Increased pressure for trade protectionism
   f. Interest rates possibly remaining high to curtail inflation and tighten the money supply, with the consequent incentive for foreign investment

TRADE BARRIERS

A. Even though individuals (as a whole) are best off under free trade, governments often establish policies designed to block the importation of certain products. Governmental devices used to control trade are
   1. **Tariffs** -- a tax on imports designed to restrict imports, e.g., tax on German beer
   2. **Import quotas** -- fixed limits on different products, e.g., French wine
      a. In the short run, import quotas will help a country's balance of payments position.
      b. In addition, domestic employment will increase.
      c. But the prices of the products produced will also increase.
   3. **Export subsidies** -- payments by the government to producers in certain industries in an attempt to increase exports
   4. **Special tax benefits to exporters** -- an indirect form of export subsidy. The best U.S. examples are Foreign Sales Corporations (FSCs), which are entities located in U.S. possessions or in countries with tax information exchange agreements with the U.S. FSCs receive an exemption of about 15% of qualified export income.
   5. **Domestic content rules** -- requirement that at least a portion of any imported product be constructed from parts manufactured in the importing nation
      a. This rule is sometimes used by capital-intensive nations. Parts can be produced using idle capacity and then sent to a labor-intensive country for final assembly.

B. The economic effect of tariffs and quotas on free trade is to shift workers from relatively efficient export industries into less efficient protected industries. Real wage rates will decline as a result, as will total world output.

C. A major reason for trade restrictions is that the costs of competition are direct and concentrated (people lose jobs and firms go out of business), but benefits of unrestricted trade are less noticeable and occur in the future (lower prices, higher wages, more jobs in export industries).
   1. Special-interest groups are strong and well organized, and they lobby effectively, getting legislation passed that is harmful to free trade.
   2. Furthermore, blocks of trading nations (e.g., the European Union) discriminate against nonmember countries.

3. **General Agreement on Tariffs and Trade (GATT)** was designed to encourage reductions in trade barriers. The signatory countries have agreed to equal treatment of all member nations, multilateral negotiations to reduce tariffs, and the abolition of import quotas. Recent emphasis has been on agricultural matters, trade in services, foreign economic investment, and intellectual property rights.

INTERNATIONAL MONETARY SYSTEM

A. In the last 50 years, international monetary crises have periodically been in the news. Economic conditions have changed rapidly. Following is a brief description of events that have helped shape today's monetary situation.

   1. The monetary system that prevailed in the post-World War II period was devised in 1944. It was a system of fixed exchange rates based on a modified gold standard. International reserves in this system included foreign currencies and the right to borrow in specified situations. The International Monetary Fund (IMF) was created and is still active today.

      a. Resources of the IMF consist of a pool of currency from which participating countries can draw during short-term balance of payments difficulties.

      b. The World Bank was created at the same time as the IMF.

         1) Its purpose is to provide credit for development purposes to underdeveloped countries.

   2. In the post-war years, the U.S. dollar became the world's key currency used for transactions and reserves.

   3. By the mid-1950s, fixed exchange rates and changing economic conditions turned the dollar shortage into a dollar glut. Holders tried to convert dollars to other currencies, causing the dollar to decline in value.

   4. In the early 1970s, convertibility of gold into dollars was abolished by the U.S., breaking down the entire fixed-rate international system. Most countries agreed to allow the currencies to float to determine the new rates, but these countries would frequently intervene in support of their currencies.

   5. In 1976 the leading (noncommunist) nations developed a system called the Jamaica Agreement. This agreement moved the world to a system of managed floating exchanges. Each country had greater autonomy in managing its exchange rate.

B. **Eurodollars** are U.S. dollars held at banks outside of the U.S., either foreign banks or branches of U.S. banks. The growth in the use of Eurodollars has been spectacular because they facilitate the exchange of goods between other nations (often the exchanges use dollars even if the U.S. is not involved in the transaction).

MULTINATIONAL CORPORATIONS

A. The home country benefits from multinational operations because of improved earnings and exports of products to foreign subsidiaries. A multinational company may also be better able to obtain scarce resources than a domestic corporation. The existence of multinationals tends to benefit everyone to the extent they foster more international trade, freer trading policies, a better international monetary system, and improved international understanding.

   1. The home country, however, may suffer adverse balance of payments effects as a result of investment in foreign nations. Jobs may be lost to foreign subsidiaries, unions weakened, and tax revenues diminished. The multinational may also have a competitive advantage over domestic rivals. Furthermore, multinationals incur greater risk of expropriation and reduced flexibility of operation in a foreign political system.

B. The host country for a multinational operation reaps the advantages of the investment of capital, technology, and management abilities. Output and efficiency often improve along with exports and the balance of payments. The presence of a multinational may stimulate competition, increase tax revenues, and produce a higher standard of living.

   1. But payment of royalties, dividends, and profits can result in a net capital outflow. Multinationals sometimes establish economically unreasonable transfer prices among subsidiaries so that profits will be earned where taxes are lowest or restrictions on the export of profits are least stringent. Moreover, multinationals may engage in anticompetitive activities, such as formation of cartels.

NORTH AMERICAN FREE TRADE AGREEMENT (NAFTA)

A. NAFTA was passed by the U.S. Congress in late 1993. The agreement basically provides for free trade among the USA, Canada, and Mexico. The pact creates the world's largest free trade zone, stretching from the Yukon to the Yucatan. Three nations and 360 million people are linked into one economic unit.

B. The consensus is that Mexico will benefit the most by the agreement because many U.S. firms are likely to transfer assembly operations to Mexican subsidiaries with lower labor costs.

   1. To a great extent, NAFTA will correct the gross disparities between the open markets of the USA and the relatively closed markets of Mexico.
   2. U.S. companies should be able to sell more goods to Mexico because Mexicans will have greater disposable income due to the new industries transferring there.
   3. The biggest fear in the USA is that NAFTA will cause the loss of jobs to Mexico due to the lower labor costs and the more lax environmental standards. Supporters of NAFTA claim that the pact will create 200,000 more jobs in the USA than it eliminates over the next two years, because of the increase in exports.
   4. The financial services industry, such as mutual funds, banks, and brokers, should benefit by NAFTA since the agreement allows U.S. financial firms, for the first time, to have easy access to Mexican investors. Also, with the opening of Mexico's financial markets, more opportunities for U.S. investors will emerge.
   5. American low-tech industries, such as shoe makers and apparel manufacturers, may be hurt by increased competition from cheaper Mexican products. U.S. citrus and vegetable farmers also fear increased competition from Mexico.
   6. High-tech firms in the USA may benefit because there will be few Mexican products to compete against and exports will expand.

C. With respect to transition rules, tariffs ended on about half of the more than 9,000 products covered by the agreement. Tariffs on another 15% of the goods will end in 5 years, and the rest of the products will be duty-free at the end of 15 years.

   1. One of the biggest controversies during negotiations was determining the products to be protected with the longest tariff phaseouts. The USA won long phaseouts for such items as sneakers, household glassware, asparagus, broccoli, peanuts, and orange juice concentrate.

D. The theory behind free trade zones is that they benefit consumers by lowering prices and that manufacturers and workers gain from expanded markets for the items each country produces most efficiently.

STUDY UNIT 4
INSTITUTIONAL ENVIRONMENT OF BUSINESS

INTRODUCTION

All businesses in the United States are subject to at least one form of governmental regulation. Such regulation exists at federal, state, and local levels. However, only the federal level is tested on the CMA exam (except for the structure and operation of corporations under state law). Regulation may take the form of statutes, rules, and regulations, and their ongoing enforcement by courts, agencies, and commissions.

A phenomenon characteristic of the last 25 years is the explosion of social regulation. Social regulation is intended to benefit society as a whole. Its purpose is to reach behavior that is thought to be not purely financial or economic. The activities of such agencies as the Equal Employment Opportunity Commission, the Consumer Product Safety Commission, the Occupational Safety and Health Administration, and the Environmental Protection Agency are examples. Social regulation has increased because of heightened consumer and environmental activism, the rise of the civil rights and women's movements, and improved communications capacities. However, social regulation, like other forms of governmental intervention, has costs. The results are increased prices and inflation, reduced innovation and consumer choice, and decreased productivity. One often-expressed concern is that the marginal benefit of social regulation may not equal the marginal cost.

Part 1 of the CMA examination tests the candidates' knowledge of major federal legislation that regulates businesses, major federal agencies, rules and regulations promulgated thereunder, reasons for the enactment of the legislation or creation of an agency, and the effects of that legislation or agency on business. The effect of regulation on firms, e.g., on costs and prices, and the rationale for regulation are embodied in microeconomic theory. Turn back to the Microeconomics outline in Study Unit 1 for review of applicable concepts, e.g., monopoly, oligopoly, rate base, etc. Institutional environment of business subjects will account for approximately 10% to 15% of Part 1.

GENERAL

A. **Statutes (Legislation)**

1. A statute must be passed by a majority vote of both the House of Representatives and the Senate, and then be signed by the President.
   a. If the President does not sign, a statute can still be passed by a two-thirds vote of the House and Senate.
2. A statute is required for an agency or a commission to be created.

B. **Agencies and Commissions**

1. An agency or commission may regulate some area of all industries or may regulate a specific industry.
   a. EXAMPLES:
      1) The Occupational Safety and Health Administration (OSHA) regulates labor safety in all businesses, and the Federal Trade Commission (FTC) regulates unfair business practices and competition among almost all industries.
      2) The Federal Communications Commission (FCC) regulates use of the airwaves by broadcasters. The Federal Aviation Administration (FAA) regulates the field of aviation, and the Interstate Commerce Commission (ICC) regulates other interstate carriers.
2. Agencies and commissions may be given functions of investigation, enforcement, rule making, and adjudication.
   a. They do not have the power to impose criminal sanctions.
   b. Exam emphasis is on the promulgated rules.
3. They must act within the authority granted by the statutes authorizing their formation and function.

C. **Rules and Regulations**

1. Rules and regulations may not go beyond the scope of the statutes under which they are promulgated.
2. They may be promulgated under general grant of authority to an agency to regulate an industry.
   a. EXAMPLE: The Federal Energy Regulatory Commission (FERC) makes rules for rate setting under its authority to regulate public utilities.
3. They may be promulgated under specific grant of authority to an agency to make detailed rules carrying out objectives of a statute.
   a. EXAMPLE: The Internal Revenue Service (IRS) makes rules to carry out specific statutes, but it is not given the general authority to make rules for the collection of revenue.

D. **Courts** interpret statutes, regulations, and the actions of agencies when a dispute develops and one or both parties wish a judicial determination.

E. All of these programs are designed to implement social change.

F. Some rules, agencies, and legislation have **sunset provisions** that require periodic review and reenactment or they terminate.

G. Small businesses have sometimes been exempted from social regulation because Congress felt that compliance costs would be an excessive burden for small firms.

FINANCIAL

A. Securities Act of 1933

1. The purpose of this act is to provide complete and fair **disclosure** to potential investors. The emphasis is on disclosure.
   a. The act applies only to initial issuance of securities.
   b. Once a potential investor has complete disclosure, (s)he should be able to make a reasonable decision.
   c. Disclosure is accomplished through the requirement that a registration statement be filed with the Securities and Exchange Commission (SEC).
      1) The potential investors must receive a prospectus, the contents of which are highly regulated. It is first filed with the SEC as part of the registration.
2. Certain securities and transactions are exempt. The major exemptions are
   a. Private placement may be offered only to knowledgeable and sophisticated investors and to no more than 35 purchasers, and it may not be offered to the public.
   b. Intrastate issues may be offered and sold only to persons within one state.

B. Securities Exchange Act of 1934

1. Purposes of the act
   a. To regulate trading of securities after initial issuance
   b. To provide adequate information to investors
   c. To prevent insiders from unfairly using nonpublic information
2. Securities exchanges, brokers and dealers, securities that are traded on exchanges, and high-volume securities traded over the counter must be registered.
3. Issuers must file frequent reports.
4. Insiders (officers, directors, and 10%-or-more shareholders) must turn over to the corporation any profits earned on purchases and sales that fall within 6 months of each other. They are also prohibited from buying or selling stock based on inside information not available to the public.
5. Antifraud provisions make it unlawful to use any manipulative or deceptive practices in the purchase or sale of securities.
   a. It is unlawful to make a false statement of a material fact or to omit a material fact that is necessary for a statement not to be misleading.
6. The SEC was created to enforce securities laws and regulate the issuance and trading of securities.
7. Refer to Study Unit 14, SEC Reporting Requirements, in Chapter 6 for further background on the securities acts.

C. Blue-Sky Laws

1. Blue-sky laws are state laws designed to prevent fraudulent or misleading security issues.
2. The name comes from the fact that some of the earliest laws prohibited "everything under the blue skies which is fraudulent."

D. Wages and Prices

1. In the unregulated marketplace, price is determined by a combination of supply and demand.
   a. The greater the supply, the lower the price. It is a scarcity of products that creates price; if a product were unlimited, it would be free.
      1) Conversely, the higher the price, the greater the supply that will be offered.
   b. The greater the demand, the higher the price. Without demand for a product, no price could be charged.
      1) Conversely, the higher the price, the lower the demand. This assumes the product is not necessary or that there are substitutes.
2. Our government has undertaken to regulate the free market in certain instances when an overriding public concern exists.
   a. EXAMPLES:
      1) Wages have been regulated in terms of minimum wages and required overtime pay.
         a) The purpose is to prevent undue exploitation of segments of society and to help reduce the welfare burden of government for those at the bottom of the pay scale.
         b) In recent years, there have been proposals that employers of teenaged workers be exempt from minimum wage laws in order to encourage firms to hire these less-qualified workers.
      2) Oil and gas have been regulated presumably because they are scarce and everyone needs to use energy for heat, transportation, etc.
         a) The need for conservation has overridden other concerns, and price deregulation began in the late 1970s.
      3) Airlines have been regulated in terms of not only prices, but also routes and mergers.
         a) An argument used for years was that prices had to be maintained so that airlines could afford to operate safely. Supposedly, genuine competition would threaten safety. Much of the airline industry has now been deregulated.
         b) The initial effects of deregulation have included the entry of new low-cost competitors with low operating costs that provide strong competition to established high-cost companies, and the merger or downsizing of some airlines. Under regulation, high costs (partially caused by regulatory agencies) were passed on to the public.
      4) The ICC has regulated prices and routes of railroads and motor carriers throughout this century.
         a) Paradoxically, it was thought regulation helped to maintain competition by saving businesses as costs changed from time to time and as one method of transportation became cheaper than the other. Here, too, deregulation is in process.
      5) A phenomenon in regard to price regulation is rent control. When rents skyrocketed during inflationary periods, rent controls were instituted in some parts of the country.

a) The reasoning behind rent control is that people need to have an affordable place to live.

b) The result has been a shortage of housing (fewer housing starts) and a greater neglect of the condition of existing housing.

3. Other industries have had price controls because they are regulated monopolies. Such industries usually have inelastic demand curves, which means regulation can help control prices.

   a. EXAMPLES:

      1) Public utilities are regulated monopolies under the theory that it would be inefficient and unworkable to have more than one of each type of utility in a locality. These are sometimes called natural monopolies.

         a) As a result, the FERC regulates the wholesale rate of public utilities, and local commissions regulate consumers' rates.

         b) The **rate base** is the amount of assets (reduced by accumulated depreciation) used in the company's operations.

         c) Normally, rates are set so that the capital providers earn a reasonable return on their investment.

         d) Public utilities can exercise the power of eminent domain and, with advance approval, may also introduce new services or alter existing ones.

      2) The regulation of the telephone system is based on the same type of reasoning as that of public utilities. However, substantial deregulation has also occurred in this industry.

E. **Political Contributions**

1. Corporations and labor unions may not contribute any money directly to a federal political campaign, candidate, or party.

2. Corporations and labor unions may make independent expenditures expressing their viewpoint or even endorsing candidates.

3. The Federal Elections Commission was created to oversee federal elections and to enforce and investigate political contributions and expenditure limitations.

F. **Banks and Other Financial Institutions**

1. The banking industry is one of the most heavily regulated.

2. Most regulation aimed at banks and other financial institutions has been concerned both with the financial health of the institution and with the safety of depositors' funds.

3. Regulation Q

   a. This regulation established interest rate ceilings for banks and thrifts.

   b. It was one of the most important regulations affecting banks and thrift institutions established by the Federal Reserve.

   c. It was a cause of credit crunches. In periods of high interest rates, deposits would be lost to instruments whose rate was not regulated.

   d. Recently, these rate ceilings have been removed by deregulation to increase competition among banking institutions.

4. Government regulation of federally chartered savings and loan associations (S&Ls) saw significant changes in 1989 because of the need to bail out the capsizing savings and loan industry.
   a. Congress committed $166 billion to rescue bankrupt S&Ls.
   b. More than 500 insolvent S&Ls were closed or merged.
   c. The previous thrift industry regulatory agency, the Federal Home Loan Bank Board, has been eliminated. Its replacement was a branch of the U.S. Treasury Department known as the Office of Thrift Supervision (OTS). The OTS was recently disbanded following completion of its oversight of the savings and loan bailout.
   d. The Federal Savings and Loan Insurance Corporation (FSLIC), a bankrupt agency that formerly supplied insurance to depositors, has been replaced by the Savings Association Insurance Fund (SAIF). Both SAIF and BIF (Bank Insurance Fund) are now under the FDIC (Federal Deposit Insurance Corporation), which insures commercial bank deposits for up to $100,000 per account. Member banks provide funding through payment of deposit insurance premiums.

LABOR AND SAFETY

A. **Norris-LaGuardia Act of 1932**

1. Prior to the enactment of this act, courts would issue injunctions against strikes even without hearing the union's argument.
2. The act removed the power of federal courts to issue injunctions against unions without a showing of fraud or violence.

B. **National Labor Relations Act (NLRA) of 1935** (also known as the Wagner Act)

1. Prior to the enactment of this act, employees could be discharged or not hired if associated with a union, and employers could refuse to recognize or bargain with unions.
2. Employees were given the right to
   a. Associate with, join, or form labor unions
   b. Bargain collectively with employers
   c. Engage in concerted activities for collective bargaining (in effect, exempting unions from antitrust laws)
3. Employers were required to bargain in good faith with unions.
4. The **National Labor Relations Board (NLRB)** was formed to administer the act.
   a. It hears grievances.
   b. After employees elect a union, the board declares the winning union to be the sole bargaining agent of the employees.

C. **Labor-Management Relations Act (Taft-Hartley Act) of 1947**

1. After the NLRA, unions became very powerful, strikes were crippling, and employees were coerced by labor bosses.
2. This act placed restraints on unions that resulted in a more even balance of power between labor and management.
   a. Unions could be guilty of not bargaining in good faith.
   b. The Federal Mediation and Conciliation Service was created to mediate disputes.
   c. The President was given authority to obtain an injunction against strikes for 80 days (**cooling-off period**) if national health, welfare, or security was threatened.

d. The **closed shop** was outlawed.
   1) A closed shop required union membership as a condition of obtaining employment.
   2) However, the **union shop** is still allowed in many states. In a union shop, an employee is required to join the union after employment.
   3) Some states have right-to-work laws that allow employees to work at any job without union membership.

e. Secondary strikes and featherbedding were prohibited.

D. **Labor Management Reporting and Disclosure Act (Landrum-Griffin Act) of 1959**

1. Corruption was found in unions, and individuals' interests were not protected.
2. The act extended the NLRA to the internal affairs of unions to make them more democratic and to give members more rights.
   a. Financial records were required to be retained and reports to be made to the government.

E. **Fair Labor Standards Act (Wage and Hour Law) of 1938**

1. Low wages, long hours, and child labor were common after the Depression.
2. The act provided for minimum wages and overtime, and prohibited child labor, except as regulated.

F. **Civil Rights Act of 1964**

1. The act prohibits discrimination in employment on the basis of race, color, religion, sex, or national origin.
2. The **Equal Employment Opportunity Commission (EEOC)** was created to investigate discrimination in employment.
   a. One of the primary goals is to help companies create plans providing affirmative action protection for current and future employees.
   b. The EEOC may initiate its own investigation of company practices thought to violate the Civil Rights Act. Companies found not to be in compliance face the possible loss of government contracts.
   c. Individuals who believe they have been discriminated against in hiring may request the EEOC to initiate court action.
   d. Under the act, a pervasive pattern or practice of discrimination, the employer's adoption of a neutral rule having an adverse impact on a protected class, and the adoption of a neutral rule that perpetuates past discrimination are violations that often must be proved, at least in part, by statistical evidence.
      1) A controversial remedy sometimes adopted in such cases is an affirmative action order, which provides preferences to members of the class that previously suffered from discrimination. Affirmative action preferences apply even though the specific persons benefited are not necessarily those who were victimized by illegal discrimination.
      2) Affirmative action programs are sometimes criticized because employment preferences are often viewed as reverse discrimination. Moreover, they may not result in the hiring, retention, and promotion of the most productive workers.
3. The issue of **comparable worth** has arisen because many believe that a wage disparity between individuals in completely different occupations (different jobs needing different skills) may also be a result of sex discrimination rather than a difference in the relative worth of the activities.

G. **Occupational Safety and Health Act of 1970**

1. The act created the **Occupational Safety and Health Administration (OSHA)** to protect the health and safety of all workers.
   a. OSHA has created many regulations to promote safety. All businesses that affect interstate commerce must adhere to these regulations unless specifically exempted (governmental entities and businesses regulated under other statutes are exempt).
   b. Entities subject to the act must also adhere to a general standard, that is, to provide a workplace free of known hazards. OSHA encourages labor-management committees to formulate safety and health programs.
   c. Various reporting, record keeping, and notice requirements are established, e.g., notice to workers of hazardous conditions.
   d. OSHA may impose civil penalties and seek injunctions, and intentional violations may result in criminal sanctions. Inspections typically focus on long-term health issues.
   e. OSHA provides training programs conducted by nonenforcement personnel.

H. **Employee Retirement Income Security Act (ERISA) of 1974**

1. Pension abuses were growing and employees were not adequately protected.
2. ERISA prohibits discrimination in favor of highly paid and key employees, provides uniform rules for eligibility and vesting, and requires extensive reporting to and approval by the IRS.
3. Under provisions of ERISA, an employer must fully fund the annual cost of any retirement program.
4. Employers are not required to offer pension programs, but if such a program is offered, it is fully regulated by ERISA.

I. **Americans with Disabilities Act (ADA) of 1990**

1. The ADA bans employment discrimination against people with disabilities, provides tax incentives for compliance costs, bans discrimination against people with disabilities in transportation, and requires remodeling of facilities to provide access by individuals with disabilities.
   a. Compliance includes acquiring or modifying work equipment, providing qualified readers or interpreters, adjusting working schedules, and making existing facilities such as restrooms, telephones, and drinking fountains accessible. Automatic doors and wheelchair ramps have been the most common changes observed.
   b. Organizations with 25 or more employees are required to provide reasonable accommodations for qualified workers and job applicants with disabilities.
2. Employers are prohibited from inquiring into a job applicant's disability with questions concerning medical history, prior workers' compensation or health insurance claims, work absenteeism due to illness, past treatment for alcoholism, or mental illness.
3. The ADA defines a person with disabilities as an individual who
   a. Has a physical or mental impairment that limits one or more life activities
   b. Has a record of such an impairment
   c. Is regarded as having such an impairment
4. A qualified "worker with a disability" is defined as one who can perform the essential functions of a job, with or without reasonable accommodation.
5. No federal funds are provided for implementation of ADA by employers.
6. Penalties for violation of the ADA can reach $500,000, and thousands of charges have already been filed.

J. **The Family and Medical Leave Act (FMLA)**

1. The FMLA, which took effect in August 1993, mandates unpaid leave for child care and other family and personal needs.
   a. The law applies to companies with 50 or more employees. Eligible employees must have worked for the employer for an average of 25 hours a week for one year.
   b. The law provides up to 12 weeks of unpaid leave after the birth or adoption of a child. Both parents are eligible.
   c. Leave may also be taken to care for a sick spouse, child, or parent, or when an employee is too sick to work.
2. Employers must provide health benefits during the leave period and give returning workers the same or an equivalent job in terms of pay, responsibilities, and other working conditions.
3. In many companies, employees may substitute paid "sick leave" for unpaid leave, but this is not a requirement of the law.

ANTITRUST

A. Competition is used to control private economic power. Its purpose is to promote

1. Efficient allocation of resources (resulting in lower prices)
2. Greater choice by consumers
3. Greater business opportunities
4. Fairness in economic behavior
5. Avoidance of concentrated political power resulting from economic power

B. **Sherman Act of 1890**

1. Section 1 makes illegal every contract, combination, or conspiracy in restraint of trade in interstate or foreign commerce.
   a. The commerce clause of the Constitution has been the basis for a considerable extension of federal power in the regulatory sphere because most businesses affect interstate commerce.
   b. The **rule of reason** is applied so usually only unreasonable restraints are illegal.
      1) EXAMPLE: A covenant not to compete is enforceable so long as it is for a reasonable time and a reasonable area.
   c. Some types of arrangements between competitors are found unreasonable without inquiry. They are called **per se violations**. These include
      1) **Price fixing** (agreeing to any price)
      2) **Division of markets** (agreeing where to sell)
      3) **Group boycotts** (agreeing not to deal with another)
      4) **Resale price maintenance** (limiting a buyer's resale price)
         a) The arrangements limit competition at the expense of the consumer.
   d. Price fixing is the most prosecuted violation under the Sherman Act.
2. Section 2 prohibits the acts of monopolizing or attempting to monopolize.
   a. **Monopoly** -- the power to control prices or exclude competition
   b. The government must prove overwhelming market power and that the act of monopolizing, attempting to monopolize, or conspiring or combining to monopolize is a deliberate or purposeful act.
      1) Acquisition of power through superior skill, or having it thrust upon one, is not a violation.

C. **Clayton Act of 1914** prohibits

1. Mergers or the acquisition of stock if the effect may be to lessen competition or tend to create a monopoly. The act allows the Justice Department to prevent mergers before they occur.
    a. A horizontal merger (between competitors) is most closely scrutinized by the Justice Department because it usually has the greatest tendency to lessen competition.
    b. A vertical merger (between supplier and purchaser) may also lessen competition if each controls a substantial part of the relevant market.
    c. A conglomerate merger involves different industries or different areas of business. It is the least likely to lessen competition unless the resulting company is so large that its size alone affects competition.
2. Sales that prevent the buyer from dealing with the seller's competitors
3. Tying or tie-in sales; that is, sales in which a buyer must take other products in order to buy the first product
4. Exclusive dealing, which occurs when a seller requires a buyer to purchase only the seller's products and not buy any products from the seller's competitors
5. Price discrimination between different buyers
6. A person from sitting as a director of competing corporations if one company has capital of greater than $1,000,000 and if antitrust law would be violated if the companies ceased to be competitors

D. **Federal Trade Commission Act of 1914**

1. The act prohibits unfair methods of competition, and unfair or deceptive acts in commerce.
2. It created the Federal Trade Commission (FTC) to enforce this act and determine what is unfair competition or deceptive acts.
    a. The basic objectives of the FTC are to initiate antitrust actions and to protect the consumer public.
    b. The FTC also has broad authority to enforce the other antitrust laws in conjunction with the antitrust division of the U.S. Justice Department.
    c. The Wheeler-Lea Amendment of 1938 prohibits deceptive practices in commerce.

E. The **Robinson-Patman Act of 1936** amended the Clayton Act with respect to price discrimination.

1. Price discrimination is prohibited with respect to both buyers and sellers.
    a. Both buyer and seller can be found guilty if there is discrimination.
2. Price differentiation between customers is allowed on the basis of quantity purchased if it can be shown that there is a cost savings.
3. Rebates, commissions, discounts, etc., to special customers are prohibited.
4. The act does not apply to export sales.

F. The **Celler-Kefauver Act of 1950** amended the Clayton Act to prohibit the acquisition of assets of another corporation if the effect could lessen competition or tend to create a monopoly.

1. The Clayton Act originally applied only to stock acquisitions.

G. **Remedies for Violations of These Acts**

1. Injunctions, forced divisions, and forced divestitures may be obtained by either the public or the government.
2. Cease and desist orders may be issued by the FTC.
3. Treble (triple) damages may be recovered by the public.
4. Criminal penalties may be assessed by the government.

H. **Exemptions from Antitrust Regulation**

1. Intrastate commerce
2. Labor unions (not exempt if the union primarily intends to restrain trade or conspires with nonlabor groups to monopolize)
3. Regulated utilities
4. Reasonable noncompetition clauses between
   a. Buyers and sellers of businesses
   b. Partners in a partnership
   c. Purchasers of technology or equipment
5. Patents and copyrights
6. Agricultural and fishing organizations
7. Financial institutions
8. Transport industries
9. Major league baseball
10. Companies qualifying for certificates of antitrust immunity issued by the Commerce Department (after concurrence by the Justice Department) under the Export Trading Company Act

CONSUMER PROTECTION

A. Several statutes and commissions already discussed are oriented toward consumer protection, e.g., the SEC and the FTC.

1. The consumer movement developed as a result of consumer dissatisfaction with goods and services. The free market provides minimal incentive for firms to provide safety and environmental protection.

B. The **Fair Packaging and Labeling Act of 1967** prohibits deceptive packaging and labeling.

C. The **Consumer Credit Protection Act (Truth-in-Lending Act) of 1968** (as amended in 1982), in simple terms, requires the interest rate and the cost of credit to be disclosed.

1. It resulted in greater record-keeping requirements for lenders.
2. Also, costs of making loans increased because of the additional compliance forms required.

D. The **Consumer Product Safety Act of 1972** emphasizes safety standards for new products.

1. Information about defects is often received from consumers.
2. Section 15 of the act requires manufacturers to publicize defects to consumers and/or refund the purchase price paid for defective products.

E. The **Fair Credit Reporting Act of 1970** gives consumers the right to obtain the information reported by credit bureaus.

F. The **Equal Credit Opportunity Act of 1974** prohibits discrimination in providing credit.

G. The **Fair Credit Billing Act of 1975** provides consumers with rights in contesting billing errors and settling disputes.

H. The **Fair Debt Collection Practices Act of 1977** prohibits certain abuses of consumers' rights by collection agencies.

I. **Equal Employment Opportunity Laws**

1. There are several laws, but it is the Civil Rights Act that did the most to prohibit discrimination on the basis of race, color, national origin, religion, or sex.
2. Employers may use selection procedures in hiring as long as the procedures are not discriminatory.
3. Violation of the laws can result in loss of government contracts, court orders to correct the situation, and damage awards to aggrieved individuals.
4. The government has set goals and timetables for large employers to bring female and minority workforces up to the appropriate percentages as they relate to the available labor pool. Companies are required to create and implement a plan of affirmative action for this. However, recent Supreme Court decisions have called into question the validity of affirmative action plans.

J. The **Magnuson-Moss Warranty Act of 1975** prohibits disclaimers of implied warranties of goods unless they are written.

K. The **Food and Drug Act of 1906** as amended by the **Food, Drug, and Cosmetic Act of 1938** and much other legislation is administered by the Food and Drug Administration (FDA).

1. The FDA was created to help maintain the safety of drugs, food, cosmetics, etc.
2. The FDA oversees the requirements of the Federal Hazardous Substances Labeling Act of 1960.
3. New drugs and food additives must be thoroughly tested before they are marketed. The premarket review is based upon research supplied by the drug companies.
   a. Results in higher prices to offset increased costs
   b. The FDA can extend patent lives of pharmaceutical products to allow for time lost during the premarket FDA review.

L. **Environmental Protection Agency (EPA)**

1. The EPA prohibits manufacturers from polluting water, land, and air.
2. Environmental regulations apply to firms in all industries.
3. Effluent (smoke, liquid industrial refuse, sewage, etc.) standards set the volume or quality of waste products that can be discharged into the air, water, etc. Either the EPA or individual citizens can bring suit to enforce standards.
4. The EPA is often criticized by business as having requirements that are not cost beneficial.

5. The setting of effluent standards has often been criticized by economists as an inefficient method of pollution control. Economists prefer a sliding tax charge based on the amount of effluent emitted. This method is preferred because
   a. As effluent discharge increases, a company's tax increases, providing a strong incentive for firms to discover new methods of controlling pollution.
   b. The tax is a less direct method of economic intervention. Rather than dictating technology, the tax allows firms to seek out the technology that is most cost-effective.
   c. The Clean Air Act of 1990 allows marketable permits for pollution that firms can buy or sell like any other commodity.
   d. Beginning in November 1994, employers in large cities with air pollution were required to begin reducing the number of people who drive to work or face fines and/or criminal penalties. The law, which affects companies employing more than 100 workers, puts the onus on companies to encourage car-pooling and mass transit.

M. The **Nuclear Regulatory Commission (NRC)** licenses nuclear facilities (such as power plants) and approves the procedures for safeguarding nuclear materials, including waste products.

N. **Consumer Tactics**. Boycotts of a manufacturer's products are the most common tactic used by consumer groups to get a company to change its behavior or the nature of its advertising. Boycotts have sometimes been quite successful.
   1. Shareholder resolutions have also been made at stockholder meetings, but such resolutions have rarely been successful.
   2. Lobbying for new laws is also an often successful tactic.
   3. Occasionally, cooperating with the manufacturer to find common ground has been used.

FEDERAL COMMUNICATIONS COMMISSION (FCC)

A. The FCC is an independent agency formed in 1934 to regulate all methods of communications over the public airwaves. FCC functions include
   1. Allocating transmission frequencies
   2. Issuing transmission licenses
   3. Fostering effective and efficient use of communication resources
   4. Regulating common communications carriers engaged in interstate and foreign operations

B. Among the rules is a limitation on the number of television stations that can be owned by a television network.

LEGAL FORMS OF BUSINESS

A. **Corporations.** A corporation is a legal entity with a legal existence separate from its owners (shareholders). The formation and existence of corporations are entirely regulated by state statute.

1. Each state has a statute governing corporations that must be complied with for a corporation to exist.
2. Once a corporation exists in one state, the other states must recognize the corporation as a legal entity, but it will usually have to register to do business in other states.
3. A corporation is owned by shareholders who elect a board of directors to manage the corporation.
   a. Shares of stock are used to represent the ownership of the corporation.
      1) Common stock usually entitles the owner to vote and participate in the financial success or failure of the corporation.
      2) Preferred stock may or may not entitle the owner to vote and usually provides for fixed dividends.
   b. The board of directors elects officers to whom they delegate the daily management of the corporation.
   c. Bondholders and other creditors normally have no management rights. Their only rights are to receive payment.

B. **General Partnerships.** A general partnership comes into being whenever a business entity meets the criteria of a functioning partnership.

1. This occurs when two or more persons associate and carry on a business as co-owners, for profit. No formalities need to be observed, and the partnership may even exist though the persons involved have not so intended.
2. Under common law, a partnership (in contrast to the corporation) is not recognized as a separate legal entity. In other words, a partnership is not regarded as being separate from its owners.
3. However, a partnership is regarded as an entity for some purposes, for example, continuation of the partnership business after dissolution, each general partner's status as an agent of the partnership, bankruptcy, filing of tax returns, and qualification as an employer under workers' compensation statutes.

C. **Limited Partnerships.** A limited partnership can be created only pursuant to a statute because it is a form of business organization unknown at common law. It is useful because it permits investors to avoid personal liability and the duties of day-to-day management without submitting to the complexities of corporate formation and operation.

1. There is no maximum limit as to the number of partners (limited or general). The only requirement is that there be at least one limited and one general partner. This differs from an S corporation, which currently has a limit of 35 shareholders.
2. One of the principal advantages of the limited partnership is that persons who invest in the enterprise but do not take part in management have limited personal liability. A limited partner is liable only to the extent of his/her agreed-upon contribution of cash or other property.
3. Limited and general partnerships are tax-reporting but not tax-paying entities.
4. Limited partnership interests are considered securities, and their issuance is subject to regulation by the SEC.

D. **Proprietorships.** A proprietorship is the easiest type of business to form. Only one owner is required. The disadvantages of the proprietorship form include the limited amount of capital available to a single owner and the unlimited liability to which the owner is exposed. The proprietorship is the most common form of business organization.

STUDY UNIT 5
WORKING CAPITAL FINANCE

INTRODUCTION

This study unit and Study Unit 6, Capital Structure Finance, outline the field of managerial finance, which embraces financial analysis, planning, implementation of financial plans, and control of a firm. The approach is microanalysis. Managerial finance requires an applied, not a conceptual, approach and thus provides usable, everyday tools for managers of businesses and other entities. From a macro point of view, the efficient operation of individual firms promotes efficiency in our market system.

Working capital finance applies to short-term decisions, and capital structure finance to longer-term decisions. Working capital is defined as the excess of current assets over current liabilities.

The field of finance has evolved from a discipline with a descriptive approach to the analysis of the formation of firms (mergers, consolidations, etc.) and the contraction of firms (e.g., liquidations, reorganizations, etc.) to the current quantitative orientation. Managerial finance applies to both investing (left side of the balance sheet) and financing (right side of the balance sheet) decisions made by corporate managers. In addition to the investing and financing decisions that determine profitability, managers must resolve solvency issues through working capital management and prudent long-term financing.

This study unit begins with a discussion of the objectives of the firm that is also pertinent to capital structure finance. Each of the topics of working capital finance and capital structure finance covers 10% to 15% of Part 1 of the CMA exam.

THE OBJECTIVES OF THE FIRM AND ITS MANAGERS

A. The objective of the firm is to maximize the stockholders' wealth, i.e., to maximize the price per share of common stock. The market price of the stock is the result of the firm's investment and financing decisions within the context of legal and ethical bounds, including those relating to

   1. Product safety
   2. Minority hiring
   3. Pollution control
   4. Fair competition
   5. Fair advertising

B. Other objectives of the firm are less beneficial to stockholders than maximization of the per share price of stock.

   1. Profit maximization is not the optimal objective when it is not consistent with the maximization of stock price. For example:

      a. Investing in high-risk projects may increase profits but not be commensurate with the additional risk borne by the firm.

      b. Increasing equity investment (resulting in a lower return on equity) will lower EPS and the stock price.

      c. Delaying needed maintenance may increase accounting profits, but damage to capital may more than offset this increase in short-term profit.

   2. Sales maximization is a nonoptimal objective because it does not maximize stockholders' wealth.

      a. A firm wants to increase sales only when the marginal revenue from the sale is greater than (or equal to) the marginal cost of the sale. Only at this output (sales) level is stockholders' wealth maximized.

   3. Social responsibility is an important issue, but if it were the only objective of the firm, the firm's existence would be short.

      a. However, some mutual funds invest only in socially responsible firms. Consequently, social responsibility can increase the demand for a corporation's stocks and bonds and thus increase stockholder wealth.

C. Management must make investment decisions, i.e., obtain a proper mix of productive assets, and obtain financing of these assets with the objective of maximizing shareholders' wealth.

   1. This is a dynamic process over time and requires adjusting to changes in the factors of production and finished-goods markets.

   2. It is a multifaceted process because of the large number of markets in which most businesses deal.

      a. The interrelationships among these many markets are complex.

D. The investing and financing decisions are not independent.

   1. The amount and composition of assets are directly related to the amount and composition of financing.

      a. Investing decisions are not independent of financing decisions.

   2. Given current and expected industry and overall economic conditions, the resulting mix of assets, liabilities, and capital determines the business risk.

      a. Managerial decisions and their outcomes are related to and dependent on many "outside" (**exogenous**) variables:

         1) Technological developments

         2) Weather

         3) National fiscal policies

         4) National monetary policies

         5) International relations and their effect on particular industries

         6) Competitors' actions (may not be exogenous if they are affected by the company's decisions)

E. **Taxes** (federal, state, local, and foreign) are an important consideration because they are frequently 25% to 50% of all costs.

1. They include income, use, excise, property, legal document, payroll, and others.
2. Thus, governmental services (national defense, fire, police, etc.) are an important and costly factor of production.
3. Tax planning is very important in investment and financing decisions.
   a. Investment tax credits have at times provided direct reduction of taxes when assets were purchased for use in the business.
      1) The net effect is to decrease the cost of the asset.
      2) The amount of the credit and limitations on the tax credit on used equipment affect investment decisions.
      3) Investment tax credit is currently available for solar and geothermal property (business energy credit), for rehabilitation of historic structures, and for certain reforestation property.
   b. Accelerated depreciation is permitted on many types of business assets.
      1) Accordingly, in the early periods of an asset's life, depreciation is higher, taxable income is lower, and the rate of return on investment is higher.
   c. Corporate capital gains are taxed at regular rates, and the capital gains of individuals are taxed at a maximum rate of 28%.
   d. Special loss carryforward and carryback rules permit businesses to deduct net operating losses incurred in one period against income earned in other periods.
   e. A dividends-received deduction makes tax free 70% to 100% of dividends received by one company from investments in the stock of another company.
      1) This prevents or reduces double taxation.
      2) It also encourages (does not discourage) one company to invest in the stock of another company.
   f. Interest is a tax-deductible expense of the debtor company.
      1) But dividends on common or preferred stock are not deductible by the issuer.
4. Federal tax policy is fiscal policy that affects the overall economy, which in turn affects production and the finished-goods markets in which the company deals.
5. Government monetary policy determines the availability and cost of capital, which affects financing (and in turn, investing) decisions.
   a. Monetary policy also affects overall economic activity.
6. See Study Unit 18 for the principal outline concerning income taxes.

F. **Growth and expansion** are important to attract both personnel and capital. Creative people want an opportunity for advancement and challenge, and investors place a premium on growth companies.

1. Growth can be either internal or external.
   a. Internal growth arises from earnings retained in the business.
   b. External growth occurs through issuance of equity or debt securities.

2. Expansion occurs through
   a. New product lines
   b. Purchase of other companies
   c. Investments in other companies
   d. **Franchising**. According to the FASB in SFAS 45, *Accounting for Franchise Fee Revenue*, a franchise is a written business agreement that meets the following criteria:
      1) *The relation between the franchisor and franchisee is contractual, and an agreement, confirming the rights and responsibilities of each party, is in force for a specified period.*
      2) *The purpose is the distribution of a product or service, or an entire business concept, within a particular market area.*
      3) *Both the franchisor and the franchisee contribute resources for establishing and maintaining the franchise. The franchisor's contribution may be a trademark, a company reputation, products, procedures, manpower, equipment, or a process. The franchisee usually contributes operating capital as well as the managerial and operational resources required for opening and continuing the franchised outlet.*
      4) *The franchise agreement outlines and describes the specific marketing practices to be followed, specifies the contribution of each party to the operation of the business, and sets forth certain operating procedures that both parties agree to comply with.*
      5) *The establishment of the franchised outlet creates a business entity that will, in most cases, require and support the full-time business activity of the franchisee. (There are numerous other contractual distribution arrangements in which a local businessperson becomes the "authorized distributor" or "representative" for the sale of a particular good or service, along with the many others, but such a sale usually represents only a portion of the person's total business.)*
      6) *Both the franchisee and the franchisor have a common public identity. This identity is achieved most often through the use of common trade names or trademarks and is frequently reinforced through advertising programs designed to promote the recognition and acceptance of the common identity within the franchisee's market area.*
      7) *The payment of an initial franchise fee or a continuing royalty fee is not a necessary criterion for an agreement to be considered a franchise agreement.*

3. Legal perspective on business combinations
   a. **Merger**. Only one of the combining companies survives. The assets and liabilities of the other combining companies are merged into the surviving company.

b. **Consolidation**. A new company is organized to take over the combining companies.

c. **Acquisition**. One company exchanges its stock for the majority of the outstanding stock of another company, and both companies continue to operate separately.

4. The tax perspective on growth is to consider whether a business combination is a tax-free or a taxable event.

   a. Certain exchanges of stock are tax-free exchanges, which permit the owners of one company to exchange their stock for the stock of the purchaser without paying taxes.

   b. Inheritance-tax problems of owners force the sale of many closely held businesses.

5. The accounting perspective on growth must consider the type of accounting to be used for acquisition-type combinations -- either purchase or pooling accounting.

   a. **Purchase accounting**. The acquisition is considered to be a purchase of net assets, and the assets and liabilities of the purchased company are recorded at their fair value on the consolidated books, usually resulting in increased depreciation charges.

      1) The book value of most assets is usually less than fair value because of inflation and accounting depreciation policies.

      2) The tax issues that arise when a combination is accounted for as a purchase, e.g., whether to file a consolidated return, the determination of tax bases and book values, and whether the event is taxable, are beyond the scope of this book.

   b. **Pooling accounting**. The acquisition is considered to be a combining of ownership interests, and the assets of the combining companies retain their old book values.

      1) The result is usually a higher accounting income under the pooling method.
      2) Depreciation remains the same for tax purposes.

6. The financial perspective on growth is the most important, encompassing all the above perspectives; the legal, tax, and accounting perspectives all have economic impact.

   a. Additional factors determining the terms of business combinations

      1) Earning levels and growth rates
      2) Sales levels and growth rates
      3) Dividends
      4) Market values
      5) Book values
      6) Net current assets

   b. The exchanges of stock in business combinations involving public companies often result in a greater market value than the sum of the market values of the individual companies.

      1) Qualitative considerations not reflected in the historical financial data may operate to create a synergistic effect.

         a) For example, a firm needing stronger management expertise, a better distribution network, or a research and development capacity may seek a complementary merger partner.

7. **Holding companies** -- companies that hold investments in the stock of other operating companies
   a. The acquisition method of business combination is pertinent.
   b. Holding-company pyramiding results in control of assets with a very small percentage of ownership.
      1) The potential profits (and losses) are high.
   c. Advantages
      1) Control can often be obtained with small percentages of total stock ownership if there are no other large stockholders.
      2) Risk is isolated; i.e., if one investee has problems, it can be sold, dumped, abandoned, etc.
      3) Approval of the investment does not require the approval of stockholders or investee board of directors.
         a) The stock may be purchased in public markets or directly from present stockholders.
      4) Alternatively, a **tender offer** may be made to the stockholders of the potential investee with or without the approval of the potential investee management.
         a) If the potential investee management does not cooperate, the potential investor can advertise the offer, e.g., in the *Wall Street Journal*.
         b) A tender offer asks stockholders to tender their shares for a specified price, subject to a certain number of shares being tendered.
      5) If a question of antitrust arises, it is easier to be forced to liquidate a stock investment than an internal operating division.
   d. Disadvantage
      1) If the entity meets the criteria of a personal holding company (PHC), undistributed PHC income is subject to a 39.6% tax rate. A company is a PHC if five or fewer shareholders own 50% or more of the shares and 60% or more of the adjusted ordinary gross income is PHC income (essentially, passive income). However, certain organizations are exempt from treatment as PHCs, e.g., S corporations, banks, and insurance companies.
8. There are two methods of accounting for stock investments.
   a. **Equity method**. The investor must recognize the investor's share of investee income as the investee reports the income, that is, on the accrual basis.
      1) Stock investments that constitute between 20% and 50% of the investee's outstanding stock are accounted for by the equity method.
      2) A 20%-to-50% interest is presumed to permit substantial influence over the investee by the investor.

3) Excess of investee cost over investee book value must be amortized as an expense by the investor.

a) EXAMPLE: If 25% of a company with $7,000,000 in assets and $3,000,000 in liabilities is purchased for $1,500,000, the excess of cost over book value is $500,000. The book value of the entire company is $4,000,000 ($7,000,000 of assets – $3,000,000 of liabilities). Because 25% of $4,000,000 was purchased for $1,500,000, the excess is $500,000.

i) The $500,000 must be attributed to specific assets and amortized using one of the methods below:

- Over the estimated lives of those assets
- On a straight-line basis as general goodwill over a period not to exceed 40 years

ii) In either case, the journal entry to record the amortization is

Investment income	XXX	
Investment in investee		XXX

b. **Cost method**. The investor reports income only when cash dividends are received from the investee.

1) The cost method accounts for investee earnings on the cash basis, i.e., when received.

c. For additional discussion, turn to Study Unit 12, Financial Statement Presentation.

G. Business **contraction and liquidation** are the final stages of a corporate life.

1. Corporations can be perpetual, in contrast to partnerships (which terminate with the death, bankruptcy, etc., of a partner).

2. As product demand, available supplies, etc., decline or the rate of growth in business activity declines, the business may

a. Retrench and decline in size

1) But employee and capital retention is difficult.

b. Be sold

c. Become insolvent, i.e., unable to meet current obligations

1) A creditor can file a petition forcing the insolvent corporation into **bankruptcy**, or the insolvent corporation can file a voluntary petition admitting itself into Chapter 7 bankruptcy.

2) Assets are marshaled and sold by a **trustee in bankruptcy**, who is appointed by the court. Creditors are paid in statutory order of priority.

d. Become bankrupt, i.e., liabilities in excess of assets

1) Alternatives to straight bankruptcy are

a) **Chapter 11 reorganization**, under which finances are restructured so the debtor may continue to operate and provide jobs, pay creditors, etc.

b) Creditor **compositions**, under which creditors get together voluntarily with the debtor and adjust the amount and timing of receivables

e. One form of contraction is **divestiture**. The types of divestiture are sale of a subunit to another company, sale of a subunit to the subunit's management, piecemeal liquidation of the subunit's assets, and a **spin-off**. This last form of divestiture is characterized by establishing a new and separate entity and transferring its newly issued stock to the shareholders of the original company.

H. The topic of this study unit is working capital finance, which concerns the optimal level, mix, and use of current assets and current liabilities. **Working capital** equals current assets minus current liabilities.

1. A company that adopts a conservative working capital policy seeks to minimize liquidity risk by increasing working capital. The result is that the company forgoes the potentially higher returns available from using the additional working capital to acquire long-term assets.
2. An aggressive policy reduces the current ratio and accepts a higher risk of short-term cash flow problems.

CASH MANAGEMENT

A. The **cash budget** details projected receipts and disbursements.

1. It is based on the projected sales level.
2. Cash outflows are budgeted based on the level of sales.
3. Cash budgeting is an ongoing, cumulative activity.
   a. One always begins with a beginning balance.
   b. Budgets must be for a specified period of time.
      1) The units of time must be short enough to assure that all cash payments can be met.

B. Cash is held for three reasons:

1. As a **medium of exchange**. Cash is necessary to conduct business transactions.
2. As a **precautionary measure**. Cash or a money-market fund can be held for emergencies. Normally, investment in high-grade, short-term securities is a better alternative to holding cash.
   a. Years ago, in face of cash shortages, money was literally held, as a precaution against bank closings.
   b. Today, if the banks fail, paper money would be worthless; thus, there is no precautionary reason to hoard U.S. paper dollars.
3. For **speculation**. Cash should be held only during deflationary periods when it becomes worth more. In periods of inflation, near-cash items should be held rather than cash itself.
   a. If there are foreseeable future cash needs (e.g., new product lines, purchase of assets up for quick sale at low prices, etc.), money should be held as near money.

C. Cash inflows should be expedited.

1. Invoices should be mailed promptly.
2. Credit terms must be competitive but geared to encourage prompt payment.
   a. See also Receivables Management on page 164.

3. A **lockbox system** may be used to expedite the receipt of funds. A company maintains mailboxes, often in numerous locations around the country, to which customers send payments. A bank checks these mailboxes several times a day, and funds received are immediately deposited to the company's account without first being processed by the company's accounting system, thereby hastening availability of the funds. In addition, having several lockboxes throughout the country reduces the time a payment is in the postal system.

   a. **Concentration banking** may be useful in this context. Regional concentration banks may serve as centers for the transfer of lockbox receipts. A disbursement account at the regional center will then expedite the use of the receipts for payments in that region. Such use might be delayed if all receipts were transmitted to a national central bank.

4. Transfer of monies by wire expedites cash management.

5. **Electronic funds transfer (EFT)** and customer debit cards speed up cash inflows.

6. **Automated clearing houses (ACHs)** are electronic networks that facilitate the reading of data among banks. The 32 regional ACH associations guarantee 1-day clearing of checks. Except for the New York ACH, they are operated by the Federal Reserve.

D. Slowing cash disbursements increases available cash.

1. Payment beyond normal credit terms, however, creates vendor ill will and may incur interest charges.

2. Payments should be made within discount periods if the return is more than the firm's cost of capital. The return on taking discounts (not considering compounding effects) is approximately

   a. $$\frac{360}{(\textit{Total pay period} - \textit{Discount period})} \times \frac{\textit{Discount \%}}{(100\% - \textit{Discount \%})}$$

   b. 2/10, net/30 means the total payment period is 30 days and the discount period is 10 days. The discount is 2%.

   c. For example, 2/10, net/30 results in the following calculation:

   $$(360 \div 20) \times (2 \div 98) = 36.7\% \textit{ annualized interest}$$

   d. A more accurate calculation of the cost of not taking discounts considers the effects of compounding. In the example above, annualizing this cost means that 18 payments are deemed to occur during the year. The annual effective rate is

   $$\textit{Rate} = [1.0 + (2 \div 98)]^{18} - 1.0 = 43.8\%$$

3. Payment by **draft** (a three-party instrument in which the drawer orders the drawee to pay money to the payee) is a means of slowing cash outflows. A check is the most common draft. **Check float** arises from the delay between an expenditure or receipt by check and the clearing of the check.

   a. The effect is an interest-free loan to the payor.

   b. Accordingly, companies attempt to maximize **disbursements float** (checks written but not yet deducted from the bank balance) and minimize **collections float** (checks received but not yet credited).

4. When **compensating balances** are negotiated with banks, use of average rather than absolute compensating balances frees most of the compensating balance as a contingency fund.
   a. The flexible compensating balance can be used as a cushion for the days when cash demands are greatest and deposits fail to materialize.
5. **Zero-balancing checking accounts** are offered by some banks. The account balance is maintained at zero until a check comes in. The resulting overdraft is covered by a transfer from an account earning a high rate of interest.
   a. The disadvantage is that the bank may charge a fee for this service.

E. The amount of cash to keep on hand should be determined by cost-benefit analysis.
   1. The reduction in average cash times the interest rate (cost of capital or investment yield rate) is the benefit.
   2. Costs of having insufficient cash include incremental personnel cost, lost discounts, and lost vendor goodwill.

F. A firm's excess cash should be placed in an investment with a high return and little risk, such as those listed below.
   1. **Treasury bills** -- short-term government debt guaranteed explicitly by the U.S. government and exempt from state and local taxation. They are sold on a discount basis.
      a. Obligations of federal agencies are not guaranteed by the U.S. government but only by the agency itself.
   2. **Certificates of deposit** -- a form of savings deposit that cannot be withdrawn before maturity without a high penalty. However, negotiable CDs are traded.
   3. **Money-market accounts** -- similar to checking accounts but pay higher interest

G. Interest rate expectation theory states that long-term interest rates are usually a geometric average of expected future short-term interest rates.

MARKETABLE SECURITIES MANAGEMENT

A. Short-term marketable securities (e.g., T-bills and CDs) are sometimes held as a substitute for cash but are more likely to be acquired as temporary investments.
   1. Most companies avoid large cash balances and prefer borrowing to meet short-term needs.
   2. As temporary investments, marketable securities may be purchased with maturities timed to meet seasonal fluctuations, to pay off a bond issue, to make tax payments, or otherwise to satisfy anticipated needs.

B. Marketable securities should be chosen with a view to the risk of default (**financial risk**).
   1. U.S. government securities are the least risky.

C. **Interest rate risk** should be minimized given the reasons for holding marketable securities.
   1. Short-term securities are less likely to fluctuate in value because of changes in the general level of interest rates.

D. Changes in the general price level (inflation) determine the purchasing power of payments on investments (principal and interest) and thus the types of securities chosen and the rates charged.

E. The degree of marketability of a security determines its **liquidity**, that is, the ability to resell at the quoted market price.

F. The firm's tax position will influence its choice of securities; for example, a firm with net loss carryforwards may prefer a higher-yielding taxable security to a tax-exempt municipal bond.

G. Short-term marketable securities are usually chosen for reasons that make high-yield, high-risk investments unattractive. Hence, a higher return may be forgone in exchange for greater safety.

   1. Thus, speculative tactics, such as selling short (borrowing and selling securities in the expectation that their price will decline by the time they must be replaced) and margin trading (borrowing from a broker to buy securities) are avoided.

H. For typical short-term marketable securities, see Sources and Choices of Short-Term Funds on page 165.

INVENTORY POLICY

A. Turn to Study Unit 30, Inventory Models, in Chapter 8 for an outline that emphasizes minimizing inventory costs, which include

   1. **Ordering costs** (costs of placing and receiving orders)
   2. **Carrying costs** (insurance, security, inventory taxes, depreciation or rent of facilities, interest)
   3. **Stockout costs**

B. Although the traditional approach to inventory management has been to minimize inventory and the related carrying costs, many companies find inventory a good hedge against inflation

   1. Stockpiles of inventory also guarantee future availability of inventory.
   2. The **economic order quantity (EOQ)** model is applicable to cash management.
      a. It can be stated in terms of the following assumptions:
         1) A known demand for cash
         2) A given carrying (interest) cost
         3) The flat amount (cost) of converting other assets to cash, such as the broker's fee for sale of marketable securities (assumed to be constant regardless of the transaction size)

C. Inventory carrying costs can sometimes be transferred to either suppliers or customers.

   1. If a manufacturer has good enough control of production schedules to know exactly when materials are needed, orders can be placed so that materials arrive no earlier tha[n] when actually needed.
      a. This practice relies on a supplier who is willing to take the responsibility for storing the needed inventory and shipping it to arrive on time.
      b. Suppliers are more willing to supply this type of service when they have many competitors who can also supply the materials.
      c. **Just-in-time (JIT)** and **materials requirements planning (MRP)** are examples of systems that rely on suppliers to make deliveries just in time for the materials to enter production. The manufacturer thus has little or no investment in raw material inventories and minimizes space needed for inventory storage.

2. Customers can sometimes be persuaded to carry large quantities of inventory by allowing them special quantity discounts or extended credit terms.
3. If customers are willing to accept long lead times, inventory can be manufactured to order to avoid storing large quantities.
4. Although these measures can reduce inventory carrying costs, additional costs might be incurred by adopting them.
   a. Stockout costs may increase because customers are not always willing to wait for goods to be produced.
   b. Production shutdowns and additional shipping costs may also keep minimization of carrying costs from being cost effective.

RECEIVABLES MANAGEMENT

A. The objective of managing accounts receivable is to have both the optimal amount of receivables outstanding and the optimal amount of bad debts.
   1. This balance requires a trade-off between
      a. The benefits of credit sales, i.e., more sales
      b. The costs of accounts receivable, e.g., collection, interest, and bad debt costs
   2. Thus, a company should extend credit until the marginal benefit (profit) is zero (taking into account opportunity costs of alternative investments).

B. Credit terms, collection policies, etc., are frequently determined by competitors; i.e., they must be met by a company in order to make sales.

C. Credit policies and collection efforts should be increased (tightened) until it becomes unprofitable to do more.
   1. The objective is to maximize the accounts receivable turnover ratio, i.e., to shorten the average time they are held.
      a. **Accounts receivable turnover ratio** -- net sales divided by average accounts receivable

D. Other tools of credit such as bank charge cards should be evaluated as an alternative to charge accounts.
   1. Banks charge a fee equal to 3% to 5% of charge sales.
   2. Charge tickets can be deposited at the bank just like a customer check.
   3. Money is instantly available to the seller.

SOURCES AND CHOICES OF SHORT-TERM FUNDS

A. Short-term credit is debt scheduled to be repaid within 1 year. The main sources of this credit are

1. **Trade credit** -- a spontaneous source of financing because it arises automatically as part of the purchase transaction. The terms of payment are set by suppliers.

2. **Commercial banks**. These banks lend money that appears on the balance sheet of the borrower as a note payable.

   a. **Maturity** is usually in less than a year, which requires the company to roll over the debt frequently if needed.

   b. The **promissory note** states the terms of the loan and repayment policy.

   c. **Compensating balances**. Banks may require a borrower to keep a certain percentage of the face value of the loan in his/her account, which raises the real rate of interest to the borrower.

   d. A **line of credit** is the maximum loan that a bank will lend the borrower in a certain period.

      1) EXAMPLE: On January 1, a bank official may tell Company X that it is "good" for up to $100,000 in the coming year.

      2) This is the most practical form of financing for most small retail businesses.

   e. Cost of bank loans

      1) **Regular interest** formula $\dfrac{\textit{Interest}}{\textit{Borrowed amount}}$

      2) **Discounted interest** $\dfrac{\textit{Interest}}{\textit{Borrowed amount} - \textit{Interest}}$

      3) **Installment loan** $\dfrac{\textit{Interest}}{\textit{Average borrowed amount}}$

   f. The **prime interest rate** is the rate charged by commercial banks to their best (the largest and financially strongest) business customers. It is traditionally the lowest rate charged by banks. However, in recent years, banks have been making loans at still lower rates in response to competition from the commercial paper market.

3. **Commercial paper** -- a short-term, unsecured, note payable issued in large denominations ($100,000 or more) by large companies with high credit ratings to other companies and institutional investors, such as pension funds, banks, and insurance companies. Maturities of commercial paper are at most 270 days. No general secondary market exists for commercial paper. Commercial paper is a lower cost source of funds than bank loans. It is usually issued at below the prime rate.

   a. Advantages

      1) Provides broad and efficient distribution
      2) Provides a great amount of funds (at a given cost)
      3) Avoids costly financing arrangements

   b. Disadvantages

      1) Impersonal market

      2) Total amount of funds available limited to the excess liquidity of big corporations

4. **Factoring**. A factor purchases a company's accounts receivable and assumes the risk of collection. The company involved gets its money immediately to reinvest in new inventories. The financing cost is usually high -- about two points or more above prime, plus a fee for doing the collecting. Factoring has been traditional in the textile industry for years, but recently companies in many industries have found it an efficient means of operation.
   a. A company that uses a factor can eliminate its credit department and accounts receivable staff.
   b. Bad debts are eliminated.
   c. These reductions in costs can more than offset the fee charged by the factor.
   d. The factor can often operate more efficiently than its clients because of the specialized nature of its service.
   e. Before the advent of computers, factoring was often considered a last-ditch source of financing used only when bankruptcy was close at hand. However, the factor's computerization of receivables means it can operate a receivables department more economically than most small manufacturers. Factoring is no longer viewed as an undesirable source of financing.
   f. EXAMPLE: In recent years, the subject of factoring has appeared on several CMA exams. A typical question asks the candidates to determine the cost to the company of a proposed factoring agreement. Assume a factor charges a 2% fee plus an interest rate of 18% on all monies advanced to the company. Monthly sales are $100,000, and the factor advances 90% of the receivables submitted after deducting the 2% fee and the interest. Credit terms are net 60 days. What is the cost to the company of this arrangement?

Amount of receivables submitted	$100,000
Minus: 10% reserve	(10,000)
Minus: 2% factor's fee	(2,000)
Amount accruing to the company	$ 88,000
Minus: 18% interest for 60 days (on $88,000)	(2,640)
Amount to be received immediately	$ 85,360

The company will also receive the $10,000 reserve at the end of the 60-day period if it has not been absorbed by sales returns and allowances. Thus, the total cost to the company to factor the sales for the month is $4,640 ($2,000 factor fee + interest of $2,640). Assuming that the factor has approved the customers' credit in advance, the seller will not absorb any bad debts.

The above costs should be compared with the cost of operating a credit and collection department and also the cost of borrowing monies otherwise advanced by the factor.

5. Other types of short-term funds

   a. **Bankers' acceptances** are drafts drawn on deposits at a bank. The acceptance by the bank is a guarantee of payment at maturity.

   b. **Repurchase agreements** involve sales by a dealer in government securities who agrees to repurchase at a given time for a specific price. Maturities may be very short-term. This arrangement is in essence a secured loan.

   c. Loans secured by receivables (**pledging** receivables). A bank will often lend up to 80% of outstanding receivables.

   d. **Money-market mutual funds** invest in portfolios of short-term securities.

   e. **Warehouse financing** uses inventory as security for the loan. A third party, a public warehouse for example, holds the collateral and serves as the creditor's agent, and the creditor receives the warehouse receipts evidencing its rights in the collateral.

   f. **Agency securities** are issued by government agencies (not the Treasury), such as the Federal Home Loan Banks and other agencies that provide credit to farmers, home buyers, etc. An example is the Federal National Mortgage Association (Fannie Mae), which issues mortgage-backed securities. Agency securities may be long- or short-term.

   g. **Treasury bills** are short-term U.S. government obligations issued by the Treasury at a discount from their face value. A T-bill is highly liquid and nearly free of risk, and it is often held as a cash substitute.

   h. **Treasury notes and bonds** are long-term investments, but issues near maturity are effectively short-term securities with high liquidity.

   i. State and local governmental entities issue short-term securities exempt from taxation.

   j. **Eurodollars** are time deposits in banks located abroad.

   k. **Chattel mortgages** are loans secured by movable personal property (e.g., equipment or livestock).

   l. **Floating liens** attach to property, such as inventory, the composition of which is constantly changing.

FINANCIAL RATIOS TO EVALUATE WORKING CAPITAL MANAGEMENT

A. **Ratio analysis** is a means of evaluating the financing and investing decisions of a business, regarding

1. Solvency -- the firm's ability to meet short-term obligations
2. Activity -- how effectively the firm is using its resources
3. Leverage -- the extent to which the firm has been financed by debt
4. Profitability -- the firm's earning power
5. Per share data -- EPS, yield, and book value

NOTE: Solvency and activity ratios are relevant to working capital finance. Leverage, profitability, and per share data are relevant to capital structure finance.

B. Ratio analysis is based on norms and trends.

1. Normal or average ratios are computable for broad industrial categories.
2. Ratios for individual firms can be compared with those of competitors.
3. Changes in ratios through time provide insight about the future.
   a. Comparisons of trends in ratios of competitors are also useful.
4. Benchmarks have evolved concerning ratios.

C. **Solvency ratios** measure the short-term viability of the business, i.e., the firm's ability to continue in the short term by paying its obligations.

1. **Current ratio** -- current assets divided by current liabilities
   a. $$\frac{\textit{Current assets}}{\textit{Current liabilities}}$$
   b. The most commonly used measure of near-term solvency, it relates current assets to the claims of short-term creditors.
   c. Benchmark: Current ratio should not be less than 2.0.
      1) Companies with an aggressive financing policy will have a low current ratio.
      2) Conservative financing policies result in a higher current ratio.
2. **Acid test or quick ratio** -- cash, net receivables, and marketable securities divided by current liabilities
   a. $$\frac{\textit{Cash} + \textit{Net receivables} + \textit{Marketable securities}}{\textit{Current liabilities}}$$
   b. It measures the firm's ability to pay its short-term debts from its most liquid assets.
   c. Benchmark: Quick ratio should be greater than 1.0.
      1) Liquidity is a trade-off for profitability. Liquid investments usually do not provide as high a return as productive assets.
3. **Working capital** -- current assets minus current liabilities

D. **Activity ratios** -- measure the firm's use of assets to generate revenue and income

1. **Inventory turnover ratio** -- cost of sales divided by average inventories

   a. $$\frac{\textit{Cost of sales}}{\textit{Average inventory}}$$

   b. A high turnover implies that the firm does not hold excessive stocks of inventories that are unproductive and lessen the firm's profitability.

   c. A high turnover also implies that the inventory is truly marketable and does not contain obsolete goods.

   d. An average inventory figure should be used.

      1) If average annual inventory is cyclical, a monthly average should be used.

2. **Number of days of inventory** -- the number of days in the year divided by the inventory turnover ratio

   a. $$\frac{365,\ 360,\ \textit{or}\ 300}{\textit{Inventory turnover}}$$

   b. It measures the average number of days inventory is held before sale.

      1) It reflects the efficiency of inventory management.

   c. The number of days in a year may be 365, 360 (a banker's year), or 300 (number of business days).

   d. The lower the number of days, the better

3. **Receivables turnover ratio** -- net credit sales divided by average accounts receivable (but with net sales often used because of unavailability of credit sales data)

   a. $$\frac{\textit{Net credit sales}}{\textit{Average accounts receivable}}$$

   b. It indicates the efficiency of accounts receivable collection.

4. **Number of days of receivables** -- the number of days in the year divided by the receivables turnover ratio

   a. $$\frac{365,\ 360,\ \textit{or}\ 300}{\textit{Receivables turnover}}$$

   b. It is the average number of days to collect a receivable.

   c. It may also be computed as average accounts receivable divided by average daily sales.

      1) Average daily sales are net credit sales divided by the number of days in a year.

   d. This ratio can be compared to the seller's credit terms to determine whether most customers are paying on time.

RISK AND RETURN

A. **Risk** can be viewed in several ways. A common general definition is that risk is an investment with an unknown outcome but a known probability distribution of returns (a known mean and standard deviation). An increase in the standard deviation of returns is synonymous with an increase in the riskiness of a project. Two ways to estimate these probability distributions are

1. Subjective -- personal estimate
2. Objective -- predetermined (e.g., probability of a coin landing on heads)

B. Specific types of financial risks are

1. **Interest rate risk** -- fluctuations in the value of an asset as interest rates change
   a. EXAMPLE: If interest rates rise (fall), bond prices fall (rise).
2. **Purchasing power risk** -- the risk that a general rise in the price level will reduce the quantity of goods that can be purchased with a fixed sum of money
3. **Default risk** -- the risk that a borrower will be unable to make interest payments or principal repayments on debt
   a. EXAMPLE: The great amount of default risk inherent in the bonds of a company experiencing financial difficulty
4. **Market risk** -- the risk that changes in a stock's price will result from changes in the stock market as a whole. Prices of all stocks are correlated to some degree with broad swings in the stock market.
5. **Liquidity risk** -- the possibility that an asset cannot be sold on short notice for its market value. If an asset must be sold at a high discount, it is said to have a substantial amount of liquidity risk.
6. **Business risk** -- fluctuations in earnings before interest and taxes or in operating income. Business risk depends on factors such as
   a. Demand variability
   b. Sales price variability
   c. Input price variability
   d. Amount of operating leverage

C. In general, an asset with more risk (greater standard deviation of returns with a constant expected return) should have a higher expected (actual) return to compensate for the additional risk. If this were not the case, investors would sell the more risky asset, lowering its price, and buy the less risky asset, raising its price.

D. Risk-return analysis should not be confined to single assets only. It is important to look at portfolios and the gains from diversification.

1. These gains occur because all asset price movements are not perfectly correlated.

E. If investors do hold diversified portfolios, the relevant risk of an individual asset is its contribution to the riskiness of the portfolio.

STUDY UNIT 6
CAPITAL STRUCTURE FINANCE

INTRODUCTION

Capital structure finance concerns the amount and mixture of permanent assets used, and the methods by which they are financed. This is in contrast to the preceding study unit, Working Capital Finance, which emphasized management of current assets and short-term financing. This study unit begins with financial analysis, forecasting, and planning. The next sideheading concerns capital budgeting because it is the basis for analyzing investment decisions. The study unit continues with outlines of the sources of long-term financing, capital structure, and cost of capital. Each topic, capital structure finance and working capital finance, makes up about 10%-15% of the material tested on Part 1 of the CMA exam. In addition to the content of the next few pages, candidates should also keep abreast of current events in the field of capital structure finance by reading the *Wall Street Journal, Business Week,* or *Barron's*. Past CMA exams have often used material so recent that it does not appear in any textbook. Because many securities are regulated by the Securities and Exchange Commission (SEC), refer to Study Unit 14 to review SEC reporting requirements.

FINANCIAL RATIOS TO EVALUATE CAPITAL STRUCTURE FINANCE

A. In the preceding study unit, the ratios affecting working capital finance, solvency, and activity ratios were outlined. The following types of ratios are used to evaluate capital structure, i.e., fixed asset investing and long-term financing decisions:

1. Activity
2. Leverage
3. Profitability
4. Per share

B. **Activity ratios** measure the firm's use of assets to generate revenue and income.

1. **Fixed asset turnover** -- net sales divided by net fixed assets

   a. $\dfrac{\textit{Net sales}}{\textit{Net fixed assets}}$

   b. It measures the level of use of productive assets.

      1) Asset turnover is largely affected by the capital intensiveness of the company and its industry.

2. **Total asset turnover** -- net sales divided by average total assets

   a. $\dfrac{\textit{Net sales}}{\textit{Average total assets}}$

   b. It measures the level of capital investment relative to sales volume.

C. **Leverage ratios** measure the firm's use of debt to finance assets and operations.

1. **Debt to equity ratio** -- total debt divided by total stockholders' equity

   a. $\dfrac{\textit{Total liabilities}}{\textit{Stockholders' equity}}$

   b. It compares the resources provided by creditors with resources provided by stockholders. A high ratio means high risk.

2. **Equity ratio** -- common stockholders' equity divided by total assets

   a. $\dfrac{\textit{Common stockholders' equity}}{\textit{Total assets}}$

   b. It indicates the percent of total assets financed by common stockholders.

3. **Debt ratio** -- total liabilities divided by total assets

   a. $\dfrac{\textit{Total liabilities}}{\textit{Total assets}}$

   b. It measures the percentage of funds provided by creditors.

   c. Creditors prefer this ratio to be low as a cushion against losses.

4. **Times-interest-earned** -- income before interest and taxes, divided by interest

   a. $\dfrac{\textit{Net income} + \textit{Interest expense} + \textit{Income tax expense}}{\textit{Interest expense}}$

   b. It indicates the margin of safety over fixed interest charges.

   c. If earnings decline sufficiently, there will be no income tax expense.

D. **Profitability ratios** measure income on a relative basis.

1. **Profit margin on sales** -- net income after taxes divided by sales

   a. $\dfrac{\textit{Net income after taxes}}{\textit{Sales}}$

   b. It measures the rate of profitability on sales.

2. **Return on assets** -- net income after taxes divided by average total assets

   a. $\frac{\textit{Net income after taxes}}{\textit{Average total assets}}$

   b. It measures the productivity of assets.

   c. The book value of assets may not equal their market value.

3. **Return on stockholders' equity** -- net income after taxes divided by average common stockholders' equity

   a. $\frac{\textit{Net income after taxes}}{\textit{Average common stockholders' equity}}$

   b. It measures the rate of return on equity investment.

   c. The book value of common stockholders' equity may be below or above market values.

E. **Per share ratios** relate company financial information to each single share.

1. **Earnings per share (EPS)**

   a. $\frac{\textit{Net income available to common stockholders}}{\textit{Average shares outstanding}}$

   b. Earnings per share is net income available to common stockholders divided by the average number of shares outstanding for the period.

   c. Net income available to common stockholders is usually net income minus preferred dividends.

   d. Two EPS figures may be required by APB 15. The calculations for primary earnings per share and fully diluted earnings per share are set forth in Study Unit 12, Financial Statement Presentation, in Chapter 6.

2. **Book value per share**

   a. $\frac{\textit{Shareholders' equity}}{\textit{Shares outstanding}}$

   b. Book value per share is the amount of net assets available to the shareholders of a given type of stock divided by the number of those shares outstanding.

   c. When a company has preferred as well as common stock outstanding, the computation of book value per common share must consider potential claims by preferred shareholders, such as whether the preferred stock is cumulative and in arrears, or participating. It must also take into account whether the call price (or possibly the liquidation value) exceeds the carrying amount of the preferred stock.

3. **Yield on common stock**

   a. $\frac{\textit{Dividend per share}}{\textit{Market value per share}}$

   b. Yield is the annual dividend payment divided by the market value per share.

4. **Price-earnings ratio**

   a. $\frac{\textit{Market Price}}{\textit{EPS}}$

   b. Most analysts prefer to use fully diluted EPS.

F. Other ratios are identifiable by their titles, e.g., fixed assets to long-term debt.

1. Ratios are identified and classified as to whether they measure
   a. Solvency
   b. Activity
   c. Leverage
   d. Profitability
   e. Per share data
2. Ratios may be determined for a period of time or as of a moment in time.
3. The variables may be
   a. Before or after adjustments
   b. Gross or net
   c. Average or year-end
4. Ratios are most useful when put in context
   a. Through trend analysis of a single company
   b. By comparison with other companies or industry averages after any adjustments are made to assure that the accounting data are comparable
5. Ratios are based on accounting data, which often do not reflect current market values.

G. **Risk**

1. A discussion and an outline of the various types of risk appear at the end of Study Unit 5, Working Capital Finance.
   a. Interest rate risk
   b. Purchasing power risk
   c. Default risk
   d. Market risk
   e. Liquidity risk
   f. Business risk
      1) Demand variability
      2) Sales price variability
      3) Input price variability
      4) Degree of operating leverage
2. Risk is as pertinent to longer-term investment and financing decisions as it is to short-term decisions.

FINANCIAL FORECASTING

A. Financial forecasting, an essential element of planning, is the basis for budgeting activities.

1. The central and most important forecast is the level of activity, i.e., sales.

    a. Most other forecasts (budgets) follow from the sales forecast.
    b. Additional budgetary variables that must be forecast are

        1) The availability of the factors of production
        2) Prices of the factors of production

B. **Percent-of-sales** is the most widely used method for forecasting sales. The present level of sales is adjusted by a specified percent increase or decrease. The percent of sales method is

1. A form of trend analysis
2. Convenient and easy to apply
3. Preferred by managers

C. Other methods of forecasting sales are described in Study Unit 30, Inventory Models, and Study Unit 31, Quantitative Methods, in Chapter 8. They include

1. Time-series analysis
2. Exponential smoothing
3. Regression analysis
4. Expected value estimation

D. **Inflation Forecasting**

1. **Neutral inflation** -- a rise in all prices by the same amount (percentage)

2. **A nominal price change** occurs when the price of good A changes in the same direction and the same magnitude as the prices of all other commodities. For example, the price of good A may increase 20% when the price of all goods increases by 20%.

3. **A real price change** occurs when the price of commodity A changes with the prices of all other commodities remaining constant. For example, if the price of good A declines 10% and all other prices stay the same, there has been a real change (decrease) in the price of good A.

4. **The real risk-free rate of interest** is the return from forgoing present consumption. It assumes no fluctuations in the price level and no default risk.

5. **The nominal risk-free rate of interest** is the real risk-free rate plus an inflation premium (expected inflation for the next period)

6. The inflation premium is an average expected rate over the life of the security. It tends to be correlated, although not perfectly, with recent actual inflation rates.

E. The **term structure of interest rates** is the relationship between yield to maturity and time to maturity. It is graphically depicted by a yield curve.

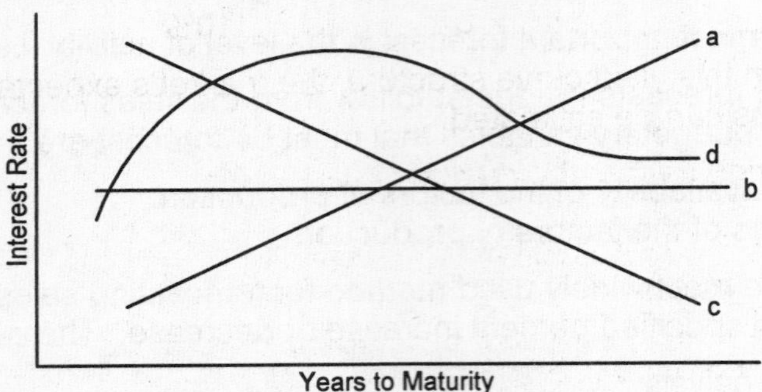

1. The graph above illustrates four common yield curves.
   a. Upward sloping
   b. Flat
   c. Downward sloping
   d. Humped
2. When plotting a yield curve, several factors are held constant:
   a. Default risk of instruments
   b. Taxability of the instruments
   c. Callability of the instruments
   d. Sinking fund provisions
3. The slopes of the foregoing yield curves depend on
   a. **Risk preference**
      1) **Interest rate risk** is the risk of loss associated with a change in bond prices caused by a change in interest rates. For a given change in rates, the price change will be greater the longer the term of the security. Thus, all other things being equal, short-term securities (and a lower interest rate) may be preferred by investors to long-term securities because their greater liquidity protects against a loss resulting from a rise in interest rates.
      2) Borrowers of funds prefer to borrow long-term (and pay a higher interest rate) to match the maturities of investments with the maturities of assets. Also, long-term borrowing avoids the expense of turning the debt over frequently.
   b. **Future expectations concerning interest rates**
      1) Most economists believe that a long-term interest rate is an average of future expected short-term interest rates. For this reason, the yield curve will slope upward if future rates are expected to rise, slope downward if interest rates are anticipated to fall, and remain flat if investors think the rate is stable. Future inflation is also incorporated into this relationship.
      2) Future interest rates are determined by the same factors that determine current rates.
      3) If the long-term rate is an average of future short-term rates, the manager can use the yield curve to derive the financial market's expectations of future interest rates.

4) EXAMPLE:

Years to Maturity	Rate
1	5%
2	8%
3	10%

Given this yield curve structure, the market's expectations for future interest rates can be estimated.

During year 1, the market is paying 5%.

For year 2, the market expects $\frac{(1.08)^2}{(1.05\ )} - 1 = 0.1109 = 11\%$

For year 3, the market expects $\frac{(1.10)^3}{(1.08)^2} - 1 = 0.1411 = 14\%$

This example shows clearly how long-term rates are created by a series of expected short-term rates.

CAPITAL BUDGETING

A. Capital budgeting is the process of planning expenditures for assets with returns expected to continue beyond 1 year.

1. Capital budgeting is tested on Part 4 of the CMA exam.
2. Study Unit 28, Capital Budgeting, is presented in Chapter 8.

SOURCES AND CHOICES OF LONG-TERM FUNDS

A. A firm may have long-term funding requirements that it cannot, or does not want to, meet using retained earnings. It must therefore issue equity or debt securities.

1. Certain hybrid forms of available financing include convertible issues and warrants. These are also used to attract long-term financing.
2. The **primary market** is the market for new stocks and bonds; i.e., investment money flows directly to the company that will use the funds to increase productive capacity.
   a. Existing securities are traded in secondary markets such as stock exchanges.
3. The **underwriting spread** is the difference between the price that an investment banker pays the issuer for a new security issue and the price at which that security is resold.

B. The principal considerations when reviewing financing options center on the cost of each type of fund (including the question of risk) and the lender's (the investor's) view of the financing device. This discussion highlights principal components of the decision:

1. **Common stock**. The common stockholders are the owners of the corporation, and their rights as owners, although reasonably uniform, depend on the laws of the state in which the firm is incorporated. Equity ownership involves risk because holders of common stock are not guaranteed a return and are last in priority in a liquidation. Stockholders' capital provides the cushion for creditors if any losses occur on liquidation.

a. Advantages

1) Common stock does not require a fixed dividend; i.e., dividends are paid from profits when available.

2) There is no fixed maturity date for repayment of the capital.

3) The sale of common stock increases the creditworthiness of the firm by providing more equity.

4) Common stock is frequently more attractive to investors than debt, because it grows in value with the success of the firm.

a) The higher the common stock value, the more advantageous equity financing is over debt financing.

b. Disadvantages

1) Control (voting rights) is usually diluted as more common stock is sold.

2) New common stock sales dilute earnings available to existing shareholders because of the greater number of shares outstanding.

3) Underwriting costs are typically higher for common stock issues.

4) Too much equity may raise the average cost of capital of the firm above its optimal level.

5) Common stock cash dividends are not deductible as an expense and are after-tax cash deductions to the firm.

c. Common stockholders ordinarily have **preemptive rights**.

1) Preemptive rights give common stockholders the right to purchase any additional stock issuances in proportion to their current ownership percentages.

2) If applicable state law or the corporate charter does not provide preemptive rights, the firm may nevertheless sell to the existing common stockholders in a **rights** offering. Each shareholder is issued a certificate or warrant that is an option to buy a certain number of shares at a fixed price.

a) Until the rights are actually issued, the stock trades **rights-on**; that is, the stock and the rights are not separable. After the rights are received, the stock trades **ex-rights** because the rights can be sold separately. The formula for the value of a stock right when the stock price is rights-on is

$$\frac{P - S}{N + 1}$$

If: P = value of a share rights-on
S = subscription price of a share
N = number of rights needed to buy a share

b) The amount recorded for stock rights is based on an allocation of the cost of the shares owned based on the relative market values of the shares and the rights.

d. **Stock warrants** (certificates evidencing options to buy stock at a given price within a certain period) may be given to employees as compensation, or they may be issued with bonds or preferred stock.

   1) The proceeds of securities issued with **detachable warrants** are allocated between the warrants and the securities based on their relative market values. If the fair value of one but not the other is known, the proceeds are allocated incrementally. If warrants are not detachable, they are not accounted for separately.

e. A stock's **par value** represents legal capital. It is an arbitrary value assigned to stock before the stock is issued. It also represents the maximum liability of a shareholder.

2. **Preferred stock**

   a. Advantages from the issuer's (firm's) view

      1) It is a form of equity and therefore builds the creditworthiness of the firm.

      2) Control is still held by common shareholders.

      3) Superior earnings of the firm are usually still reserved for the common stockholders.

   b. Disadvantages of issuing preferred stock

      1) Preferred stock cash dividends are not deductible as a tax expense and are paid with taxable income. The result is a substantially greater cost relative to bonds.

      2) In periods of economic difficulty, accumulated (past) dividends may create major managerial and financial problems for the firm.

   c. Typical provisions of preferred stock issues

      1) **Priority** in assets and earnings; i.e., if the firm goes bankrupt, the preferred stockholders have priority over common stockholders.

      2) **Cumulative dividends**. All past preferred dividends must be paid before any common dividends can be paid.

      3) **Convertibility**. Preferred stock issues may be convertible into common stock at the option of the shareholder.

      4) **Participating** preferred stock participates with common in excess earnings of the company. For example, 8% participating preferred stock might pay a dividend each year greater than 8% when the corporation is extremely profitable. But nonparticipating preferred stock will receive no more than is stated on the face of the stock.

   d. Holding preferred stock rather than bonds provides corporations a major tax advantage: at least 70% of the dividends received from preferred stock is tax deductible, whereas all bond interest received is taxable.

      1) The **dividends received deduction** also applies to common stock.

3. **Bonds.**

a. Advantages of bonds to the issuer

1) Basic control of the firm is not shared with the debtholder.

2) Cost of debt is limited. Bondholders usually do not participate in the superior earnings of the firm.

3) Ordinarily, the expected yield of bonds is lower than the cost of common stock.

4) Interest paid on debt is tax deductible as an expense.

5) Debt may add substantial flexibility in the financial structure of the corporation through the insertion of call provisions in the bond indenture.

b. Disadvantages of bonds to the issuing firm

1) Debt has a fixed charge. Therefore, if the earnings of the firm fluctuate, there is a risk of not meeting the fixed interest obligations, which could lead to the demise of the firm.

2) Debt adds risk to a firm. Stockholders will consequently demand higher capitalization rates on equity earnings, which may result in a decline in the market price of stock.

3) Debt usually has a maturity date.

4) Debt is a long-term commitment, a factor that can affect risk profiles. Debt originally appearing to be profitable may become a burden and drive the firm into bankruptcy.

5) Certain managerial prerogatives are usually given up in the contractual relationship outlined in the bond's indenture contract.

a) For example, specific ratios must be kept above a certain level during the term of the loan.

6) There are clear-cut limits to the amounts of debt available to the individual firm. Generally accepted standards of the investment community will usually dictate a certain debt-equity ratio for an individual firm. Beyond this limit, the cost of debt may rise rapidly, or debt may not be available.

c. Basic types of bonds

1) **Mortgage** -- a pledge of certain assets for a loan. It is usually secured by real property as a condition of the loan.

2) **Debenture** -- a long-term bond not secured by specific property. It is a general obligation of the borrower. Only companies with the best credit ratings can issue debentures because holders will be general creditors. They will have a status inferior to that of secured parties and creditors with priorities in bankruptcy.

3) **Income** -- a bond that pays interest only if the issuing company has earnings. Such bonds are riskier than other bonds.

4) **Serial** -- bonds with staggered maturities. These bonds permit investors to choose the maturity dates that meet their needs.

d. Contractual clauses in bond contracts include those discussed below:

   1) **Call provisions** give the corporation the right to call in the bond for redemption. This is an advantage to the firm but not for the investor. If interest rates decline, the company can call in the high-interest bonds and replace them with low-interest bonds.

   2) **Sinking fund** requires that the firm retire a certain portion of its bonds each year or that money be set aside for repayment in the future. It increases the probability of repayment for bondholders but requires the use of capital by the firm.

e. **Zero-coupon bonds** pay no interest but sell at a deep discount from face value. A relatively new type of bond, these instruments are very useful to investors and investees.

   1) The need to reinvest the periodic payments renders the final return available from normal coupon bonds uncertain because future reinvestment rates are uncertain. But the investor knows the exact return on a zero-coupon bond. Investors might therefore be willing to pay a premium for them, which in turn might lead firms to issue them.

   2) The lack of interest payments means the firm faces no additional insolvency risk from the issue until it matures.

f. **Junk bonds** are very high-risk, high yield securities issued to finance leveraged buyouts and mergers. They are also issued by troubled companies. They exploit the large tax deductions for interest payments made by entities with high debt ratios.

g. International bonds are of two types: **foreign bonds** and **Eurobonds**. Foreign bonds are denominated in the currency of the nation in which they are sold. Eurobonds are denominated in a currency other than that of the nation where they are sold.

   1) Foreign bonds issued in the United States and denominated in dollars must be registered with the SEC, but such extensive disclosure is not required in most European nations. Thus, an American company may elect to issue Eurobonds denominated in dollars in a foreign nation because of the convenience of not having to comply with governmental registration requirements.

4. Numerous financing arrangements are used by corporate management to increase investor interest in corporate securities. The objective is to have a lower interest rate on bonds or a higher selling price for stocks.

   a. **Warrants** permit a holder to share in a company's prosperity by permitting a future purchase of stock at a special low price.

   b. **Convertibility**. Bonds or preferred stock may be exchangeable (by the investor) into common stock under certain conditions.

   c. Both warrants and a conversion feature offer a corporation a means of delayed equity financing when market prices are unfavorable. When the market price rises above the conversion price, holders will presumably exercise the warrants or convert the securities.

   d. **Subordinated debentures** possess a feature undesirable to investors: They are subordinated to (inferior to) the claims of other general creditors as well as secured parties and persons with priorities in bankruptcy. The indenture specifies the claims (senior debt) to which these bonds are subordinate. They are usually issued only when the company has some debt instrument outstanding that prohibits the issuance of additional regular bonds. Subordinated debentures will normally pay a higher rate of interest than secured bonds.

5. **Employee stock ownership plans (ESOPs)** are established by a corporation under federal income tax laws. Under such a plan, an employee stock ownership trust (ESOT) acquires qualifying employer securities, which may be outstanding shares, treasury shares, or newly issued shares. It holds the stock in the name of the company's employees. The trust typically obtains the cash to buy the stock by borrowing from a bank, and the corporation typically cosigns the note to the bank. Each year, the corporation makes contributions to the ESOT as a deductible contribution to a qualified retirement plan. Similarly, the employees themselves might make deposits to the ESOT.
   a. The corporation receives the benefit of the bank loan by selling stock to the ESOT. Moreover, the corporation in effect repays the bank loan through deductible contributions (with pretax dollars) to the ESOT. Thus, use of a leveraged ESOP allows the corporation to obtain a deduction for the principal as well as the interest on the loan.
   b. Another advantage of an ESOP is that employees should be motivated to perform better because they have a financial interest in the success of the company (although, if the market price of the stock declines, morale may be harmed).
   c. Some small business owners have found that an ESOP is an effective way to transfer ownership (to employees) when no other buyer can be found.
6. **Dividend reinvestment plans (DRPs)**. Any dividends due to shareholders are automatically reinvested in shares of the same corporation's common stock. In recent years, many corporations have adopted such plans. Broker's fees on such purchases of stock are either zero (the costs absorbed by the corporation) or only a few cents per stockholder because only one purchase is made and the total fee is divided among all shareholders participating.
   a. Initially, dividends were reinvested in stock bought by a trustee (typically a large bank) on the open market. Many plans are still of this type.
   b. More recently, corporations have seen the opportunity to use DRPs as a source of financing. Thus, many plans now involve a sale of newly issued stock to the trustee to fulfill the requirements of the plan. The corporation benefits because it can issue stock at the current market value without incurring underwriting and issue costs.
7. **Intermediate-term financing** refers to debt issues having approximate maturities of greater than 1 but less than 10 years. The principal types of intermediate-term financing are term loans and lease financing. Major lenders under term agreements are commercial banks, life insurance companies, and, to some extent, pension funds.
   a. **Term loans**. One possible feature of term loans is tying the interest payable on the loan to a variable rate of interest. This **floating rate**, usually stated as some percentage over the prime, creates the potential for extremely high borrowing costs.
      1) This risk must be traded off against
         a) The need of the firm to obtain the loan
         b) The flexibility inherent in term borrowing
         c) The ability of the firm to borrow in the capital market
         d) Other available types of debt financing
         e) The amount of privacy desired
      2) Term loans are private contracts between private firms, whereas long-term debt securities quickly involve the SEC and massive disclosure.

3) Variable or floating rate loans are advantageous to lenders because they permit better matching of interest costs and revenues. The market values of these loans also tend to be more stable than those for fixed rate loans.

a) The disadvantages include a heightened risk of default, losses of expected revenues if interest rates decline or if market rates rise above the ceiling specified in the agreement, and the difficulty of working with a more complex product.

4) Borrowers may benefit from the lower initial costs of these loans but must accept increased interest rate risk, the difficulty of forecasting cash flow, a possible loss of creditworthiness if interest rates are expected to rise, and the burden of more complex financing arrangements.

5) If the interest rate is variable but the monthly loan payment is fixed, an increase in the rate means that the interest component of the payment and the total interest for the loan term will be greater.

a) The term of the loan will also be extended, and the principal balance will increase because amortization is diminished. Indeed, negative amortization may occur if the interest rate increase is great enough.

b) Floating or variable rate loans have an impact on monetary policy because they render analyses more complex. These loans give the Federal Reserve less control over the money supply and credit. The economy is now more sensitive to interest rate fluctuations, and political pressure to avoid rate increases will become greater.

b. **Lease financing** must be analyzed by comparing the cost of owning to the cost of leasing. Whereas the principal advantage of leasing used to be the tax advantages allowed, leasing has become a major means of financing because it offers a variety of other benefits. If leases are not accounted for as installment purchases, they provide off-balance-sheet financing. The three principal forms of leases are discussed below:

1) A **sale-leaseback** is a financing method. A firm seeking financing sells an asset to an investor (creditor) and leases the asset back, usually on a noncancelable lease. The lease payments consist of principal and interest paid by the lessee to the lessor.

2) **Service or operating leases** usually include both financing and maintenance services.

3) **Financial leases**, which do not provide for maintenance services, are noncancelable and fully amortize the cost of the leased asset over the term of the basic lease contract; i.e., they are installment purchases.

8. **Maturity matching**. The desirability of maturity matching (equalizing the life of an asset acquired with the debt instrument used to finance it) is an important factor in choosing the source of funds. Financing long-term assets with long-term debt allows the company to generate sufficient cash flows from the assets to satisfy obligations as they mature.

9. **Venture capital**. Venture capital firms invest in new enterprises that might not be able to obtain funds in the usual capital markets due to the riskiness of new products. Placements of securities with venture capital firms are usually "private placements" and not subject to SEC regulation.

a. Venture capitalists risk low liquidity for their investments and high risk.
b. The payoff may be substantial if the company does succeed.

FINANCIAL STRUCTURE, LEVERAGE, AND THE COST OF CAPITAL

A. **Financial structure** refers to the entire right-hand side of the balance sheet, which indicates the way the firm's assets are financed.

1. Capital structure is the permanent financing of the firm and is represented principally by
    a. Long-term debt
    b. Preferred stock
    c. Common stockholders' equity
        1) Common stock
        2) Capital surplus
        3) Retained earnings
2. Permanent financing includes long-term debt.
    a. Most firms renew (roll over) their long-term obligations.
    b. Thus, long-term debt is often effectively permanent.

B. The following factors influence financial structure:

1. Growth rate of future sales
2. Stability of future sales
3. Competitive structures in the industry
4. Asset makeup of the individual firm
5. Attitude toward risk of owners and management
6. Control position of owners and management
7. Lenders' attitude toward the industry and a particular firm

C. **Leverage** -- the relative amount of the fixed cost of capital, principally debt, in a firm's capital structure

1. Leverage, by definition, creates financial risk, which relates directly to the question of the cost of capital.
    a. The more leverage, the higher the financial risk, and the higher the cost of debt capital
    b. **The degree of financial leverage (DFL)** -- the percentage change in earnings available to common stockholders that is associated with a given percentage change in net operating income
    c. $$\text{DFL} = \frac{\%\ \Delta \textit{ in net income}}{\%\ \Delta \textit{ in net operating income}}$$
        1) Net income means earnings available to common stockholders.
        2) Operating income equals earnings before interest and taxes (EBIT). The following is another version of the DFL formula (I = interest, P = preferred dividends, t = tax rate):

$$\frac{EBIT}{EBIT - I - [P \div (1 - t)]}$$

    d. The more financial leverage employed, the greater the DFL, and the riskier the firm

2. Whenever the return on assets is greater than the cost of debt, additional leverage is favorable.

3. Operating leverage is a related concept based on the degree that fixed costs are used in the production process. A company with a high percentage of fixed costs is more risky than a firm in the same industry that relies more on variable costs to produce.

   a. **The degree of operating leverage (DOL)** -- the percentage change in net operating income associated with a given percentage change in sales

   b. $$\text{DOL} = \frac{\%\ \Delta\ \textit{in net operating income}}{\%\ \Delta\ \textit{in sales}}$$

   c. Given that Q equals units sold, P is unit price, V is unit variable cost, and F is fixed cost, the DOL can also be calculated from the following formula:

$$\frac{Q(P - V)}{Q(P - V) - F}$$

4. **The degree of total leverage (DTL)** -- summarizes the total risk for sales variability

   a. It is the percentage change in net income that is associated with a given percentage change in sales.

   b. $$\text{DTL} = \frac{\%\ \Delta\ \textit{in net income}}{\%\ \Delta\ \textit{in sales}}$$

   c. The degree of total leverage is also equal to the degree of operating leverage times the degree of financial leverage.

$$\text{DTL} = \text{DOL} \times \text{DFL}$$

      1) For this reason, firms with a high degree of operating leverage do not usually employ a high degree of financial leverage and vice versa. One of the most important considerations in the use of financial leverage is the amount of operating leverage.

   d. EXAMPLE: A firm has a highly automated production process. Because of automation, the degree of operating leverage is 2. If the firm wants a degree of total leverage not exceeding 3, it must restrict its use of debt so that the degree of financial leverage is not more than 1.5. If the firm had committed to a production process that was less automated and had a lower DOL, more debt could be employed, and the firm could have a higher degree of financial leverage.

D. **Cost of Capital.** Managers must know the cost of capital in making investment (long-term funding) decisions because investments with a return higher than the cost of capital will increase the value of the firm (stockholders' wealth). The theory underlying the cost of capital applies to new, long-term funding because long-term funds finance long-term investments. Short-term funds are used to meet working capital and other temporary needs. Cost of capital is of less concern for short-term funding.

1. The cost of capital is a weighted average of the various debt and equity components.
   a. The **cost of debt** equals the interest rate times (1 – marginal tax rate) because interest is a tax deduction.
   b. The **cost of retained earnings** -- the rate required by investors equal to the rate they could obtain elsewhere, given the same risk. The cost of internally generated funds is an imputed cost.
   c. The **cost of new external equity** is higher than the cost of retained earnings because of stock flotation costs.
2. Standard financial theory states that there is an **optimal capital structure**.
   a. The optimal capital structure minimizes the **weighted average cost of capital** and thereby maximizes the value of the firm.
   b. The optimal capital structure usually involves some debt but not 100% debt.
   c. The relevant relationships are depicted below.

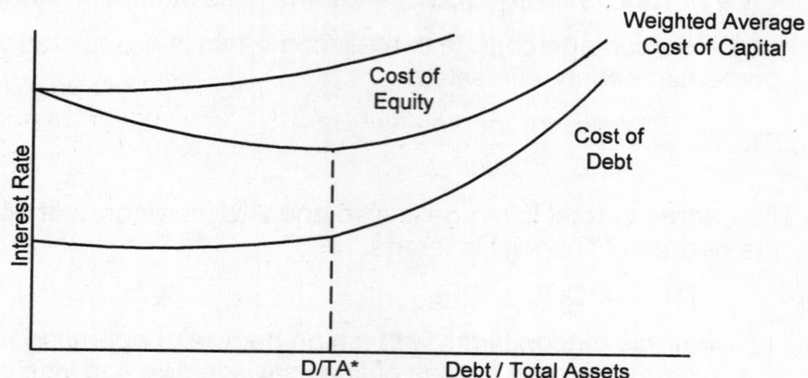

   D/TA* represents the lowest weighted average cost of capital and is therefore the firm's optimal capital structure.

   d. Ordinarily, firms will not be able to identify this optimal point precisely. The best they can find is an optimal range within which to maintain the capital structure.
3. The required rate of return on equity capital (R) can be determined by the
   a. **Capital asset pricing model** -- adds the risk-free rate (determined by government securities) to the product of the beta coefficient (a measure of the firm's risk) and the difference between the market return and the risk-free rate

$$R = RF + \beta(RM - RF)$$

      1) The **market risk premium** (RM – RF) is the amount above the risk-free rate for which investors must be compensated to induce them to invest in the market.
      2) The **beta coefficient** of an individual stock is the correlation between the volatility (price variation) of the stock market and the volatility of the price of the individual stock.
         a) EXAMPLE: If an individual stock goes up 10% and the stock market goes up 10%, the beta coefficient is 1.0. If the stock goes up 15% and the market only 10%, beta is 1.5.

b. **Bond plus approach** -- adds a percentage to the company's long-term interest rate
   1) A 4% premium is a frequently used figure.

c. **Gordon growth model**
   1) Three elements required to estimate the cost of equity are
      a) Dividends per share
      b) Expected growth rate
      c) Market price
   2) Formula for calculating the equity cost
      a) $K_s = \frac{D_1}{P_0} + G$

         If: P_0 = current price
         D_1 = next dividend
         K_s = required rate of return
         G = growth rate in dividends per share (but the model assumes that the dividend payout ratio, retention rate, and therefore the EPS growth rate are constant).

      b) To incorporate the flotation cost of new stock, the growth model can be slightly altered.

$$K_s = \frac{D_1}{P_0\ (1 - \textit{Flotation cost})} + G$$

         As the flotation costs rise, K_s rises accordingly.
   3) The Gordon Growth Model is also used for stock price evaluation. The formula can be restated in terms of P_0 as follows:

$$P_0 = \frac{D_1}{K_s - G}$$

   4) How is the stock price affected by the dividend payout ratio? Some investors may want capital gains, but others may prefer current income. Individual investor preference is important. Thus, investors will choose stocks that give the proper mix of capital gains and dividends.
   5) Stock dividends are not genuine dividends. They simply divide the pie into a greater number of slices but do not change the wealth positions of the stockholders.

4. The **marginal cost of capital**

a. The cost of capital to the firm for the next dollar of new capital increases because lower-cost capital sources are used first.

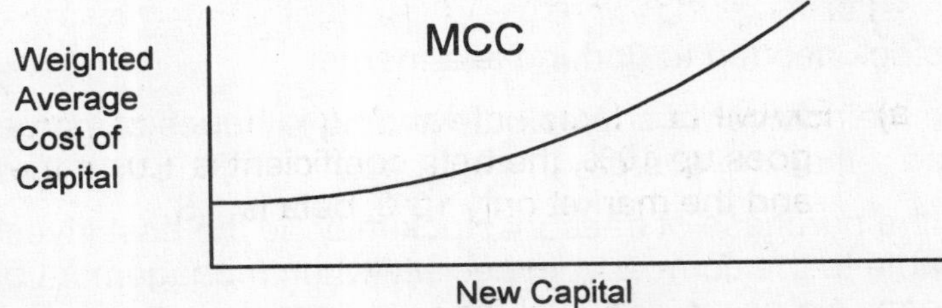

5. The **marginal efficiency of investment**

   a. The return on additional dollars of capital investment decreases because the most profitable investments are made initially.

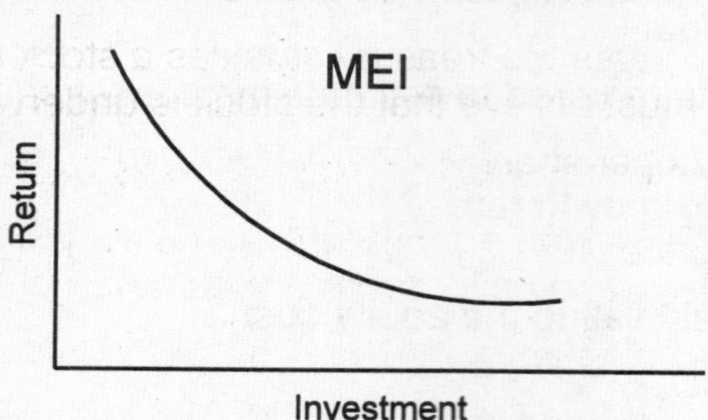

6. Combining the MCC and MEI schedules (graphs) produces the equilibrium investment level for the firm (and the capital budget).

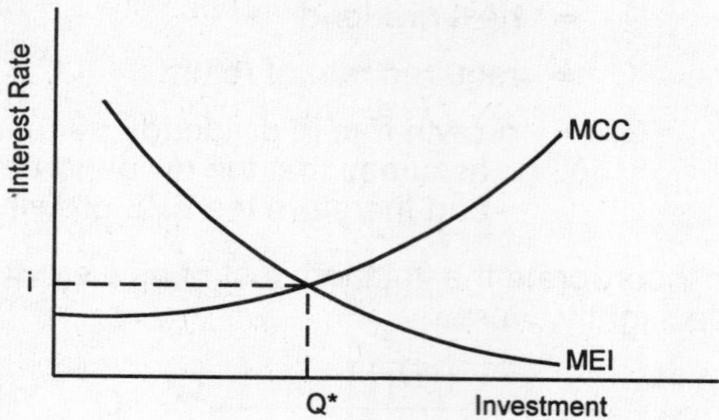

TREASURY STOCK

A. **Treasury stock** is a corporation's own stock that it has reacquired. It is usually purchased on the open market at the current market price.

   1. Treasury stock is not an asset of a corporation.

      a. A corporation cannot own itself.

   2. Treasury stock is shown as a reduction of stockholders' equity (a contra-equity account). Such stock is considered issued, but not outstanding.

B. A corporation might buy back its own stock for a number of reasons:

   1. To have sufficient stock on hand to meet employee stock option and bonus plan requirements
   2. To buy out a particular stockholder when the stock cannot be sold on the open market (or when such a sale would be so large that the market price would be adversely affected)
   3. To attempt to support the market for the company's stock
   4. To reduce the size of the business
   5. To acquire stock needed to undertake a merger
   6. To decrease the number of shares outstanding in hopes of increasing the earnings per share on the remaining shares

      a. Thus, the purchase of treasury stock may be the best investment opportunity available to the company, especially when management believes that the company's stock is undervalued.

7. To increase the book value per share of the remaining shares outstanding
   a. The market value must be less than the book value.
8. To hold the shares until the market goes up again, at which time the stock will be resold
   a. Management thereby treats the treasury stock as a stock market investment.
   b. Again, management must believe that the stock is undervalued.
9. To provide a quick and simple means of adjusting a firm's capital structure.
   a. A repurchase of shares using debt financing is an even more dramatic way of quickly changing the relationship between debt and equity in the capital structure.

C. Dividends are not paid on treasury stock.

D. Treasury stock does not have any voting rights.

E. The purchase of treasury stock is sometimes criticized as being a selective dividend to those stockholders who sell their stock.
   1. Like a dividend, purchase of treasury stock decreases stockholders' equity.
   2. Such dividends are usually not taxed as dividends but rather as capital gains. This is an advantage if the capital gains rate is less than the marginal tax rate of the shareholder.

F. Disadvantages of buying treasury stock include
   1. A higher debt-equity ratio, which may increase the difficulty of obtaining loans
   2. An increase in the company's susceptibility to acquisition by another corporation because fewer shares are outstanding (But a treasury stock purchase can thwart a hostile takeover. If the price is above market, this practice is known as "paying greenmail.")
   3. Liquidity problems because cash is being paid out to shareholders

G. To prohibit a corporation from using all of its capital (including borrowed capital) to buy treasury stock and then liquidating once all stock has been acquired, most states stipulate that legal capital (paid-in capital) cannot be reduced by treasury stock purchases.
   1. A company can buy treasury stock only to the extent it has retained earnings.

H. In addition to buying treasury stock on the open market, a corporation planning a large purchase may make a tender offer for a certain number of shares. The tender offer may specify a specific price, or it may be effected by a Dutch auction.
   1. A tender offer asks stockholders to offer their shares for sale.
   2. Some stockholders may prefer regular tender offers over regular dividends in that those owners in need of money can tender some of their shares and receive cash at favorable tax rates. Those shareholders who do not need cash can ignore the tender offer.
   3. In a Dutch auction involving a solicitation to buy stock, each seller specifies the number of shares (s)he wishes to sell and a minimum price. Given the number of shares tendered and the prices offered by the selling shareholders, the lowest price that enables the buyer to acquire the requisite total of shares is set as the purchase price.
      a. One variation is for the tender offer to specify a range of acceptable prices.

STOCK DIVIDENDS AND STOCK SPLITS

A. Stock dividends and splits involve issuance of additional shares to existing stockholders.

1. Stockholders do not really receive any increase in the value of their holdings. The previous holdings are simply divided into more pieces (additional shares).
2. A **stock dividend** is an issuance of stock and entails the transfer of a sum from the retained earnings account to a paid-in capital account.
   a. Usually, the corporation wants to give something to the shareholders but without paying out a cash dividend because the funds are needed in the business.
   b. Casual investors may believe they are receiving something of value when in essence their previous holdings are merely being divided into more pieces.
   c. Stock dividends are often used by growing companies that wish to retain earnings in the business while placating stockholders.
3. A **stock split** does not involve any accounting entries. Instead, the existing shares are divided into more pieces so that the market price per share will be reduced.
   a. EXAMPLE: If a corporation has 1 million shares outstanding, each of which sells for $90, a 2-for-1 stock split will result in 2 million shares outstanding, each of which sells for about $45.
   b. **Reverse stock splits** reduce the shares outstanding.
4. Advantages of issuing stock splits and dividends
   a. Because more shares will be outstanding, the price per share will be lower. The lower price per share will induce more small investors to purchase the company's stock. Thus, because demand for the stock is greater, the price may increase.
      1) EXAMPLE: In the example above, the additional investors interested in the company at the lower price may drive the price up to $46 or $47, or slightly higher than the theoretically correct price of $45. Consequently, current stockholders will benefit from the split (or dividend) after all.
   b. A dividend or split can be a publicity gesture. Because stockholders will think they are getting something of value (and maybe indirectly they are), they will have a better opinion of their company.
   c. Moreover, the more shares a corporation has outstanding, the larger the number of stockholders, who are usually good customers for their own company's products.
5. On rare occasions, a company will have a reverse stock split in an attempt to raise the market price per share. For example, a 1-for-10 stock split would require stockholders to turn in ten old shares in order to receive one new share.

DIVIDEND POLICY

A. **Dividend policy** -- the determination of what portion of a corporation's net income should be distributed to stockholders and what portion kept in the business for expansion purposes

1. A high dividend rate means a slower rate of growth.
2. A high growth rate usually means a low dividend rate.
3. Because both a high growth rate and a high dividend rate are desirable, the financial manager is in a quandary.
4. Normally, corporations try to maintain a stable level of dividends, even though profits may fluctuate considerably, because many stockholders buy stock with the expectation of receiving a certain dividend every year. Hence, management tends not to raise dividends if the payout cannot be sustained.
   a. The desire for stability has led theorists to propound the **information content or signaling hypothesis**: a change in dividend policy is a signal to the market regarding management's forecast of future earnings.
5. This stability often results in a stock that sells at a higher market price because stockholders perceive less risk in receiving their dividends.

B. Various factors influence a company's dividend policy.

1. **Legal restrictions.** Dividends ordinarily cannot be paid out of paid-in capital. A corporation must have a balance in its retained earnings account before dividends can be paid.
2. **Stability of earnings.** A company whose earnings fluctuate greatly from year to year will tend to pay out a smaller dividend during good years so that the same dividend can be paid even if profits are much lower. For example, a company with fluctuating earnings might pay out $1 every year whether earnings per share are $10 (10% payout rate) or $1 (100% payout rate).
3. **Rate of growth.** A company with a faster growth rate will have a greater need to finance that growth with retained earnings. Thus, growth companies usually have lower dividend payout ratios.
   a. Stockholders hope to be able to obtain larger capital gains in the future.
4. **Cash position.** Regardless of a firm's earnings record, cash must be available before a dividend can be paid. No dividend can be declared if all of a firm's earnings are tied up in receivables and inventories.
5. **Restrictions in debt agreements.** Bond indentures and other debt agreements often place restrictions on the amount of dividends that a company can declare.
6. **Tax position of stockholders.** In closely held corporations, the stockholders may not want regular dividends because the individual owners are in such high tax brackets. They may want to forgo dividends in exchange for future capital gains or wait to receive dividends in future years when they are in a lower tax bracket.
7. Possibility of being assessed an **accumulated earnings tax**. The IRS does not like stockholders to postpone paying taxes on their dividends. They can assess an accumulated earnings tax if a corporation has accumulated retained earnings beyond its reasonably expected needs.
8. **Residual theory of dividends.** The amount (residual) of earnings paid as dividends depends on the available investment opportunities and the debt-equity ratio at which cost of capital is minimized. The rational investor should prefer reinvestment of retained earnings when the return exceeds what the investor could earn on investments of equal risk. However, the firm may prefer to pay dividends when investment opportunities are poor and the use of internal equity financing would move the firm away from its ideal capital structure.

C. **Important Dates Concerning the Declaration of Dividends**

1. **Date of declaration** -- the date the directors meet and formally vote to declare a dividend. On this date, the dividend becomes a liability of the corporation.
2. **Date of record** -- the date as of which the corporation determines the stockholders who will receive the declared dividend. Essentially, the corporation closes its stockholder records on this date. Only those stockholders who own the stock on the date of record will receive the dividend. It typically falls anywhere from 2 to 6 weeks after the declaration date.
3. **Date of payment** -- the date on which the dividend is actually paid (when the checks are put into the mail to the investors). The payment date is usually from 2 to 4 weeks after the date of record.
4. **Ex-dividend date** -- a date established by the stock exchanges, such as 4 days before the date of record. Unlike the other dates mentioned above, it is not established by the corporate board of directors. The period between the ex-dividend date and the date of record gives the stock exchange members time to process any transactions so that new stockholders will receive the dividends to which they are entitled. An investor who buys a share of stock before the ex-dividend date will receive the dividend that has been previously declared. An investor who buys the stock after the ex-dividend date (but before the date of record or payment date) will not receive the declared dividend. Instead, the individual who sold the stock will receive the dividend because (s)he owned it on the ex-dividend date.
   a. Usually, a stock price will drop on the ex-dividend date by the amount of the dividend because the new investor will not receive it.

INTEREST RATE FUTURES

A. A financial manager can protect a company against adverse changes in interest rates by hedging in the interest rate futures market.

1. **Hedging** -- the process of using offsetting commitments to minimize or avoid the impact of adverse price movements
   a. EXAMPLE: In the commodities market, a manufacturer might have a contract with a farmer to buy soybeans at a future date. The price is agreed upon as the current price. The company would lose money if the soybean prices declined before the beans were delivered. So, to avoid any loss (or gain), the corporation could sell soybeans in the future, but at today's price. If the price of soybeans does decline before the delivery date, the company will lose money on the beans bought from the farmer, but will gain money on the beans sold under the futures contract by buying cheap beans in the future to cover the delivery.

2. Interest rate futures contracts involve risk-free bonds, such as treasury bonds, T-bills, Ginnie-Maes, and money-market certificates.
   a. The quantity traded is either $100,000 or $1 million, depending on which market is used.
   b. Because commodities can be bought and sold with very little down payment, considerable leverage is involved.
      1) This high degree of leverage is most beneficial to the speculator who is looking for large returns and is willing to bear the risk to get them. For hedgers, however, the small down payment is useful only because the risk can be hedged away without tying up a large amount of cash.
3. EXAMPLE: If a corporation wants to borrow money in 6 months for a major project, but the lender refuses to commit itself to an interest rate, the interest rate futures market can be used to eliminate the risk that interest rates might go up in the interim. The company agrees to sell T-bills, or another type of bonds, in 6 months. If the interest rates do increase over the period, the value of the T-bills will decline. Then the company can buy T-bills in 6 months and use them to cover the delivery that it had promised in the futures contract. Because the price of T-bills has declined over the period, the company will make a profit on the delivery of the T-bills. The interest rates that the company will have to pay on the upcoming loan will be higher, however. It has cost the company money to wait 6 months for the loan. The profit from the futures contract should thus approximately offset the loss resulting from the higher interest loan. Alternatively, if interest rates had declined, the company would have had the benefit of a lower interest loan but lost money on the T-bills. The goal of any such hedging operation is to break even on the change in interest rates.
   a. By hedging, the financial manager need not worry about fluctuations in interest rates but can instead concentrate on the day-to-day operations of the company.

FINANCING AFTER A BUSINESS FAILURE

A. A financially troubled business can restructure its debts under **Chapter 11 of the Federal Bankruptcy Act**.
   1. This is a voluntary alternative to liquidation proceedings in bankruptcy (Chapter 7 of the Federal Bankruptcy Act).
   2. The corporation submits a plan of reorganization to restructure its debts and take any other appropriate action, including a change in management.
   3. The corporation remains in business and does not lose all its assets.
   4. The plan of reorganization must be approved by the court. First, a majority of creditors of each class of debt must approve the plan, or only one class of creditors need approve the plan if it is fair and equitable.
B. An alternative to the bankruptcy proceedings is a **composition among creditors**.
   1. It is simply an agreement between the debtor and the creditors.
   2. The creditors agree to extend time for payment, take lesser sums in satisfaction of the debts owed, or accept some other plan of financial adjustment.
   3. The debtor continues in business under this method also unless the parties agree to a liquidation.

LEVERAGED BUYOUTS

A. A leveraged buyout arrangement is a financing technique by which a company is purchased using very little equity.

1. A leveraged buyout is often used when a company is sold to management or some other group of employees.
2. The new owners put down very little initial equity.
3. The company assets are used as collateral for a loan to finance the purchase.
    a. Junk bonds are often used to finance a leveraged buyout or merger (and may also be issued by troubled companies).
        1) Junk bonds are high-risk and therefore high-yield securities that are normally issued when the debt ratio is very high. Thus, the bondholders will have as much risk as the holders of equity securities.
            a) Junk bonds have been accepted because of the tax deductibility of interest paid by the restructured companies. Given the high debt ratios of these concerns, after-tax cash flows increase.
4. Characteristics of firms that are candidates for a leveraged buyout include
    a. An established business with proven operating performance
    b. Stable earnings and cash flows
    c. Very little outstanding debt
    d. Quality asset base that can be used as collateral for a new loan
    e. Stable technology that will not require large expenditures for research and development
5. The high degree of risk in leveraged buyouts results from the fixed charges for interest on the loan and the lack of cash for expansion.

TENDER OFFERS

A. A tender offer is often used in corporate takeover attempts.

1. An acquisition-minded investor offers to buy outstanding shares of an investee by tendering an open offer to all stockholders at a specified price.
2. A tender offer can be either friendly (approved by the corporate board of directors) or hostile (opposed by the board).

B. **Greenmail** is a defensive tactic to protect against takeover. First, an acquirer buys a large number of shares on the open market and then makes (or threatens to make) a tender offer. If management and the board are opposed to the takeover (i.e., a hostile tender offer), the potential acquirer is offered the opportunity to sell his/her already acquired shares back to the corporation at an amount substantially above market value (i.e., paying greenmail).

C. **Other Takeover Defenses**

1. **Staggered election of directors**. New stockholders must wait several years before being able to place their own people on the board of directors.
2. **Golden parachutes** are provisions passed by a board of directors requiring large payments to specified executives if they are not still employed following a takeover.
   a. A 1984 change in the tax law created a 20% excise tax on such payments and nondeductibility by the corporation. It was specifically designed to reduce the use of golden parachutes.
   b. Stockholders have often been unhappy with golden parachute payoffs and have filed suit to stop such payments.
3. **Fair price provisions** (shareholder rights plans) have become popular.
   a. Warrants are issued to stockholders that permit purchase of stock at a small percentage (often half) of market price in the event of a takeover attempt.
   b. The plan is intended to protect stockholder interests if the corporation is confronted with a coercive or unfair takeover attempt.
   c. The objective is not to deter takeovers but to ensure that all stockholders are treated equally.
   d. In the event of a friendly tender offer, the outstanding stock rights (warrants) may be repurchased by the corporation for a few cents per share, thus paving the way for the takeover.
   e. In many cases, these rights are not even issued in certificate form to stockholders because they are not immediately exercisable and are not traded separately from the common stock.

PORTFOLIO THEORY

A. Portfolio theory concerns the composition of an investment portfolio that is efficient in balancing risk and return.
   1. An investment portfolio is a combination of investment assets.

B. The expected rate of return of a portfolio is the weighted average of the expected returns of the individual assets in the portfolio.

C. The variability of a portfolio's return is determined by the correlation of the returns of individual portfolio assets.
   1. To the extent the returns are uncorrelated, the variability is decreased.

D. Company-specific (investee-specific) risk is associated with a specific company's (investee's) operations: new products, patents, acquisitions, competitors, activities, etc.
   1. This risk can be reduced (eliminated) by proper diversification of investments.
   2. The relevance of an individual security's individual risk is its contribution to the overall risk of a portfolio.
   3. When most of a security's risk can be eliminated by diversification, the relevant risk is low. A security has high relevant risk when its risk cannot be largely eliminated through diversification.

E. The risk that cannot be eliminated through diversification is **market risk** and is measured by the **beta coefficient**.

1. A security that moves with the general market is said to have a beta of 1.0; e.g., if the market increases 20% in value, the security increases 20% in value.
2. A beta of less than 1.0 is less volatile than the market; e.g., if the market increased 20% and a security price increased only 10%, the security would have a .5 beta.
3. A beta over 1.0 indicates a volatile security; e.g., if the security increases 30% when the market as a whole increases 15%, it would have a beta of 2.0.
4. The word "beta" comes from the equation for regressing the return of an individual security to the overall market return (the beta coefficient is the slope of the regression line).

F. Market risk premium is the increased return necessary to compensate investors for holding more risky investments.

G. The **security market line** is the graphed relationship between risk (beta values on the horizontal axis) and returns (percentages on the vertical axis). In the example graph to the right, 8% is the risk-free rate of return.

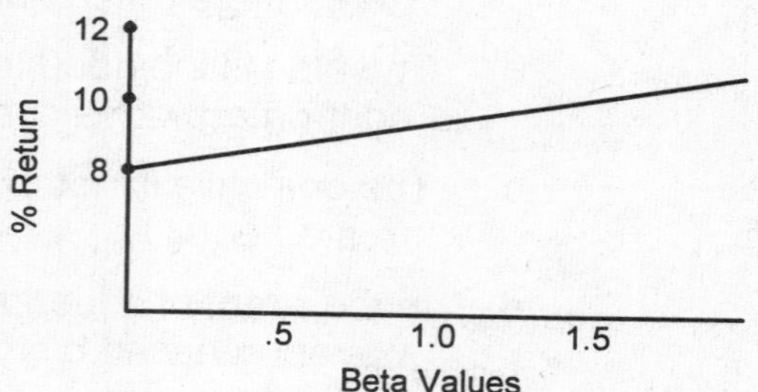

H. The **Capital Asset Pricing Model** (CAPM) specifies that a security's required rate of return is the risk-free rate of return plus a risk premium.

1. Risk is measured by the beta coefficient.

EFFICIENT MARKETS HYPOTHESIS (EMH)

A. The EMH is a stock market theory stating that stock prices reflect all publicly available information.

B. The conclusion is that it is impossible to beat the market consistently with either fundamental or technical analysis.

1. Fundamental analysis -- evaluation of a security's future price movement based upon sales, internal developments, industry trends, the general economy, and expected changes in each
2. Technical analysis -- evaluation of a security's future price based on the sales price and number of shares traded in a series of recent transactions

C. Under the EMH, the expected return of each security is equal to its required return.

1. Also, the stock price equals its just value as perceived by investors.
2. Thus, each security is said to be in equilibrium.

D. The EMH has three forms (versions).

1. **Strong form**. All public and private information is instantaneously reflected in securities' prices; thus, insider trading is assumed not to result in abnormal returns.
2. **Semistrong form**. All publicly available data are reflected in security prices, but private or insider data are not immediately reflected; i.e., insider trading can result in abnormal returns.
3. **Weak form**. Current securities' prices reflect all recent past price movement data; i.e., technical analysis will not provide a basis for abnormal returns in securities trading.

STUDY UNIT 7
ORGANIZATION THEORY

Organization and Management Theory covers 20% to 30% of Part 1. We cover this topic in the following study units:

Study Unit 7: Organization Theory
Study Unit 8: Motivation and the Directing Process

Study Unit 23, The Controlling Process, is also relevant. Prior to December 1990, the CMA exam had five parts (now four). Part 2, Organization and Behavior, Including Ethical Considerations, was eliminated in the new format. Organizational topics were included in new Part 1, and the control and behavioral topics in new Part 3. Ethics issues are tested in all four parts.

HISTORY OF MANAGEMENT

A. **Scientific School of Management** -- the first major school to develop

1. Scientific management focuses on the production process and ways to make it more efficient.
2. It is based on the work of Frederick W. Taylor, the father of scientific management in the United States. Taylor advocated a systematic quantitative approach to getting a job done, primarily at the shop level.
    a. Taylor's four principles of scientific management are
        1) Scientific analysis of work
        2) Scientific selection, training, and development of workers
        3) Cooperation between work planners and operators
        4) Equal sharing of responsibility by labor and management, each doing that for which it is best suited
    b. Taylor also pioneered the use of time and motion analysis, stopwatch measurement, and systematic shop management.

c. Scientific management holds that there is a best way to do each job and that it is up to management to discover the best way and teach the workers.

1) Each job/task should be designed for maximum efficiency.

2) Management should teach workers new habits. Old habits are often inefficient.

d. Taylor designed incentive programs based on the prevailing management philosophy that the best way to get worker cooperation in performing the job in the prescribed efficient manner was to offer monetary rewards.

1) If workers produce more, they should share in benefits.

2) Productivity increased because the workers' incremental bonus usually was less than their productivity increase.

e. The scientific approach is now classified as a type of the Theory X management system (see G.3.a. on page 201).

3. Frank and Lillian Gilbreth, a husband-and-wife team who paralleled much of Taylor's work, are credited with the development of time and motion study using stopwatches and motion pictures.

4. Scientific management is largely oriented towards individual job design.

a. The scientific approach led to one best way of performing each task.

1) Separation of tasks into simple subtasks created greatest efficiency and productivity.

2) Low reliance on worker skills created greater control and freedom for management.

b. Once the one best way was developed, it was management's job to keep the worker doing it that way.

c. Few early industrialists knew how to develop cooperation or understood the philosophy of shared responsibility, so their solution to ensuring worker performance was close supervision.

d. Simple, repetitive tasks, close supervision, and reliance on economic motivation are all characteristics of the classical school later attacked by human relations researchers.

B. **Administrative School of Management** -- a school emphasizing the principles, concepts, and ideas from past organizational experience. It parallels the scientific school of management in seeking one best way to organize (often called the classical school of organization).

1. It attempts to distill universal principles from practical experience.

a. A principle is a statement of valid causal relationships that is useful in predicting the outcome of a pending relationship. The administrative school believes there are valid principles of organization, such as the following:

1) **Principle of span of control**. The number of subordinates a superior can effectively supervise is limited.

2) **Principle of unity of command**. Each subordinate should have only one superior (though a superior may have as many subordinates as allowed by the superior's span of control). Violation of this principle (unity of command) leads to confusion and frustration for the subordinate.

b. The value of a management principle is to give the manager guidelines for

1) Improving decisions
2) Minimizing inefficiency
3) Reducing unnecessary conflict

c. Principles based on successful practices or careful observation did help managers to learn and apply useful knowledge about organizational design and structuring.

2. The administrative school of management is considered mechanistic in that it seeks to build static models of organizations and the people in them (as opposed to organic or dynamic models).

3. It tends to reflect the same lack of concern with human relations as the scientific school of management does.

4. It assumes away the need of the organization to adapt to human, social, and technological changes.

5. The difficulty with administrative school of management principles is that they do not always hold true in actual organizations. For example, different organizations use different spans of control and are still successful.

6. It focuses on overall organization in an effort to scientifically develop an optimal organizational structure as opposed to Taylor's focus on shop management and individual workers (i.e., the scientific school of management).

C. Henri Fayol (a Frenchman publishing in 1916), sometimes called the father of administration, advocated the separation of administration from technical, commercial, financial, and accounting operations.

1. Fayol's writings are similar to those of the classical school because his concepts are based on his own managerial experience. Fayol's work was largely unknown in the U.S. until it was translated from the French in 1949.

2. Fayol's **functions of management** form the foundation for the modern functional or process approach to classifying a manager's activities. The functions, as Fayol identified them, are

a. Planning
b. Organizing
c. Commanding
d. Coordinating
e. Controlling

D. **Fayol's 14 Principles of Management**

1. **Division of labor**. Groups of people must divide their work and specialize to accomplish work most efficiently.

2. **Authority and responsibility**. Authority is the right to command and the power to make oneself obeyed. It includes both authority of position and authority of personality. Responsibility follows from authority; i.e., with authority to get the job done comes responsibility to do the job.

3. **Discipline** is degree of conformity; a subordinate's willingness to go along with rules set up by leaders.

4. **Unity of command**. It is desirable to have only one person giving orders. Otherwise, contradictory orders and priorities result.

5. **Unity of direction** -- "one manager and one plan." An organization should not contain separate groups, with separate managers, if their objectives are the same.

6. **Subordination of individual interests** to the common good. Individual interests should not take precedence over the common good; e.g., the individual's interests are served if his/her own pay is maximized, but the common good (that of the organization) requires that pay be competitive and equitable.

7. **Remuneration**. Pay should be fair and satisfactory to the employee and employer, based on reward for successful effort, within reasonable limits.

8. **Centralization of management**. The degree of an organization's centralization or decentralization depends on the given undertaking.

9. **Hierarchy** (the scalar principle) -- a ranking of authority. The scalar principle describes the division of work among the various levels of the organizational structure. However, horizontal communication is useful to facilitate effective communication and to enable subordinates to exercise initiative.

10. **Order**. Human resources should be carefully deployed according to organizational needs as well as each individual's abilities.

11. **Equity**. There must be a fair balancing of the needs of the organization with a friendly approach to the needs of the individual.

12. **Stability of tenure**. The situation determines the length of time needed for an employee to adjust to the job and to begin to perform at his/her best. Successful firms normally have more stable staffs.

13. **Initiative**. Performance and satisfaction are greatly improved when the employees are encouraged to conceive and carry out their own ideas.

14. **Esprit de corps**. Harmony and unity provide strength to organizations. An extension of the principle of unity of command, this principle emphasizes the need for teamwork and the importance of communication.

E. The scientific and the administrative schools are often termed classical because they were among the earliest efforts to systematize management. Their approaches are also deemed to be classical because they assume that all organizations can follow the same set of organizing principles.

1. The scientific school emphasizes a micro approach (how to manage a specific worker or shop).

2. The administrative school emphasizes a macro approach (how to manage a total organization).

F. Henry Mintzberg believed that the functional approach for describing what managers do was inadequate. He developed a system based on managerial roles.

1. The **interpersonal roles** (figurehead, leader, liaison) are necessary because, given his/her authority and status, a manager has substantial interpersonal contacts, particularly with peers and subordinates.

2. The **informational roles** (nerve center, disseminator, spokesperson) reflect the importance of information to organizational activity. Managers must receive and transmit information to parties both within and outside the organization.

3. The **decisional roles** (entrepreneur, disturbance handler, resource allocator, negotiator) require managers to make choices and balance divergent interests. Decisions involve developing strategies and implementing them.

G. The **behavioral school** views management as accomplishing results through people, both as individuals and in groups. Therefore, the stress is on applying findings from psychology, anthropology, and sociology.

1. Elton Mayo (working in the 1920s and 1930s) is referred to as the father of human relations.
   a. His initial experiments studied the relationship of workshop lighting levels to levels of productivity.
   b. These experiments, conducted at the Hawthorne plant of Western Electric from 1927 to 1932, are known as the Hawthorne experiments.
   c. The results astounded researchers by revealing that increased worker productivity resulted from the workers' willingness to cooperate, not from the level of lighting.
   d. The researchers concluded that
      1) The workers' individual needs and their social relationships with peers on the job were more important to productivity than the physical working conditions.
      2) Work is a group activity.
      3) Informal relationships are important parts of organizational systems.
2. Chester Barnard, a former telephone company president who wrote *The Functions of the Executive* (1938), argued that authority derives from subordinates' acceptance of management's direction, in direct contrast to the classical belief.
3. Douglas McGregor (1960s) described his Theory X and Theory Y concepts as extremes in management style.
   a. A **Theory X** manager believes that people inherently dislike working, are motivated by fear and greed, and will do as little as possible for the largest possible wage.
   b. A **Theory Y** manager believes that people like to work, will do a good job if given the opportunity, and seek satisfaction in their jobs.
   c. McGregor advocated the Theory Y approach to management as yielding the greatest efficiency and effectiveness.
4. Rensis Likert (1967) described and studied four systems of management to determine the optimal management style.
   a. The systems studied ranged from Exploitive-Autocratic to Participative.
   b. Data indicated that more participative organizations were the most effective.
5. Key elements recognized by the behavioral school
   a. Participation
      1) Permits more involvement of subordinates in the organization
      2) Encourages communication up as well as down the organization hierarchy
      3) Leads to better decisions
   b. Group influences
      1) Informal communication processes are important.
      2) Group pressure shapes individual behavior, beliefs, values, and job attitudes

c. Individual needs

1) Individuals are not solely motivated by financial incentives.
2) People get bored doing routine, simple, and repetitive jobs.
3) People have a variety of needs that the job setting should satisfy.

H. The **systems school** stresses interrelationships and interdependence of managerial problems. Emphasizes chains of events and how components relate to one another. It is considered the modern approach to management.

1. Systems approach defined

a. An organizational system is a group or set of things that are interrelated or interdependent so as to form a part of a larger whole.

1) The systems school recognizes that it is impossible to understand an organization without considering the larger context or system of which it is a part.

2) It seeks to include the concerns and the focus of both classical school and behavioral school in finding one best way by considering both people issues and structural issues.

b. Systems may be closed or open.

1) **Closed systems** are closed to the external environment. There are few truly closed systems, but boundaries may be artificially drawn in order to facilitate analysis by treating a system as if it were closed.

a) EXAMPLE: A thermostat connected to a furnace may be considered a closed system. However, it must be located within a house, the air must change temperature, fuel oil must be delivered, etc. The thermostat cannot function isolated from other, larger systems.

b) A closed system, unable to draw in new resources from the outside, will eventually deteriorate and die (entropy).

c) Classical viewpoints treated management as a closed system and ignored most things external to the organization. Such policy is limited and dangerous in that effective management of a social system is neither deterministic nor mechanistic.

2) **Open systems** are open to and have interaction with an external environment. The system boundaries are drawn to reflect external inputs and system outputs.

2. **Contingency approach**, derived from systems thinking, stresses the idea that the search for answers to organizational problems depends on contingencies that can be discovered and studied.

a. Because this approach argues for situationally determined answers to management concerns, the key is finding the relevant factors in the organization's environment.

b. The same argument applies to individuals' motivations, needs, and wants because people are subsystems within the larger organizational social system.

3. Management should be studied as an open social system because the continual interaction between the organization and its external environment must be considered.

a. This interaction has several dimensions: social, technological, psychological, political, etc.

1) Technological change
2) Social responsibilities to other social institutions
3) Relationships of employee needs to organizational requirements
4) Organizational growth and development
5) Individual and organizational reasons for resisting change

b. A closed system suffers entropy, but an open system seeks replenishment through its boundaries with the larger system (environment).

c. Closed-systems management writers viewed environment as beyond their concern; open-systems writers see the environment as vital to organizational thinking.

1) Rather than looking for universal principles of management or rigid adherence to humanistic beliefs, the systems thinkers look for situationally optimal answers to managerial questions.

4. The recognition of social responsibilities is a logical outgrowth of systems thinking.

a. If the organization is part of a larger social system, it must recognize its subordination to and interdependence with this larger system.

b. This recognition requires accepting the responsibility to make decisions with thoughtful consideration of their impact on the larger system, i.e., society.

I. **Nature of Management**

1. Management can be characterized in many ways, each view reflecting one or more aspects of the development of management theory.

a. Management is getting work done through people.

b. Management is the process of planning, organizing (staffing), directing, and controlling resources to reach organizational goals.

c. Management is making and implementing decisions in an organizational setting.

J. **Behavior modification** is an attempt to condition an individual by varying the response to his/her behavior.

1. Management assumes that behavior leading to a positive consequence tends to be repeated, whereas behavior leading to a negative consequence is less likely to be repeated.

a. A positive consequence or reinforcement (e.g., a bonus) is a reward for desired behavior.

b. Negative reinforcement can be accomplished by rewarding behavior by removing an unpleasant consequence.

c. A negative consequence punishes undesired behavior.

2. Extinction occurs when a behavior has no consequences. When no reinforcement occurs, the behavior will eventually disappear.

3. Consequences, whether positive or negative, should always be timely to ensure maximum impact.

4. Behavior modification is sometimes criticized because it threatens personal autonomy and is seen as a form of bribery. An emphasis on extrinsic rewards may detract from intrinsic motivations.

NATURE OF THE ORGANIZING PROCESS

A. Organizing is the design and structuring of tasks and roles to accomplish organizational goals.

   1. The roles define the relationships among individuals and groups of individuals within an organization.

   2. The structuring reflects the division of activities into subactivities.

   3. Structuring also coordinates or integrates these divided activities into a cohesive whole.

B. The **traditional approach** (also known as classical, structural, or formal) emphasizes authority, responsibility, tasks, hierarchy, span of control, etc.

   1. The traditional approach to organizing sets up prescribed (or dictated) relationships and then places people in them.

   2. "The person is selected to fill the job."

C. The **behavioral approach** emphasizes the limits, strengths, availability, and interests of the people available.

   1. The participants provide feedback in the role-definition process.
   2. "The job is designed to fit the person."

D. The **modern (contingency) approach** emphasizes the tailoring of the organization to its unique situation.

   1. Optimal organization depends or is contingent on situational forces, e.g.,

      a. Environmental influences
      b. Technical considerations
      c. Nature of the workforce
      d. Size and age of the organization

   2. The modern approach is less deterministic than the behavioral approach because group dynamics and the feelings of subordinates are included in the process.

   3. The contingency approach is the logical outgrowth of systems theory.

   4. It combines the classical and behavioral aspects of organizing problems into the best design or structural solution.

   5. "The job and the person must fit each other."

BASIC PRINCIPLES OF ORGANIZATION STRUCTURE AND DESIGN

A. A number of relationships are present in the structure of an organization. These include authority, responsibility, and accountability. Classical theory stresses the need for balance between authority and responsibility.

   1. **Authority** -- the right to direct and exact performance from others. Includes the right to prescribe the means and methods by which the work will be done.

      a. Classical approach says that the right to give the order is vested in the position. Based on rational criteria, the organization has rationally determined where a decision is best made, given the authority to make the decision to that position, and filled the position with the person most suited for the position.

b. Behavioral approach says that the right to direct is only as good as the receiver's willingness to carry out the order, i.e., only as good as one individual's willingness to accept direction from another.

1) This view is based on the acceptance theory of Chester Barnard.

2) It emphasizes the willingness of followers to be directed as opposed to the classical focus on the right of a leader to command.

3) Belief in this approach necessitates a change in the attitude of the leader toward subordinates by focusing on the leader's need to secure compliance from followers rather than an assumption of blind obedience to commands.

c. Power is the ability to enforce one's commands. Power sources are by virtue of

1) Position (the legitimate power of the boss)
2) Expertise (the one who knows how)
3) Friendship ("I like you, so I'll do it.")
4) Controlling rewards ("I'll give you this if you do it.")
5) Coercion ("If you don't, I'll punish you.")

d. The greater number of sources a boss has (e.g., having the power to hire and fire, being the legitimate boss, being liked, and knowing what the job is), the more likely an employee will be inclined to accept authority.

2. **Responsibility** -- the obligation to perform

a. In the classical view, this obligation formally comes down from a superior position and is inherent in any job (it has its origins in the rights of private property as defined by the appropriate laws).

b. In the behavioral view, responsibility must and should be delegated; i.e., there is a successive dividing and passing down of obligation.

1) The appropriate amount of authority or power must be delegated with the responsibility.

2) However, a higher position can never rid itself of ultimate responsibility.

3. **Accountability** -- the duty to account for the fulfillment of the responsibility. In practice, accountability is

a. The duty to report performance to one's superior

1) The principle of single accountability or unity of command means that each subordinate should report to only one superior.

2) The principle of unity of command permits more than one person to act as a subordinate's superior only under conditions in which there is complete coordination of plans so that no conflicting or contradicting instructions are given.

b. The physical means for reporting or being able to substantiate performance, i.e., record keeping

4. In summary

a. **Authority** is the power to direct (delegate) that a task be done.
b. **Responsibility** is the obligation to do it.
c. **Accountability** is the liability for failure to fulfill the obligation.

B. **Unity of Objective**. An organizational structure is effective if it facilitates the contribution of individuals toward the attainment of enterprise objectives. Hence, organizational objectives must have been clearly formulated in the planning process.

1. In other words, the purpose of organizing is to ensure that all individuals in the organization are working toward the same organizational goals.
2. Organizing also allows management to determine when goals are not achieved and where the problems exist within the organization (e.g., monitoring, feedback).

C. **Efficiency**. An organizational structure is efficient if it facilitates the accomplishment of organizational objectives with minimum resources and fewest unsought consequences. An efficient organizational structure

1. Maximizes output for a given amount of input
2. Uses all resources required, whether physical, financial, or human

D. **Effectiveness**. An organization that reaches its goals is effective. However, effectiveness does not consider the cost-benefit criterion. Thus, a process may be both very effective and very inefficient.

1. Goals usually include being efficient.
2. Effectiveness concerns accomplishing goals.
   a. Efficiency means accomplishing goals economically. In other words, the input-output ratio is favorable.
3. Goals may include human goals.

DEPARTMENTATION

A. Division of labor breaks complex processes into their simpler components. However, dividing labor creates a need for efficient coordination of those performing the separate tasks. One response to the problem is departmentation, which is a form of organizational integration intended to promote coordination. It is the grouping of related activities into significant organizational subsystems.

1. Departmentation methods include
   a. **Departmentation by function** -- This method is the most widely used. It is found in almost every organization at some level whether profit-making or nonprofit. The most common departments in profit-making organizations are marketing, production, and finance (though other terms may be used). These often extend upward in the organizational chart to the level below the chief executive.
      1) Advantages
         a) Occupational specialization
         b) Simplified training
         c) Representation of primary functions at the top level of the organization
      2) Disadvantages
         a) Difficulties for companies with many locations (e.g., coordination)
         b) Lack of coordination between primary functions
         c) Absence of profit centers within the organization

b. **Departmentation by territory** -- favored by national or multinational firms and government agencies with scattered offices or plants

1) Advantages

a) Quicker reaction to local market changes
b) Greater familiarity with local problems or unique geographic concerns
c) Logistical savings in freight costs and travel time

2) Disadvantages

a) Usually requires more delegation of authority to regional managers
b) Problems of control for headquarters
c) Duplication of service functions (personnel, purchases, etc.)

c. **Departmentation by product** -- growing in importance for multiline, large-scale enterprises. It is often an outgrowth of functional departmentation and permits extensive authority for a division executive over a given product or product line.

1) Advantages

a) Better use of specialized capital and skills
b) Ease of coordination of the activities for a given product
c) Simpler assignment of profit responsibility
d) Compatible with decentralization strategy
e) Provides, through product profit centers, a basis for allocating capital efficiently to products likely to achieve the best returns

2) Disadvantages

a) Requires greater number of persons with managerial ability
b) Duplication of staff functions
c) Difficulty in maintaining top management control over operations

d. **Departmentation by customer** -- service to a particular customer provided under the management of a department head. This form of departmentation seldom appears at the top level of an organizational structure, but it is often found at middle levels (e.g., the loan officer of a large bank who handles one account exclusively). Customer departmentation is often found within the sales department of a firm organized by function.

1) Advantages

a) Increased customer service as a result of the expertise gained in that customer's business
b) Ease in identifying contributions to profit made by different types and locations of customers

2) Disadvantages

a) Difficulties in coordination with other units in the organization
b) Pressure to give preferential treatment to any given manager's customers

e. **Project departmentation** -- for experimental or one-time activities, e.g., the construction of a ship, a large building, or a major design project (such as a military weapons system)

1) Advantages

a) Degree of specialization possible

b) Ease of communication and coordination of efforts required within a particular project

2) Disadvantages

a) Need for reorganization at the end of the project
b) Problems of recruitment at the start of the project
c) Difficulty of maintaining control at the central office

f. **Matrix organization** -- usually seen as a combination of any of the above-mentioned approaches to departmentation, such as functional-product in manufacturing. It is a compromise between functional and product departmentation. A manager for each product is appointed and draws on personnel who are organized by function and who simultaneously report to a manager for each function. This form is used in research and development and in project management.

1) The emphasis or focus of the arrangement is on the result or the product.

2) The functional organization remains, while parts of it are temporarily lent or assigned to a given project.

3) The project may be to make a product indefinitely or to accomplish a limited but lengthy task, such as construction of a submarine.

4) Advantages

a) Matrix organization provides the security and accountability of the functional form while providing expert personnel to the project only when needed and only to the extent required. It allows personnel as well as functions to be most effectively and efficiently used.

b) Technical ability of employees is better appraised by the functional managers than by the project manager.

c) Practical applications skills can be appraised by the project manager on-site.

d) Unnecessarily large swings in levels of personnel and equipment are minimized.

5) EXAMPLE: An engineering consulting firm draws from a variety of functionally grouped engineering talents to serve on a variety of projects. This process permits great flexibility in using people.

a) The major disadvantage is that the principle of unity of command is violated by this type of departmentation. It is important that the authority, responsibility, and accountability of the parties involved be clearly defined to avoid confusion and employee dissatisfaction.

b) A second disadvantage is the possible inefficient use of employees. Individuals may be idle while waiting for project assignments that require their specific talents.

6) It is difficult for large organizations to use matrix organization because they typically have many levels (both vertical and horizontal), thus slowing communications.

2. The method of departmentation chosen is contingent upon

   a. Organizational plans, programs, policies, and purpose
   b. Environmental constraints
   c. Training and preferences of available personnel

LINE AND STAFF RELATIONSHIPS

A. Major Approaches to Line and Staff Distinctions

1. The classical approach views **line** activities as those directly responsible for the primary function, product, or service of the organization, whereas staff members provide support services.

   a. Production is ordinarily classified as a line activity, although more current writers include sales (marketing) and sometimes finance, depending on the goals of the organization.

   b. **Staff** activities are those necessary to the organization but secondary or peripheral to the line functions. These functions assist or advise the line function.

      1) EXAMPLES:

         a) In a manufacturing firm, accounting and research would be staff.

         b) In accounting firms, the editing and typing of reports would be staff.

         c) In research and development, the machinery, production scheduling, material stores, etc., would be staff.

   c. Confusion arises from this concept because most staff activities are, in fact, essential to the accomplishment of the organization's purpose as recognized in modern (systems) theory.

   d. Because early classical writers were describing production organizations, the holders of formal line authority were those producing the product.

   e. Staff were merely hired hands to take the burden of secondary tasks off the shoulders of the production people.

2. Behavioral theorists' concerns with authority and its acceptance distinguish their approach to line/staff relationships.

   a. The behavioral school sees exercise of informal authority as a very important constraint on formal chains of command.

   b. Advice offered by senior staff members is akin to a command because they have access to top management and can exercise more informal authority than a junior-level line manager.

   c. Staff assistants may be perceived as spies rather than assistants.

   d. Even the classical school acknowledged the dilemma of how to ensure adoption of specialized staff advice without subverting line authority.

      1) If line management refuses to accept staff's advice, what can top management do?

e. A staff group with **advisory** authority can only offer suggestions, prepare plans for consideration by line managers, and study and evaluate organizational performance.

   1) A staff member often has an area of technical expertise, such as law, industrial labor relations, operations research, or personnel.
   2) Line managers are not obligated to follow staff advice.
   3) The staff member's goal is the approval (or rejection) of a complete recommended solution, but a line manager may want a quick fix to a problem rather than a complete solution.
   4) Consultation by staff members with line personnel while preparing a solution is essential.
   5) The concept of completed staff work requires that all loose ends be tied down by the staff member.

f. A staff group may be given **concurrent** authority, meaning that line management is required to induce the staff experts in specified areas to agree to an action or decision.

   1) EXAMPLE: A line production manager may be required to obtain a second signature on a lease agreement from the law department, which must concur with terms in the lease.

g. A staff group may be given complete authority in a specialized area, and their specialized activities are separated from line.

   1) Unlike advisory activities, the line manager in this case has no choice but must acquire the service from the staff organization.
   2) Examples
      a) Information systems
      b) Purchasing
      c) Personnel

h. A staff group may occasionally be given **control** authority. Thus, line authority may be superseded by that of the specialist staff designated by higher levels of management to make certain decisions in the area of staff expertise.

   1) Control staff authority appears to violate classical principles of unity of command.
   2) Ideally, however, there is no violation because the control staff act as agents for the higher-level line manager, who has delegated authority to the staff.
      a) EXAMPLE: Quality-control inspectors have the authority to reject marginal products, but because this authority is exercised on behalf of the manufacturing manager, the chain of command actually remains intact.

i. If the organization adopts Total Quality Management concepts with an emphasis on internal as well as external service, line managers and staff personnel may be viewed as having a customer-service provider relationship.

B. A hybrid of the control authority relationship of staff and line is called a **functional** relationship.

1. Functional authority exists when an individual is given authority outside the normal chain of command for certain specified activities. The individual may be either a line or a staff manager who is a specialist in a particular field.
   a. EXAMPLE: The vice president in charge of sales may be given functional authority over manufacturing executives in scheduling customer orders, packaging, or making service parts available.
2. Functional authority may be created for numerous reasons when a line manager is not the person best suited to oversee a given activity. Examples are a lack of special knowledge, a lack of ability to supervise processes, a danger of diverse interpretations of policies, etc.
   a. EXAMPLE: The vice president for industrial labor relations may have functional authority over the production manager for the purpose of negotiating a new labor contract, though no line relationship exists at other times.
3. Functional specialists have the authority to determine the appropriate standards in their own field of specialization and to enforce those standards.
   a. EXAMPLE: The chief engineer of an airline may have the authority to remove airplanes from service, overriding the wishes of the vice president for operations.

C. **Line and Staff Conflicts**

1. Conflict between line and staff personnel is almost inevitable given the considerable difference in their backgrounds and activities.
   a. These individuals tend to have different training and education, perspectives on the organization, and career and other objectives.
   b. Line and staff personnel also tend to have different temperaments.
      1) Line managers are immediately responsible for operating activities. Thus, they place an emphasis on decisive action.
      2) Staff members have a preference for thorough research and analysis of problems.
2. Operating executives with line authority often see a high potential for harm in staff activity. A staff member with vaguely defined authority from a chief executive effectively usurps the authority of departmental managers.
3. Staff are not responsible for the success of a line department but only for generating suggestions. If an implemented suggestion fails,
   a. Line managers will blame the suggestion.
   b. Staff will blame the poor implementation of the suggestion.
4. Setting staff apart from line responsibilities gives them the time and environment in which to think.
   a. Unfortunately, this separation can also lead to thinking in a vacuum and resultant impracticable or inappropriate suggestions by staff.
5. Excessive staff activity may violate the principle of unity of command.
   a. Subordinates may become confused and wonder whether they are primarily responsible to the staff member or to their line manager.

D. Line-staff conflicts may be minimized by

1. Clearly defining areas of activity and authority
2. Sharply defining the nature and place of line and staff. For example,
   a. Line may have authority and responsibility.
   b. Staff may be required to sell their ideas to line.
3. Stressing the systems approach to all employees, whether line or staff, to encourage them to work together towards organizational goals
4. Minimizing areas of possible conflict, e.g.,
   a. Keeping functional authority to a minimum
   b. Providing feedback to staff of line's reaction to proposals
5. Using the concept of completed staff work if possible
   a. Recommendations should be complete enough to make possible a simple yes-or-no response from line managers.
   b. Staff members should be problem solvers, not problem creators.
      1) Incomplete or vague advice creates problems for line managers.
   c. The essential task of staff is to make the line manager involved look good. This result cannot be accomplished by staff members who insist on taking credit for the success of their ideas.

E. The modern approach to line and staff is based on systems thinking.

1. Every position and every task must contribute to the organizational purpose or it should not exist.
2. Distinctions between producers and helpers are therefore irrelevant.
3. The changing nature of work environments from predominantly production firms to predominantly service providers makes it harder to pinpoint who exactly is responsible for producing.
   a. EXAMPLE: At a motor inn with the purpose of people pleasing, who is line and who is staff?

SPAN OF CONTROL

A. **Span of Control** -- the principle that there is an upper limit to the number of subordinates who can be effectively supervised by one person

1. Beyond a certain number of subordinates, the effectiveness and efficiency of supervision decreases.

B. Span of control is also known as **span of management** and **span of authority**. Consideration of span of control is one of the oldest principles of management.

C. The classical view holds that the universal span of control is five or six subordinates.

D. The behavioral school advocates expanding the span of control if possible. The advantages are

1. Increasing the autonomy and morale of individual workers by reducing the time available to a manager to direct them (the more subordinates per manager, the less time available per subordinate)
2. Decreasing communication problems by reducing organizational levels (given a fixed number of employees, the narrower the span of control, the taller the organization, and the greater the number of levels)

E. The modern or contingency approach to span of control identifies the situational variables that determine the span of control, including

1. The supervisor's
    a. Training
    b. Interests
    c. Abilities
    d. Personality
    e. Time available to supervise, etc.
2. The subordinates'
    a. Interests
    b. Drives
    c. Commitment to the job
    d. Training
    e. Attitudes
    f. Aptitudes
3. The work situation
    a. The technological process used (job shop, mass production, continuous process)
    b. Frequency of change in job method
    c. Complexity of the task
    d. Interdependence on the work of others
    e. Supervision required
4. The organization's environment
    a. How rapidly it is compelled to change by technological innovation or market pressure
    b. Amount of uncertainty in environment
5. Current research indicates that the appropriate span of control varies widely depending on the situation as defined by the factors above.

F. The number of levels in an organization will be greatly influenced by the span of control.

G. **Flat** organizational structures have relatively few levels from top to bottom. Thus, they have wide spans of control.

1. Flat structures have the following advantages:
    a. Fast information flow from top to bottom of the organization
    b. Increased employee satisfaction.

H. **Tall** organizational structures have many levels between top and bottom. Hence, they have relatively narrow spans of control.

1. Tall structures are faster and more effective at problem resolution than flat structures for the following reasons:
    a. Increased frequency of interaction between superior and subordinate
    b. Greater order imposed by the hierarchical structure
2. Studies do not indicate great advantages for either flat or tall structures.

CENTRALIZATION AND DECENTRALIZATION

A. Centralization deals with the concentration of authority in an organization and the degree and levels at which it occurs.

B. Centralization and decentralization are relative terms. Absolute centralization or decentralization is impossible.

C. Classicists view decentralization with some distrust because they seek to avoid any dilution of control by top managers.

D. Behavioralists view decentralization in the same way as delegation, that is, as a good way to improve motivation and morale of lower-level employees.

E. The modern or contingency view is that neither centralization nor decentralization is good or bad in itself. The degree to which either is stressed depends upon the requirements of a given situation.

   1. Information. Decisions cannot be decentralized to those who do not have necessary information, e.g., knowledge of job objectives or measures for evaluation of job performance.

   2. Ability. Decisions cannot be decentralized to people who do not have training, experience, knowledge, or ability to make them.

   3. Timeliness. Decisions requiring a quick response should be decentralized to those near the action.

   4. Degree of coordination. Do not decentralize below the organization level at which coordination must be maintained (e.g., each foreman on an assembly line cannot be allowed to decide reporting time for employees).

   5. Significance of decision. Do not decentralize to lower levels any decisions that are of critical importance to the survival of the organization.

   6. Morale. When possible, decentralize because of the positive influence on morale.

F. Decentralization is a philosophy of organizing and managing. Careful selection of which decisions to push down the hierarchy and which to hold at the top is required. There will be a greater degree of decentralization if

   1. The greater number of decisions are made lower down the management hierarchy.
   2. The more important decisions are made lower down the management hierarchy.
   3. Most functions are affected by decisions made at lower levels.
   4. Review or prior approval is required before implementation of a decision.

G. **Implementing Decentralization**

   1. Decentralized structures typically use **return on investment** (ROI) or **profit center** accounting methods.

      a. ROI gives an objective measure of the performance of individual managers of decentralized units.

      b. ROI allows monitoring of performance through **management by exception**.

      c. ROI permits comparison of performance of decentralized divisions.

      d. ROI facilitates allocation of resources and rewards to the decentralized divisions.

e. ROI measures for decentralized divisions have some limitations, as do other profit-center approaches.

1) ROI measures encourage short-run performance to the detriment of long-run survival.

2) They encourage division managers to maximize subunit goals to the possible detriment of the total organization.

3) Transfer prices between units may be unjust.

4) Top management may adversely influence divisional performance by indirect cost allocation decisions.

5) Some parts of an organization do not lend themselves to 1-year evaluations (e.g., new product divisions).

6) Annual profit objectives in a cyclical industry or economy may be difficult to determine.

7) It is frequently impossible to assign responsibilities for deviations from profit objectives beyond the manager's control.

2. Decentralization is most easily implemented in organizations with product departmentation based on clearly divisible units.

a. Eliminates extensive transfer-price problems
b. Easier to allocate and isolate overhead

H. **Advantages of Decentralization**

1. Allows greater speed in making operational decisions

2. Encourages better communication

3. Necessitates understanding of goals throughout the organization (goal congruence)

4. Enables identification and training of good decision makers at lower levels

5. Builds a large pool of experienced management talent

6. Provides many behavioral advantages

a. Gains advantages of participation in management
b. Gives responsibility and authority to lower-level managers

1) Job autonomy is desired by many employees.
2) Specific feedback is important for goal-directed people.

c. Provides objective feedback

7. Frees top management from operating problems, thus allowing them to concentrate on long-term strategy

8. Provides a mechanism for allocating resources to profit centers based on ROI applications

9. Permits determination of a single comprehensive figure, e.g., ROI or net income, that measures the financial status of the decentralized unit

I. **Disadvantages of Decentralization**

1. Strong tendency to focus on short-run results to the detriment of long-run health
2. Increased risk of loss of control by top management
3. More difficulty in coordinating highly interdependent units
   a. EXAMPLE: A conglomerate that is highly decentralized, i.e., operates its divisions as totally separate companies, will find it difficult to establish a transfer price for goods manufactured in one division and consumed in another. The consuming division will not believe market prices are equitable, and the producing division will not want to sell for less.
4. Greater danger of **satisficing** decisions (those that satisfy or suffice but are not optimal) made by a manager who is unable or unwilling to see overall organizational goals and is rewarded for maximizing the performance of the decentralized unit
5. Less cooperation and communication between competing decentralized unit managers

J. Delegation of authority is the formal process of passing power downward from one individual to a subordinate. Delegation is similar to decentralization in philosophy, process, and requirements.

1. The classical approach is to avoid delegation because the superior is deemed to be both responsible and knowledgeable. Delegation avoids responsibility, i.e., passes the buck to a subordinate.
2. The behavioral view sees delegation as useful in every organization because no one has time to make every decision and subordinates like to make decisions affecting their work.
3. The modern approach is to view delegation as dependent on the situation and the people involved. Delegation requires
   a. Skill, self-confidence, and knowledge of organizational goals
   b. Feedback system to allow objective assessment of delegated decision performance
   c. Faith in subordinates' abilities
   d. Clear recognition of the basic need to delegate (because of span of control and expertise limitations)
   e. Willingness to accept risk
   f. Desire to develop and train subordinates
4. The delegation process involves
   a. Determination of results expected
   b. Assignment of tasks and responsibilities
   c. Delegation of authority for accomplishing these tasks
   d. Recruitment of responsible subordinates for the accomplishment of these tasks
   e. Clear communication of what is expected in reasonably objective terms to subordinates
   f. Follow-up because ultimate responsibility still resides with the delegator

K. **The Scalar Principle** -- the chain of direct authority relationships from superior to subordinate throughout the organization, i.e., the chain of command. This kind of authority is found in all organizations as an uninterrupted scale, or series of steps, from the superior to the subordinate, from that subordinate to the next subordinate, and so on. The clearer the line of authority from top management to every subordinate position, the more effective the responsible decision making and organizational communication will be. Failure to define the chain of command with care leads to inefficiency.

COMMITTEES

A. A committee is a group that considers a particular problem or class of problems. The committee's objective is educating, informing, or making a decision relative to the problem.

B. The committee is one of the most universal, and most controversial, devices of the organization. Other names include task force, team, commission, and board.

C. The classical position is to avoid the committee. The behavioral position is to encourage its use because of positive morale benefits. The modern position is to determine both the type and the nature of committees by situational factors.

D. Committees may

1. Undertake managerial functions
2. Make decisions
    a. Or participate in one or more parts of the decision process (e.g., problem identifying, searching for alternatives, evaluating alternatives, making recommendations, helping find ways to implement choices)
3. Be formed merely to receive information, without making decisions or recommendations
4. Be either line or staff, depending upon authority
5. Be formal, if designated an established part of the organizational structure
    a. Formal committees can be
        1) Standing (permanent) or
        2) Ad hoc (temporary), i.e., formed to consider a one-time situation
6. Be informal, if organized without specific delegation of authority
    a. Informal committees are often formed by individuals desiring a variety of inputs for decision making in the form of advice from other managers or specialists.

E. **Examples of Standing Committees**

1. Budget
2. Salary
3. Safety
4. Make-or-buy
5. Corrective action
6. Warranty
7. Housekeeping
8. Minority employment
9. U.S. Savings Bond sales

F. **Examples of Subjects Considered by Temporary or Ad Hoc Committees**

1. New plant location
2. Selection of a new consultant
3. Bidding on a government contract

G. An informal committee is much more casual.

1. EXAMPLE: A manager who needs to buy a new copying machine asks other managers. Not getting sufficient specific information from them, (s)he asks the secretaries about the performance of the machines they operate. From them, the manager learns about the machines that break down most, give the clearest copies, etc.

H. **Principles Relative to the Use of Committees**

1. **Balance**. Members should be selected to obtain optimum input bearing on the problem; the selection entails consideration of members' knowledge, time, and communication skills.
2. **Efficiency**. The benefits expected from the committee should exceed the cost.
3. **Time**. Scheduling and time away from regular work should be considered.
4. **Objective**. The objective should guide the committee and limit its actions in solving a problem, coordinating activities, selling an idea, education, etc.
5. **Leadership**. The chair should act as a moderator and not be considered threatening or overbearing by the members.
6. **Groupism**. A tendency toward mediocrity and compromise should be avoided. **Groupthink**, i.e., the tendency to conform and ignore relevant individual input that is at variance with the perceived group opinion, is to be avoided. At the same time, consensus or agreement by the majority is desirable.
7. **Size**. The size of a committee is determined by its needed input, but in any event it should be kept small. Five members are often considered maximum for effective work.
8. **Individualism**. An overriding question is whether an individual should make the decision rather than the committee.

I. Misuse of committees has caused some organizations to neglect this form of management. The following abuses of committees should be avoided:

1. The committee should not be used as a managing device. Leadership is essentially a quality of individuals rather than groups. Clear, prompt decisions subject to unquestioned responsibility are better made by individuals.
2. Use of the committee for research or study is ineffective. The primary purpose of a committee is to discuss or exchange views on information already known to the members. A committee may use a research staff if research and study are needed.
3. Unimportant decisions are not appropriate for the committee forum. The feeling that time is being wasted on insignificant matters frustrates and alienates intelligent managers and specialists.
4. One of the most common abuses of committees is to make decisions that are beyond the authority of the participants. Delays occur while matters are referred to the appropriate superior authority, and much of the advantage of group decision making is lost.
5. The consolidation of divided authority is better accomplished through changes in the organizational structure than through the use of committees.

INFORMAL GROUPS

A. Informal groups, ignored by classical school writers, became the major focus of the behavioral school.

B. People naturally seek association and group acceptance and tend to form both formal and informal groups as a result. Thus, effective managers recognize, accept, and take advantage of informal organization.

   1. Informal groups are created within organizations because of

      a. Authority interrelationships that cannot be charted
      b. Unwritten rules of conduct
      c. Group preferences

C. **Characteristics of Informal Groups** (informal organization)

   1. Almost all employees, including managers, are members of some informal group(s).
   2. Members of informal groups react to the pressures of these groups.

      a. These pressures are difficult to resist, and most members do tend to conform.

   3. These groups tend to be small and

      a. Are often very complex

      b. Tend to develop their own leaders

      c. Exist to fill the needs of the members

      d. Usually result from the frequent interaction among individuals in the course of their work

D. **Favorable Effects of Informal Groups**

   1. Reduce tension and encourage production
   2. Improve coordination and reduce supervision required
   3. Aid in problem-solving situations
   4. Provide another channel of communication (in addition to the formal ones)

      a. The grapevine is the informal, unofficial communication system found in every kind of organization.

         1) The emergence of computer networks in the workplace has only served to strengthen the grapevine.

   5. Provide social satisfactions that supplement job satisfactions

E. **Some Potential Unfavorable Effects of Informal Groups**. They can

   1. Work to circumvent managerial actions

   2. Serve to reduce production levels (slowdowns caused by counterproductive social interactions)

   3. Generate dissension in the formal organization

   4. Spread rumors and distort information

   5. Add to the cost of doing business

   6. Pressure members to adopt group norms that may be contrary to the main goals of the organization

QUALITY CIRCLES

A. A quality circle is a group, usually from five to ten employees (management and/or subordinates), doing similar work who volunteer to meet at a specified time (e.g., once a week) to discuss and solve problems associated with their work areas.

1. The objectives of quality circles
    a. Using employee capabilities more fully
    b. Building a more congenial workplace
    c. Contributing to the improvement and development of both the company and individual employees

B. The mechanics of a quality circle include the following problem-solving steps:

1. Circle members bring problems before the group.
2. The problems or projects are analyzed.
3. Solutions are developed.
4. Solutions are presented to management.
5. Management follows up on the suggestions by either approving or disapproving the ideas, with feedback to circle members.

C. **Advantages of Quality Circles**

1. Easy implementation without major organizational change
2. More efficient and effective operation of the company
3. Better-quality products
4. Improved employee morale and better cohesion among coworkers

D. **Disadvantages of Quality Circles**

1. Objections from unions
2. Reduced morale if suggestions are not accepted by management and management fails to adequately explain nonacceptance
3. Potential loss of management control

E. **Self-managed teams** are a facet of total quality management. They are autonomous groups that go beyond quality circles because they represent a major organizational change.

1. Team members are not volunteers but have been assigned to the teams.
2. Teams are assembled to produce a complete product or service. Accordingly, they are empowered to perform traditional management tasks, such as scheduling, ordering materials, and even hiring.
3. The benefits of teams flow from the principle that employee self-management is the best management.
    a. Motivation is improved because decision making is decentralized. The increased authority of autonomous work groups is intended to create a sense of ownership in the work product. Better decision making, productivity, quality, and goal congruence should be the results.
    b. An advantage of cross-functional teams is improved communication because all members have a better understanding of all facets of team activities.
    c. If teams are staffed appropriately and have the necessary resources and support from management, they should be able to improve the processes of production. The individuals who perform the work have the power to make decisions about the way it is done.

ADDITIONAL CONCERNS OF MODERN ORGANIZATIONAL THEORY

A. Classical theory is largely a closed model concerned with internal design issues.

B. Behavioral theory opens up the closed system by including human variation and informal group influences.

C. Modern (contingency) theory includes both classical and behavioral concerns but adds environmental forces to the factors that must be considered in constructing the optimal organizational structure for a particular situation.

   1. Technological forces. The nature of the technological process used in producing the product or service affects design.

      a. Joan Woodward classified these processes into

         1) Job shop
         2) Mass production
         3) Continuous process

      b. Woodward concluded that organizations with more complex technology have more management levels, more administrative and clerical personnel, more coordination by committees, and a larger span of control at the chief-executive level.

   2. Other factors

      a. Size of an organization will influence its design.

      b. Stage in life cycle. Older organizations take on structures different from new ones.

      c. Uncertainty. Organizations that must cope with high levels of uncertainty, or rates of change, require design strategies different from those of stable organizations.

D. The key to the contingency approach is that the answer to any organizational design question rests on finding the optimal match between a structural strategy and the array of factors that influence the organization and vary from one setting to another.

ORGANIZATIONAL CHARTS

A. Organizational charts, used to represent the organizational structure, normally resemble a pyramid, with the chief executive on top and the operating workforce on bottom. The typical organizational chart can be designed to

   1. Reflect classical, formal authority channels (chain of command)
   2. Show reporting relationships and task groupings (departmentation)
   3. Describe communication channels
   4. Identify location of sources of organizational expertise
   5. Show promotional or career tracks
   6. Depict span of control and number of organizational levels
   7. Show major functions and their respective relationships

B. **Shortcomings in Organizational Charts**

1. Limited presentation of information
    a. This limitation can be overcome by supplementing the chart with a detailed manual.
2. Tendency to become quickly obsolete because of rapid change
    a. Also, there is the problem of who has the authority to make changes.
3. Failure to show informal communication, influence, power, or friendships
4. Tendency to ignore informal job trade-offs between titles on the chart
5. Possibility of misleading management by giving an appearance of structure and order that might not exist
6. Possibility of position titles being misleading as to functions actually performed

C. An organization manual is becoming more popular than the chart because it can provide more details.

ORGANIZATIONAL CHANGE

A. Organizational change may anticipate expected changes in circumstances or may be a reaction to the unexpected. The nature of the change may be incremental, or it may entail a strategic alteration of the structure or purpose of the organization.

1. The implementation of organizational and procedural changes often meets with resistance from the individuals and groups affected. Resistance to change may be caused by simple surprise or by inertia, but it also may arise from fear of
    a. Personal adjustments that may be required
        1) Real concern about usefulness
        2) Apparent lack of concern for workers' feelings
        3) Fear about the outcome
        4) Deviations from past procedures for implementing change (especially if procedures used are less participative than before)
        5) Downgrading of job status
    b. Social adjustments that may be required
        1) Potential violation of the behavior norms set up by informal groups
        2) Disruption of the social situation within groups
    c. Economic adjustments
        1) Potential economic loss
        2) Insecurity based on perceived threats to jobs
    d. In general, any perceived deterioration in the work situation that is seen as a threat to needs -- economic, social, and/or psychological

2. Resistance to change may be overcome by a participative management approach that
   a. Uses full communication to reduce fear of personal, social, or economic adjustments
      1) EXAMPLE: When management announces the intention to install a new computer system, a group meeting could be held with the employees of the accounting department to gain employee feedback about the proposed improvement. This meeting can do much to reduce insecurity ("Will I be replaced by a computer?") and to avoid the impression that the change is being "crammed down their throats" with no concern for employee feelings.
   b. Avoids arbitrary, capricious, or prejudicial actions
   c. Times the change so ample notice is given
   d. Gives notice of change, including
      1) The reasons for the change (reasons that have meaning to those affected)
      2) The precise nature of the change
      3) Expected outcomes or results of the change
   e. Allows maximum participation in the implementation of changes by those affected
   f. Includes informal and formal conferences, consultations, and problem-solving groups
   g. Provides express guarantees against economic loss
   h. In general, anticipates and accommodates the perceived impact of a proposed change on the needs -- economic, social, or psychological -- of those involved

CORPORATE STRUCTURE

A. At the top of a corporate organizational chart are the stockholders. They elect directors as their representatives.
   1. The board of directors hires the management of the company.
   2. The board
      a. Plans for management succession
      b. Appoints corporate officers
      c. Monitors management performance
   3. Inside directors are those who are also employees or officers of the corporation.
      a. Inside directors cannot objectively evaluate their own performance.
   4. Outside directors are not employees of the corporation; they have no responsibility for day-to-day operations of the company.
      a. Outside directors should possess expertise needed by the corporation.
      b. Because of liability problems, many corporations have had difficulty recruiting qualified outside directors. As a result, most major corporations now provide liability insurance policies for directors.
      c. Outside directors usually sit on the audit committee.

5. Committees of directors are often formed to facilitate the activities of the board. Typical committees are
   a. The audit committee -- the board's liaison with both internal and external auditors. Ideally, the director of internal audit should report directly to the audit committee.
   b. The nominating committee -- recommends individuals for membership on the board as well as nominates board officers and corporate officers
   c. The executive committee -- reviews the long-range goals and plans of the corporation and makes suggestions for solving major problems brought to its attention

B. The corporate officers include a president, one or more vice presidents, a treasurer, and a secretary.
   1. The treasurer maintains custody of corporate assets by directing cash management, risk management (insurance), credits and collections, banking arrangements, and investor relations.
   2. The controller (comptroller) or financial vice president is the chief accountant of the corporation. Duties include general accounting; cost accounting; internal, external, and government reporting; tax preparation; and establishment of accounting information systems, including internal control.

NETWORK CORPORATIONS

A. The relative independence of the various firms in a network differentiates it from a vertically integrated organization.
   1. A network is not based on the price mechanism or on a hierarchical relationship but on coordination through adaptation.
   2. It is a long-term, strategic relationship based on implicit contracts without specific legal ties.
   3. A network allows member firms to gain a competitive advantage against competitors outside the network.

B. A network corporation can be viewed as a group of activities involving suppliers and customers that add value. Each activity can be performed internally at an internal cost or subcontracted at an external cost.
   1. When an activity is subcontracted, a transaction cost will be incurred.
   2. A technological restriction on the existence of a network is that external costs must be less than internal costs. The firms in the network must be able to reduce the transaction costs so that the combination of external and transaction costs is less than internal costs.
   3. The difference between a network and a normal market is that transaction costs in the market are low enough for any player.
      a. In a network, the participating firms reduce initially high transaction costs through cooperative efforts.

STUDY UNIT 8
MOTIVATION AND THE DIRECTING PROCESS

Organization and Management Theory covers 20% to 30% of Part 1. The study units related to this topic are

Study Unit 7: Organization Theory
Study Unit 8: Motivation and the Directing Process

NATURE OF THE DIRECTING PROCESS

A. Directing or leadership is the managerial function of encouraging and motivating people in an organized enterprise to be willing and able to contribute effectively and efficiently toward the accomplishment of enterprise goals.

1. Unlike raw materials, machinery, etc., the individuals who supply the human resources are not merely another asset to be purchased as required. Effective leadership requires the realization that

    a. Individuals are members of social systems, both internal and external to the enterprise in which they work.

    b. Individuals have complex needs, desires, and attitudes.

2. Effective leaders do not treat the feelings and morale of people as secondary considerations.

    a. Managers must be very concerned with the human side of their subordinates.

B. Directing is jointly dependent on the leader's ability to direct and on the motivation of those directed. The motive to perform rests upon several factors.

1. The background, motivations, needs, training, and expectations of the **individual**
2. The characteristics and influences of the **group** with which the individual works
3. The **work situation**, including

    a. Complexity of task
    b. Stability of employment
    c. Educational or training requirements
    d. The leader and his/her behavior
    e. Rewards available to the individual for performing, and the expectation that the rewards will indeed be given for performance

C. The key to directing is in the manager's (leader's) ability to make the appropriate need-fulfilling rewards available to subordinates and to link these rewards with the desired behavior. The leader must

1. Identify rewards that are desirable to individual members
2. Create reasonable expectations for obtaining those rewards
3. Define the precise circumstances under which rewards will be given (i.e., precisely defining the task and level of desired performance)
4. Relate the task to individual abilities (be sure that the attainment of rewards through task performance lies within the individual's abilities)

EARLY APPROACHES TO DIRECTING

A. A philosophy or viewpoint about the nature of human beings is eventually developed by every person in a position of leadership. The manager's viewpoint determines the approach to motivation of subordinates, as well as the reaction of subordinates to the manager's individual leadership style.

B. The traditional approach to directing adopted by the classical school is based on military command patterns.

1. Orders are issued (dictated) by a commander.
2. The subordinate is obligated to obey out of
   a. Loyalty
   b. Fear of the consequences of disobeying
   c. Respect for the right of the leader to lead
3. Authority flows down from the top of the organization while responsibility flows up from the bottom.

C. Consideration of subordinates and their behavioral needs is an outgrowth of the behavioral school of thought.

1. The **Golden Rule** was an early attempt to meet the needs of the individual in human relationships. The weakness of this approach is the assumption that all others want what the leader wants, i.e., that all people are alike.
2. Classical management concentrated on the one best way to do a job. This was primarily an industrial engineering approach using time-motion studies.
3. The Hawthorne studies in the 1920s and early 1930s showed that workers did not respond directly to a physical change but rather to their perception of the change. Feelings resulting from change determined employee response to change. Social acceptance was found to be more important than wages in determining individual output.

D. Chester Barnard (1930s and 1940s), a corporate president, provided many behavioral insights based on executive experiences.

1. Distinctions should be made between formal and informal organization.
   a. The latter is essential and always present.
2. The executive must provide the linkage between the individual's needs and the organization's requirements.

3. Authority is real only if subordinates accept its existence.
   a. The communication of a directive will be effective if four conditions are met. The directive must be
      1) Understood by the subordinate
      2) Compatible with the purpose of the organization as the subordinate sees it
      3) Compatible with the subordinate's own interests
      4) Compatible with the subordinate's own abilities and skills
   b. Authority is usually accepted because
      1) Most managers do not send communications that violate the four preconditions.
      2) Employees have a **zone of acceptance** covering the typical areas of organizational authority within which they do not question the right of the superior to issue orders (e.g., "type a letter" is perceived to be a legitimate order directed to a secretary).
      3) Group pressure is exerted by those who adhere to organizational policies on those who challenge authority.

INDIVIDUAL DYNAMICS

A. Individual dynamics is concerned with the psychological model of a single personality, in contrast to group dynamics, which attempts to explain the behavior of people in groups.

1. Abraham Maslow (1940s and 1950s) presented one of the most widely cited theories of motivation. He saw human needs as a hierarchy, from lowest to highest. Lower-level needs must be satisfied before higher-level needs can influence the individual. He concluded that as the set of needs on each level was satisfied, those needs ceased to be a motivator.
2. Maslow's hierarchy from lowest to highest is
   a. **Physiological needs** -- the basic requirements for sustaining human life, such as water, food, shelter, sleep, and sexual satisfaction. Maslow took the position that until these needs are satisfied to the degree needed to maintain life, higher-level needs will not serve as motivators.
   b. **Security or safety needs** -- freedom from physical danger, or from loss of job, property, food, and/or shelter
   c. **Affiliation or acceptance needs** -- the need of people as social beings to belong to groups and be accepted by others
   d. **Esteem** -- the need to be valued, including the need for esteem from both one's self and others. These needs are satisfied by power, prestige, status, and self-confidence.
   e. **Self-actualization** -- the highest need in the hierarchy: the desire to become what one is capable of becoming, to realize one's potential and accomplish to the limit of one's ability

3. Research does not support the concept of a strict hierarchy in all situations (beyond the requirement that biological needs must be satisfied before other needs begin to serve as motivators).
   a. Physiological and safety needs tend to decrease in importance as managers advance in organizations, whereas needs for acceptance, esteem, and self-actualization tend to increase.
   b. Higher-level needs, esteem and self-actualization, are variable in their identity, depending upon the individual.
4. Maslow's hierarchy does not apply equally to all situations. It is dependent on the social, cultural, and psychological backgrounds of the people involved.
   a. People of different cultures respond differently.
   b. Professional workers, skilled workers, and unskilled workers react differently.
   c. Other social, ethnic, and cultural factors make people react differently.
   d. The hierarchy is not a smooth, step-by-step path; it is a complicated, intermingled, and interdependent set of relationships.
      1) However, the tendency to move upward as lower needs are satisfied does exist.

GROUP DYNAMICS

A. Many problems in management stem from group behavior patterns, attitudes, and desires.
   1. Any organized enterprise is also a social structure that includes a number of subunits.
      a. Each social structure is a complex of interacting attitudes, pressures, and conflicts arising from the cultural background of the individuals making up the subunit.
   2. Some problems arise from the work group (inside the enterprise).
   3. Other problems result from the differing backgrounds of people (outside of the enterprise), i.e., attitudes they bring with them to work. Examples are the prejudices people have about race or religion.

B. Kurt Lewin (late 1930s) identified **group dynamics** as a working model for describing human behavior. He stressed studying people where they were, not where someone believed they ideally should have been.
   1. Lewin's work provided the theoretical framework for modern **sensitivity training** and training laboratories.

C. Several common characteristics of groups should be noted, as they all influence behavior.
   1. Leadership. All groups have leaders, formal and/or informal, who initiate interrelationships and act as communication centers.
   2. Norms. From earliest observations, groups have been found to be guided by self-set standards of performance and behavior, usually based on a composite of the personal and social backgrounds of the individuals on the job as well as those of people outside the group and outside the job.
   3. Status systems. There is a ranking within the group; it may be based on skill, age, ethnic background, seniority, and/or personality.
   4. Roles. Certain behavior patterns are expected of the individual by the group.

5. Goals. The group becomes an entity and develops its own goals, its own survival and recognition needs, etc.
6. Activity. Action by the members of the group identify them as a group.
7. Bias. The group shares common beliefs and values about the world in which the group operates.

D. **Group behavior** is a distinct phenomenon. It is not merely the sum of the behaviors of the individuals making up the group.

1. A group as a whole tends to be more emotional than most of its individuals.
2. A group has values of its own, as expressed by group behavior.
3. Groups tend to normalize behavior, bringing deviant individuals into line through pressure to conform to group norms.
    a. The strength of this normalizing pressure is correlated to group cohesiveness, i.e., the strength of the bonds among members. Increased cohesiveness may either increase or decrease productivity.
    b. Workers who exceed the group norm will also be pressured to conform so as not to embarrass the other group members.
    c. Workers who produce below the norm will be pressured to improve so as not to overburden the others.
    d. Cohesiveness in the organization of a labor union may allow the group to halt production completely until their demands are met.
4. Work groups have a positive effect on the organization if management arranges for congruence between group goals and organizational goals.
    a. Management may encourage the development of a **corporate or organizational culture**, that is, a sense of shared customs, values, rituals, history, and style. It may operate through both formal procedures and implicit means of social control.
        1) An organizational culture should enhance stability, goal congruence, morale, and performance.
        2) Organizational socialization is the formal or informal process of training new employees to conform to the organizational culture.

E. **Role playing** is an important concept that emerged from the group dynamics theory. A role is the behavior expected of a person who occupies a particular position. Everyone is expected to play or assume different roles in different situations.

1. EXAMPLES: Consider the differences in behavior expected in the following roles:
    a. Parent
    b. Spouse
    c. Employee in the parking lot looking for a scarce space
    d. Auto driver on a freeway hurrying home from work
    e. Auto driver taking a grandparent for a Sunday outing
    f. Management accountant talking to
        1) His/her superior
        2) The head of a department
        3) The president of the company
        4) A competitor with whom (s)he is seeking a job

F. **Role conflict** emerges when two or more roles, making conflicting demands, are simultaneously expected of, or imposed on, a person.

1. EXAMPLES:
   a. A manager expects an employee to work late (employee role) on the night of his/her child's birthday party (parent role).
   b. A person is promoted to supervisor (employer role) of a department in which (s)he was previously on the same level with other members (peer or co-worker role).
2. Types of role conflict
   a. Conflict between role and self -- personal characteristics incompatible with expected role
   b. Interrole conflict -- having two different roles, each with different behavioral expectations
   c. Intersender conflict -- being expected to behave differently by different people, although having the same role, e.g., a manager who has to be a leader (of subordinates) and a follower (of top management)
   d. Intrasender conflict -- being sent different **messages** (roles) by the same person (e.g., a manager who expects an employee to behave one way one day and another the next)

G. Ambiguous or contradictory role demands cause stress to the individual. Recognition of the causes of role conflict helps to minimize its effect.

MOTIVATION AS THE KEY TO DIRECTION

A. **Motivation** is a general term used to describe an entire class of drives, desires, needs, fears, and similar forces that cause behavior.

1. The ideal management action motivates subordinates by structuring situations and requiring behaviors of subordinates that will simultaneously satisfy both the subordinates' needs and the organization's requirements.
2. There is no reason that the organization's needs and those of the individual **must** conflict.
3. Level of motivation is determined by individuals' opportunity to satisfy their needs and wants within the organizational setting (i.e., the greater the ability to satisfy these needs, the greater the motivational level).
   a. The inducements that an organization offers an individual member should be matched with the contributions expected from that individual (i.e., each is willing to give up something to get something it wants).
   b. The task of a leader is to make available the kinds and amounts of inducements an individual requires as a trade for the kinds and amounts of contributions the organization requires.

B. Classical views stress fear and economics as motivators, i.e., the carrot-and-stick approach. For example,

1. Economic incentive programs or bonuses (carrots)
2. Losing one's job or being demoted (sticks)

C. Behavioralists believe that these motivational strategies are effective only for the short run or for people who don't have job alternatives. The behavioralist approach focuses on participation and personal involvement in the work situation as motivational factors.

1. Chris Argyris (1964) proposed a theory of motivation that involves integrating the needs of the individual with those of the organization.

   a. Conflict arises when a mature, independent adult who seeks self-actualization joins a highly structured, demanding, and limiting organization.

      1) EXAMPLE: A highly competent aeronautical engineer who takes a job with the federal government may find his/her attempts to pursue technical excellence through intellectual effort stifled by the rules and procedures that are characteristic of a bureaucracy.

      2) Self-actualization is the process of accomplishing goals to the limit of one's ability because of the personal need to excel.

2. **Douglas McGregor's Theory X and Theory Y** (1960s) -- simplified models deliberately defining the extremes of managers' views on employee conduct so that a manager can evaluate his/her own tendencies when attempting to improve techniques of management

   a. **Theory X** -- the viewpoint of the autocratic manager. It is thought to be very common.

      1) "Average human beings have an inherent dislike of work and will avoid it if possible."

      2) "Because of this dislike for work, most people must be coerced, controlled, directed, and threatened with punishment to get them to put forth adequate effort toward the achievement of organizational objectives."

      3) "Average human beings prefer to be directed, have relatively little ambition, and want security above all."

   b. **Theory Y** -- the opposite extreme of Theory X. The permissive manager assumes that

      1) "The expenditure of physical and mental effort in work is as natural as play or rest -- to average human beings."

      2) "External control and the threat of punishment are not the only means for bringing about individual effort toward organizational objectives. Employees will exercise self-direction and self-control in their efforts to accomplish goals thought to be worthwhile."

      3) "Commitment to objectives is proportional to the rewards associated with their achievement."

      4) "Average human beings learn, under proper conditions, not only to accept responsibility, but to seek it."

      5) "The capacity to exercise a relatively high degree of imagination, ingenuity, and creativity in the solution of organizational problems is widely, not narrowly, distributed in the population."

      6) "Under the conditions of modern industrial life, the intellectual potentialities of the average human being are only partially realized."

   c. McGregor did not suggest that Theory Y was the only correct manager behavior. He suggested these theories as starting points from which a manager can examine his/her own views about human nature.

3. **Frederick Herzberg's two-factor theory of human behavior** (late 1950s) postulated that there are two classes of factors in the job situation.

   a. **Dissatisfiers (maintenance or hygiene factors)**. These factors are found in the job context. Their presence will not especially motivate people, but their absence will lead to diminished performance. They include

      1) Company policy and administration
      2) Supervision
      3) Working conditions
      4) Interpersonal relations
      5) Salary
      6) Status
      7) Job security

   b. **Satisfiers (motivational factors)**. These factors relate to job content. Their absence will not diminish performance, but their addition or availability will motivate employees. These include

      1) Achievement
      2) Recognition
      3) Challenging work
      4) Advancement
      5) Growth in the job
      6) Responsibility

   c. If Herzberg is correct, considerable attention should be given to upgrading job content through the use of job enrichment strategies.

   d. Herzberg's work has not gone unchallenged, and there is concern over his experimental methods. Other researchers have found hygiene factors to be potent in yielding both satisfaction and dissatisfaction, and therefore motivation.

      1) Nevertheless, Herzberg's ideas have been well received by practicing managers because many of them hold similar beliefs about motivation.

      2) Using Herzberg's two factors, it is obvious that some jobs do not contain many motivators, whereas others have more than are being fully used by management.

         a) EXAMPLES:

            i) Routine, low-status work like mail sorting has few motivators.

            ii) A company that may be paying above the industry average (maintenance factor) could also increase satisfaction by openly acknowledging sales or other efforts by initiating a salesperson of the week recognition program.

4. Rensis Likert (1967) stressed participation as the key to motivation. The manager is the **supportive mechanism** or device used in building toward the environment most conducive to participation and a resulting increase in productivity. He outlined four systems of management, the effects of which range from low productivity to high productivity.

   System 1 -- Exploitive-authoritative
   System 2 -- Benevolent-authoritative
   System 3 -- Consultative
   System 4 -- Participative

a. As the management style moves from System 1 to System 4 (from autocratic to participative), some of the following shifts in variables are observed:

1) Motivational forces move

a) From security, fear, threats, conflict of goals, responsibility felt only at the top, and subservience

b) To group processes in goal-setting, a high level of satisfaction, feelings of responsibility, high satisfaction with achievement

2) Communications move

a) From little, all downward, inaccuracy, no questioning

b) To up-and-down freely, initiated by all levels as needed, accuracy, no supplementary means needed

3) Personal interaction (influence) moves

a) From little interaction, fear, distrust, no teamwork

b) To friendliness, trust and confidence, much teamwork. Effective participation is impossible if either party feels threatened.

4) Decision-making process moves

a) From decisions made at top without lower inputs, made by individuals only, made at too-high levels

b) To decision making spread throughout organization, full information inputs, group decisions

5) Goal-setting moves

a) From goals by edict and orders from the top, rejection by many
b) To group participation, inputs from all levels, full acceptance

6) Control processes move

a) From top-heavy concentration, inaccurate measurements
b) To concern felt throughout, widespread responsibility

5. Job enrichment versus job enlargement

a. **Job enrichment** -- attempts to apply the findings of Maslow, Likert, and McGregor by structuring the job so that each worker participates in planning and controlling. The purpose is to maximize the satisfaction of both social and ego needs and avoid the disadvantages of routine, highly specialized work. Job enrichment includes

1) Allowing and encouraging more worker discretion over work methods, sequence, and pace.

2) Encouraging interactions between workers

3) Giving workers a feeling of personal responsibility for their tasks

4) Making sure workers understand how their tasks contribute to the finished product

5) Giving people feedback on their job performance

6) Involving workers in changes in physical aspects of the work environment

b. **Job enlargement** -- primarily a technique for combating boredom at repetitive or highly paced jobs through the assignment of a wide variety of tasks. Job enrichment may result from job enlargement.

6. **Quality of work life (QWL)** -- emerging concept building on participatory ideas similar to job enrichment
   a. Involves workers in quality-improvement round-table discussions
   b. Gains advantages of participation in decision making
7. **Expectancy theory** (Victor Vroom, 1960s) -- a commonsense notion that people have expectations of rewards derived from their unique personal motive structure (achievement, affiliation, power, etc.), from their beliefs as to what is important (a trip to Acapulco, a gold watch, a pat on the back), and from their expectations of getting these incentives if they exert effort (probability assessments, such as, "If I do this, will I get that reward?").
   a. High effort expended, ability, and accurate role assessment will lead to a high performance level (e.g., putting the effort into the task and having the right amount of ability to do it will lead to high performance).
      1) Not having proper ability will impede performance despite effort.
      2) Executing a task that is not desired or is improperly performed according to role definition will impede performance despite effort or ability.
   b. Motivation is a product of the values an individual seeks and his/her estimation of the probability that a certain action will lead to those values. This relationship can be expressed as the following equation:

      Motivation = Valence x Expectancy

   c. **Valence** is the strength of an individual's preference for one outcome in relation to others. Valence is a personal value unique to each employee that cannot be controlled by management.
   d. **Expectancy** results from past experiences and measures the strength of belief that a particular act will be followed by a specific outcome.
   e. Management is more able to control the expectancy factor than the valence factor because expectations are based on past experiences. A consistent management policy will reinforce employee expectations.
   f. Performance leads to rewards.
      1) Individuals evaluate rewards on the basis of equity ("Did I get what I deserved for what I did?") compared to others in similar jobs.
      2) If inequity exists, individuals react, usually negatively.
   g. Perception of the equity of rewards leads to satisfaction ("I got what I earned.")
   h. Level of satisfaction or dissatisfaction feeds back into the next cycle's estimates of reward values, individual abilities, and role perceptions.
8. Satisfaction and productivity
   a. "A happy worker is a good worker" has **not** been supported by research. Evidence tends to indicate that increased rewards bring increased satisfaction, but not necessarily increased productivity.
   b. Increased productivity, when followed by increased rewards, has been shown to produce increased satisfaction. Productivity is affected by many factors other than satisfaction; i.e., there is no direct relationship between satisfaction and productivity.
   c. Job satisfaction has an economic importance only indirectly related to productivity. Satisfied workers exhibit lower rates of absenteeism and turnover, and reduced tardiness, apathy, and sabotage.
   d. It remains a basic belief of the human relations position that satisfaction and productivity must bear some relationship despite the lack of empirical evidence.

LEADERSHIP

A. Leadership is the act or process of influencing people so that they will strive willingly toward the achievement of group goals. Effective leadership is achieved when the followers perform.

1. The classical position focuses on the idea that authority, decision making, and responsibility may all be decentralized in the organization to some extent, but leadership is a characteristic of the individual's personality and cannot be subdivided.

2. **Traitist approach** -- characteristic of studies before 1949, in which attempts were made to identify the traits possessed by leaders. Starting with the "great man" theory, that leaders are born, not made, attempts were made to identify the physical, mental, and psychological traits of various leaders. The traitist approach has produced such a long list of leadership traits that, in effect, it identifies nothing. A few traits do have significant correlation with leadership effectiveness, however.

   a. Intelligence
   b. Maturity
   c. Social participation and interest
   d. Socioeconomic status (in comparison to nonleaders)

B. With so little useful guidance from the leader characteristics approach, behavior-oriented researchers examined **leader behavior** to see if leaders conducted themselves in certain ways.

1. **Styles of leadership** -- emphasized in behavioral approaches. The behaviorists believe that leadership traits are not hereditary, except for physical characteristics, such as stature or health.

   a. Autocratic. The manager dictates all decisions to the employees.

   b. Consultative. The manager takes the employee's view into account, but still makes the decisions.

   c. Participative (also known as democratic). The employee has a definite input into decision making, and the manager must include subordinates' views in the decision.

   d. Free-rein. The employees make their own decisions.

2. **Employee versus task orientation**. A greater concern for people than for task accomplishment (though a certain degree of task orientation is vital) is believed to be more productive. The leader must balance the personal needs of subordinates with task accomplishment.

3. **Structuring versus consideration behavior**. Two behavior patterns that are consistently found in the study of leadership are the initiation of structure and the initiation of consideration by the leader (also called **production centered** versus **employee centered**).

   a. Structuring behavior is directed towards accomplishing tasks. Structure includes

      1) Defining duties
      2) Establishing procedures
      3) Planning and organizing the work

   b. Consideration behavior is the establishment of a personal relationship between the leader and the subordinate. **High** consideration by the leader includes

      1) Warmth toward the employee as a person
      2) Psychological support for the employee
      3) Helpfulness with problems in the work

c. Both structure and consideration are present in all job situations, and the relative amounts of each must be appropriate to the situation.

1) EXAMPLES:

a) A highly structured situation (such as assembly-line work) may respond negatively to further structure initiated by the manager but positively to increased consideration.

b) A manager of research and development may find the initiation of structure much more productive than increased consideration. Creative personnel working on a disorganized project may find a better-defined project plan much more satisfying than a demonstration of concern by the manager.

C. In looking for even better answers to "What is an effective leader?" or "How do we train and identify leaders?," the modern view follows a contingency approach; i.e., what are the forces in the situation, and who is the effective leader?

1. **Fred E. Fiedler's contingency theory** (mid 1960s). People become leaders not only because of personality attributes but also because of various situational factors and the interaction between the leaders and the situation.

a. For example, the right person at the right time may rise to a position of leadership if his/her personality and the needs of the situation complement each other. The same person might not rise to leadership in different circumstances because of failure to interact successfully with that situation.

b. There are three dimensions to the contingency theory model.

1) **Position power** is a function of the formal authority structure and is the degree to which the position held enables a leader to evaluate, reward, punish, or promote the group members in the absence of other sources of power, such as personality or expertise.

2) **Task structure** is how clearly and carefully the worker's responsibilities for various tasks are defined. Quality of performance is more easily controlled when tasks are clearly defined.

3) **Leader-member relations** is the extent to which group members like and trust and are willing to follow a leader.

a) Most important dimension from the leader's point of view because position power and task structure may be largely under the control of the enterprise

c. Research showed two types of leaders.

1) Task oriented -- most effective style when the situation is very favorable or very unfavorable

2) Relationship oriented -- most effective in the middle, less extreme situations

d. There is an optimal leadership style for each leadership situation.

e. The most effective leadership style (from directive-task orientation to permissive-people orientation) is contingent upon the definition of the three dimensions defined above.

f. Leadership is therefore as much a responsibility of the organization's placement of leaders as it is of the leaders themselves. An organization should identify leadership situations and its managers' leadership styles and engineer the job to suit the manager if necessary.

MANAGEMENT AND ORGANIZATIONAL DEVELOPMENT

A. Management development is a progressive process designed to improve the abilities of a manager. Higher level managers are responsible for providing training to their subordinates as part of their directing function.

   1. Managers benefit from the preparation and presentation to subordinates.
   2. Training provided by managers can be tailored to employees' needs and abilities.

B. Some of the techniques used include the following:

   1. **Planning a career progression**. The general path expected for a manager's progress in the enterprise is laid out in advance at the hiring or the first promotion. This schedule is geared to the short term rather than the long term. Advantages accrue from the increased knowledge of what is expected, both from the manager's point of view and from that of superiors.

   2. **Job rotation**. A manager's knowledge and skills are broadened when (s)he serves in a number of different capacities. Though popular with managers, this technique often suffers from lack of continuity, both for the subordinates and for superiors, and from confusion about the training process.

   3. **Formal management training programs**

      a. Certain managerial positions, which are a regular part of the organizational structure, are designated for training purposes and are filled by a succession of managerial trainees.

      b. In-house training programs are geared toward passing national certification examinations, e.g., the CIA, CMA, and CPA examinations.

   4. **Special assignments**. These appointments, such as acting manager or project management responsibilities, may be temporary.

   5. **Special training**

      a. Attendance at regional or national conferences gives managers exposure to other ideas and approaches, and develops skills in presentation and interaction.

      b. Continuing education

         1) For example, evening classes toward an MBA degree

      c. Refresher courses offered by professional groups

         1) For example, the management development seminars offered by the American Management Association aimed at practicing managers

      d. Role-playing situations

C. Sensitivity training (also known as **encounter groups**, **T-group training**, or **laboratory training**) has been an effective tool in psychological therapy for many years. However, it is a fairly new approach to managerial training and is somewhat controversial.

   1. Sensitivity training has as its objective the development of **awareness** of the feelings of oneself and others.

   2. Techniques, especially adapted to managerial development, vary widely, but they all seem to have some common aspects.

      a. Groups of managers (not necessarily from the same department or even the same company) meet with a person trained in the techniques.

      b. There may be no agenda and little or no directive guidance.

      c. The group members interact and then gain an understanding of how they appear to others from the feedback they receive from the trainer and the rest of the group.

3. The advantages claimed for sensitivity training are the development of
   a. Better skill in listening
   b. Tolerance for individual differences
   c. Awareness of the impact of one's personality on others
   d. Greater understanding of the group process
   e. Awareness of others' perception of one's own personality
   f. Greater awareness of others at the feeling level
   g. Better decisions because of increased ability to deal with actual feelings rather than mere surface appearances
   h. Reduced prejudices from various sources
4. The disadvantages claimed for sensitivity training are
   a. Difficulty of administration
   b. Lack of competent trainers
   c. Cost in time and resources
   d. Difficulty of relating training to improved job productivity
   e. Difficulty in reestablishing lines of authority (if coworkers attend the same session)
   f. Adverse results back on the job, e.g., difficulty in resuming roles after emotional confrontations (if coworkers attend the same session)
   g. Possible damage to egos and individual defense mechanisms
   h. The need for such training at all levels of management to be effective

D. **Organizational development (OD)** is a contemporary expression that refers to planned change in an organization. These changes are massive and long term. OD is an attempt to make earlier behavioral approaches (such as sensitivity training) more pragmatic and relevant to business situations.

1. It requires a commitment by top management.
   a. Conscious, planned, directed, structured change
   b. Special emphasis on behavioral aspects
   c. The behavioral approach as the focal point in implementing any change
2. Grid training is a popular method.
   a. Developed by Robert Blake and Jane Mouton
   b. Postulates two dimensions of managing on a 9 x 9 grid
      1) Concern for production on the X axis
      2) Concern with people on the Y axis
   c. Most people tend to be either too concerned with one while ignoring the other, or not concerned enough about either.
   d. Organizational development training develops maximum concern for both dimensions (a 9.9 manager).

MANAGEMENT BY OBJECTIVES (MBO)

A. MBO is a behavioral, communications-oriented, responsibility approach to employee self-direction.

  1. MBO is based on the philosophy that
     a. Employees want to work hard if they know what is expected.
     b. Employees like to understand what their jobs actually entail.
     c. Employees are capable of self-direction and self-motivation.
  2. MBO requires
     a. Top management participation and commitment to the program. They must
        1) Determine overall direction and objectives for the organization
        2) Communicate these effectively in operational or measurable terms
        3) Coordinate subordinate managers' goals with overall goals
        4) Follow up at end of time period to reward performance and review problems
     b. Integration of the objectives for all subunits into a compatible, balanced system directed toward accomplishment of the overall goals
     c. Provisions for regular periodic reporting of performance toward attainment of the objectives
     d. Free and honest communications between manager and subordinate
     e. A commitment to a Theory Y philosophy on the part of managers
     f. An organizational climate that encourages mutual trust and respect

B. Early definition of MBO was made by Peter Drucker (1954). He emphasized that

  1. Objectives are needed in every area where performance and results directly and vitally affect the survival and prosperity of the business.
  2. The performance that is expected of the manager must be derived from the performance goals of the business.
  3. A manager's performance should be measured by the contribution (s)he makes to the success of the enterprise.
  4. Traditional systems were inadequate in fulfilling the two major requirements of a good performance appraisal program.
     a. Performance appraisals should identify good performers for rewards and promotions.
     b. Performance appraisals should serve as a feedback mechanism to show employees' strengths and weaknesses.
     c. Evaluations used as a basis for compensation frequently conflict with use as objective feedback, and, consequently, they become merely documents to justify pay or promotion decisions.
     d. See D. on page 245 under the Human Resource Policies and Procedures sideheading for further discussion of evaluations.

5. Traditional appraisals are inadequate because
   a. They focus on past events rather than future direction.
   b. Trait appraisals measure traits, not job performance.
   c. They focus on personal traits that are irrelevant to what an employee needs to know to correct actual job performance deficiencies (e.g., a poor score on the **trait** "appearance" may be of little use to an employee who is seeking information on job **behavior**).
   d. Traditional trait appraisals do not easily encourage the employee and the manager to communicate about job performance expectations, career development needs, or job context and objectives (how the subordinate's job fits into the big picture).
   e. Traditional appraisal systems encourage the manager to "look over the subordinates' shoulders to see how they are doing" rather than clarifying what to accomplish and letting them do it on their own.
6. MBO fulfills the need for a new method by
   a. Allowing employee self-direction with specific tasks and concrete feedback
   b. Encouraging the manager to be a facilitator rather than a director
   c. Promoting positive morale by allowing participation, good communication, mutual trust, and job autonomy

C. **The Steps Necessary to Implement an MBO Program**

1. First, ask for the subordinate's own job objectives and the specific actions (s)he would like to take over the next time period to help reach those job objectives.
2. Review the subordinate's goals and activities within the context of the goals at higher levels.
3. When the subordinate's goals are at odds with upper-level goals, initiate a coaching session to review them.
   a. The review frequently represents the acid test of the MBO because the manager must avoid dictating the subordinate's goals if the spirit of participation is to be preserved.
   b. If the subordinate's goals are deemed by the supervisor to be inappropriate, and the subordinate cannot be **coached** out of them, the supervisor can either
      1) Let the subordinate learn by failing in doing the job his/her way, or
      2) Overrule on this particular issue.
   c. Commitment to Theory Y, trust in subordinates, and the supervisor's job security (the confidence to allow subordinates still more latitude) will play important roles.
   d. The clearer the definition of job objectives and organizational purposes and the greater the degree of trust and communication between supervisor and subordinate, the easier it is to avoid these dilemmas in implementing MBO.
4. Mutually set and agree on a realistic program of activities that can be accomplished by the end of the period.
5. Maintain flexibility during the period to accommodate unforeseen changes.
6. Review the results, analyzing and discussing differences, and using the discussion as learning and performance feedback (not as correctional, disciplinary, etc.).
7. Repeat the process to set new goals and objectives.

D. **Benefits of MBO**

1. Opens up communication between manager and subordinate
2. Allows subordinate to participate in setting job objectives
3. Forces specification of organizational objectives throughout the organization
4. Allows subordinates to be measured on what they do, not on personality traits
5. Facilitates employee development

E. MBO has excited the interest of managers everywhere and has been successful in providing improved leadership. However, MBO can fail for the following reasons:

1. Failure of managers to accept the Theory Y philosophy behind MBO
2. Failure to give goal setters adequate guidelines
3. Difficulty in setting truly verifiable goals
4. Tendency for goals to be short-term only
5. Tendency for plans under MBO to become inflexible, making it difficult to adapt to change
6. Lack of precise management knowledge of a task, resulting in a supervisor allowing a subordinate to set inappropriate goals

F. The effectiveness of MBO depends on how well it is administered in light of the above problems.

PLANNING

A. Planning is the determination of **what** is to be done, and of **how, when, where**, and **by whom** it is to be done. Plans serve to direct the activities that all organizational members must undertake and successfully perform to move the organization from where it is to where it wants to be (i.e., toward its goals).

1. Planning must be completed before undertaking any other managerial function.
2. Planning establishes the means to reach organizational ends or goals.

B. **The Planning Process**

1. Long-range (strategic) planning is from one to ten years or more. It is the concern of top management and is based on
    a. Identifying and specifying organizational goals and objectives, i.e., the future course of the organization consistent with its mission statement
    b. Evaluating the strengths and weaknesses of the organization (e.g., what it does well and/or poorly)
    c. Assessing risk levels
    d. Forecasting the future direction and influences of environmental factors relevant to the organization (e.g., market trends, changes in technology, international competition, and social change)
    e. Deriving the best strategy for reaching the objectives, given the organization's strengths and weaknesses and the relevant future trends
2. Strategic plans are translated into measurable and achievable intermediate and operational plans.
    a. Intermediate plans (6 months to 2 years) are the province of middle management.
    b. Operational plans (1 week to 1 year) are developed by lower-level managers.
3. Intermediate and operational plans must be retranslated into policies, procedures, and rules.

C. The terms **objectives** and **goals** are most often used interchangeably. However, some writers distinguish between overall organizational objectives and individual, departmental, or subunit goals.

1. The determination of organizational objectives is the first step in actual planning.
2. Organizations usually have multiple objectives, which are often contradictory.
   a. The objective of maximizing profit and the objective of growth could be mutually exclusive within a given year. Maximizing short-term profit might hamper or preclude future growth.
   b. Conflict among an organization's objectives is common.
3. Objectives vary with the organization's type and stage of development.
4. Each subunit of an organization may have its own goals.
   a. Because subunit goals may detract from or conflict with overall organizational objectives, considerable effort needs to be made to achieve goal congruence.
   b. Subunit goals are frequently needed to translate broad overall corporate objectives into meaningful and measurable terms for the subunit members.
      1) Broad objectives should be established at the top and retranslated in more specific terms as they are communicated downward in a means-end hierarchy.
5. Objectives and goals should be
   a. Clearly stated in specific terms. General or poorly defined objectives are not useful for guiding the action of managers or measuring their performance.
   b. Easily communicated to all concerned. The executives who determine objectives have not had the desired impact on the organization until they have successfully communicated the objectives to all from whom action is required.
   c. Accepted by the individuals concerned. An objective is unlikely to be attained if it is thought to be unachievable by those affected.

D. After objectives, goals, and premises are formulated, the next step in the planning process is the development of policies, procedures, and rules to deal with repetitive situations. These elements are necessary at all levels of the organization and overlap both in definition and in practice.

1. **Policies** are general statements that guide thinking and action in decision making.
2. **Procedures** are specific directives that define how work is to be done.
   a. Usually consist of a set of specific steps in chronological order
3. **Rules** are specific, detailed guides that restrict behavior.

HUMAN RESOURCE POLICIES AND PROCEDURES

A. Human resource planning consists of forecasting future employment requirements. It includes the hiring, training, and monitoring of employees.

B. **Recruitment, Selection, and Testing**

1. Recruitment

   a. Sources

      1) Advertising in media (e.g., newspapers)
      2) Word-of-mouth referral by current employees
      3) Walk-ins
      4) Internal job posting and computerized staff inventories of existing employees
      5) Targeted recruiting sources, e.g., colleges and universities
      6) Temporary placement and part-time employees

   b. Governmental constraints and restrictions on recruiting practice

      1) Employment laws

         a) Title VII of the 1964 Civil Rights Act, including its subsequent amendments, prohibits discrimination on the basis of race, color, religion, sex, or national origin by private employers of 15 or more persons, unions, employment agencies, joint labor-management committees controlling apprenticeships or training programs, state and local governments, and educational institutions.

            i) Discrimination is permissible on the basis of a **bona fide occupational qualification**; e.g., clergy can be selected on the basis of religious faith.

            ii) The Equal Employment Opportunity Commission has the right to bring discrimination suits against employers in federal courts.

         b) The Age Discrimination in Employment Act of 1967 prohibits discrimination on the basis of age (as amended in 1978).

         c) Summary of compliance criteria

            i) Does the employment practice have an unequal impact on the groups covered by law?

            ii) Is the practice justified by job-related (bona fide occupational qualification) requirements or is it otherwise legally defensible as necessary to the organization?

      2) Governmental reviews evaluate compliance with employment law by checking

         a) Sources of employees recruited for each job category

         b) Advertising

         c) Estimates of employees needed for coming year

         d) Statistics on number of applicants processed by sex, race, etc. for each job category and level

c. The following cannot be done in recruiting interviews:

1) Make notation of sex
2) Ask marital status (may ask after hiring)
3) Ask for number of children (may ask after hiring)
4) Ask for height and weight
5) Ask for criminal record (only for security clearance)
6) Ask type of military discharge
7) Ask age

2. Using temporary or part-time workers gives management the flexibility to adjust quickly to changing market conditions.

a. Such workers can often be paid lower salaries and given fewer benefits than full-time workers.

b. Disadvantages of hiring temporary or part-time workers include the lack of long-term benefits to the company from training programs and less employee loyalty to the firm.

c. These workers can improve the morale of permanent employees, however, by relieving overtime pressures or by performing the more tedious and less desirable tasks.

1) On the other hand, they may reduce the morale of permanent employees who might desire more overtime work or who might feel that their jobs are threatened.

d. Leasing employees has a variety of administrative benefits because the lessor prepares payrolls, pays the employees, files tax returns, etc. (S)he also assumes liability for unemployment claims.

1) However, the behavioral disadvantages of directly hiring temporary or part-time workers also apply to employee leasing.

3. Employee selection

a. Requirements should come from job specifications developed from each job description and include

1) Education
2) Experience
3) Physical characteristics, e.g., strength and stamina
4) Personal characteristics, e.g., personality, confidence, and skills

b. All requirements, to be legal, must be based on their relationship to the ability to perform successfully in a specific job category.

4. Employee testing

a. Testing applicants for jobs with quantifiable output (e.g., jobs requiring clerical skills or manual dexterity) is easier than testing for positions with a less tangible work product (e.g., public relations director or human resource manager).

b. All tests must be validated in each organization and for minority and nonminority groups before they can be predictive of successful performance.

c. Tests must be given to all applicants for the same job category.

d. It is not easy or inexpensive to validate a test.

e. Test validity is the capacity to measure accurately what it was designed to measure.

f. Test reliability is the ability of a test to obtain the same scores in repeated administrations, regardless of validity.

5. Lie detector tests and drug tests are currently significant issues. The validity, legality, etc., of these tests have not yet been determined.

C. **Training and Development**

1. Training -- organizational programs to prepare employees to perform currently assigned tasks (e.g., on-the-job training, formal programs, etc.)
2. Development -- organizational programs to prepare people to do future tasks and acquire new skills
    a. Mostly focused on management and organizational development to develop human relations skills
        1) Organizational development is a systematic development of managerial concern for both people and production.
        2) Increasing recognition of need to realize human potential in future productivity gains

D. **Evaluation**

1. Purpose
    a. Performance criteria identify job-related abilities necessary to do the job.
    b. Performance goals help employees direct their energies toward what the organization expects without constant supervision.
    c. Performance outcomes allow employee satisfaction in knowing when jobs are completed and done well.
    d. Evaluation distinguishes effective from ineffective job performance.
    e. The organization can develop employee strengths and identify weaknesses.
2. Problems
    a. Design of evaluation system can be faulty if the
        1) Criteria for evaluations are poor or inappropriate.
        2) Technique is cumbersome or not understood by users.
        3) Criteria focus on wrong attributes causing emphasis on wrong things (e.g., personal appearance rather than job accomplishments).
        4) Top management does not lend support.
    b. Evaluation-based problems
        1) **Halo effect**. Manager's judgment on one trait (either negative or positive) affects rating on other traits.
        2) **Central tendency**. All employees are rated within the same narrow range; e.g., "All my people are good."
        3) **Recency effect**. Most recent behavior overshadows overall performance.
        4) **Hard versus easy ratios**. Some managers have stricter standards than others, making cross-departmental comparisons difficult.
        5) **Personal bias**. Because traits may not reflect actual job performance, appraisal can be biased by the degree to which the manager likes the subordinate.
        6) Some traits, e.g., dependability or industriousness, may have little to do with the job expected of an employee and may be very subjective.
        7) Trait scales tend to equate both pertinent and nonperformance traits subjectively (e.g., quality of work and appearance are equal on many scales in influencing total appraisal score).
        8) The once-a-year process tends to affect the usefulness and accuracy of any job-related information.

3. Major types of appraisals
   a. Rating scales on personal traits
   b. Management by objectives (see sideheading on page 239)
   c. Critical incident technique -- listing of critical aspects of job that is used to evaluate employee performance
   d. Behaviorally anchored rating scales (BARS) -- similar to critical incident technique in which descriptions of good and bad performance are developed for a number of specific job-related behaviors and then used for evaluation of employees
4. Characteristics of effective evaluation systems
   a. Relevant. Reliable and valid criteria that are closely related to actual job performance and output should be used.
   b. Unbiased. Systems should be based on performance of job, not on unrelated personal characteristics.
   c. Significant. System should focus on the important part of the job rather than what is convenient to evaluate. This focus avoids misdirection or confusion of employee effort.
   d. Practical. System should be as objective, easy-to-use, clearly understood, and efficient as possible.
5. Criteria for effective appraisal
   a. Employees must understand the appraisal.
   b. They must believe appraisal is fair.
   c. They must believe it is important to them and their jobs.

REVIEW OF KEY NAMES

A. Argyris: Motivation as means of reconciliation of individual needs with organization's needs.
B. Barnard: Distinguishing between formal and informal organization.
C. Blake and Mouton: Developed grid training method of organizational development.
D. Drucker: The need to set verifiable objectives.
E. Fiedler: Contingency theory. Leadership ability/success varies with the situation.
F. Follett: Leadership is a function of acceptance by subordinates.
G. Herzberg: Two-factor theory (maintenance/hygiene factors, and motivators/satisfiers).
H. Lewin: Studied group dynamics, which underlies sensitivity training.
I. Likert: Participation is the key to motivation.
J. McGregor: Theory X (autocratic manager) and Theory Y (permissive manager).
K. Maslow: Hierarchy of need from physiological through security, affiliation or acceptance, and esteem to self-actualization.
L. Taylor: Father of Scientific Management; time-motion studies.
M. Vroom: Developed expectancy theory.

SUMMARY

The study of leadership has revealed much more about how not to lead than it has about how to lead. Valid generalized principles of leadership have not yet been discovered. The trait approach does not help select leaders without reference to the situation. There is no support for the idea that leaders are born, not made. The leader cannot be described in isolation from the group being led. Reciprocal causation forces the leader-group pair to be considered simultaneously. Leaders are not autonomous; they are influenced by superiors, peers, subordinates, the work climate, and the work itself. There is no one best way to lead.

STUDY UNIT 9
COMMUNICATION

Communication is the secret to the success of any manager. A manager's ability to understand other people, and their ability to understand the manager, are crucial to accomplishing organizational objectives. Communication is the link that ties an organization together and transforms a diverse group of people into a cohesive whole. Being a good communicator does not ensure that a person will be a good manager, but virtually every good manager is a good communicator. Communication should not be viewed as a separate managerial activity. Every aspect of management requires effective communication.

Communication covers 10% to 15% of Part 1 of the CMA exam.

NATURE OF COMMUNICATION

A. **Communication** is the process of conveying meaning or understanding from one person to another. It permeates all segments of an organization and moves in many directions.

1. **Formal communication** is conducted through the formal structure of the organization, e.g., budgets, bonus programs.
2. Informal communication (the **grapevine**) operates outside of formal structural channels.
   a. The grapevine exists wherever there are people.
   b. Although the grapevine is usually accurate, it can carry gossip and rumor.
   c. The effective manager stays tuned in to the grapevine and uses it constructively.
3. **Written communication** provides a permanent record of the message and tends to be accurate but can be time consuming to prepare. An inherent weakness of written communication is that it inhibits feedback because the sender and the receiver are not in simultaneous communication.
4. **Oral communication** is less formal and less accurate than written communication but permits immediate feedback. It also permits messages to be transmitted rapidly.
   a. Most managers spend more of their time in oral than in written communication. However, modern technology (e.g., voice mail and e-mail) blurs the distinction between written and oral communications.

B. **Directions of Communication**

1. **Downward** (from superior to subordinate) -- orders, instructions, notices, memos, bulletins, newsletters, handbooks, loudspeakers, chain of command

2. **Upward** -- morale surveys, grievance procedures, interviews, conferences. Upward communication must overcome more barriers and is slower than downward communication.

3. **Horizontal** (from one peer to another)

C. The communication process has five elements (the mnemonic is SSMRF).

1. **Sender**, who originates the message
2. **Symbols**, in which the message is encoded
3. **Medium**, the channel through which the message flows
4. **Receiver**, the person who decodes the message and interprets the sender's meaning
5. **Feedback**, acknowledging to the sender that the message was correctly understood

D. The effectiveness of communication can be determined only when the sender seeks feedback and observes the impact of the communication on the receiver.

1. The sender is obligated to solicit feedback to ensure the communication process is complete.

2. The receiver is obligated to give feedback to the sender.

3. The importance of feedback to check on the effectiveness of the communication process indicates the limitations of one-way communications (e.g., memos).

E. Managers must consider the nature of the message receiver. Receivers vary in their perception of messages because of language, education, culture, attitudes toward the sender and job, etc. This variance may result in communication distortion.

1. EXAMPLES:

   a. In some cultures, to move toward a person while speaking is expected; in others, it is considered an act of aggression.

   b. In some cultures, consistently being late to appointments means laxness, lack of concern, discourtesy, and disinterest; in others, it is normal and expected, and carries no particular meaning.

APPROACHES TO COMMUNICATIONS THEORY

A. **Traditional or classical management** stresses the sending of one-way communications from top management down to the subordinates. This military model of organization is autocratic or mechanistic and ignores the need for feedback.

B. **Participative management** stresses multidirectional communication. All parts of the organization are allowed and expected to communicate with each other, and not merely along lines of authority.

C. **Systems theory** stresses the importance of feedback in determining the effectiveness of communications. Without a channel from the receiver back to the sender, the sender has no idea how the information has affected the performance or actions of the receiver, if at all.

COMMUNICATIONS NETWORKS

A. Research shows that communications networks have various characteristics.

1. A **wheel** network, which is a fast and accurate means of information flow, channels all communication to a central supervisor.
   a. The result is lower satisfaction among participants, but the circumstances favor the emergence of a leader.
2. Extensive cross-communication in an **all-channel network** results in moderate accuracy but with
   a. Free-flow
   b. More innovation
   c. Member satisfaction
3. **Chain-type** communication is slower.
   a. Accuracy is high, but member satisfaction is moderate.

PROBLEMS IN COMMUNICATION

A. **Poorly Encoded Messages**

1. Inappropriate choice of words or phrases for the receiver
   a. For example, using technical accounting in speaking with a lay person
2. Careless omissions of key ideas
3. Lack of coherence in forming the message
4. Inconsistency between verbal and nonverbal messages
5. Incomplete ideas or ideas out of receiver's context
6. Projection, which is the tendency of the sender to attribute his/her traits, values, and emotions to the receiver, and vice versa
7. Filtering the message so that it reflects more favorably on the sender, a typical problem in upward communication

B. **Faulty Channel Selection**

1. Trying to speak while a loud airplane flies overhead
2. Gesturing to someone who cannot see the gesture

C. **Noise in the communications channel** is an outside disruption that impedes the flow of a message, for example,

1. Asking for a raise in the middle of a discussion of an operations problem
2. Random events that cause a breakdown in communication (lost mail, phone service disruption, etc.)

D. **Perceptual Problems**

1. Sender's dislike of receiver or vice versa
2. Distortion created by personal enthusiasm for embellishing good news and downplaying the bad, or vice versa
3. Status differences between people that impede free and open communication
   a. Few people are secure enough to tell a superior that what was just said was not understood.

4. Emotions, prior experiences, and expectations that affect the receiver's perception of the message
   a. Perception is selective.
   b. Moreover, people necessarily must narrow their perception to avoid sensory overload. Such screening is required to organize and interpret experience.

E. **Use of Communication Channels for Enhancement of Personal Status**

1. Some lower-level employees who have the ear of management become influential among their peers.

F. **Loss in Transmission and Poor Retention**

1. Research shows that as much as 30% of the information in oral communication is lost in each transmission. Even written communications are subject to some loss. After passing through a chain of command, little of the message may have been retained.
2. Poor retention. One study found that as little as 50% of communicated information was retained by employees.

G. **Nonreception**. The receiver commonly fails to receive any communication.

1. Inattention or disinterest in the message
2. Information overload. The receiver is already receiving so many messages that (s)he cannot process what (s)he is hearing.
3. Confusing messages. The sender is not sending enough information to fully communicate thoughts, and the receiver must allocate too much time to interpreting what the sender is saying.

H. **Formal Organization Channel Breakdowns**

1. EXAMPLE: Omissions from mailing lists

SOLUTIONS TO COMMUNICATION PROBLEMS

A. The message should be in the context of the receiver's perceptions.

1. Explaining an accounting concept to a nonaccountant will require terms different from those used with someone who has an accounting background.

B. The sender must monitor channels to ensure they are free from distortion or breakdown.

C. The sender must actively solicit feedback to ensure reception and understanding.

D. The organizational climate should encourage the elimination of interpersonal barriers to communication.

E. The sender should look for nonverbal cues or feedback (body language).

F. The sender must remember that it is his/her responsibility to deliver the communication with appropriate symbols over appropriate channels and never to make assumptions about the receiver's reaction.

G. Two-way communication should be used whenever possible to permit ease of feedback.

H. Communication can be improved through redundancy, that is, by repeating the message in several different formats and in several media.

LISTENING

A. **Listening** is the responsibility of both the speaker (sender) and the listener (receiver). Listening is one of the problems in communication that can be improved by the manager. The art of listening must be exercised effectively to

1. Gain more information about the work situation
2. Have a positive effect on both superiors and subordinates through showing concern for their views

B. **Problems in Listening**

1. People can listen several times faster than words can be spoken, which may result in inattention and mind-wandering.
2. Prejudgment of the message, before or during the communication process, may reduce the ability to listen objectively.
3. Concentration may be focused on the words used to the exclusion of the ideas.

C. **Guides to More Effective Listening**

1. **Empathy** -- the process of mentally putting oneself in another person's position to better understand his/her feelings, attitudes, and thoughts. Empathy
   a. Enables the sender and the receiver to take into account each other's backgrounds, biases, beliefs, and values
   b. Aids in anticipating others' reactions to messages
   c. Aids in effective communication by guiding the choice of
      1) Words used and their meanings
      2) Word inflection and emphasis
      3) Tone of voice and gestures
2. **Sensitivity training** can sometimes give managers a greater awareness of, or sensitivity to, their own attitudes, feelings, and beliefs. This understanding permits them to perceive how their behavior affects the people with whom they communicate.
   a. Such training is designed to result in better listening skills, tolerance for individual differences, and an awareness of the impact of one's personality on other people.
   b. The disadvantage is that some managers may spend a disproportionate amount of time focusing on relationships rather than on the day-to-day problems of the job.
3. **Interpersonal communications training.** Supervisors and their subordinates receive formal training in how to give and receive both written and oral communication. The advantage is that everyone has the same training and can practice working together using specific problems.
4. **Conflict management** trains both supervisors and subordinates in various forms of conflict management, such as confronting, smoothing, negotiating, and compromise.

OTHER FORMS OF COMMUNICATION

A. Audit reports and other documents are forms of communication.

1. Internal audit reports are expected to communicate audit results to management and create desired actions.
2. Audit reports should be timely, clear, concise, objective, and constructive.
3. A corporate annual report is a one-way communication device.
   a. Clarity and conciseness must be emphasized because no immediate feedback from readers is possible.
   b. A logical organization of the report's contents facilitates transmission of the message.

B. Employee handbooks and accounting manuals are also forms of communication.

1. The employee handbook communicates company policies and provides employees and management with quick and consistent answers to employment-related questions.
   a. It provides a store of knowledge and outlines the responsibilities and levels of authority within an organization.
   b. It can be the basis of a contract between the company and its employees.
   c. It should contain information about
      1) Benefit packages
      2) Holiday and vacation policies
      3) Sick pay provisions
      4) Severance policy
      5) Retirement benefits
      6) Grievance procedures
      7) Promotion and transfer policies
      8) Other matters
2. An accounting manual promotes equitable and consistent treatment of similar transactions.
   a. It should define accounting and technical terms in language that all employees can understand.
3. Both employee handbooks and accounting manuals should be prepared so that revisions and updates are facilitated (e.g., kept in a ring binder).
   a. Specific individuals should be responsible for periodic updating of handbooks and manuals.

C. **Nonverbal communication** consists of nonverbal nuances, whether or not accompanied by verbal communication. Examples of nonverbal communication include tone of voice, eye contact, the positioning of furniture in a person's office, the physical distance between the speaker and the listener, facial expressions, gestures, posture, and appearance.

D. **Telecommuting**. People who are computer literate have in recent years begun working from their homes. They correspond with their offices by means of telecommunication.

1. Problems associated with these employees include a tendency to fall behind in their fields of specialization, a lack of strong working relationships with other employees, a loss of career opportunities, and inadequate organizational socialization.
2. The primary strength of these individuals, however, has been their communication skills.

STUDY UNIT 10
ETHICS AND THE MANAGEMENT ACCOUNTANT

Ethics questions may appear on any part of the examination. Ethical issues will appear on at least two parts of each examination and will be addressed within the context of specific subject areas. Over the four parts of an examination, the ethical issues content will not be less than the equivalent of one 30-minute question or more than two 30-minute questions, i.e., from 3% to 6% of each overall CMA examination. The presence of this study unit in Part 1 has no significance. It must be studied in conjunction with each chapter because ethics will be tested on all four parts of the CMA exam.

Ethical standards are vital to the accounting profession. Thus, management accountants must continually be alert to situations that might compromise those standards.

RECENT HISTORY OF SOCIAL RESPONSIBILITY

A. The late 1950s and early 1960s saw a rapid rise in society's expectations for more than merely economic performance by business organizations.
   1. This rise reflected the general belief that economic problems were under control and that it was time to move on to solve social ills.
   2. Also, scholars recognized the inadequacy of classical economic controls on large-scale corporations and industries. Classical economists had assumed the following conditions existed:
      a. There was no awareness of one business by another because there were many small firms in the market.
      b. Entry into and exit from the industry was easy: excess profits would attract new competition and low profits would drive inefficient firms out.
      c. Information was equally available to all competitors.
      d. Competition would reward the efficient users of society's resources (and punish the inefficient).
   3. The media and general public became aware that the actions of large corporations were newsworthy, causing closer observation of all corporate activities.

B. The general increase in the education level of the population brought a concurrent increased interest in overall social concerns, including the social responsibilities of business.

C. Growth and pervasiveness of large social institutions led to the competition of these institutions for the hearts and minds (i.e., attention) of the public (the concept of pluralism).

D. International markets and corporations grew more complex.

E. Technological advances in communications made instant monitoring of all social institutions, including business, possible. What a company does at noon can be seen nationally on the 6 o'clock news.

F. Development of the systems viewpoint encouraged the investigation of complex interdependencies of society's institutions.

G. Increased separation of ownership (stockholders) of business from management led to revision of the philosophy that managers should only manage on behalf of the owners' private property interests; i.e., now they may have other objectives.

SOME DEFINITIONS OF SOCIAL RESPONSIBILITY

A. "The obligations of businessmen to pursue those policies, to make those decisions, and to follow those lines of action that are desirable in terms of the objectives and values of our society." (Howard Bowen)

B. "The substance of social responsiveness is that it is concerned with the consequences of organizational acts as they might affect the interests of others." (Keith Davis)

C. **Activities Considered as the Domain of Social Responsibility**

1. Ecology and environmental quality
2. Philanthropy
3. Minority hiring and training
4. Community service and urban problems
5. Product quality and safety
6. Consumer complaints
7. Employee health, safety, and welfare
8. Ethical and moral concerns (e.g., refusing to do business in countries where the government violates human rights)
9. Commitment to presenting honest, fair, and open information to shareholders and owners

D. The major difficulty with any definition is operationalizing or measuring what actually represents socially responsible behavior.

COMMON ARGUMENTS FOR CORPORATE INVOLVEMENT IN SOCIALLY RESPONSIBLE BEHAVIOR

A. **Business Accountability**

1. Corporations are legal persons and should be expected to behave as responsibly as any good citizen.
2. If corporations expect to maintain their corporate power, they must exercise the responsibility of any powerful institution or lose their power.
3. Because business has been responsible for creating many social problems (e.g., pollution), business should underwrite the social costs of remedying those problems.

B. **Long-run Advantages to Business**

1. Socially responsible behavior may lead to long-run profit maximization for a business that treats customers, owners, employees, etc., fairly and thus creates goodwill.
   a. Large corporations especially can afford to defer short-run profits in the interests of long-run profit and survival.
   b. Potential competition can be avoided if a business establishes a strong public image and customer satisfaction.
   c. EXAMPLE: A petroleum company emphasizes its socially redeeming qualities in gasoline advertisements to induce consumers to buy its gas -- a product that is often undifferentiated among consumers.
2. Governmental intrusion in decision making can be avoided by socially responsible behavior.
3. Community involvement enables a business to avoid adverse local political decisions and to build employee relations (e.g., giving funds or lending executives to local school systems can help in recruiting new outside employees and in building the educational competence of existing staff).

C. Some socially responsible activities are profitable in themselves.

1. EXAMPLE: Installing a pollution control smokestack may recapture an otherwise lost precipitated material that can be sold for profit.
2. EXAMPLE: Some investors (e.g., many pension funds and university endowment funds) will invest only in the securities of socially responsible companies. Also, in recent years mutual funds have been started that invest only in socially responsible companies. Thus, being socially responsible results in an indirect support of the market price of a corporation's securities.

COMMON ARGUMENTS AGAINST CORPORATE INVOLVEMENT IN SOCIALLY RESPONSIBLE BEHAVIOR

A. "The business of business is business."

1. The only responsibility of a business is "to use its resources and engage in activities designed to increase its profits so long as it stays within the rules of the game, which is to say, engages in open and free competition, without deception or fraud." (Milton Friedman)
2. Managers are responsible to stockholders, not to a vague public image.
3. Corporate managers are trained to make business decisions, not social welfare decisions.

4. Diverting executive energies from business concerns to social concerns is a poor use of executive time, talent, and training.
5. Business persons are rewarded for making good business decisions but are seldom held accountable for the quality of their social decisions in the way that a specifically created social institution would be.
6. Business may frequently have a potential conflict of interest with socially responsible behavior (e.g., an accounting firm may have a conflict if it donates funds to a college that buys accounting services).

B. "Business lacks social authority." To say that business must act responsibly to avoid losing its social power implies that it should be allowed to have social power in the first place. Many argue that it should have no such power.

C. "Plurality is essential." In a society with many social institutions competing for people's attention, loyalty, and resources, any encroachment of one institution (industry) on the activities or domain of another (social) is bad.

D. **Negative Aggregate Impact**. Evidence shows socially responsible activities are economically procyclical -- they tend to increase in good times and decrease in bad times when they are most needed.

E. **Competitive Disadvantage**. If two firms are now in a competitive market, for one firm to incur costs of socially responsible activities would put it in an uncompetitive position.

NOTE: Positions both for and against corporate social responsibility are defensible, but the long-run favorable arguments are most easily supported.

ETHICS

A. **Definitions**

1. Corporate ethics -- an organization's policies and standards established to assure certain kinds of behavior by its members
2. Individual ethics -- principles of conduct adhered to by an individual

B. **Increased Concern for Business Ethics**

1. Electrical-equipment conspiracy cases in 1960 caused public concern and creation of Business Ethics Advisory Council (BEAC) in 1961 under the Secretary of Commerce.
2. BEAC pointed out areas needing self-evaluation by the business community:
    a. General business understanding of ethical issues
    b. Compliance with laws
    c. Conflicts of interest
    d. Entertainment and gift expenses
    e. Relations with customers and suppliers. Should gifts or kickbacks be given or accepted?
    f. Social responsibilities
3. BEAC's recommendations generated business interest, especially from big business, in problems of ethical behavior.

C. **Factors That May Lead to Unethical Behavior**

1. In any normal population, some people have less than desirable levels of ethics. If these people hold leadership positions, they will adversely influence subordinates.
2. Organizational factors
   a. Pressures for short-run performance in decentralized return on investment (ROI) centers may inhibit ethical behavior.
   b. Emphasis on strict adherence to chain-of-command authority may provide excuses for ignoring ethics when following orders.
   c. Informal work-group loyalties may subvert ethical behavior.
   d. Committee decision processes may make it possible to abstain from or dodge ethical obligations.
3. External factors
   a. Pressure of competition may compromise ethics in the interest of survival.
   b. Unethical behavior of others may force a compromise of ethics.
   c. Definitions of ethical behavior may vary from one culture to another.
      1) Bribes to overseas officials or buyers may be consistent with some countries' customary business practices, but such a practice is not considered ethical among U.S. purchasing agents.
         a) Bribes are now considered illegal under the Foreign Corrupt Practices Act of 1977. See Legal Aspects of Social Responsibility on page 260.
      2) The propriety of superimposing our cultural ethical standards (by refusing to bribe) on another culture is debatable.

D. **General Guides to Ethics**

1. Golden Rule -- Do unto others as you would have others do unto you.
2. Maximize good -- Act to provide the greatest good for the greatest number.
3. Fairness -- Act in ways that are fair or just to all concerned.
4. Maximize long-run outcomes -- Act to provide the best long-range benefits to society and its resources.
5. General respect -- Act to respect the planet all humans share and the rights of others because corporate and individual decisions affect them.

E. **Simplified Criteria for Evaluating Ethical Behavior**

1. Would this behavior be acceptable if people I respect knew I was doing this?
2. What are the consequences of this behavior for myself, other employees, customers, and society?

F. Ethics are individual and personal, influenced by

1. Life experiences (rewards for doing right, punishment for wrong)
2. Friendship groups (professional associations, informal groups)
3. Organizational pressures (responsibilities to superiors and the organization)

CODES OF ETHICAL CONDUCT

A. An organization's code of ethical conduct is the established general value system the organization wishes to apply to its members' activities through
   1. Communicating organizational purposes and beliefs
   2. Establishing uniform ethical guidelines for members
      a. Including guidance on behavior for members in making decisions

B. Laws and written rules cannot cover all situations. However, organizations can benefit from having an established ethical code because it
   1. Effectively communicates acceptable values to all members
      a. Including recruits and subcontractors
   2. Provides a method of policing and disciplining members for violations
      a. Through formal review panels
      b. Through group pressure (informal)
   3. Establishes high standards against which individuals can measure their own performance
   4. Communicates to those outside the organization the value system from which the organization's members must not be asked to deviate

C. A typical code for accounting activities (note similarities to the Standards for the Professional Practice of Internal Auditing, GAAP, GAAS, etc.) holds that a management accountant must have
   1. Independence from conflicts of economic interest
   2. Independence from conflicts of professional interest
      a. Responsibility to present information fairly to stockholders/owners and not intentionally protect management
      b. Responsibility to present all data to all appropriate managers and not play favorites with information or cover up bad news
      c. Responsibility to exercise an ethical presence in the conduct of professional activities
         1) Ensuring organizational compliance with spirit as well as letter of pertinent laws and regulations
         2) Conducting oneself according to the highest moral and legal standards
         3) Reporting to appropriate internal or external authority any illegal or fraudulent organizational act
   3. Integrity in not compromising professional values for the sake of personal goals
   4. Objectivity in presenting information, preparing reports, and making analyses

IMA CODE OF ETHICS

A. The National Association of Accountants (now the Institute of Management Accountants or IMA), through its Management Accounting Practices Committee, issued a code of ethics for management accountants in July 1983. This code reflects the official position of the organization. CMA candidates are urged to study the provisions of the code closely because it is extensively tested. The code is printed on the following pages in its entirety. (Source: Statement on Management Accounting 1C, Objectives: Standards of Ethical Conduct for Management Accountants, *Management Accounting*, June 1983, pp. 69-70). The mnemonic CCIO (competence, confidentiality, integrity, and objectivity) is useful. The final section, Resolution of Ethical Conflict, is especially significant.

STANDARDS OF ETHICAL CONDUCT FOR MANAGEMENT ACCOUNTANTS

Management accountants have an obligation to the organizations they serve, their profession, the public, and themselves to maintain the highest standards of ethical conduct. In recognition of this obligation, the Institute of Management Accountants has promulgated the following standards of ethical conduct for management accountants. Adherence to these standards is integral to achieving the objectives of management accounting. Management accountants shall not commit acts contrary to these standards nor shall they condone the commission of such acts by others within their organizations.

Competence

Management accountants have a responsibility to:

- *Maintain an appropriate level of professional competence by ongoing development of their knowledge and skills.*
- *Perform their professional duties in accordance with relevant laws, regulations, and technical standards.*
- *Prepare complete and clear reports and recommendations after appropriate analyses of relevant and reliable information.*

Confidentiality

Management accountants have a responsibility to:

- *Refrain from disclosing confidential information acquired in the course of their work except when authorized, unless legally obligated to do so.*
- *Inform subordinates as appropriate regarding the confidentiality of information acquired in the course of their work and monitor their activities to assure the maintenance of that confidentiality.*
- *Refrain from using or appearing to use confidential information acquired in the course of their work for unethical or illegal advantage either personally or through third parties.*

Integrity

Management accountants have a responsibility to:

- *Avoid actual or apparent conflicts of interest and advise all appropriate parties of any potential conflict.*
- *Refrain from engaging in any activity that would prejudice their ability to carry out their duties ethically.*
- *Refuse any gift, favor, or hospitality that would influence or would appear to influence their actions.*
- *Refrain from either actively or passively subverting the attainment of the organization's legitimate and ethical objectives.*
- *Recognize and communicate professional limitations or other constraints that would preclude responsible judgment or successful performance of an activity.*
- *Communicate unfavorable as well as favorable information and professional judgments or opinions.*
- *Refrain from engaging in or supporting any activity that would discredit the profession.*

Objectivity

Management accountants have a responsibility to:

- *Communicate information fairly and objectively.*
- *Disclose fully all relevant information that could reasonably be expected to influence an intended user's understanding of the reports, comments, and recommendations presented.*

Resolution of Ethical Conflict

In applying the standards of ethical conduct, management accountants may encounter problems in identifying unethical behavior or in resolving an ethical conflict. When faced with significant ethical issues, management accountants should follow the established policies of the organization bearing on the resolution of such conflict. If these policies do not resolve the ethical conflict, management accountants should consider the following courses of action:

- *Discuss such problems with the immediate superior except when it appears that the superior is involved, in which case the problem should be presented initially to the next higher managerial level. If satisfactory resolution cannot be achieved when the problem is initially presented, submit the issues to the next higher managerial level.*

  If the immediate superior is the chief executive officer, or equivalent, the acceptable reviewing authority may be a group such as the audit committee, executive committee, board of directors, board of trustees, or owners. Contact with levels above the immediate superior should be initiated only with the superior's knowledge, assuming the superior is not involved.
- *Clarify relevant concepts by confidential discussion with an objective advisor to obtain an understanding of possible courses of action.*
- *If the ethical conflict still exists after exhausting all levels of internal review, the management accountant may have no other recourse on significant matters than to resign from the organization and to submit an informative memorandum to an appropriate representative of the organization.*

Except where legally prescribed, communication of such problems to authorities or individuals not employed or engaged by the organization is not considered appropriate.

CONFLICT OF INTEREST

A. Conflict of interest is a conflict between the private and the official responsibilities of a person in a position of trust, sufficient to affect judgment, independence, or objectivity in conducting the affairs of the business.

B. **Examples of Conflict of Interest**

1. Having a substantial financial interest in a supplier, customer, or distributor
2. Using privileged information gained from one's official position to enter transactions for personal gain

C. **Methods for Control**

1. Provide a code of conduct provision applying to conflicts of interest.
2. Require full financial disclosure by managers.
3. Require prior notification of any transaction that may raise conflict of interest.
4. Prohibit financial ties to any supplier, customer, or distributor.
5. Encourage adherence to strong ethical behavior in corporate actions, policies, and public communications.

LEGAL ASPECTS OF SOCIAL RESPONSIBILITY

A. **Foreign Corrupt Practices Act (FCPA) of 1977** regulates payments by U.S. firms operating in other nations.

1. The act is a reaction to publicity over questionable foreign payments.
2. It makes it a criminal offense to make payments to a foreign government or representative thereof to secure or retain business.
3. It prohibits payments of sales commissions to independent agents, if the commissions are knowingly passed to foreign officials.
4. Corporations are required to establish internal accounting controls to assure that all overseas payments are proper.

5. The FCPA applies even if payment is legal in the nation where it is made.
6. The rationale for the FCPA is that the international reputation of the United States is affected by its international business conduct, which should reflect the best of United States' ethics.

B. The SEC mandates that the composition of boards of directors include outside directors.

1. To create diversity and broaden the overview of a company's place in the market and in society

C. Courts are increasingly willing to hold boards of directors and auditors liable for problems.

SOCIAL AUDITS

A. The systematic study and evaluation of an organization's social performance, as distinguished from its economic performance, leads to a **social performance report** for management's use in decision making.

B. The social audit can be difficult to conduct.

1. It requires both qualitative and quantitative data.
2. Generally accepted standards are hard to establish.

C. The social audit is also hard to evaluate.

1. Social results are usually intangible, at least with present techniques for measurement.
2. Results are often arguable, and individual value judgments are often the basis for evaluation of results as good or bad.

D. The benefits can outweigh the difficulties because a social audit of an organization

1. Allows evaluation
   a. Of social programs against organizational objectives
   b. Of competing social programs against each other
2. Encourages greater concern for social responsibility within the organization
3. Compiles information on social commitments for publicity or governmental reports

E. The social audit typically focuses on

1. Community involvement
   a. Activities undertaken to benefit the social, economic, and physical environment of the firm
   b. EXAMPLES: Philanthropy and urban renewal
2. Human resources
   a. Activities that lead to improving the quality of work life for employees
   b. EXAMPLES: Job enrichment, safety programs, and affirmative action
3. Physical resources and environmental contributions
   a. Activities that maintain or improve the quality of the environment
   b. EXAMPLES: Pollution control and aesthetic programs
4. Product or service contribution
   a. Activities that go beyond the strict letter of the law in providing a service or product, fairly advertising it, and backing up the warranty
   b. EXAMPLES: Consumer arbitration, consumer hot lines, and prompt attention to consumer complaints

F. One type of social audit, an environmental audit, is becoming more common, particularly among companies in Europe.

REPORT OF THE NATIONAL COMMISSION ON FRAUDULENT FINANCIAL REPORTING

The Treadway Commission (named after its chairman) was sponsored by the American Accounting Association, the American Institute of CPAs, the Financial Executives Institute, The Institute of Internal Auditors, and the National Association of Accountants. The commission was established in 1985 and gave its final report in 1987 regarding allegations of widespread financial reporting fraud by public companies.

A. The objectives were to
   1. Consider the causes and effects of fraudulent financial reporting and how to prevent and detect it
   2. Examine the roles of both the internal auditor and the independent auditor in preventing and detecting fraudulent financial reporting
   3. Identify those attributes of corporate structure that may contribute to fraudulent reporting or to failure in detection

B. As a result of research, public hearings, etc., the commission drafted a report containing recommendations regarding
   1. Public companies
   2. Independent public accountants
   3. The SEC and other regulatory bodies
      a. Improvement in the regulatory and legal environment
   4. Education

C. **Recommendations for the Public Company**
   1. The tone at the top
      a. Management should perform an ongoing fraud-risk assessment.
      b. All public companies should maintain internal controls that provide reasonable assurance of the prevention or early detection of fraudulent financial reporting.
      c. All public companies should establish effective written codes of conduct including guidelines on
         1) Conflicts of interest
         2) Compliance with domestic and foreign laws
         3) Confidentiality of proprietary information
      d. All public companies should maintain accounting functions that are designed to meet their financial reporting obligations.
      e. The SEC should require that management acknowledge in the annual report to shareholders its responsibility for the financial statements and internal controls.
   2. The internal audit function
      a. The director of internal auditing should have unrestricted and direct access to both the audit committee and the CEO.
      b. Internal auditors should coordinate their work with the independent public accountants.

3. The audit committee

   a. The board of directors of every public company should develop and approve a written charter describing the audit committee's duties and responsibilities.

   b. Audit committees should review the independence of the independent public accountant.

   c. The SEC should require that the annual report to stockholders include a letter from the audit committee chair describing the committee's responsibilities and activities during the year.

   d. Audit committees should monitor compliance with codes of conduct.

   e. Audit committees should have necessary resources available.

   f. The audit committee should oversee the quarterly reporting process.

   g. Audit committees should monitor instances in which management seeks second opinions on significant accounting issues.

4. Standards for internal control

   a. The Treadway Commission recommends that its sponsoring organizations set up an interdisciplinary body to integrate internal control concepts and develop a common reference point.

   b. Currently, varying interpretations and philosophies on internal control exist, which cause managements, independent public accountants, and internal auditors to disagree sometimes about the adequacy of internal controls.

D. **Recommendations for the Independent Public Accountant**

1. The Auditing Standards Board of the AICPA should clarify the independent public accountant's responsibility for fraud detection.

2. To enhance their ability to detect fraud, CPAs should be required to use analytical procedures in all audit engagements.

3. Existing quality assurance procedures should be improved to recognize the risk inherent in audits of new clients.

4. Guidance as to qualifications of concurring, or second, partners and timing of their reviews should be enhanced.

5. Independent public accounting firms should recognize and control the pressures that might reduce audit quality.

6. The auditor's standard report should be revised to clarify the auditor's responsibility for fraud detection.

7. The auditor's standard report should be revised to explain the extent of the auditor's review and evaluation of the system of internal accounting control. (NOTE: The auditor's standard report does not contain such language.)

8. The AICPA should reorganize the Auditing Standards Board to provide full-time members.

E. **Recommendations to the SEC and Others**

1. SEC resources should be increased to enhance its enforcement activities and its oversight of the financial reporting system.
2. The SEC should seek to expand its enforcement remedies (including increased criminal prosecution) to provide more severe penalties and more effective tailoring of penalties to individual cases.
3. When a public company changes independent public accountants, the SEC should require public disclosure of the nature of any material accounting or auditing issues discussed with its old or new auditors during the 3-year period preceding the change.
4. The SEC should require independent public accounting firms that audit public companies to be members of professional organizations that have peer review and independent oversight functions.
5. Federal agencies responsible for public companies not reporting to the SEC should be encouraged to implement the commission's SEC recommendations.
6. The exchange of information between financial institution regulatory agencies and independent public accountants should be improved.
7. State boards of accountancy should be encouraged to establish programs for monitoring the quality of services provided by accountants they license.
8. The SEC should reconsider, for independent directors, its position that corporate indemnification of directors for liabilities arising under the Securities Act of 1933 is against public policy and thus unenforceable.
9. The implications of the perceived liability crisis on long-term audit quality should be assessed by parties charged with responding to various tort reform initiatives.

F. **Education**

1. Educators should foster knowledge and understanding of the factors that may cause fraudulent financial reporting and the strategies that can lead to reduction in its incidence.
2. The business and accounting curricula should promote a better understanding of the function and the importance of internal controls, including the control environment.
3. Business and accounting students should be well-informed about the regulation and enforcement activities by which government and private bodies safeguard the financial reporting system and thereby protect the public interest.
4. The business and accounting curricula should help students develop stronger analytical, problem-solving, and judgment skills.
5. Business schools should encourage business and accounting faculty to develop their own personal competence as well as classroom materials for conveying information, skills, and ethical values that can help prevent, detect, and deter fraudulent financial reporting.
6. Professional certification examinations should be revised to test for an understanding of the complexities involved in fraudulent financial reporting.
7. Continuing professional education programs should incorporate the issues involved with fraudulent financial reporting.

CHAPTER SIX
EXAM PART 2
FINANCIAL ACCOUNTING AND REPORTING

This chapter covers Part 2, Financial Accounting and Reporting. It consists of eight study units numbered 11 through 18.

Study Unit 11: Financial Accounting: Development of Theory and Practice
Study Unit 12: Financial Statement Presentation
Study Unit 13: Special Financial Reporting Problems
Study Unit 14: SEC Reporting Requirements
Study Unit 15: Ratio and Accounts Analysis
Study Unit 16: Internal Control
Study Unit 17: External Auditing
Study Unit 18: Income Taxes

The ICMA Content Description of Part 2 follows:

A. ***Financial Statements (30% - 40%)***
Objectives of external financial reporting; types, purposes, and timing of principal financial statements; external users of financial statements and their needs; conceptual framework of financial accounting; generally accepted accounting principles governing the recognition and valuation of assets, liabilities, owners' equity, revenue, and expense; limitations of financial statement information.

B. ***Reporting Requirements (30% - 40%)***
Public reporting standards regulating financial reporting; disclosure requirements in financial statements; the annual report; accounting for corporate income taxes; accounting standard setting organizations and the processes by which standards are set; the SEC and its reporting requirements.

C. ***Analysis of Accounts and Statements (15% - 20%)***
Interpretation and analysis of financial statements including activity ratio analysis and comparative analysis; analysis of accounts including aging accounts receivable and uncollectible accounts, inventory valuation and control, and analysis and valuation of fixed and intangible assets, depreciation, and depletion.

D. ***External Auditing (10% - 15%)***
External audit services; auditor and management responsibilities; professional standards of the external auditor; evidence and procedures used by external auditors; audit reports.

With the 1990 revision of the CMA exam (effective as of the December 1990 exam), the ICMA published a content specification outline for Part 2 that expanded the above content description for Part 2.

A. ***Financial Statements (30% - 40%)***

1. *Objectives of external financial reporting*
2. *Types of principal financial statements and their purposes*
    a. *Statement of Financial Position (Balance Sheet)*
    b. *Statement of Earnings (Income Statement)*
    c. *Statement of Cash Flow*
3. *Timing of financial statements*
    a. *Annual financial statements*
    b. *Interim financial statements*
4. *External users of financial statements and their needs*
    a. *Users of financial statements*
    b. *Needs of external users*
5. *Conceptual framework underlying financial accounting*
    a. *Basic objectives*
    b. *Qualitative characteristics of accounting information*
    c. *Elements of financial statements*
    d. *Recognition and measurement concepts*
6. *Generally accepted accounting principles governing recognition and valuation*
    a. *Asset recognition and valuation*
    b. *Liability recognition and valuation*
    c. *Owners' equity recognition and valuation*
    d. *Revenue recognition and valuation*
    e. *Expense recognition and valuation*
7. *Limitations of financial statement information*
    a. *Historical cost*
    b. *Entity segmentation*

B. **Reporting Requirements (30% - 40%)**

1. *Public reporting standards regulating financial reporting*

   a. *Pronouncements issued by the Financial Accounting Standards Board (FASB)*
   b. *Opinions of the Accounting Principles Board (APB)*
   c. *Pronouncements issued by the Government Accounting Standards Board (GASB)*
   d. *Accounting Research Bulletins of the Committee on Accounting Procedure (CAP)*
   e. *Reporting issues for multinational companies*
   f. *Major task forces influencing financial reporting*

2. *Disclosure requirements in financial statements*

   a. *Disclosures which can be made either in the body of the statements or in the notes*
   b. *Note disclosure*

3. *The annual report*

   a. *Financial statements and notes to the financial statements*
   b. *Management's responsibilities for financial statements*
   c. *Independent auditor's report*
   d. *Other areas included in the annual report*

4. *Accounting for corporate income taxes*

   a. *Differences between book and tax income arising from differences between tax regulations and GAAP*
   b. *Deferred income taxes*
   c. *Accounting for net operating losses*
   d. *Tax rate considerations*
   e. *Other special issues regarding deferred income taxes*

5. *Development of accounting standards*

   a. *User groups which influence accounting standards*
   b. *Organizational structure for setting accounting standards*
   c. *Influence of the SEC on standard setting*
   d. *Due process of developing standards by the FASB*

6. *The SEC and its reporting requirements*

   a. *Acts establishing SEC and its powers*
   b. *SEC accounting standards and policies*
   c. *Disclosure requirements*
   d. *Reporting requirements*

C. **Analysis of Accounts and Statements (15% - 20%)**

1. *Interpretation and analysis of financial statements*

   a. *Ratio analysis*
   b. *Comparative analysis*
   c. *Percentage (common-size) analysis*

2. *Interpretation and analysis of accounts*

   a. *Accounts receivable aging and uncollectible accounts*
   b. *Inventory valuation and control*
   c. *Analysis of fixed assets*
   d. *Intangible assets*

D. ***External Auditing (10% - 15%)***

1. *Types of services offered by external auditors relating to financial reporting*

   a. *Audit of financial statements*
   b. *Review of financial statements*
   c. *Compilation of financial statements*

2. *Definition of auditor and management responsibilities*

   a. *Responsibilities and functions of external auditors*
   b. *Relationship between external auditors and management through the audit committee*
   c. *Relationship between external auditors and internal auditors*
   d. *Engagement letter*
   e. *Representation letter*
   f. *Management letter*

3. *Professional standards of external auditor*

   a. *Generally Accepted Auditing Standards*
   b. *Public accounting code of ethics*
   c. *Statements on Auditing Standards*

4. *Evidence required by the external auditor*

   a. *Competency of audit evidence*
   b. *Sufficiency of audit evidence*
   c. *Evaluation of evidence*
   d. *Types of evidence*

5. *Procedures of the external auditor*

   a. *Factors affecting procedures*
   b. *Types of audit procedures*

6. *Audit reports*

   a. *Standard audit report*
   b. *Modifications of the standard audit report*
   c. *Special reports requiring maximum levels of assurance*
   d. *Special reports requiring limited levels of assurance*
   e. *Special reports requiring minimum levels of assurance*

The topics and subject areas above may include ethical considerations in financial accounting and reporting of concern to management accountants.

Statement on Management Accounting No. 1C, Standards of Ethical Conduct for Management Accountants

-- Competence
-- Confidentiality
-- Integrity
-- Objectivity

Fraudulent reporting
External auditor's responsibility for detecting fraud

The ICMA lists four topics (A-D above) in Part 2, and we have eight study units. We cover ICMA's topics A and B with four study units (11-14) and topic D with two study units (16 and 17). We have added an income tax study unit (18). Our Study Unit 15, Ratio and Accounts Analysis, corresponds with ICMA topic C, Analysis of Accounts and Statements.

Ethics will be covered on at least two parts of the examination and will have between 30 and 60 total minutes of coverage (out of the 16 hours of testing), i.e., 3% to 6% of the total exam.

STUDY UNIT 11
FINANCIAL ACCOUNTING: DEVELOPMENT OF THEORY AND PRACTICE

In Part 2, the ICMA specifies 60% to 80% coverage of financial statements and reporting.

Financial Statements	30%–40%
Reporting Requirements	30%–40%

We further differentiate this material by dividing it into four study units.

Study Unit 11: Financial Accounting: Development of Theory and Practice (FAD)
Study Unit 12: Financial Statement Presentation (FS)
Study Unit 13: Special Financial Reporting Problems (SPE)
Study Unit 14: SEC Reporting Requirements (SEC)

INTRODUCTION

Financial accounting concerns reporting the results of operations (income statement) and financial position (balance sheet). The other two primary financial statements are the statement of cash flows and the statement of retained earnings. A separate statement of changes in stockholders' equity may also be presented if these changes are not disclosed in the other statements or in the footnotes. Although financial statements can be prepared for any entity, this study unit concerns the body of knowledge regarding financial statement preparation for business enterprises and the underlying accounting theory. Study Units 12 and 13 cover the procedural aspects of financial reporting. Study Unit 14 concerns disclosures to the SEC.

Business enterprises operate in a market system. They purchase the factors of production in their respective markets and sell their finished goods, services, etc. (which may be factors of production for another business). The objective is to be as efficient as possible in order to maximize profit. Financial accounting systems measure efficiency in terms of net income. In the diagram on the next page, sales dollars and payments for the factors of production (including interest and dividends for financial capital) flow from right to left. The goods and services flow from left to right.

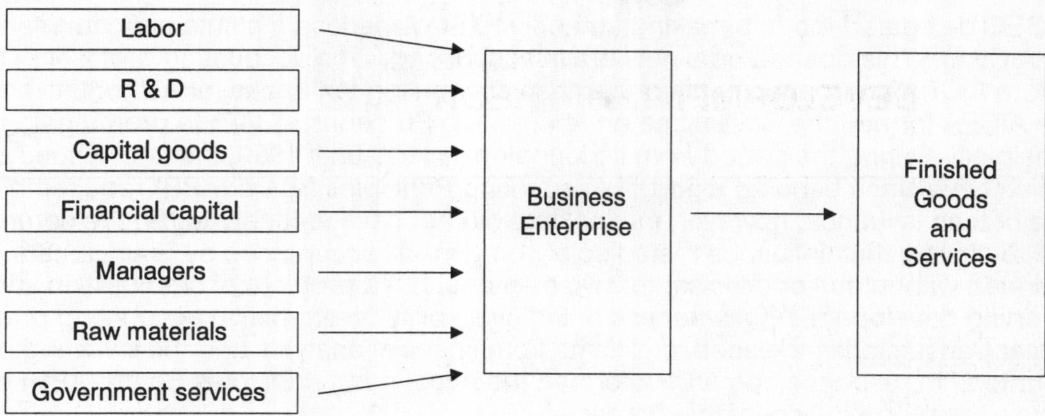

Businesses that are more efficient, i.e., have higher income and prospects thereof, have access to more capital (and at a lower cost) from creditors and investors than companies with lower incomes. Accordingly, accounting methodology measures the efficiency of business enterprises, which, in turn, is a means of allocating financial capital in the market system. Because each business enterprise operates its own accounting system, it is capable of manipulating the results, e.g., of overstating income for reports to investors and creditors and understating income for tax purposes. As a result, the accounting profession has emerged to provide an independent attest function. CPAs attest to the fairness of the presentation of financial statements under generally accepted accounting principles (GAAP).

GAAP include those procedures, practices, etc., that the Financial Accounting Standards Board (FASB) and its predecessors, the Accounting Principles Board and the Committee on Accounting Procedure (two now-defunct AICPA committees), have deemed preferable in their official pronouncements. They also include statements and interpretations of the Governmental Accounting Standards Board (GASB). In the absence of officially established accounting principles, GAAP are deemed to include such sources of established principles as FASB and GASB Technical Bulletins, AICPA Audit and Accounting Guides, and practices widely recognized and prevalent in industry. If no sources of established principles exist, other accounting literature (e.g., Statements of Financial Accounting Concepts) may furnish guidance.

THE ACCOUNTING PROFESSION

A. During the early 1900s, there was little need for accounting rule making in the United States because little, if any, reporting of financial condition was required. Borrowing was based on personal character or collateral rather than financial statements, and relatively few people invested in the stock market.

B. In 1917, the American Institute of Accountants and the Federal Reserve Board issued a publication on financial statements that provided a better basis for lending money as well as some uniformity in reporting. World War I was followed by the booming 20s. Industrial capacity was not sufficient to satisfy the sudden increase in demand and companies went to the marketplace for equity capital. The Great Depression wiped out many of these equity investments. The combination of the Depression and the publicity surrounding several large stock fraud schemes (especially that of Ivar Kreuger) led to Congressional passage of the securities acts of 1933 and 1934 that delegated the right of accounting rule making for publicly held companies to the Securities and Exchange Commission (SEC) and required most publicly held companies to be audited by independent CPAs.

C. The SEC delegated the rule-making authority to the American Institute of Accountants (later the AICPA). This opened up a new era in accounting. The accounting profession began to look to AICPA pronouncements rather than accounting textbooks for authoritative support. The AICPA formed the Committee on Accounting Procedure (CAP) to promulgate accounting principles. During the period from its founding in 1939 until 1959, the CAP issued 51 bulletins (which have since become a part of Accounting Principles Board (APB) requirements). At the time of their issuance, however, the Institute did not have authority to require compliance with CAP bulletins; their influence rested solely on general acceptance by practitioners. The CAP operated without major criticism for two decades, but a problem of credibility in financial reporting developed. As awareness of the availability of alternative accounting practices for similar transactions increased, criticisms from financial analysts and the investing public mounted. In response, the AICPA formed the Accounting Principles Board (APB) in 1959 to narrow the range of acceptable practice.

D. The APB was composed of 18 to 21 members who were appointed for 3-year terms by the president of the AICPA, with the approval of the board of directors. The APB was composed of members of the AICPA who were, for the most part, practicing public accountants. The APB issued 31 opinions during its 15-year life.

E. Unfortunately, when the APB was formed, the extent of the problem was underestimated. A part-time voluntary board of CPAs, primarily from public practice, was inadequate to address the increasing number of financial reporting issues demanding attention. In 1971, the president of the AICPA appointed the Wheat Committee to examine the situation and propose a more effective method of establishing accounting principles. A little over a year later, the Wheat Report was adopted. The APB was terminated, and the Financial Accounting Standards Board (FASB) was established.

F. The FASB has seven salaried members, all having extensive experience in financial accounting, with four required to be CPAs. Each member severs all other business affiliations during his/her term. Two related organizations assist the FASB. The first is a foundation to select the board members, appoint an advisory council, raise supporting funds, and review the whole plan and operation periodically. The second group is an advisory council to help the Board maintain contact with the realities of the business world.

G. Following its formation, the FASB outlined its operating procedures. A majority of the Board decides on its agenda. They determine which subjects require attention and the order of their importance. A separate task force is appointed to consider each subject on the agenda. It is the duty of the task force to see that the entire problem is discussed (in a discussion memorandum) rather than to select from among the possible solutions.

H. Public hearings are held on each issue. A 60-day notice of the hearings is given so that anyone wishing to prepare presentations will have sufficient time. A written position or outline must be submitted to the Board by those who wish to participate in the hearing.

I. All proposed statements of the Board must be exposed to the public (by means of an exposure draft) for 60 days before being made official. Official pronouncements require five or more affirmative votes from the seven-member Board. All dissenting opinions of board members must be published along with the statement. Each pronouncement includes the opinion of the Board, background on the research results and the various solutions considered, the effective data, and the date of implementation.

J. FASB procedures may be summarized as follows:

1. A project is placed on the Board's agenda.
2. A task force of experts defines specific problems.
3. The FASB conducts research.
4. A discussion memorandum is drafted and released.
5. A public hearing is held (at least 60 days after the discussion memorandum is released).
6. Public response is evaluated by the Board.
7. The Board deliberates on various issues and prepares an exposure draft of a proposed Statement of Financial Accounting Standards.
8. The exposure draft is released.
9. There is at least a 60-day waiting period for public comment.
10. All letters and comments are evaluated by the Board.
11. The Board revises the draft if necessary.
12. The Board gives final consideration to the draft.
13. The Board votes on the issuance of the statement.

K. Subsequently, the Board may issue formal interpretations of its own statements. Like the original pronouncement, interpretations require at least five affirmative votes. Unlike the AICPA's accounting interpretations, FASB interpretations are developed and voted upon by the Board itself and have the same status as Statements of Financial Accounting Standards. Accounting Research Bulletins (ARBs) issued by the CAP and APB Opinions continue to be authoritative until they are amended or superseded by FASB pronouncements.

THE SEC

A. As mentioned earlier, the SEC was granted the authority to establish accounting practices and procedures by the securities acts of 1933 and 1934. The SEC originally delegated this authority to the accounting profession. With the creation of the FASB, the SEC issued Accounting Series Release No. 150, which acknowledged that the SEC would continue to look to the private sector (through the FASB) for leadership in establishing and improving accounting principles. However, the release also stated that the SEC would identify areas for which additional information is needed and would determine the appropriate methods of disclosure to meet those needs. Study Unit 14 of this book deals specifically with the SEC's disclosure requirements.

EMERGING ISSUES TASK FORCE

A. In 1984, the FASB created the Emerging Issues Task Force (EITF) to develop principles of accounting for new or unusual accounting issues. The EITF is composed of 17 members, one of whom is a representative from the FASB. In order to reach a consensus, at least 15 of the 17 members must agree on how to account for new types of transactions. The purpose of the EITF is to resolve new accounting issues quickly. Essentially, the EITF identifies controversial accounting issues as they arise and comes up with a generally accepted solution more quickly than the FASB could act. Items on which the EITF cannot reach a consensus may later be addressed by the FASB. Basically, the EITF works on short-term issues, leaving the FASB more time to concentrate on long-term issues.

ACCOUNTING STANDARDS EXECUTIVE COMMITTEE (AcSEC)

A. Following the demise of the Accounting Principles Board, the AICPA created a new standing committee to address accounting standard issues. This committee, known as AcSEC, is a 15-member committee that issues pronouncements on accounting standards that have not been addressed by the FASB. These pronouncements are called Statements of Position (SOP) and usually are rather narrow in scope. Some SOPs are so narrow that they cover accounting problems in a single industry. SOPs are developed in a manner similar to an FASB pronouncement. A task force puts together an exposure draft, which is issued by the full AcSEC. Accountants and others respond to various aspects of the exposure draft. Following analysis of responses, the exposure draft will be either abandoned or issued as a formal SOP in its original form or in a revised form.

INTERNATIONAL ACCOUNTING STANDARDS COMMITTEE (IASC)

A. The IASC was established to harmonize accounting standards used by member countries. Currently, 13 nations are voting members, and 31 standards have been issued. However, IASC pronouncements are not binding.

COST ACCOUNTING STANDARDS BOARD

A. Probably the least known organization promulgating accounting principles is the Cost Accounting Standards Board (CASB). The CASB was created by Congress in 1970 with the objective of establishing cost accounting principles for federal defense contractors and subcontractors. The creation of the CASB was a response to complaints about inconsistent accounting practices of companies that had cost-plus contracts with the government. Many state governments also require adherence to CASB standards in cost-plus contract situations.

B. The standards established by the CASB are not necessarily acceptable for financial statement reporting purposes. They are required only for price-setting.

C. Once the CASB standards are approved, they are published twice in the *Federal Register*. The standards become law 60 days after the second publication if Congress does not enact a contrary resolution.

D. The original CASB had five members, including the Comptroller General of the United States. Although the CASB was only a part-time board, it had a large staff of full-time employees. With its objectives significantly accomplished, the CASB was abolished by a sunset review in 1980. Many standards that were promulgated by the original CASB are still law and must be followed by government contractors.

   1. In 1988, Congress reestablished the CASB as an independent body in the Office of Federal Procurement Policy. It has "exclusive authority to make, promulgate, amend, and rescind cost accounting standards and interpretations thereof" for negotiated contracts and subcontracts over $500,000.

   2. CASB standards are incorporated into Federal Acquisition Regulations (FARs).

GOVERNMENTAL ACCOUNTING STANDARDS BOARD

A. The Governmental Accounting Standards Board (GASB), the newest authoritative body for setting accounting standards, establishes standards for state and local governmental entities. It consists of five members and issues statements and interpretations. GASB pronouncements have the status of GAAP. As of December 1995, the GASB has issued 29 statements.

1. Until changed by a GASB pronouncement, all currently effective statements from the National Council on Governmental Accounting and the AICPA remain in force.
2. The GASB uses Technical Bulletins to clarify, explain, or elaborate an underlying statement or interpretation. Technical Bulletins apply to issues that are too specific to be addressed by a statement.

OTHER GROUPS

A. Other groups that have some influence on the development of accounting principles include the American Accounting Association (AAA), Institute of Management Accountants (IMA, formerly the National Association of Accountants or NAA), Financial Executives Institute (FEI), Congress, and the Internal Revenue Service (IRS).

1. The AAA affects the development of accounting theory through the influence of its members on future accountants. Many of the AAA's members are accounting professors who shape future principles by their current teaching activity. The AAA has had a pronounced effect on accounting principles, but many years may elapse before those effects become obvious.
2. The IMA and FEI affect the development of accounting principles through publication of monthly magazines and various research studies.
3. The U.S. Congress has affected accounting principles through the Internal Revenue Code. For example, many firms adopted LIFO inventory valuation for financial reporting purposes when it became acceptable for tax purposes (but only if the same method was used for financial reporting).
   a. The IRS also has the power to influence accounting principles by adopting regulations affecting various practices for tax reporting purposes.

AUTHORITATIVE PRONOUNCEMENTS

A. Generally accepted accounting principles (GAAP) have a variety of sources. The following is the GAAP hierarchy for nongovernmental entities:

1. Established accounting principles
   a. Officially established accounting principles consisting of FASB Statements and Interpretations, APB Opinions, and AICPA Accounting Research Bulletins
   b. FASB Technical Bulletins and, if cleared by the FASB, AICPA Industry Audit and Accounting Guides and AICPA Statements of Position
   c. Consensus positions of the FASB Emerging Issues Task Force and AICPA Practice Bulletins
   d. AICPA accounting interpretations, "Qs and As" (Questions and Answers) published by the FASB staff, as well as industry practices widely recognized and prevalent
2. Other accounting literature
   a. FASB Concepts Statements; APB Statements; AICPA Issue Papers; International Accounting Standards Committee Statements; GASB Statements, Interpretations, etc.; textbooks, handbooks, articles, etc.

THE ACCRUAL METHOD OF ACCOUNTING

A. While the timing of changes in the legal rights and obligations represented by assets and liabilities is relatively straightforward, the recognition points of revenues and expenses are not so easily determined.

   1. Legally, changes in asset and liability ownership are usually considered to be instantaneous (the legal approach is followed for recording assets and liabilities).

   2. However, the earning of revenue is usually the culmination of a long process. Each of the following steps may be undertaken to earn revenue:

      a. Business is formed, incorporated, etc.
      b. Products or services are designed.
      c. Employees are hired.
      d. Physical facilities and assets are acquired.
      e. Raw materials are purchased.
      f. Production is undertaken.
      g. Product is sold.
      h. Cash and receivables are collected.
      i. Warranty protection is provided.

B. Under cash-basis accounting, income is recognized when cash is received.

   1. Expenses are recognized when paid.

   2. Cash-basis accounting is subject to manipulation by arranging payments or receipts before or after year-end.

   3. The cash basis cannot properly reflect multiperiod transactions in which cash expenditures or receipts relate to several financial reporting periods.

C. To overcome the problems of cash-basis accounting, accrual-basis accounting is used.

   1. Revenue is recognized at the point of sale (title transfer) or upon performance of service.

      a. Exceptions

         1) Revenue is recognized at the time of production when the goods are immediately marketable and have a guaranteed selling price, e.g., precious metals and agricultural products.

         2) Revenue is recognized at production stages when there is no way to allocate costs, such as in the meat packing business.

            a) Meat is valued at its net realizable value (selling price minus selling costs).

         3) Revenue is recognized at the point of collection when collection of receivables is in serious doubt, e.g., by use of the installment method.

   2. Expense is recognized when there is a consumption of benefit. There are three pervasive expense-recognition principles.

      a. SFAC 6 defines **matching** as "simultaneous or combined recognition of the revenues and expenses that result directly and jointly from the same transactions or events."

      b. Immediate recognition is appropriate for some expenses, such as advertising, that cannot feasibly be directly or indirectly associated with particular revenues.

      c. Systematic and rational allocation to future periods expected to be benefited is the applicable principle if the costs and revenues are indirectly related.

         1) Depreciation is an example.

3. Most accounting transactions are recorded when cash is received or paid (or a specific commitment to pay or receive cash is made or received).
   a. As a result, **adjusting entries** are made at year-end to assure that there has been proper revenue and expense recognition during the year.
      1) Reversing entries are then made at the beginning of the next period.
   b. When revenue has been earned or expense incurred but the cash has not been received or paid, the revenue or expense must be accrued.
      1) **Accruals of revenue** are made when revenue has been earned but not received.

Receivable	$XXX	
Revenue		$XXX

      2) **Accruals of expense** are recorded when expense has been incurred but not paid.

Expense	$XXX	
Payable		$XXX

      3) Accrual entries are usually reversed at the beginning of the next period.
   c. When cash has been received or paid but the revenue has not been earned or the expense incurred, the revenue or expense must be deferred.
      1) Deferrals of expense occur when expenses have been prepaid.

Prepaid expense	$XXX	
Expense		$XXX

         a) The above year-end entry assumes that the expense account was debited when the cash was paid.
         b) If the asset account (prepaid expense) was debited, the following adjusting entry is appropriate:

Expense	$XXX	
Prepaid expense		$XXX

      2) Deferrals of revenue occur when revenue has been received in advance. The adjusting entry is

Revenue	$XXX	
Unearned revenue		$XXX

         a) The above year-end entry assumes that the revenue account was credited when the cash was received.
         b) If the liability account (unearned revenue) was credited, the following adjusting entry is appropriate:

Unearned revenue	$XXX	
Revenue		$XXX

CONCEPTUAL FRAMEWORK OF ACCOUNTING

A. As part of its project to develop a conceptual framework for accounting, the Financial Accounting Standards Board (FASB) has issued a series of Statements on Financial Accounting Concepts (SFACs). The first six are

1. *Objectives of Financial Reporting by Business Enterprises*
2. *Qualitative Characteristics of Accounting Information*
3. SFAC 3 has been superseded by SFAC 6.
4. *Objectives of Financial Reporting by Nonbusiness Organizations*
5. *Recognition and Measurement in Financial Statements of Business Enterprises*
6. *Elements of Financial Statements*

B. The objectives (SFAC 1) are concerned with the underlying goals and purposes of accounting.

1. Information provided should be useful to those making investment and credit decisions, assuming that those individuals have a reasonable understanding of business and economic activities.
2. Information provided should be helpful to present and potential investors, creditors, and other users in assessing the amount, timing, and uncertainty of future cash flows.
3. Information should be provided about economic resources, claims to those resources, and the changes therein.
4. SFAC 1 also states the following:
   a. Financial reporting objectives are determined by the legal, political, economic, and social environment.
   b. Financial accounting information relates to companies rather than industries or the overall economy.
   c. Information often is based upon approximations, not exact measures.
   d. Financial reports are based on historical transactions.
   e. Financial accounting reports are only one source of information about a business enterprise.
   f. Financial reports are provided and used at a cost.
   g. External users lack the authority to prescribe information they want.
   h. The objectives of general purpose financial statements are broad, rather than narrow, and directed to the common interests of many users (including investment advisors).
   i. The primary focus is on earnings and its components.
   j. A financial accounting report does not report the value of a business enterprise but may be useful in determining the value.
   k. Management knows more about the enterprise than any external party and can increase the usefulness of information by providing explanations of various relevant events.
   l. Information based on accrual accounting generally provides a better indication of an entity's present and future cash flows than information based solely on cash transactions.

C. In SFAC 2, the FASB has identified the fundamental qualitative characteristics of accounting information. These qualities apply to both business enterprises and not-for-profit organizations. The purpose is to allow preparers of accounting information to distinguish useful from less useful information. The first two characteristics are decision-specific. The next two are interactive qualities. Additionally, SFAC 2 states user-specific qualities such as relevance to individuals.

1. **Relevance**. Information must be capable of making a difference in a decision.
   a. **Predictive value** enables users to predict the outcome of future events.
   b. **Feedback value** permits users to confirm or correct their prior expectations.
   c. **Timeliness.** Information must be made available to decision makers while that information still has the capacity to influence decisions.
2. **Reliability**. Information is reliable if users can depend upon that information to represent economic events or conditions accurately. Reliability entails freedom from error and bias.
   a. **Verifiability**. The information can be verified by independent measurers using the same methods.
   b. **Neutrality**. Reliable information must be unbiased; it cannot favor one statement user over another.
   c. **Representational faithfulness**. The financial statements and the events they are supposed to represent are in agreement.
3. **Comparability**. Financial statements must be comparable with those of other entities.
4. **Consistency**. A firm must be consistent in its selection of accounting methods from one period to the next.
5. **Constraints**
   a. **Cost-benefit constraint**. The usefulness of accounting information has to be weighed against the cost of providing that information.
   b. **Materiality constraint**. There is a certain threshold for recognition at which inaccuracies are unimportant because they are immaterial to the decisions made by financial statement users.

D. SFAC 4 establishes the objectives of general purpose financial reporting by nonbusiness organizations.

1. It is not necessary to develop an independent conceptual framework for any particular category of entities.
2. A final decision on whether these objectives apply to state and local governmental units has been deferred.
3. The FASB believes that the objectives of general purpose external financial reporting for government-sponsored hospitals, universities, utilities, etc., engaged in activities not unique to government should be similar to those of business enterprises or other nonbusiness entities engaged in similar activities.

4. Nonbusiness entities are distinguished by receipts of significant resources from those who do not expect economic benefits in return, by nonprofit operation, and by the absence of defined ownership interests. The results are transactions that are infrequent in businesses, such as contributions, and an absence of dealing with owners.

5. Borderline cases may exist in which an entity possesses some of the characteristics of a nonbusiness enterprise but not others. Examples include private nonprofit hospitals and schools that receive small amounts of contributions but are essentially dependent on debt issues and user fees. For such enterprises, the objectives of SFAC 1 may be more appropriate.

6. The objectives stem from the needs of those who provide resources to nonbusiness entities, especially external users who cannot prescribe the information they want. Nonbusiness entities often have no single indicator of performance comparable to a business enterprise's net income. Thus, other performance indicators are needed.

7. Information on performance is not subject to the test of market competition; other controls are therefore necessary, such as donor restrictions. Information about departures from such mandates is important to assess management's stewardship.

8. The objectives of financial reporting for nonbusiness entities and business enterprises have certain similarities.
   a. The objectives of financial reporting are affected by the economic, legal, political, and social environment in which financial reporting takes place.
   b. The operating environments of nonbusiness and business enterprises are similar (they both use scarce resources to produce and distribute goods and services).

9. The manner in which resources are obtained is the primary difference between nonbusiness and business enterprises.

10. The objectives are affected by the characteristics and limitations of financial information (see SFAC 1).

11. Financial reporting should provide information useful to present and potential resource providers in making resource allocation decisions.

12. Financial reporting should provide information to assist in assessing the services that a nonbusiness organization provides and its ability to continue providing services.

13. Financial reporting should provide information useful in evaluating how well managers have discharged their stewardship responsibilities.

14. The financial reporting for both business and nonbusiness organizations should provide information about economic resources, liabilities, changes in resources and interests therein, sources and uses of cash, and borrowing activities. In addition, financial reporting should include explanations to help users understand the information provided.

15. Financial reporting should provide performance information. The most useful is periodic measurement of changes in net resources combined with information about service efforts and accomplishments.

E. SFAC 5 concerns recognition and measurement criteria for items to be included in income statements.

1. Financial statements are the primary means of communicating financial information to external parties.
2. Additional information is provided by financial statement notes, supplementary information, and other types of disclosures.
3. Recognition means incorporating transactions into the accounting system so as to report them in the financial statements as assets, liabilities, revenues, expenses, etc.
4. When items meet the criteria for recognition, disclosure by other means is not a substitute for recognition in the financial statements.
   a. The **four fundamental recognition criteria** are
      1) The item meets the definition of an element of financial statements.
      2) The item has an attribute measurable with sufficient reliability.
      3) The information is relevant.
      4) The information is reliable.
   b. Revenue should be recognized when it is **realized or realizable** and **earned**.
      1) Gains ordinarily do not culminate an earning process, so the condition of being realized or realizable is usually sufficient for their recognition.
   c. An expense or loss is recognized if previously recognized future economic benefits have been reduced, or a liability has been incurred or increased, without associated economic benefits.
5. Items reported in financial statements are measured by different attributes. The unit of measurement is money unadjusted for changes in purchasing power over time. According to SFAC 5, the use of different attributes is expected to continue.
   a. **Historical cost** is the amount of cash or its equivalent paid to acquire an asset. Historical cost is the attribute at which assets such as property, plant, and equipment and most inventories are measured and reported.
      1) Liabilities that involve obligations to provide goods or services to customers are usually reported as historical proceeds. **Historical proceeds** is the amount of cash or its equivalent received when the obligation was incurred. It may be adjusted after acquisition for amortization or other allocations.
   b. **Current (replacement) cost** is the attribute used to measure and report some inventories. It is the cash or its equivalent that would have to be paid if the same or an equivalent asset were acquired currently.
   c. **Current market value** is the amount of cash or its equivalent that could be obtained by selling an asset in orderly liquidation. Some investments in marketable securities and certain liabilities for marketable commodities and securities are reported at current market value.
   d. **Net realizable value** is the undiscounted amount of cash or its equivalent into which an asset is expected to be converted in due course of business minus direct cost, if any, necessary to make that conversion. Short-term receivables and some inventories are examples.
      1) **Net settlement value** is the undiscounted amount of cash or its equivalent expected to be paid to liquidate an obligation in the due course of business, including any direct costs necessary to making the payment. Examples are trade payables and warranty obligations.

e. Long-term receivables are measured and reported at the **present or discounted value of future cash inflows** into which they are expected to be converted in the due course of business, minus the present value of cash outflows necessary to obtain those inflows.

   1) The present value of future cash outflows is used to measure long-term payables. This amount is the present value of future cash outflows expected to be required to satisfy the liability in due course of business.

6. A recognized item is shown in both words and numbers with the amount included in statement totals.

7. A full set of financial statements discloses

   a. Financial position (balance sheet)
   b. Earnings
   c. Comprehensive income
   d. Cash flows
   e. Owner transactions

      1) Investments
      2) Distributions

8. Financial statements must be considered collectively, but the parts of a financial statement also help meet the objectives of financial reporting. Indeed, the parts may sometimes be more useful to those who make investment and credit decisions than the whole.

   a. Financial statements help to simplify and make useful great masses of data, but focusing attention almost exclusively on a highly simplified condensation (such as EPS) should be avoided.

9. The **statement of financial position** (balance sheet) provides information concerning assets, liabilities, equity, and their relationships at a moment in time.

   a. This statement does not purport to show value but will enable users to make their own estimates of value.

   b. Estimates of value are a part of financial analysis, not financial reporting, but financial accounting assists financial analysis.

10. Statements of earnings and comprehensive income together show the amount and ways by which equity changed during a period.

   a. **Earnings** are essentially net income with exclusion of certain accounting adjustments, such as the cumulative effect of a change in principle.

   b. **Comprehensive income** is a broad measure of all recognized changes that affect equity, other than transactions with owners.

11. The full set of financial statements is based on the concept of **financial capital maintenance**.

   a. An enterprise receives a return on investment only after its capital has been maintained or recovered.

   b. A return on financial capital occurs if the financial (money) amount of net assets at period-end exceeds the amount at the beginning of the period after excluding owner transactions.

12. A **statement of cash flows** should show, either directly or indirectly, the major sources of cash receipts and major uses of cash during a period.
13. SFAC 5 does not suggest radical changes in present practice. Instead, it endorses current GAAP while allowing for gradual evolutionary change.
14. SFAC 5 led the FASB to require companies to issue statements of cash flows.
    a. The requirement (see SFAS 95) was consistent with what was already becoming common practice.
15. SFAC 5 does not resolve the dilemma concerning the relative importance of current value and historical cost. The Board expects the use of different measurement attributes to continue.

F. SFAC 6 replaced SFAC 3. It concerns the classes of items contained in financial statements. SFAC 6 expands upon the earlier SFAC 3 by encompassing not-for-profit organizations.

1. Ten interrelated elements of financial statements are defined.
    a. **Assets** are probable future economic benefits obtained or controlled by an entity resulting from past transactions or events.
    b. **Liabilities** are probable future sacrifices of economic benefits resulting from present or past transactions or events.
    c. **Equity**, or **net assets**, is the residual interest in assets remaining after deducting liabilities. In a nonbusiness organization, equity is divided into three categories: permanently restricted, temporarily restricted, and unrestricted.
    d. **Investments by owners** are increases in equity resulting from transfers of something valuable to an entity to increase ownership interests.
    e. **Distributions to owners** are decreases in equity resulting from transfers by the entity to owners.
    f. **Comprehensive income** is the change in equity during a period that does not arise from investments by or distributions to owners.
    g. **Revenues** are inflows or other enhancements of assets or settlements of liabilities from activities that constitute the entity's ongoing major operations.
    h. **Expenses** are outflows or other consumption of assets or incurrences of liabilities from activities that constitute the entity's ongoing major operations.
    i. **Gains** are increases in equity from all transactions and events affecting the entity except those increases resulting from revenues from or investments by owners.
    j. **Losses** are decreases in equity from peripheral or incidental transactions of an entity and from all other transactions and other events and circumstances affecting the entity except those decreases resulting from expenses or distributions to owners.

2. SFAC 6 defines three classes (permanently restricted, temporarily restricted, and unrestricted) of net assets of not-for-profit organizations. Each class is composed of revenues, expenses, gains, and losses affecting the class and of reclassifications from or to other classes.
3. SFAC 6 defines or describes various other concepts closely related to the elements and classes.
4. SFAC 6 does not define earnings. That term was defined in SFAC 5 as excluding certain cumulative accounting adjustments and other nonowner changes in equity that are included in comprehensive income.
5. The FASB does not expect this statement to lead to broad upheavals in present practice, but in due time it may lead to evolutionary changes in practice or in the way certain items are viewed.

G. There are several approaches to understanding the theoretical basis for accounting practice. The following discussion concerns assumptions, principles, and constraints.

1. **Assumptions**. These refer to the underlying environment in which the reporting entity operates.
   a. **Entity** assumption. Every business is a separate entity. The affairs of the business are kept separate from the personal affairs of the owners.
   b. **Going concern** assumption (business continuity). Unless stated otherwise, every business is assumed to be a going concern that will continue operating indefinitely. As a result, liquidation values are not important because it is assumed that the company is not going to be liquidated in the near future.
   c. **Unit-of-money** assumption. Accounting records are kept in terms of money. Using money as the unit of measure is the best way of providing economic information to users of financial statements. Also, the changing purchasing power of the monetary unit is assumed not to be significant.
   d. **Periodicity** (time period) assumption. Even though the most accurate way to measure an entity's results of operations is to wait until it liquidates and goes out of business, this method is not followed. Instead, financial statements are prepared periodically throughout the life of a business to ensure the timeliness of information. The periodicity assumption necessitates the use of estimates in the preparation of financial statements.
2. **Principles** are guidelines that the accountant follows when recording financial information.
   a. **Historical cost** principle. Transactions are recorded at cost because that is the most objective determination of value. It is a reliable measure.
   b. **Revenue recognition** principle. Revenue is recognized (recorded) when the earning process is essentially complete. Revenue is recorded when the most important event in the earning of that revenue has occurred.
      1) **Sales basis**. Normally, revenue is recorded when the sale is made because it is the making of the sale (the customer agrees to accept the product and to pay for it) that is usually the most critical event in the earning process.
      2) **Cash basis** (installment sales basis). In some cases, the making of a sale is no guarantee that the seller will be paid. Thus, the most important event in the earning process is the actual receipt of cash. Consequently, no revenue is recorded until the cash is actually received. Medical doctors, for instance, have traditionally used the cash basis of revenue recognition.

3) **Production basis**. Revenue is recognized as goods are produced; e.g., inventory is recorded at net realizable value when goods are fungible and an established market exists. Examples are some agricultural products and rare minerals.

4) **Percentage-of-completion basis**. Sometimes neither the sales basis nor the cash basis is appropriate. For instance, a contractor who is building a bridge over a 3-year period would recognize no revenue over the first 2 years of the contract if either the cash or sales basis were used. Therefore, contractors traditionally use the percentage-of-completion basis under which some revenue is recognized each year over the life of a contract.

c. **Matching** principle. Revenues and expenses should be matched with the periods to which they apply. Expenses should follow the revenues that they are expected to produce. For example, if a cost is not expected to produce any future benefit to a firm, that cost should be written off as an expense. However, if a cost (such as the cost of a large piece of equipment) is expected to result in revenues in the future, that cost should be capitalized and written off against future revenues.

1) According to SFAC 6, however, the term matching is best and most narrowly defined as "simultaneous or combined recognition of the revenues and expenses that result directly and jointly from the same transactions or other events." Thus, it corresponds to the pervasive expense recognition principle of associating cause and effect as defined in APB Statement 4.

d. **Full disclosure** principle. This principle permits financial statement users to assume that anything they need to know about a company is shown in the financial statements. As a result, many footnotes are typically presented with the financial statements to provide information that is not shown on the face of the statements.

3. **Constraints** (doctrines). There are certain constraints on the amount and type of information that is shown in the financial statements. The cost-benefit and materiality constraints were mentioned earlier in the discussion on qualitative characteristics. Two additional doctrines are discussed below.

a. **Conservatism** constraint. The conservatism doctrine originally directed accountants, when faced with two or more acceptable choices, to show the lowest amount for an asset or income. The modern approach to conservatism is to regard it as a "prudent reaction to uncertainty to try to ensure that uncertainties and risks inherent in business situations are adequately considered" (SFAC 2). Such prudence does not condone introducing bias into the financial statements through deliberate understatement of assets and profits. If different estimates are available and are equally likely, conservatism dictates using the less optimistic estimate; if they are not equally likely, conservatism does not necessarily require use of the less optimistic rather than the more likely estimate.

b. **Industry practices** constraint. Occasionally, GAAP are not followed in an industry because adherence to them would generate misleading or unnecessary information. For instance, banks and insurance companies typically value marketable equity securities at market value, regardless of cost. Market value and liquidity are most important to these industries.

STUDY UNIT 12
FINANCIAL STATEMENT PRESENTATION

In Part 2 the ICMA specifies 60% to 80% coverage of financial statements and reporting.

Financial Statements	30%-40%
Reporting Requirements	30%-40%

We further differentiate this material by dividing it into four study units.

Study Unit 11: Financial Accounting: Development of Theory and Practice (FAD)
Study Unit 12: Financial Statement Presentation (FS)
Study Unit 13: Special Financial Reporting Problems (SPE)
Study Unit 14: SEC Reporting Requirements (SEC)

Review the topical coverage in this study unit listed above, and compare it with the topics you will be studying in Study Unit 13 (listed below).

Segmental Disclosures
Accounting Changes
Consignment Sales
Partnership Accounting
Installment Sales
Accounting for Changing Prices
Foreign Currency Issues
Consolidations
Interperiod Tax Allocation

BASIC FINANCIAL STATEMENTS

A. **Income Statement** -- presents revenues earned and expenses incurred over a period of time (the period)

1. Revenue and expense transactions of a business enterprise are held in their respective accounts until the end of the period.
   a. Revenue and expense accounts are temporary holding (nominal) accounts.
      1) The accountant need not close each revenue and expense transaction directly to capital.
   b. Their net effect is income or loss that is closed to the capital accounts in the balance sheet at the end of the period.
2. **Single-step format**. All revenues and gains are aggregated, and the aggregate of all expenses and losses is subtracted from total revenue to obtain net income.

Revenues and gains		
Net sales	$XXX	
Other revenues	XXX	
Gains	XXX	
Total revenues and gains		$ XXX
Expenses and losses		
Cost of goods sold	$XXX	
Selling and administrative expenses	XXX	
Interest expense	XXX	
Losses	XXX	
Income tax expense	XXX	
Total expenses and losses		$(XXX)
Net income		$ XXX

3. **Multiple-step format**. The multiple-step format has operating and nonoperating sections and an intermediary calculation of gross profit (income before operating expenses and nonoperating items). It also classifies expenses by function.

Net sales		$ XXX
Cost of goods sold		(XXX)
Gross profit		$ XXX
Operating expenses		
Selling expenses	$XXX	
Administrative expenses	XXX	(XXX)
Operating profit		$ XXX
Other revenues and gains		XXX
Other expenses and losses		(XXX)
Pretax income from continuing operations		$ XXX
Income taxes		(XXX)
Net income from continuing operations		$ XXX

a. The items below net income from continuing operations (discontinued operations, extraordinary items, and the cumulative effect of a change in accounting principle) are presented in the same way in single- and multiple-step income statements.

1) An intraperiod allocation of income tax expense (or benefit) for the year is made among income from continuing operations, discontinued operations, extraordinary items, and items taken directly to shareholders' equity (SFAS 109).

2) Intraperiod and interperiod tax allocations are discussed in the next study unit.

b. Disclosure of earnings per share (EPS) information is required only for public companies. An entity that makes these disclosures must present per share amounts for income from continuing operations, net income, income before extraordinary items, and cumulative effect of changes in accounting principle. Presentation of EPS data for discontinued operations and gain or loss on disposal of a segment is optional.

1) See the Shareholders' Equity sideheading on page 319.

B. **Balance Sheet** -- a listing of assets and liabilities and shareholders' equity of an enterprise at a certain moment in time

1. Assets minus liabilities equals capital (shareholders' equity).
2. Recognition of assets and liabilities is based on legal ownership and debt rules.
3. There are three general formats for balance sheets.

a. The account form has two columns, with assets in the left and liabilities and capital in the right.

b. The report form has one column, with assets over liabilities and capital.

c. The financial position form subtracts current liabilities from current assets to obtain working capital. Noncurrent assets are added and noncurrent liabilities are subtracted from working capital to obtain **net assets**, which is equal to capital.

Account

Assets	Liabilities & Capital
$XXX	$XXX
XXX	XXX
XXX	XXX
$XXX	$XXX

Report

Assets	$XXX
	XXX
	XXX
	$XXX
Liabilities	XXX
Capital	XXX
	$XXX

Financial Position

Current assets	$XXX
- Current liabilities	XXX
Working cap.	$XXX
+ Other assets	XXX
- Other liabilities	XXX
Net assets	$XXX
Capital	$XXX

4. A classified balance sheet also distinguishes between current and noncurrent assets and liabilities.

a. "**Current assets** are cash and other assets or resources reasonably expected to be realized in cash or sold or consumed during the normal operating cycle of the business" (ARB 43, Ch. 3A).

1) Besides cash, examples of current assets include receivables, trading securities, inventories, and prepaid expenses.

b. "**Current liabilities** are obligations whose liquidation is reasonably expected to require the use of existing resources properly classifiable as current assets or the creation of other current liabilities" (ARB 43, Ch. 3A).

c. Current is defined in terms of the next operating cycle or 1 year, whichever is greater.

   1) An **operating cycle** is the average time between acquisition of raw materials, production of goods for sale, and realization of cash from their sale.

5. The rest of the sideheadings in this study unit contain descriptions of how various assets and liabilities are valued and recognized in the financial statements. The following measurement attributes for assets are used:

   a. The basic rule is to record assets at **historical cost**, which is the cost of assets at the time they were purchased.

      1) Changing price levels or changes in fair value are not reflected.

      2) If cost is not known (e.g., in a barter transaction), the new asset is recorded at the book value of the asset given up.

      3) Prepaid expenses are reported at cost minus the expired or used portion.

   b. **Current (replacement) cost (entry value)** is the cost to replace assets.

      1) It is difficult to determine objectively because of changing technology.

      2) The **lower of cost or market** rule for inventory defines replacement cost as the market price (with some exceptions for floor and ceiling).

   c. **Fair value** is the amount at which an asset can be exchanged in a current transaction between willing parties, other than in a forced or liquidation sale.

      1) This amount is often hard to determine objectively when there are no arm's-length transactions.

      2) Fair value can be objectively applied to trading and available-for-sale securities.

   d. **Price-level adjusted (constant dollar) values** are historical cost data adjusted for changes in the purchasing power of the monetary unit.

      1) Usually, these are only supplemental data that do not appear in the principal financial statements.

   e. **Present (discounted cash flow) values** are based on the present value of future cash flows from assets.

      1) Future cash flows and interest rates must be estimated.
      2) Long-term receivables and payables are reported at present value.

   f. Accounts receivable are reported at **estimated net realizable value**.

C. **Statement of Retained Earnings** -- reconciles the beginning balance of retained earnings with the ending balance

1. Net income is added to the beginning balance and dividends are subtracted.
2. Prior-period adjustments are corrections of errors from prior-period financial statements. They are reported net of applicable taxes.
3. Format of retained earnings statement

Statement of Retained Earnings	
Beginning balance	$ X
± Prior periods' adjustments	X
Adj. beginning balance	$ X
± N.I. (loss)	X
– Dividends	X
Ending balance	$ X

4. Changes in stockholders' equity accounts (in addition to retained earnings) should be reported in a separate statement, in the basic statements, or in footnotes thereto.

D. **Statement of Cash Flows**

1. The growing awareness of the importance of cash flow information is indicated by the following statement in SFAC 5: "A full set of financial statements for a period should show cash flows during the period." Because practice regarding the statement of changes in financial position was characterized by ambiguity in terms and lack of comparability arising from varying statement formats and definitions of funds, SFAS 95 required a statement of cash flows as part of a full set of financial statements. It applies to all business entities (both publicly held and privately held) and to not-for-profit organizations. This statement replaces the statement of changes in financial position.
   a. A cash flow statement must be provided by any business enterprise or not-for-profit organization that reports financial position and results of operations for any period for which results of operations are presented.
2. The primary purpose of a statement of cash flows is to provide information about the cash receipts and payments of an entity during a period. A secondary purpose is to provide information about investing and financing activities.
   a. If used with information in the other financial statements, the statement of cash flows should help users to assess
      1) The entity's ability to generate positive future net cash flows,
      2) The entity's ability to meet its obligations and pay dividends,
      3) The entity's needs for external financing,
      4) The reasons for differences between income and associated cash receipts and payments, and

5) The cash and noncash aspects of the entity's investing and financing activities.

   a) Information about transactions that do not directly affect cash flow for the period must be disclosed, but SFAS 95 does not retain the **all financial resources concept** required by APB 19. SFAS 95 excludes all noncash transactions from the body of the statement of cash flows. The purpose of this exclusion is to avoid undue complexity and detraction from the objective of providing information about cash flows. Instead, information about all noncash financing and investing activities affecting recognized assets and liabilities shall be reported in related disclosures.

3. The changes during the period in cash and in cash equivalents are to be explained in a statement of cash flows.

   a. If an entity invests its cash in excess of immediate needs in short-term, highly liquid investments (cash equivalents), it should use the descriptive term **cash and cash equivalents**. Otherwise, the term **cash** is acceptable. Terms such as funds or quick assets may not be used.

      1) Usually, only investments with original maturities of 3 months or less qualify as cash equivalents. Money market funds, CDs, commercial paper, and treasury bills are examples.

4. A statement of cash flows should report the cash effects of an entity's operations, its investing transactions, and its financing transactions during the period. The effects of investing and financing transactions that do not directly affect cash should also be disclosed.

   a. **Operating activities** include all transactions and other events not classified as investing and financing activities. In general, the cash effects of transactions and other events that enter into that determination of income are to be classified as operating activities.

      1) SFAS 102 classifies the following as operating items: cash flows from certain securities and other assets acquired for resale and carried at market value in a trading account and cash flows from loans acquired for resale and carried at lower of cost or market.

      2) Moreover, SFAS 115 states that cash flows from purchases, sales, and maturities of trading securities are cash flows from operating activities.

   b. **Investing activities** include the lending of money and the collecting of those loans, and the acquisition, sale, or other disposal of securities that are not cash equivalents and of productive assets that are expected to generate revenue over a long period of time.

      1) Cash flows from purchases, sales, and maturities of available-for-sale and held-to-maturity securities are cash flows from investing activities and are reported gross for each class of security (SFAS 115).

   c. **Financing activities** include the issuance of stock, the payment of dividends, the receipt of donor-restricted resources to be used for long-term purposes, treasury stock transactions, the issuance of debt, and the repayment or other settlement of debt obligations.

      1) However, dividend income is a cash flow from an operating activity.

5. In general, cash inflows and outflows should be reported separately at gross amounts in a statement of cash flows. In certain instances, however, the net amount of related cash receipts and payments may provide sufficient information for certain classes of cash flows.
   a. If the turnover of an item is quick, amounts are large, and the maturity is short, or if the entity is essentially holding or disbursing cash for customers, net reporting is proper.
      1) Examples are demand deposits of a bank and customer accounts payable of a broker-dealer.
      2) SFAS 104 permits banks, thrifts, and credit unions to report net cash receipts and payments for deposits, time deposits, and loans.
6. The statement also requires translation of foreign currency cash flows.
   a. A weighted-average exchange rate may be used if the result is substantially the same as would be obtained by using rates in effect when the flows occurred.
   b. The effect of exchange rate fluctuations must be separately reported as part of the reconciliation of cash and cash equivalents.
7. The statement of cash flows may report operating activities in the form of either an indirect or a direct presentation, but SFAS 95 encourages use of the direct method.
   a. The **direct presentation** reports the major classes of gross operating cash receipts and payments and the differences between them.
      1) SFAS 95 prescribes minimum requirements for the classes of operating cash flows to be shown.
   b. The **indirect presentation** reconciles the net income of a business enterprise or the change in net assets of a not-for-profit organization with the net operating cash flow. It removes the effects of all past deferrals of operating cash receipts and payments, all accruals of expected future operating cash receipts and payments, and all items not affecting operating cash flows to arrive at the net cash flow from operating activities.
      1) The sole difference between the direct and indirect presentations lies in the treatment of operating cash flows.
      2) Examples of deferrals of past operating cash items are changes in inventory and deferred income.
      3) Examples of accruals of expected future operating cash items are changes in receivables and payables.
      4) Examples of nonoperating items affecting net income or the change in net assets are depreciation; goodwill amortization; amortization of bond premium or discount; and gains or losses on sales of PPE, on discontinued operations, or on debt extinguishment.

c. The same net operating cash flow will be reported under both methods. Moreover, the reconciliation of net income or the change in net assets to net operating cash flow must be disclosed regardless of the presentation chosen.

1) EXAMPLE: Tune Company's income statement for the year ended December 31 reported net income of $90,000. The financial statements also disclosed the following information:

Depreciation	$20,000
Increase in net accounts receivable	35,000
Increase in inventory	12,000
Decrease in accounts payable	19,000
Increase in wages payable	7,000
Dividends paid	30,000

a) The $20,000 of depreciation should be added to net income because depreciation is included in the determination of net income but has no effect on cash.

b) The increase in the accounts receivable balance of $35,000 should be deducted because it indicates that sales revenue (which is included in the determination of net income) was greater than cash collections from customers.

c) The changes in inventory and accounts payable together explain the difference between cost of goods sold and cash paid to suppliers. The increase in inventory indicates that purchases are $12,000 greater than cost of goods sold. The decrease in accounts payable indicates that the cash disbursements to suppliers is $19,000 greater than purchases. The total change in these accounts of $31,000 should be subtracted from net income because it indicates that cash paid to suppliers is $31,000 greater than cost of goods sold.

d) The increase in wages payable of $7,000 indicates that wages expense is greater than cash paid to workers. To reflect cash paid to workers, the $7,000 should be added as an adjustment to net income.

e) Dividends paid is not an operating activity and therefore would not be an adjustment to net income.

f) The total adjustment to net income is a net decrease of $39,000 (+$20,000 – $35,000 – $12,000 – $19,000 + $7,000). Cash flow from operating activities would thus be $51,000 ($90,000 net income – $39,000 net adjustments).

E. The basic financial statements are prepared in accordance not only with GAAP but also with certain basic assumptions (entity, unit-of-money, periodicity, and going concern) discussed in Study Unit 11.

1. For example, if the going-concern assumption is invalid, a company would prepare a statement of affairs based on liquidation values rather than the usual attributes normally used to measure financial statement items.

ACCOUNTS AND NOTES RECEIVABLE

A. Accounts receivable are recorded when title passes in a sale of goods or when services are performed. The balance sheet presentation is based on the net realizable value of the receivables.

B. **Bad Debts**. There are two approaches to bad debts: the direct write-off method and the allowance method.

1. The **direct write-off method** expenses bad debts as uncollectible when they are determined to be uncollectible. The direct write-off method is subject to manipulation because the determination that debts are bad can be moved from one period to another at the discretion of management.

2. The **allowance method** records bad debt expense systematically as a percentage of either sales or the level of accounts receivable on an annual basis.

   a. The credit is to an allowance account (an account contra to accounts receivable).

   b. As accounts receivable are written off, they are charged to the allowance account. The write-off of a bad debt has no effect on working capital or total assets because the asset account (accounts receivable) and the contra account are reduced by equal amounts.

   c. If bad debt expense is computed as a percentage of sales (e.g., 1% of sales), bad debts are considered a function of sales on account. This is an income-statement-oriented approach.

   d. If the allowance is adjusted to reflect a percentage of accounts receivable (e.g., 10% at year-end), bad debt expense is a function of both sales and collections. This is a balance-sheet-oriented approach.

      1) A common method of estimating bad debt expense is to develop an analysis of accounts receivable known as an **aging schedule**. Stratifying the receivables according to the time they have been outstanding permits the use of different percentages for each category. The result should be a more accurate estimate than if a single rate is used.

C. The **installment method** recognizes profit on a sale when cash is collected rather than when the sale occurs.

1. The method can be used only when collection of the sales price is not reasonably assured.

2. Gross profit is deferred until cash is collected.

3. Special deferred gross profit and installment receivable accounts must be established for each year because the gross profit rate usually changes yearly.

D. The **cost recovery method** may be used when receivables are collected over an extended period, considerable doubt exists as to collectibility, and a reasonable estimate of the loss cannot be made.

1. Profit is recognized only after collections exceed cost. Subsequent receipts are treated entirely as revenues.

E. **Discounting Notes Receivable.** When a note receivable is discounted (usually at a bank), the holder is borrowing the maturity value (principal + interest at maturity) of the note. The bank usually collects the maturity value from the maker of the note.

1. Thus, the steps are to
   a. Compute the maturity value.
   b. Compute the interest on the loan from the bank (the bank's interest rate times the maturity value of the note).
   c. Subtract the bank's interest charges from the maturity value to determine the loan proceeds.
2. The entries to record the transaction are

Cash	\$(amount received from the bank)	
Interest expense or revenue	\$(the difference dr or cr)	
Notes receivable		\$(carrying value)

3. The discounted note receivable must be disclosed as a contingent liability. If the maker dishonors the note, the bank will collect from the person or entity that discounted the note. Alternatively, the credit in the above entry is sometimes made to notes receivable discounted, a contra-asset account, and would be shown on the balance sheet as a deduction from notes receivable.
4. When computing yearly interest, the day the note is received, made, etc., is not included, but the last day of the note is counted.
   a. EXAMPLE: A 30-day note dated January 17 matures on February 16. There are 14 days (31–17) left in January, and there would have to be 16 days in February for a 30-day note. Accordingly, the maturity date is February 16.

F. Notes receivable should be recorded at their present value. Thus, noninterest-bearing notes and notes bearing interest rates other than the market rate should be revalued to their present value.

1. EXAMPLE: A 10-year \$10,000 note paying 10% annually has a present value of \$5,813 when issued if the current market rate of interest is 20% at issuance. Determine the present value of the maturity value of \$10,000 by multiplying the \$10,000 times the present value of an amount, 20%, n = 10, which is .162. Determine the present value of the 10 \$1,000 interest payments by multiplying the \$1,000 by the present value of an annuity, 20%, n = 10, which is 4.193.

\$10,000 x 0.162 =		\$1,620
\$ 1,000 x 4.193 =		4,193
Present value of note		\$5,813

   a. When the note is received, it should be recorded at \$5,813.
   b. The value of the note is not changed for subsequent interest rate changes.
   c. The discount (\$10,000 – \$5,813) is amortized over the 10-year life by the interest method.

THE INTEREST METHOD OF AMORTIZING DISCOUNT AND PREMIUM

A. The interest method results in a constant rate of return on a receivable or payable.

1. It is in contrast to straight-line amortization, which results in a constant amount of discount or premium being amortized for each period.

   a. The interest method results in an increasing (if amortization of discount) or decreasing (if amortization of premium) amortization.

B. The interest method is applicable to receivables (payables), bond investments (bonds payable), lease and pension accounting, etc.

1. The basic principle is the application of the effective rate of interest to the net book value of the receivable or payable.

2. The effective rate is the rate of interest being earned.

   a. EXAMPLE: Look back to the note receivable example on the previous page. A 10-year, 10% note is issued when the market rate of interest is 20%. The present value of the note is $5,813.

   b. The contract or nominal rate is the rate being paid, e.g., 10% on the note in the previous example.

C. The basic rule of the interest method is that **interest expense** or **interest revenue** is the effective interest rate times the net book value of the receivable or payable.

1. If the receivable or payable is interest bearing, the cash received or paid is the contract (nominal) rate of interest times the face value of the receivable or payable.

2. The difference between the two items above is the amortization of discount or premium.

3. The journal entry is

*Interest expense	(Effective rate x Net book value)	
**Discount or premium	(Forced debit or credit)	
Cash or interest payable		(Contract rate x Face value)

* Assumes a payable; a receivable would have a debit to cash and a credit to interest income with the same computations.

** May be debited or credited directly to the payable if it is carried net of the premium or discount.

D. EXAMPLE: Assume a 10%, 10-year, $10,000 note (interest paid annually) with a present value of $5,813 and a 20% effective rate.

1. Year 1. Interest income is $1,163 (20% of $5,813).

   a. Cash received is $1,000 (10% of $10,000).
   b. Discount amortization is $163 ($1,163 – $1,000).

Cash	$1,000	
Notes receivable	163	
Interest income		$1,163

2. Year 2. Interest income is $1,195, which is 20% of ($5,813 + $163).

   a. Cash received is $1,000.
   b. Discount amortization is $195.

3. The amortization increases because 20% is applied to an increasing book value.

INVENTORY

A. Inventory is a frequently tested topic on the CMA exam. It is an important financial accounting topic because there are many methods of valuing inventory.

B. Inventory quantities are usually determined by either physical counts at the end of reporting periods (known as the periodic system) or perpetual records, which keep running totals of the number of items on hand.

   1. In **perpetual systems**, every time goods are purchased they are added to the total, and every time they are sold they are deducted.

      a. Sometimes dollar values of inventory are also included in the perpetual records, i.e., a running total of inventory cost.

   2. However, goods not physically on hand may properly be included in inventory. For example, goods out on consignment are effectively part of the inventory.

      a. Moreover, whether goods recently purchased or sold and currently in transit are properly included in inventory may be a function of the shipping terms in the relevant contract.

         1) The term **FOB shipping point** means that title passes to the buyer at the time and place of shipment.

         2) The term **FOB destination** means that title passes when the goods arrive at their destination.

C. In a **periodic system**, purchases and beginning inventory are debited, and the ending inventory is credited, to the cost of goods sold account.

   1. In other words, cost of goods sold is simply purchases adjusted for the change in inventory.

   2. The entry to record cost of goods sold under a physical inventory system:

	Debit	Credit
Inventory	$(ending of the period amount)	
Cost of goods sold	$(forced figure)	
Purchases		$(for the period)
Inventory		$(amount at the beg. of period)

   3. If perpetual records include dollar amounts (rather than just units), the entries to record purchases and sales are

	Debit	Credit
Inventory	$XXX	
Cash, accounts payable		$XXX
Cost of goods sold	$XXX	
Inventory		$XXX

D. The following methods are used to cost ending inventory (and therefore CGS):

1. **Weighted average** divides the total cost of beginning inventory and all purchases by the sum of the number of units in beginning inventory plus those purchased to obtain a weighted-average cost of goods in ending inventory (and the weighted average of goods sold).

   a. EXAMPLE:

	Units	Price per Unit	Amount
BI	20	$5	$100
PUR	10	6	60
PUR	20	8	160
	50		$320

   b. Ending inventory (and CGS) would be priced at $6.40 per unit ($320 ÷ 50 units).

2. **First-in, first-out (FIFO)** considers the first goods purchased to be the first goods sold. Accordingly, ending inventory consists of the latest purchases. Cost of goods sold consists of goods purchased at the beginning of the current period and in prior periods.

   a. Ending inventory is considered to be priced at the cost of the latest purchase if the number of units in ending inventory is equal to or less than the number of units in the latest purchase.

   b. The valuation will be the same regardless of whether the inventory is valued at the end of the period (a periodic system) or on a perpetual basis.

   c. EXAMPLE: In the above example, an ending inventory of 15 units would be priced at $8 per unit. 25 units would be priced at two levels: 20 at $8, and 5 at $6.

3. **Last-in, first-out (LIFO)** considers the most recent purchases to be sold first. Accordingly, ending inventory is priced at the cost of beginning inventory and the earliest purchases if inventory increases.

   a. EXAMPLE: In the example above, a LIFO ending inventory of 20 units or less would be priced at $5 per unit. Inventory in excess of 20 units but less than 30 units would be priced at $6 per unit.

   b. Physical and perpetual systems will yield different results under a LIFO assumption. If perpetual records include cost data, the results of the examples for LIFO would probably be different depending on when sales were made; i.e., if a sale were made on the first day of the period, it would be made out of beginning inventory.

   c. Variations in LIFO valuation include **dollar value LIFO** and **retail dollar value LIFO**.

   d. The dollar value LIFO method eliminates some of the clerical problems of the unit LIFO method by using pooled quantities as its measurement basis.

      1) Increases or decreases in inventory levels are based upon comparison of dollar values adjusted by price indexes rather than by changes in the number of units.

      2) EXAMPLE: A company began using dollar value LIFO when the price index was 100%. The beginning inventory was $10,000 consisting of many different items valued at numerous prices. At the end of year 1, the ending inventory was $14,400 valued at year-end prices. The year-end price index had risen to 120%. The first step is to convert the value of the ending inventory to base-year prices. This is done by dividing the current dollar figures by the price index.

$14,400 ÷ 1.20 = $12,000 inventory at base-year prices

The second step is to determine the increment in inventory for the period: \$12,000 – \$10,000 = \$2,000 increment. Because LIFO is being used, the objective is to report the inventory at its original costs. The oldest costs are the \$10,000 from beginning inventory. The incremental layer of \$2,000 at base-year costs is converted into year-end dollars by multiplying the base-year dollars times the ratio of year-end price level over the base-year price level. \$2,000 x 120% = \$2,400. The ending inventory consists of two layers.

\$10,000 x 100%	=	\$10,000
2,000 x 120%	=	2,400
		\$12,400

At the end of year 2, the inventory at year-end prices was \$24,000 when the price index had risen to 150%. The calculations are

\$24,000 ÷ 1.50 = \$16,000
Increment = \$4,000 (\$16,000 – \$12,000)

Ending inventory at dollar value LIFO consists of the following three LIFO layers:

\$10,000 x 100%	=	\$10,000
2,000 x 120%	=	2,400
4,000 x 150%	=	6,000
		\$18,400

e. The dollar value LIFO method requires the following steps:

1) Determine inventory value at year-end prices.
2) Convert year-end value to base-year prices.
3) Determine incremental layer (positive or negative).
4) Convert increment (if inventory increases) to year-end prices.
5) Add value of inventory layers.

f. Some companies use LIFO for external reporting but another method for internal reporting. In this case, a **LIFO reserve** may be established. It is an account contra to inventory stated using the other valuation method. At year-end, it should reflect the difference between LIFO and that method.

4. **Lower of cost or market** is a method of assuring that, if inventory is written down from cost to market, neither a loss nor more than a normal profit will be recognized in the future.

a. The procedure is to use the **replacement cost** as **market**, subject to floor and ceiling limitations.

1) The **ceiling** limitation is **net realizable value** (selling price minus cost to complete and selling cost).

a) If an inventory cost in excess of net realizable value is deferred, a loss will be incurred in a subsequent period.

2) The **floor** is **net realizable value minus normal profit**.

a) If less than net realizable value minus a normal profit is deferred, a profit greater than normal profit will be recognized in a subsequent period.

b. EXAMPLE:

Part No.	Cost	Replacement Cost	Sales Price	Disposal Cost	Normal Profit	Market
11E	$8.50	$8.75	$10.00	$1.75	$1.00	$8.25*
14A	$7.25	$6.25	$10.00	$1.50	$2.00	$6.50*
67Z	$3.25*	$4.75	$ 7.00	$1.00	$1.50	$4.75

1) Part 11E: Market of $8.25 (ceiling: $10.00 – $1.75) is lower than cost of $8.50.

2) Part 14A: Market of $6.50 (floor: $10.00 – $1.50 – $2.00) is lower than cost of $7.25.

3) Part 67Z: Market of $4.75 (between ceiling and floor) is more than cost of $3.25.

4) The * denotes lower of cost or market. The replacement cost had to be adjusted to the ceiling for Part 11E and to the floor for Part 14A.

c. An inventory loss may be recorded by a credit to inventory and a debit to cost of sales. However, a preferable procedure is to debit a separate loss account (e.g., loss due to market decline). This account appears on the income statement as a reduction of gross profit.

5. **Moving average** is a weighted average to date that can be used only with perpetual inventory records in which inventory values are also included.

   a. After each purchase, a new weighted average is computed of the cost of merchandise then on hand.

   b. Sales prior to the next purchase are then removed from credited inventory at the previously computed weighted average.

6. **Simple average** is an average of the beginning inventory unit cost and the unit cost of each purchase with no regard for the number of items in beginning inventory or any purchase. It is appropriate when beginning inventory and all purchases have approximately the same number of units.

7. **Specific identification** requires determining which specific items are sold. It can be used for various blocks of investment securities or special inventory items such as electric motors, automobiles, heavy equipment, etc. It does allow manipulation since inventory items costing more could be considered sold if profit is to be lowered, and inventory items with lower historical cost could be considered sold if management wished a higher profit.

8. **Retail method** is a method of converting ending inventory at retail to cost. The advantage is that a physical inventory can be taken at retail and then converted to cost. The cost ratio used to convert retail to cost depends upon the flow assumption used. If a **weighted-average** flow is assumed, the cost ratio should be goods available at cost over goods available at retail. If a **FIFO** assumption is used, the cost ratio should be cost of purchases over purchases at retail. If a **LIFO** flow assumption is used, the cost of ending inventory depends on the cost of beginning inventory. If ending inventory is less than beginning inventory, the cost ratio should be cost of beginning inventory over beginning inventory at retail. Any increase (stated at retail) should be valued at the ratio of cost of purchases over purchases at retail.

Also, the **lower-of-cost-or-market** concept may be applied to the retail method. In this approach, markups are added to beginning inventory and purchases at retail to obtain goods available at retail. Markdowns are not subtracted. This results in a higher denominator in the cost-retail ratio, which results in a lower ending inventory figure.

a. EXAMPLE:

	At Cost	At Retail
Beginning inventory	$ 90,000	$130,000
Purchases	330,000	460,000
Markups		10,000
Markdowns		40,000
Sales		480,000

b. Ending inventory at retail is thus $80,000 ($130,000 + $460,000 + $10,000 – $40,000 – $480,000).

c. The cost-retail ratio for retail method weighted average is 420 ÷ 560. Include both markups and markdowns in goods available at retail.

d. The cost-retail ratio for the retail method FIFO is 330 ÷ 430, assuming all markups and markdowns applied to goods purchased this period. Under FIFO, all inventory would come from current period purchases.

e. The cost-retail ratio for the retail method LIFO is 90 ÷ 130 because ending inventory of $80,000 retail is less than beginning inventory of $130,000. If there had been an increase in inventory, the increment would be valued using a cost-retail ratio of 330 ÷ 430.

f. The cost-retail ratio for the retail method LCM, assuming weighted average, is 420 ÷ 600 because markups, not markdowns, are included in the calculation of the percentage. This method is typically used if LIFO is not used. The exclusion of markdowns from the ratio results in a valuation that approximates the lower of cost or market.

g. The dollar value LIFO method can also be used in conjunction with the retail inventory method.

1) EXAMPLE:

	Cost	Retail
Beginning inventory	$12,000	$ 16,800
Purchases	70,000	100,000
Sales		90,000
Ending inventory at retail		$ 26,800

The beginning price index was 100%; the year-end index is 134%. The first step is to convert the year-end inventory to base-year prices: $26,800 ÷ 1.34 = $20,000. Determine the increment: $20,000 – $16,800 = $3,200. Convert the increment back to year-end prices: $3,200 x 134% = $4,288. The next step is to convert the retail prices to cost and then add the layers:

$16,800 x 100% (price index) x 71.43% (cost ratio) =	$12,000.24
3,200 x 134% (price index) x 70% (cost ratio) =	3,001.60
	$15,001.84

h. The retail dollar value LIFO method requires the following steps:
   1) Determine inventory value at year-end retail prices.
   2) Convert year-end values to base-year prices.
   3) Determine incremental layer (positive or negative).
   4) Convert increment (if inventory increases) to year-end prices.
   5) Convert retail prices to cost.
   6) Add cost of inventory layers.

9. **Gross profit method** is a method of computing ending inventory given sales figures. The gross profit is taken out of sales to determine cost of sales. The gross profit method is not acceptable for tax purposes. It can, however, be used when the inventory has been destroyed or stolen. It is also often used in the preparation of interim statements.
   a. EXAMPLE: Assume beginning inventory of $10,000, purchases of $20,000, and sales of $50,000, given a 100% markup on cost. Because the cost of goods sold was $25,000 (50% of sales), ending inventory was $5,000 ($30,000 goods available – $25,000 CGS). The easy way to work this type of problem is to prepare the cost of goods sold section of an income statement and solve algebraically for those amounts that are not known.

10. **Market costing** values ending inventory at its current market rate, e.g., the current price of wheat or gold.

11. **Cost apportionment by relative sales value** is a means of allocating cost of common products or a group of items purchased together by their relative sales values. Thus, the lots in a real estate subdivision would be valued at a percentage of the total cost, that is, the ratio of the market value of an individual lot to the total estimated market value of all the lots.

12. **Direct costing** is a method of costing inventory arising from production processes that does not include fixed overhead. It is not acceptable for financial reporting purposes. It is a responsibility accounting approach. See the discussion in Study Unit 20, Variable and Absorption Costing, in Chapter 7.

13. **Standard costing** is a means of pricing inventory at budgeted, predetermined costs. Standard costing is an acceptable means of pricing inventory if, for financial reporting purposes, the standard costs approximate the actual costs. If actual costs are significantly different from standard costs, the ending inventory and cost of goods sold must be adjusted to actual cost. See the discussion in Study Unit 24, Standard Costs and Variance Analysis, in Chapter 7.

14. **Completed-contract** and **percentage-of-completion** are methods of accounting for long-term contracts (see the next sideheading).

LONG-TERM CONSTRUCTION CONTRACTS

A. The **completed-contract method** defers all contract costs until the project is completed and then matches the costs of completing the contract with the revenues from the project; i.e., the profit from a contract is recognized in the year of completion.

B. The **percentage-of-completion method** recognizes profit based upon the estimated total profit, the percentage of completion, and the profit recognized to date. The percentage of completion is multiplied times the total expected profit, and the profit recognized in prior periods is subtracted from the expected profit to date to determine the profit to be recognized in the current period.

C. Under both the percentage-of-completion and completed-contract methods, all of the loss on any project is reflected in the accounts as soon as the loss is anticipated.

D. EXAMPLE: A contractor has a contract to build a bridge that will take 3 years to complete. The contract price is $2,000,000. The contractor expects total costs to be $1,200,000. The following information applies to the costs incurred and expected to be incurred during the 3 years:

	Year 1	Year 2	Year 3
Costs incurred during year	$300,000	$600,000	$550,000
Costs expected in future	900,000	600,000	0

1. By the end of the first year, the contractor has incurred 25% of all costs expected to be incurred on the project. Therefore, if the percentage-of-completion method is being used, the contractor will recognize 25% of the profit that will be earned on the project. The total profit is expected to be $800,000 ($2,000,000 – $1,200,000). Therefore, 25% x $800,000 = $200,000 of profit to be recognized in the first year.
2. At the end of the second year, the company has incurred total costs of $900,000 ($300,000 in the first year and $600,000 in the second year). An additional $600,000 of cost is expected to be incurred in the future. Therefore, the total cost of the project is expected to be $1,500,000. The new estimate of total profit is $500,000 ($2,000,000 contract price – $1,500,000 of costs). The project is 60% complete after year 2 ($900,000 ÷ $1,500,000). Therefore, 60% of all profit should be recognized by the end of year 2, or $300,000 (60% x $500,000). Since $200,000 was already recognized in the first year, $100,000 remains to be recognized in year 2.
3. At the end of the third year, total costs have been $1,450,000. Thus, the total profit is known to be $550,000. Since a total of $300,000 has been recognized in the first 2 years, $250,000 is recognized in year 3.
4. Journal entries

		%-of-Completion		Completed-Contract	
Year 1:	Construction in progress	$ 300,000		$ 300,000	
	Cash or accounts payable		$ 300,000		$ 300,000
	Construction in progress	$ 200,000			
	Construction revenue		$ 200,000	No entry	
Year 2:	Construction in progress	$ 600,000		$ 600,000	
	Cash or accounts payable		$ 600,000		$ 600,000
	Construction in progress	$ 100,000			
	Construction revenue		$ 100,000	No entry	
Year 3:	Construction in progress	$ 550,000		$ 550,000	
	Cash or accounts payable		$ 550,000		$ 550,000
	Cash	$2,000,000		$2,000,000	
	Construction in progress		$1,750,000		$1,450,000
	Construction revenue		250,000		550,000

5. The above entries assume payment was made at the end of the contract. Ordinarily, progress billings are made and payments are received during the term of the contract. Accounts receivable is debited and **progress billings** is credited. Neither billing nor the receipt of cash affects net income. As cash is received, accounts receivable is credited. Progress billings is an offset to **construction in progress** (or vice versa) on the balance sheet. The difference between construction in progress (costs and recognized income) and progress billings to date is shown as a current asset if construction in progress exceeds total billings, and as a current liability if billings exceed construction in progress.

   Another variation of the foregoing entries is to credit the gross amount of revenue (costs + gross profit recognized) rather than the net amount each period. The offsetting debits are to cost of revenue earned and construction in progress (for the gross profit recognized).

INVESTMENTS

A. Short-term investments are current assets. They must be readily marketable and be intended to be converted into cash within the next year or operating cycle, whichever is longer. Bonds, other debt instruments, and stocks are typical investments.

   1. The accounting value of debt securities includes brokerage fees paid, but not accrued interest. Discounts or premiums on debt securities (e.g., bonds) are not amortized because the securities are expected to be sold within 1 year.

B. SFAS 115 applies to investments in equity securities with readily determinable fair values and all investments in debt securities. It does not apply to investments in equity securities accounted for under the equity method, investments in consolidated subsidiaries, enterprises with specialized accounting practices that include accounting for all investments at fair or market value, and not-for-profit organizations.

   1. When acquired, debt and equity securities should be classified as held-to-maturity, trading, or available-for-sale.

      a. **Held-to-maturity securities** include debt securities, but only if the reporting enterprise has the positive intent and ability to hold the securities to maturity.

         1) Held-to-maturity securities are reported at amortized cost.

         2) Changes in circumstances may cause a change in the above-mentioned intent "without calling into question the intent to hold other debt securities to maturity in the future."

         3) Classifying securities as held-to-maturity is inappropriate if their sale may result from such factors as need for liquidity, changes in market rates, changes in foreign currency risk, changes in the yield of alternative investments, or changes in funding sources and terms.

         4) Securities are deemed to be held to maturity in the following circumstances:

            a) Sale near enough to the maturity or call date (e.g., within 3 months) so that interest rate risk (change in the market rate) does not have a significant effect on fair value

            b) Sale after collection of 85% or more of the principal

      b. **Trading securities** include debt securities that are not classified as held-to-maturity or available-for-sale and certain equity securities with readily determinable fair values.

         1) Trading securities are bought and held primarily for sale in the near term. They are frequently purchased and sold.

         2) **Unrealized holding gains and losses** for trading securities are determined by the difference between recorded cost and **fair value** at year-end and are included in earnings.

         3) To retain historical cost in the accounts, a valuation allowance may be established for each security or at the portfolio level (if records for individual securities are maintained).

      c. **Available-for-sale securities** include equity securities with readily determinable fair values that are not classified as trading securities, and debt securities that are not classified as held-to-maturity or trading securities.

         1) Unrealized holding gains and losses on available-for-sale securities, including those classified as current assets, are determined by the difference between recorded cost and fair value at year-end. They are excluded from earnings and reported at a net amount in a separate component of shareholders' equity until realized, net of tax effect.

d. Income from dividends and interest, including amortization of premium or discount, continues to be included in earnings. Realized gains and losses on held-to-maturity and available-for-sale securities also continues to be included in earnings.

   1) SFAS 115 does not affect the methods of accounting for dividends and interest income.

e. Transfers between categories are at fair value.

f. **Impairment**. If a decline in fair value of an individual held-to-maturity or available-for-sale security is other than temporary, its cost basis is written down to fair value as a new cost basis.

   1) The write-down is a realized loss and is included in earnings.

   2) The new cost basis is not affected by subsequent recoveries in fair value.

   3) Subsequent changes in fair value of available-for-sale securities are included in the separate component of equity, except for other-than-temporary declines.

g. Trading securities are current assets, but individual held-to-maturity and available-for-sale securities may be current or noncurrent.

C. **Stock dividends** and **stock splits** are not considered income when received by the investors. They decrease the unit cost of the securities; i.e., more securities are owned, and their total cost is not affected.

   1. No entries are made to record the receipt of stock dividends or splits; however, a memorandum entry should be made in the investment account to record the additional shares owned.

D. When **stock rights** (options to purchase additional shares) are received, the cost of the stock on which the rights were issued is allocated between the rights and the stock.

   1. The journal entry is

Investment in stock rights	$XXX	
Investment in stock		$XXX

   2. Allocation is based on the relative market values of the rights and stock.

   3. The rights are either sold or exercised, or they expire on their expiration date.

E. Long-term debt securities (e.g., bonds) are carried at their historical cost (including brokerage fees but excluding accrued interest at purchase), and any discount or premium (difference between the purchase price and maturity value) is amortized over the remaining life of the debt instrument.

   1. If the amounts are not material, the straight-line method may be used.
   2. In all other cases, the effective-rate-of-interest method must be used.

      a. The effective-rate-of-interest method requires that the effective interest rate at the time of the instrument's purchase be multiplied by the book value of the security to determine the interest revenue for that period. The difference between the interest revenue and the amount of cash debited on the receipt of the contract rate of interest is amortization of discount or premium.

F. **The Equity Method of Accounting for Investments in Common Stock**

   1. The equity method recognizes both distributed and undistributed income arising from an investment in an investee.

   2. This is in contrast to the **cost method**, which recognizes only dividends from investees as income. The cost method is essentially a cash-basis method of accounting for investments in common stock (income from the investment is recognized as it is received).

3. Under the equity method, investor income is recorded as the investee reports income. The investor's share of investee income is recorded by the investor.

Investment in investee	$XXX	
Income from investee		$XXX

Then, as dividends are received, the entry is

Cash	$XXX	
Investment in investee		$XXX

The net effect is

Cash	$(distributed income)	
Investment in investee	(undistributed income)	
Income from investee		$(total income)

4. The excess of the cost of the investment over the equity in the book value of the investee's net assets should be amortized in the same way as goodwill. However, if the excess is attributable to specific undervalued assets it should be amortized as appropriate for those assets, for example, over the remaining life of the equipment. Also, intercompany profit items should be eliminated as in consolidations. See Consolidations in Study Unit 13, page 386.
5. The equity method is required (by APB 18) whenever an investor exercises significant influence over the investee. Significant influence is assumed in the absence of contrary evidence when 20% or more of the voting stock of the investee is held. If more than 50% of the stock is held, however, consolidated statements are usually prepared (see SFAS 94).

G. The **cash surrender value** of life insurance policies on key executives is shown in the investment section of the balance sheet.

1. The annual premium for life insurance typically involves an allocation between expense and the cash surrender value (CSV), which is an asset. For the payment of a $1,000 premium, which results in an $800 increase in CSV, the entry is

Life insurance expense	$200	
Cash surrender value	800	
Cash		$1,000

2. If the key executive died shortly after the above entry was made and the company collected $50,000, the entry would be

Cash	$50,000	
Cash surrender value		$ 800
Gain from insurance		49,200

FIXED ASSETS

A. The costs of fixed assets (plant and equipment) are all costs necessary to acquire these assets and to bring hem to the condition and location required for their intended use. These costs include shipping, installation, pre-use testing, sales taxes, interest capitalization, etc.

1. All costs of internally constructed assets are usually capitalized. The asset costs should not exceed what the asset could be purchased for; i.e., the cost of the asset is not recorded in excess of fair value.
    a. An issue arises as to whether fixed overhead costs should be considered part of the asset cost.
        1) Given idle capacity, fixed costs probably should not be included in asset costs.
        2) If the construction of the asset displaced other production, the fixed overhead costs should be capitalized.
            a) However, the cost of the asset should not exceed fair value.
            b) Any excess cost would be written off in the period of construction as a loss.
2. Criteria must be established to differentiate between capitalizable costs and expense-type costs. If costs are going to benefit more than one period, they should theoretically be capitalized and expensed in the periods they will benefit.
    a. Ordinarily, if expenditures are for recurring maintenance, they are expensed.
    b. Also, costs below a certain amount, e.g., for wastebaskets, are expensed by most companies.
    c. Major asset improvements are usually capitalized.
        1) If a major existing section of an asset is rebuilt, replaced, etc., it is most often capitalized as the full cost of the asset section, and the remaining book value (original cost minus accumulated depreciation) of the section of the asset is expensed as a loss on removal.
3. Occasionally, a company will receive a gift of land or a factory building from a governmental unit such as a county or city. The purpose of such a donation is usually to provide more local employment opportunities.
    a. Under a strict interpretation of the historical cost principle, an asset that has no cost would be recorded at zero.
    b. However, under SFAS 116, **contributions received** in this context are recognized as assets and as revenues or gains in the period received.

B. **Depreciation** is the method of amortizing costs of fixed assets to subsequent accounting periods that are benefited by the fixed assets. Usually, all the costs of fixed assets minus salvage value are expensed (this amount is the **depreciation base**).

1. In theory, costs of removing the asset should be included in the depreciation base.
2. The useful life of assets is determined by
    a. Normal physical usage
    b. Normal time of obsolescence
    c. Rapid technological change

3. **Amortization** is defined broadly in SFAC 6 as the process of reducing a liability recorded as a result of a cash receipt by recognizing revenues or of reducing an asset recorded as a result of a cash payment by recognizing expenses or costs of production.
   a. Thus, amortization includes depreciation and depletion. Other examples of amortizations include expenses for insurance and intangible assets and the recognition of subscriptions revenue.
4. **Depletion** is amortization of the costs of natural resources.
   a. It is most often based on the number of recoverable units, e.g., tons of coal. Thus, the depletion base (capitalized costs of acquisition, exploration, and development, minus residual value adjusted for restoration costs) is divided by the number of economically recoverable units to determine the depletion rate.

C. **Depreciation Methods**

1. **Straight-line** depreciation (S-L) allocates the depreciation base evenly over the estimated useful life of an asset.
   a. EXAMPLE: S-L depreciation is calculated by dividing the useful life, e.g., 5 years, into the asset cost, e.g., $9,000, resulting in an annual depreciation change of $1,800. This calculation assumes that the asset cost $10,000 and had a $1,000 salvage value.
2. **Declining-balance** depreciation allocates a series of decreasing depreciation charges over the asset's life.
   a. It is an accelerated method because larger amounts are charged in early years of the asset's life.
   b. A percentage (usually 200%, which is called double-declining-balance or DDB) of the straight-line rate is multiplied by the asset's book value each year.
      1) The asset is depreciated until the book value (cost minus accumulated depreciation) is equal to the salvage value.
      2) DDB EXAMPLE: Using the data in the S-L example, twice the straight-line ratio is 40%, which is multiplied times the book value.

Year	Book Value	Depreciation
1	$10,000	$4,000
2	6,000	2,400
3	3,600	1,440
4	2,160	864
5	1,296	296

(Not below salvage value)

3. **Sum-of-the-years'-digits** (SYD) is another accelerated depreciation method that gives results similar to those of the declining-balance method. The depreciation base is allocated based on a fraction.
   a. The numerator is the years remaining in the asset's life.
   b. The denominator is the sum of all the years in an asset's life.

c. EXAMPLE: Using the S-L example in C.1. on the previous page, the sum of years 1 through 5 is 15 (1 + 2 + 3 + 4 + 5), and the depreciation base is $9,000.

Year	Fraction	Depreciation
1	5 ÷ 15	$3,000
2	4 ÷ 15	2,400
3	3 ÷ 15	1,800
4	2 ÷ 15	1,200
5	1 ÷ 15	600

d. For larger numbers, the denominator can be determined by the formula

$$n\left(\frac{n + 1}{2}\right)$$

For n = 7,

$$7\left(\frac{7 + 1}{2}\right) = 28$$

4. **Physical usage** depreciation is an allocation based on a fraction each year.
   a. The numerator is the amount used, e.g., hours, miles, etc.
   b. The denominator is the total expected usage, e.g., hours, miles, etc.
   c. EXAMPLE: If total expected usage is 100,000 miles, 10% of the asset's cost would be expensed in a year when 10,000 miles were driven.
   d. This approach is taken for most depletion computations.
5. Other depreciation methods
   a. **Replacement**. Original asset cost is kept on the books and the cost of replacing the asset is expensed. It is sometimes used for assets such as utility poles, which are numerous and have long lives and low unit cost.
   b. **Retirement**. Asset cost is expensed when the asset is retired. It is also sometimes used for utility poles.
   c. **Composite and group**. The composite method relates to groups of dissimilar assets with varying useful lives. The group method concerns similar assets. Both depreciate a group of assets based on a weighted average of their useful lives.
      1) Depreciation is computed on the entire group of assets as if they were one.
      2) Because depreciation applies to the entire group of assets, there are no fully depreciated assets, regardless of their age.
      3) When a component asset of the group is disposed of, no gain or loss is recorded regardless of the amount received for the asset. The amount received is a debit, and the original cost of the asset is a credit, with the difference recorded in accumulated depreciation.

4) EXAMPLE: A company bought four similar trucks with an average service life of 5 years at a total cost of $100,000. The four trucks are carried in one asset account, and only one accumulated depreciation account is used for the group. Assuming zero salvage value, the depreciation recorded at the end of the first year is $20,000 ($100,000 ÷ 5). The entry for years 1 and 2 is

Depreciation expense	$20,000	
Accumulated depreciation		$20,000

a) On the first day of year 3, one of the trucks was destroyed. It was uninsured. No loss is recorded.

Accumulated depreciation	$25,000	
Trucks ($100,000 ÷ 4 trucks)		$25,000

b) At the end of year 3, the balance of the trucks account is only $75,000. The 20% per year depreciation rate is applied, and the depreciation expense on the remaining three trucks is $15,000 (20% x $75,000).

c) The balance in accumulated depreciation at the end of year 3 is $30,000 ($20,000 + $20,000 – $25,000 + $15,000).

D. Nonmonetary Exchanges

1. Nonmonetary exchanges are exchanges of assets other than cash, e.g., an exchange of land for a fixed asset. Frequently, cash (**boot**) is involved, as in the trade-in of an old asset on the purchase of a new asset.

a. The asset received is usually recorded at the fair value of the asset surrendered, but the fair value of the asset received is used if it is more clearly evident. A gain or loss is recognized.

b. Fair value is not used if the fair values are not reasonably determinable.

c. If the exchange is not the culmination of an earning process, that is, if it is an exchange of similar inventory or of similar productive assets, losses but not gains are recognized.

1) EXAMPLE: An old truck, which had cost $10,000 and had a book value of $2,000, was traded in on a new truck. The cash paid for the new truck was $13,500, and the fair value of the old truck was $1,500. The following entry would result:

Truck (new)	$15,000	
Accumulated depreciation	8,000	
Loss on exchange	500	
Truck (old)		$10,000
Cash		13,500

2) If the fair value of the old truck in the preceding example had been $2,500, the entry would have been as follows:

Truck (new)	$15,500	
Accumulated depreciation	8,000	
Truck (old)		$10,000
Cash		13,500

d. Even if fair value is **not** to be recognized, a portion of the gain is recognized when cash (boot) is also received in an exchange of similar nonmonetary assets.

1) Although the general rule is that gains on exchanges of like-kind assets are not to be recorded, there is an exception.

2) When cash is received in an exchange of like-kind items, a part of the asset is considered sold and gain is recognized in the proportion of the boot received to the total amount received.

$$\frac{\textit{Boot received (cash)}}{\textit{Boot and fair value of asset received}} \times \textit{Total gain} = \textit{Gain recognized}$$

3) EXAMPLE: Assume that a company has an auto that originally cost $10,000 and has been depreciated a total of $6,000 (remaining book value is $4,000). The old auto is traded for another auto with a fair value of $5,000. In addition to receiving the new auto, boot is received in the amount of $1,000. In other words, the company has had a gain of $2,000 ($6,000 of assets received – $4,000 book value of assets given up). The portion of the $2,000 gain to be recognized would be computed as follows:

$$\frac{\$1{,}000\ (\textit{boot received})}{\$1{,}000 + \$5{,}000} \times \$2{,}000 = \$333$$

The entry to record the exchange would be

	Debit	Credit
New auto	$3,333	
Cash	1,000	
Accumulated depreciation	6,000	
Old auto		$10,000
Gain on exchange		333

E. **Intangible Assets**

1. Intangible assets are differentiated from fixed assets in that they are nonphysical. They are also noncurrent (e.g., accounts receivable are not considered intangibles because they are current). Intangibles often convey a right to do something that gives its holder some form of economic benefit.

   a. Goodwill
   b. Licenses
   c. Patents
   d. Leaseholds and leasehold improvements that cannot be removed
   e. Copyrights
   f. Organizational costs
   g. Franchises
   h. Trademarks and trade names
   i. Future advertising benefits
   j. Water rights
   k. Human resources

2. The costs of intangibles are **amortized** (rather than depreciated or depleted).

   a. The credit is usually directly into the asset account; no accumulated amortization account is used.

3. Goodwill arises only from the purchase of another business. It is the excess of cost over the fair value of the net identifiable assets acquired.

4. Under APB 17, *Intangible Assets*, all intangibles must be amortized over a period of 40 years or less. The straight-line method should be used unless another method is more appropriate.

   a. For example, the legal duration of a patent is now 20 years, but its amortization period may be much less as a result of obsolescence, contractual agreements, or other factors. Furthermore, the amount amortized includes the initial costs of obtaining the patent and legal fees incurred in a successful defense of the patent.

F. **Impairment**

1. SFAS 121 applies to **long-lived assets and certain identifiable intangibles** (excluding certain assets for which specialized accounting principles have been prescribed).

   a. Under SFAS 121, when events or changes in circumstances indicate that the recoverability of the carrying amount of **assets to be held and used** is in doubt, the entity should determine whether the sum of the undiscounted estimated future cash inflows from the assets is less than the carrying amount.

      1) If this test is met, an **impairment loss** is recognized equal to the **excess of the carrying amount over the fair value**.

      2) The reduced carrying amount resulting from recognition of an impairment loss is the new cost.

         a) Restoration of an impairment loss is not allowed.

      3) Goodwill associated with assets subject to an impairment loss is eliminated before the carrying amount of the impaired assets is reduced.

2. **Long-lived assets and certain identifiable intangibles to be disposed of** are reported at the **lower of the carrying amount** or **fair value minus cost to sell**.

   a. Costs to sell include such items as broker commissions, title fees, and closing costs.

   b. Assets to be disposed of are not depreciated or amortized while held for disposal.

   c. A revision in the estimated fair value minus cost to sell is an adjustment of the carrying amount of the asset to be disposed of. However, the revised carrying amount cannot exceed the carrying amount prior to the adjustment made to reflect the disposal decision.

   d. SFAS 121 does not apply to assets that constitute a segment of a business to be disposed of. Under APB 30, such assets are measured at the lower of the carrying amount or net realizable value.

CURRENT AND LONG-TERM LIABILITIES

A. **Current liabilities** are obligations for which liquidation is reasonably expected to require the use of existing resources properly classifiable as current assets or the creation of other current liabilities. Current liabilities include

1. Trade accounts payable and payables for cash dividends declared, notes, payroll, vacation pay, taxes, etc.
   a. Cash dividends are a liability when declared.
   b. A checking account overdraft is a current liability.
   c. Stock dividends are not current liabilities; they are a shareholders' equity item.
   d. Current liabilities are ordinarily recorded at net settlement value (undiscounted amount of cash or its equivalent expected to be paid to liquidate the obligations in the ordinary course of business).
2. Portions of long-term debt payable in the next year (or operating cycle if longer) are current, unless they are to be repaid from a noncurrent asset, e.g., a bond sinking fund.
3. Short-term debt cannot be reclassified as noncurrent debt unless there is both an intent and a creditor commitment to refinance the debt.
4. Property taxes vary as to assessment, lien, and payment dates from jurisdiction to jurisdiction.
   a. Property taxes should be expensed over the fiscal year of the taxing authority, or the tax liability should be recorded when it is due.
5. Advances from customers should be recorded as deferred revenue and recognized in the income statement as earned.
6. Some liabilities are estimated, such as liabilities for product warranties and redemption coupons. Warranty expense is usually based on some percentage of sales.
   a. EXAMPLE: A canning company offers a free toy to customers who submit 50 labels from the company's products. The toys cost $5 each. At year-end, no premiums have been given out, but from past experience the company knows that about 20% of all labels will be returned. Thus, if sales for the period were 100,000 cans, 20,000 labels are expected to be returned. It takes 50 labels to earn one premium; therefore, the company expects to give away 400 premiums (20,000 ÷ 50). The adjusting entry to record the liability for premiums is

	Debit	Credit
Premium expense	$2,000	
Liability for premiums		$2,000

B. **Long-term liabilities** consist primarily of bonds and term loans. A discount is a subtraction from the carrying amount of the bond payable. A premium increases the carrying amount.

1. Discounts and premiums are accounted for by the interest method.

C. **Contingencies** should be accrued and reported as liabilities if two conditions are met:

1. It must be probable that a liability has been incurred.
2. The amount of the liability can be reasonably estimated.
   a. Other contingencies are only disclosed.
   b. See the outline of SFAS 5, *Accounting for Contingencies*, on page 338.

LEASES

A. A lease is a rental or sub-purchase arrangement between a lessor (the owner or seller of the property) and lessee (the renter or purchaser of the property).

1. The issue in all leases is whether the rights and risks of ownership have been transferred from the lessor to the lessee; if so, the lease should be accounted for as a sale-purchase, i.e., a **capital lease**.

    a. If the rights and risks of ownership have not transferred, the lease is a rental arrangement and called an **operating lease**.

2. If any one of four criteria is met, the lease is accounted for as a sale-purchase, i.e., a capital lease.

    a. The lease transfers title to lessee.

    b. The lease has a bargain purchase option.

    c. The lease term is 75% of the useful life of the leased asset.

    d. The present value (PV) of the minimum lease payments is 90% or more of the asset's fair value.

    NOTE: Criteria c. and d. cannot be applied in the last one-fourth of the asset's useful life.

3. Definitions

    a. **Minimum lease payments** -- payments required by the lease agreement, including

        1) Bargain purchase options

        2) Guaranteed residual value (lessee guarantee of leased-asset sales price at the end of the lease)

        3) Lease termination penalty

    b. **Discount rate** to determine present value of the minimum lease payments for the lessee -- the lessee's incremental borrowing rate, unless the lessee knows the lessor's implicit rate and it is lower

    c. **Implicit rate of return** (used by the lessor) -- the rate of return on capital leases. It is the discount rate that equates the minimum lease payments to the lessor's cost of the leased asset.

B. **Lessee Accounting for Capital Leases**

1. Lessee records the leased asset and related liability at the present value of the minimum lease payments. This entry is essentially the same as if the asset had been purchased on an installment contract.

Leased equipment	$XXX	
Lease liability payable		$XXX

2. The effective interest method is used.
3. The asset is depreciated over its useful life to its net salvage value.
   a. If the lease does not contain a bargain purchase option, transfer of title, etc., the asset should not be depreciated over a period longer than the lease term.
4. If the lessor retains responsibility for **executory costs** (such as insurance and maintenance), a portion of each lease payment represents executory costs. The executory costs should be excluded in computing the present value of lease payments because such costs are not for the acquisition of the asset.

C. **Lessor Accounting for Capital Leases**

1. Two additional criteria must be met before leases are accounted for as capital leases by lessors.
   a. The lease payments have to be collectible with reasonable predictability.
   b. The lease has to be without important uncertainties, e.g., unusual guarantees, work to be completed, etc.
2. Capital leases are either direct financing or sales-type leases.
   a. **Direct financing leases** provide only interest income to the lessor.
   b. **Sales-type leases** result in a selling profit as well as interest income for the lessor; e.g., a manufacturer or dealer leasing goods both sells and finances the goods.
   c. This distinction is made by lessors, but not by lessees.
3. Direct financing leases are recorded by the lessor at the gross amount of the minimum lease payments.
   a. The cost of the asset is credited, and the difference is the unearned lease revenue.

Lease receivable	$XXX	
Asset to be leased		$XXX
Unearned lease revenue		XXX

   b. The unearned lease revenue is recognized over the life of the lease under the effective-interest-rate method.

Cash	$XXX	
Unearned lease revenue	XXX	
Lease receivable		$XXX
Lease revenue		XXX

4. EXAMPLE: A capital lease involves a piece of equipment leased under a contract that provides for 10 annual payments of $1,000 each. The payments are due at the beginning of each year, with the first payment due immediately. Assuming a direct financing lease and an applicable interest rate of 15%, the entries to record the lease would appear as follows on the books of the lessee and lessor:

LESSEE'S BOOKS		
Leased equipment	$5,771.58	
Lease liability payable		$4,771.58
Cash		1,000.00

The $5,771.58 is the present value of an annuity due of 10 payments of $1,000 at 15%.

LESSOR'S BOOKS		
Cash	$1,000.00	
Lease receivable	9,000.00	
Equipment		$5,771.58
Unearned lease revenue		4,228.42

The entries for the second $1,000 payment would be

LESSEE'S BOOKS		
Lease liability payable	$ 284.26	
Interest expense (15% x $4,771.58)	715.74	
Cash		$1,000.00

LESSOR'S BOOKS		
Cash	$1,000.00	
Unearned lease revenue	715.74	
Lease receivable		$1,000.00
Lease revenue		715.74

5. For sales-type leases, the present value of the minimum lease payments is recorded as sales.

   a. Cost of sales is the cost of the leased asset minus the present value of any unguaranteed residual value.

Lease receivable	$XXX	
Cost of goods sold	XXX	
Sales		$XXX
Leased asset		XXX
Unearned interest		XXX

   b. The lease receivable is debited for the total to be received plus the unguaranteed residual value; i.e., interest is earned on the net receivable plus the adjusted book value of the residual value.

PENSIONS (to reflect SFAS 87 and 88; see outlines on pages 356-359)

A. Pension benefits are a form of compensation to employees and are intended to provide them with retirement income.

1. The central issue in pension accounting is the determination of the annual amount of **net periodic pension cost (NPPC)**.
2. All pension costs, even for years of service credited prior to a plan's inception, must be recognized on an accrual basis. No charges are made to retained earnings.
3. The pension fund is a separate entity from the employer. The fund assets and/or liabilities do not appear on the employer's financial statements.
4. Vested benefits are pension benefits earned by employees that are not contingent upon continued employment.
5. The most significant parts of the FASB pronouncements on pensions concern defined benefit plans.
   a. The employer promises to provide retirement payments according to the plan's benefit formula, which may contain such variables as
      1) How long the employee and his/her survivors live
      2) Years of service by the employee
      3) The employee's compensation
   b. Plans may also be contributory (employees pay into the plan).
6. Although the employee may have completed service and retired, the total benefit to be paid and its cost cannot be determined precisely but must be estimated using the benefit formula and assumptions about future events that will determine the amount and timing of the benefit payments.
   a. Moreover, the cost of the benefits must be attributed to individual years of service.
7. Changes in the pension obligation (including those resulting from plan amendments) and in the value of plan assets are not recognized as they occur but rather systematically and rationally over subsequent periods as net cost components or as liabilities or assets.
8. The recognized consequences of events and transactions affecting the plan are reported as a single net amount in the financial statements. Thus, compensation cost of promised benefits, interest cost resulting from deferred payment of benefits, and results of investing are aggregated.
9. Recognized values of assets contributed to a plan and liabilities for pensions recognized as net pension cost of past periods are shown net (as one amount) in the employer's balance sheet as accrued/prepaid pension cost (see the entries in C. on page 318).
10. The standardized method for measuring NPPC recognizes compensation over the employee's approximate service period and relates it to the actuarial terms of the plan.
11. A **minimum liability** must be recognized when the **accumulated benefit obligation (ABO)** exceeds the **fair value of plan assets**, but the offsetting amount will be recognized as an intangible asset or as a reduction of equity.
    a. The ABO is the actuarial PV of benefits (vested or not) attributed by the benefit formula to employee service and compensation before a specified date.
    b. The **projected benefit obligation (PBO)** differs in that it is measured according to assumptions about future compensation levels if the plan benefits are based, for instance, on career average pay or final pay.

B. The net periodic pension cost has the following elements:

1. **Service cost** -- the actuarial PV of benefits attributed by the benefit formula to services rendered during the period
2. **Interest cost** on the PBO
3. **Expected return on plan assets**
4. **Amortization of unrecognized prior service costs**
   a. Retroactive benefits arising from plan initiation or amendments are assigned to the future service periods of active employees (a straight-line or another acceptable method may be allowed).
5. **Gains and losses** (to the extent recognized) -- changes in the PBO or plan assets resulting from experience different from that assumed or from changes in assumptions
   a. Recognition is not required in the period in which the changes (i.e., the gains or losses) occur.
6. **Amortization of the unrecognized net asset or obligation** existing at the time SFAS 87 is applied

C. The following are typical journal entries:

1. The entry to record NPPC is

NPPC	$XXX	
Accrued/prepaid pension cost		$XXX

2. The entry to record a contribution is

Accrued/prepaid pension cost	$XXX	
Cash		$XXX

3. The entry to record a required minimum liability when unrecognized prior service cost is less than the minimum liability is

Excess of additional pension liability over unrecognized pension cost (an offset to equity)	$XXX	
Intangible asset	XXX	
Additional liability		$XXX

If in the next year the plan assets exceed the ABO, this entry would be reversed.

SHAREHOLDERS' EQUITY

A. Shareholders' equity consists of contributed capital and retained earnings.

1. Contributed capital

Preferred stock	$XXX		
Paid-in capital in excess of par	XXX	$XXX	
Donated capital		XXX	
Common stock subscribed		XXX	
Common stock dividends distributable		XXX	
Stock warrants outstanding		XXX	
Common stock	XXX		
Paid-in capital on common	XXX	XXX	
Total contributed capital			$XXX
Earnings retained in the business			
Retained earnings appropriated		$XXX	
Unappropriated retained earnings		XXX	
Total retained earnings			$XXX
Treasury stock (cost method)			(XXX)
Total shareholders' equity			$XXX

2. An important concept is legal capital, which is the par or stated value of preferred and common stock.

B. Relatively few transactions directly affect stockholders' equity. They include

1. Issuance of stock
2. Retirement of stock
3. Treasury stock purchases and sales
4. Stock dividends
5. Cash dividends
6. Stock splits
7. Issuance of stock warrants
8. Net income or loss
9. Appropriation of retained earnings
10. Valuation of available-for-sale securities at fair value
11. Unrecognized gain or loss on translation of foreign investee financial statements into domestic currency units
12. Preferred stock transactions

C. **Other Issues in Stockholders' Equity Transactions**

1. Rights of shareholders
   a. Common shareholders have a right to share proportionately in declared dividends (but only after payment to preferred shareholders, including any cumulative preferred dividends)
   b. They have the voting rights conferred by the classes of stock held.
   c. They share in corporate assets upon liquidation (but only after other claims, including the preferences of preferred shareholders, have been satisfied).
   d. They may have a preemptive right regarding new issues of stock of the same class.

2. Upon issuance of stock, cash is debited and common stock is credited for the par or stated value.
   a. The difference is credited to paid-in capital.
   b. A discount is unlikely but would be debited to stock discount.
3. When stock is retired, cash is credited and stock debited for the par or stated value.
   a. A credit difference goes to paid-in capital.
   b. A debit difference goes to paid-in capital to the extent paid-in capital exists from the original stock issuance.
   c. Any remaining debit goes to retained earnings.
4. **Treasury stock** is common stock acquired by the issuer but not retired. Treasury stock is purchased to facilitate possible acquisitions, to allow shareholders to receive capital gains rather than dividends, to meet obligations under stock option agreements, to avoid hostile takeovers, to eliminate dissident shareholders, to support the stock's market price, to increase EPS and book value per share, and to reduce the size of the business.
   a. Treasury stock (with a debit balance) is a contra shareholders' equity account (not an asset). It is an unallocated amount deducted from total shareholders' equity if it is accounted for at cost.
   b. Treasury stock (TS) is accounted for by either of the following methods:
      1) **Cost method**, in which TS is debited and carried at cost
      2) **Par value method**, in which TS is debited and carried at par value
   c. Gains on TS are credited to paid-in capital.
      1) No dividends are paid on TS.
   d. Losses on TS are debited to paid-in capital from previous TS transactions and thereafter to retained earnings.
      1) This treatment is also followed in the par value method because fair value is usually in excess of par value.
   e. Cost method example
      1) If 1,000 shares of $10 par stock were reacquired at $20 per share, the entry under the cost method would be

	Debit	Credit
Treasury stock	$20,000	
Cash		$20,000

      2) If 500 shares of the above stock are sold at $22, the entry would be

	Debit	Credit
Cash	$11,000	
Treasury stock		$10,000
Paid-in capital from treasury stock		1,000

      3) If the remaining 500 shares are later sold for $17 per share, the entry would be

	Debit	Credit
Cash	$8,500	
Paid-in capital from treasury stock	1,000	
Retained earnings	500	
Treasury stock		$10,000

4) Losses on treasury stock transactions are charged to the paid-in capital account if that account has a balance from previous transactions. If there an insufficient balance to absorb the loss, the difference is charged to retained earnings.

f. If the par value method had been used, the treasury stock would have been debited for $10,000 on acquisition. The remaining $10,000 would have been debited to paid-in capital (from issuance) to the extent it existed, with the remainder being debited to retained earnings.

1) On each sale, all amounts received over par are credited to paid-in capital.

5. Cash dividends are recorded by debiting retained earnings and crediting a liability on the declaration date.

a. Unlike stock dividends, they cannot be rescinded.

6. **Stock dividends** are issuances of additional shares of a corporation's own stock.

a. **Small stock dividends** are debited to retained earnings for the market value of the stock to be issued if the dividend is less than 20% to 25% of shares already outstanding.

1) The par or stated value of the stock is credited to common stock.
2) The difference is a credit to paid-in capital.

b. **Large stock dividends** are split-ups in the form of stock dividends. They are in excess of 20% to 25% of the stock outstanding.

1) The debit to retained earnings is at least equal to the legal requirement in the state of incorporation (usually the par or stated value).

7. A **stock split** involves a corporation calling in its outstanding stock, reducing the par value or stated value, and issuing a proportionate number of new shares.

a. EXAMPLE: A corporation with 10,000 shares of $20 par stock outstanding issues a 2-for-1 stock split. After the split, 20,000 shares of $10 par stock are outstanding. In practice, the old stock is not retired. Instead, additional shares are issued and mailed to the stockholders. The par value is printed incorrectly on the old shares, but they are still valid.

b. No journal entry is required to record a stock split (other than a memorandum entry noting that more shares are outstanding).

c. A stock split has no effect on any account or on the proportionate shareholdings of any individual.

d. The purpose of the stock split is effectively to reduce the market price of the stock by increasing the number of shares on the market. The hope is that the lower price will attract additional investors.

e. Not only will having additional investors drive up the price of the shares, but also new investors can help the company by becoming customers of the company's products.

8. **Stock warrants** are certificates evidencing the right to buy stock at a specified price. They may be issued with other securities, such as bonds, to provide an additional inducement for investors.
   a. Under APB 14, if detachable warrants are issued with bonds, the proceeds are allocated to the warrants and bonds based on their relative fair value.
   b. If the fair value of one security but not the other is known, the allocation is incremental, not proportional. Thus, the one security is recorded at its fair value, with the balance of the proceeds allocated to the other security.
   c. If the warrants are not detachable, no allocation is made.
9. A company may decide to sell additional shares of a class of stock already outstanding. Accordingly, it may issue **stock rights** evidenced by warrants to current shareholders. These rights permit them to maintain their proportionate ownership at a stipulated exercise price.
   a. Until the rights are issued, the stock will sell **rights on**. After issuance, the stock sells **rights off**.
   b. The investor must allocate the cost of the stock to the stock and the rights.
   c. Under SFAS 115, stock rights, warrants, and options are trading securities or available-for-sale securities and must be accounted for at fair value at the balance sheet date.
10. Net income or loss is closed to retained earnings at the end of the period.
11. **Retained earnings** are sometimes **appropriated** to a special account to disclose that earnings retained in the business (not paid out in dividends) are being used for special purposes.
    a. The only effect is to decrease **unappropriated** retained earnings available for dividend payout.
    b. Retained earnings are sometimes appropriated in the same amount as the cost of treasury stock (this treatment may be required by state statute).
12. **Available-for-sale securities** are accounted for at fair value at the balance sheet date, with holding gains or losses recorded directly in a shareholders' equity account. They are not included in earnings.
13. When foreign investee accounts or statements are **translated** into domestic currency units, unrecognized gains and losses are reported (cumulatively) in shareholders' equity.
    a. They are written off (included in the sale entry) upon sale, liquidation, etc., of the foreign entity.
    b. The account title might be "deferred foreign currency translation gain or loss for consolidation purposes."
14. Preferred stock transactions include sales, repurchases, and dividends.
    a. Sales and repurchases can affect a separate paid-in capital account for preferred stock.
    b. Preferred dividends are debited to retained earnings as are common stock dividends.

D. **Earnings per Share (EPS)**

1. Earnings per share is a frequently reported financial statistic for publicly traded companies.
   a. It is a ratio of $\dfrac{\textit{Adjusted net income}}{\textit{Adjusted shares outstanding}}$
   b. EPS must be reported on the face of the income statement for each period that financial statements are presented.
   c. If there is 3% or more potential dilution of EPS from convertible securities, stock options, etc., the following two EPS figures are required.
      1) Primary EPS
      2) Fully diluted EPS
2. General guidelines for EPS calculations
   a. The numerator is net income minus preferred dividends.
   b. The denominator is the weighted-average number of shares outstanding during the period.
3. **Primary EPS (PEPS)** reflects adjustments to the numerator and denominator for each of the following categories if they exist and if they are dilutive (i.e., have the effect of decreasing EPS):
   a. All options and warrants
   b. Contingent issues that will be issued
   c. Convertible securities
      1) Only if they are **common stock equivalents (CSE)**, i.e., were issued at an effective yield less than 66⅔% of the current average Aa corporate bond yield at time of issuance
4. **Fully diluted EPS (FDEPS)** reflects adjustments for each of the following if dilutive:
   a. Options and warrants
   b. Contingent issuances of stock
   c. Convertible securities, whether or not they are common stock equivalents
5. **Options and warrants** are assumed to be exercised at the beginning of the year or when issued, with the hypothetical proceeds used to repurchase treasury stock (at the average price of the year for PEPS).
   a. For FDEPS, the year-end price is used, if higher.
   b. Under the **treasury stock method**, if the shares obtainable from the exercise of all outstanding options and warrants exceed 20% of the common shares outstanding at the end of the period, all options and warrants are assumed to be exercised. Furthermore, the hypothetical repurchase is limited to 20% of the actual common stock outstanding. The remaining proceeds are deemed to be used to decrease short-term debt and then long-term debt, and finally to purchase government securities.
6. **Contingent issuances** of stock should be added to the denominator.
7. The **if-converted method** applies to **convertible securities**. These securities are assumed to be converted at the beginning of the period or when issued, which adds interest savings minus tax effect to the numerator and shares to the denominator.

E. EPS EXAMPLES: A corporation began the year with 50,000 shares of common stock outstanding and 10,000 shares of 10%, $10-par preferred shares outstanding. On April 1, 10,000 shares of common stock were sold. On October 1, an additional 60,000 shares of common stock were issued pursuant to a 2-for-1 stock split. Based on these figures, calculate the company's primary EPS assuming a net income of $100,000.

1. The amount of income available to common shareholders is net income minus preferred dividends (in the case of cumulative preferred stock, this subtraction is made regardless of whether the dividends were actually declared). The preferred dividend requirement is $1 per share (10% of $10) times 10,000 shares outstanding, or $10,000. The amount of income available to common shareholders is $90,000 ($100,000 – $10,000).

2. For the denominator of the EPS ratio, the calculation of shares outstanding, ignoring the split, is

50,000 shares for 3 ÷ 12 of the year	=	12,500
60,000 shares for 9 ÷ 12 of the year	=	45,000
		57,500

Had there been no stock split, the number of shares in the denominator would have been 57,500.

   a. Stock splits and dividends are always treated as if they occurred at the beginning of the year. Thus, the above number of shares (57,500) is doubled to account for the stock split. As a result, PEPS = $90,000 ÷ 115,000 shares = $.78.

3. Continuing with the preceding data, assume the same facts except that the company also had outstanding a convertible bond issue of $100,000 (which is a CSE because its yield is less than 662/3% of the average Aa corporate bond yield at issuance). Each $1,000 denomination bond was convertible into 100 shares of common stock. Thus, if the bonds were all converted, an additional 10,000 shares of stock would have to be issued. Interest on the bonds was 5%, and the company's combined federal and state income tax rate was 50%. The calculation for EPS assumes that conversion actually took place at the beginning of the year (if the effect of conversion would be to lower EPS).

   a. In computing the numerator of the equation, the aftertax savings of $2,500 is added to the net income minus preferred dividends. Thus, the numerator would be $92,500 ($90,000 previously).

   b. The denominator would be the number of shares computed in the previous example plus the additional 10,000 shares to be issued as a part of the conversion, or 125,000 (115,000 + 10,000).

   c. PEPS = $92,500 ÷ 125,000 shares = $.74

4. Continuing with the above data, suppose stock rights were outstanding to purchase 10,000 shares at $10 when the average price of the stock for the year was $20 and the year-end price was $25.

   a. Consider the rights as exercised at the beginning of the year, i.e., adding 10,000 shares to the EPS denominator. The proceeds of $100,000 (10,000 shares at $10) are further assumed to have been used to repurchase 5,000 shares ($100,000 ÷ $20 per share), and the net effect is to increase the denominator from 125,000 shares to 130,000 shares (125,000 + 10,000 – 5,000).

b. There was no effect on the numerator because not over 20% of the stock outstanding at the end of the period would have been reacquired. If the 20% limit were exceeded, only 20% of the stock would be considered to be reacquired, and the remaining funds (from the assumed option exercise) would then be assumed to be used to decrease debt. The aftertax interest savings are added to the numerator.

c. PEPS = $92,500 ÷ 130,000 shares = $.71

5. FDEPS follows the previous calculations except it presents a more conservative (lower) EPS by assuming maximum dilution.

a. It includes all possible issuances of stock that would be dilutive, i.e., not only common stock equivalents.

b. When applying the treasury stock method for stock options, rights, etc., the year-end price is used to compute repurchased shares if it is higher than the average stock price for the year. In the previous example (4.a.), $25 rather than $20 would be used, resulting in only 4,000 shares (rather than 5,000) being hypothetically repurchased.

DIGEST OF CURRENT APB AND FASB PRONOUNCEMENTS

CMA candidates should have a basic knowledge of all APB Opinions and FASB Statements that have not been superseded. Candidates should also be especially knowledgeable about recent pronouncements. The outlines on the following pages summarize the basic conclusions of ARB, APB, and FASB pronouncements. Those that have been superseded or are largely irrelevant are omitted. The unsuperseded Accounting Research Bulletins are not identified by number and/or chapter, but rather summarized in one outline. Most pronouncements contain lists of required disclosures that are not given in these outlines. These disclosures are impossible to memorize. The best approach is to rely on common sense to guess what would be reasonable disclosures for a certain type of transaction (as a financial analyst, ask yourself what you would want disclosed).

Because the following outlines reiterate many of the definitions laid out earlier in the study unit, they constitute a good review and overview of financial statement presentation.

ACCOUNTING RESEARCH BULLETINS (ARBs)

A. Normally, gross profit is recognized at the time of sale. Sales are recorded when title passes or a service is performed. Related costs are recognized in the same period.

1. If collection is not reasonably assured, installment sales or cost recovery methods should be used to account for income.

2. Under the installment sales method, gross profit is deferred and recognized as cash is collected (e.g., if 30% of a cash sale is collected in one year, 30% of the gross profit would then be recognized).

3. The cost recovery method recognizes profit only after all costs have been recovered.

B. Paid-in capital is charged for losses (and deficits in retained earnings) only in quasi-reorganizations. A **quasi-reorganization** is a statutorily prescribed procedure by which a company may eliminate a deficit in retained earnings by writing down assets to fair values and then charging paid-in capital (and perhaps even reducing the par or stated value of stock). The result is a retained earnings account with a zero balance.

1. Disclosure of a quasi-reorganization must be made in the footnotes to the financial statements for the following 10 years.

C. Treasury stock is a contra shareholders' equity item. No dividends are paid on treasury stock. Profits on sales (and purchases of) treasury stock are additions to paid-in capital, not income.

D. Current assets are cash and other assets expected to be realized in cash, sold, or consumed during the normal operating cycle of the business.

1. Current liabilities are obligations requiring the use of current assets or creation of other current liabilities during the operating cycle of the business.

2. The operating cycle is the time between the expenditure of cash for materials and services and the receipt of cash for the sale of those materials and services.

E. Inventory contains finished goods, work-in-process, and raw materials.

1. The cost flow method used should be the one that most clearly reflects periodic income.

2. All overhead must be contained in inventory; i.e., variable costing is not in accordance with GAAP.

3. Lower of cost or market defines market as replacement cost.

   a. Replacement cost cannot be more than net realizable value (upper limit).

      1) Net realizable value is selling price minus cost to complete and disposal costs.

   b. Replacement cost cannot be less than net realizable value minus normal profit (lower limit).

   c. These limits on replacement cost preclude deferring inventory costs at values that would seriously over- or understate inventory and therefore result in losses or abnormal gains in subsequent periods.

4. Inventory may be stated above cost only when there is no basis for cost allocation and both the disposal price and sale are assured.

5. Any losses on firm purchase commitments should be recognized in the period that they occur when the market price declines below the commitment price. These losses are measured in the same way as inventory losses.

6. Required disclosures include the basis for stating inventories, the nature and effects of any significant changes, any goods stated above cost, and accrued net losses on firm purchase commitments.

F. The distinction between stock dividends and stock splits is based on the magnitude of the increase in the number of shares outstanding.

1. Dividends of less than 20% to 25% are considered small stock dividends. Those in excess of 20% to 25% are large stock dividends.

2. Small stock dividends are accounted for by debiting retained earnings and crediting capital stock for the fair value of shares issued. A large stock dividend (a split-up effected in the form of a dividend) requires capitalization of retained earnings equal only to the amount established by the state of incorporation. This amount is usually the par value.

   a. The SEC treats an issuance of 25% or more as a split-up effected in the form of a dividend.

3. Splits are normally considered an adjustment to the par or stated value of the stock, and only a memo entry is made. If the par or stated value is not adjusted in a stock split, the par or stated value of the stock issued should be debited to retained earnings and credited to paid-in capital.

G. Assets should not be written up to appraisal values. But if they are, depreciation should be recorded on the written-up amount.

H. Real and personal property tax assessment, billing, collection, etc., vary from jurisdiction to jurisdiction. Tax expense should be recognized by monthly accrual over the fiscal period of the taxing authority.

I. When stock options are issued and the fair value of the stock exceeds the stock option price, compensation expense should be recognized over the period of the option contract. It is not recognized if the options are issued either to raise capital or to encourage wider holdings by employees.

J. Accelerated depreciation (including declining-balance and sum-of-the-years'-digits) is systematic and rational and is acceptable under GAAP.

K. The percentage-of-completion method is recommended (instead of the completed-contract method) when total costs and percentage of completion may be reasonably estimated.

L. Consolidated financial statements shall be issued when one company owns over 50% of another, unless control is temporary or does not rest with the majority owner, e.g., because the subsidiary is in legal reorganization or bankruptcy or operating under foreign exchange restrictions, controls, or severe governmentally imposed uncertainties.

   1. Differing fiscal periods of parents and subsidiaries of up to 3 months are acceptable; otherwise, interim statements must be used to prepare the consolidated worksheet.

   2. Intercompany balances and the effects of intercompany transactions should be eliminated in the consolidated statements.

ACCOUNTING PRINCIPLES BOARD OPINIONS (APBs)

A. The Accounting Principles Board was the predecessor of the FASB. It issued 30 Opinions, of which the following are still relevant:

   1. **APB 4**, *Accounting for the Investment Credit*, allows an investment tax credit (ITC) to be recognized either as a reduction in tax expense in the year of asset purchase or as a reduction of the cost of the asset. The latter treatment essentially results in deferral of the tax credit and recognition over the useful life of the asset.

      a. Carrybacks of an ITC can be shown as a receivable, but carryforwards should not be recognized until earned.

      b. The ITC was repealed by the Tax Reform Act of 1986, but APB 4 continues to be pertinent because of the strong potential for reenactment.

   2. **APB 6**, *Status of Accounting Research Bulletins*, revised several of the Accounting Research Bulletins.

      a. Accounts and notes receivable should be reported net of finance charges, unearned interest, etc.

      b. Receipt of stock dividends and stock splits is not a receipt of income.

      c. Gains on treasury stock transactions are paid-in capital (not income).

         1) Losses may be charged to paid-in capital, to the extent it exists for that class of stock, and then to retained earnings, or entirely to retained earnings.

      d. Noncurrent assets should not be written up to fair values (but if they have been, depreciation should be based on the written-up values).

3. **APB 9**, *Reporting the Results of Operations*, presents the format for the preparation of the income statement.
   a. There should be a section for the results of normal operations and a section for extraordinary items.
   b. Prior-period adjustments appear only on the retained earnings statement.
4. **APB 10**, *Omnibus Opinion-1966*, is an omnibus opinion used to clarify previously issued pronouncements and handle miscellaneous matters.
   a. Liabilities and assets are not to be offset against each other unless a right of offset exists.
   b. Revenues should be recognized when goods are sold unless the collectibility of receivables is in doubt.
   c. Preferred stock liquidation rights and dividends in arrears should be fully disclosed.
   d. Deferred tax credits (arising from interperiod tax allocation) should not be presented at their present value, i.e., no discounting.
5. **APB 12**, *Omnibus Opinion-1967*, is an omnibus opinion.
   a. Full disclosure should be made of depreciation methods and practices, including
      1) Depreciation expense for the period
      2) Balances of major classes of depreciable assets by nature or function
      3) Accumulated depreciation either by major class or in total
      4) Description of depreciation methods for each class of assets
   b. Explanation of changes in all stockholders' equity accounts (i.e., not just retained earnings) should be disclosed.
   c. Deferred compensation contracts that are equivalent to a postretirement income plan or health or welfare benefit plan should be accounted for in accordance with SFAS 87 or SFAS 106, respectively.
      1) Other deferred compensation contracts should be accounted for individually on an accrual basis.
   d. Allowance accounts, e.g., for bad debts, depreciation, etc., should be shown as a deduction from, i.e., contra to, the related asset account.
6. **APB 14**, *Convertible Debt and Debt Issued with Stock Purchase Warrants*, concerns convertible debt and debt issued with stock warrants.
   a. A convertible debt security is convertible into common stock of the issuer or affiliate.
   b. None of the proceeds of a convertible bond should be attributed to the conversion factor when the security is inseparable from the conversion feature; i.e., all proceeds are considered received for issuance of debt.
   c. Bonds issued with detachable stock warrants should be accounted for as both debt and stockholders' equity. The allocation of proceeds received between the debt and warrants should be based on the relative fair value of each at the date of issuance.

7. **APB 15**, *Earnings per Share*, requires earnings per share information to be reported on the face of the income statement for both income before extraordinary items and net income.
   a. There are two types of capital structures.
      1) Simple capital structures have few potentially dilutive securities, e.g., no options or warrants, no contingent share agreements, no convertible bonds or convertible preferred stock. Maximum allowable EPS dilution from any of the foregoing is 3%.
      2) Complex capital structures contain potentially dilutive securities. Dilution is potential reduction of EPS on outstanding weighted-average common shares in excess of 3%.
   b. Dual presentation of EPS is required for complex capital structures.
      1) Primary earnings per share (PEPS) is based on outstanding common stock and common stock equivalents (CSE).
         a) Potential CSE are those securities that are equivalent to common stock or entitle the holders to become common stockholders. Potential common stock equivalents include
            i) Convertible debt and convertible preferred stock
               - If issued at a price to yield less than 66 2/3% of the average Aa corporate bond yield at the time of issuance
            ii) All stock options and warrants
            iii) Contingent issuances
            iv) Participating securities and two-class common stock
      2) Fully diluted earnings per share (FDEPS) is based upon all shares outstanding and all contingent issues that might have a dilutive effect. It presents the maximum dilution of EPS.
   c. This APB applies only to publicly held companies.
8. **APB 16**, *Business Combinations*, prescribes accounting for business combinations.
   a. Purchase accounting and pooling accounting are appropriate in certain circumstances.
   b. Pooling accounting is to be used if all 12 of the following criteria are met (otherwise use purchase accounting):
      1) The combining companies are autonomous; i.e., one has not been a subsidiary of the other during the past 2 years.
      2) Not more than 10% of the stock of any combining company is held by the other combining companies before the pooling.
      3) The combination is effected in a single transaction within 1 year after the plan is initiated.
      4) Only common stock of the surviving company is issued for at least 90% of the outstanding voting stock of the other combining companies.
      5) The combining companies do not change the composition of shareholders' equity or the amount of common stock in contemplation of the combination.

6) The combining companies reacquire treasury stock only for purposes other than the business combination.

7) The ratio of ownership of individual common stockholders to that of other common stockholders remains the same after the exchange of stock; i.e., each stockholder maintains his/her relative percentage of ownership.

8) The new stockholders are not deprived of or restricted in exercising the voting rights of their stock.

9) The combination is resolved when initiated, and there are no provisions for contingent issuances of securities or for the payment of other contingent consideration.

10) There is no plan to retire any stock issued to effect the combination.

11) No special financial arrangements are made to benefit former stockholders of the combining companies.

12) There is no plan to dispose of a significant amount of the combining companies' assets for the 2 years following the combination, except to eliminate duplicate facilities or excess capacity.

c. Pooling accounting assumes that a combining of ownership interests has occurred (not a purchase); hence, there is no basis for revaluing assets. In poolings, the accounts and financial statements of the pooled entities are added together.

d. Purchase accounting assumes a purchase of net assets; thus, the assets are recorded at their cost to the acquiring company.

9. **APB 17**, *Intangible Assets*, concerns intangible assets.

a. Intangible assets purchased from others are to be recorded at their cost.

b. Costs of internally developed intangibles that are not specifically identifiable (such as goodwill) are to be expensed when incurred.

c. Intangible assets acquired from others are to be amortized over their useful or legal lives, not to exceed 40 years.

d. Straight-line amortization should be used unless another method is more appropriate (but see SFAS 72 for goodwill amortization arising from acquisitions of banks and thrifts).

10. **APB 18**, *Equity Method for Investments in Common Stock*, indicates that the equity method should be used for all subsidiaries, foreign and domestic, as well as corporate joint ventures.

a. It should also be used when significant influence can be exercised over investees. This is presumed of investments between 20% and 50%.

b. If an investment falls below the 20% level, the investor should discontinue the equity method (unless significant influence can still be exercised) but should not make any retroactive adjustment.

c. Intercompany profits should be eliminated from the investor's share of investee income.

d. If an investment rises above the 20% level, the investment account and retained earnings of the investor should be adjusted retroactively to reflect balances as if the equity method had been used from the first purchase of the stock.

e. The difference between the net book value purchased and the cost of the investment should be handled as in consolidations, i.e., amortized over the undervalued asset's useful life.

11. **APB 20**, *Accounting Changes*, states that accounting changes include changes in accounting principles, estimates, and accounting entities.
    a. Changes in principles are normally effected by using the new principle in the period of change and determining the cumulative effect of the change on all prior periods (i.e., on beginning retained earnings) and presenting the cumulative effect of the accounting change (net of the tax effect) as the last item in the income statement.
        1) Thus, for most accounting changes, the financial statements are not retroactively adjusted. However, a pro forma presentation of net income from continuing operations and final net income and related EPS figures for all years presented must be made.
        2) APB 20, as amended, mentions five special changes that require retroactive adjustment and a special exemption from cumulative-effect treatment: Changing
            a) From LIFO to another inventory method
            b) From the completed-contract to the percentage-of-completion method or vice versa
            c) To or from the full-cost method of accounting used in the extractive industries
            d) From one acceptable principle to another when an initial public offering of securities is made in specified circumstances
            e) The method of accounting for railroad track structures
    b. Changes in estimates must be made prospectively, i.e., without retroactive adjustment.
    c. Changes in accounting entities require restatement of the financial statements for all periods presented.
    d. Corrections of errors are accounted for as prior-period adjustments, i.e., to the beginning balance of retained earnings, and do not appear in the income statement.
12. **APB 21**, *Interest on Receivables and Payables*, applies to receivables and payables that will not mature for at least 1 year and whose face value differs from their present value.
    a. It does not apply to
        1) Ordinary payables and receivables that are normally settled in less than 1 year
        2) Amounts that do not require repayment in the future
        3) Transactions whose interest rates are legally fixed
        4) Security deposits
        5) Customary transactions of those whose primary business is lending money
        6) Transactions between parents and subsidiaries
        7) Contingent claims, such as warranties

b. Receivables and payables should be recorded at their present value.

1) When a note is exchanged only for cash, the present value is the cash payment.

2) The general presumption when a note is exchanged for property, goods, or services in an arm's-length transaction is that the rate of interest is fair and adequate.

a) If the rate is not stated or the stated rate is unreasonable, the note and the asset should be recorded at the fair value of the asset or of the note, whichever is more clearly determinable.

b) In the absence of these values, the present value of the note should be used as the basis for recording both the note and the asset.

i) This present value is obtained by discounting all future payments on the note using an imputed rate of interest.

ii) Many factors, such as credit standing, security provided, and tax considerations, should be weighed in choosing the imputed rate.

c. Any bond discount or premium should be amortized using the effective interest method.

1) Discount or premium should be offset against the related receivable or payable on the balance sheet.

2) Debt issue costs may be disclosed separately as deferred charges.

13. **APB 22**, *Disclosure of Accounting Policies*, requires disclosure of accounting policies in a separate summary of significant accounting policies or as the initial footnote to the financial statements.

a. The disclosure should emphasize selection of an alternative accounting principle, accounting principles peculiar to a particular situation or industry, and innovative or unusual applications.

b. The disclosure should include accounting principles adopted and the method of applying them.

c. EXAMPLES:

1) Depreciation and amortization methods
2) Inventory pricing and composition (classification)
3) Consolidation method (purchase or pooling)
4) Franchising, leasing, etc., activities
5) Long-term construction contract accounting

14. **APB 23**, *Accounting for Income Taxes-Special Areas*, contains certain exceptions to the requirements for recognition of deferred taxes (as amended by SFAS 109).

15. **APB 25**, *Accounting for Stock Issued to Employees*, defines compensation from issuance of stock options to employees as the best estimate of market value minus the amount that the employee has to pay for the stock. This must be determined on the measurement date, which is the date on which both the number of shares and the option price are known.

   a. APB 25 does not apply to noncompensatory plans if

      1) All full-time employees participate.
      2) The stock available to each employee is equal or based on salary.
      3) The option exercise period is reasonable.
      4) The discount from market is not great, i.e., similar to stock sold to shareholders.

   b. For compensatory plans, recognize expense in the period the employee provides service.

      1) The amount is market value minus option price.
      2) The employee service period is frequently over several periods before or after the measurement date.
      3) This requires deferral or accrual of estimated expenses.
      4) Any adjustments of these expenses are made prospectively; e.g., overaccrual in a prior period reduces current and future periods' expense.

   c. Because expense is not tax deductible to the corporation until income is reported by the employee, deferred tax accounting must be used.

      1) Differences between recorded deferred tax amounts and actual tax deductions should be closed to the related paid-in capital accounts arising from the issuance of the stock, which was presumably issued above par value.

16. **APB 26**, *Early Extinguishment of Debt*, applies to all extinguishments of debt except for troubled debt restructurings and conversions to equity securities of the debtor pursuant to conversion privileges granted at the date of issuance of the debt. It requires the difference between the net carrying amount (book value) and the reacquisition price of an extinguished debt to be recognized in income in the period the debt is extinguished.

   a. SFAS 76, *Extinguishment of Debt*, defines qualifying transactions (see page 353).

      1) The net carrying amount is the amount due at maturity, adjusted for unamortized premium, discount, and cost of issuance.
      2) The reacquisition price is the amount paid on extinguishment, including a call premium and miscellaneous costs of reacquisition. If extinguishment is achieved by a direct exchange of new securities, the reacquisition price is the total present value of the new securities.

   b. SFAS 4 requires such a gain or loss to be recorded as an extraordinary gain or loss of the period in which the reacquisition occurred.

      1) But gains and losses on early extinguishment of debt to satisfy sinking-fund requirements are not extraordinary (reiterated in SFAS 64).

c. SFAS 76 permits debt to be accounted for as having been extinguished if the debtor irrevocably places essentially risk-free monetary assets in a trust.

1) The trust assets must be used solely for the payment of the debt.

2) Either the debtor must be relieved of primary liability for the debt as a result of the deposit or the possibility of having to make further payments must be remote.

17. **APB 28**, *Interim Financial Reporting*, sets forth the principles of interim financial reporting. Interim financial statements are considered a part of the annual period. Only a few modifications to the criteria for the recognition of revenue and expense for annual reporting purposes are permitted.

a. Revenue recognition criteria are the same as for annual statements.

b. Modifications of expense recognition are inconsequential.

1) Gross profit methods can be used to estimate inventory.

2) Declines in inventory value may be ignored if they are temporary.

3) Liquidation of LIFO base-period inventory may be accounted for at current prices if the inventory will be replaced prior to year-end.

c. The main concern is to prorate nonrecurring annual charges equitably to interim periods, e.g., year-end bonuses, vacation pay, major repairs, etc.

1) Seasonal variations should be disclosed in footnotes and/or by use of 12-month, year-to-date statements.

2) Extraordinary items are reported separately in the interim period in which they occur.

d. Taxes are based on the expected annual effective rate after all tax-planning tools are implemented and include the effect of credits, special deductions, etc. This rate also includes the effect of any expected year-end valuation allowance for deferred tax assets related to originating deductible temporary differences and carryforwards during the year (FASB Interpretation No. 18 and SFAS 109).

1) Each interim period's tax is the revised annual tax rate times year-to-date income, minus tax expense recognized in prior interim periods.

2) SFAS 109 amended APB 28 and FASB Interpretation No. 18. Among other things, it provides that a tax benefit is recognized for a loss arising early in the year if the benefits are expected to be (a) realized during the year or (b) recognizable as a deferred tax asset at year-end. A tax benefit is recognized for a loss arising in an interim period if realization is more likely than not. Also, a valuation allowance must be recognized if it is more likely than not that some portion of a deferred tax asset will not be realized. The foregoing principles are applied in determining the estimated tax benefit of an ordinary loss for the fiscal year used to calculate the annual effective tax rate and the year-to-date tax benefit of a loss.

3) Taxes on all items other than continuing operations (e.g., cumulative effect of accounting changes, extraordinary items, etc.) are determined at incremental rates; i.e., their marginal effect on taxes is calculated.

e. Accounting changes in interim periods are governed by SFAS 3.

   1) Cumulative-effect-type changes are reported as occurring in the first interim period, and all subsequent interim periods reflect the new principle. All interim periods are restated no matter when the change was made.

      a) The cumulative effect is computed on the beginning retained earnings of the first interim period.

   2) Restatement-type accounting changes are the same as for changes in annual statements, i.e., per APB 20, *Accounting Changes*.

   3) All disclosures required by APB 20 for accounting changes in annual statements are required in interim statements.

f. Part II of APB 28 requires certain minimum disclosures of interim data by public companies: sales, provisions for income taxes, extraordinary items, cumulative effect of accounting changes on net income, primary and fully diluted EPS, seasonal revenues, costs, expenses, significant changes in estimates or income tax expenses, disposal of a segment, contingent items, changes in accounting principles or estimates, and significant cash flows.

18. **APB 29**, *Accounting for Nonmonetary Transactions*, provides that the exchange of nonmonetary assets or items is not a culmination of the earnings process; e.g., the exchange of like assets should be recorded at book value.

   a. Monetary assets and liabilities are assets and liabilities whose amounts are fixed in terms of units of currency by contract or otherwise, e.g., cash, payables.

      1) Nonmonetary items are all other items.

   b. APB 29 **does** apply to

      1) Nonreciprocal transfers to or from owners and other parties
      2) Nonmonetary exchanges

   c. APB 29 does **not** apply to

      1) Business combinations
      2) Companies under common control
      3) Acquisition of assets with stock
      4) Stock dividends or stock splits

   d. Nonmonetary transfers should be accounted for at their fair value.

      1) An exception exists when fair value cannot be determined or when the exchange is not the culmination of the earnings process, such as the exchange of similar inventory or productive assets.

      2) In that case, no gain is recognized, and the asset received is recorded at the cost or book value of the asset given up.

         a) Gain should not be recognized on liquidation distributions to owners.

   e. When boot (cash) is received in a transaction that is not the culmination of an earning process, a gain may be recognized in the ratio of the cash received to the total consideration received.

      1) This ratio multiplied times the total gain (total consideration received minus total book value given up) is the gain that can be recognized.

   f. Fair value is based on quoted market prices, appraisals, similar transactions, etc.

19. **APB 30**, *Reporting the Results of Operations*, concerns reporting results of operations.
    a. Both the gain (loss) on the disposal of a segment of a business and the results of its operations should be separately reported on the income statement between normal operating income and extraordinary items.
    b. Any estimated loss from disposal of discontinued operations (including results during the phase-out period) should be reported with the results of discontinued operations.
        1) The expected gain (loss) calculation includes operating results during the phase-out period, direct costs of disposal, and the gain or loss on the actual disposal (difference between net realizable value and carrying amount). The estimate should be made on the measurement date (the date on which management commits itself to a plan to dispose of a segment either by sale or by abandonment).
            a) Presumably, the measurement date will not precede the final disposition date by more than one year.
        2) Any gain on disposal should be recognized when realized.
            a) Operating results during the phase-out period may offset the gain (loss) on the disposal itself.
    c. Extraordinary items
        1) Both of the following criteria must be met to classify items as extraordinary:
            a) Unusual in nature -- must possess a high degree of abnormality and be clearly unrelated, or only incidentally related, to ordinary activities, considering the environment in which the entity operates
            b) Infrequency of occurrence -- must not be expected to recur in the foreseeable future, considering the environment in which the entity operates
        2) If only one criterion is met, the item should be separately disclosed as part of continuing operations but not net of tax.
    d. Any gain or loss from extraordinary items should be presented net of tax after discontinued operations.
        1) Descriptive captions and the amounts for individual material extraordinary items should be presented, preferably on the income statement, if practicable, and otherwise in the footnotes.
    e. Certain gains or losses should not be reported as extraordinary items except in rare situations:
        1) Write-downs of receivables, inventories, etc.
        2) Translation of foreign exchange
        3) Disposal of a business segment
        4) Sale of productive assets
        5) Effects of strikes
        6) Accruals on long-term contracts
    f. Under APB 30, disclosure of EPS data for results of discontinued operations and the gain or loss on disposal is optional.
        1) However, EPS disclosure is mandatory for income from continuing operations, net income, and income before extraordinary items.
        2) APB 20 requires disclosure of the EPS amount for the cumulative effect of changes in accounting principle.

STATEMENTS OF FINANCIAL ACCOUNTING STANDARDS (SFASs)

A. SFASs are the principal pronouncements issued by the FASB. To date, 123 have been promulgated.

1. **SFAS 2**, *Accounting for Research and Development Costs*, prescribes accounting for research and development (R&D).

   a. Research is "planned search or critical investigation aimed at discovery of new knowledge with the hope that such knowledge will be useful in developing a new product or service or a new process or technique or in bringing about a significant improvement to an existing product or process."

   b. Development is "the translation of research findings or other knowledge into a plan or design for a new product or process or for a significant improvement to an existing product or process whether intended for sale or use."

   c. All R&D costs should be expensed as incurred.

      1) Such costs are not to be capitalized as intangible assets.

      2) Only expenditures for a tangible asset that has an alternative future use may be capitalized (and then must be depreciated to R&D expense as it is used).

   d. The following are examples of activities typically included in R&D unless conducted for others under a contract (reimbursable costs are not expensed):

      1) Laboratory research aimed at discovery of new knowledge

      2) Searching for applications of new research findings or other knowledge

      3) Conceptual formulation and design of possible product or process alternatives

      4) Testing in search for or evaluation of product or process alternatives

      5) Modification of the formulation or design of a product or process

      6) Design, construction, and testing of preproduction prototypes and models

      7) Design of tools, jigs, molds, and dies involving new technology

      8) Design, construction, and operation of a pilot plant that is not of a scale economically feasible to the enterprise for commercial production

      9) Engineering activity required to advance the design of a product to the point that it meets specific functional and economic requirements and is ready for manufacture

   e. The following are examples of activities that typically are not classified as R&D:

      1) Engineering follow-through in an early phase of commercial production

      2) Quality control during commercial production including routine testing of products

      3) Troubleshooting in connection with breakdowns during commercial production

      4) Routine, ongoing efforts to refine, enrich, or otherwise improve upon the qualities of an existing product

5) Adaptation of an existing capability to a particular requirement or customer's need as part of a continuing commercial activity

6) Seasonal or other periodic design changes to existing products

7) Routine design of tools, jigs, molds, and dies

8) Activity, including design and construction engineering, related to the construction, relocation, rearrangement, or start-up of facilities or equipment other than pilot plants and facilities or equipment whose sole use is for a particular R&D project

9) Legal work in connection with patent applications or litigation and the sale or licensing of patents

f. The statement does not cover R&D costs incurred under a contract for the benefit of others.

1) If R&D is performed for others, revenues and expenses should be recorded in the traditional manner. This assumes the risk has been transferred to others. If the risk is retained, i.e., if payment for R&D depends on the results, R&D expenditures performed for others should be expensed.

2. **SFAS 3**, *Reporting Accounting Changes in Interim Financial Statements*, covers cumulative-effect-type accounting changes. If an accounting change occurs in other than the first quarter of the enterprise's fiscal year, the proper treatment is to calculate the cumulative effect on retained earnings at the beginning of the year and include it in restated net income presented in the first quarter financial statements. In addition, all previously issued interim financial statements of the current year must be restated to reflect the new accounting method.

3. **SFAS 4**, *Reporting Gains and Losses from Extinguishment of Debt*, clarified that gains or losses from extinguishment of debt should be reported as extraordinary items (see APB 26 on page 333).

4. **SFAS 5**, *Accounting for Contingencies*, prescribes accounting for contingencies.

a. Definitions

1) A contingency is "an existing condition, situation, or set of circumstances involving uncertainty as to possible gain or loss to an enterprise that will ultimately be resolved when one or more future events occur or fail to occur."

2) Probable -- Future events are likely to occur.

3) Reasonably possible -- Chance of occurrence is more than remote, but less than probable.

4) Remote -- Chance of occurrence is slight, i.e., less than reasonably possible.

b. Estimated losses from contingencies should be charged to income (and the liability or asset impairment should be recorded) when

1) Information available prior to issuance of financial statements indicates that it is probable that an asset was impaired or a liability was incurred (as of year-end), and

2) The amount of loss can be reasonably estimated.

a) According to FASB Interpretation No. 14, *Reasonable Estimation of the Amount of Loss*, if the estimate is stated within a given range and some amount within the range appears to be the best estimate, that amount should be accrued.

i) However, if no amount within the range is a better estimate than any other, the minimum of the range should be accrued.

b) If the amount cannot be estimated and no accrual is made, full disclosure is required.

c. If an accrual is not made, disclosure of the contingency should be made when there is a reasonable possibility that a loss will occur.

1) Some remote contingencies, e.g., guarantees of others' indebtedness, should always be disclosed.

d. Examples of contingencies include bad debts, warranty obligations, expropriations, pending or threatened litigation, risk of casualty losses by insurers, and repurchase agreements.

1) However, no loss contingency is accrued for general business risks (e.g., fire loss) because no asset has been impaired or liability incurred.

e. Gain contingencies should be disclosed but are not recognized until realized.

5. **SFAS 6**, *Classification of Short-Term Obligations Expected to Be Refinanced*, states that short-term liabilities expected to be refinanced should be reported as current liabilities unless the firm both plans to refinance and has the ability to refinance the debt on a long-term basis.

a. The ability to refinance on a long-term basis is evidenced by a post-balance-sheet-date issuance of long-term debt or a financing arrangement that will clearly permit long-term refinancing.

b. The amount of the short-term liability excluded from current liabilities should not exceed the

1) Net proceeds of debt or securities issued
2) Net amounts available under refinancing agreements

c. Any current liabilities that are repaid after year-end but prior to receipt of funds from long-term debt are not considered refinanced; they are current liabilities because they required use of current assets.

6. **SFAS 7**, *Accounting and Reporting by Development Stage Enterprises*, prescribes accounting and reporting by development stage companies.

a. Development stage companies, divisions, etc., have

1) Substantially all their efforts devoted to establishing the business, or
2) Principal operations under way but have not produced significant revenues.

b. Development stage companies account for all transactions in the same manner as any other enterprise; that is, no special accounting principles apply.

c. Some additional disclosures are required in the financial statements:

1) An extra column showing cumulative amounts from inception of the enterprise in the income statement and statement of cash flows

2) Dates of securities issuances and amounts received

7. **SFAS 13**, *Accounting for Leases*, covers accounting for leases on the books of both the lessee and the lessor.

   a. For the lessee, there are two classifications, capital leases and operating leases.

      1) **Capital lease** -- in reality, a purchase of an asset. It should be treated in a manner similar to a purchase.

         a) An asset and a liability should be recorded for the present value of the minimum lease payments.

            i) Minimum lease payments are the payments to be made during the lease term consisting of any guaranteed residual value, bargain purchase option, penalties for failure to renew, and other similar payments.

         b) Interest expense should then be recognized over the life of the lease based on the effective interest rate times the lease liability.

            i) The effective interest rate is that which equates all of the minimum lease payments to the present value recorded as the initial liability.

         c) The asset's cost should be amortized (depreciated) over the useful life of the asset (if the lease will transfer ownership). Otherwise, amortize over the life of the lease.

      2) **Operating lease** -- usually shorter term. It is a rental contract and is accounted for as such.

         a) No entry is made to record the lease. Lease payments are expensed as incurred.

         b) Expense is recognized as the services are used; if lease payments are not reasonably aligned with service obtained, accruals or deferrals must be used.

   b. For a lease to be recorded by the lessee as a capital lease, it must meet at least one of the following four criteria:

      1) Title reverts to the lessee at the end of the lease.

      2) There is a bargain purchase option.

      3) The lease term is 75% or more of the useful economic life of the property.

      4) Present value of the minimum lease payments equals 90% or more of the fair value of the leased property.

   c. Classification of leases by lessors

      1) A **sales-type lease** provides both sales profit and interest revenue for a manufacturer or dealer-lessor and transfers ownership rights and responsibilities to the lessee.

      2) A **direct financing lease** transfers ownership rights and responsibilities to the lessee and provides interest revenue to the lessor, but does not provide sales profit.

      3) A **leveraged lease** is similar to a direct financing lease, but there is a substantial leverage; i.e., the lessor finances the leased asset with nonrecourse debt.

      4) An **operating lease** is any lease that is, in effect, a rental agreement.

d. For the leases to be recorded (by the lessor) as sales-type, direct financing, or leveraged leases, they must meet one of the four criteria for lessee capital leases (see b. on page 340), and meet both of the following criteria:

   1) Be collectible with reasonable predictability
   2) Have no material uncertainties, such as unusual guarantees

e. Sales-type leases are recorded by debiting a lease receivable for the total amount of all payments to be received (at gross). This amount includes any residual value, whether or not guaranteed. The sales account is credited.

   1) The cost of the leased asset is credited. Also credited is the deferred interest income (total payments to be received minus cost of lease asset and gross profit on the sale). The debit is to cost of sales.

      a) If the residual value is unguaranteed, cost of sales and sales revenue are reduced by the present value of the residual value, but other amounts are unaffected.

         i) The reason for this procedure is that realization of an unguaranteed residual value is not deemed to be assured, and therefore its "sale" is not recognized.

   2) Initial direct costs of the lease are also expensed as cost of sales on sales-type leases. See SFAS 91 for the full definition of initial direct costs.

f. A direct financing lease is accounted for as a financing transaction with a debit to lease receivable for the total payments to be received, a credit to the asset cost, and a credit to the deferred interest income.

   1) Under SFAS 98, the initial direct costs of a direct financing lease are included in the gross investment. The net investment equals the gross investment, plus unamortized initial direct costs, minus unearned income. Unearned income equals the gross investment minus the carrying amount. The unearned income and the initial direct costs are amortized over the lease term to provide a constant periodic rate of return on the net investment.

g. Operating leases are rental agreements under which lease payments are revenues earned. The leased asset remains on the lessor's books, and all related expenses (e.g., taxes, insurance, maintenance, etc.) are lessor expenses.

   1) The initial direct costs of operating leases are deferred and allocated over the lease term in proportion to the recognition of rental income by the lessor.

h. Real estate leases

   1) Land leases are considered capital leases only if they transfer title or have a bargain purchase option.

   2) A lease of land and a building is separated into land and building portions. The present value of the minimum lease payments minus executory costs is allocated based on the fair values of the land and building at the inception of the lease.

      a) However, if the lease has neither a title transfer provision nor a bargain purchase option and the land value is less than 25% of total value, the lease should be accounted for as a single item over the lease term.

   3) When real estate leases include equipment, the equipment portion should be accounted for separately as an equipment lease.

i. Sales-leasebacks (See SFAS 98 on page 361 regarding sales-leasebacks involving real estate.)

   1) Lessor accounts for this kind of lease as an asset purchase and then records the lease as either direct financing or operating.

   2) Lessee recognizes any loss on sale immediately but defers gain recognition and amortizes over the life of the lease.

      a) If the seller gives up use of more than 90% of the property, gain can be recognized at sale.

      b) If seller continues to lease 10% to 90% of the property, gain is recognized to the extent the gain exceeds the present value of the operating lease payments (or the amount of the lease asset if one of the four criteria for a capital lease is met).

j. Related party leases follow the same rules except when their substance varies from their form (due to the related party relationship) -- then they should be restated.

   1) All leasing subsidiaries are consolidated.
   2) All related party transactions must be disclosed.

k. In a sublease, the original lessee accounts for the transaction as a lessor unless (s)he is relieved of the lease obligation.

   1) Sublessee accounts for the transaction as for any other lessee.

l. Because of tax advantages (the reason leveraged leases developed), leveraged leases usually have negative book values on the lessor's books during the early years.

   1) The net investment in the lease (lease receivable) is net of the nonrecourse debt (the reason for the term leveraged lease).

   2) Lessor recognizes income using the interest method only in periods when the net investment in the lease has a positive book value.

   3) Lessee accounts for the lease as for any other lease.

8. **SFAS 14**, *Financial Reporting for Segments of a Business Enterprise*, requires disclosures about operations in different industries, foreign operations and export sales, and major customers. It does not apply to interim statements.

   a. The criteria for separate industry segment disclosures

      1) Revenue of the segment is 10% or more of combined revenue (including intersegment revenue).

      2) Absolute amount of operating profit or loss is 10% or more of the greater of the combined operating profit of all segments that did not have an operating loss, or the combined operating loss of all segments that did have an operating loss.

         a) Based on traceable expenses, not general corporate expenses, etc.

      3) Identifiable assets exceed 10% of the combined identifiable assets.

         a) Excludes central administration assets

         b) Excludes investments in and loans to other segments except financial segments

   b. The reportable segments should account for 75% of total sales to nonaffiliated customers. The maximum number of reportable segments is 10.

c. Disclosure requirements for each segment

1) Sales to nonaffiliated customers
2) Revenue from intersegment sales
3) Operating profit or loss for each segment
4) Carrying amounts of identifiable assets

d. Other related disclosures

1) These include

a) The aggregate amount of depreciation, depletion, and amortization for each reportable segment

b) The amount of capital expenditures, by segment, for the period

c) The equity in the net income and investment in unconsolidated subsidiaries and other equity method investees whose operations are vertically integrated with the operations of that segment

i) Disclosure shall also be made of the geographic areas in which those vertically integrated equity method investees operate.

2) The effect on the segment of all changes in accounting principles should be disclosed. This latter provision is simply an expansion of the reporting requirements prescribed in APB 20.

3) There is no requirement that inventory composition and amount be reported for each segment; however, the aggregate carrying value of identifiable assets must be disclosed.

e. If foreign operations' revenue from sales to unaffiliated customers is 10% or more of combined revenue, or if the identifiable assets of foreign operations are 10% or more of consolidated assets, disclosure of foreign revenue, operating profit, and asset data is required.

f. If a major customer accounts for 10% or more of revenue, disclosure should be made and the segment making the sales identified. The customer need not be named.

g. This SFAS applies only to public companies and only to annual statements (SFAS 18 eliminated the requirement to report segment information in interim reports).

1) Segment data are also not required for statements of consolidated investees, presented with the consolidated financial statements.

2) If segment disclosures are made for other (interim or nonpublic) financial statements, however, they must conform to this SFAS.

9. **SFAS 15**, *Accounting by Debtors and Creditors for Troubled Debt Restructurings*, prescribes the accounting by debtors and creditors in a restructuring of troubled debt. Troubled debt restructurings are those in which a creditor, for economic or legal reasons related to the debtor's financial difficulties, grants a concession to the debtor that it would not otherwise consider.

a. Debtors should recognize a gain when creditors settle a debt by accepting assets with a fair value less than the book value of the debt.

1) If equity securities are issued to settle a debt, the issuance should be recorded at fair value.

2) SFAS 114, concerning creditor accounting for impaired loans, amended SFAS 15 to require that all loans restructured in a troubled debt restructuring involving a modification of terms be measured in accordance with the provisions of SFAS 114. Under this pronouncement, impairment is measured based on the present value of the expected future cash flows discounted at the effective interest rate, or at the loan's observable market price or the fair value of the collateral.

b. Creditors should account for assets received as full payment of debt at fair value. However, when long-lived assets that will be sold are received, they should be accounted for at fair value minus cost to sell, as that term is defined in SFAS 121.

   1) When the restructuring involves only a modification of terms, the creditor accounts for the transaction in accordance with SFAS 114.

c. Repossessions are accounted for as the receipt of assets in full satisfaction.

d. Debt restructuring expenses are expensed as incurred, except when debtors issue equity securities (reduce paid-in capital by the amount of restructuring expenses).

e. Material gains or losses are extraordinary for debtors because an extinguishment of debt has occurred.

f. Debtors must disclose

   1) The principal changes in terms, the major features of settlement, or both
   2) Aggregate gain on restructuring and related tax effect
   3) Aggregate net gain or loss on asset transfers
   4) Per share aggregate gain on restructuring, net of tax
   5) In subsequent periods, the extent to which contingent amounts are included in the carrying value of restructured payables

g. Creditors must disclose the amount of commitments to lend additional monies to troubled debtors owing receivables whose terms have been modified.

10. **SFAS 16**, *Prior Period Adjustments*, (as amended by SFAS 109) permits only the correction of an error in a statement for a prior period to be accounted for as a prior-period adjustment, i.e., as an adjustment to beginning retained earnings.

   a. On interim statements, however, the adjustments listed below identified with a prior interim period of the current fiscal year should result in the retroactive restatement of each prior interim period:

      1) This includes adjustments arising from litigation, income taxes, contract negotiations, and rate regulation of utilities.
      2) Any adjustment relating to prior fiscal periods should be included as a prior-period adjustment in the first interim period.
      3) Full disclosure must be made in all interim statements.
      4) These adjustments only affect interim reporting. In annual statements, these items are reported in current income.

11. **SFAS 18**, *Financial Reporting for Segments of a Business Enterprise - Interim Financial Statements*, eliminates the requirement to present segment information in interim financial statements.

12. **SFAS 19,** *Financial Accounting and Reporting by Oil and Gas Producing Companies*, **SFAS 25,** *Suspension of Certain Accounting Requirements for Oil and Gas Producing Companies*, and **SFAS 69**, *Disclosures about Oil and Gas Producing Activities*, concern accounting by oil- and gas-producing companies.
    a. Both the full-cost method and the successful-efforts method of accounting are acceptable.
        1) Full-cost accounting capitalizes all costs related to the discovery of oil and gas (e.g., exploration, leasing, carrying, and development costs).
        2) Successful-efforts accounting capitalizes costs that result directly in the discovery of oil or gas (successful wells), but the same costs are expensed for a dry hole (unsuccessful well).
        3) All companies (public and private) must disclose how costs of oil- and gas-producing activities are accounted for and how capitalized costs are amortized.
    b. The following are required disclosures by publicly held companies if 10% or more of revenues or income (loss) is derived from oil- and gas-producing activities:
        1) Proved oil and gas reserves at beginning and end of year
        2) Aggregate capitalized costs and accumulated depreciation on oil and gas property
        3) Oil and gas costs for the period
        4) Operating results in the aggregate and by each area for which reserve data are disclosed
        5) Discounted future cash flows from proven reserves
    c. Authors' note: The SEC once proposed reserve recognition accounting (RRA).
        1) Revenue was to be recognized when reserves were discovered.
        2) The future estimated cash flows from these reserves would be discounted back to the present.
        3) Changes in the present value of the future cash flows would be recognized in income in the period of change.
        4) The SEC abandoned the RRA method because of procedural difficulties (it was difficult to estimate reserves, and the process was subject to manipulation).
13. **SFAS 21**, *Suspension of the Reporting of Earnings per Share and Segment Information by Nonpublic Enterprises*, eliminates these requirements for nonpublicly held companies. Thus, segment information must now be disclosed only in the annual financial statements of publicly held companies.
14. **SFAS 22**, *Changes in the Provisions of Lease Agreements Resulting from Refundings of Tax-Exempt Debt*, applies when the lessor refunds tax-exempt debt; the advantages of the refunding are passed through to the lessee; and the lessee classifies the revised agreement as a capital lease, or the lessor classifies it as a direct-financing lease.
15. **SFAS 23**, *Inception of the Lease*, defines the inception of the lease as occurring at the date of the earlier of the lease agreement or commitment, not at the date that construction is completed or the property is acquired by the lessor. It also redefines the "fair value of the leased property" for a lease with a cost-based or escalator provision.

16. **SFAS 24**, *Reporting Segment Information in Financial Statements That Are Presented in Another Enterprise's Financial Report*, eliminates the requirement to disclose segment information in the separate statements of a parent or investee company when consolidated or combined financial statements accompany those statements.
17. **SFAS 27**, *Classification of Renewals or Extensions of Existing Sales-Type or Direct Financing Leases*, requires a lessor to classify a renewal or an extension of a sales-type or direct financing lease as a sales-type lease if the lease otherwise qualifies as a sales-type lease and the renewal or extension occurs near the end of the lease term.
18. **SFAS 28**, *Accounting for Sales with Leasebacks*, requires the seller to recognize some profit or loss when the seller retains the use of only a minor part of the property or a minor part of its remaining useful life through the leaseback, or when the seller retains more than a minor part but less than substantially all of the use of the property and the profit on the sale exceeds the present value of the minimum lease payments for an operating lease or the recorded amount of the leased asset for a capital lease.
19. **SFAS 29**, *Determining Contingent Rentals*, defines contingent rentals as the changes in lease payments that result from changes subsequent to the inception of the lease in the factors on which lease payments are based. Lease payments that depend on a factor that exists and is measurable at the inception of the lease are included in minimum lease payments. Lease payments that depend on a factor that does not exist or is not measurable at the inception of the lease are contingent rentals and are excluded.
20. **SFAS 30**, *Disclosure of Information about Major Customers*, amends SFAS 14 to require disclosure of sales to an individual domestic government or foreign government when those revenues are at least 10% of total revenues. Disclosure of sales to a governmental customer is the same as that to any other customer.
21. **SFAS 34**, *Capitalization of Interest Cost*, requires capitalization of material interest costs for certain assets constructed for internal use and those constructed as discrete units (e.g., real estate projects and ships).
    a. It does not apply to products routinely produced for inventory, assets in use or ready for use, assets not being used or being prepared for use, and idle land.
    b. Because interest cost is an integral part of the total cost of acquiring a qualifying asset, its disposition should be the same as that of other components of asset cost.
    c. Capitalize interest costs that could have been avoided if the asset had not been constructed.
        1) Use the average accumulated expenditures for the asset during the period.
        2) An enterprise may use the interest rate on new borrowings for the asset.
            a) To the extent average accumulated expenditures exceed new borrowings associated with the asset, a weighted average of the rates on other borrowings must be used.
        3) The interest cost capitalized cannot exceed the amount incurred.
    d. The capitalization period begins when the following three conditions are present:
        1) The company has made expenditures for the asset.
        2) Work on the asset is in progress.
        3) Interest cost is incurred.
    e. The capitalization period ends when the asset is substantially complete.

22. **SFAS 35**, *Accounting and Reporting by Defined Benefit Pension Plans*, requires that financial statements of defined benefit pension plans (excluding those of state and local governments) be prepared on an accrual basis and disclose the following:
    a. Net assets available for benefits at year-end with reasonable detail of
        1) Contributions receivable
        2) Investments
        3) Operating assets
    b. Changes in net assets during the year
        1) Net appreciation (depreciation) of each class of investment
        2) Investment income
        3) Contributions
            a) Employer
            b) Employee
            c) Other, e.g., government
        4) Benefits paid
        5) Payments to insurance companies
        6) Administrative expenses
    c. Actuarial present value of benefits at the beginning or end of the year based on
        1) Employee pay and length of employment
        2) Expected continued employment
        3) Future benefit increases
        4) Other factors affecting future payments
    d. Factors affecting changes in the actuarial present value of plan benefits that are assumptions about the future, including
        1) Rate of return
        2) Inflation
        3) Employee continued service
        4) Investment current value
        5) Method of computing benefit present value
    e. Further description, if applicable, of
        1) The plan agreement
        2) Significant plan amendments
        3) The priority order of participants' claims to the assets of the plan upon plan termination and benefits guaranteed by the Pension Benefit Guaranty Corporation (PBGC)
        4) The funding policy and any changes in such policy
        5) The policy regarding purchase of contracts with insurance companies that are excluded from plan assets
        6) The federal income tax status of the plan, if a favorable letter of determination has not been obtained
        7) Investments that represent 5% or more of the net assets available for benefits
        8) Significant real estate or other transactions with related parties

23. **SFAS 37**, *Balance Sheet Classification of Deferred Income Taxes*, states that deferred taxes are classified the same as the related asset or liability. If they are not related to an asset or liability, they are classified according to the expected reversal date of the temporary difference (SFAS 109 reinstated SFAS 37, which had been superseded by SFAS 96).

24. **SFAS 38**, *Accounting for Preacquisition Contingencies of Purchased Enterprises*, specifies the accounting by an acquiring enterprise for contingencies of an acquired enterprise that existed at the purchase date and for subsequent adjustments resulting from those contingencies. Amounts that can be reasonably estimated for contingencies that are probable are part of the allocation of the purchase price. Subsequent adjustments are included in net income when the adjustments are determined with limited exceptions.

25. **SFAS 42**, *Determining Materiality for Capitalization of Interest Cost*, amends SFAS 34 to delete ambiguous language that might be construed to allow capitalization of interest to be avoided in some cases and to clarify that SFAS 34 does not establish new tests of materiality.

26. **SFAS 43**, *Accounting for Compensated Absences*, describes accounting for compensated future absences such as sick leave, holidays, and vacations.

    a. Usually, only vacation pay is sufficiently material to be accrued.
    b. Criteria for accrual

        1) Obligation arises for past services.
        2) Employee rights vest or accumulate.

            a) Sick pay benefits need not be accrued unless they vest.

        3) Payment is probable.
        4) Amount can be reasonably estimated.

    c. SFAS 43 as amended by SFAS 112 explicitly does not apply to postemployment benefits provided through a pension or postretirement benefit plan (see SFASs 87, 88, and 106), individual deferred compensation arrangements (see APB 12), special or contractual termination benefits (see SFASs 88 and 106), and stock compensation plans (see APB 25).

27. **SFAS 44**, *Accounting for Intangible Assets of Motor Carriers*, requires that the unamortized costs of intangible assets representing interstate rights to transport goods with limited competition be charged to income and, if material, reported as an extraordinary item.

28. **SFAS 45**, *Accounting for Franchise Fee Revenue*, requires that franchisors recognize franchise-fee revenue when all material services have been performed and all material conditions have been met.

    a. Defer initial fees if they are large in relation to subsequent fees or future related services are promised, e.g., if bargain purchase prices exist for supplies.

        1) Recognize the portion of the franchise fee applicable to any tangible assets provided to the franchisee based on the fair values.

    b. Repossession of franchise or refund of franchise fee is a reduction of revenue in the current period.

        1) If a refund is made to franchisee, consider previously recognized revenue to be a contra revenue in the current period.

        2) If no refund is made, bad debts and other expenses are recognized as expenses, and associated deferred revenues should be recognized in the current period.

    c. Disclose all franchisor obligations and commitments.

29. **SFAS 47**, *Disclosure of Long-Term Obligations*, requires disclosure of unconditional purchase obligations associated with suppliers and future payments required by long-term debt and redeemable stock agreements.

   a. Unconditional purchase obligations (which are unrecorded) are those requiring payment for future goods or services and are not cancelable or, if so, provide for a substantial penalty.

   b. Disclosures required for **unrecorded** obligations

      1) Nature and term
      2) Determinable payments in total and for each of the next 5 years
      3) Nature of variable payments
      4) Amounts purchased in current period

   c. Disclosures for **recorded** obligations

      1) Total liability recognized for unconditional purchase obligations
      2) Aggregate maturities and sinking fund requirements for all long-term debt
      3) Aggregate amount of capital stock redeemable at fixed amounts

30. **SFAS 48**, *Revenue Recognition When Right of Return Exists*, requires sales revenue and cost of sales to be reduced by expected returns when goods are sold with a right of return (all related expected costs should be accrued in accordance with SFAS 5).

   a. This pronouncement states that the sale may be recognized at the time of sale if all of the following conditions are met:

      1) The seller's price is substantially fixed or determinable.
      2) The buyer has paid the seller, or the buyer is obligated to pay, and the obligation is not contingent on resale.
      3) The buyer's obligation to the seller is unchanged by damage to or theft or destruction of the product.
      4) The buyer has economic substance apart from the seller.
      5) The seller does not have any significant obligations regarding resale of the product by the buyer.
      6) The amount of future returns can be reasonably estimated.

   b. If these conditions are not met, revenue recognition is deferred until they are met or the return privilege expires.

31. **SFAS 49**, *Accounting for Product Financing Arrangements*, states that product financing arrangements (to finance inventory) should be accounted for as borrowings rather than as sales.

   a. EXAMPLES:

      1) Product is sold to another with an agreement from the seller to repurchase it.
      2) Seller establishes separate entity for the above purpose(s).
      3) Seller guarantees debt of buyer.
      4) Financed product is to be used or sold by seller.

b. Money received is accounted for as a liability rather than as a sale.

1) Financing and inventory holding costs are to be imputed. Usually, the selling price to the buyer is less than the repurchase price to cover these costs.

2) The SFAS calls the seller (i.e., the party seeking the financing) the **sponsor**.

c. If another firm purchases inventory for repurchase by a sponsor, the repurchaser-sponsor should record asset and liability when the other firm makes the purchase.

32. **SFAS 50**, *Financial Reporting in the Record and Music Industry*, **SFAS 51**, *Financial Reporting by Cable Television Companies*, **SFAS 53**, *Financial Reporting by Producers and Distributors of Motion Picture Films*, **SFAS 60**, *Accounting and Reporting by Insurance Enterprises*, **SFAS 61**, *Accounting for Title Plant*, **SFAS 63**, *Financial Reporting by Broadcasters*, and **SFAS 65**, *Accounting for Certain Mortgage Banking Activities*, contain specialized accounting principles and practices extracted from AICPA Statements of Position and issued by the FASB in SFASs after appropriate due process. The purpose is to establish that these principles are preferable for purposes of justifying accounting changes. However, this explicit adoption of the principles in SOPs and Guides is no longer necessary because of the promulgation of SAS 69 (AU 311), which established a GAAP hierarchy.

33. **SFAS 52**, *Foreign Currency Translation*, prescribes the functional currency translation approach for all foreign currency translation.

a. The functional currency is that of the primary environment in which an entity operates, i.e., usually the currency in which cash is generated and expended by the entity whose financial statements are being translated.

b. Steps in the functional currency translation approach

1) Identify functional currency.

2) Measure (present) statements in the functional currency; e.g., a Swiss company may prepare its statements in Swiss francs even though it conducts most of its business in German marks (the German mark is the functional currency).

a) In such a case, the statements are **remeasured** into the functional currency using the temporal rate method. This method applies the current rate to all items except common nonmonetary accounts and their related revenues, expenses, gains, and losses, which are remeasured at historical rates.

b) Remeasurement presents statements as if they had been originally prepared in the functional currency.

3) Use a current rate to **translate** assets and liabilities in terms of the functional currency to the reporting currency if different (revenues and expenses at average rates for the year).

a) EXAMPLE: If a German subsidiary of a U.S. company operates primarily in Germany, its statements should be prepared in terms of German marks and then translated into U.S. dollars for purposes of the consolidated financial statements.

4) When translating foreign currency statements into the reporting currency for consolidation, neither foreign exchange gain nor loss is reported in the income statement. Rather, these gains and losses are accumulated in a separate shareholders' equity account to be recognized in income upon the sale or liquidation of the foreign entity.

c. Foreign currency gains and losses on transactions with foreign customers, suppliers, etc., are recognized by applying the current rate (the spot rate).

1) For forward exchange transactions (hedging), discount or premium (difference between the spot rate and the forward rate) should be amortized over the life of the hedging contract.

2) On hedging contracts related to a particular foreign exchange commitment, gains should be deferred and recognized as part of the underlying transaction.

a) EXAMPLE: If a forward contract is bought to hedge against a payable due in a foreign currency, the hedging gain is netted with settlement of the liability (note that the purpose of hedging is to eliminate or offset gain or loss on holding the liability).

b) Losses that will not be offset by gains should be recognized immediately, not deferred.

34. **SFAS 57**, *Related Party Disclosures*, requires disclosure of related party transactions except compensation agreements, expense allowances, and other similar items; and transactions eliminated in consolidated or combined financial statements.

a. Related parties include equity method investees, trusts for benefit of employees, principal owners and management and their immediate families, and others who can significantly influence such transactions.

b. Required disclosures include

1) Relationship of related parties
2) Description of the transactions
3) Dollar amounts of the transactions for each period presented
4) Amounts due to or from the related parties

c. All situations in which an individual, organization, etc., controls another must also be disclosed.

35. **SFAS 58**, *Capitalization of Interest Cost in Financial Statements That Include Investments Accounted for by the Equity Method*, amends SFAS 34 to limit capitalization of consolidated interest to qualifying assets of the parent and consolidated subsidiaries. Investments by the investor qualify if they are accounted for by the equity method during the period that "the investee has activities in progress necessary to commence its planned principal operations provided that the investee's activities include the use of funds to acquire qualifying assets for its operations."

36. **SFAS 62**, *Capitalization of Interest Cost in Situations Involving Certain Tax-Exempt Borrowings and Certain Gifts and Grants*, amends SFAS 34 to require capitalization of interest cost of restricted tax-exempt borrowings minus interest earned on their temporary investment from the date of borrowing until the qualifying assets are ready for their intended use. It also prohibits capitalization of interest on qualifying assets acquired using restricted gifts or grants.

37. **SFAS 64**, *Extinguishments of Debt Made to Satisfy Sinking-Fund Requirements*, amends SFAS 4 to provide that gains and losses from extinguishments of debt made to satisfy sinking-fund requirements that must be met within one year of the extinguishment are not extraordinary items. Furthermore, the classification of gains and losses from extinguishments made to satisfy sinking-fund requirements is to be determined regardless of the means used for the extinguishment.

38. **SFAS 66**, *Accounting for Sales of Real Estate*, deals with accounting for sales of real estate.
    a. When accounting for sales of land other than at retail, the full accrual method is used if the following criteria are met:
        1) The sale is consummated.
        2) The buyer's investments (both initial and continuing) indicate a commitment to pay for the property.
        3) Seller's receivable is not subject to subordination.
    b. If the above criteria are not met, then one of the following five methods should be used:
        1) Installment method
        2) Cost-recovery method
        3) Accounting for receipts as deposits until certain conditions are met
        4) Reduced-profit method
        5) Financing or leasing agreement instead of a sale
    c. Retail land sales also should use the full accrual method if several criteria are met.
        1) If criteria are not met, then the percentage-of-completion, the installment, or the deposit method should be used.
39. **SFAS 67**, *Accounting for Costs and Initial Rental Operations of Real Estate Projects*, covers the accounting for costs and initial rental operations of real estate projects, including acquisition, development, construction, selling, and rental costs associated with such projects.
    a. Preacquisition costs, such as surveying, may be capitalized as are taxes and insurance during the development stage.
    b. Amortization of capitalized costs may be done on the basis of relative fair value before construction, relative sales value, or land area, or by means of specific identification.
40. **SFAS 68**, *Research and Development Arrangements*, prescribes the accounting for an obligation under an arrangement for the funding of R&D by others. If the enterprise is obligated to repay the other parties, it credits a liability and debits R&D costs to expense as incurred.
41. **SFAS 71**, *Accounting for the Effects of Certain Types of Regulation*, applies to the general purpose financial statements of regulated enterprises.
    a. Rates are normally set by an independent, third-party regulator and are designed to recover the enterprise's costs and a return on capital.
    b. Enterprises subject to this statement shall apply it instead of any conflicting provisions of other authoritative pronouncements.
        1) The assumption is that, if a rate-maker's definition of an asset is different from that under GAAP, the rate-maker will permit the future realization of that asset in an amount equal to the carrying value.
        2) EXAMPLE: Some public utilities are permitted to capitalize interest during construction based on the cost of debt capital (permitted under SFAS 34) and equity capital (not permitted by SFAS 34). In such a case, a utility would apply SFAS 71 instead of SFAS 34.

c. Also, utilities are often not permitted to record deferred income taxes, but SFAS 71 (as amended) requires recognition of a deferred tax liability or asset for the deferred tax consequences of temporary differences in accordance with SFAS 109.

d. Refunds to customers should be recognized in the statements in accordance with SFAS 5, *Accounting for Contingencies*.

e. Leases should be accounted for under SFAS 13, *Accounting for Leases*. See page 340.

42. **SFAS 72**, *Accounting for Certain Acquisitions of Banking or Thrift Institutions*, concerns accounting for the excess of the fair value of liabilities assumed over the fair value of net identifiable assets obtained (goodwill) in an acquisition of a bank or thrift institution. This "excess" is amortized by the interest method. The amortization period is to be no longer than that period over which the discount on the long-term interest-bearing assets acquired is to be recognized as interest income.

43. **SFAS 73**, *Reporting a Change in Accounting for Railroad Track Structures*, amends APB 20 to require that a change to depreciation accounting for railroad track structures be reported by restating financial statements of all prior periods presented.

44. **SFAS 75**, *Deferral of the Effective Date of Certain Accounting Requirements for Pension Plans of State and Local Governmental Units*, amends SFAS 35 to defer indefinitely its application to pension plans of state and local governmental units.

45. **SFAS 76**, *Extinguishment of Debt*, concerns in-substance defeasance transactions.

a. Debt will be considered extinguished for accounting purposes, if

1) The debtor pays the creditor and is relieved of all obligations.

a) This includes reacquisition of debt in the public securities markets.

2) The debtor places cash or risk-free securities (those issued by the U.S. government or backed by U.S. government securities) in an irrevocable trust to be used solely for satisfying scheduled payments of a specific debt. This is in-substance defeasance.

a) The possibility must be remote that the debtor will be required to make future payments with respect to the debt.

b) The cash flow of the trust must coincide with debt service requirements.

3) The debtor is legally released from its primary obligation, and it is probable that the debtor will not have to make any future payments.

b. There are several reasons for in-substance defeasance, including removing a liability from the books without actually paying it off.

1) For instance, a high call premium may make repurchase of bonds undesirable.

2) Taxes on reacquisition gains can be avoided or postponed.

46. **SFAS 77**, *Reporting by Transferors for Transfers of Receivables with Recourse*, deals with the accounting by transferors for transfers of receivables with recourse.
    a. Transferors are required to report a sale of receivables with recourse as a sale (e.g., a factoring arrangement) if the transferor surrenders control of future economic benefits of the receivables, the transferor can reasonably estimate its liability under the recourse provisions, and the transferee cannot require the transferor to repurchase except under the recourse provisions.
        1) An assignment of receivables with recourse is to be accounted for in the same manner as a factoring of receivables.
        2) The amount received from the buyer of the receivables is to be treated as the proceeds from a sale and not as a liability.
        3) Any gain or loss on transfer is to be reported in the period of transfer rather than over the period that the receivables remain outstanding.
        4) When a floating interest rate is used to determine the selling price of receivables, SFAS 77 requires that the sales price be estimated by use of the market interest rate at the transfer date. Later changes in the rate are treated prospectively as a change in estimate, not as interest expense or income.
        5) When the transfer does not qualify as a sale
            a) A liability is credited for the total proceeds.
            b) Cash is debited for the amount received.
            c) A receivable is debited for any amount still due from the transferee.
            d) The balance is treated as a cost of borrowing by debiting it to discount on transferred receivables.
                i) This cost is amortized to interest expense over the life of the receivables.

47. **SFAS 78**, *Classification of Obligations That Are Callable by the Creditor*, requires a debtor, who is in violation of a long-term loan agreement that makes the debt callable, to classify the obligation as a current liability.
    a. Long-term debts need not be classified as current if it is probable that a violation existing at the balance sheet date will be cured within a specified grace period.
        1) If the creditor formally waives the right to demand repayment for a period of more than a year from the balance sheet date, the debt need not be classified as current.
        2) Reclassification is not required if the debtor expects and has the ability to refinance the obligation on a long-term basis.
    b. The provisions of this statement also apply to debts that by their terms are callable within the year (or normal operating cycle, if longer).

48. **SFAS 79**, *Elimination of Certain Disclosures for Business Combinations by Nonpublic Enterprises*, amends APB 16 to eliminate the requirement for nonpublic enterprises to disclose pro forma results of operations for business combinations accounted for by the purchase method.

49. **SFAS 80**, *Accounting for Futures Contracts*, addresses accounting for futures contracts.

    a. A gain or loss must be recognized in the period in which a change in the market value of a contract occurs.

    b. Exceptions are made for contracts that are hedges of existing assets, liabilities, firm commitments, or anticipated transactions.

        1) To qualify as a hedge, a futures contract must meet three criteria at inception:

            a) The item to be hedged should expose the company to price or interest rate risk.

            b) The futures contract should reduce that exposure.

            c) The contract should be designated as a hedge.

        2) No exception is allowed and immediate recognition of gain or loss is required if the contract is intended to hedge an item reported at fair value.

    c. A change in market value not reported as a gain or loss because the contract qualifies as a hedge is usually

        1) Reported as an adjustment of the carrying amount of an existing asset or liability that is hedged

        2) Included in the measurement of a transaction that satisfies a firm commitment

        3) Included in the measurement of a subsequent anticipated transaction

    d. SFAS 80 does not apply to foreign currency futures contracts.

50. **SFAS 84**, *Induced Conversions of Convertible Debt*, deals with the accounting treatment of incentives given to induce conversion of convertible debt to equity securities of the debtor.

    a. An expense must be recognized equal to the fair value of the sweetener, i.e., the additional securities or other consideration given to induce conversion.

    b. The expense should not be treated as an extraordinary item.

51. **SFAS 85**, *Yield Test for Determining Whether a Convertible Security Is a Common Stock Equivalent*, changes the yield test for determining whether a convertible security is a common stock equivalent.

    a. Previously, a cash yield test was used to determine whether a convertible security should be classified as a common stock equivalent in the calculation of primary earnings per share. An effective yield test is now required for convertible securities issued after March 31, 1985.

    b. The popularity of zero coupon bonds led to this change in the common stock equivalency test.

        1) Because zero coupon bonds have no annual interest payments, they were automatically common stock equivalents under the cash yield test.

        2) This treatment was inconsistent with the economic substance of such securities and with the objectives of APB 15, *Earnings per Share*.

    c. Under the new test, for a convertible bond to be classified a common stock equivalent, it must have an effective yield (including accrual of interest) of less than 66⅔% of the average Aa corporate bond yield at issuance.

52. **SFAS 86**, *Accounting for the Costs of Computer Software to Be Sold, Leased, or Otherwise Marketed*, concerns the cost of computer software to be sold, leased, or otherwise marketed, whether developed internally or purchased.

   a. Costs are expensed as R&D until technological feasibility has been established for the product.

   b. Thereafter, costs (limited to net realizable value) should be capitalized and amortized using the straight-line method over the estimated remaining life of the product.

      1) Capitalization ends when the product is available for general release.

53. **SFAS 87**, *Employers' Accounting for Pensions*, concerns employers' accounting for pensions. SFAS 87 is a very complicated document with a number of confusing calculations. The objective of this overview is to cut through the minutiae to several basic concepts in SFAS 87.

   a. Basically, SFAS 87 specifies

      1) A standardized method of calculating annual pension expense. Previously, annual pension expense was required to lie between maximum and minimum figures, the elements of which differed.

      2) That the assignment of pension cost to individual periods is to be based on the pension plan's benefit formula. Previously, the periodic cost of the plan could be calculated using "any acceptable actuarial cost method."

      3) Recording an immediate liability if the pension obligation is underfunded. Previously, no pension liability was required to be recognized except to the extent that recognized pension cost exceeded funding for the period.

      4) More extensive disclosures with emphasis on reconciling the funded status of the pension plan with the amounts reported in the employer's financial statements. Previously, such matters as the reconciliation of the funded status of the plan and the components of net periodic pension cost did not have to be disclosed.

   b. Annual pension expense is now called **net periodic pension cost (NPPC)**. It consists of

      1) **Service cost**, which is the present value of the future benefits earned in the current period (as calculated according to the plan's benefit formula). This amount is provided by the plan's actuary.

      2) **Interest cost**, which is the increase in the projected benefit obligation (PBO). Multiply PBO at the beginning of the year times the current discount rate (e.g., the interest rate at which annuities could be purchased to settle pension obligations). This discount rate may change with changes in interest rates.

         a) Definitions

            i) **Projected benefit obligation (PBO)** -- the actuarial present value of all future benefits attributed to past employee service at a moment in time. It is based on assumptions as to future compensation if the pension plan formula is based on future compensation; e.g., the plan might base benefits on the highest level of compensation earned during the employee's period of service.

            ii) **Accumulated benefit obligation (ABO)** -- the same as the PBO, but limited to past and current compensation levels

         b) The PBO and the discount rate are provided by the plan's actuary.

3) **Actual return on plan assets**. SFAS 87 includes the "actual return on plan assets" as a component of NPPC, but this amount is usually not used in calculating the NPPC figure reported in the income statement.

   a) Instead, the **expected return on plan assets** is used. It is the market-related value of plan assets at the beginning of the period multiplied by the expected long-term rate of return.

4) **Amortization of actuarial gains and losses**. These include changes in valuation of the PBO and asset gains and losses (difference between the expected return on assets for a period and the actual return for that period).

5) **Amortization of prior service cost**. If a pension plan is amended to grant additional benefits for past periods of service, the cost of the retroactive benefits is allocated to the future periods of service of employees active at the date of the amendment who are expected to receive benefits.

6) **Amortization of any unrecognized net obligation or net asset arising when SFAS 87 is first applied**. The net obligation or net asset is essentially the difference between the PBO of the plan and the fair value of the plan assets adjusted for any recognized accrued liability or prepaid asset. Straight-line amortization is to be over the average remaining service period of participating employees (if less than 15 years, the employer may elect a 15-year amortization period).

   a) For example, if a plan is underfunded by $125,000 (the excess of the PBO over plan assets) but an accrued liability of $50,000 has already been credited because the periodic pension cost of prior periods exceeded funding, the unrecognized net obligation is $75,000. This $75,000 would be amortized over the remaining service period of participating employees.

c. An additional minimum pension liability may now be required to be recognized. Recognized pension liabilities may already exist prior to application of SFAS 87 and can arise when funding is less than the NPPC.

   1) The amount is based on the unfunded amount of the ABO rather than the PBO.

   2) The amount reported in the balance sheet is the net of the additional minimum liability and any previously recognized accrued liability or prepaid asset. The net liability must equal the excess of the ABO over the fair value of the plan assets.

   3) Recognition has no effect on earnings because an intangible asset will be debited to the extent that unrecognized prior service cost exists. If that amount is not adequate, a separate component of equity is debited.

d. SFAS 87 requires extensive disclosures about

   1) The plan, its coverage, and benefit formula

   2) The components of the NPPC

   3) Schedules reconciling the plan's funded status with amounts shown, with separate disclosure of various gains, losses, liabilities, assets, and obligations

   4) Assumed discount (interest) rates used in the pension expense and liability calculations

54. **SFAS 88**, *Employers' Accounting for Settlements and Curtailments of Defined Benefit Pension Plans and for Termination Benefits*, concerns employer's accounting for settlement of defined benefit pension obligations, curtailment of defined benefit plans, and termination benefits.

   a. It is applicable within the framework created by SFAS 87.

      1) Settlement refers to a payoff of the pension obligation, such as by purchase of an annuity from an insurance company.

      2) Curtailment refers to a reduction in benefits resulting in a decrease in the pension obligation.

   b. If all or part of the PBO is settled, gain or loss is immediately recognized equal to an appropriate proportion of the combined amounts of the unrecognized gain or loss arising subsequent to application of SFAS 87 and any remaining unrecognized net asset arising at the transition to SFAS 87.

      1) EXAMPLE: A company settles 80% of its $100,000 PBO by purchasing a nonparticipating annuity contract for $80,000. The unrecognized net loss subsequent to transition was $30,000, and the unrecognized net asset at transition was $40,000. The maximum gain is therefore $10,000 ($40,000 net asset – $30,000 net loss). The settlement gain is $8,000 (80% settlement percentage x $10,000 maximum gain).

      2) Definition recap

         a) The unrecognized gain or loss arising subsequent to application of SFAS 87 is an actuarial gain or loss.

         b) The unrecognized net asset arising at the transition to SFAS 87 equals pension plan assets minus the PBO, plus any pension liability, or minus any prepaid pension costs on the employer's balance sheet.

   c. If a curtailment occurs, the net gain or loss will be equal to the combined amount of unrecognized prior service cost associated with years of service no longer expected to be rendered (a loss) and the change in the PBO (a curtailment gain or loss) that is not a reversal of previously unrecognized gains or losses.

      1) For this purpose, any remaining unrecognized net obligation arising from the transition to SFAS 87 is treated as unrecognized prior service cost.

      2) A net loss is recognized when it is probable that a curtailment will occur and its effects are reasonably estimable.

      3) A net gain is recognized when the related employees terminate or the plan suspension or amendment is adopted.

   d. Special benefits for termination of employment are those offered for a short time, and contractual termination benefits are those required by a plan only if a specified event occurs.

      1) The liability and loss are recognized when the employees accept special benefits or when it is probable that employees will be entitled to contractual benefits and the amount is reasonably estimable.

      2) The amount includes any lump-sum payment plus the present value of expected future payments.

e. The gain or loss measured in accordance with the above should be included in the gain or loss upon disposal of a segment if a direct relation exists.

f. A description of the nature of the event(s) and the amount of gain or loss recognized should be disclosed.

g. If an employer entered into an asset reversion transaction (plan assets in excess of obligations reverted to the employer) prior to the effective date of SFAS 88 and recognized a deferred credit for the amount withdrawn, it should recognize a gain as the cumulative effect of a change in accounting principle when SFAS 88 becomes effective (which is at the date SFAS 87 is first applied).

55. **SFAS 89**, *Financial Reporting and Changing Prices*, revokes all required supplementary disclosures about inflation accounting.

   a. SFAS 89 applies to disclosures specified in

      1) SFAS 33, *Financial Reporting and Changing Prices*
      2) SFAS 39, *Financial Reporting and Changing Prices: Specialized Assets -- Mining and Oil and Gas*
      3) SFAS 40, *Financial Reporting and Changing Prices: Specialized Assets -- Timberlands and Growing Timber*
      4) SFAS 41, *Financial Reporting and Changing Prices: Specialized Assets -- Income-Producing Real Estate*
      5) SFAS 46, *Financial Reporting and Changing Prices: Motion Picture Films*
      6) SFAS 54, *Financial Reporting and Changing Prices: Investment Companies*
      7) SFAS 69, *Disclosures about Oil and Gas Producing Activities*, paragraphs 35-38.
      8) SFAS 70, *Financial Reporting and Changing Prices: Foreign Currency Translation*
      9) SFAS 82, *Financial Reporting and Changing Prices: Elimination of Certain Disclosures*

   b. Appendix A of SFAS 89 contains disclosure guidelines for companies that voluntarily make available supplementary information about the effects of price level changes.

56. **SFAS 90**, *Regulated Enterprises - Accounting for Phase-in Plans, Abandonments, and Disallowances of Plant Costs*, concerns costs of abandoned utility plants and disallowed costs of newly completed plants.

   a. Probable future revenue from the rate-making process based on recovery of costs of abandoned plants should be reported at its present value.

      1) Any excess of the plant's cost over that present value is a loss.

   b. Any disallowance in the rate-making process of cost of newly completed plants shall be recognized as a loss.

   c. An allowance for funds used during construction should be capitalized only if its inclusion in allowable costs for rate-making purposes is probable.

57. **SFAS 91**, *Accounting for Nonrefundable Fees and Costs Associated with Originating and Acquiring Loans*, concerns nonrefundable loan fee revenue and loan origination costs applicable to any loan and any lender or purchaser of a loan (banks, S&Ls, insurance companies, etc.).

   a. Loan origination fees and direct loan origination costs (incremental direct costs and certain costs directly related to specified lender activities) are offset. The net amount is deferred and amortized using the interest method.

   b. Estimated prepayments may not be anticipated in the amortization schedules unless the enterprise holds a large number of similar loans and reasonable estimates of future prepayments can be made.

   c. With certain exceptions, loan commitment fees are deferred and recognized as additional interest over the life of the loan (under the interest method).

      1) Expired unused commitment fees are taken immediately to income.

   d. A refinancing is considered a new loan if terms are as favorable to the lender as the original terms. The unamortized costs (revenues) are taken to income when the new loan is granted.

      1) If the terms are not as favorable, the unamortized fees or costs are carried forward as part of the new loan basis.

   e. Unamortized loan origination, commitment, or other fees and costs and purchase premiums and discounts amortized under the interest method should be included in the loan balance.

   f. SFAS 91 also applies to initial direct costs of leases.

      1) Initial direct costs have two components: (1) the lessor's external costs to originate a lease incurred in dealings with independent third parties, and (2) the internal costs directly related to specified activities performed by the lessor for that lease, e.g., to evaluate the lessee's financial condition, to evaluate guarantees and collateral (security arrangements), to negotiate lease terms, to prepare and process lease documents, and to close the transaction.

      2) Initial direct costs do not include the cost of advertising and other solicitation, servicing of existing leases, establishing and monitoring of credit policies, supervision, and administration.

58. **SFAS 92**, *Regulated Enterprises - Accounting for Phase-in Plans*, specifies the accounting for phase-in plans of regulated enterprises.

   a. A phase-in plan is adopted by a regulator when conventional rate-making would provide for a substantial increase in rates upon completion of a new plant. The purpose of the plan is to defer allowable costs that would otherwise be expensed under GAAP to permit graduated rate increases while the utility recovers its costs, including a return on investment.

   b. If substantial construction was performed or the plant was completed prior to 1988, all allowable costs deferred by the regulator under the plan should be capitalized as a deferred charge provided all the following conditions are met:

      1) Costs are deferred under a formal plan accepted by the regulator.

      2) The plan states the timing of cost recovery.

      3) Deferred costs are recovered within 10 years of the time deferrals begin.

      4) The scheduled percentage rate increase for any plan year is not greater than that for the preceding year.

59. **SFAS 93**, *Recognition of Depreciation by Not-for-Profit Organizations*, requires all nonprofit organizations to recognize depreciation on long-lived tangible assets and to make related disclosures. An exception is made for certain art works and historical treasures.

60. **SFAS 94**, *Consolidation of All Majority-Owned Subsidiaries*, is an amendment to ARB 51, APB 18, and ARB 43, Chapter 12. It eliminates certain exceptions to the requirement that all majority-owned subsidiaries be consolidated. Henceforth, foreign subsidiaries, those with large minority interests, or those with nonhomogeneous operations should be consolidated unless control is temporary or is not held by the majority owner.

61. **SFAS 95**, *Statement of Cash Flows*, replaces the statement of changes in financial position with a statement of cash flows.
    a. The statement of cash flows must use terms such as cash or cash and cash equivalents rather than ambiguous terms such as funds because it is intended to explain the change in cash and cash equivalents for the period.
    b. The statement must classify cash receipts and disbursements depending on whether they are from operating, investing, or financing activities.
    c. SFAS 95 encourages use of the direct method of reporting major classes of operating cash receipts and payments.
        1) However, net cash flow from operations may be shown indirectly by reconciling net income or the change in net assets with the same amount of net cash flow that would have been reported under the direct method. The reconciliation should remove
            a) Deferrals of past operating cash receipts and payments and accruals of future operating cash receipts and payments
            b) Items not affecting operating cash receipts and payments
        2) If the direct method is used, the above-mentioned reconciliation must still be provided.
    d. The statement also requires translation of foreign currency cash flows.
        1) A weighted-average exchange rate may be used if the result is substantially the same as would be obtained by using the rates in effect when the flows occurred.
        2) The effect of exchange rate fluctuations must be separately reported as part of the reconciliation of cash and cash equivalents.
    e. Noncash financing and investing activities are excluded from the statement but are required to be separately disclosed.

62. **SFAS 97**, *Accounting and Reporting by Insurance Enterprises for Certain Long-Duration Contracts and for Realized Gains and Losses from the Sale of Investments*, concerns accounting and reporting for certain long-duration insurance contracts and for realized gains and losses on the sale of investments. This SFAS deals with new types of insurance policies, e.g., universal life contracts, developed since the issuance of SFAS 60 (which covered insurance accounting).

63. **SFAS 98**, *Accounting for Leases - Sale-Leaseback Transactions Involving Real Estate; Sales-Type Leases of Real Estate; Definition of the Lease Term; Initial Direct Costs of Direct Financing Leases*, specifies the accounting by a seller-lessee for a sale-leaseback involving real estate. Among other amendments, it also modifies the definition of the lease term given in SFAS 13, the accounting by a lessor for a sales-type lease of real estate that transfers title, and the accounting for initial direct costs of direct financing leases.

64. **SFAS 101**, *Regulated Enterprises - Accounting for the Discontinuation of Application of FASB Statement No. 71*, specifies how a regulated enterprise that no longer meets the criteria for applying SFAS 71 should report that event in its general-purpose financial statements.
65. **SFAS 102**, *Statement of Cash Flows - Exemption of Certain Enterprises and Classification of Cash Flows from Certain Securities Acquired for Resale*, amends SFAS 95. Defined benefit pension plans and certain other employee benefit plans need not provide a statement of cash flows. This exemption also applies to certain highly liquid investment companies. SFAS 102 also classifies as operating items cash flows (1) from certain securities and other assets acquired for resale and carried at market value in a trading account or (2) from loans acquired for resale and carried at lower of cost or market.
66. **SFAS 104**, *Statement of Cash Flows - Net Reporting of Certain Cash Receipts and Cash Payments and Classification of Cash Flows from Hedging Transactions*, amends SFAS 95 to permit banks, thrifts, and credit unions to report certain transactions in net rather than gross amounts. It also permits classification of cash flows from hedging transactions in the same category as the items hedged.
67. **SFAS 105**, *Disclosures of Information about Financial Instruments with Off-Balance-Sheet Risk and Financial Instruments with Concentrations of Credit Risk*, states disclosure requirements for all entities with regard to the extent, nature, and terms of financial instruments with off-balance-sheet credit or market risk of accounting loss; the credit risk of financial instruments with off-balance-sheet credit risk of accounting loss; and concentrations of credit risk of all financial instruments. SFAS 105 is the result of the initial phase of the FASB's project on financial instruments and off-balance-sheet risk.
68. **SFAS 106**, *Employers' Accounting for Postretirement Benefits Other than Pensions*, establishes accounting standards for employers' accounting for postretirement benefits other than pensions, with an emphasis on health benefits. The required accounting principles are similar to those described in SFASs 87 and 88. This was a very controversial statement because it made such a major impact on many companies' financial statements. Many economists have worried that the promulgation of SFAS 106 would have substantial social impact because employers might be enticed to provide fewer benefits to their retirees in order to minimize the postretirement liability on the books.
69. **SFAS 107**, *Disclosures about Fair Value of Financial Instruments*, requires all entities to disclose the fair value of financial instruments, whether or not they are recognized in the balance sheet, if it is practicable to estimate such fair values. If it is not, descriptive information relevant to estimation of the fair values should be provided. However, certain financial instruments are exempted, and entities with assets of less than $150,000,000 need not comply with SFAS 107 until fiscal years beginning after December 15, 1995.
70. **SFAS 109**, *Accounting for Income Taxes*, is an important pronouncement that provides new standards of accounting and reporting for the effects of income taxes. It changes the acceptable accounting for interperiod tax allocation from the deferred method to the asset and liability method. SFAS 109 supersedes SFAS 96, which was never permitted to go into effect because of controversy about its complexity and its treatment of deferred tax assets. For a full outline, see the Interperiod Tax Allocation sideheading in Study Unit 13 on page 389.

71. **SFAS 110**, *Reporting by Defined Benefit Pension Plans of Investment Contracts*, concerns reporting by defined benefit pension plans of investment contracts. It amends SFAS 35 to require that all investment contracts, including those with insurance companies, be reported at fair value. However, an exception is made for insurance contracts that incorporate mortality or morbidity risk. SFAS 35 requires plan investments to be reported at fair value, but it formerly created an exception for insurance contracts. This exception has now been narrowed.

72. **SFAS 111** rescinds SFAS 32, *Specialized Accounting and Reporting Principles and Practices in AICPA Statements of Position and Guides on Accounting and Auditing Matters*. The guidance in SFAS 32, which specifies that the specialized accounting principles and practices contained in AICPA SOPs and Guides are preferable for purposes of justifying a change in accounting principles, is no longer needed. SAS 69 (AU 411), *The Meaning of "Present Fairly in Conformity With Generally Accepted Accounting Principles" in the Independent Auditor's Report*, now requires an entity to adopt the accounting principles in pronouncements whose effective date is after March 15, 1992. An entity initially applying an accounting principle after that date (including those making an accounting change) must follow the hierarchy in SAS 69. An entity following an established accounting principle effective as of March 15, 1992 need not change its accounting until a new pronouncement is issued.

73. **SFAS 112**, *Employers' Accounting for Postemployment Benefits*, concerns accounting standards for employers who provide benefits to former or inactive employees after employment but before retirement. Postemployment benefits are all benefits provided to former or inactive employees, their beneficiaries, and covered dependents. Those benefits include, but are not limited to, salary continuation, supplemental unemployment benefits, severance benefits, disability-related benefits (including workers' compensation), job training and counseling, and continuation of benefits such as health care benefits and life insurance coverage.

    a. SFAS 112 requires employers to recognize the obligation to provide postemployment benefits if the obligation is attributable to employees' services already rendered, employees' rights accumulate or vest, payment is probable, and the amount of the benefits can be reasonably estimated. If all those conditions are not met, the employer should accrue an estimated loss from a loss contingency when it is probable that an asset has been impaired or a liability has been incurred and the amount can be reasonably estimated. If an obligation for postemployment benefits is not accrued solely because the amount cannot be reasonably estimated, the financial statements should disclose that fact.

74. **SFAS 113**, *Accounting and Reporting for Reissuance of Short-Duration and Long-Duration Contracts*, concerns accounting by insurance enterprises for the reinsuring (ceding) of insurance contracts. It amends SFAS 60 to eliminate reporting assets and liabilities relating to reinsured contracts net of the effects of reinsurance. Reinsurance receivables (including amounts related to claims incurred but not reported and liabilities for future policy benefits) and prepaid reinsurance premiums should be reported as assets. Estimated reinsurance receivables are recognized in a manner consistent with the liabilities relating to the underlying reinsured contracts.

    a. SFAS 113 states the requirements for a contract with a reinsurer to be accounted for as reinsurance and prescribes standards for those contracts. The accounting treatment depends on whether the contract is long duration or short duration and, if the latter, on whether it is prospective or retroactive. Immediate recognition of gains is precluded unless the ceding enterprise's liability is extinguished. Contracts that do not result in the reasonable possibility that the reinsurer may realize a significant loss from the insurance risk assumed ordinarily do not qualify for reinsurance accounting and are to be accounted for as deposits.

75. **SFAS 114**, *Accounting by Creditors for Impairment of a Loan*, concerns creditor accounting for impairment of certain loans. It applies to all creditors and to all loans, except large groups of smaller-balance homogeneous loans that are collectively evaluated for impairment, loans that are measured at fair value or at the lower of cost or fair value, leases, and debt securities as defined in SFAS 115. It applies to all loans that are restructured in a troubled debt restructuring involving a modification of terms.

    a. Impaired loans are to be measured based on the present value of expected future cash flows discounted at the effective interest rate or, alternatively, at the loan's observable market price or the fair value of the collateral.

    b. SFAS 114 clarifies that a creditor should evaluate the collectibility of contractual interest and contractual principal of all receivables when assessing the need for a loss accrual. It also requires a creditor to measure all loans that are restructured in a troubled debt restructuring involving a modification of terms in accordance with SFAS 114.

76. **SFAS 115**, *Accounting for Certain Investments in Debt and Equity Securities*, concerns investments in equity securities with readily determinable fair values and investments in debt securities. These investments are to be classified as held-to-maturity, trading, or available-for-sale. Debt securities that the enterprise has the positive intent and ability to hold to maturity are **held-to-maturity securities** and are reported at amortized cost. Debt and equity securities that are bought and held principally for the purpose of sale in the near term are **trading securities** and are reported at fair value, with unrealized holding gains and losses included in earnings. Debt and equity securities not classified as held-to-maturity securities or trading securities are **available-for-sale securities** and are reported at fair value, with unrealized holding gains and losses excluded from earnings and reported in a separate component of shareholders' equity.

77. **SFAS 116**, *Accounting for Contributions Received and Contributions Made*, established accounting standards for contributions received by both for-profit and not-for-profit entities. Generally, contributions received, including unconditional promises to give, are recognized as revenues in the period received at their fair values. Contributions made are recognized as expenses in the period made at their fair value.

    a. Conditional promises to give, whether given or received, are reported when the conditions have been substantially met.

    b. Contributions received that increase permanently restricted net assets, temporarily restricted net assets, or restricted net assets should each be reported separately.

    c. If donor-imposed restrictions expire, such expiration should be recognized at the time of expiration.

    d. The statement allows exceptions for contributions of services, works of art, historical treasures, and similar assets. Service contributions are recognized only when services received create or enhance nonfinancial assets or require specialized skills that would normally be purchased if not provided by donation.

    e. Donations of works of art and historical treasures need not be reported as revenue and capitalized if the donated items are added to collections held for public exhibition, education, or research. However, such donations should be disclosed in the financial statements.

78. **SFAS 117**, *Financial Statements of Not-for-Profit Organizations*, establishes standards for general-purpose financial statements of not-for-profit organizations. It requires those financial statements to focus on the entity as a whole and to meet the needs of external users of those statements.

   a. A statement of financial position (balance sheet) is required, as is a statement of activities and a statement of cash flows.

   b. The statement of activities reports the change in an organization's net assets.

   c. Assets, revenues, expenses, gains, and losses are to be classified relative to the existence or absence of donor-imposed restrictions.

   d. Assets are to be classified according to whether they are permanently restricted, temporarily restricted, or unrestricted.

   e. SFAS 95, *Statement of Cash Flows*, is extended to not-for-profit organizations, and its description of cash flows from financing activities is expanded to include certain donor-restricted cash that must be used for long-term purposes.

79. **SFAS 118**, *Accounting by Creditors for Impairment of a Loan - Income Recognition and Disclosures*, amends SFAS 114, *Accounting by Creditors for Impairment of a Loan*, to allow a creditor to use existing methods for recognizing interest income on an impaired loan. Thus, it eliminates the provisions in SFAS 114 that described how a creditor should recognize, measure, and display income on an impaired loan.

   a. SFAS 118 also amends the disclosure requirement in SFAS 114 to require information about the recorded investment in certain impaired loans and about how a creditor recognized interest income related to those impaired loans.

80. **SFAS 119**, *Disclosure about Derivative Financial Instruments and Fair Value of Financial Instruments*, requires disclosures about derivatives and other instruments with similar characteristics.

   a. SFAS 119 requires disclosures about amounts, nature, and terms of derivatives that are not subject to SFAS 105 because they do not result in off-balance-sheet risk. It distinguishes between instruments held or issued for trading purposes and those held or issued for other purposes. It also amends SFASs 105 and 107 to require that distinction in certain disclosures required by those SFASs.

   b. Entities that hold or issue derivatives for trading purposes must disclose average fair value and net trading gains or losses. Entities that hold or issue derivatives for other purposes must disclose those purposes and the manner in which the instruments are reported. Entities that hold or issue derivatives and account for them as hedges of anticipated transactions must disclose the anticipated transactions, the classes of derivatives used to hedge those transactions, the amounts of hedging gains and losses deferred, and the transactions or other events that result in recognition of the deferred gains or losses in earnings.

   c. SFAS 119 amends SFAS 105 to require disaggregation of information about instruments with off-balance-sheet risk by class, business activity, risk, or other category consistent with the entity's management of those instruments. It also amends SFAS 107 to require that fair value information be presented without combining, aggregating, or netting the fair value of derivatives with the fair value of nonderivatives. Also, fair value information should be presented with the related carrying amounts in the body of the financial statements, in a single footnote, or in a summary table in a form clarifying whether the amounts are assets or liabilities.

81. **SFAS 120**, *Accounting and Reporting by Mutual Life Insurance Enterprises and by Insurance Enterprises for Certain Long-Duration Participating Contracts*, extends the requirements of SFAS 60, *Accounting and Reporting by Insurance Enterprises*, SFAS 97, *Accounting and Reporting by Insurance Enterprises for Certain Long-Duration Contracts and for Realized Gains and Losses from the Sale of Investments*, and SFAS 113, *Accounting and Reporting for Reinsurance of Short-Duration and Long-Duration Contracts*, to mutual life insurance enterprises, assessment enterprises, and fraternal benefit societies.

    a. The accounting for certain participating life insurance contracts of mutual life insurance enterprises in SOP 95-1, *Accounting for Certain Insurance Activities of Mutual Life Insurance Enterprises*, should be applied to those contracts that meet the conditions in SFAS 120. Stock life insurance enterprises are also permitted to apply the provisions of the SOP to participating life insurance contracts that meet those conditions.

82. **SFAS 121**, *Accounting for the Impairment of Long-Lived Assets and for Long-Lived Assets to Be Disposed Of*, establishes the accounting for the impairment of long-lived assets, certain identifiable intangibles, and goodwill related to assets to be held and used and for long-lived assets and certain identifiable intangibles to be disposed of.

    a. Long-lived assets and certain identifiable intangibles to be held and used should be reviewed for impairment whenever events or changes in circumstances indicate that the carrying amount may not be recoverable. The review for recoverability entails estimating the future cash flows expected from the use and disposal of the asset. If the undiscounted sum of those flows is less than the carrying amount, an impairment loss is recognized. The impairment loss is based on the fair value of the asset.

    b. Long-lived assets and certain identifiable intangibles to be disposed of should be reported at the lower of carrying amount or fair value minus cost to sell, except for assets involved in the disposal of a business segment, which continue to be reported at the lower of carrying amount or net realizable value.

    c. SFAS 121 also requires that a rate-regulated enterprise recognize an impairment for the costs excluded when a regulator excludes all or part of a cost from the enterprise's rate base.

83. **SFAS 122**, *Accounting for Mortgage Servicing Rights*, amends SFAS 65, *Accounting for Certain Mortgage Banking Activities*, to require that a mortgage banking enterprise recognize as separate assets rights to service mortgage loans for others. Such an entity may acquire mortgage servicing rights (MSR) through the purchase or origination of mortgage loans. If it sells or securitizes those loans but retains the MSR, it should allocate the total cost of the loans to the MSR and the loans (without the MSR) based on their relative fair values if it is practicable to estimate those fair values. If it is not, the entire cost should be allocated to the loans. A mortgage banking enterprise must assess its capitalized MSR for impairment based on their fair values. It should stratify its MSR that are capitalized after the adoption of SFAS 122 based on one or more of the predominant risk characteristics of the underlying loans. Impairment is recognized through a valuation allowance for each stratum.

84. **SFAS 123**, *Accounting for Stock-Based Compensation*, recommends but does not require that stock-based compensation be accounted for using a fair-value-based method. However, entities may continue to apply APB 25, *Accounting for Stock Issued to Employees*. Entities that elect to apply APB 25 must nevertheless make certain fair-value-based disclosures. (Effective for fiscal years beginning after December 15, 1995.)

85. **SFAS 124**, *Accounting for Certain Investments Held by Not-for-Profit Organizations*, primarily applies to certain investments of nonprofit entities. Equity securities with readily determinable fair values and all debt securities must be reported at fair value, with gains and losses included in the statement of activities. (Effective for annual statements issued for fiscal years beginning after December 15, 1995, with earlier application encouraged.)

STATEMENTS OF GOVERNMENTAL ACCOUNTING STANDARDS (SGASs)

A. **SGAS 1**, *Authoritative Status of NCGA Pronouncements and AICPA Industry Audit Guide*

1. When the GASB was organized, it was agreed that its predecessors' standards, "Governmental Accounting and Financial Reporting Principles Statement 1," which was issued by the National Council on Governmental Accounting (NCGA); other currently effective NCGA statements and interpretations; and AICPA pronouncements would continue in force as GAAP for governmental agencies until changed by the GASB. NCGA Statements 1 and 6 and SFAS 35 are also recognized as acceptable alternatives for pension reporting.

B. **SGAS 2**, *Financial Reporting of Deferred Compensation Plans Adopted under the Provisions of Internal Revenue Code Section 457*

1. Regardless of what entity holds the assets, the plan's fund balance and related liability should be shown in the agency fund of a governmental employer using governmental accounting that has legal access to the assets. The amounts should also be reported in the balance sheet of an employer using proprietary fund accounting. Complete disclosure is required.

C. **SGAS 3**, *Deposits with Financial Institutions, Investments (including Repurchase Agreements), and Reverse Repurchase Agreements*

1. Carrying amounts and fair value of investments (including repurchase agreements and reverse repurchase agreements) must be disclosed, including contractual and legal requirements for deposits or investments. Also, assets and liabilities of reverse repurchase agreements cannot be offset (nor can related interest revenue and expense).

D. **SGAS 4**, *Applicability of FASB Statement No. 87, Employers' Accounting for Pensions, to State and Local Governmental Employers* (to be superseded by SGAS 27)

1. SFAS 87 is not a basis for pension reporting by governmental entities. The GASB has its own pension project. See SGAS 5 below.

E. **SGAS 5**, *Disclosure of Pension Information by Public Employee Retirement Systems and State and Local Governmental Employers* (to be superseded by SGASs 25 and 27)

1. The pension benefit obligation of a defined benefit plan is to be calculated by a standardized measure: the actuarial present value of credited projected benefits prorated on service and reflecting salary progression and step-rate benefits. Certain small employers and retirement systems are granted an exemption from disclosure of the standardized measure.

2. Required disclosures include a plan description, accounting policies, actuarial assumptions, required and actual contributions, and a 10-year summary of supplemental information (including net assets available for benefits, accrued pension obligations, and a revenue-expense comparison).

F. **SGAS 6**, *Accounting and Financial Reporting for Special Assessments*

1. This statement provides standards of accounting and reporting for a local governmental unit's liability for debt arising from the financing of services and capital improvements by special assessments. It prescribes the particular fund accounting to be employed for the transactions, the related fixed assets, if any, and long-term debt. The accounting and reporting will vary depending on whether the governmental unit is obligated in some manner, on the nature of the obligation, and on the nature of the benefit (capital improvement or services) extended to the particular property owner or group of property owners subject to the special assessment.

G. **SGAS 7,** *Advance Refundings Resulting in Defeasance of Debt*

1. This statement provides standards of accounting and reporting for both legal and in-substance defeasance of debt incurred by all types of funds. Much of SGAS 7 is based on SFAS 76, *Extinguishment of Debt*.

H. **SGAS 8,** *Applicability of FASB Statement No. 93, Recognition of Depreciation by Not-for-Profit Organizations, to Certain State and Local Governmental Entities*

1. This statement provides that certain state and local governmental entities that use certain specialized industry accounting and reporting principles and practices should not change their accounting and reporting for capital asset depreciation as a result of SFAS 93. But governmental colleges and universities may still depreciate capital assets under an option provided by the AICPA Industry Audit Guide, *Audits of Colleges and Universities.*

I. **SGAS 9**, *Reporting Cash Flows of Proprietary and Nonexpendable Trust Funds and Governmental Entities That Use Proprietary Fund Accounting*

1. SGAS 9 establishes standards for cash flow reporting but exempts some entities from the requirement.

J. **SGAS 10**, *Accounting and Financial Reporting for Risk Financing and Related Insurance Issues*

1. This statement essentially requires public entity risk pools to follow SFAS 60, *Accounting and Reporting by Insurance Enterprises*.

K. **SGAS 11**, *Measurement Focus and Basis of Accounting -- Governmental Fund Operating Statements*

1. This statement was initially intended to be effective for periods beginning after June 15, 1994, but the effective date has been deferred pending issuance of an implementing standard. It establishes basic standards for developing the guidance to be provided by the other projects in the GASB's reevaluation of governmental accounting and financial reporting. These standards concerning measurement focus and basis of accounting apply to governmental and expendable trust fund operating statements. SGAS 11 also applies specifically to many governmental fund transactions, especially revenues, and to balance-sheet reporting of general long-term capital debt, but not to reporting of operating debt or long-term debt from the accrual of governmental fund expenditures.
2. See the summary for SGAS 17 on page 370.

L. **SGAS 12**, *Disclosure of Information on Postemployment Benefits Other than Pension Benefits by State and Local Governmental Employers*

1. All state and local employers that furnish such benefits must describe the benefits provided, the employees covered, and the obligations for contributions of the employer and participants; the authority for establishment of benefit provisions and obligations; accounting and funding policies; and the expenditures/expenses for benefits recognized during the period and certain related data. At this time, however, no changes in accounting and financial reporting for these benefits are necessary.

M. **SGAS 13**, *Accounting for Operating Leases with Scheduled Rent Increases*

1. This statement applies without regard to the fund type reporting the transaction. If the payment pattern is systematic and rational, the terms of the lease will control the accounting. But if payment requirements in a year are artificially low, measurement should either be on a straight-line basis or be based on the fair value of the rental. The accrual basis is required for recognition of operating lease revenue and expenditures/expense, but, until SGAS 11 becomes effective, entities reporting these transactions in governmental and similar trust funds should use the modified accrual basis.

N. **SGAS 14**, *The Financial Reporting Entity*

1. This statement provides standards for defining and reporting on the financial reporting entity and for reporting participation in joint ventures.

O. **SGAS 15**, *Governmental College and University Accounting and Financial Reporting Models*

1. Governmental colleges and universities should follow the accounting and reporting model established either by the AICPA (the AICPA College Guide model) or by NCGA Statement 1 (the governmental model), as modified by subsequent relevant pronouncements.

P. **SGAS 16**, *Accounting for Compensated Absences*

1. This statement applies regardless of the reporting model or fund type used by the state or local government to report the transactions.
2. Benefits for vacation leave and other similar compensated absences should be accrued as a liability as they are earned if the leave is attributable to past service and it is probable that the employer will compensate the employees through paid time off or some other means, such as payment at termination or retirement.
3. Benefits for sick leave should be accrued as a liability as they are earned but only to the extent it is probable that the employer will compensate the employees through cash payments conditioned on the employees' termination or retirement. An alternative is to measure the liability based on the sick leave accumulated by employees currently eligible to receive termination payments and other employees expected to become eligible. These accumulations should be reduced to the maximum allowed as a termination payment.
4. The compensated absences liability ordinarily is measured using the pay rates in effect at the balance-sheet date. Other amounts should be accrued for certain items related to compensated absences, e.g., the employer's share of Social Security and Medicare taxes.
5. For governmental and similar trust funds, the current portion of the liability should be reported in the funds. The long-term portion is reported in the general long-term debt group of accounting. The basis of accounting is the modified accrual method.

Q. **SGAS 17**, *Measurement Focus and Basis of Accounting -- Governmental Fund Operating Statements: Amendment of the Effective Dates of GASB Statement No. 11 and Related Statements*

1. The effective date of SGAS 11 is deferred to periods beginning approximately 2 years after an implementation standard is issued. SGAS 17 also established an effective date (periods beginning after June 15, 1994) for Statement 10, for entities other than pools, that is independent of the effective date of SGAS 11. It also established that entities that report risk financing activities in governmental and similar trust funds should use the modified accrual basis of accounting.

R. **SGAS 18**, *Accounting for Municipal Solid Waste Landfill Closure and Postclosure Care Costs*

1. An EPA rule issued in 1991 established closure requirements for all municipal solid waste landfills. The rule also established 30-year postclosure care requirements. The effect of the rule and similar laws or regulations is to require owners and operators to perform certain closing functions and postclosure monitoring and maintenance functions. SGAS 18 applies to state and local governmental entities that are required to incur these closure and postclosure care costs.

S. **SGAS 19**, *Governmental College and University Omnibus Statement*

1. Governmental colleges and universities that follow the AICPA College Guide model must report Pell grants in a restricted current fund. Furthermore, if a single fund is used to account for risk financing, it should be reported as an unrestricted current fund.

T. **SGAS 20**, *Accounting and Financial Reporting for Proprietary Funds and Other Governmental Entities That Use Proprietary Fund Accounting*

1. Pending GASB issuance of pronouncements on the accounting and financial reporting model for proprietary activities, SGAS 20 provides interim guidance on these matters.
2. Proprietary activities should apply all applicable GASB pronouncements as well as pronouncements issued on or before November 30, 1989 that constitute promulgated GAAP unless they conflict with GASB pronouncements.
3. A proprietary activity may also apply all SFASs and FASB Interpretations issued after November 30, 1989, except for those that conflict with GASB pronouncements.

U. **SGAS 21**, *Accounting for Escheat Property*

1. Property escheats when it reverts to a governmental entity absent any legal claimants. SGAS 21 specifies the fund types to be used to report such property and the standards governing reporting of liabilities and interfund transfers.

V. **SGAS 22**, *Accounting for Taxpayer-Assessed Tax Revenues in Governmental Funds*

1. Revenue from such taxes as sales and income taxes, net of estimated refunds, should be recognized in governmental funds when they become susceptible to accrual, i.e., when they are measurable and available to finance expenditures of the fiscal period.

W. **SGAS 23**, *Accounting and Financial Reporting for Refundings of Debt Reported by Proprietary Activities*

1. This pronouncement applies to current refundings and advance refundings resulting in defeasance of debt reported by proprietary activities, i.e., proprietary funds and other governmental entities that use proprietary fund accounting.
2. SGAS 23 requires that the difference between the reacquisition price and the net carrying amount of the old debt be deferred and amortized as interest expense in a systematic and rational manner over the shorter of the remaining life of the old debt or the life of the new debt. The deferred amount should be reported as a deduction from, or an addition to, the new debt liability.

X. **SGAS 24**, *Accounting and Financial Reporting for Certain Grants and Other Financial Assistance*

1. Recipient governments should recognize all cash pass-through grants as revenue and expenditures or expenses in a governmental, proprietary, or trust fund. If the recipient is merely a cash conduit, the grant should be reported in an agency fund.
2. Distributions of food stamp benefits are revenues and expenditures in the general fund or a special revenue fund. Food stamp balances are an asset offset by deferred revenue.
3. On-behalf payments for fringe benefits and salaries are direct payments made by one entity to a third-party recipient for the employees of another, legally separate entity. Employer governments must recognize revenue and expenditures or expenses for on-behalf payments. Revenue equals the amounts that third-party recipients have received and that are receivable at year-end. If the employers are not legally responsible for the payments, expenditures or expenses equal revenues. If they are legally responsible, they should follow accounting standards for that type of transaction. On-behalf payments should be classified in the same manner as similar cash grants. (Effective for periods beginning after June 15, 1995. Earlier application is encouraged.)

Y. **SGAS 25**, *Financial Reporting for Defined Benefit Pension Plans and Note Disclosures for Defined Contribution Plans*

1. SGAS 25 applies to pension trust funds included in the financial reports of plan sponsors or employers and to the stand-alone financial reports of pension plans or the public employee retirement systems that administer them. Reduced disclosures are acceptable when a stand-alone plan financial report is publicly available and contains all required information.
2. Financial reporting for defined benefit pension plans distinguishes between current information about plan assets and financial activities and actuarially determined information, from a long-term perspective, about funded status and the accumulation of assets.
3. Current information is given in a statement of plan net assets and a statement of changes in plan net assets. The notes should include a plan description, a summary of accounting policies, and information about contributions, legal reserves, and investment concentrations.
4. Actuarial information should be included, for a minimum of 6 years, in supplementary information: a schedule of funding progress and a schedule of employer contributions. Note disclosures should include the actuarial methods and significant assumptions used. Plans may elect to report one or more years of the information required for the schedules in additional financial statements or in the notes.

5. Actuarially determined information should be in accordance with certain parameters, including requirements for the frequency and timing of valuations and for the methods and assumptions that are acceptable for financial reporting. When the methods and assumptions meet the parameters, the same methods and assumptions are required for financial reporting by both a plan and its participating employer(s).

6. The notes to the financial statements of defined contribution plans must include a plan description, a summary of accounting policies, and information about contributions and investment concentrations. (Effective for periods beginning after June 15, 1996. Early implementation is encouraged; and SGAS 26, if applicable, should be implemented in the same year.)

Z. **SGAS 26**, *Financial Reporting for Postemployment Healthcare Plans Administered by Defined Benefit Pension Plans*

1. This interim pronouncement was issued pending completion of the GASB's project on accounting and financial reporting for other postemployment benefits.

2. Defined benefit plans that administer postemployment healthcare plans must present a statement of postemployment healthcare plan net assets, a statement of changes in postemployment healthcare plan net assets, and notes to the financial statements, all in accordance with the pension plan reporting standards. SGAS 26 also establishes certain requirements for plans that elect to provide historical trend information about the funded status of the postemployment healthcare plan and the employer's required contributions to the plan. (Effective for periods beginning after June 15, 1996. Early implementation is encouraged, and SGAS 25 should be implemented in the same fiscal year.)

AA. **SGAS 27**, *Accounting for Pensions by State and Local Governmental Employers*

1. SGAS 27 provides standards for employer measurement, recognition, and display of pension expenditures/expense and related liabilities, assets, note disclosures, and, if applicable, required supplementary information.

2. With regard to single-employer and agent multiple-employer defined benefit pension plans, employers must measure and disclose annual pension cost on the accrual basis, regardless of the amount recognized. Annual pension cost is the annual required contributions (ARC), unless a net pension obligation (NPO) for past under- or overcontributions exists (including a transition amount).

3. The ARC are based on certain parameters: requirements for the frequency and timing of actuarial valuations and for the actuarial methods and assumptions acceptable for financial reporting. When the methods and assumptions that determine funding requirements meet the parameters, the same methods and assumptions are required for financial reporting by a plan and the employer(s).

4. Given an NPO, annual pension cost equals the ARC, one year's interest on the NPO, and an adjustment to the ARC to offset actuarial amortization of past under- or overcontributions. The transition amount is calculated similarly.

5. Pension expenditures of entities that apply governmental fund accounting are recognized on the modified accrual basis. An NPO liability is recognized in the GLTDAG; an asset is not recognized but should be disclosed. Pension expense of entities that apply proprietary fund accounting and expenditures of entities that apply the AICPA College Guide model are recognized on the accrual basis; NPO balances are fund liabilities or assets.

6. Employers in cost-sharing multiple-employer defined benefit pension plans recognize pension expenditures/expense for contractually required contributions and a liability for unpaid contributions. Recognition is on the modified accrual or accrual basis. Previously recognized liabilities are adjusted to the transition amount.
7. Employers that participate in defined contribution plans recognize pension expenditures/expense for the required contributions to the plan and a liability for unpaid contributions. Recognition is on the modified accrual or accrual basis.
8. SGAS 27 also includes guidance for employers that participate in insured plans, for entities legally responsible for contributions to plans covering employees of other entities, and for sole and agent employers that elect to apply the pension measurement provisions to postemployment healthcare benefits on an interim basis. (Effective for periods beginning after June 15, 1997. Earlier application is encouraged.)

BB. **SGAS 28**, *Accounting and Financial Reporting for Securities Lending Transactions*

1. In securities lending transactions, governmental entities transfer their securities to broker-dealers and other entities for collateral and agree to return it for the same securities in the future. The securities lent, cash collateral, and investments made with that cash should be reported as assets. Securities received as collateral also should be reported as assets if the entity can pledge or sell them without a borrower default. Resulting liabilities should be recognized.
2. The costs of securities lending transactions, such as borrower rebates (interest costs) and agent fees, should be reported as expenditures or expenses. These costs should not be netted with interest revenue or income.
3. SGAS 28 requires a variety of disclosures and provides guidance for classifying securities lending collateral and the underlying securities in the categories of custodial credit risk required by SGAS 3. (Effective for periods beginning after December 15, 1995. Earlier application is encouraged.)

CC. **SGAS 29**, *The Use of Not-for-Profit Accounting and Financial Reporting Principles by Governmental Entities*

1. SGAS 29 provides interim guidance pending other GASB pronouncements on this subject.
2. Governmental entities that have applied not-for-profit accounting and financial reporting principles stated in AICPA pronouncements should apply the governmental model or the AICPA not-for-profit model. The latter consists of the principles contained in SOP 78-10 or *Audits of Voluntary Health and Welfare Organizations* (except for provisions relating to the joint costs of informational materials and activities that include a fund-raising appeal) as modified by FASB pronouncements issued through November 30, 1989 and by GASB pronouncements.
3. SGAS 29 also provides guidance for proprietary funds and other governmental entities that use proprietary fund accounting. They should apply only those FASB pronouncements issued after November 30, 1989 that are developed for business enterprises. They should not apply pronouncements that are limited to not-for-profit organizations or that address issues concerning primarily such organizations (e.g., SFASs 117 and 116, respectively). (Effective for periods beginning after December 15, 1994; the modification of the AICPA model for certain GASB pronouncements is effective for periods beginning after December 15, 1995. Earlier application is encouraged.)

STUDY UNIT 13
SPECIAL FINANCIAL REPORTING PROBLEMS

In Part 2, the ICMA specifies 60% to 80% coverage of financial statements and reporting.

Financial Statements	30%-40%
Reporting Requirements	30%-40%

We further differentiate this material by dividing it into four study units.

Study Unit 11: Financial Accounting: Development of Theory and Practice (FAD)
Study Unit 12: Financial Statement Presentation (FS)
Study Unit 13: Special Financial Reporting Problems (SPE)
Study Unit 14: SEC Reporting Requirements (SEC)

SEGMENTAL DISCLOSURES

A. Segmental disclosures are required in the annual statements of public companies that operate in different industries. Each segment contributing 10% or more to total sales, assets, or income is required to disclose certain sales, assets, and income data. Also, disclosure of foreign operations, export sales, and major customer data is required.

1. The purpose of these disclosures is to allow users of the financial statements to evaluate the operations of the distinct components of large, conglomerate-type enterprises.

2. The example below illustrates segmental disclosures. The income statement is based on a contribution approach and includes intersegment sales.

XYZ COMPANY
Information about the Company's Operations in Different Industries
Year Ended December 31, 19XX

	Industry A	Industry B	Industry C	Other Industries	Eliminations	Consolidated
Sales to unaffiliated customers	$1,000	$2,000	$1,500	$ 200		$ 4,700
Intersegment sales	200		500		$(700)	
Total revenue	$1,200	$2,000	$2,000	$ 200	$(700)	4,700
Operating profit	$ 200	$ 290	$ 600	$ 50	$ (40)	$ 1,100
Equity in net income of Zu Co.						100
General corporate expenses						(100)
Interest expense						(200)
Income from continuing operations before income taxes						$ 900
Identifiable assets at December 31	$2,000	$4,050	$6,000	$1,000	$ (50)	$13,000
Investment in net assets of Zu Co.						400
Corporate assets						1,600
Total assets at December 31						$15,000

Intersegment sales, ownership of Zu, major customers, etc., should be explained in footnotes. See the outline of SFAS 14 beginning on page 342.

ACCOUNTING CHANGES

A. Accounting changes are defined as changes in the application or implementation of accounting principles (e.g., changing from the LIFO to the FIFO inventory method).

1. The issue in reporting accounting changes is whether to restate the previous financial statements to provide consistency through time.

    a. If financial statements of prior periods presented comparatively are restated, they will be consistent with those of the current period.

    b. Restatement, however, involves changing prior years' net income and related EPS figures, which may undermine stockholders' confidence in the accounting methodology.

2. Accounting changes are accounted for by retroactive restatement only in special cases. The following changes in principle require (unless otherwise noted) a retroactive restatement of financial statements with full footnote disclosure in the year of the change:

    a. Change from LIFO to another inventory pricing method

    b. Change from the completed-contract to the percentage-of-completion method (or vice versa)

    c. Change to or from the full-cost method used in the extractive industries

    d. Change in the reporting entity (e.g., from a business combination or spinoff)

        1) APB 20 defines this change as a "special type of change in accounting principle."

    e. Change from retirement-replacement-betterment accounting to depreciation accounting for railroad track structures (See SFAS 73 on page 353.)

    f. Change from one acceptable principle to another by a closely held company when its financial statements are issued for the first time for any of the following purposes: obtaining additional equity capital, effecting a business combination, or registering securities

        1) Under APB 20, retroactive restatement is permitted (not required) in these circumstances as a one-time exemption from cumulative-effect treatment.

    g. Change to the method of accounting required by a new pronouncement

        1) A pronouncement may include a transition rule that not only mandates use of a new principle but also requires its retroactive application. Examples are

            a) APB 18, *The Equity Method of Accounting for Investments in Common Stock*

            b) SFAS 11, *Accounting for Contingencies -- Transition Method*

            c) SFAS 13, *Accounting for Leases*

        2) When changing from the deferred method to the asset-liability method of accounting for income taxes required by SFAS 109, an entity may elect either the retroactive or the cumulative-effect method.

3. For all other changes in accounting principles or application thereof, the cumulative effect of the change is included in the income statement in the year of change (minus related tax effects). This cumulative effect is to be shown in a separate section of the income statement after extraordinary items.
   a. The new accounting method is used in the year of change.
   b. Supplementary disclosure of pro forma income and related EPS figures based on retroactive application of the new accounting principle is made on the face of the income statement.
      1) Thus, even though the financial statements are not retroactively restated, the effect of restatement is disclosed.
4. Changes in accounting estimates, e.g., length of useful life or salvage value of fixed assets, are accounted for prospectively; prior years' financial statements are not restated. Only the current and future statements are affected.

B. Retroactive restatement is also required for error corrections (net of related tax effects). The effect of errors on periods prior to the statements for the earliest period presented is reported as an adjustment to beginning retained earnings in the retained earnings statement. In other words, these are prior-period adjustments and have no impact on the income statement for the current period.

1. Accountants and auditors correct errors discovered in the period of the error in three steps.
   a. Determining that an error was made
   b. Reversing the erroneous journal entry
   c. Recording the correct journal entry
2. In periods subsequent to the error, the same analysis is undertaken, but any correcting entries normally made to nominal revenue or expense accounts are made instead to retained earnings.
3. Accounting errors are classified as correcting and noncorrecting. Correcting errors are errors in transactions that only affect 2 years.
   a. EXAMPLE: If ending inventory is misstated at the end of a period, it will affect that period and the subsequent period, but no other periods. This error is correcting because after two periods the statements will be correct.
   b. Multi-year transactions (e.g., purchase of a building) recorded in error will affect the incomes of several periods. These errors are noncorrecting.

C. The possible treatments of accounting changes are summarized in the following table:

Treatment	Change in Principle (General Rule)	Change in Principle (Exceptions)	Book-keeping Error	Change in Estimate	Change in Entity
Report currently in special section of income statement	X				
Prospective basis				X	
Prior-period adjustment of retained earnings			X		
Retroactive adjustment		X			X

D. EXAMPLE: The following is taken from Appendix A of APB 20. The data illustrate disclosures of the effects of a change in depreciation methods.

1. Changing from accelerated depreciation to straight-line depreciation is a cumulative-effect type change. The cumulative effect on Year 2 beginning retained earnings is included in the Year 2 income statement.

2. Through Year 1, the excess of accelerated over straight-line depreciation was $250,000 ($125,000 net of direct tax effects). Items shown below are net of tax effects. Assume that the effect of a hypothetical application of the change to Year 1 was to increase income before the extraordinary item by $13,500 (reflecting the change in depreciation, the tax effect, and a change in the provision for incentive compensation).

3.

	Year 2	Year 1
Income before extraordinary item and cumulative effect of a change in accounting principle	$1,200,000	$1,100,000
Extraordinary item (description)	(35,000)	100,000
Cumulative effect on prior years (to December 31, Year 1) of changing to a different depreciation method	125,000	
Net income	$1,290,000	$1,200,000
Per share amounts (1,000,000 shares outstanding):		
EPS -- assuming no dilution:		
Income before extraordinary item and cumulative effect of a change in accounting principle	$1.20	$1.10
Extraordinary item	(0.04)	0.10
Cumulative effect on prior years (to December 31, Year 1) of changing to a different depreciation method	0.13	
Net income	$1.29	$1.20
EPS -- assuming full dilution [bonds paying $25,000 interest (net of tax) that are not CSE can be converted to 100,000 shares]:		
Income before extraordinary item and cumulative effect of a change in accounting principle	$1.11	$1.02
Extraordinary item	(0.03)	0.09
Cumulative effect on prior years (to December 31, Year 1) of changing to a different depreciation method	0.11	
Net income	$1.19	$1.11
Pro forma amounts assuming the new depreciation method is applied retroactively:		
Income before extraordinary item	$1,200,000	$1,113,500
EPS -- assuming no dilution	$1.20	$1.11
EPS -- assuming full dilution	$1.11	$1.04
Net income	$1,165,000	$1,213,500
EPS -- assuming no dilution	$1.17	$1.21
EPS -- assuming full dilution	$1.08	$1.13

CONSIGNMENT SALES

A. A consignment sale is an arrangement between the owner of goods and a sales agent. Goods on consignment are not sold to the sales agent but rather consigned for possible sale.

1. Title remains with the consignor (owner), and risk of loss does not transfer to the consignee (sales agent).
2. Sales are recorded on the books of the consignor only when the goods are sold to third parties by the consignee.
3. Inventory shipped on consignment should thus not be reported as a sale by a consignor but rather included in inventory.
4. The consignee records sales commissions when the goods are sold and at no time shows the inventory as an asset.

B. **Accounting by the Consignee**

1. The initial acquisition of inventory is not recorded in the ledger accounts, although a supplementary memorandum entry may be made.
2. Sales are recorded with a debit to cash (or accounts receivable) and credits to commission income and accounts payable to the consignor.
3. Any expenses incurred by the consignee on behalf of the consignor (such as freight-in or service costs) are reductions of the payable to the consignor.
4. Periodic remittances to the consignor result in a debit to accounts payable and a credit to cash.

C. **Accounting by Consignor**

1. The initial shipment is recorded with a debit to consigned goods out and a credit to inventory for the cost of the merchandise.
2. Periodic remittances and notification of expenses incurred by the consignee are recorded by debits to cash, delivery expense, commission expense, and cost of goods sold, and credits to sales and consigned goods out.

D. **Example Entries on the Books of the Consignor and Consignee**

1. 100 units, costing $50 each, are shipped to a consignee:

CONSIGNOR'S BOOKS			CONSIGNEE'S BOOKS		
Consigned goods out	$5,000		Only memorandum entry		
Inventory		$5,000			

2. Consignee pays $120 for freight-in:

CONSIGNOR'S BOOKS			CONSIGNEE'S BOOKS		
No entry at this time			Payable to consignor	$120	
			Cash		$120

3. 80 units are sold at $80 each. Consignee is to receive a 20% commission on all sales:

CONSIGNOR'S BOOKS			CONSIGNEE'S BOOKS		
No entry at this time			Cash	$6,400	
			Payable to consignor		$5,120
			Commission income		1,280

4. Consignee sends monthly statement to consignor along with balance owed:

CONSIGNOR'S BOOKS			CONSIGNEE'S BOOKS		
Cash	$5,000		Payable to consignor	$5,000	
Commission expense	1,280		Cash		$5,000
Delivery expense	120				
Cost of goods sold	4,000				
Sales		$6,400			
Consigned goods out		4,000			

5. The consignee may use consignment in rather than payable to consignor. Consignment in is a receivable/payable account.

6. If the consignor uses a physical inventory system, the credit on shipment would be to consignment shipments, a contra cost of sales account. The balance in this account is closed at the end of the period when the inventory adjustments are made.

PARTNERSHIP ACCOUNTING

A. **Partnership Defined.** A partnership, as defined by the Uniform Partnership Act, is "an association of two or more persons to carry on, as co-owners, a business for a profit."

B. **Liability.** Unlike corporations, general partnerships do not insulate a partner from liability to creditors. Each general partner has unlimited liability for partnership debts. The partners may agree among themselves to limit a partner's liability, but such a provision cannot limit direct liability to creditors.

C. **Partnership Accounts.** Partnership capital accounts make up the residual equity section of the partnership balance sheet. Partnership drawing accounts are nominal accounts that are closed to partnership capital at the end of each period along with the profit and loss account.

D. **Profit and Loss.** Common law and the Uniform Partnership Act both provide that profit and loss are to be distributed equally among partners unless the articles of copartnership provide otherwise. The equal distribution should be based on the number of partners rather than be in proportion to partner capital balances.

E. **Admission of Partners.** The goodwill and bonus methods are two means of adjusting for differences between the net book value and the fair value of partnerships when new partners are admitted. The goodwill method revalues assets to adjust the total value of partnership capital. The bonus method simply readjusts capital accounts and makes no changes in existing asset accounts.

F. **Retirement of Partners.** When partners retire, the transaction is in essence a buy-out by the remaining partners. Accordingly, the same issues exist as to valuation of the partnership and individual partner capital accounts as when a new partner is admitted.

G. **Liquidation of Partnerships**. Prior to liquidation, a schedule of possible losses is frequently prepared to determine the amount of cash that may be safely distributed to the partners. It presents a series of incremental losses to indicate the amount of loss in a liquidation that will eliminate each partner's capital account. The presumption is that losses or partner capital deficits will not be repaid.

1. Under the UPA, the assets of the partnership are made available first to the partnership creditors. Only after creditors' claims are fully satisfied will the personal creditors of the partners be able to proceed against the partnership assets. Similarly, the personal creditors of each general partner have first claim to the personal assets of that general partner. The Bankruptcy Reform Act of 1978, however, alters the marshaling of assets concept with regard to the personal assets of a bankrupt partner when the partnership is also bankrupt. The trustee of a bankrupt partnership would share pro rata with the other general unsecured creditors of a bankrupt general partner.

INSTALLMENT SALES

A. As outlined in ARB 43 and upheld in APB 10, the proper accounting treatment of installment sales is to recognize gross profit as cash is received. Gross profit is deferred at the time of sale and recognized as income in the accounting periods in which cash is received.

1. EXAMPLE: Assume that a TV costing $600 is sold on the installment basis for a price of $1,000 on November 1, Year 1. A down payment of $100 was received and the remainder is due in nine monthly payments of $100 each. The entry for the sale is

Cash	$100	
Installment receivable (Year 1)	900	
Inventory		$600
Deferred gross profit (Year 1)		400

2. In December when the first installment is received, the entry is

Cash	$100	
Installment receivable (Year 1)		$100

3. At December 31, the deferred gross profit must be adjusted to report the portion that has been earned. Given that 20% ($200 ÷ $1,000) of the total price has been received, 20% of the gross profit has been earned. The entry is

Deferred gross profit (Year 1)	$80	
Realized gross profit		$80

4. Net income should include only the $80 realized gross profit for the period. The balance sheet showed a receivable of $800 minus the deferred gross profit of $320. Thus, the net receivable is $480.

5. In Year 2, the remaining $800 is received, and the $320 balance of deferred gross profit is recognized. If only $400 were received in Year 2 (if payments were extended), the December Year 2 statements would have a $400 installment receivable and $160 of deferred gross profit.

B. Installment receivables are shown as current assets regardless of the due date. Even though the receivable may be due in more than 1 year, the stipulation that a current receivable is one that will be collected within the normal operating cycle makes installment receivables current assets.

C. Normally, there is also an interest component, and APB 21, *Interest on Receivables and Payables*, applies. The recognition of deferred gross profit is based on receipt of principal.

D. If the TV in the previous example had to be repossessed because no payments after the down payment were made by the buyer, the used TV would be recorded at its net realizable value minus a resale profit. Assume that fair value at the time of repossession was only $500 because the TV had been damaged and that repair costs and sales commissions will amount to $100.

Inventory of used merchandise	$400	
Deferred gross profit	360	
Loss on repossession	140	
Installment receivable		$900

1. The loss on repossession represents the difference between the $400 net realizable value ($500 fair value – $100 repair and sales costs) and the $540 book value ($900 remaining on the contract – $360 deferred gross profit) of the receivable.

E. **Cost-Recovery Method**. The cost-recovery method may be used when receivables are collected over an extended period, considerable doubt exists as to collectibility, and a reasonable estimate of the loss cannot be made. Under the cost-recovery method, profit is recognized only after collections exceed the cost of the item sold. Subsequent amounts are treated entirely as revenues. This method is more conservative than the installment method.

1. EXAMPLE: In 1994, Creditor Co. made a $100,000 sale accounted for using the cost-recovery method. The cost of the item sold was $70,000, and 1994 collections equaled $50,000. In 1995, collections equaled $25,000, and $10,000 of the receivable was determined to be uncollectible. As a result of these transactions, the net receivable (receivable-deferred profit) was $0 at the end of 1995. The following entries were made in 1994 and 1995:

1994:	Receivable	$100,000	
	Inventory		$70,000
	Deferred gross profit		30,000
	Cash	$50,000	
	Receivable		$50,000
1995:	Cash	$25,000	
	Deferred gross profit	5,000	
	Receivable		$25,000
	Realized gross profit		5,000
	Deferred gross profit	$10,000	
	Receivable		$10,000

ACCOUNTING FOR CHANGING PRICES

A. Basic financial statements are not adjusted to reflect the changes in the value of the monetary unit.

   1. Also, basic financial statements ordinarily report historical cost, not current cost.

B. **Constant purchasing power accounting** is a method of adjusting the financial statements so they are stated in units of currency, each of which has the same (constant) general purchasing power (as of the end of the latest period).

   1. All financial statement items are adjusted by a TO-FROM ratio.
   2. The TO-FROM ratio uses the price level at the end of the latest reporting period in the numerator, and the price level when the transaction originated in the denominator. For example, a 1990 cost would be adjusted to end-of-1995 dollars.
   3. **Purchasing power gains and losses** reflect changes in the unit of measure as determined by a general price index.
      a. Purchasing power gains or losses are calculated for monetary items only.

C. **Current cost accounting** requires assets and the expenses associated with their use or sale to be reported at their current costs or lower recoverable amounts at year-end or at the date of use or sale. The adjustments are determined by reference to specific price indexes.

   1. Changes in current costs or lower recoverable amounts are **unrealized holding gains or losses**.

D. Current cost/constant purchasing power accounting adjusts for both general and specific price-level changes.

   1. Holding gains and losses are calculated for nonmonetary items only.
   2. EXAMPLE: Land with a historical cost of $100,000 had a current cost of $200,000 when the applicable general price index was 176 (the asset was purchased when the general price index was 110). The historical cost adjusted for general price-level changes is $160,000 [$100,000 x (176 ÷ 110)], and the unrealized holding gain is $40,000 ($200,000 – $160,000).
      a. No purchasing power gain or loss results because land is not a monetary item.

E. SFAS 33, *Financial Reporting and Changing Prices*, which formerly required large public companies to disclose certain constant dollar and current cost data, was superseded by SFAS 89. These disclosures are now completely voluntary.

FOREIGN CURRENCY ISSUES

A. Currently, accounting data for foreign operations are consolidated into domestic financial statements using a functional currency approach.

   1. An entity's **functional currency** is the currency of the primary economic environment in which it operates. The functional currency is normally that of the environment in which the entity primarily expends and generates cash. For example, the functional currency of a French subsidiary would be the franc.
      a. If the subsidiary's financial statements are not maintained in the functional currency, they must be **remeasured** into that currency using the temporal rate method. The current exchange rate is used to remeasure all accounts except those specified in SFAS 52, *Foreign Currency Translation*. Historical rates should be used for these accounts, which include common nonmonetary balance sheet items and related revenue, expense, gain, and loss accounts, e.g., inventory, cost of sales, intangible assets, amortization of intangibles, and common stock.

b. Exchange gains and losses arising from remeasurement of monetary assets and liabilities are recognized currently in income.

2. An entity can be in any form, including subsidiary, division, branch, or joint venture.
3. A highly inflationary currency (3-year inflation rate of 100% or more) is not considered stable enough to be a functional currency.
   a. Instead, the more stable currency of the parent corporation should be used as the functional currency.
4. Once the financial statement elements (i.e., assets, liabilities) have been measured in terms of the functional currency, a current exchange rate (at the balance sheet date) is used to **translate** assets and liabilities from the functional currency into the reporting currency of the parent.
   a. In theory, revenues, expenses, gains, and losses should be translated at the rate in effect at the date those elements were recognized, but they are so numerous that a weighted-average rate for the period may be used.
5. Translation adjustments are not included on the income statement for the period but instead are shown as a cumulative amount in a separate component of stockholders' equity.

B. When a foreign currency transaction gives rise to a receivable or a payable that is fixed in terms of the amount of foreign currency to be received or paid, a change in the exchange rate between the functional currency and the currency in which the transaction is denominated results in a gain or loss that ordinarily should be included as a component of income from continuing operations in the period in which the exchange rate changes. **Transaction gains and losses** are reported in the aggregate in the income statement.

1. EXAMPLE: Assume that inventory was purchased for 10,000 French francs at a time when the franc was worth $.25. The entry for the purchase would be

Purchases	$2,500	
Accounts payable		$2,500

   a. If the franc strengthens compared with the dollar before the payment date, the company will have to pay more to obtain the 10,000 francs necessary to make payment to the French supplier. If the price of the franc rises to $.26, the entry for payment will be

Accounts payable	$2,500	
Transaction loss	100	
Cash		$2,600

   b. If the dollar becomes stronger during the intervening period, the company will record a gain. If, for instance, the franc falls to a rate of $.22, the entry for payment will be

Accounts payable	$2,500	
Cash		$2,200
Transaction gain		300

2. Companies with a large number of transactions denominated in foreign currencies avoid transaction gains and losses by engaging in hedging activities, that is, by purchasing or selling forward exchange contracts in appropriate amounts.

   a. A **forward exchange contract** is defined in SFAS 52 as "an agreement to exchange at a specified future date currencies of different countries at a specified rate (forward rate)."

      1) A difference between the contract (future) rate and the spot (current) rate at the date of the contract's inception is a **discount** or **premium**.

         a) A discount or premium should be accounted for separately from the gain or loss on the contract and included in net income over the contract's term.

            i) An exception to this amortization requirement is a hedge of an identifiable foreign currency commitment. In this case, the discount or premium related to the commitment period may be included in the related foreign currency transaction when recorded.

            ii) Moreover, if a foreign currency transaction is designated and effective as an economic hedge of a net investment in a foreign entity, the discount or premium may be included with translation adjustments arising from consolidation as a separate component of consolidated owners' equity.

      2) A **speculative forward contract** is a contract that does not hedge any exposure to foreign currency fluctuations; it creates the exposure.

         a) Both the receivable from the broker and the liability to the broker are recorded at the forward exchange rate existing at the date of the contract.

            i) The receivable or liability denominated in the foreign currency is adjusted to reflect the forward rate at each ensuing balance sheet date and at the date of settlement with a corresponding recognition of gain or loss.

         b) For forward exchange contracts other than speculative contracts, the asset or liability denominated in U.S. dollars is recorded at the forward rate, and the item denominated in a foreign currency is recorded at the spot rate.

      3) When a foreign currency forward exchange contract is intended and is effective as an economic hedge against an exposed net asset or net liability position (e.g., an outstanding receivable or liability), any transaction gain or loss on the forward contract will offset any exchange gain or loss on the exposed net asset or net liability position.

         a) Thus, no transaction gain or loss will result.

      4) An **identifiable future commitment** is a commitment for a future sale or purchase that will be denominated in a foreign currency.

         a) SFAS 52 provides for a gain or loss on a forward contract that is considered a hedge of an identifiable foreign currency commitment to be deferred and included in the measurement of the related foreign currency transaction (the purchase or sale).

CONSOLIDATIONS

A. Consolidations occur whenever one company acquires a controlling interest (i.e., over 50%) in another entity. Consolidated statements are prepared under the assumption that two or more corporate entities are in reality only one economic entity. Consolidated financial statements are prepared after the statements of each of the individual corporations have been completed. Consolidated statements are usually prepared with the aid of a worksheet. The consolidated statements are prepared by combining the account balances of the individual firms after certain adjusting and eliminating entries are made.

1. The previous paragraph describes an acquisition in which the subsidiary continues to operate as a separate entity. Consolidating worksheets have to be prepared every time consolidated statements are prepared. This situation is emphasized in advanced accounting courses and on the professional accounting exams, including the CMA exam.

2. Parent companies shall prepare consolidated statements with their subsidiaries if more than 50% ownership is held unless control is only temporary or does not rest with the majority owner, e.g., because of bankruptcy, legal reorganization, or severe governmentally imposed uncertainties (see SFAS 94 on page 361).

3. Whether a subsidiary is consolidated makes little difference to the bottom line of the income statement of the parent company. APB 18, *Equity Method for Investments in Common Stock*, requires the equity method to be used whenever the investor can exercise significant influence over the investee. Ownership of 20% or more of the investee's voting stock creates a presumption of **significant influence**. Thus, if consolidated statements are not prepared, the equity method will give similar results.

   a. APB 18 also requires users of the equity method to eliminate intercompany profits and amortize any goodwill (see the outline for APB 18 on page 330).

B. If the acquiring company absorbs the acquired company (a merger) or a new company is formed to absorb both the acquirer and the acquired companies (a consolidation), one journal entry (or series of entries) records the business combination, and no consolidated worksheet is necessary because only one company is operating.

1. In a consolidation, the new company records the assets and liabilities transferred from the parent and subsidiary and the issuance of securities (i.e., the books of the parent and the subsidiary are permanently closed). The entry on the books of the new company is

Assets	$XXX	
Liabilities		$XXX
Stock		XXX
Paid-in capital		XXX

2. In a merger, the parent makes the above entry to record the assets received, liabilities assumed, and securities issued (i.e., the former subsidiary's books are permanently closed).

C. **Purchase versus Pooling**

1. Purchase accounting assumes a purchase of net assets, so the assets are recorded at their cost to the acquiring company.

   a. Direct fees paid related to the combination are added to the consideration given.

   b. Costs of registering and issuing equity securities reduce the otherwise determinable value of the securities.

   c. Indirect acquisition expenses are included in the determination of net income when incurred.

2. Pooling accounting assumes a combining of ownership interests, not a purchase, and thus no basis exists for revaluing assets. In poolings, the accounts and financial statements of the pooled entities are added together. APB 16, *Business Combinations*, restricts the applicability of pooling to certain instances that meet 12 criteria (listed in the outline of APB 16 on page 329).
   a. All expenses related to effecting a business combination accounted for as a pooling of interests are deducted in determining income when incurred.

D. Accounting for the excess of cost over the sum of the assigned costs (fair values) of the identifiable net assets acquired applies only in purchase accounting.

1. **Goodwill** is this excess. It is computed by comparing the cost of an investment with the product of the percentage of the company acquired times the fair value of the acquired company's identifiable net assets (assets minus liabilities).
   a. Cost is allocated to specific asset and liability accounts on the consolidated worksheet.
2. The excess of the current fair value of the net identifiable assets acquired over the cost is **negative goodwill**. It should be allocated proportionately to all noncurrent assets except long-term marketable securities. Any excess remaining after noncurrent assets are adjusted to zero should be classified as a deferred credit and amortized over not more than 40 years.
3. EXAMPLE: Assume 100% of a company is purchased for $600,000, and the book value of the company is $500,000. All assets and liabilities are recorded at fair value except a patent with a fair value of $80,000 in excess of book value. The $100,000 excess of cost over total book value would be allocated to the patent and to goodwill on the consolidated worksheet. Thus, the patent will be assigned a cost equal to $80,000 plus its book value, the other assets and liabilities will be recorded at their book values (also their fair values), and goodwill of $20,000 will be recognized. The $80,000 increase in the recorded amount of the patent will be amortized over its remaining life. The $20,000 of goodwill is amortized under APB 17, *Intangible Assets* (probably over 40 years, straight-line).

E. **Basic Worksheet Entries in Purchase Accounting**

1. The first step is to establish reciprocity between the parent's investment account and the subsidiary's (sub's) shareholders' equity accounts. They should be equal after reconciling amortization of goodwill in prior years (the parent, if applying the equity method correctly, should be amortizing the goodwill by debiting investment income and crediting the investment account).
   a. If the parent has not amortized the goodwill, a correcting entry on the parent's or the consolidated books should be made.
2. The second step is to eliminate the investment account and the subsidiary's (sub's) shareholders' equity accounts. The entry is

Sub's stock	$XXX	
Sub's paid-in capital	XXX	
Sub's retained earnings	XXX	
Parent's investment account		$XXX

   a. If there is a minority interest,

Sub's stock	$XXX	
Sub's paid-in capital	XXX	
Sub's retained earnings	XXX	
Parent's investment account		$XXX
Minority interest		XXX

b. If the worksheet contains nominal accounts, the investment account probably should be adjusted back to the beginning of the year (and the entry in E.2.a. is then to the sub's beginning retained earnings and the parent's investment account at the beginning of the year).

Parent's income from investee	$XXX	
Sub's dividend payment		$XXX
Parent's investment account		XXX

3. The third step is to eliminate all other reciprocal accounts between the parent and sub, such as receivables-payables, sales-purchases, and interest revenue-interest expense.

a. The worksheet entries are to debit the credits, e.g., payables, sales, etc., and credit the debits, e.g., purchases, receivables, etc.

Sales	$XXX		A/P	$XXX	
Purchases		$XXX	A/R		$XXX

b. Nominal accounts reflect the cumulative amounts of transactions during the year. Real accounts reflect year-end balances.

4. The fourth step is to eliminate intercompany profit arising from parent-sub transactions in inventory, fixed assets, and intercompany bond transactions.

a. For inventory and fixed assets, intercompany sales usually result in recognition of profit prior to its being earned through sale to third parties. Beginning inventory was overstated by intercompany profit, so the adjusting entry is

Retained earnings	$XXX	
Cost of sales		$XXX

b. For the amount of intercompany profit in ending inventory

Cost of sales	$XXX	
Inventory		$XXX

c. In the year of intercompany sale of fixed assets

Gain on sale of FA	$XXX	
Fixed assets		$XXX
Accumulated depreciation	$(amount taken on FA write-up)	
Depreciation expense		$XXX

d. If the consolidation occurred in a subsequent year

Retained earnings	$(amount of original gain)	
Fixed assets		$XXX
Accumulated depreciation	$(amount to date on FA write-up)	
Depreciation expense		$(current year)
Retained earnings		(plug)

5. For bonds, there are five entries.
   a. Eliminate the bonds payable and investment in bonds at maturity value.
   b. Eliminate the bonds interest payable and receivable at year-end.
   c. Eliminate the bonds interest income and interest expense for the year.
   d. Eliminate the discount or premium of the issuer at year-end and the amortization thereof for the year, with the plug figure to retained earnings.
   e. Eliminate the discount or premium of the investor at year-end and the amortization thereof for the year, with the plug figure to retained earnings.

F. **Pooling Accounting Procedures**

1. In poolings, no readjustment of asset and liability values is necessary except to conform accounting principles among the pooled companies.
2. Frequently, the legal capital (par or stated value) that is issued by the surviving company is different from the legal capital of the combining companies. Thus, an adjustment to capital stock on the books of the surviving company is necessary to make debits equal credits.
   a. EXAMPLE: A company may issue $700,000 of par value stock for 100% of the stock of a company with $450,000 of stock outstanding. If the issuing (surviving) company records the accounts of the combining company on its books, it will have to reduce paid-in capital and/or retained earnings to make the entry balance. Here, the credit to paid-in capital would be reduced by $250,000. It can only be reduced to zero. Any further debit is a reduction of retained earnings.

	Debit	Credit
Assets	$(book value)	
Liabilities		$XXX (book value)
Stock		700,000
Paid-in capital		(plug)
RE		(book value)

INTERPERIOD TAX ALLOCATION

A. **SFAS 109** is an important pronouncement that provides new standards of accounting and reporting for the effects of income taxes in accordance with the asset and liability method.

1. SFAS 109 supersedes APB 11, which prescribed the deferred method of accounting for interperiod tax allocation.
2. SFAS 109 also supersedes SFAS 96, which initially prescribed the asset and liability method. However, SFAS 96 was never permitted to go into effect because of controversy about its complexity and its treatment of deferred tax assets.
3. SFAS 109 applies to taxes based on income, whether foreign, federal, state, or local. It does not apply to
   a. The investment tax credit
   b. Discounting
   c. Income tax accounting for interim periods except for the
      1) Standards for recognition of tax benefits
      2) Effects of enacted tax law changes
      3) Changes in valuation allowances

B. Tax consequences are a transaction or event's effects on current and deferred income taxes. Income taxes currently payable or refundable for a particular year usually include the tax consequences of most of the events recognized in the financial statements for the same year.

1. However, certain significant exceptions exist. As a result, income taxes currently payable or refundable for a year either may include the tax consequences of some events that are recognized in financial income in an earlier year or later year or may not include the tax consequences of some events that are recognized in the financial statements in the current year.

    a. Because of these differences, income taxes currently payable or refundable may differ from (exceed or be less than) income tax expense or benefit. The accounting for these differences is interperiod tax allocation.

C. **Objectives of SFAS 109**. Accrual accounting should recognize taxes payable or refundable for the current year.

1. It should also recognize deferred tax liabilities and assets for the future tax consequences of events that have been recognized in the enterprise's financial statements or tax returns.

D. **Basic Principles of Income Tax Accounting**

1. A current tax liability (asset) is recognized for the estimated taxes payable (refundable) on current-year tax returns.
2. A deferred tax liability or asset is recognized for the estimated future tax effects attributable to temporary differences and carryforwards.
3. Measurement of tax liabilities and assets is based on enacted tax law; the effects of future changes in that law are not anticipated.
4. A deferred tax asset is reduced by a valuation allowance if it is more likely than not that some portion will not be realized.

E. **Temporary differences (TDs)** include differences between the tax basis of an asset or liability and its reported amount in the financial statements that will result in taxable or deductible amounts in future years when the reported amount of the asset is recovered or the liability is settled.

1. A future taxable amount (deferred tax liability) will result from recovery of an asset related to a revenue or gain that is taxable subsequent to being recognized in financial income.

    a. An example is a receivable from an installment sale, which is recognized at the time of sale in financial income and at the time of collection in taxable income.

2. A future taxable amount (deferred tax liability) also results from the recovery of an asset related to any expense or loss that is deductible for tax purposes prior to being recognized in financial income.

    a. An example is a long-term asset that is depreciated for tax purposes more quickly than it is depreciated for financial reporting.

3. A future deductible amount (deferred tax asset) results from the settlement of a liability related to an expense or loss that is deductible for tax purposes subsequent to being recognized in financial income.

    a. An example is a warranty liability, which is recognized as an expense in financial income when a product is sold and recognized in taxable income when the expenditures are made in a later period.

4. A future deductible amount (deferred tax asset) also results from the settlement of a liability related to a revenue or gain that is taxable prior to being recognized in financial income.

   a. An example is subscriptions revenue received in advance, which is recognized in taxable income when received and recognized in financial income when earned in a later period.

5. TDs may also result from events that have been recognized in the financial statements and will result in taxable or deductible amounts in future years based on provisions in the tax laws but that cannot be identified with a particular asset or liability for financial reporting purposes.

   a. An example is organizational costs expensed when incurred for financial reporting purposes (written off rather than recognized as an asset) but deferred for tax purposes.

   b. Another example is a long-term contract accounted for by the percentage-of-completion method for financial reporting (recognition of both an asset and a liability, not just one asset or one liability) and the completed-contract method for tax purposes.

6. A **permanent difference** is an event that is recognized either in pretax financial income or in taxable income but never in the other.

   a. An example is payment of the premium for life insurance covering a key executive. This amount is expensed for financial reporting purposes but is not deductible for income tax purposes.

   b. Goodwill acquired after August 10, 1993, is tax deductible on a pro rata basis over 15 years. It does not result in a permanent difference. Goodwill acquired on or before that date is not tax deductible and therefore constitutes a permanent difference.

F. **Recognition and Measurement**. Because recovery of assets and settlement of liabilities are inherent assumptions of GAAP, accrual accounting must recognize deferred tax consequences of TDs (temporary differences).

1. Basic definitions

   a. **Income tax expense or benefit** is the sum of the current tax expense or benefit and deferred tax expense or benefit.

   b. **Current tax expense or benefit** is the amount of taxes paid or payable (or refundable) for the year.

   c. **Deferred tax expense or benefit** is the net change during the year in an enterprise's deferred tax liabilities and assets.

   d. A **deferred tax liability** records the deferred tax consequences attributable to taxable TDs.

   e. A **deferred tax asset** records the deferred tax consequences attributable to deductible TDs and carryforwards.

   f. **Temporary differences** include differences between the tax basis of an asset or a liability and its reported amount in the financial statements that will result in taxable or deductible amounts in future years when the reported amount of the asset is recovered or the liability is settled.

   g. A **valuation allowance** is a contra account to a deferred tax asset.

2. A valuation allowance is used to reduce a deferred tax asset if the weight of the available evidence, both positive and negative, indicates that it is more likely than not (that is, the probability is more than 50%) that some portion will not be realized. The allowance should be sufficient to reduce the deferred tax asset to the amount that is more likely than not to be realized.
   a. The valuation allowance is based on information about future years as well as past performance. Its recognition ultimately depends on the existence of sufficient taxable income of the proper character (ordinary income or capital gain) within the carryback and carryforward period (for example, the 3-year carryback and 15-year carryforward periods for federal corporate net operating losses). The sources of taxable income permitting realization of the tax benefit of a deferred tax asset include
      1) Reversals of taxable TDs
      2) Future taxable income without regard to reversing differences and carryforwards
      3) Taxable income in the carryback period
      4) Tax-planning strategies, for example, those that accelerate taxable amounts to permit use of an expiring tax credit carryforward, change the character of income or loss, or switch from tax-exempt to taxable items of income
3. **Determination of deferred taxes.** The process below is followed for each taxpaying entity in each tax jurisdiction:
   a. Identify TDs (types and amounts), and operating loss and tax credit carryforwards for tax purposes (nature and amounts, and length of the remaining carryforward period).
   b. Measure the total deferred tax liability for taxable TDs using the applicable tax rate.
      1) The tax rate used in the measurement is the flat rate if graduated rates are not significant to the enterprise. Otherwise, an average of the graduated rates applicable is used.
   c. Measure the total deferred tax asset for deductible TDs and operating loss carryforwards using the applicable tax rate.
   d. Measure deferred tax assets for each type of tax credit carryforward.
   e. Recognize a valuation allowance if necessary.
4. The basic entry to record taxes in accordance with the asset and liability method required by SFAS 109 is

Income tax expense (or benefit) debit (or credit)	$XXX	
Income tax payable (or refundable) credit (or debit)		$XXX
Deferred income tax liability (or asset) credit (or debit)		XXX

G. SFAS 109 requires **intraperiod tax allocation**. This means that income tax expense (benefit) shall be allocated to continuing operations, discontinued operations, extraordinary items, and items taken directly to shareholders' equity.
   1. Thus, intraperiod tax allocation requires an allocation of a period's income tax expense to various components of the period's income but does not affect that income.

H. **Enacted changes** in the tax law or rates require an adjustment of a deferred tax liability or asset in the period of the enactment of the tax law or rate. The effect is included in income from continuing operations.

I. **Change in Tax Status.** When an enterprise changes its tax status, the resulting effect on the deferred tax accounts is recognized.

1. When an enterprise changes from nontaxable to taxable status, a deferred tax liability or asset reflecting temporary differences that exist at the time of the change is recognized.
2. When an enterprise changes its status from taxable to nontaxable, any existing deferred tax liability or asset ordinarily is eliminated at the date of the change.
3. The effect of recognizing or eliminating the deferred tax liability or asset is treated as a component of income from continuing operations.

J. **Financial Statement Presentation**. Deferred tax liabilities and assets should be separated into current and noncurrent components.

1. Classification as current or noncurrent depends on the classification of the related asset or liability.
   a. If a deferred tax liability or asset is not related to an asset or liability for financial reporting, it is classified according to the expected reversal date of the TD.
   b. A valuation allowance is allocated pro rata between current and noncurrent deferred tax assets.
   c. For a given tax-paying entity and within a specific jurisdiction, current deferred tax assets and liabilities are netted. Noncurrent deferred tax assets and liabilities are also offset and shown as a single amount.

K. **Basic Examples**

1. **Deferred tax liability**. In Pitou Co.'s first year of existence, its pretax financial income is $520,000, and its taxable income is $500,000. The $20,000 difference is attributable solely to recognition of earned revenue from installment sales that will result in future taxable amounts when the receivables are collected. Pitou's applicable tax rate is 34%. Thus, the deferred tax liability is $6,800 (34% x $20,000 taxable TD), and the deferred tax expense is also $6,800 ($6,800 year-end deferred tax liability – $0 balance at the beginning of the year). Income tax payable (current tax expense) is $170,000 (34% x $500,000 taxable income). Accordingly, income tax expense is $176,800 ($170,000 current tax expense + $6,800 deferred tax expense). The year-end entry is

Income tax expense	$176,800	
Income tax payable		$170,000
Deferred income tax liability		6,800

In its second year, Pitou Co. has taxable income of $450,000, which includes the collection of $8,000 of installment receivables previously recognized in financial accounting income. There is no other difference between pretax financial income and taxable income. Hence, the taxable TD is reduced to $12,000 ($20,000 – $8,000), the year-end deferred tax liability is $4,080 (34% x $12,000), and the decrease in the deferred tax liability (the deferred tax benefit arising from reduction in the liability) is $2,720 ($6,800 at the beginning of the year – $4,080 at year-end). Current tax expense (tax payable) is $153,000 (34% x $450,000 taxable income). Consequently, total income tax expense for the year is $150,280 ($153,000 current tax expense – $2,720 deferred tax benefit). The year-end entry is

Income tax expense	$150,280	
Deferred income tax liability	2,720	
Income tax payable		$153,000

2. **Deferred tax asset**. Lunes Co. began operations in the year just ended. It has taxable income of $400,000 and pretax financial income of $385,000. The difference is solely attributable to receipt of unearned subscription revenue (a liability) that was included as revenue in the tax return in the year of collection. Lunes will recognize $9,000 of this unearned revenue as earned in its second year of operations and $6,000 in the third year. The applicable tax rate is 34%. Thus, the deferred tax asset is $5,100 (34% x $15,000 deductible TD), and the deferred tax benefit is also $5,100 ($5,100 year-end deferred tax asset – $0 balance at the beginning of the year). Income tax payable (current tax expense) is $136,000 (34% x $400,000 taxable income). Accordingly, income tax expense is $130,900 ($136,000 current tax expense – $5,100 deferred tax benefit). Based on the evidence (taxable income), no valuation allowance is required for the deferred tax asset. Thus, the year-end entry is

Income tax expense	$130,900	
Deferred income tax asset	5,100	
Income tax payable		$136,000

In its second year of operations, Lunes has taxable income of $600,000, with income tax payable (current tax expense) of $204,000 (34% x $600,000). Taxable income and pretax financial income differ only in that $9,000 of unearned revenue collected in the preceding year is included in the determination of pretax financial income. At the end of the second year, the deferred tax asset is therefore $2,040 [34% x ($15,000 – $9,000)], and the deferred tax expense (the decrease in the deferred tax asset) is $3,060 ($5,100 – $2,040). Total income tax expense is $207,060 ($204,000 current tax expense + $3,060 deferred tax expense). Based on the evidence (taxable income), no valuation allowance is required for the deferred tax asset. Thus, the year-end entry is

Income tax expense	$207,060	
Income tax payable		$204,000
Deferred income tax asset		3,060

3. **Deferred tax asset -- valuation allowance.** Mardi Co. has a $6,000 deductible TD at the end of its current year. The applicable tax rate is 34%. Consequently, Mardi recorded a deferred tax asset of $2,040 (34% x $6,000). However, after weighing all the evidence, Mardi Co. has decided that it is more likely than not (more than 50% probable) that $4,000 of the deductible temporary difference will not be realized. To reflect this determination, a valuation allowance (a contra account) should be credited. The offsetting debit is to income tax expense. The amount of the valuation allowance should be sufficient to reduce the deferred tax asset to the amount that is more likely than not to be realized. Accordingly, Mardi should recognize a $1,360 valuation allowance to reduce the $2,040 deferred tax asset to $680 (34% x $2,000). The entry is

Income tax expense	$1,360	
Valuation allowance		$1,360

STUDY UNIT 14
SEC REPORTING REQUIREMENTS

In Part 2, the ICMA specifies 60% to 80% coverage of financial statements and reporting.

Financial Statements	30%–40%
Reporting Requirements	30%–40%

We further differentiate this material by dividing it into four study units.

Study Unit 11: Financial Accounting: Development of Theory and Practice (FAD)
Study Unit 12: Financial Statement Presentation (FS)
Study Unit 13: Special Financial Reporting Problems (SPE)
Study Unit 14: SEC Reporting Requirements (SEC)

SECURITIES AND EXCHANGE COMMISSION (SEC)

A. The SEC was created in 1934 by the Securities Exchange Act to regulate the trading of securities and carry out the 1933 and 1934 securities acts.

1. The basic purposes of the securities laws are to
   a. Prevent fraud and misrepresentation
   b. Require full and fair disclosure so investors can evaluate investments on their own
2. Under the **Securities Act of 1933**, disclosure is made before the initial issuance of securities through registration (i.e., initial filing) and disseminating a prospectus to prospective investors.
3. Under the **Securities Exchange Act of 1934**, disclosure is made for subsequent trading of securities by requiring periodic reports to be filed that are available for review.
4. The SEC requires the registration and the reports to comply with certain accounting standards and policies.
   a. **Regulation S-X** governs the reporting of financial statements, including footnotes and schedules.
   b. **Regulation S-K** provides disclosure standards, including many of a nonfinancial nature. S-K also covers certain aspects of corporate annual reports to shareholders.
   c. **Financial Reporting Releases (FRRs)** announce accounting and auditing matters of general interest.
      1) They provide explanations and clarifications of changes in accounting or auditing procedures used in reports filed with the SEC.
      2) These and **Accounting and Auditing Enforcement Releases (AAERs)** replace what used to be called Accounting Series Releases.

d. AAERs disclose enforcement actions involving accountants.

e. **Staff Accounting Bulletins (SABs)** are promulgated as interpretations to be followed by the SEC staff in administering disclosure requirements.

1) SABs are not requirements to be followed by registrants.

5. See Study Unit 4, Institutional Environment of Business, in Chapter 5 for exemptions from SEC regulation.

B. **Integrated Disclosure System**

1. In 1982, a revised disclosure system became effective.

a. Previously, disclosures were duplicative, i.e., required similar information in different formats under the 1933 and 1934 acts.

b. To alleviate this problem, the integrated disclosure system

1) Standardizes the financial statements

2) Uses a Basic Information Package (BIP) common to most of the filings

3) Allows incorporation by reference from the annual shareholders' report to the annual SEC report (Form 10-K)

2. Standardized financial statements are required.

a. They must be audited and include

1) Balance sheets for the two most recent fiscal year-ends

2) Statements of income, cash flows, and changes in stockholders' equity for the three most recent fiscal years

b. They are required in the annual shareholders' report as well as in forms filed with the SEC.

c. The accountant certifying the financial statements must be independent of the management of the filing company. The accountant is not required to be a CPA, but (s)he must be registered by a state.

3. The **Basic Information Package (BIP)** includes the following:

a. Standardized financial statements

b. Selected financial information

1) Columnar format for preceding 5 fiscal years

2) Presentation of financial trends through comparison of key information from year to year

c. **Management's discussion and analysis** of financial condition and results of operations

1) This information includes liquidity, capital resources, results of operations, risk associated with any repurchase agreement, effect of the 1986 Tax Reform Act, and impact of inflation and changing prices.

2) Forward-looking information (a forecast) is encouraged, but not required.

d. Market price of securities and dividends
   1) Principal market in which security is traded
   2) High and low sales prices for each quarter in the last 2 years
   3) Most recent number of shareholders
   4) Frequency and amount of dividends in the last 2 years
   5) Any restrictions on the payment of dividends

e. Description of business
   1) Fundamental developments for past 5 years, e.g., organization, reorganizations, bankruptcies, major dispositions or acquisitions of assets, etc.
   2) Financial information of industry segments, and also foreign and domestic operations
   3) Narrative description including
      a) Principal products or services for each industry segment and principal markets for them
      b) Total revenues of each class of products equaling or exceeding 10% or more of consolidated revenue (15% if consolidated revenue is not in excess of $50 million)
      c) Other information material to the business on the basis of industry segments

f. Description of properties

g. Legal proceedings

h. Management
   1) General data for each director and officer
   2) Financial transactions with the corporation involving in excess of $60,000
   3) Remuneration for the five highest paid directors and officers whose compensation exceeds $50,000 (including personal benefits, i.e., perks)

i. Security holdings of directors, officers, and those owning 5% or more of the security

C. **Registration (Initial Filing)**

1. The issuer must register new issuances of securities with the SEC.
   a. **Form S-1** is used for the registration statement for companies that have never registered securities.
      1) Incorporation by reference is usually not allowed, and all material must be included.
   b. **Form S-2** is a shorter form for companies that have been reporting to the SEC (Form 10-K, etc.) for at least 3 years and have done so on a timely basis.
      1) Allows BIP to be incorporated by reference from the latest annual shareholders' report

c. **Form S-3** is another short form for companies that meet the requirements for Form S-2 and have at least $50 million value of stock held by nonaffiliates (or at least $100 million with an annual trading volume of 3 million or more shares).

   1) Allows most information to be incorporated by reference from other filings with the SEC

d. Other forms

   1) **Form S-4** is a simplified form for business combinations.

      a) **Form F-4** is to be used by foreign registrants in business combinations.

      b) **Form N-14** is to be used by investment companies to register securities in business combinations.

   2) **Form S-8** is for securities offered to employees under a stock option or other employee benefit plan.

   3) **Form S-11** is used by real estate investment trusts and real estate companies.

   4) **Form S-18** is for small companies not required to report annually to the SEC. The offering limit is now $7,500,000.

e. Filings become public information.

f. Securities may not be offered for sale to the public until the registration is effective.

   1) The registration statement is examined by the Division of Corporation Finance.

   2) Registration becomes effective 20 days after filing unless an amendment is filed or the SEC issues a stop order.

   3) A preliminary prospectus is allowed that contains the same information as a regular prospectus (prices are omitted) but is clearly marked in red to be preliminary (therefore called a **red herring prospectus**).

2. Registration forms requirements (especially Form S-1)

   a. Basic information package

   b. Plan of distribution, name of underwriter, use of broker, and commissions

   c. Use of proceeds and details of offerings other than cash

   d. Capital structure of registrant including details of current securities being registered

   e. Risk factors

   f. Signatures of

      1) Issuer
      2) Principal executive, financial, and accounting officers
      3) Majority of board of directors

3. The **prospectus** is part of the registration statement.

   a. Its purpose is to provide investors with information to make an informed investment decision.

   b. However, it usually may be presented in a more condensed or summarized form than Form S-1.

D. **Form 10** is used to register securities under the 1934 act.

1. Securities must be registered if they are traded in one of the ways listed below.
   a. On a national securities exchange
   b. Over the counter if the issuer has assets in excess of $5 million and there are 500 or more shareholders
2. An issuer may voluntarily register its securities.
3. An issuer may deregister its securities if its shareholders decrease to fewer than 300 or if its shareholders are fewer than 500 and it had less than $5 million in assets for each of the three most recent fiscal year-ends.
4. Banks must also register their securities, but they file with the appropriate banking authority, not with the SEC.
5. Its required contents are
   a. Basic information package
   b. Other information required for Form S-1

E. **Form 10-K** is the annual report to the SEC. It must be

1. Filed within 90 days of corporation's year-end
2. Certified by an independent accountant
3. Signed by the following:
   a. Principal executive, financial, and accounting officers
   b. Majority of the board of directors
4. Presented with the basic information package
   a. Additional information is required but the CMA exam has not tested it.
   b. Information contained in the annual report to shareholders may be incorporated by reference.
   c. Information contained in proxy statements may also be incorporated by reference into Form 10-K because the proxy statement is a published source readily available to the shareholders and investing public.

F. **Form 10-Q** is the quarterly report to the SEC.

1. It must be filed for each of the first three quarters of the year within 45 days after the end of each quarter.
2. Financial statements need not be certified by an independent accountant, but they must be prepared in accord with APB 28, *Interim Financial Reporting*.
3. Also required are changes during the quarter, for example,
   a. Legal proceedings
   b. Increase, decrease, or change in securities or indebtedness
   c. Matters submitted to shareholders for a vote
   d. Exhibits and reports on Form 8-K
   e. Other material events not reported on Form 8-K

G. **Form 8-K** is a current report to disclose material events.

1. It must be filed within 15 days after the material event takes place. Also, a change in independent accountants or the resignation of a director must be reported within 5 business days.

2. Material events
   a. Change in control
   b. Acquisition or disposition of a significant amount of assets not in the ordinary course of business
   c. Bankruptcy or receivership
   d. Resignation of directors
   e. A change in independent accountants, the reporting requirements for which are listed below:
      1) Date
      2) Disclosure of any disagreements in the prior 2 years
      3) Disclosure certain reportable events, e.g., the former accountants' concerns about internal control or the reliability of management's representations
      4) Disclosure prior consultations with the new accountants
      5) Whether a disagreement or reportable event was discussed with the audit committee
      6) Whether the company authorized the former accountants to respond fully to the new accountants' inquiries about disagreements
      7) Whether the former accountants were dismissed, resigned, or refused to seek reemployment
      8) Disclosure any qualification of reports in the prior 2 years
      9) Letter from the former accountant indicating agreement (or disagreement) with the above. The letter must be submitted within 10 business days.
      10) Whether the decision to change was recommended or approved by the audit committee or the board of directors
   f. Other events, e.g., major legal proceedings, default on securities or debt, write-down or write-off of assets, change of more than 5% of ownership of a security

H. **Proxy Solicitations**

1. A proxy is a grant of authority by a shareholder allowing the holder of the proxy to vote for the shareholder at a meeting.
2. A formal proxy statement must be sent before or with any proxy solicitation.
   a. A proxy solicitation is a request by any person (usually management or someone trying to take over the management) to a shareholder for that shareholder's proxy to vote at a corporate meeting.
3. The proxy statement must
   a. Contain disclosure of all material facts of matters to be voted upon at the meeting
   b. Include an annual shareholders' report if the solicitation is on behalf of the present management at a meeting at which directors are to be elected
   c. Be filed with the SEC
4. Management must mail proxy materials of insurgents, if so requested and the insurgents pay the expenses.

I. **Shareholder Proposal Rules**

1. Minority shareholders are permitted to submit proposals in a proxy statement to be voted upon at meetings of shareholders.
2. However, the SEC has placed limitations on this right of shareholders because of abuses.
   a. For example, without these restrictions, an owner of one share of stock can submit a proposal supporting his/her favorite political cause. Although the proposal may be certain to be defeated, the shareholder may receive much free publicity for his/her cause.
3. To submit a proposal, a shareholder or group of shareholders must have owned at least 1% of the voting shares or $1,000 in market value of voting securities, whichever is less, for at least 1 year and must continue to own them through the date of the meeting.
4. A shareholder may submit only one proposal per meeting to an issuer.
5. Persons engaged in proxy contests (persons who deliver written proxy materials to holders of more than 25% of a class of voting securities) are ineligible to use the shareholder proposal process.
6. Proposals may be rejected if
   a. They are not a proper subject for shareholder voting under state law.
   b. They relate to operations that account for less than 5% of an issuer's total assets or less than 5% of its net earnings and gross sales for the current year, and are not otherwise significant to the business.
7. To be resubmitted to shareholders in a proxy statement, proposals that have been previously voted down must be approved by at least 5% of the shareholders if submitted once before, 8% if submitted twice before, and 10% if submitted three times before.

J. **Shelf Registration.** SEC Rule 415 (under the Securities Act of 1933) allows corporations to file registration statements covering a stipulated amount of securities that may be issued over the 2-year effective period of the statement. The securities are placed on the shelf and issued at an opportune moment without the necessity of filing a new registration statement, observing a 20-day waiting period, or preparing a new prospectus. The issuer is only required to provide updating amendments or to refer investors to quarterly and annual statements filed with the SEC. It is most advantageous to large corporations that frequently offer securities to the public.

SEC ACCOUNTING AND DISCLOSURE REQUIREMENTS

A. The SEC has the authority to regulate the form and content of all financial statements, notes, and schedules filed with the SEC, and also the financial reports to shareholders if the company is subject to the Securities Act of 1934.

1. Accounting principles to be followed are those with substantial authoritative support.
   a. The SEC recognizes GAAP and has stated that financial statements conforming to standards set by the FASB will be presumed to have substantial authoritative support.
2. However, the SEC reserves the right to substitute its principles for those of the accounting profession and to require such additional disclosures as it deems necessary.
   a. This is achieved through Regulation S-X and Financial Reporting Releases (FRRs). A summary of the major areas of increased disclosure follows.

B. **Materiality**

1. If an amount is not material, it need not be separately set forth.
2. Material information is significant to a reader or decision maker.
3. Even if dollar amounts are small, the following items are deemed material:
   a. Amounts due to and from officers and directors
   b. Various types of surplus and important reserve accounts
   c. Accrued liability for taxes
   d. Income from dividends and equity method income if there are large investments in other companies
   e. Items amounting to more than 10% of a general category on a balance sheet (e.g., deferred charges) or more than 5% of total assets

C. **Cash Flow (FRR 202)**

1. Cash flow is sometimes presented to help show the economic performance of certain types of companies.
2. When such measurement models differing from conventionally computed income are used, explanations and data should be presented in the following manner:
   a. So as not to give them greater authority or prominence than conventionally computed earnings
   b. On a consistent basis for all segments
3. It should not be used for per share data.

D. **Compensating Balances and Short-Term Borrowing Arrangements (FRR 203)**

1. Compensating balances are amounts kept in financial institutions to support present and future credit, and also bank services.
   a. These amounts should be disclosed, even if they cannot be specified with precision because they affect the company's liquidity.
2. Funds maintained for future credit availability (short- and long-term) should be disclosed.
3. Unused lines of credit should be disclosed.

E. **Income tax expense (FRR 204)** requires disclosure of

1. The components of income tax expense, including
   a. Current taxes payable
   b. Net effects of temporary differences
   c. Operating losses
   d. Net deferred investment tax credits. Note that the investment tax credit was phased out after 1985.
   e. Domestic and foreign taxes, which are separately stated
2. Reasons for, and tax effects of, temporary differences
3. Any estimates that taxes payable will exceed tax expense for the next 3 years
4. Reconciliation between total income tax expense and income before taxes times the income tax rates

F. **LIFO Inventory Method (FRR 205)**

1. LIFO may be applied differently for book and tax purposes.
2. The excess of replacement or current cost over the LIFO value on the balance sheet must be disclosed.
3. A material amount of income recorded as a result of a LIFO inventory liquidation should be disclosed.

G. **Defense and other long-term contracts (FRR 206)** require disclosure of

1. Receivables
   a. Amounts of retainage, i.e., amounts withheld until work is completed
   b. Amounts not billed and expected to be collected after 1 year
   c. Amounts of claims or similar items subject to uncertainty concerning their ultimate realization
2. Inventories
   a. Description of cost elements included in inventory
   b. Amount of costs relating to long-term contracts included in inventory
   c. Assumptions used to develop estimates of costs in inventory when estimates are made, e.g., especially for general and administrative costs
   d. Claims or similar items included in inventory if subject to uncertainty

H. When **notes to the financial statements** contain information required by the SEC but not required by GAAP, cross-references to the notes must appear on the face of the financial statements **(FRR 208)**.

I. **Property, plant, and equipment (PP&E) (FRR 209)** must be disclosed in detailed supplemental schedules.

1. This disclosure is not required if the company's PP&E, net of accumulated depreciation, depletion, and amortization, is less than 25% of its total assets at both the beginning and end of the year.

J. **Redeemable preferred stocks (FRR 211)** must be presented separately in the balance sheets as to

1. Preferred stocks not redeemable or redeemable solely at the option of the issuer
2. Preferred stocks that are subject to mandatory redemption requirements or whose redemption is outside the control of the issuer

K. **Material related party transactions** affecting the financial statements **(FRR 212)** must be disclosed prominently on the face thereof.

L. **Unusual Risks and Uncertainties**

1. Significant changes in business certainty or circumstances that create unusual risks and uncertainties must be reported in the financial statements.
   a. At such times, the conventional financial statements alone may not adequately inform investors.
2. The SEC has identified examples of uncertainties requiring disclosure; however, they are not all-inclusive.
   a. Declines in loan loss reserves of financial institutions
   b. Declines in the value of marketable securities
   c. Uncertainty as to recovery of deferral of fuel cost by public utilities
   d. Significant dependence upon a small number of projects
   e. Cost of raw materials when the price is still under negotiation
3. Disclosure should include
   a. Description of the situation
   b. Impact on current and prospective earnings
   c. Assumptions made by management in this evaluation
4. Methods of disclosure are
   a. Narrative discussion as part of the statement of accounting policies
   b. Separate footnotes to the financial statements
   c. Parenthetical statement on the face of the financial statements

M. **Forecasts (Forward-Looking Information)**

1. The SEC does not require forecasts but has encouraged companies to publish projections of future performance.
2. If a company does elect to publish forecast data, it may not present only those items that appear favorable or that might give a misleading impression.
3. The SEC has established safe harbor rules for forecasts prepared in a reasonable manner and in good faith to encourage the publication of forecast information in SEC filings.

N. **Other FRRs**

1. FRR 14 -- Oil and gas producers may exclude costs of unevaluated properties from the amortization base until the property is shown to have proven reserves or to be impaired.
2. FRR 16 -- In an accountant's report filed in registration statements, a going concern modification no longer precludes a company from making a public offering of securities if the company makes full disclosure. Forms 10-K and 10-Q reports are affected by these disclosure guidelines.
3. FRR 17 -- A company using the full-cost method may not recognize income on sales of oil and gas properties unless the sales significantly alter the relationship between capitalized costs and proven reserves. Guidance is also provided as to when management fees and contract services income may be recognized.

4. FRR 20 -- Additional disclosures by property/casualty insurers are required concerning loss reserves. Also, Form 10-K should now include a new schedule showing items such as premiums written and earned, claims paid and incurred, unpaid claim reserves, and deferred policy acquisition costs. A new exhibit presenting reserves is to be included in Form 10-K.

5. FRR 23 -- Oral and written guarantees are equally important for financial reporting. Hence, oral guarantees should be disclosed pursuant to SFAS 5, *Accounting for Contingencies*. An important factor in the disclosure decision is whether a lender relied on the oral guarantee when deciding to extend credit.

6. FRR 24 -- When the higher of the carrying amount or market value of assets sold under repurchase agreements (sales of securities with agreements to repurchase) or the carrying amount of reverse repurchase agreements exceeds 10% of total assets, the liability or asset must be separately disclosed as a line item on the balance sheet.

7. FRR 26 -- In the Management's Discussion and Analysis, the potential material effects of the Tax Reform Act of 1986 must be discussed but need not be quantified.

8. FRR 28 -- Lenders should document use of a systematic method each period for estimating loan losses and the basis supporting the determination that reported amounts are adequate. Also, fair values must be considered when loan collateral has been substantively repossessed, and current market values are deemed more appropriate than derived amounts when valuing collateral for purposes of determining the allowance for loan losses.

9. FRR 29 -- A registered, open-end investment company preparing financial statements as part of a registration statement or shareholder report must include as an expense in its Statement of Operations all costs incurred under a plan adopted under Rule 12b-1 of the Investment Company Act of 1940. A 12b-1 plan allows a fund to use its assets to finance the distribution of shares. Also, a contingent deferred sales load (CDSL) paid to a fund to offset initial Rule 12b-1 plan costs is treated as 12b-1 expense reimbursement, not as income.

10. FRR 30 -- Regulation S-K, Form 20-F, and the Codification of Financial Reporting Policies are amended to make voluntary the disclosure of supplemental information on the effects of inflation and other changes in prices. Previously, these disclosures were required under SFAS 33.

11. FRR 31 -- More complete disclosures are required concerning the circumstances surrounding a change in accountants. Certain issues discussed with the newly engaged auditor during the registrant's 2 most recent fiscal years and any subsequent interim period prior to engagement must be disclosed. Disagreements with the former auditor must also be disclosed. The purpose is to reduce opinion shopping.

12. FRR 32 -- Companies engaged in the defense business should review on an ongoing basis the need for appropriate disclosure in connection with government investigations into illegal or unethical activity in the procurement of defense contracts. Material pending legal proceedings involving a company or its subsidiaries must be disclosed. Legal proceedings involving any director, nominee, executive officer, promoter, and/or control person should likewise be disclosed if material to the ability or integrity of such person(s). Any additional material information that is necessary to assure that the required statements are not misleading must also be disclosed.

13. FRR 33 -- Letters to the SEC that request its staff's views on an accountant's independence, together with the staff's response thereto, will be available for public inspection and copying unless confidential treatment is granted.
14. FRR 34 -- The time period for a registrant to file a Form 8-K announcing a change in its independent certifying accountant or the resignation of a director is reduced from 15 calendar days to 5 business days. The time period for the former accountant to file a report is reduced from 30 calendar days to 10 business days.
15. FRR 35 -- An issuer changing its fiscal year must report both the date of its determination to change its fiscal year-end and the date of its new fiscal year-end. The issuer is required to begin filing quarterly reports on the new fiscal year basis with the quarterly report for the first quarter of the new fiscal year ending after the issuer determined to change its fiscal year-end.
16. FRR 36 -- In the Management's Discussion and Analysis, additional disclosure matters must be considered by registrants. Also, additional disclosures are required by investment companies that invest in, or are permitted to invest in, securities issued in highly leveraged transactions, even though investment companies are not subject to MD&A disclosure requirements.

FEDERAL TRADE COMMISSION (FTC)

A. The FTC, in addition to monitoring antitrust laws (see Study Unit 4, Institutional Environment of Business, in Chapter 5), also has some reporting requirements.
   1. About 15,000 randomly selected corporations must submit quarterly financial statements of their consolidated domestic activity.
      a. The data are used by the Department of Commerce to monitor business profits and develop macroeconomic statistics.
      b. A corporation is usually required to participate for a period of 2 years, at which time it is replaced by another corporation.
   2. Large manufacturing corporations must submit financial statements by line of business (industry segment).
      a. It only applies to domestic business.
      b. SFAS 14 requires this form of reporting for financial accounting purposes.

STOCK EXCHANGE LISTING REQUIREMENTS

A. A company must file an application with both the exchange and the SEC.
   1. Both must approve the application before the company's securities can be listed.
B. Each stock exchange has minimum standards that must be met.
   1. These standards include minimum amounts of assets or earning power, number of shares outstanding, number of shareholders, and wide distribution of the securities to provide an adequate market.
   2. The standards vary, but the New York Stock Exchange has the most stringent standards.

STUDY UNIT 15
RATIO AND ACCOUNTS ANALYSIS

Accounts and statement analysis covers 15% to 20% of Part 2. Much of the material implicit in this topic is covered in the first three study units in this chapter. Refer also to the study units on Working Capital Finance and Capital Structure Finance. Ratio analysis, by itself, is a straightforward and relatively narrow topic. Most ratio titles describe the numerator and denominator, e.g., debt-equity ratio.

RATIO ANALYSIS

A. Ratio analysis is a means of evaluating the financing and investing decisions of a business, regarding

   1. Solvency -- the firm's ability to meet short-term obligations
   2. Activity -- the firm's effectiveness in using its resources
   3. Leverage -- the extent to which the firm has been financed by debt
   4. Profitability -- the firm's earning power
   5. Per share data -- EPS, yield, and book value

B. Ratio analysis is based on norms and trends.

   1. Normal or average ratios are computable for broad industrial categories.
   2. Ratios for individual firms can be compared with those of competitors.
   3. Changes in ratios over time provide insight about the future (trend analysis).
      a. Comparisons of trends in ratios of competitors are also useful.
   4. Benchmarks have evolved for the use of ratios; e.g., a current ratio should not be less than 2.

C. **Solvency (liquidity) ratios** measure the short-term viability of the business, i.e., the firm's ability to pay its obligations in the short term and thus to continue operations.

   1. **Current ratio** (sometimes called working capital ratio) -- current assets divided by current liabilities

      a. $\dfrac{\textit{Current assets}}{\textit{Current liabilities}}$

      b. The most commonly used measure of near-term solvency, it relates current assets to the claims of short-term creditors.

      c. A current ratio can be either too high or too low. A low ratio indicates a possible solvency problem. An overly high ratio indicates that management may not be investing idle assets in the most productive manner.

2. **Acid test or quick ratio** -- cash, net receivables, and trading securities divided by current liabilities

   a. $$\frac{\textit{Cash} + \textit{Net receivables} + \textit{Trading securities}}{\textit{Current liabilities}}$$

   b. It measures the firm's ability to pay off its short-term debt from its most liquid assets.

   c. The primary difference between current and quick ratios is that the latter excludes inventory.

3. **Working capital** is the excess of current assets over current liabilities.

D. **Activity ratios** measure the firm's use of assets to generate revenue and income. Thus, they also relate to liquidity.

1. **Inventory turnover ratio** -- cost of sales divided by average inventories

   a. $$\frac{\textit{Cost of sales}}{\textit{Average inventory}}$$

   b. A high turnover implies that the firm does not hold excessive stocks of inventories that are unproductive and that lessen the firm's profitability.

   c. A high turnover also implies that the inventory is truly marketable and does not contain obsolete goods.

   d. An average inventory figure should be used.

      1) If the average of the beginning and ending inventory is not representative because of cyclical factors, a monthly average should be used.

2. **Number of days of inventory** (days' sales in average inventory) -- the number of days in the year divided by the inventory turnover ratio

   a. $$\frac{\textit{365, 360, or 300}}{\textit{Inventory turnover ratio}}$$

   b. It measures the average number of days that inventory is held before sale.

      1) It reflects the efficiency of inventory management.

   c. The number of days in a year may be 365, 360 (a banker's year), or 300 (number of business days).

3. **Receivables turnover ratio** -- net credit sales divided by average accounts receivable. (However, net sales is often used because credit sales data may be unavailable.)

   a. $$\frac{\textit{Net credit sales}}{\textit{Average accounts receivable}}$$

   b. It indicates the efficiency of accounts receivable collection.

   c. The higher the turnover, the better

4. **Working capital turnover** -- net sales divided by average working capital

5. **Number of days of receivables** (days' sales in average receivables or the average collection period) -- the number of days in the year divided by the receivables turnover ratio

   a. $\dfrac{\text{365, 360, } \textit{or} \text{ 300}}{\textit{Receivables turnover ratio}}$

   b. It is the average number of days to collect a receivable.

   c. It may also be computed as average accounts receivable divided by average daily sales.

      1) Average daily sales are net credit sales divided by the number of days in a year.

   d. The number of days of receivables should be compared with the company's credit terms to determine whether the average customer is paying within the credit period.

   e. The operating cycle of an enterprise may be estimated by adding days' sales in average inventory to days' sales in average receivables.

6. **Fixed asset turnover** -- sales divided by net fixed assets

   a. $\dfrac{\textit{Net sales}}{\textit{Net fixed assets}}$

   b. It measures the level of use of property, plant, and equipment.

      1) It is largely affected by the capital intensiveness of the company and its industry.

   c. A high turnover is preferable to a low turnover.

7. **Total asset turnover** -- net sales divided by average total assets

   a. $\dfrac{\textit{Net sales}}{\textit{Average total assets}}$

   b. It measures the level of capital investment relative to sales volume.

   c. For all turnover ratios, high turnover is preferable to low turnover.

E. **Leverage ratios** measure the firm's use of debt to finance assets and operations.

1. **Debt-equity ratio** -- total debt divided by total stockholders' equity

   a. $\dfrac{\textit{Total liabilities}}{\textit{Stockholders' equity}}$

   b. It compares the resources provided by creditors to resources provided by common stockholders.

2. **Equity ratio** -- common stockholders' equity divided by total assets

   a. $\dfrac{\textit{Common stockholders' equity}}{\textit{Total assets}}$

   b. It indicates the percentage of total assets financed by common stockholders.

3. **Times-interest-earned** -- income before interest and taxes, divided by interest
   a. $$\frac{\textit{Net income} + \textit{Interest expense} + \textit{Income tax expense}}{\textit{Interest expense}}$$
   b. It indicates the margin of safety for payment of fixed interest charges.
   c. Interest is tax deductible. Hence, interest and tax must be added to net income to determine the amount available to pay interest.
4. The question of what constitutes a safe level for debt and equity ratios depends on the nature of the industry in which a company operates.
   a. A low-risk industry (such as banking) can accept a very low equity ratio (less than 10%).
   b. A high-risk industry (such as uranium mining) requires a high equity ratio (perhaps 90%).
5. **Degree of financial leverage**
   a. This ratio is sometimes expressed as the percentage change in EPS available to holders of common stock associated with a given percentage change in earnings before interest and taxes (EBIT).
   b. Assuming no preferred stock, this formula may also be expressed as

$$\frac{\textit{EBIT}}{\textit{EBIT} - \textit{Interest}}$$

F. **Profitability ratios** measure income on a relative basis.

1. **Profit margin on sales** -- net income after taxes divided by sales
   a. $$\frac{\textit{Net income after taxes}}{\textit{Sales}}$$
   b. It measures the rate of profitability on sales.
2. **Return on assets** -- net income after taxes divided by average total assets
   a. $$\frac{\textit{Net income after taxes}}{\textit{Average total assets}}$$
   b. It measures the rate of return on investment, including that of both shareholders and creditors.
   c. The book value of assets may differ from their fair value.
3. **Return on stockholders' equity** -- net income after taxes divided by common stockholders' equity
   a. $$\frac{\textit{Net income after taxes}}{\textit{Average common stockholders' equity}}$$
   b. It measures the rate of return on stockholders' investment.
   c. The book value of common stockholders' equity may differ from its fair value.
   d. If the return on stockholders' equity is greater than the return on assets, the company is using leverage effectively. Thus, the company is earning a higher rate of return on assets than the interest rate paid to its creditors.

G. **Per share ratios** relate company financial information to each share.

1. **Earnings per share (EPS)**

   a. $\frac{\textit{Net income available to common stockholders}}{\textit{Average outstanding shares}}$

   b. EPS is net income available to common stockholders divided by the average number of shares outstanding.

   c. Net income available to common stockholders is ordinarily net income minus preferred dividends.

   d. In some cases, two EPS figures are required by APB 15. The calculations for primary EPS and fully diluted EPS are explained in Study Unit 12, Financial Statement Presentation.

2. **Book value per share**

   a. $\frac{\textit{Shareholders' equity}}{\textit{Shares outstanding}}$

   b. Book value is the amount of net assets available to the shareholders of a given type of stock divided by the number of those shares outstanding.

   c. When a company has preferred as well as common stock outstanding, the computation of book value per common share must consider potential claims by preferred shareholders, such as whether the preferred stock is cumulative and in arrears, or participating. It must also take into account whether the call price (or possibly the liquidation value) exceeds the carrying amount of the preferred stock.

   d. Book value per share is ordinarily based on historical cost expressed in nominal dollars. Accordingly, it may be misleading because book values may differ materially from fair values.

3. **Yield on common stock**

   a. $\frac{\textit{Dividend per share}}{\textit{Per share market value}}$

   b. Yield is the annual dividend payment divided by the market value per share.

4. **Price-earnings ratio** -- market price divided by EPS

   a. $\frac{\textit{Market price}}{\textit{EPS}}$

   b. Most analysts prefer to use fully diluted EPS.

   c. Growth companies are likely to have high P-E ratios.

5. **Dividend payout ratio**

   a. $\frac{\textit{Dividends per share}}{\textit{Earnings per share}}$

   b. Dividend policy is a crucial aspect of financial management. Companies and investors prefer stable dividends.

H. Other ratios are usually identifiable by their titles, e.g., fixed assets to long-term debt.

1. You should be able to identify ratios and classify them as to whether they measure
   a. Solvency (liquidity)
   b. Activity
   c. Leverage
   d. Profitability
   e. Per share data
2. You must also determine whether each value is for a period of time or a moment in time.
3. Also consider whether the variables are
   a. Before or after adjustments
   b. Gross or net
   c. Average or year-end
4. Ratios are most useful when put in context.
   a. Through trend analysis of a single company
   b. By comparison with other companies or industry averages
      1) After any adjustments are made to assure that the accounting data are comparable
5. Always remember that ratios are based on accounting data, which normally do not reflect current fair values.

I. **Common-size financial statements** are used to compare the components of different companies' financial statements.

1. Common-size financial statements are expressed in percentages.
2. Common-size statements permit evaluation of the efficiency of various aspects of operations of different businesses.
3. Expressing financial statement items as percentages of corresponding base-year figures is a **horizontal** form of common-size (percentage) analysis that is useful for evaluating trends. The base amount is assigned the value of 100%, and the amounts for other years are stated in percentages of the base.
   a. **Vertical** common-size (percentage) analysis presents figures for a single year expressed as percentages of a base amount on the balance sheet (e.g., total assets) and on the income statement (e.g., sales).

J. **Sources of Accounting Data to Compute Ratios**

1. Financial statements of individual companies
2. Dun & Bradstreet financial statements
3. Federal Trade Commission and Securities and Exchange Commission quarterly data on manufacturing companies
4. Various investment services, e.g., Standard & Poor's, Value Line, and Moody's Investors Service

ACCOUNTS ANALYSIS

A. Accounts analysis and interpretation consider the nature of the components of an ending balance: the beginning balance and the transactions for the period. A classic example is the aging of accounts receivable.

1. For more about specific accounts, see Study Unit 12, Financial Statement Presentation.
   a. The related topic of inventory control is covered in Study Unit 30.

STUDY UNIT 16
INTERNAL CONTROL

INTRODUCTION

This study unit begins with the AICPA's approach to internal control stated in SAS 55 (AU 319), *Consideration of the Internal Control Structure in a Financial Statement Audit*, as amended to incorporate the definition stated in *Internal Control Integrated Framework* published by the Committee of Sponsoring Organizations (COSO). SAS 55 redefines internal control, broadens the auditor's responsibility to consider it, and integrates internal control principles with those of audit risk and audit evidence.

The balance of this study unit concerns matters that may have relevance beyond the scope of the financial statement audit. Also see Study Unit 33, Internal and Operational Auditing. Internal auditors and management accountants share the CPA's concern for reliable financial data and safeguarding of assets, but are also interested in a much broader range of controls. Thus, SMA 2A, *Management Accounting Glossary*, defines internal control as follows:

> *The whole system of controls (financial and otherwise) established by management to carry on the business of the enterprise in an orderly and efficient manner, to ensure adherence to management policies, safeguard the assets, and ensure as far as possible the completeness and accuracy of the records.*

INTERNAL CONTROL ACCORDING TO THE AICPA

A. **Introduction**. The crucial pronouncement is AU 319. Audits in accordance with generally accepted auditing standards (GAAS) require the auditor to obtain an understanding of the five components of the internal control structure (ICS) and to assess control risk.

1. AU 319 revised the second standard of field work (GAAS) as follows:

   > "A sufficient understanding of the ICS is to be obtained to plan the audit and to determine the nature, timing, and extent of tests to be performed."

2. As amended, AU 319 defines internal control as follows:

   > *Internal control is a process--effected by an entity's board of directors, management, and other personnel--designed to provide reasonable assurance regarding the achievement of objectives in the following categories: (a) reliability of financial reporting, (b) compliance with applicable laws and regulations, and (c) effectiveness and efficiency of operations.*

a. ICS policies and procedures most likely to be relevant to an audit pertain to the entity's objective of preparing financial statements for external purposes that are fairly presented in conformity with GAAP or another comprehensive basis of accounting.

b. Certain ICS policies and procedures ordinarily are not relevant and need not be considered, for example, policies and procedures concerning the effectiveness, economy, and efficiency of certain management decisions, such as product pricing or some expenditures for R&D or advertising.

B. **Components of an ICS**. For a financial statement audit, the ICS consists of five components: the control environment, risk assessment, control activities, information and communication, and monitoring.

1. "**The control environment** sets the tone of an organization, influencing the control consciousness of its people. It is the foundation of all other components of the ICS, providing discipline and structure." It includes the following factors:

   a. Management's philosophy and operating style
   b. Organizational structure
   c. Board of directors or audit committee
   d. Assignment of authority and responsibility
   e. Integrity and ethical values
   f. Commitment to competence
   g. Human resource policies and practices

2. "**Risk assessment** is the entity's identification and analysis of relevant risks to achievement of its objectives, forming a basis for determining how the risks should be managed."

   a. This process considers internal and external matters that may adversely affect the entity's ability to record, process, summarize, and report financial data consistent with financial statement assertions.

   b. The entity's risk assessment is distinct from the auditor's assessment of inherent and control risk.

3. "**Control activities** are the policies and procedures that help ensure that management directives are carried out. They help ensure that necessary actions are taken to address risks to achieve the entity's objectives." Control activities relevant to a financial statement audit consist of internal controls related to

   a. Performance reviews
   b. Information processing

      1) General controls
      2) Application controls

   c. Physical controls
   d. Segregation of duties

4. "**Information and communication** are the identification, capture, and exchange of information in a form and time frame that enable people to carry out their responsibilities." An effective information system provides for

   a. Identifying and recording all valid transactions

   b. Timely and sufficiently detailed descriptions of transactions to permit proper classification

   c. Proper measurement of transactions

   d. Recording transactions in the appropriate periods

   e. Proper financial statement presentation

5. "**Monitoring** is a process that assesses the quality of the ICS's performance over time."
   a. An ICS should be monitored by management to provide reasonable assurance that objectives are achieved. Management considers whether the ICS is properly designed and operating as intended and modifies it to reflect changing conditions.
   b. Internal auditors and external parties, such as customers and regulators, contribute to the monitoring process.

C. **Limitations of an ICS**

1. **Reasonable assurance**. An ICS should be designed and operated to provide reasonable assurance that an entity's objectives are achieved. Thus, costs should not exceed benefits.
2. **Inherent limitations** of an ICS include the following:
   a. Mistakes in applying ICS policies and procedures may arise from misunderstanding of instructions, mistakes of judgment, or personal carelessness, distraction, or fatigue.
   b. Segregation of duties can be circumvented by collusion.
   c. Management may override certain ICS policies and procedures.

D. **Understanding the ICS in Planning an Audit**. The auditor should obtain a sufficient understanding of the ICS components to plan the audit, including knowledge about the design of relevant ICS policies and procedures and whether they have been placed in operation.

1. Such knowledge should be used to
   a. Identify types of potential misstatements
   b. Consider factors that affect the risk of material misstatements
   c. Design substantive tests
2. **Placed in operation** differs from **operating effectiveness.**
   a. Placed in operation means the entity is using the policy or procedure.
   b. Operating effectiveness is concerned with how and by whom the policy or procedure was applied and the consistency of application. For example, a budgetary reporting system may produce adequate reports that are not acted upon.
      1) Knowledge about operating effectiveness need not be obtained as part of the understanding of the ICS.
3. The understanding may raise doubts about auditability.
   a. Concerns about management integrity may lead to the conclusion that the risk of misrepresentations precludes an audit.
   b. The nature and extent of records may indicate that sufficient competent evidence is unlikely to be available.
4. In obtaining the understanding of the ICS, the auditor considers
   a. Knowledge obtained from other sources, such as previous audits and the understanding of the industry
   b. Assessments of inherent risk
   c. Judgments about materiality
   d. Complexity and sophistication of operations and systems, including whether data processing depends on the computer

5. **Understanding the control environment component** requires sufficient knowledge to understand the attitude, awareness, and actions of management and the board.
6. **Understanding the risk assessment component** requires sufficient knowledge of how management considers risks relevant to financial reporting objectives, estimates their significance, assesses their likelihood, and decides about appropriate actions.
7. **Understanding the control activities component.** The auditor's understanding of the other components may provide some knowledge about control activities. The knowledge thus obtained should be considered in determining the additional attention required for understanding control activities.
8. **Understanding the information and communication component** requires sufficient knowledge of the information system relevant to financial reporting to understand
   a. Major classes of transactions and how they are initiated
   b. The accounting records, supporting documents, and specific accounts involved in processing and reporting
   c. The accounting process from initiation to inclusion in the financial statements
   d. The financial reporting process, including significant estimates and disclosures
9. **Understanding of the monitoring component** requires sufficient knowledge of the major activities used to monitor the ICS, including how they are used to initiate corrective action.
10. **Documentation of the understanding** is required. Its form and extent are influenced by the size and complexity of the entity and the nature of the ICS.

E. **Consideration of the ICS in Assessing Control Risk**

1. **The risk of material misstatement** in a financial statement assertion consists of the following:
   a. "**Inherent risk** is the susceptibility of an assertion to a material misstatement assuming there are no related ICS policies or procedures."
   b. "**Control risk** is the risk that a material misstatement that could occur in an assertion will not be prevented or detected on a timely basis by the entity's ICS policies or procedures."
   c. "**Detection risk** is the risk that the auditor will not detect a material misstatement that exists in an assertion."
2. **The assessment of control risk** is an evaluation of the effectiveness of the ICS in preventing or detecting material misstatements. It is
   a. Made in terms of financial statement assertions
   b. Stated quantitatively [such as from 0% to 100% (0 to 1.0)] or nonquantitatively (such as a range from maximum to minimum)
      1) For example, the auditor may decide that the probability is 10% that the ICS policies and procedures relevant to an assertion will not prevent or detect a possible material misstatement of that assertion. However, absent any relevant ICS policies and procedures, control risk is 1.0 (100%); that is, failure to prevent or detect is certain.
3. After obtaining the understanding of the ICS, the auditor may **assess control risk at the maximum** (1.0 or 100%) because
   a. Policies and procedures are unlikely to pertain to an assertion,
   b. Policies and procedures are unlikely to be effective, or
   c. Evaluating effectiveness would be inefficient.

4. **Assessing control risk at below the maximum** requires

   a. Identifying specific policies and procedures relevant to specific assertions that are likely to prevent or detect misstatement

   b. Testing of controls to evaluate effectiveness

      1) **Tests of controls** are "directed toward the design or operation of an ICS policy or procedure to assess its effectiveness in preventing or detecting material misstatements in a financial statement assertion."

5. The lower the assessed level of control risk (the more closely it approaches zero), the more assurance audit evidence must provide that ICS policies and procedures relevant to an assertion are effective.

6. The ultimate purpose of assessing control risk (and inherent risk) is to contribute to the evaluation of the overall risk that the financial statements contain material misstatements. The assessed levels of control risk and inherent risk determine the acceptable level of detection risk for financial statement assertions.

   a. Based on the level to which the auditor seeks to restrict the risk of a material misstatement and the assessed levels of inherent risk and control risk, substantive tests restrict detection risk to an acceptable level.

      1) The risk of material misstatement of an assertion (AR) can be expressed algebraically as the product of inherent risk (IR), control risk (CR), and the acceptable detection risk (DR). Accordingly, if the auditor decides to restrict the risk of misstatement (that is, the risk of incorrect acceptance) to 5% and assesses inherent risk and control risk at 50% and 30%, respectively, the following calculation determines the acceptable level of detection risk:

$$AR = IR \times CR \times DR$$

$$DR = \frac{AR}{IR \times CR}$$

$$DR = \frac{5\%}{50\% \times 30\%}$$

$$DR = 33\tfrac{1}{3}\%$$

      2) The acceptable level of detection risk determines the nature, timing, and extent of substantive tests (procedures to detect material misstatements in assertions).

         a) Because its relation to control risk is inverse, a lower acceptable level of detection risk increases the assurance to be provided by substantive tests. Thus, the auditor may

            i) Change their nature to a more effective procedure, such as directing tests toward independent parties rather than parties within the entity

            ii) Change timing, such as from interim dates to year-end

            iii) Change their extent, such as using a larger sample

7. **Documentation of the assessed level of control risk** is required.

   a. When control risk for an assertion is assessed at the maximum, the auditor should document the conclusion but need not document its basis.

INTERNAL CONTROL ACCORDING TO IIA PRONOUNCEMENTS

A. Internal control is the basis for the field of internal auditing. According to the Statement of Responsibilities of Internal Auditing, "The audit objective includes promoting effective control at reasonable cost."

   1. The controls envisioned extend beyond those relevant to the traditional financial statement audit conducted by external auditors.

B. General Standard 300 of the Standards for the Professional Practice of Internal Auditing defines the scope of work of internal auditors largely in terms of internal control.

   "The scope of internal auditing should encompass the examination and evaluation of the adequacy and effectiveness of the organization's system of internal control and the quality of performance in carrying out assigned responsibilities."

   1. Adequacy concerns whether reasonable assurance is given that objectives and goals will be met efficiently and economically.
   2. Effectiveness concerns whether the system is functioning as intended.
   3. The five primary objectives of internal control listed in Standard 300 (CARES) must be considered by internal auditors. However, only c. and e. below are normally relevant to an audit performed as a basis for expressing an opinion on financial statements.

      a. ***C**ompliance with policies, plans, etc.*
      b. ***A**ccomplishment of objectives and goals*
      c. ***R**eliability and integrity of information*
      d. ***E**conomical and efficient use of resources*
      e. ***S**afeguarding of assets*

C. SIAS 1, *Control: Concepts and Responsibilities*, defines control with an emphasis on the roles of the participants, especially the management functions of planning, organizing, and directing.

   A control is any action taken by management to enhance the likelihood that established objectives and goals will be achieved. Management plans, organizes, and directs the performance of sufficient actions to provide reasonable assurance that objectives and goals will be achieved. Thus, control is the result of proper planning, organizing, and directing by management.

   1. In the aggregate, the internal auditors' evaluations of the processes of planning, organizing, and directing permit appraisal of the system of internal control.

INTERNAL CONTROL FLOWCHARTING

A. Flowcharting is a useful tool for systems development as well as understanding the internal control structure. A flowchart is a pictorial diagram of the definition, analysis, or solution of a problem in which symbols are used to represent operations, data flow, equipment, etc.

   1. The processing is presented as sequential from the point of origin to final output distribution.

      a. Processing usually flows from top to bottom and left to right in the flowchart.

   2. Areas of responsibility (e.g., data processing or purchasing) are usually depicted in vertical columns or areas.
   3. A **system flowchart** provides an overall view of the inputs, processes, and outputs of a system.
   4. A **document flowchart** depicts the flows of documents through an entity.
   5. A **program flowchart** represents the specific steps in a program and the order in which they will be carried out.

      a. Macro- and microflowcharts describe a program in less or greater detail, respectively.

6. Commonly used flowcharting symbols

Starting or ending point or point of interruption

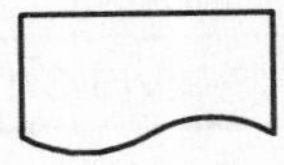

Input or output in the form of a document or report

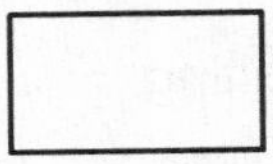

Computer operation or group of operations

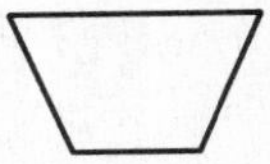

Manual processing operation, e.g., keypunching

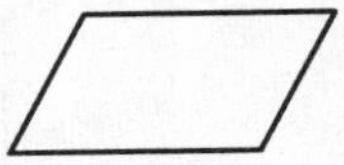

Generalized symbol for input or output used when the medium is not specified

Magnetic tape used for input or output

Magnetic disk used for storage

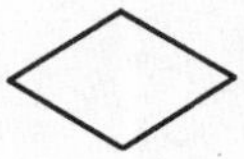

Decision symbol indicating a branch in the flow

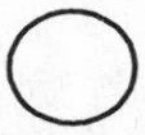

Connection between points on the same page

Connection between two pages of the flowchart

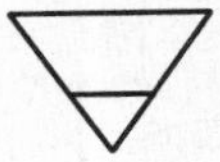

Storage (file) that is not immediately accessible by computer

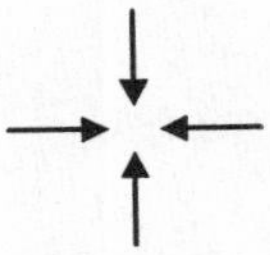

Flow direction of data or processing

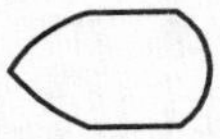

Display on a video terminal

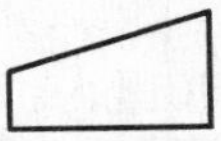

Manual input into a terminal or other online device

Adding machine tape (batch control)

Auxiliary operation performed offline, e.g., payroll records used in a cost system after payroll is complete

Online storage

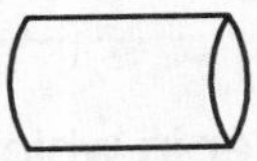

Keying operation

Storage on punched paper tape

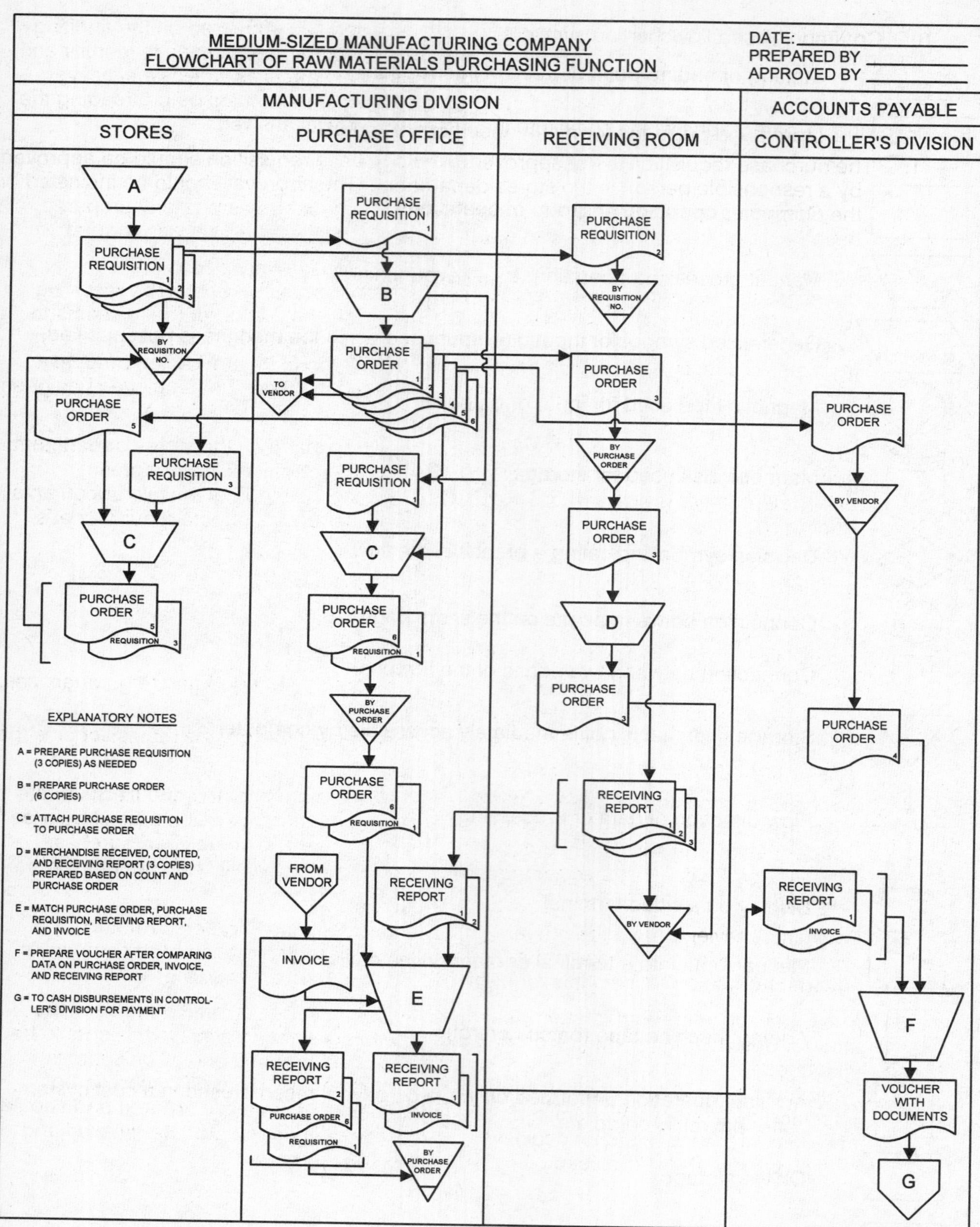
MEDIUM-SIZED MANUFACTURING COMPANY
FLOWCHART OF RAW MATERIALS PURCHASING FUNCTION
DATE:
PREPARED BY
APPROVED BY
MANUFACTURING DIVISION
ACCOUNTS PAYABLE
STORES
PURCHASE OFFICE
RECEIVING ROOM
CONTROLLER'S DIVISION
A
PURCHASE REQUISITION
BY REQUISITION NO.
PURCHASE ORDER
C
B
TO VENDOR
BY PURCHASE ORDER
BY VENDOR
D
RECEIVING REPORT
FROM VENDOR
INVOICE
E
F
VOUCHER WITH DOCUMENTS
G
EXPLANATORY NOTES
A = PREPARE PURCHASE REQUISITION (3 COPIES) AS NEEDED
B = PREPARE PURCHASE ORDER (6 COPIES)
C = ATTACH PURCHASE REQUISITION TO PURCHASE ORDER
D = MERCHANDISE RECEIVED, COUNTED, AND RECEIVING REPORT (3 COPIES) PREPARED BASED ON COUNT AND PURCHASE ORDER
E = MATCH PURCHASE ORDER, PURCHASE REQUISITION, RECEIVING REPORT, AND INVOICE
F = PREPARE VOUCHER AFTER COMPARING DATA ON PURCHASE ORDER, INVOICE, AND RECEIVING REPORT
G = TO CASH DISBURSEMENTS IN CONTROLLER'S DIVISION FOR PAYMENT

B. The flowchart of a raw materials purchasing function on page 420 appeared on the auditing section of the November 1975 CPA exam. The question required candidates to identify and explain the internal control weaknesses, including missing controls as well as ineffective ones. You should study the flowchart, noting weaknesses, for 5 minutes before reading the following 17 paragraphs which constitute the AICPA's unofficial answer.

1. The purchase requisition is not approved. The purchase requisition should be approved by a responsible person in the stores department. The approval should be indicated on the purchase requisition after the approver is satisfied that it was properly prepared based on a need to replace stores or the proper request from a user department.

2. Purchase requisition number two is not required. Purchase requisitions are unnecessarily sent from the stores department to the receiving room. The receiving room does not make any use of the purchase requisitions and no purpose seems to exist for the receiving room to obtain a copy. A copy of the requisition might be sent from stores directly to accounts payable where it can be compared to the purchase order to verify that the merchandise requisitioned by an authorized employee has been properly ordered.

3. Purchase requisitions and purchase orders are not compared in the stores department. Although purchase orders are attached to purchase requisitions in the stores department, there is no indication that any comparison is made of the two documents. Prior to attaching the purchase order to the purchase requisition, the requisitioner's function should include a check that

   a. Prices are reasonable.

   b. The quality of the materials ordered is acceptable.

   c. Delivery dates are in accordance with company needs.

   d. All pertinent data on the purchase order and purchase requisition (e.g., quantities, specifications, delivery dates, etc.) are in agreement.

   Since the requisitioner will be charged for the materials ordered, the requisitioner is the logical person to perform the steps.

4. Purchase orders and purchase requisitions should not be combined and filed with the unmatched purchase requisitions in the stores department. A separate file should be maintained for the combined and matched documents. The unmatched purchase requisitions file can serve as a control over merchandise requisitioned but not yet ordered.

5. Preliminary review should be made before preparing purchase orders. Prior to preparation of the purchase order, the purchase office should review the company's need for the specific materials requisitioned and approve the request.

6. The purchase office should attempt to obtain the highest quality merchandise at the lowest possible price, and the procedures that are followed to achieve this should be included on the flowchart. There is no indication that the purchase office submits purchase orders to competitive bidding when appropriate. That office should be directly involved with vendors in determining the cost of materials ordered and should be primarily responsible for deciding at what price materials should be ordered and which vendor should be used.

7. The purchase office does not review the invoice prior to processing approval. The purchase office should review the vendor's invoice for overall accuracy and completeness, verifying quantity, prices, specifications, terms, dates, etc. If the invoice is in agreement with the purchase order, receiving report, and purchase requisition, the purchase office should clearly indicate on the invoice that it is approved for payment processing. The approved invoice should be sent to the accounts payable department.
8. The copy of the purchase order sent to the receiving room ordinarily should not show quantities ordered, thus forcing the department to count goods received. In addition to counting the merchandise received from the vendor, the receiving department personnel should examine the condition and quality of the merchandise upon receipt.
9. There is no indication of the procedures in effect when the quantity of merchandise received differs from what was ordered. Procedures for handling over-shipments and short-shipments should be clearly outlined and included on the flowchart.
10. The receiving report is not sent to the stores department. A copy of the receiving report should be sent from the receiving room directly to the stores department along with the materials received. The stores department, after verifying the accuracy of the receiving report, should indicate approval on that copy and send it to the accounts payable department. The copy sent to accounts payable will serve as proof that the materials ordered were received by the company and are in the user department.
11. There is no indication of control over vouchers in the accounts payable department. In the accounts payable department a record of all vouchers submitted to the cashier should be maintained, and a copy of each voucher should be filed in an alphabetical vendor reference file.
12. There is no indication of control over dollar amounts on vouchers. Accounts payable personnel should prepare and maintain control sheets on the dollar amounts of vouchers. Such sheets should be sent to departments posting transactions to general and subsidiary ledgers.
13. There is no examination of documents prior to voucher preparation. In addition to the matching procedure, the mathematical accuracy of all documents should be verified prior to preparation of vouchers.
14. The controller should not be responsible for cash disbursements. The cash disbursement function should be the responsibility of the treasurer, not the controller, so as to provide proper division of responsibility between the custody of assets and the recording of transactions.
15. There is no indication of the company's procedures for handling purchase returns. Although separate return procedures may be in effect and included on a separate flowchart, some indications of this should be included as part of the purchases flowchart.
16. Discrepancy procedures are not indicated. The flowchart should indicate what procedures are followed whenever matching reveals a difference between the information on the documents compared.
17. There is no indication of any control over prenumbered forms. All prenumbered documents should be accounted for.

PLANNING CONTROL

A. Planning precedes all other managerial functions by establishing the

- Organizational objectives (goals)
- Policies
- Procedures
- Rules
- Programs

1. Planning determines what, how, when, where, and by whom.
2. Planning is performed by all managers.
   a. The higher the management level, the more time spent planning
3. See Study Unit 21, Planning, and Study Unit 22, Budgeting, in Chapter 7.

B. **Planning control** is the process of reevaluating plans after they have been implemented.

1. Feedback provides a basis for
   a. Improving plans
   b. Changing the planning process
      1) See the organizational control sideheading beginning on page 424.
2. The information and communication component of the ICS may also be involved.
   a. Faulty planning may have been based on poorly collected or otherwise misleading data
3. Management accountants and auditors must be conversant with the management process in general and planning in particular, with emphasis on planning's interrelationships with organizing, directing, and controlling.

C. Planning controls are measured by evaluating their existence and success.

1. Short-range plans such as production schedules and budgets (capital, expense, cash, etc.) should be analyzed.
   a. Have plans been achieved?
      1) How, why, when, and by whom?
   b. When objectives are not met, why not?
      1) What was the planning problem?
      2) If objectives were unattainable, why?
         a) Poor coordination with other managerial processes
         b) Unrealistic objectives
         c) Inadequate information
         d) Other causes
   c. Plans should be evaluated to determine if they are aggressive enough.
      1) Standards for whether a plan is adequate may be derived from other departments, divisions, competitors, industry norms, etc.
2. Long-range planning is difficult to undertake, control, and evaluate.
   a. The difficulty of projecting current controls to future periods is the problem.

b. Long-range planning is a top-management function that may present difficulties in analysis; i.e., it may be difficult to second guess top management.

   1) However, it provides an opportunity to work with top management.
   2) The long-range planning process should be formally established.

      a) It should be adequately documented and regularly updated.
      b) Responsibility and authority should be assigned.
      c) The involvement of the board of directors is required.

c. Review and analysis of the process involve determining whether

   1) Sufficient resources are devoted to the function based upon cost-benefit analysis.
   2) The process is being followed.
   3) New (additional) information is being used as it becomes available to modify or extend the plans.
   4) Long-range plans are revised or extended and how often.
   5) Changes in expectations are anticipated (sought out) or whether they are surprises.
   6) Long-range planning personnel use enough independent data (obtained outside the company) regarding competition, technology, national and international politics, and availability of resources.

ORGANIZATIONAL CONTROL (largely from IIA Research Committee Report 18)

A. Organization is the way individual work efforts within an entity are assigned and integrated for achievement of the organization's goals.

   1. Assignments are defined in terms of job descriptions.

      a. To avoid confusion and conflict of work efforts

   2. Integration is accomplished through specific organizational arrangements in a structure of roles, including

      a. Coordinating committees
      b. Requirements for review and approval
      c. Specific assignment of authority and responsibility

B. **Organizational control** is the means of achieving the most effective possible use of organizational arrangements. Organizational control

   1. Is part of the larger control process
   2. Relates to the special control aspects of the organizing activity
   3. Consists of

      a. Design of arrangements to meet a particular entity's objectives
      b. Continuous reappraisal and modification of the design

   4. The general elements of systems of control, applicable to procedural efforts, include

      a. Establishing standards for the operation to be controlled
      b. Measuring performance against the standards
      c. Examining and analyzing deviations
      d. Taking corrective action
      e. Reappraising the standards based on experience (sometimes not listed separately)

C. Some examples of the major types of organizational problems and conflicting issues may be useful in understanding the organizational process and its controls.

1. Objectives are accomplished by people, and therefore the organizational relationships must be among people.

    a. Emphasizing activity-authority relationships among individuals

2. Activity is divided into pieces, i.e., job assignments. The job assignments are then integrated to achieve the organization's goals.

3. The design of organizational activity and its implementation are separate phases.

    a. However, they are interrelated.
    b. In the design phase, the rationale (including objectives) is more important.
    c. In the implementation phase, the human dimension is more important.

4. Organizational arrangements require judgment.

5. Many organizational arrangements are based on trade-offs between alternatives.

6. Assignment of organizational responsibilities sometimes results in conflict between different responsibilities, personalities, etc.

7. Organizational arrangements must be based upon management goals and objectives.

D. In implementing organizational structures, numerous application problems are encountered in

1. Grouping activities effectively

    a. How much specialization?
    b. How much internal control for protection and efficiency?
    c. Functional or nonfunctional departmentation?
    d. How much decentralization?
    e. Can profit responsibility be fixed?
    f. How much staff?
    g. How many service departments?
    h. How is balance of emphasis achieved?
    i. What should be the span of control?
    j. How much formal coordination?

2. Achieving effective operational relationships

    a. Effectiveness of delegating
    b. Quality of supervision
    c. Adequacy of the information provided
    d. Adequacy of participation
    e. Effectiveness of staff use
    f. Proper recognition of common objectives
    g. Fairly defined rewards and punishments
    h. Quality of leadership

3. Additional considerations

    a. Formal organizational charts are necessary, but the informal organization must be monitored, understood, and modified as needed to encourage conformity with the organization's goals.

    b. Human resources and their interrelationships must be administered effectively.

    c. Organizational arrangements should be

        1) Adapted to managerial style
        2) Tied to the total management process
        3) Responsive to changing conditions

E. **Maintaining Organizational Control**

1. Organizational control should be reappraised continually.
   a. Reappraisal of organizational arrangements is the basic element of the organizational control process.
2. Managers should be responsible for organizational control.
   a. A manager should initiate actions deemed appropriate, putting them into effect to the extent of his/her authority.
   b. A manager should channel information and proposals for change to the appropriate people responsible for the particular organizational arrangement.
   c. A considerable amount of a manager's time must be devoted to the paperwork of administering the department being supervised. This includes coordination with other departments. For example,
      1) New employees must be added to the payroll.
      2) Verified time sheets must get to the proper department.
      3) In short, the manager is a funnel for transactions up and down the organizational chart.
3. Special staff function for organizational control provides personnel who
   a. Have the overall responsibility of coordinating current organizational changes and studying ongoing organizational needs
   b. Assist managers with organizational arrangements
   c. Provide company-wide control and coordination over all organizational arrangements
4. Role of the internal auditor in organizational control
   a. The internal audit function is part of management's concern for the total control process. Auditors
      1) Assist in providing organizational control
      2) Monitor organizational changes
   b. Auditors must be familiar with organizational arrangements.
      1) To understand the nature of the relations between particular operations to be reviewed and the related company organizational arrangements
         a) Establishes a reference point for later determining how the organizational arrangements actually operate
   c. Auditors must relate operational arrangements to operational deficiencies. Auditors should
      1) Understand the basic organizational concepts for appraising the soundness of organizational arrangements
      2) Probe for factors leading to the deficiency
      3) Consider the extent to which existing organizational arrangements are the cause of operational deficiencies
   d. Organizational control within the internal audit department
      1) The internal audit department should implement the same degree of organizational control within its own department as it expects to find throughout the organization.

OPERATING CONTROL

A. Operating controls are used in the management processes of directing and controlling.

1. This study unit has classified controls according to the elements in the management process.

   a. See the sideheadings on Planning Control and Organizational Control on pages 423 and 424.

2. Other categories (and dimensions) of control include

   a. Security
   b. Quality
   c. Information systems
   d. Procedural
   e. Personnel
   f. Budgetary

3. Adherence versus adaptive controls

   a. Adherence controls require conformity with original plans.

      1) Required in the short run

   b. Adaptive control permits adaptation of plans to changed conditions.

      1) Required in the long run

B. Like organizational controls, operating controls are based on the **control loop**, which consists of

1. Establishing proper standards for the particular operation to be controlled
2. Measuring performance against the standards
3. Examining and analyzing deviations
4. Taking needed corrective action
5. Reappraising the standards on the basis of further experience

   a. This last step is sometimes not listed separately.

C. Thus, the control loop should be applied to each activity and responsibility in the organization.

1. As the activity or responsibility becomes more conceptual, i.e., less mechanical, the standards become more difficult to determine.

2. The internal auditor's function is to see that the control loop is functioning effectively.

   a. At every level
   b. For each responsibility or activity

D. Informational controls include the information and communication component of the ICS and operational controls.

1. Information systems that lead to the authorization of transactions (the decision-making process) are operational informational controls.

   a. Under these criteria, budgets and their implementation are parts of the planning and controlling processes.

2. Computer controls have the same objectives as other informational controls.

   a. But the computer systems organization and specific procedures for accomplishing its control objectives are usually different.

   b. See Study Unit 32, Information Systems, in Chapter 8.

FRAUD DANGER SIGNALS

A. Even the best ICS can sometimes be circumvented, such as by collusion of two or more employees or by management override. Thus, an auditor or management accountant must be sensitive to certain conditions that might indicate the existence of fraud, including

1. High personnel turnover
2. Low employee morale
3. Paperwork supporting adjusting entries not readily available
4. Bank reconciliations not completed promptly
5. Increases in the number of customer complaints
6. Deteriorating income trend when the industry or the company as a whole is doing well
7. Numerous audit adjustments of significant size
8. Write-offs of inventory shortages with no attempt to determine cause
9. Unrealistic performance expectations
10. Low-paid employees driving high-priced cars
11. Major illness in an employee's family

MEANS OF ACHIEVING CONTROL

A. Sawyer and Summers, *Sawyer's Internal Auditing* (Altamonte Springs, FL: The Institute of Internal Auditors, 1988), pages 100-105, defines control and lists eight means of achieving control (the list was adapted from a GAO audit manual). Sawyer defines control as

> *The employment of all the means devised in an enterprise to promote, direct, restrain, govern, and check upon its various activities for the purpose of seeing that enterprise objectives are met. These means of control include, but are not limited to, form of organization, policies, systems, procedures, instructions, standards, committees, charts of accounts, forecasts, budgets, schedules, reports, records, checklists, methods, devices, and internal auditing.*

The eight means of control are

1. *Organization. Organization, as a means of control, is an intentional structure of roles assigned to people within the enterprise so as to achieve the objectives of the enterprise efficiently and economically.*
   a. *Responsibilities should be divided so that no one person will control all phases of any transaction.*
   b. *Each manager should have the authority to take the action necessary to discharge his or her responsibility.*
   c. *Individual responsibility should always be clearly defined so that it can neither be sidestepped nor exceeded.*
   d. *An official who assigns responsibility and delegates authority to subordinates should have an effective system of follow-up to make sure that tasks assigned are properly carried out.*
   e. *The individuals to whom authority is delegated should be required to exercise that authority without close supervision. But they should check with their superiors in case of exception.*

f. *People should be required to account to their superiors for the manner in which they have discharged their responsibilities.*

g. *The organization should be flexible enough to permit changes in its structure when operating plans, policies, and objectives change.*

h. *The organizational structures should be as simple as possible.*

i. *Organization charts and manuals should be prepared to help in planning, controlling changes in, and providing better understanding of the form of organization, chain of authority, and assignments of responsibilities.*

2. *Policies. A policy is any rule which requires, guides, or restricts action. Policies should follow certain principles.*

   a. *Policies should be clearly stated in writing and systematically organized in handbooks, manuals, or other publications.*

   b. *They should be systematically communicated to all officials and employees of the organization.*

   c. *They must conform with applicable laws and regulations, and they should be consistent with objectives and general policies prescribed at higher levels.*

   d. *They should be designed to promote the conduct of authorized activities in an effective, efficient, and economical manner and to provide a satisfactory degree of assurance that the resources of the enterprise are suitably safeguarded.*

   e. *They should be periodically reviewed, and they should be revised when circumstances change.*

3. *Procedures. Procedures are methods employed to carry out activities in conformity with prescribed policies. The same principles applicable to policies are also applicable to procedures. In addition,*

   a. *To reduce the possibility of fraud and error, procedures should be so coordinated that one employee's work is automatically checked by another who is independently performing his or her own prescribed duties. In determining the extent to which automatic internal checks should be built into the system of control, such factors as degree of risk of loss or error, cost of preventive procedures, availability of personnel, and feasibility should be considered.*

   b. *For nonmechanical operations, prescribed procedures should not be so detailed as to stifle the use of judgment.*

   c. *To promote maximum efficiency and economy, prescribed procedures should be as simple and as inexpensive as possible.*

   d. *Procedures should not be overlapping, conflicting, or duplicative.*

   e. *Procedures should be periodically reviewed and improved as necessary.*

4. *Personnel. People hired or assigned should have the qualifications to do the jobs assigned to them. The best form of control over the performance of individuals is supervision. Hence, high standards of supervision should be established. The following practices help improve control.*

a. *Employees should be given training and refresher courses to provide the opportunity for improving competence and to keep them informed of new policies and procedures.*

b. *Employees should be given information on the duties and responsibilities of other segments of the organization so that they may better understand how and where their jobs fit into the organization as a whole.*

c. *The performance of all employees should be periodically reviewed to see whether all essential requirements of their jobs are being met. Superior performance should be given appropriate recognition. Shortcomings should be discussed with employees so that they are given an opportunity to improve their performance or upgrade their skills.*

5. *Accounting. Accounting is the indispensable means of financial control over activities and resources. It furnishes a framework which can be fitted to assignments of responsibility. It is the financial scorekeeper of the enterprise. The problem lies in what scores to keep. Here are some basic principles for accounting systems.*

   a. *Accounting should fit the needs of managers for rational decision making rather than the dictates of some textbook or canned check list.*

   b. *It should be based on lines of responsibility.*

   c. *Financial reports of operating results should parallel the organizational units responsible for carrying out operations.*

6. *Budgeting. A budget is a statement of expected results expressed in numerical terms. As a control, it sets a standard of what should be achieved.*

   a. *Those who are responsible for meeting a budget should participate in its preparation.*

   b. *They should be provided with adequate information that compares budgets with actual events and shows reasons for any significant variances.*

   c. *All subsidiary budgets should tie into the overall budget for the enterprise.*

   d. *Budgets should set measurable objectives; they are meaningless unless managers know what they are budgeting for.*

   e. *They should help sharpen the organizational structure because objective budgeting standards are difficult to set in a confused combination of subsystems. Budgeting is therefore a form of discipline.*

7. *Reporting. In most organizations, management functions and makes decisions on the basis of the reports it receives. Reports should therefore be timely, accurate, meaningful, and economical. Here are some principles for establishing a satisfactory internal reporting system.*

   a. *The reports should be made in accordance with assigned responsibilities.*

   b. *Individuals or units should be required to report only on those matters for which they are responsible.*

   c. *The cost of accumulating data and preparing reports should be weighted against the benefits to be obtained from them.*

   d. *Reports should be as simple as possible, and consistent with the nature of the subject matter. They should include only information which serves the needs of the readers. Common classifications and terminology should be used as much as possible to avoid confusion.*

e. *When appropriate, performance reports should show comparisons with predetermined standards of cost, quality, and quantity.*

f. *When performance cannot be reported in quantitative terms, the reports should be designed to emphasize exceptions or other matters requiring management attention.*

g. *Reports should be timely to be of maximum value. Timely reports based partly on estimates may be more useful than delayed reports that are more precise.*

h. *Report recipients should be polled periodically to see if they still need the reports they are receiving.*

8. *Internal Review. The uninspected inevitably deteriorates. All operations should be periodically reviewed by people who are independent of those operations. Internal auditing is one such form of review. Here are some principles for a system of internal review.*

   a. *Top management should devise an internal review system and organization that will best suit its needs.*

   b. *All types of review activity within an organization, such as inspections and internal audits, should be coordinated. The work done by each review group should be clearly defined to avoid duplication and jurisdictional disputes.*

   c. *Organizational needs for internal review vary. The scope of work cannot, therefore, be standardized, but should be set by each company's management.*

   d. *The duties, responsibilities, and the stature of the review agency should be clearly defined so that the review authority is recognized.*

   e. *Review authority should be independent of the operations reviewed. Thus, the manager of quality control should not report to the director of manufacturing.*

   f. *The internal review operation should not replace line authority and responsibility. Operating managers must remain responsible for doing and supervising their own jobs.*

   g. *Internal review is a staff function. Internal reviewers should not control or direct action - their responsibility is advisory: to provide information as a basis for decision making and action.*

   h. *Review work should be planned, and the plans should be approved by top management.*

   i. *All internal review work should meet professional standards of competence, reliability, and objectivity.*

   j. *Internal reviewers should place primary emphasis on promoting improvement of operations, rather than on fault finding.*

   k. *Findings should be reviewed with the people whose work is being appraised except where the possibility of fraud requires different treatment.*

   l. *Suitable follow-up procedures should be devised to see whether findings and recommendations have been considered, corrective action has been taken, and results are satisfactory.*

STUDY UNIT 17
EXTERNAL AUDITING

INTRODUCTION

Auditing coverage on the CMA exam is very broad. The following are the relevant study units:

Study Unit 16: Internal Control
Study Unit 17: External Auditing
Study Unit 32: Information Systems
Study Unit 33: Internal and Operational Auditing

The following outlines are longer and more detailed than in many of the other study units. Most CMA candidates have been away from auditing longer than from other topics and require more assistance in this area.

Study Unit 17 provides an overview of the attest function performed by independent public accountants (CPAs). It contains the standard audit report, the 10 generally accepted auditing standards (GAAS), outlines of the AICPA *Code of Professional Conduct* and Statements on Auditing Standards (SASs), a section on audit evidence, and material on audit sampling methods. It also includes outlines of pronouncements governing services other than the traditional audit of financial statements. Nevertheless, the financial statement audit remains the most vital function of independent accountants.

The objective of financial audits is to express an opinion on whether the financial statements are fairly presented, in all material respects, in conformity with generally accepted accounting principles (GAAP). CPAs conduct audits in accordance with GAAS. Under GAAS, CPAs must obtain an understanding of an entity's internal control structure (ICS) to determine the nature, timing, and extent of the additional auditing procedures necessary to gain reasonable assurance that the company's financial statements are fairly presented.

These additional procedures must include tests of controls if the auditor desires to assess control risk at less than the maximum level. The assessment of control risk is required; that is, the auditor must both understand the ICS and assess control risk. The assessment is necessary to determine the acceptable detection risk and therefore the nature, timing, and extent of substantive tests. Audit testing provides the evidence on which the audit report is based.

AUDITOR'S STANDARD REPORT

Independent Auditor's Report

We have audited the accompanying balance sheet of X Company as of December 31, 19XX, and the related statements of income, retained earnings, and cash flows for the year then ended. These financial statements are the responsibility of the Company's management. Our responsibility is to express an opinion on these financial statements based on our audit.

We conducted our audit in accordance with generally accepted auditing standards. Those standards require that we plan and perform the audit to obtain reasonable assurance about whether the financial statements are free of material misstatement. An audit includes examining, on a test basis, evidence supporting the amounts and disclosures in the financial statements. An audit also includes assessing the accounting principles used and significant estimates made by management, as well as evaluating the overall financial statement presentation. We believe that our audit provides a reasonable basis for our opinion.

In our opinion, the financial statements referred to above present fairly, in all material respects, the financial position of X Company as of [at] December 31, 19XX, and the results of its operations and its cash flows for the year then ended in conformity with generally accepted accounting principles.

[Signature]

[Date]

GENERALLY ACCEPTED AUDITING STANDARDS (GAAS)

A. The 10 GAAS are categorized as general, field work, and reporting standards.

B. **General Standards**

1. The audit is to be performed by a person or persons having adequate technical training and proficiency as an auditor.
2. In all matters relating to the assignment, an independence in mental attitude is to be maintained by the auditor or auditors.
3. Due professional care is to be exercised in the performance of the audit and the preparation of the report.

C. **Standards of Field Work**

1. The work is to be adequately planned and assistants, if any, are to be properly supervised.
2. A sufficient understanding of the internal control structure is to be obtained to plan the audit and to determine the nature, timing, and extent of tests to be performed.
3. Sufficient competent evidential matter is to be obtained through inspection, observation, inquiries, and confirmations to afford a reasonable basis for an opinion regarding the financial statements under audit.

D. **Standards of Reporting**

1. The report shall state whether the financial statements are presented in accordance with GAAP.
2. The report shall identify circumstances in which GAAP have not been consistently observed in the current period in relation to the preceding period.
3. Informative disclosures in the financial statements are to be regarded as reasonably adequate unless otherwise stated in the report.
4. The report shall contain either an expression of opinion regarding the financial statements, taken as a whole, or an assertion to the effect that an opinion cannot be expressed. When an overall opinion cannot be expressed, the reasons therefor should be stated. In all cases in which an auditor's name is associated with financial statements, the report should contain a clear-cut indication of the character of the auditor's work, if any, and the degree of responsibility the auditor is taking.

AICPA CODE OF PROFESSIONAL CONDUCT

A. The *Code of Professional Conduct* was formally adopted on January 12, 1988. It consists of two sections: Principles and Rules. The Principles are goal-oriented and aspirational but nonbinding. The Rules are mandatory. When the Code was adopted, the AICPA membership also voted to make changes regarding quality review, membership requirements, the disciplinary process, and CPE standards.

1. The following are the Principles:

   Article I - Responsibilities. "In carrying out their responsibilities as professionals, members should exercise sensitive professional and moral judgments in all their activities."

   Article II - The Public Interest. "Members should accept the obligation to act in a way that will serve the public interest, honor the public trust, and demonstrate commitment to professionalism."

   Article III - Integrity. "To maintain and broaden public confidence, members should perform all professional responsibilities with the highest sense of integrity."

   Article IV - Objectivity and Independence. "A member should maintain objectivity and be free of conflicts of interest in discharging professional responsibilities. A member in public practice should be independent in fact and appearance when providing auditing and other attestation services."

   Article V - Due Care. "A member should observe the profession's technical and ethical standards, strive continually to improve competence and the quality of services, and discharge professional responsibility to the best of the member's ability."

   Article VI - Scope and Nature of Services. "A member in public practice should observe the Principles of the Code of Professional Conduct in determining the scope and nature of services to be provided."

2. The following are the Rules:

   Rule 101 - Independence. "A member in public practice shall be independent in the performance of professional services as required by standards promulgated by bodies designated by Council."

   Rule 102 - Integrity and Objectivity. "In the performance of any professional service, a member shall maintain objectivity and integrity, shall be free of conflicts of interest, and shall not knowingly misrepresent facts or subordinate his or her judgment to others."

   Rule 201 - General Standards. "A member shall comply with the following standards and with any interpretation thereof by bodies designated by Council:

   Professional Competence. Undertake only those professional services that the member or the member's firm can reasonably expect to be completed with professional competence.

   Due Professional Care. Exercise due professional care in the performance of professional services.

   Planning and Supervision. Adequately plan and supervise the performance of professional services.

   Sufficient Relevant Data. Obtain sufficient relevant data to afford a reasonable basis for conclusions or recommendations in relation to any professional services performed."

   Rule 202 - Compliance with Standards. "A member who performs auditing, review, compilation, management advisory, tax, or other professional services shall comply with standards promulgated by Council."

Rule 203 - Accounting Principles. "A member shall not (1) express an opinion or state affirmatively that the financial statements or other financial data of any entity are presented in conformity with generally accepted accounting principles or (2) state that he or she is not aware of any material modifications that should be made to such statements or data in order for them to be in conformity with generally accepted accounting principles, if such statements or data contain any departure from an accounting principle promulgated by bodies designated by Council to establish such principles that has a material effect on the statements or data taken as a whole. If, however, the statements or data contain such a departure and the member can demonstrate that, due to unusual circumstances, the financial statements or data would otherwise have been misleading, the member can comply with the rule by describing the departure, its approximate effects, if practicable, and the reasons why compliance with the principle would result in a misleading statement."

Rule 301 - Confidential Client Information. "A member in public practice shall not disclose any confidential client information without the specific consent of the client. This rule shall not be construed (1) to relieve a member of his or her professional obligations under rules 202 and 203, (2) to affect in any way the member's obligation to comply with a validly issued and enforceable subpoena or summons, or to prohibit a member's compliance with applicable laws and government regulations, (3) to prohibit review of a member's professional practice under AICPA or state CPA society or Board of Accountancy authorization, or (4) to preclude a member from initiating a complaint with, or responding to any inquiry made by, the ethics division or trial board of the Institute or a duly constituted investigative or disciplinary body of a state CPA society or Board of Accountancy.

Members of any of the bodies identified in (4) above and members involved with professional practice reviews identified in (3) above shall not use to their own advantage or disclose any member's confidential client information that comes to their attention in carrying out those activities. This prohibition shall not restrict members' exchange of information in connection with the investigative or disciplinary proceedings described in (4) above or the professional practice reviews described in (3) above."

Rule 302 - Contingent Fees. "A member in public practice shall not:

(1) Perform for a contingent fee any professional services for, or receive such a fee from, a client for whom the member or the member's firm performs:

(a) an audit or review of a financial statement; or,

(b) a compilation of a financial statement when the member expects, or reasonably might expect, that a third party will use the financial statement and the member's compilation report does not disclose a lack of independence; or,

(c) an examination of prospective financial information; or,

(2) Prepare an original or amended tax return or claim for a tax refund for a contingent fee for any client.

The prohibition in (1) above applies during the period in which the member or the member's firm is engaged to perform any of the services listed above and the period covered by any historical financial statements involved in any such listed services.

Except as stated in the next sentence, a contingent fee is a fee established for the performance of any service pursuant to an arrangement in which no fee will be charged unless a specified finding or result is attained, or in which the amount of the fee is otherwise dependent upon the finding or result of such service. Solely for purposes of this rule, fees are not regarded as being contingent if fixed by courts or other public authorities, or, in tax matters, if determined based on the results of judicial proceedings or the findings of governmental agencies.

A member's fees may vary depending, for example, on the complexity of services rendered."

Rule 501 - Acts Discreditable. "A member shall not commit an act discreditable to the profession."

Rule 502 - Advertising and Other Forms of Solicitation. "A member in public practice shall not seek to obtain clients by advertising or other forms of solicitation in a manner that is false, misleading, or deceptive. Solicitation by the use of coercion, overreaching, or harassing conduct is prohibited."

Rule 503 - Commissions and Referral Fees

"A. Prohibited commissions

A member in public practice shall not for a commission recommend or refer to a client any product or service, or for a commission recommend or refer any product or service to be supplied by a client, or receive a commission, when the member or the member's firm also performs for that client:

(a) an audit or review of a financial statement; or

(b) a compilation of a financial statement when the member expects, or reasonably might expect, that a third party will use the financial statement and the member's compilation report does not disclose a lack of independence; or

(c) an examination of prospective financial information.

This prohibition applies during the period in which the member is engaged to perform any of the services listed above and the period covered by any historical financial statements involved in such listed services.

B. Disclosure of permitted commissions

A member in public practice who is not prohibited by this rule from performing services for or receiving a commission and who is paid or expects to be paid a commission shall disclose that fact to any person or entity to whom the member recommends or refers a product or service to which the commission relates.

C. Referral fees

Any member who accepts a referral fee for recommending or referring any service of a CPA to any person or entity or who pays a referral fee to obtain a client shall disclose such acceptance or payment to the client."

Rule 505 - Form of Organization and Name. "A member may practice public accounting only in a form of organization permitted by state law or regulation whose characteristics conform to resolutions of Council.

A member shall not practice public accounting under a firm name that is misleading. Names of one or more past owners may be included in the firm name of a successor organization. Also, an owner surviving the death or withdrawal of all other owners may continue to practice under a name which includes the name of past owners for up to two years after becoming a sole practitioner.

A firm may not designate itself as 'Members of the American Institute of Certified Public Accountants' unless all of its owners are members of the Institute."

NOTE: According to the pertinent resolution of the AICPA Council, at least 66 ⅔% of the firm's ownership must belong to CPAs, and each non-CPA owner must be actively engaged in providing services to clients as his/her principal occupation. A CPA must have ultimate responsibility for all the services provided by the firm and by each business unit performing attest and compilation services. Moreover, non-CPA owners must abide by the Code and complete CPE requirements.

AICPA STATEMENTS ON AUDITING STANDARDS

A. The Auditing Standards Board of the AICPA issues Statements interpreting the 10 GAAS. These Statements are considered to have the status of GAAS. Accordingly, they must be followed by independent auditors. They are issued as separate pronouncements in sequence but are also codified and organized into the following sections.

100 Statements on Auditing Standards - Introduction
200 The General Standards
300 The Standards of Field Work
400 The First, Second, and Third Standards of Reporting
500 The Fourth Standard of Reporting
600 Other Types of Reports
700 Special Topics
800 Compliance Auditing
900 Special Reports of the Committee on Auditing Procedure

Auditing Interpretations are integrated into the foregoing sections.

B. The following summaries of the SASs are listed by their codified numbers for ease of reference to the AICPA Professional Standards. Although the summaries do not need to be memorized, the basic concept set forth in each pronouncement should be noted; it may be a topic on the CMA exam.

AU SECTIONS

110 - Responsibilities and Functions of the Independent Auditor

The object of independent audits is to express an opinion on whether the financial statements, in all material respects, are presented fairly in conformity with GAAP. Both the financial statements and the internal control structure are the responsibility of management. Auditors must comply with professional standards and have adequate education and experience.

150 - Generally Accepted Auditing Standards (GAAS)

Standards concern the quality of performance of audit procedures and the objectives to be attained by the use of those procedures. The 10 GAAS are given in a separate sideheading of this study unit.

161 - The Relationship of Generally Accepted Auditing Standards to Quality Control Standards

Under Conduct Rule 202, individual auditors are responsible for complying with GAAS. Firms of auditors should also establish quality control policies and procedures. The type and extent of these procedures are dependent upon the firm's size, organizational structure, nature of the practice, cost-benefit considerations, and the separation between personnel and practice departments. Whereas GAAS relate to individual audits, quality control standards relate to overall audit practice, but quality control should affect both individual audits and overall practice.

201 - Nature of the General Standards

They refer to the qualifications of the auditor and the quality of his/her work.

210 - Training and Proficiency of the Independent Auditor

Both education and experience, as well as proper supervision, are necessary. An auditor must have experience and seasoned judgment to accept final responsibility for an audit opinion. Objectivity and independent judgment are necessary in the preparation of the audit opinion.

220 - Independence

An auditor must always have an independent state of mind. (S)he must also be independent in appearance. The Securities and Exchange Commission (SEC) also stresses the independence of auditors. Many companies encourage independence by having the auditors appointed by the board of directors or elected by stockholders.

230 - Due Care in the Performance of Work

Due care relates to the auditor's activities and how well (s)he performs them. There should be critical review of personnel and practices at all levels of supervision. A professional who offers his/her services must exercise both skill and reasonable care. If a specialized skill is a prerequisite, (s)he should possess the common level of skill, but no one guarantees faultless work.

310 - Relationship between the Auditor's Appointment and Planning

It is more efficient and effective to appoint the auditor as early as possible. If appointment comes near or after the close of the period being audited, the auditor must determine whether an adequate audit can be made or if a qualified opinion or a disclaimer is necessary. Early appointment allows a significant portion of the audit to be carried out before year-end.

311 - Planning and Supervision

Planning and supervision relate to the first standard of field work with respect to preparing audit programs, obtaining knowledge of the client's business, and dealing with differences of opinion among firm personnel. Audit planning requires developing an overall strategy for the audit. The nature, extent, and timing of planning varies with the size of the entity and other factors. A written audit program aids and instructs assistants in work to be done, and details necessary audit procedures. The audit program should be based on the auditor's knowledge of the client's business, including the methods used by the entity for computer processing of significant accounting information. The auditor may need to consider whether specialized skills are needed, e.g., to consider the effects of computer processing. Supervision, the directing and evaluating of subordinates, relates to all aspects of an audit. Assistants should know what is expected of them and procedures to follow concerning disagreements on accounting and auditing issues. Procedures should be adequate for the documentation and resolution of such disagreements.

312 - Audit Risk and Materiality in Conducting an Audit

Audit risk and materiality relate to the nature, timing, and extent of audit procedures and their evaluation. Audit risk is the risk that the auditor may unknowingly fail to modify the opinion on materially misstated financial statements. It includes inherent risk, the susceptibility of an assertion to material misstatement assuming that there are no related internal control structure policies and procedures. It also includes control risk, the risk that a material misstatement could occur that will not be prevented or detected by the internal control structure. A third aspect of audit risk is detection risk, the risk that the auditor will not detect a material misstatement that exists in an assertion.

Financial statements are materially misstated if they contain misstatements that, singly or in the aggregate, are important enough to cause them not to be fairly presented, in all material respects, in conformity with GAAP. Materiality is based on the auditor's professional judgment as to the needs of a reasonable person who will rely on the financial statements. The FASB defines it as the "magnitude of an omission or misstatement of accounting information that, in the light of surrounding circumstances, makes it probable that the judgment of a reasonable person relying on the information would have been changed or influenced by the omission or misstatement."

Auditors must consider audit risk and materiality during the entire audit. These factors especially affect the standards of field work and reporting. The audit should be planned to limit risk to a level low enough to permit issuing an opinion. Audit planning should take into account the auditor's preliminary judgment about materiality levels. The auditor must balance the inherent risk and control risk believed to exist and the acceptable detection risk. The auditor should consider this balance when evaluating the fairness of the financial statements in view of the aggregation of likely misstatements.

313 - Substantive Tests prior to the Balance Sheet Date

Application of substantive tests at interim dates, i.e., prior to year-end, increases the risk that undetected misstatements may exist at year-end. Accordingly, auditors should apply some substantive tests to the remaining period (from the date substantive tests were performed to year-end). But, if control risk is assessed at the maximum, the auditor must consider whether the effectiveness of the tests covering the remaining period will be impaired. Also, all auditing procedures must be coordinated, e.g., those applied to related party transactions. In other words, the tests applied during the remaining period and at year-end need to be based on the interim work.

315 - Communications between Predecessor and Successor Auditors

Prospective successor auditors are required to communicate with predecessor auditors before accepting auditing engagements. With permission from the client, successor auditors should inquire of predecessor auditors about management's integrity, client disagreements about accounting principles, etc., and the reason for changing auditors. Additionally, the successor should communicate with the predecessor auditor concerning beginning balances, consistency of application of GAAP, etc.

316 - The Auditor's Responsibility to Detect and Report Errors and Irregularities

This section requires that the auditor assess the risk that material misstatements will occur and design the audit to provide reasonable assurance of detecting them. It identifies factors that may indicate the existence of errors and irregularities and the characteristics thereof. It also defines the auditor's appropriate attitude toward material misstatements (professional skepticism) and explains how that attitude affects audit planning and performance.

317 - Illegal Acts by Clients

This section requires the auditor to design the audit to provide reasonable assurance of detecting illegal acts that have a direct and material effect on the financial statements. This responsibility is the same as that for material errors and irregularities. The auditor's responsibility for illegal acts having material but indirect financial statement effects is to be aware that they may have occurred. However, the auditor is not obligated to apply specific procedures to detect them unless information comes to his/her attention indicating their existence.

319 - Consideration of the Internal Control Structure in a Financial Statement Audit

See the Internal Control According to the AICPA sideheading in Study Unit 16 on page 413.

322 - The Auditor's Consideration of the Internal Audit Function in an Audit of Financial Statements

External auditors may consider the existence of an internal audit function in determining the nature, timing, and extent of audit work. The auditor should obtain an understanding of the internal audit function as part of the understanding of the internal control structure. The purpose is to identify internal audit activities relevant to a financial statement audit. If some of those activities are relevant, the auditor should determine whether it is efficient to consider further how the internal audit function may affect the audit work. If it is efficient, the auditor should assess the competence and objectivity of the internal audit function. (S)he must also evaluate and test the internal auditors' work that significantly affects the auditor's procedures. Even if the internal auditors' work is expected to affect the audit procedures, the reporting responsibility continues to rest solely with the external auditor. Moreover, the external auditor must make judgments about whether and to what extent (s)he must directly test financial statement assertions after considering the work of the internal auditors. Issues of materiality, inherent and control risk, and the subjectivity involved in the evaluation of audit evidence must be weighed. Even if the internal audit function is deemed not to be relevant to the audit, the external auditor must assess the competence and objectivity of the internal auditors and evaluate and supervise their work if their direct assistance is sought.

324 - Reports on the Processing of Transactions by Service Organizations

This section concerns the audit of an entity that uses a service organization to process certain transactions. It also describes the responsibilities of independent auditors whose reports on the processing of transactions by service organizations are to be used by other independent auditors. The guidance in this pronouncement applies when a service organization executes client transactions and maintains the recorded accountability, when it records transactions and processes related data, or both. The user auditor must consider the effect of the service organization on the ICS of the user entity. The user auditor must also consider the availability of evidence to obtain an understanding of the user entity's ICS, to assess control risk at the user entity, and to perform substantive tests. This section also describes the considerations involved in using a service auditor's report.

325 - Communication of Internal Control Structure Related Matters Noted in an Audit

An auditor must communicate all reportable conditions related to any of the ICS components. Reportable conditions constitute a broader category than material weaknesses. However, AU 325 does not change the definition of material weaknesses except to extend it to all ICS elements. The report states the purpose of an audit, defines reportable conditions (and possibly material weaknesses), describes deficiencies found, and includes a restriction on distribution. No report is issued if no reportable conditions were identified in the audit.

326 - Evidential Matter

Management assertions represented in the financial statements include existence or occurrence, completeness, rights and obligations, valuation or allocation, and presentation and disclosure. Auditors develop audit objectives and design substantive tests based on these assertions. Objectives do not vary depending on whether processing is manual or by computer, but audit procedures are influenced by the type of processing. The basic evidential matter supporting the financial statements are the underlying accounting data and corroborating information. Accounting data include the books of original entry, ledgers, accounting manuals, worksheets, and reconciliations. Corroborating information includes documentary items, e.g., checks, invoices, contracts, and minutes of meetings; confirmations and other written representations; evidence obtained through inquiry, observation, inspection, and physical examination; and any other available information that permits the auditor to reach conclusions through valid reasoning.

329 - Analytical Procedures

This standard is intended to improve the effectiveness of audits by requiring that analytical procedures be applied in the planning and overall review phases of an audit. Use of analytical procedures as substantive tests of particular financial statement assertions is discretionary. Analytical procedures consist of evaluations of financial information made by a study of plausible relationships among both financial and nonfinancial data. They entail comparisons of recorded amounts, or ratios developed therefrom, with expectations developed by the auditor.

330 - The Confirmation Process

Confirmation is "the process of obtaining and evaluating a direct communication from a third party in response to a request for information about a particular item affecting financial statement assertions." This pronouncement defines confirmation, relates confirmation procedures to the assessment of audit risk, discusses the assertions addressed by confirmations, describes the design of the confirmation request (positive or negative) and the performance of procedures, describes alternative procedures, states the factors used in evaluating the evidence obtained, and provides specific guidance with respect to confirmation of accounts receivable. The presumption is that material accounts receivable will be confirmed unless confirmation would be ineffective or the combined assessed level of inherent risk and control risk and the evidence provided by analytical procedures and other substantive tests of details together reduce audit risk to an acceptably low level.

331 - Inventories

Observation of physical inventories is a generally accepted auditing procedure. Auditors must make test counts when observing physical inventories. Inventories in public warehouses may be verified by direct confirmation. In addition, if the inventories are material, the auditors must evaluate the warehouse's internal control structure (or obtain a report thereon from an independent accountant).

332 - Long-Term Investments

Independent auditors are concerned with carrying values, investor shares of investee earnings, and related disclosures about long-term investments. Audited statements are adequate evidence for carrying value and investor earnings. Auditors should be concerned that the proper choice between the cost and equity methods was made. Intercompany profit and loss items should be appropriately eliminated when using the equity method.

333 - Client Representations

Auditors are required to obtain written representations from management. These representations vary with the circumstances but ordinarily include such items as availability and completeness of all financial data, management's acceptance of responsibility for compliance with GAAP, related party transactions, subsequent events, absence of unrecorded transactions, irregularities, gain and loss contingencies, repurchase agreements, losses on sales commitments, capital stock requirements, unasserted claims, title to collateral, violations of laws or regulations, and plans affecting carrying values of assets and liabilities. If management refuses to provide written representations, an unqualified audit opinion cannot be expressed.

334 - Related Parties

SFAS 57, *Related Party Disclosures*, requires material related party transactions to be disclosed in the financial statements. Also, these transactions should be accounted for to reflect their substance. Auditors must therefore undertake procedures, e.g., inquiries of management, to determine the existence of related parties and to identify and examine related party transactions.

336 - Using the Work of a Specialist

Specialists under this section include appraisers; engineers; actuaries; attorneys not engaged to provide services related to litigation, claims, or assessments; geologists; etc. The auditor may decide to use a specialist for various reasons, for example, to establish valuation, determine physical characteristics, determine amounts derived through special techniques, and interpret technical requirements, regulations, or agreements. The auditor must consider the specialist's qualifications, obtain an understanding of his/her work, and evaluate any relationship the specialist may have with the client. When using the work of the specialist, the auditor must understand the methods and assumptions used, test the data given to the specialist (in the light of the assessed control risk), and evaluate whether the findings of the specialist support the related assertions in the financial statements. An auditor ordinarily should not refer to the work or findings of a specialist. However, "The auditor may, as a result of the report or findings of the specialist, decide to add explanatory language to his/her standard report or depart from an unqualified opinion." The specialist may be identified "if the auditor believes the reference will facilitate an understanding of the reason for the explanatory paragraph or the departure from the unqualified opinion."

337 - Inquiry of a Client's Lawyer Concerning Litigation, Claims, and Assessments

Auditors should question management about the existence of contingent liabilities. The client should send a letter to its attorney describing all contingent liabilities (litigation, claims, and assessments), including unasserted claims. The letter should request that the attorney confirm the correctness of the client's understanding regarding these claims (reflected in the letter of audit inquiry). The letter should also ask for confirmation that the attorney will advise the client when unasserted claims require disclosure.

339 - Working Papers

Working papers assist auditors in performing audit procedures, supporting the audit opinion, and documenting compliance with GAAS. Working papers include analyses, confirmations, client document abstracts, memoranda, representations, and audit programs. Working papers are the records of the conclusions reached based upon procedures and tests undertaken. The structure and content of working papers are dependent upon the type of audit report presented; the nature of the financial statements, schedules, and other information reported on; the nature and condition of the client's records; the assessed level of control risk; and review and supervision requirements. Working papers may also be in the form of data stored on tapes, films, or other media. Working papers are the property of the auditor, and disclosure of the contents is limited by client confidentiality (Conduct Rule 301).

341 - The Auditor's Consideration of an Entity's Ability to Continue as a Going Concern

This standard requires the auditor to evaluate whether "there is a substantial doubt about the entity's ability to continue as a going concern for a reasonable period of time." Whereas the auditor need not apply auditing procedures specifically designed for this purpose, (s)he may have to obtain additional evidence as well as information about management's plans to mitigate the effects of the conditions or events indicative of the substantial doubt. A substantial doubt requires an explanatory paragraph following the opinion paragraph. The terms substantial doubt and going concern must be included in the explanatory paragraph.

342 - Auditing Accounting Estimates

Accounting estimates are specifically addressed in the scope paragraph of the standard audit report (see AU 508). AU 342 defines accounting estimates, gives examples, describes management's responsibilities, and provides guidance for the auditor's evaluation.

350 - Audit Sampling

The internal control structure (ICS) should prevent or detect most monetary misstatements or deviations from ICS policies and procedures. Substantive tests should detect many of the remaining material misstatements. Sampling risk is the possibility that samples do not represent populations; nonsampling risk encompasses all aspects of audit risk not due to sampling. Regarding sampling risk for a substantive test of details, auditors should be concerned with both incorrect rejection and incorrect acceptance (the critical risk). They must also be concerned with two aspects of sampling risk for a test of controls: the risk of assessing control risk too high or too low (the critical risk). The scope of substantive testing varies inversely with assessed control risk. Dual-purpose tests are both tests of controls and substantive tests. They may be used both to assess control risk and to test the correctness of monetary amounts of transactions. Both judgmental and statistical sampling are appropriate. Statistical sampling permits efficient sampling plans and quantification of sample precision and reliability. If AR is overall allowable audit risk, IR is inherent risk, CR is control risk, and AP is the risk that analytical procedures and other substantive tests will not detect material misstatements occurring in an assertion that are not detected by the ICS, the risk of incorrect acceptance for a specific substantive test of details (TD) may be expressed as $TD = AR \div (IR \times CR \times AP)$.

380 - Communication with Audit Committees

This standard is intended to improve internal reporting by requiring that certain audit matters be communicated to those who oversee the entity's financial reporting process. It applies if the entity has an audit committee or its equivalent or if the audit constitutes an SEC engagement. Among the matters to be communicated are (1) the auditor's responsibility under GAAS; (2) selection of, changes in, or application of significant accounting policies; (3) management's judgments about sensitive accounting estimates; (4) significant audit adjustments; (5) other information in documents containing audited financial statements; (6) disagreements with management; (7) management's consultations with other accountants; (8) major issues discussed with management prior to accepting the engagement; and (9) difficulties in performing the audit.

390 - Consideration of Omitted Procedures after the Report Date

This statement provides guidance for an auditor who, subsequent to the date of the report on audited financial statements, concludes that one or more necessary auditing procedures were omitted from the audit, but there is no indication that those statements are not fairly presented in conformity with GAAP or with another comprehensive basis of accounting. Once (s)he has reported, an auditor has no responsibility to carry out any retrospective review. However, reports and working papers relating to particular engagements may be subjected to post-issuance review for various reasons, and the omission of a necessary procedure may be disclosed. When the auditor concludes that a necessary procedure was omitted, (s)he should assess its importance. If the auditor concludes that the omission of a necessary procedure impairs his/her current ability to support the previously expressed opinion, and (s)he believes there are persons currently relying, or likely to rely, on the report, (s)he should promptly undertake to apply the omitted procedure(s) that would provide a satisfactory basis for the opinion. If (s)he cannot apply the omitted procedure, (s)he should seek advice about his/her legal responsibilities.

410 - Adherence to GAAP

Generally accepted accounting principles include methods of application as well as accounting principles and practices. External auditors must express an opinion as to whether the client's financial statements adhere to GAAP.

411 - The Meaning of "Present Fairly in Conformity with GAAP" in the Independent Auditor's Report

This section defines GAAP as the "conventions, rules, and procedures necessary to define accepted accounting practice at a particular time." GAAP include both the broad guidelines and the detailed practices and procedures that provide a standard to measure financial presentations. Judgments about fairness are applied within the framework of GAAP. AU 411 states the sources of GAAP and establishes a hierarchy of accounting principles for nongovernmental entities and for state and local governments.

420 - Consistency of Application of GAAP

If comparability among periods has been materially affected by changes in accounting principles, the auditor should appropriately modify the report. Consistency is not mentioned in the report, however, if no change with a material effect has occurred. Accounting changes that affect consistency and require recognition in audit reports include changes in principle, changes in the reporting entity, correction of an error in principle, and changes in principle that are inseparable from a change in estimate.

Modification of the report for an inconsistency is necessary when a pooling of interests is not accounted for by restating prior-period financial statements presented comparatively or when single-year statements do not include adequate disclosure of the pooling. The departure from GAAP in these cases also requires qualification of the opinion. A change in the policy for determining the items treated as cash equivalents in a statement of cash flows is a change in principle requiring retroactive restatement. The audit report should recognize this change in an explanatory paragraph. Changes that do not affect consistency and do not require modification of the audit report include changes in estimate, error corrections not involving accounting principles, changes in classification, substantially different transactions or events, and changes having a material future but not current effect.

431 - Adequacy of Disclosure in Financial Statements

Fairness contemplates adequate disclosure relating to form, content, arrangement of statements, terminology, classifications, and detail. If disclosure is not adequate, the auditor must express a qualified or adverse opinion.

435 - Segment Information

SFAS 14, *Financial Reporting for Segments of a Business Enterprise,* requires disclosure of segment sales, operating profit, and assets for segments that have more than 10% of total sales, total operating profit or loss, or assets. Auditors should modify their auditing procedures so as to evaluate the classification of entries of the various segments. The methods, procedures, and systems to develop segment data should be evaluated, and analytical procedures should be applied to segment data. Auditors do not refer to segment data in the report unless the financial statements contain omissions or material misstatements.

504 - Association with Financial Statements

An accountant is associated with financial statements when his/her name is used in a report or document containing the financial statements. This section is based on the fourth standard of reporting, which is intended to prevent misinterpretation of the accountant's responsibility when his/her name is associated with those statements. Accountants should not allow their names to be associated with unaudited financial statements unless the statements are clearly marked "unaudited" and an indication is provided that the accountants do not express an opinion. Negative assurance should never be given if a disclaimer of opinion is expressed. A disclaimer of opinion is appropriate when an accountant is not independent.

508 - Reports on Audited Financial Statements

This section prescribes the auditor's standard report (see the Auditor's Standard Report sideheading in this study unit) and the conditions for its modification . The standard report states an unqualified opinion. Departures from the standard report include the addition of explanatory language that does not affect the unqualified opinion, a qualified opinion (stating that, except for the effects of the matter(s) to which the qualification relates, the statements are presented fairly), an adverse opinion (stating that the statements are not presented fairly), and a disclaimer of opinion (stating that the auditor does not express an opinion). Explanatory language not affecting an unqualified opinion must be added in circumstances that include the following: The opinion is based in part on the report of another auditor, the statements contain a departure from GAAP necessary to prevent them from being misleading, an uncertainty not susceptible of reasonable estimation affects the statements*, substantial doubt about the going concern assumption exists, GAAP is applied inconsistently, and the auditor chooses to emphasize a matter. A qualified opinion is expressed when a lack of sufficient evidence or a scope limitation precludes an unqualified opinion but the auditor has chosen not to disclaim an opinion or when a material departure from GAAP exists but the auditor has decided not to express an adverse opinion. Departures from GAAP include use of a principle at variance with GAAP, inadequate disclosure, and an accounting change if the newly adopted principle is not generally accepted, the method of accounting for the change is not in conformity with GAAP, or the change is not reasonably justified. An adverse opinion is expressed when the financial statements as a whole are not presented fairly in conformity with GAAP. A disclaimer of opinion is expressed because the audit has not been sufficient in scope to permit the formation of an opinion.

530 - Dating of the Independent Auditor's Report

Audit reports should be dated as of the last day of field work. If events or transactions that occur after completion of the field work are reflected in the financial statements, the report should be dual-dated, i.e., dated as of the last day of field work except for the additional disclosure, which is dated as of its discovery. If audit reports are reissued, they should use the last day of field work.

*NOTE: An Exposure Draft dated 7/20/95 has been issued that eliminates the requirement that, when certain criteria are met, the auditor add an explanatory paragraph for an uncertainty. However, the auditor has the option to add an explanatory paragraph to emphasize a matter, e.g., unusually important risks or uncertainties associated with contingencies, significant estimates, or concentrations.

534 - Reporting on Financial Statements Prepared for Use in Other Countries

A U.S. auditor may be engaged to report on the financial statements of a U.S. entity that have been prepared in conformity with accounting principles accepted in another country for use outside the U.S. The auditor should understand, and obtain written representations about, the purpose and uses of such financial statements. If the auditor uses the standard report of another country, and the financial statements will have general distribution in that country, (s)he should consider whether any additional legal responsibilities are involved. The auditor should perform the procedures that are necessary to comply with the general and field work standards of U.S. GAAS, although they may need to be modified because the assertions in the statements differ from those prepared according to GAAP. The auditor should understand the accounting principles generally accepted in the other country. The auditor may also be requested to apply the auditing standards of the other country and should thus comply with that nation's general and field work standards. A modified U.S.-style report or the report form of the other country may be used. The auditor may report on two sets of statements for the entity: one based on GAAP and the other on principles generally accepted in the other country. The other country's reporting standards must be complied with.

543 - Part of Audit Performed by Other Independent Auditors

When an audit is conducted by two or more auditors, the principal auditor must determine whether his/her participation in the audit is sufficient for recognition as the principal auditor. For this purpose, (s)he must have knowledge of the overall statements and an understanding of the individual components. The principal auditor makes a basic decision whether to accept responsibility for the other auditor. If responsibility is accepted, there is no mention of the other auditor in the audit report. If the auditor wishes to divide responsibility, the audit report indicates the magnitude of the portion of the financial statements audited by the other auditor as a percentage of total assets, income, or other criterion. Reference to the work of another auditor does not affect the nature of the opinion expressed by the principal auditor. If no reference is made to the other auditor, the principal auditor must gain assurance of the independence, professional reputation, and quality of the other auditor's work. Whether or not (s)he refers to the other auditor, the principal auditor should make inquiries of the professional reputation of the other auditor and obtain assurances about his/her independence. Furthermore, the other auditor must understand his/her relationship with the principal auditor.

544 - Lack of Conformity with GAAP

If financial statements of regulated companies depart from GAAP, a qualified or adverse opinion will ordinarily be expressed. However, an additional paragraph of the report should express an opinion as to conformity with the basis of accounting prescribed by the regulatory body.

550 - Other Information in Documents Containing Audited Financial Statements

The auditor should read the other financial information in the annual reports to determine that there is no inconsistency between the other material and the financial statements. Any material misstatements, inconsistencies, etc., require modification by the client, modification of the audit report (an additional paragraph), or withdrawal.

551 - Reporting on Information Accompanying the Basic Financial Statements in Auditor-Submitted Documents

Auditors should report on all information included in the documents submitted to clients that include audited financial statements. The auditor's report should identify the other information and state that the information is not part of the basic financial statements. The audit opinion should be modified to cover the other information. If the auditor disclaims an opinion on the other information, it should be clearly marked "unaudited."

552 - Reporting on Condensed Financial Statements and Selected Financial Data

This pronouncement concerns reporting in a client-prepared document on condensed statements derived from audited statements of a public entity required to file complete audited statements with a regulatory agency. It also concerns reporting on selected financial data derived from audited statements of any entity presented either in a client-prepared document that includes audited statements or, with respect to a public entity, in a client-prepared document that incorporates audited statements by reference to regulatory agency filings. The auditor's report on condensed statements or selected data should indicate that the auditor has audited and expressed an opinion on the complete statements, the type of opinion expressed, and an opinion as to whether the information set forth is fairly stated in all material respects in relation to the complete statements from which it was derived. In the case of condensed statements, the report should also indicate the date of the report on the complete statements. If the selected data include other information not derived from the complete statements, the auditor should specifically identify the data on which (s)he is reporting.

558 - Required Supplementary Information

This standard recognizes supplementary information required by both the FASB and the GASB. Auditors report (i.e., add an additional paragraph to the standard report) on the supplementary disclosures required by the FASB or GASB only when they are omitted, they contain material misstatements, the auditor is unable to complete the prescribed procedures, the auditor is unable to remove substantial doubts about whether the information conforms to prescribed guidelines, or the supplementary data are not clearly marked "unaudited." Auditors should determine whether supplementary information is required and whether it meets the prescribed guidelines.

560 - Subsequent Events

There are two types of subsequent events: (1) those that require reflection in the financial statements and (2) those that require disclosure only. Events that merely confirm situations existing at the balance sheet date should be reflected in the financial statements; e.g., the receivables of a bankrupt debtor should be written off on the statements even though the debtor went bankrupt after the year-end. Other events should be merely disclosed, e.g., the bankruptcy of a debtor arising from a fire that occurred after year-end. Subsequent events may be detected during cutoff tests and post-balance-sheet date evaluation of assets and liabilities. Reading interim statements, inquiring of officers and other executives, reading minutes, inquiring of legal counsel, and obtaining a representation letter are among the other procedures that might detect subsequent events.

561 - Subsequent Discovery of Facts Existing at the Date of the Auditor's Report

Subsequent to the date of the report, an auditor may become aware of information affecting the financial statements and/or the audit report that existed at the report date. In these circumstances, the report should be reissued. If the client refuses to cooperate, the auditor should notify the client, regulatory agencies, and others relying on the statements.

622 - Special Reports -- Applying Agreed-upon Procedures to Specified Elements, Accounts, or Items of a Financial Statement

Reports based upon the application of agreed-upon procedures to one or more items in financial statements, such as rents or royalties, are not subject to the second and third standards of field work and the standards of reporting. A special report should be issued indicating the specific element, etc., to which procedures were applied, the intended recipients of the report, the procedures performed, and the accountant's findings. It should disclaim an opinion on the specific element, etc., and no opinion should be expressed on any financial statements.

623 - Special Reports

This pronouncement establishes the auditor's responsibility for reports on financial statements that are prepared in conformity with a comprehensive method of accounting other than GAAP. It also provides guidance for an engagement to express an opinion on specified elements, accounts, or items of a financial statement. Other topics covered are compliance reports required by contractual agreements and regulatory agencies (however, AU 801 applies when the auditor tests compliance with laws and regulations in accordance with *Government Auditing Standards*), special-purpose financial presentations required by contractual agreements or regulatory agencies, and financial information presented in prescribed forms or schedules.

625 - Reports on the Application of Accounting Principles

AU 625 applies to an accountant in public practice (reporting accountant), either in connection with a proposal to obtain a new client or otherwise, when preparing a written report on the application of accounting principles to specified transactions, either completed or proposed. It also applies when the accountant is requested to provide a written report on the type of opinion that may be rendered on a specific entity's financial statements. Another application is in the preparation of a written report to intermediaries on the application of accounting principles not involving facts or circumstances of a particular principal. AU 625 also governs oral advice on the application of accounting principles to a specific transaction and the type of opinion that may be rendered on an entity's financial statements when the reporting accountant concludes the advice is intended to be used by a principal to the transaction as an important decision factor.

The reporting accountant should exercise due care, have adequate training and proficiency, plan the engagement adequately, and supervise the work of assistants, if any. (S)he must also accumulate sufficient information to provide a reasonable basis for the professional judgment described in the report. Moreover, the reporting accountant considers the one requesting the report, the circumstances under which the request is made, the purpose of the request, and the requester's intended use of the report. Also, the continuing accountant should be consulted.

634 - Letters for Underwriters and Certain Other Requesting Parties

AU 634 deals with several issues related to comfort letters. First, in a number of areas involving professional standards, it states whether it is proper for independent accountants acting in their professional capacity to comment on specified matters, and, if so, what the form of comment should be. Second, practical suggestions are offered on such matters as forms of comfort letters suitable to various circumstances, the way in which a particular form of letter may be agreed upon, the dating of letters, and the steps to be taken when information that may require special mention in a letter comes to the accountants' attention. Third, ways are suggested to reduce or avoid the uncertainties regarding the nature and extent of accountants' responsibilities in connection with a comfort letter.

711 - Filings under Federal Securities Statutes

An accountant has a defense against lawsuits regarding false or misleading statements if (s)he had reasonable grounds, after reasonable investigation, to believe and did believe that statements were true and not misleading at the effective date of the registration statement. The accountant should extend procedures from the date of the report to the effective date of the registration statement. The investigation consists of reading statements, making inquiries, and obtaining a written representation letter from the client about subsequent events. Although the accountant has not expressed an opinion on the unaudited interim information, (s)he still must comment on any noncompliance with GAAP in the report. A predecessor accountant also has subsequent event responsibility and must read the applicable portions of any prospectus and registration statement.

722 - Interim Financial Information

The review of interim financial information provides the accountant, based on application of his/her knowledge of reporting practices to significant accounting matters of which (s)he becomes aware through inquiries and analytical procedures, with a basis for reporting whether material modifications should be made for such information to conform with GAAP (negative assurance). This objective differs significantly from that of an audit, which is to provide a basis for expressing an opinion. This pronouncement provides guidance on the procedures to be applied and on the appropriate reports to be prepared. It also establishes requirements for communication with audit committees.

801 - Compliance Auditing Considerations in Audits of Governmental Entities and Recipients of Governmental Financial Assistance

AU 801 provides general guidance on the auditor's responsibilities in applying AU 317, *Illegal Acts by Clients*, as it relates to misstatements resulting from illegal acts having direct and material effects on financial statements and to audits of governmental entities or recipients of federal financial assistance. It also provides guidance on performing audits under Government Auditing Standards, performing a single or organization-wide or program-specific audit under federal requirements, and communicating with management when the auditor learns that the entity is subject to audit requirements not within the terms of the engagement.

901 - Public Warehouses -- Internal Control Structure Policies and Procedures and Auditing Procedures for Goods Held

This pronouncement describes public warehouse activities and internal control structure policies and procedures that should be in existence for public warehouse companies. It provides audit programs and procedures for auditors of public warehouses.

STATEMENTS ON STANDARDS FOR ATTESTATION ENGAGEMENTS (SSAEs)

AICPA bodies issue standards for a variety of attest services other than the traditional financial statement audit. The AICPA's codification of SSAEs covers pronouncements on attestation standards (AT 100), financial forecasts and projections (AT 200), reporting on pro forma financial information (AT 300), reporting on an entity's internal control structure over financial reporting (AT 400), and compliance attestation (AT 500). SSAE 1 includes AT 100, 200, and 300. SSAE 2 and SSAE 3 are codified as AT 400 and AT 500, respectively. The summaries of the standards given below are presented in their codified numerical AT sequence.

AT SECTIONS

100 - Attestation Standards

An attest engagement is one in which a practitioner (a CPA in the practice of public accounting) expresses a conclusion about the reliability of a written assertion that is the responsibility of another party based on an examination, a review, or the application of agreed-upon procedures. AT 100 permits two levels of attest assurance in general distribution reports. Positive assurance should be given in reports that express conclusions on the basis of an **examination**. Negative assurance should be given in reports that express conclusions on the basis of a **review**. Standards for all attest engagements, which are a natural extension of (but do not supersede) the 10 GAAS, are given as follows.

General Standards

a. *The engagement shall be performed by a practitioner or practitioners having adequate technical training and proficiency in the attest function.*

b. *The engagement shall be performed by a practitioner or practitioners having adequate knowledge in the subject matter of the assertion.*

c. *The practitioner shall perform an engagement only if (s)he has reason to believe that the following two conditions exist:*

   1) *The assertion is capable of evaluation against reasonable criteria that either have been established by a recognized body or are stated in the presentation of the assertion in a sufficiently clear and comprehensive manner for a knowledgeable reader to be able to understand them.*

      a) For example, an engagement to attest that "workers recorded an average of 40 hours per week on a project" could be accepted by a CPA because "recorded" and "40 hours" are measurable (objectively determinable).

      b) However, an engagement to attest that "workers worked very hard on the project" could not be accepted because "very hard" is not measurable.

   2) *The assertion is capable of reasonably consistent estimation or measurement using such criteria.*

      a) Others applying the same measurement criteria to the issues should reach substantially the same conclusions.

d. *In all matters relating to the engagement, independence in mental attitude shall be maintained by the practitioner(s).*

e. *Due professional care shall be exercised in the performance of the engagement.*

Standards of Field Work

a. *The work shall be adequately planned and assistants, if any, shall be properly supervised.*

b. *Sufficient evidence shall be obtained to provide a reasonable basis for the conclusion that is expressed in the report.*

Standards of Reporting

a. *The report shall identify the assertion being reported on and state the character of the engagement.*

b. *The report shall state the practitioner's conclusion about whether the assertion is presented in conformity with the established or stated criteria against which it was measured.*

c. *The report shall state all of the practitioner's significant reservations about the engagement and the presentation of the assertion.*

d. *The report on an engagement to evaluate an assertion that has been prepared in conformity with agreed-upon criteria or on an engagement to apply agreed-upon procedures should contain a statement limiting its use to the parties who have agreed upon such criteria or procedures.*

200 - Financial Forecasts and Projections

An accountant who either (1) submits to clients or others prospective financial statements (PFSs) that (s)he has assembled or assisted in assembling or (2) reports on PFSs should either compile, examine, or apply agreed-upon procedures to them if those statements are, or reasonably might be, expected to be used by another (third) party.

A **financial forecast** presents an entity's expected financial position, results of operations, and changes in financial position. It is based on the responsible party's assumptions reflecting conditions it expects to exist and the course of action it expects to take. It may be expressed in specific monetary amounts as a single point estimate of forecasted results or as a range, if the responsible party selects key assumptions to form a range within which it reasonably expects, to the best of its knowledge and belief, the item or items subject to the assumptions to actually fall. Certain minimum presentation guidelines apply.

A **financial projection** differs from a forecast in that it is based on the responsible party's assumptions reflecting conditions it expects would exist and the course of action it expects would be taken, given one or more hypothetical assumptions. A projection is sometimes prepared to present one or more hypothetical courses of action for evaluation, as in response to a question such as "What would happen if . . . ?"

300 - Reporting on Pro Forma Financial Information

This pronouncement is applicable to an accountant who examines or reviews and reports on pro forma financial information (PFFI). It does not apply to post-balance-sheet-date transactions reflected in the historical financial statements or to PFFI required by GAAP.

PFFI indicates what the effects on historical information might have been if a consummated or proposed transaction or event, such as a business combination, had occurred earlier.

An accountant may report on an examination (positive assurance) or review (negative assurance) of PFFI if three conditions are met.

1. The appropriate complete historical financial statements are included in the document.
2. The pertinent historical financial statements have been examined or reviewed, and the assurance given by the accountant is commensurate with that given on those statements.
3. The reporting accountant has appropriate knowledge of the accounting and reporting practices of each significant constituent part of the combined entity.

400 - Reporting on an Entity's Internal Control Structure over Financial Reporting

This SSAE is primarily concerned with engagements to examine and report on management's written assertion about the effectiveness of an entity's ICS over financial reporting. It states the conditions for performance of the engagement, describes the components of one possible definition of an ICS (the components of the entity's ICS depend on management's definition), and describes the limitations of that structure. This pronouncement also provides guidance for planning an engagement to express an opinion on management's assertion, obtaining an understanding of the ICS, evaluating the design effectiveness of ICS policies and procedures, testing and evaluating the operating effectiveness of ICS policies and procedures, and forming an opinion. In addition, AT 400 establishes reporting standards and describes the practitioner's responsibility to communicate deficiencies of which (s)he becomes aware.

500 - Compliance Attestation

This SSAE describes compliance attestation engagements and the accompanying reporting obligations. These engagements should be conducted in accordance with the basic standards set forth by AT 100. The practitioner may perform either agreed-upon procedures or an examination leading to an opinion on management's written assertion concerning (a) the entity's compliance with specified requirements (e.g., covenants of a contract either financial or otherwise) or (b) the effectiveness of the entity's control structure over compliance.

The standard does not relate to engagements subject to *Government Auditing Standards*, which require reporting on an entity's compliance with laws and regulations as well as on the internal control structure.

If the practitioner performs an examination on management's written assertion presented in a separate report that will accompany the practitioner's report, the practitioner's report need not be limited in use. In all other cases, the practitioner's report should be limited in use to management or others with specific knowledge about the limitations of the report.

AUDIT EVIDENCE AND PROCEDURES

The third standard of field work states, "Sufficient competent evidential matter is to be obtained through inspection, observation, inquiries, and confirmations to afford a reasonable basis for an opinion regarding the financial statements under audit." Similarly, internal auditors are expected to collect, analyze, interpret, and document sufficient, competent, relevant, and useful information to support audit results. Thus, this section applies to both external and internal auditing.

A. The fundamental pronouncement on audit evidence, AU 326, *Evidential Matter*, is the basis for most of this outline. According to AU 326, the audit work consists primarily of obtaining and evaluating evidence about the assertions in the financial statements.

1. **Evidence** is anything that provides a basis for belief; it tends to prove or disprove something.

2. **Assertions** are explicit or implicit management representations contained in the financial statements. They are classified in the following categories:

   a. **Existence or occurrence**
   b. **Completeness**
   c. **Rights and obligations**
   d. **Valuation or allocation**
   e. **Presentation and disclosure**

B. **Audit objectives** are determined with regard to the assertions.

1. Audit objectives also depend on the nature of the auditee's economic activity, industry accounting practices, and other specific circumstances of the engagement.

2. **Audit procedures** do not necessarily have a one-to-one correspondence with audit objectives; one procedure may bear upon several objectives, or several procedures may be needed to attain one objective.

C. **Substantive tests** must be designed to achieve the audit objectives.

1. Substantive tests are tests of details and analytical procedures intended to detect material misstatements.

2. The nature, timing, and extent of substantive tests will depend on audit risk (inherent, control, and detection risk) and materiality (AU 312). Considerations will include the

   a. Effectiveness of the particular procedures
   b. Efficiency of the particular procedures (cost-benefit ratio)
   c. Nature of items tested
   d. Kinds and competence of available evidence
   e. Nature of the specific objective
   f. Type of processing (manual or computer) of the accounting data
   g. Effectiveness of the auditee's internal control structure

D. As noted above, the audit effort devoted to gathering evidence through substantive tests is determined in part by the evidence obtained regarding the effectiveness of the internal control structure.

1. Evidence must be gathered permitting assessment of inherent risk and control risk. These assessments permit determination of the allowable level of detection risk for a particular assertion given the level to which the auditor seeks to restrict overall audit risk.

2. If control risk is to be assessed at less than the maximum, **tests of controls** must be performed.

   a. These tests are directed toward the design or operation of specific internal control structure policies or procedures. Their purpose is to obtain evidence permitting an assessment of effectiveness in preventing or detecting material misstatements.

3. The reasonable basis for the opinion is therefore a body of evidence provided by a combination of the consideration of the internal control structure and substantive tests.

E. Evidence may also be viewed as consisting of the underlying accounting data and corroborating information.

1. However, the books of original entry, ledgers, accounting manuals, and informal records (e.g., worksheets and reconciliations) are not sufficient evidence.
2. Corroboration comes from documents, such as checks, invoices, contracts, and minutes; from confirmations and other written representations; from the auditor's own inquiry, observation, inspection, and physical examination; and from any other information permitting conclusions to be drawn.
3. The auditor analyzes and reviews the accounting data, retraces the steps in the accounting process and in the preparation of worksheets and allocations, recalculates amounts, and performs reconciliations.
4. The foregoing procedures permit the auditor to determine whether the accounting system has the internal consistency that is persuasive evidence of the fair presentation, in all material respects, of the financial statements.

F. Evidence must be both **competent** and **sufficient**.

1. Professional judgment is the measure of the validity of audit evidence.
   a. The auditor is permitted a broad discretion not available in the consideration of legal evidence, which is narrowly limited by admissibility criteria.
2. Competent evidence is valid and relevant.
   a. Pertinence, objectivity, timeliness, and the existence of corroborating matter are aspects of the competence of audit evidence.
   b. Evidence is more likely to be reliable if
      1) It is gathered from independent sources external to the auditee.
      2) The internal control structure is effective.
      3) It is obtained directly through the auditor's own physical examination, observation, computation, and inspection.
3. What constitutes sufficient evidence to provide a reasonable basis for the opinion is a matter of professional judgment.
   a. Judgment and attention to the unique circumstances of a specific audit are necessary because obtaining convincing rather than merely persuasive evidence to support the opinion is often not feasible.
   b. Evidence gathering is subject to time and cost constraints, and the auditor must adhere to a cost-benefit criterion.
      1) However, the difficulty and expense of an audit procedure are not, by themselves, grounds for its omission.

G. The evaluation of audit evidence entails determining whether audit objectives have been attained and considering relevant evidence regardless of whether it supports or contradicts assertions in the financial statements.

1. The auditor must avoid forming an opinion until (s)he has obtained sufficient competent evidence to remove substantial doubt about the assertion.

AUDIT SAMPLING (AU 350)

A. **Definition**. Audit sampling applies an audit procedure to less than 100% of the items within an account balance or class of transactions for the purpose of evaluating some characteristic of the balance or class.

B. **Statistical and Nonstatistical Sampling** (for definitions of these and other terms, see Sampling Terminology on page 457). Both types of sampling require the auditor to exercise judgment in planning, performing, and evaluating a sample and in relating the evidence produced by the sample to other evidence when forming a conclusion about the related balance or class.

1. Either approach, properly applied, can provide sufficient evidence.
   a. The sufficiency of evidence is related to the design and size of the sample. The necessary size depends on the objectives and the efficiency of the sample. For a given objective, efficiency relates to design; one sample is more efficient than another if it achieves the same objective with a smaller size. In general, careful design can produce more efficient samples.
   b. The competence of evidence is a matter of judgment and is not determined by the design and evaluation of the sample. The sample evaluation relates only to the likelihood that existing misstatements or deviations are proportionately included in the sample. Thus, the choice of nonstatistical or statistical sampling does not directly affect the auditor's decisions about the auditing procedures to be applied, the competence of the evidence obtained with respect to individual sample items, or the actions that might be taken given the nature and cause of particular misstatements or deviations.

C. **Uncertainty**. Some uncertainty is implied in the "reasonable basis for an opinion" language in the third standard of field work.

1. The justification for accepting uncertainty arises because of the need to balance such factors as the cost and time required to examine all data against the adverse consequences of examining only a sample. If these factors do not justify some uncertainty, the only alternative is a complete audit.
2. The uncertainty inherent in audit procedures is **audit risk**. Audit risk consists of inherent risk, control risk, and detection risk.
   a. The risk that these adverse events will occur jointly is a function of the respective individual risks. Using professional judgment, the auditor assesses inherent risk and control risk (assessing control risk at less than the maximum requires tests of controls), and performs substantive tests (analytical procedures and tests of details of balances or classes) to limit detection risk.
   b. Audit risk includes uncertainties caused by sampling and nonsampling uncertainties.
      1) **Sampling risk** arises from the possibility that the auditor's conclusions may differ from the conclusions reached if the test were applied in the same way to all items in the balance or class. Hence, a sample may contain proportionately more or less misstatements or deviations than exist in the balance or class as a whole. Given a specific design, sampling risk varies inversely with sample size.
      2) **Nonsampling risk** embraces all aspects of audit risk that are not caused by sampling. Nonsampling risk includes selecting audit procedures that are not appropriate to achieve the specific objective and failing to recognize misstatements included in documents examined.
         a) Nonsampling risk can be reduced through adequate planning, supervision, and quality control.

D. **Sampling Risk.** The auditor should apply professional judgment in assessing sampling risk.

1. In performing substantive tests of details, the auditor is concerned with
   a. **The risk of incorrect acceptance**, which "is the risk that the sample supports the conclusion that the recorded account balance is not materially misstated when it is materially misstated"
   b. **The risk of incorrect rejection**, which "is the risk that the sample supports the conclusion that the recorded account balance is materially misstated when it is not materially misstated"
2. The auditor is also concerned with two aspects of sampling risk in performing tests of controls.
   a. **The risk of assessing control risk too low**, which "is the risk that the assessed level of control risk based on the sample is less than the true operating effectiveness of the control structure policy or procedure"
   b. **The risk of assessing control risk too high**, which "is the risk that the assessed level of control risk based on the sample is greater than the true operating effectiveness of the control structure policy or procedure"
3. The risks of incorrect rejection and of assessing control risk too high relate to audit efficiency.
4. The risks of incorrect acceptance and of assessing control risk too low relate to audit effectiveness.

E. **Sampling and Substantive Tests**

1. Planning the sample requires consideration of
   a. The relevant audit objectives and characteristics of the population
   b. Preliminary materiality judgments
      1) **Tolerable misstatement** for a balance or class is defined in view of the maximum misstatement that may exist without causing the financial statements to be materially misstated.
   c. Allowable risk of incorrect acceptance
      1) As the assessed levels of inherent risk, control risk, and detection risk for other substantive procedures directed toward the same audit objective decrease, the auditor's allowable risk of incorrect acceptance for the substantive test of details increases and the required sample size decreases.
2. Sample selection should be conducted so that the sample represents the population. Consequently, all items should have an opportunity to be chosen.
   a. Random-based selection (random sampling, stratified random sampling, etc.) is one appropriate method.
3. Performance and evaluation
   a. Appropriate procedures are applied to each sample item.
      1) If documentation for selected items is missing, the auditor must consider the impact on the evaluation of the sample and the possible need for alternative procedures.
   b. The auditor must project the quantitative misstatement results of the sample to the population and compare it with tolerable misstatement.
      1) Qualitative aspects of misstatements should also be considered.

c. Projected misstatements, known misstatements detected by nonsampling tests, and other audit evidence should be considered in the aggregate in determining whether the financial statements are materially misstated.

F. **Sampling and Tests of Controls**

1. Planning the sample requires consideration of the
   a. Relation of the sample to the objective of the test
      1) Some tests of controls do not involve sampling.
   b. **Tolerable rate** of deviations that would support the assessed level of control risk
      1) The auditor must consider the planned assessed level of control risk and the degree of assurance sought from the evidence in the sample. (S)he must also consider that deviations from policies or procedures do not necessarily cause misstatements.
   c. Allowable risk of assessing control risk too low
   d. Characteristics of the population
2. Sample selection should be representative, and all items should have an opportunity to be selected.
   a. The selection method should have the potential for choosing items from the entire period.
3. Performance and evaluation
   a. The effects of limitations on tests of controls should be considered.
   b. The sample deviation rate is the best estimate of the population deviation rate.
      1) Qualitative aspects of the deviations should also be considered.
   c. If the sample does not support the planned assessed level of control risk for an assertion, the nature, timing, and extent of substantive procedures may need to be reevaluated.

SAMPLING TERMINOLOGY

A. Textbooks, firm literature, auditing standards, professional exams, and professors often use different vocabulary for the same statistical concepts. After working through the questions and answer explanations in the corresponding study unit in Volume II, you should be able to deal effectively with such differences. In particular, the following two terms cause considerable misunderstanding:

1. **Confidence level** or **reliability** is specified by the auditor. It is the percentage of times that the sample is expected to be representative of the population. For example, a confidence level of 90% should result in samples that adequately represent the population 90% of the time. Confidence level is related to audit risk because the auditor is accepting a risk of 10% (100% – 90%) that the sample will not represent the population. In sampling for variables (substantive testing), the primary concern is **the risk of incorrect acceptance**. In sampling for attributes (tests of controls), the primary concern is **the risk of assessing control risk too low** (see Sampling Risk definitions on page 456). These wrong conclusions are also called Type II or beta errors.

2. **Precision** or **confidence interval** is the allowance for sampling risk. It is an interval around the sample statistic (for example, the mean) that is expected to include the true value of the population. Precision is based upon tolerable misstatement determined by materiality considerations. In sampling for attributes (tests of controls), precision is determined by subtracting the expected deviation rate from the tolerable rate. In sampling for variables (substantive testing), precision is determined by considering tolerable misstatement in conjunction with the confidence level (an effectiveness issue) as well as the risk of incorrect rejection. **The risk of incorrect rejection** (see Sampling Risk definitions on page 456) is a Type I or alpha error. It relates to efficiency rather than effectiveness issues because the auditor will likely continue auditing until the balance is finally supported. A table is typically consulted to determine the appropriate precision for various risk levels. A benchmark often used is to set precision at 50% of tolerable misstatement.

B. **Other Definitions**

1. **Acceptance sampling** is useful for quality control. Acceptance sampling for attributes involves sampling from a lot to determine what percentage of items have a specified attribute (e.g., defective or not defective). Acceptance sampling for variables is used when the characteristic being tested is continuously measurable. For example, a lot of ball bearings may be accepted or rejected depending on whether the mean of the sizes of the sample items is within the tolerance limits.
2. **Alpha (Type I) error** is the rejection of a correct hypothesis. The risk of incorrect rejection of an account balance and the risk of assessing control risk too high both relate to alpha error. These risks are aspects of sampling risk that involve efficiency issues.
3. **Attribute sampling** enables the auditor to estimate the occurrence rates of deviations from internal control structure policies and procedures and/or to determine whether the estimated rates are within an acceptable range.
4. **Beta (Type II) error** is the failure to reject an incorrect hypothesis. The risk of incorrect acceptance of an account balance and the risk of assessing control risk too low both relate to beta error. These risks are aspects of sampling risk that involve effectiveness issues.
5. **Block sampling** (also termed **cluster sampling**) selects groups of items rather than individual items. For this plan to be effective, dispersion within clusters should be greater than dispersion among clusters. An example of block sampling is the inclusion in the sample of all cash disbursements for a particular month. If blocks of homogeneous samples are selected, the sample will be biased.
6. **Confidence level (reliability)**. See A.1. on the preceding page.
7. **Difference estimation** of population error entails determining the differences between the audit and book values for items in the sample, adding the differences, calculating the mean difference, and multiplying the mean by the number of items in the population. An allowance for sampling risk is also calculated.
8. **Discovery sampling** is a form of attribute sampling used for the identification of critical errors or irregularities in a population. The occurrence rate is assumed to be 0%, and the method cannot be used to evaluate results statistically if errors are found in the sample. Hence, discovery sampling may be used for testing controls. However, it is appropriate only when a single error would be critical.

9. **Hypothesis testing** involves a predetermined rule for evaluating the auditee figure. Strictly speaking, the auditor either rejects the hypothesis or is unable to do so. In auditing literature, however, a hypothesis that cannot be rejected is often said to be accepted. This usage is followed even though a sample is never a sufficient basis for concluding that the hypothesis is in fact true. For example, in hypothesis testing for mean-per-unit estimation, the auditor prespecifies the level of significance and the materiality limits around the auditee's proposed amount; i.e., the auditor determines the acceptable risk of incorrect rejection and the acceptable range (the nonrejection region) about the auditee's value. The auditor accepts (is unable to reject) the book value if the sample precision interval is within the auditor's prespecified materiality limits about the auditee's reported amount. The auditor rejects the auditee's figure if the sample precision interval is sufficiently outside the precision limits. The sample tests the null hypothesis that there is a null or zero difference between the true value and the recorded amount. The null hypothesis will consist of an equality (H_o = a given value) if a two-tailed test is involved (relatively large or small values will be rejected). If a one-tailed test is involved (extreme values on one side can be ignored), the null hypothesis will be an inequality ($H_o \geq$ or $\leq$ a given value).

10. **Judgment (nonstatistical) sampling** uses the auditor's subjective judgment to determine the sample size (number of items examined) and sample selection (which items to examine). This subjectivity is not always a weakness. The auditor, based on other audit work, may be able to test the most material and risky transactions and to emphasize the types of transactions subject to high control risk. Probability (random) sampling provides an objective method of determining sample size and selecting the items to be examined. Unlike judgment sampling, it also provides a means of quantitatively assessing precision (how closely the sample represents the population) and reliability (confidence level, the percentage of times the sample will reflect the population).

11. **Mean-per-unit (MPU) sampling** and stratified MPU are considered less efficient than either ratio or difference estimation. MPU averages the audit values of the sample items and multiplies them by the number in the population to estimate the population value. An allowance for sampling risk is then determined.

12. **Nonsampling risk** embraces all aspects of audit risk not caused by sampling, e.g., failure to apply an appropriate procedure or to recognize a misstatement in a document the auditor examines.

13. **PPS sampling** (also known as dollar-unit sampling) is a modified version of attribute sampling that relates error rates to dollar amounts. It uses the dollar as the sampling unit. PPS sampling is appropriate for testing account balances, such as those for inventory and receivables, in which some items may be far larger than others in the population. In effect, it stratifies the population because the larger account balances have a greater chance of being selected. PPS is most useful if few errors are expected and overstatement is the most likely kind of error. One disadvantage of PPS sampling is that it is designed to detect overstatements. It is not effective for estimating understatement errors.

14. **Precision** or **confidence interval**. See A.1. on page 457.

15. **Probability sampling** is possible if every item in the population has a known and nonzero chance of being drawn.

16. **Ratio estimation** is similar to difference estimation except that it estimates the population error by multiplying the book value of the population by the ratio of the total audit value of the sample items to their total book value. It has been demonstrated that ratio or difference estimation is both reliable and efficient when small errors predominate and the errors are not skewed.

17. **Risk of assessing control risk too high**. See D.2.b. on page 456.
18. **Risk of assessing control risk too low (AU 350)**. See D.2.a. on page 456.
19. **Risk of incorrect acceptance (AU 350)**. See D.1.a. on page 456.
20. **Risk of incorrect rejection (AU 350)**. See D.1.b. on page 456.
21. **Sample** is the set of items to be chosen from the population being tested.
22. **Sample size formulas**
    a. The standard equation for a mean-per-unit application of **variables sampling** can be stated as

$$n_1 = \frac{C^2\sigma^2}{P^2}$$

n_1 equals the preliminary sample size, C is the desired confidence coefficient, σ is the estimated standard deviation of the population, and P is the specified average precision or allowance for sampling risk (per item). A variant of the formula multiplies the numerator by N (the population), with P equal to the total precision. The same equation may be used for difference and ratio estimation, although σ will be the estimated standard deviation of the population of differences between audit and book values. n_1 gives the sample size assuming sampling with replacement. It can be adjusted by a correction factor to allow for sampling without replacement. An approximation of the adjusted sample size is

$$n = n_1\sqrt{\frac{N - n_1}{N}}$$

n equals the modified sample size, n_1 equals the sample size determined in the formula above, and N is the finite population.

    b. The formula for **attribute sampling** is

$$n = \frac{C^2pq}{P^2}$$

C is the confidence coefficient, p is the expected error rate, q is 100% – p, P is the desired precision, and n is the sample size.

23. **Sampling risk** arises from the possibility that the auditor's conclusions may be different from those reached if the test were applied in the same way to all items in the account balance or class of transactions. A sample may thus contain more or fewer monetary errors or control deviations than exist in that population as a whole (AU 350).
24. **Sampling without replacement** means not returning a sample item to the population to prevent its being selected more than once. Audit sampling is customarily done without replacement.
25. **Sampling with replacement** means returning a sample item to the population so that it has a chance to be chosen more than once.
26. **Simple random sampling** is a special case of probability sampling in which every possible sample of a given size has the same probability of being chosen. Random selection can be used for stratified and other samples in which sample items do not have an equal chance of being selected.

27. **Standard deviation** is a measure of the degree of compactness of the values in a population. This measure is used by the auditor to help determine appropriate sample sizes. The first formula given below is for the population standard deviation (σ). It is the square root of the quotient of the sum of the squared deviations from the mean (μ), divided by the number of items in the population (N). The sample standard deviation is found using the second formula given below. The sample standard deviation is s, the mean of the sample is $\bar{x}$, and the sample size is n.

$$\sigma = \sqrt{\frac{\Sigma\,(x_i - \mu)^2}{N}} \qquad s = \sqrt{\frac{\Sigma\,(x_i - \bar{x})^2}{n - 1}}$$

28. **Standard error of the mean** is the standard deviation of the distribution of sample means and is calculated as population standard deviation (sigma or σ) divided by the square root of n (sample size).

29. **Statistical sampling** is the use of a sample to estimate the parameters of a population in such a way that sampling risk can be measured and controlled.

30. **Stop-or-go sampling** is a special case of attribute sampling. The objective is to examine the smallest number of items, i.e., minimize sample size. Thus, the auditor looks at only enough sample items to be able to state that the deviation rate is below a prespecified rate with a prespecified confidence level. Unlike discovery sampling, the auditor can achieve the result even if one or more deviations are discovered by enlarging the sample size sufficiently. In contrast, acceptance and discovery sampling have fixed sample sizes.

31. **Stratified sampling** divides a population into subpopulations, thereby permitting application of different sampling techniques to each subpopulation or stratum. Stratifying allows for greater emphasis on larger or more important items. Stratification also reduces the effect of high variability. Reducing the variance within each subpopulation allows the auditor to sample a smaller number of items while holding precision and confidence level constant.

32. **Systematic sampling** is accomplished by selecting a random start and taking every nth item in the population. The value of n is computed by dividing the number in the population by the size of the sample. The random start should be in the first interval.

33. **Tolerable misstatement** is the amount of monetary misstatement in an account balance or class of transactions that may exist without causing the financial statements to be materially misstated. It is a planning concept related to preliminary judgments about materiality levels (AU 350).

34. **Tolerable rate** is the maximum rate of deviations from a prescribed internal control structure policy or procedure that the auditor is willing to accept without changing his/her assessment of control risk for the assertions related to the policy or procedure (AU 350).

35. **Variables sampling** is used to estimate the value of a population. In auditing, this process entails estimating the monetary value of an account balance or other accounting total. The result is often in terms of a point estimate, plus or minus a stated dollar value (the range of precision at the desired level of confidence).

36. **Variance** is the square of the standard deviation.

PROBABILITY-PROPORTIONAL-TO-SIZE SAMPLING

A. The AICPA's Audit and Accounting Guide, *Audit Sampling,* popularized PPS (probability-proportional-to-size) sampling. This approach to variables sampling is distinct from the classical approach. It uses attribute sampling methods to reach a conclusion regarding the probability of overstating an account balance by a specified amount of dollars.

1. PPS sampling is based on the Poisson distribution, which is used in attribute sampling to approximate the binomial distribution.

B. The classical approach uses items (e.g., invoices, checks, etc.) as the sampling units.

1. PPS sampling uses a dollar as the sampling unit, but the item containing the sampled dollar is selected for audit.
2. PPS sampling is appropriate for account balances that may include only a few overstated items, such as may be expected in inventory and receivables.
3. In contrast, the classical approach to variables sampling is not always appropriate.
   a. When only a few differences between book and audit figures are found, difference and ratio estimation sampling may not be efficient.
   b. Mean-per-unit estimation sampling may also be difficult in an unstratified sampling situation.

C. The following simplified sample size formula is used when anticipated misstatement is zero:

$$n = \frac{BV \times RF}{TM}$$

If:
- n = sample size
- BV = book value of the account, e.g., inventory, accounts receivable
- RF = risk or reliability factor based on the Poisson distribution and the auditor's specified risk of incorrect acceptance
- TM = tolerable misstatement

1. Tolerable misstatement (TM) must be specified by the auditor. It is the maximum misstatement in an account balance or class of transactions that may exist without causing the financial statements to be materially misstated.
2. The risk or reliability factor (RF) is a multiplier, the value of which is determined by a Poisson factor found in a standard table. RF is always determined for zero misstatements, irrespective of the misstatements actually anticipated.
   a. The table below is a simplified version taken from the Audit and Accounting Guide, *Audit Sampling*.

Reliability Factors for Overstatements

Number of Overstatements	Risk of Incorrect Acceptance 1%	5%	10%	15%	20%
0	4.61	3.00	2.31	1.90	1.61
1	6.64	4.75	3.89	3.38	3.00
2	8.41	6.30	5.33	4.72	4.28

3. Example sample size calculation. A company's inventory balance is expected to have few if any errors of overstatement. The following information relates to an audit of the balance using PPS sampling:

Tolerable misstatement	$15,000
Anticipated misstatement	$0
Risk of incorrect acceptance	5%
Recorded amount of accounts receivable	$300,000
Overstatements discovered:	

	Recorded Amount	Audit Amount
1st	$ 400	$ 320
2nd	500	0
3rd	6,000	5,500

Accordingly, the sample size is 60 items.

$$n = \frac{BV \times RF}{TM} = \frac{\$300{,}000 \times 3.0}{\$15{,}000} = 60 \textit{ dollar items}$$

a. Alternatively, the dollar sampling interval can be determined by dividing the TM by the RF ($15,000 ÷ 3.0 = $5,000).

4. The auditor selects the sample items by looking at a listing of cumulative inventory value subtotals and selecting the item including every 5,000th dollar ($300,000 ÷ 60).

a. To apply PPS selection, the inventory listing must contain cumulative totals by item so that the items in which each 5,000th dollar occurs can be selected for inspection, count, valuation, etc.

Description	Inventory on Hand	Unit Value	Amount	Cumulative Amount
Item A	90	$105	$ 9,450	$ 9,450
B	30	16	480	9,930
C	70	40	2,800	12,730
D	46	111	5,106	17,836
E	300	7	2,100	19,936
F	390	2	780	20,716
•	•	•	•	•
•	•	•	•	•
•	•	•	•	•
				$300,000

$5,000 x 1 = $ 5,000
x 2 = $10,000
x 3 = $15,000
x 4 = $20,000

1) Thus, items A, C, D, F . . . will be inspected, counted, valued, etc.

5. If no misstatements are found in the 60 items, the auditor concludes that the auditee's balance has a maximum overstatement of $15,000 at the specified risk of incorrect acceptance.

6. If misstatements do occur, the average amount of misstatement must be projected to the entire population.

a. A tainting percentage [(book value – audit value) ÷ book value] is calculated for each misstatement in a sample item when the item is smaller than the sampling interval. This percentage is then applied to the interval to estimate the projected misstatement or taint (population misstatement in that interval).

b. The sum of the projected misstatements is the total estimated misstatement in the population.

c. If the sample item is greater than the sampling interval, the difference between the book value and audited value is the projected misstatement for that interval (no percentage is computed).

d. The total projected misstatement based on the information in C.3 on page 463 is $6,500.

Book Value	Audit Value	Tainting %	Sampling Interval	Projected Misstatement
$ 400	$ 320	20%	$5,000	$1,000
500	0	100%	5,000	5,000
6,000	5,500	--	--	500
				$6,500

e. The calculation of the upper misstatement limit (UML) based on the preceding information is more complex. The first component of the UML is basic precision: the product of the sampling interval ($5,000) and the risk factor (3.00) for zero misstatements at the specified risk of incorrect acceptance (5%). The second component is the total projected misstatement ($6,500). The third component is an allowance for widening the precision gap as a result of finding more than zero misstatements. This allowance is determined only with respect to logical sampling units with book values less than the sampling interval. If a sample item is equal to or greater than the sampling interval, the degree of taint for that interval is certain, and no further allowance is necessary. The first step in calculating this allowance is to determine the adjusted incremental changes in the reliability factors (these factors increase, and precision widens, as the number of misstatements increases). The factors are from the 5% column in the table. To prevent double counting of amounts already included in basic precision, in projected misstatement, and in the adjustments for higher-ranked misstatements, the preceding reliability factor plus 1.0 is subtracted from each factor. The projected misstatements are then ranked from highest to lowest, each adjusted incremental reliability factor is multiplied by the related projected misstatement, and the products are summed. In this case, the UML is found to exceed TM.

Basic precision ($5,000 x 3.00)		$15,000
Total projected misstatement		6,500
Allowance for precision gap widening:		
(4.75 – 3.00 – 1.00) x $5,000 =	$3,750	
(6.30 – 4.75 – 1.00) x $1,000 =	550	4,300
UML		$25,800

7. Because the sample size formula was based on a presumed 0% misstatement rate, the sample size may have to be increased.

a. The following is the modified sample size formula when anticipated misstatement is not zero:

$$n = \frac{BV \times RF}{TM - (AM \times EF)}$$

If: AM = anticipated misstatement
EF = an expansion factor derived from the following table (Source: Audit and Accounting Guide, *Audit Sampling*):

	Risk of Incorrect Acceptance				
	1%	5%	10%	15%	20%
Factor	1.9	1.6	1.5	1.4	1.3

D. Advantages of PPS are that it
   1. In effect stratifies samples because it selects sample items in proportion to their dollar values
   2. Is unaffected by population item variability
   3. May result in a smaller sample size if there are few or no errors
   4. Is easier to implement than classical approaches

E. Disadvantages of PPS are that
   1. It is designed primarily to detect overstatements.
   2. Zero balance or negative sign items are presumed not to occur in PPS populations.
   3. It is a cookbook approach that is not intuitively as appealing to auditors as classical approaches.

COMPILATION ENGAGEMENTS AND REVIEW ENGAGEMENTS

A. CPAs may not be associated with unaudited financial statements of nonpublic companies unless they are reviewed or compiled.
   1. Unaudited statements of public companies are covered by AU 504.
   2. The AICPA has issued to date seven Statements on Standards for Accounting and Review Services (SSARSs) that apply to unaudited statements of nonpublic entities. These have been codified in section AR of AICPA Professional Standards (Vol. II).

B. **AR 100**, *Compilation and Review of Financial Statements*
   1. CPAs may compile financial statements from client data without performing any auditing or other procedures.
      a. This write-up work simply involves presenting management's assertions without expressing any assurance on the statements.
      b. The accountant need only be familiar with the client and its business, read the statements, and check clerical accuracy.
      c. A compilation report consists of two paragraphs.
         1) The first states that the statements were compiled in accordance with SSARSs.
         2) The second states what a compilation is, that no audit or review was undertaken, and that no opinion or other assurance is expressed.
   2. When CPAs undertake review engagements, they express limited assurance based upon inquiry and analytical procedures.
      a. A review does not include
         1) Evaluation of internal control
         2) Tests of transactions and account balances
         3) Other auditing procedures
      b. An accountant's review report consists of three paragraphs.
         1) The scope paragraph states that a **review** was performed in accordance with SSARSs and that the information is the representation of management.
         2) A review consists principally of inquiries of company personnel and analytical procedures applied to the financial data. The accountant is also required to obtain a representation letter from management. It does not constitute an audit in accordance with GAAS, and thus no opinion is expressed.
         3) The accountant states that (s)he is not aware of any material modifications that should be made to the financial statements to conform with GAAP.

3. If accountants undertaking compilation and review engagements believe that the financial statements are not in conformity with GAAP, they must have the client make necessary corrections or make the necessary disclosures in their compilation or review report.

C. **AR 200**, *Reporting on Comparative Statements,* establishes standards for reporting on comparative financial statements of nonpublic entities when financial statements of one or more periods presented have been compiled or reviewed.

D. **AR 300**, *Compilation Reports on Financial Statements Included in Certain Prescribed Forms,* provides an alternative compilation report for financial statements included in a prescribed form (e.g., of a regulatory body) that calls for a departure from GAAP. It also provides further guidance applicable to reports on financial statements included therein.

E. **AR 400**, *Communications between Predecessor and Successor Accountants,* concerns communications by a successor accountant with his/her predecessor regarding acceptance of an engagement to compile or review financial statements of a nonpublic entity.

F. **AR 600**, *Reporting on Personal Financial Statements Included in Written Personal Financial Plans,* provides an exemption from AR 100 for personal financial statements included in written personal financial plans prepared by an accountant if the statement will be used solely by the client and his/her advisers and will not be used for any other purpose than to develop the client's personal financial goals and objectives.

OTHER AUDIT REPORT CONCEPTS

A. Financial statements that disclose segment data (see SFAS 14, *Financial Reporting for Segments of a Business Enterprise*) require special audit procedures and appropriate reflection in the audit report.

B. If a qualified opinion or disclaimer of opinion is expressed, negative assurance is inappropriate. Thus, a statement that "nothing has come to our attention indicating the financial statements are not fairly presented" should not be included.

C. Audit reports are usually dated as of the last day of field work.

D. Auditors have a responsibility to determine that other data appearing in documents containing audited financial statements do not conflict with the data in the audited statements.

E. Auditors are responsible for events occurring subsequent to year-end, and prior to the issuance of the audit report.

F. Auditors also have a responsibility for making disclosures after issuance of audit reports if information comes to their attention that would have affected their audit report had they known it at the time of issuance.

G. Instead of the standard report, a longer, more analytical report may be issued.

H. Auditors may issue reports on

1. Financial statements prepared on a comprehensive basis of accounting other than GAAP
2. Specific elements, accounts, or items of statements
3. Compliance with contractual or regulatory provisions
4. Information on prescribed forms
5. Internal control
6. The application of accounting principles

I. Auditors may be requested to issue special letters to underwriters that are issuing securities of a client.

J. Accountants may undertake limited reviews of interim statements based on inquiry and analytical procedures.

STUDY UNIT 18
INCOME TAXES

INTRODUCTION

Taxes are tested in Parts 1, 2, and 4. The intended emphasis by the ICMA is now on a user's rather than a preparer's point of view. Prior to 1991, CMA tax questions were very much like CPA corporate tax questions. Now, they focus on how to account for income tax expense and the tax implications for business decisions.

Part 1 - Tax code provisions that affect financing and capital structure decisions, such as deductibility of payments for use of capital and after-tax cost of capital

Part 2 - Accounting for corporate income taxes

a. Differences between book and tax income arising from differences between tax regulations and GAAP

b. Deferred income taxes

c. Accounting for net operating losses

d. Tax rate considerations

e. Other special issues regarding deferred income taxes

Part 4 - The impact of income taxes on operational decisions, including operating income subject to income taxes, gains and losses subject to income taxes, and tax credits

This study unit provides an overview of what we believe will be tested as tax and tax-related questions in Parts 1, 2, and 4. Deferred taxes is a financial accounting topic covered in Study Unit 13, Special Financial Reporting Problems, which begins on page 374. Also see the following sideheadings: The Objectives of the Firm and Its Managers (page 153) and Financial Structure, Leverage, and the Cost of Capital (page 184).

The ICMA Content Specification Outlines do not specify income taxes as a separate topic. Rather, tax issues are buried in the Content Specification Outlines for Parts 1, 2, and 4 as explained above. The two-page outline beginning on page 469 is designed to provide you with the necessary knowledge to respond to CMA tax-related questions.

The following two questions have been the only tax multiple-choice questions since December 1990. They appear complete with explanations in Study Unit 18 of Volume II.

(CMA 1291, 2-11) None of the following items is deductible in calculating taxable income except

a. Bad debt expense computed under the reserve method.

b. Estimated liabilities for product warranties expected to be incurred in the future.

c. Dividends on common stock declared but not payable until next year.

d. Bonus accrued but not paid by the end of the year to a cash-basis 90% shareholder.

e. Vacation pay accrued on an employee-by-employee basis.

(CMA 1291, 2-12) All of the following are adjustments/preference items to corporate taxable income in calculating alternative minimum taxable income except

a. Gains or losses from long-term contracts.

b. All of the gain on an installment sale of real property in excess of $150,000.

c. Mining exploration and development costs.

d. A charitable contribution of appreciated property.

e. Sales commission earned in 1990 but paid in 1991.

The following MACRS depreciation table appeared in a capital budgeting problem *(CMA 1290, 4-5)* that required an understanding of MACRS depreciation. Similar questions appeared on the 1993 exams.

	MACRS 3-Year	Present Value of $1 Received at the End of the Period		Present Value of an Ordinary Annuity of $1 Received at the End of Each Period	
Year	Rate	12%	20%	12%	20%
1	33.3%	.89	.83	.89	.83
2	44.5%	.80	.69	1.69	1.52
3	14.8%	.71	.58	2.40	2.10
4	7.4%	.64	.48	3.04	2.58
5	--	.57	.40	3.61	2.98

A problem requiring conversion of an income statement to taxable income appeared on the December 1992 exam. It required the knowledge that only actual bad debts, warranty expense, and losses on investments can be deducted for tax purposes. Candidates also needed to understand the dividends-received deduction and the deductibility of interest expense that finances investments in tax-exempt bonds. This computational question is in Study Unit 18 of Volume II.

GENERAL PRINCIPLES AND DEFINITIONS

A. A C corporation is subject to tax liability imposed on its income.

B. **Gross income** means all income from whatever source derived (unless excluded by statute).

1. Income is considered realized when certain transactions occur.
   a. Mere increases in value (appreciation) do not create income.
      1) EXAMPLE: Land owned by a corporation increases in value from $5,000 to $20,000 per acre. There is no income until the land is sold or exchanged.
   b. Transactions are normally in the form of a sale, an exchange, or the rendering of services.
   c. Taxation of realized income may be excluded or deferred, for example, upon exchange of like-kind property.
   d. The term "recognized" is used when income is realized and also taxed.
   e. Nonresident aliens (including foreign corporations) are, generally, subject to federal income tax on U.S.-source income.

C. **Deductions** are those expenses and other statutorily prescribed items that are subtracted from gross income to determine taxable income.

1. Deductions should be distinguished from **exclusions**. Exclusions are never included in gross income (e.g., interest on tax-exempt bonds).

D. **Taxable income** is gross income minus deductions.

1. Taxable income is analogous to net income.
2. The tax rates are applied to taxable income to determine the tax liability.

E. **Credits** are subtracted from the tax liability.

1. Credits directly reduce taxes, while deductions reduce taxable income upon which the taxes are computed.

F. **Book Income versus Taxable Income**

1. CMA candidates are required to understand the difference between book income and taxable income. Problems may begin with book income, list numerous transactions, and require the adjustments necessary to arrive at taxable income.
2. The following adjustments are necessary to adjust book income to taxable income:
   a. Add to book income
      1) Federal income tax
      2) Excess of capital losses over capital gains
      3) Taxable income not reported on books
      4) Expenses reported on books but not deducted on tax return (e.g., charitable contributions in excess of limit)
   b. Subtract from book income
      1) Income reported on books but not included on tax return (e.g., interest income from tax-exempt municipal bonds)
      2) Deductions on tax return but not reported on books (e.g., dividends-received deduction)

3. These adjustments are the fundamental differences between net income for financial accounting purposes (book income) and taxable income. Therefore, the discussion of income and deductions in this study unit will concentrate on these differences and assume that candidates can already compute book (i.e., accrual accounting) income.

4. According to generally accepted accounting principles (SFAS 109), accounting for income taxes (interperiod tax allocation) is based on the asset and liability method (see Study Unit 13).

G. **Temporary Differences**

1. Depreciation expense arises from using different methods for tax and book purposes.

2. Bad debt expense. Direct write-off method is used for tax purposes and allowance method (estimating expenses) is used for book purposes.

3. Warranty expense. For tax purposes, it is deductible only when paid, even if reserves based on estimates are used for book purposes.

4. Charitable contributions exceeding 10% of corporate taxable income before charitable contributions and special deductions are deductible during the 5 succeeding tax years.

5. Capital losses in excess of capital gains are not deductible in the current year. Instead, a net capital loss must be carried back 3 years (as a short-term capital loss) and applied towards any capital gains. Any loss remaining can be carried forward for 5 years. Capital losses can be used only to offset capital gains (i.e., ordinary income is unaffected).

6. Prepaid rent income is included in taxable income when received. Prepaid rent expense is deductible in computing taxable income for the period to which it is attributable.

7. The cost of certain intangibles (e.g., goodwill) acquired in connection with the conduct of a trade or business or income-producing activity is amortized over a 15-year period, beginning with the month in which the intangible is acquired.

8. Organization costs are amortizable over not less than 60 months for tax purposes.

H. **Permanent Differences**

1. Life insurance premiums paid on key persons are not deductible if the corporation is the beneficiary. Proceeds from the policy are not taxed.

2. Dividends-received deduction. 70% of dividends received from taxable domestic corporations are deductible by a distributee corporation that owns less than 20% of the stock of the distributing corporation. The percentage deductible is 80 if the distributee owns 20% to 80% of the distributing corporation. A 100% dividend-received deduction is permitted for dividends received among members of an affiliated group of corporations (80% ownership).

3. Federal income tax expense is not deductible in computing taxable income.

4. Tax-exempt interest is included in book income. Expense attributable to earning it is not deductible for tax purposes.

5. Business gifts exceeding $25 are generally not deductible for income tax purposes.

6. Compensation in excess of $1 million paid to the chief executive officer and certain other employees is not deductible in computing taxable income. Premiums, tax-free benefits, and compensation based on performance goals are excluded from the $1 million limit.

CHAPTER SEVEN
EXAM PART 3
MANAGEMENT REPORTING, ANALYSIS, AND BEHAVIORAL ISSUES

The ICMA Content Description of Part 3 follows:

A. ***Cost Measurement (20% - 30%)***
Cost concepts, flows and terminology; alternative cost objectives; cost measurement concepts; cost accumulation systems including job order costing, process costing, and activity-based costing; overhead cost allocation to cost objectives.

B. ***Planning (20% - 30%)***
Strategic plans; purposes of budgeting; budgeting concepts; annual profit plans and supporting schedules; financial budgeting including fixed assets, cash flow, and statement of financial position.

C. ***Control and Performance Evaluation (20% - 30%)***
Factors to be analyzed for control and performance evaluation including revenues, costs, profits, and investment in assets; techniques to control and evaluate operations including variance analysis based on flexible budgets and standard costs; techniques to evaluate and report performance including responsibility accounting for revenue, cost, contribution and profit centers.

D. ***Behavioral Issues (20% - 30%)***
Alignment of managerial and organizational goals; behavioral issues in developing and using budgets and standards; behavioral and communication issues in reporting and performance evaluation including segment reporting, transfer pricing, and allocation of common costs.

With the 1990 revision of the CMA exam, the ICMA has published a content specification outline for Part 3 that expands the above Content Description for Part 3.

Cost Measurement (20% - 30%)

1. *Cost concepts and flows*
   a. *Alternative cost objectives*
   b. *Cost terminology*
2. *Cost measurement concepts*
   a. *Cost behavior*
   b. *Method of charging to cost objects*
   c. *Alternative measurement concepts*
   d. *Joint product and by-product costing*
   e. *Historical versus replacement cost*
3. *Cost accumulation systems*
   a. *Operation costing*
   b. *Constant flow manufacturing*
   c. *Activity-based costing*
   d. *Job order costing*
   e. *Process costing*
4. *Alternative methods for accumulating and assigning overhead costs to products and services*
   a. *Considerations in measuring and assigning overhead*
   b. *Plant-wide versus departmental overhead*
   c. *Allocation of service department costs*

A. ***Planning (20% - 30%)***

1. *Hierarchy of planning*
   a. *Mission and strategic goals*
   b. *Strategic objectives and plans*
   c. *Tactical objectives and plans*
   d. *Operational objectives and plans*
   e. *Contingency plans*
2. *Purposes of budgeting*
   a. *Plan operations and performance goals*
   b. *Implement plans and motivate people*
   c. *Frame of reference for performance evaluation*
   d. *Communicate and coordinate activities among organizational units*
   e. *Authorize action*
3. *Budget concepts*
   a. *Relating planning to organizational structure*
   b. *The budget process*
   c. *Mechanics in budgeting*
   d. *Types of budget systems*

4. *Annual profit plan and the supporting schedules*
   a. *Sales budget*
   b. *Production budget*
   c. *Direct materials budget*
   d. *Direct labor budget*
   e. *Overhead budget*
   f. *Cost of goods sold budget*
   g. *Selling and administrative budget*
   h. *Budget for acquisition of capital assets*
   i. *Cash budget and cash management plans*
   j. *Pro forma income statement*
   k. *Pro forma statement of financial position*
   l. *Pro forma statement of cash flows*

B. ***Control and Performance Evaluation (20% - 30%)***
   1. *Factors to be analyzed for control and performance evaluation*
      a. *Regular operations*
      b. *Investment base and financing costs*
      c. *Product quality*
   2. *Techniques to control and evaluate operations*
      a. *Comparison of actual results to the annual budget*
      b. *Use of flexible budgets to analyze performance*
      c. *Types of variation measures*
      d. *Use of standard cost systems*
   3. *Techniques to evaluate and report performance*
      a. *Type of responsibility segments*
      b. *Factors needed to exercise control*
      c. *Reporting in a responsibility setting*
      d. *Divisional performance measures*

C. ***Behavioral Issues (20% - 30%)***
   1. *Alignment of managerial and organizational goals*
      a. *Goal congruence with respect to purpose and use of budgets and standards*
      b. *Establishing authority and responsibility for activities*
   2. *Behavioral issues in developing budgets and standards*
      a. *Approaches to development of budgets and standards*
      b. *Advantages to participatory development*
      c. *Potential problems of participatory development*
   3. *Behavioral issues in reporting and performance evaluation*
      a. *Frequency and form of performance feedback*
      b. *Controllability of costs for accountability*
      c. *Arbitrary allocations of common costs*
      d. *Use of flexible budgets rather than static budgets*
      e. *Multiple measures of performance*
      f. *Specific issues related to segment reporting*

The topics and subject areas above may include ethical considerations in management reporting, analysis, and behavioral issues of concern to management accountants.

Statement on Management Accounting No. 1C, Standards of Ethical Conduct for Management Accountants

• Competence • Confidentiality • Integrity • Objectivity

Manipulation of analyses and results
Unethical behavior in developing budgets and standards

The ICMA's content specification outline indicates 20% to 30% of Part 3 will be devoted to behavioral issues related to goal congruence, budgeting and other standard setting activities, reporting, and performance evaluation. We do not present separate outlines for this major topic because behavioral issues should logically be integrated with a variety of related technical subjects. We believe the ICMA is likely to combine technical and behavioral matters in a single essay question.

The following contain substantial behavior-oriented material: Study Unit 7: Organization Theory, Study Unit 8: Motivation and the Directing Process, Study Unit 21: Planning, Study Unit 22: Budgeting, Study Unit 23: The Controlling Process, and Study Unit 25: Responsibility Accounting.

Ethics will be covered on at least two parts of the examination and will have between 30 and 60 total minutes of coverage (out of 16 hours of testing), i.e., 3% to 6% of the total exam.

STUDY UNIT 19
PROCESS AND JOB-ORDER COSTING

INTRODUCTION

Cost and managerial accounting are obviously important topics on the CMA examination. Questions and problems on cost measurement, planning, and control and performance evaluation are expected to account for 60% to 90% of Part 3. The balance of coverage concerns related behavioral issues (and possibly ethics questions). Managerial accounting is essential to planning and controlling operations. For example, standard costing permits the monitoring and controlling of production efficiency. Traditional cost accounting is also important for both internal and external reporting. However, standard costing and variable costing are sufficiently significant to be treated in separate study units.

COST AND MANAGERIAL ACCOUNTING DEFINITIONS

Abnormal spoilage is spoilage that is not expected to occur under normal, efficient operating conditions. The cost of abnormal spoilage should be separately identified and reported to management. Abnormal spoilage is typically treated as a period cost (a loss) because of its unusual nature.

Absorption (full) costing is the accounting method that considers all manufacturing costs as product costs. These costs include variable and fixed manufacturing costs whether direct or indirect.

Activity-based costing "identifies the causal relationship between the incurrence of cost and activities, determines the underlying driver of the activities, establishes cost pools related to individual drivers, develops costing rates, and applies cost to product on the basis of resources consumed (drivers)" (SMA 2A).

Applied (absorbed) overhead is factory (manufacturing) overhead allocated to products or services, usually on the basis of a predetermined rate. Overhead is over- or underapplied (absorbed) when overhead charged is greater (less) than overhead incurred.

Avoidable costs are those that may be eliminated by not engaging in an activity or by performing it more efficiently.

Breakeven analysis is a means of predicting the relationships among revenues, variable costs, and fixed costs at various production levels. It allows management to discern the probable effects of changes in sales volume, sales price, costs, product mix, etc.

Budgeting is the formal quantification of management's plans. Budgets are usually expressed in quantitative terms and are used to motivate management and evaluate its performance in achieving goals. In this sense, standards are established.

Budget variance (also known as the flexible-budget variance or spending variance) is the difference between actual and budgeted fixed overhead in a four-way analysis of overhead variances. In three-way analysis, the spending variance combines the variable overhead spending variance and the fixed overhead budget variance. In two-way analysis, the budget (flexible-budget or controllable) variance is that part of the total overhead variance not attributed to the production volume variance.

By-products are products of relatively small total value that are produced simultaneously from a common manufacturing process with products of greater value and quantity (joint products).

Committed costs result when a going concern holds fixed assets (property, plant, and equipment). Examples are insurance, long-term lease payments, and depreciation.

Common (joint) costs are incurred in the production of two or more inseparable products up to the point at which the products become separable (the split-off point).

Contribution margin is calculated by subtracting all variable costs from sales revenue. Variable costs include both manufacturing variable costs and variable selling and general costs. Fixed costs (whether manufacturing or not) are not deducted. The contribution margin ratio equals unit contribution margin divided by unit sales price.

Controllable costs are directly regulated by management at a given level of production within a given time span; e.g., fixed costs are not controllable.

Controller (or comptroller) is a financial officer having responsibility for the accounting functions (management and financial) as well as budgeting and the internal control structure.

Conversion costs are direct labor and factory overhead, the costs of converting raw materials into finished goods.

Cost. In SMA 2A, the IMA defines cost as follows: "(1) In management accounting, a measurement in monetary terms of the amount of resources used for some purpose. The term by itself is not operational. It becomes operational when modified by a term that defines the purpose, such as acquisition cost, incremental cost, or fixed cost. (2) In financial accounting, the sacrifice measured by the price paid or required to be paid to acquire goods or services. The term 'cost' is often used when referring to the valuation of a good or service acquired. When 'cost' is used in this sense, a cost is an asset. When the benefits of the acquisition (the goods or services) expire, the cost becomes an expense or loss."

Cost accounting includes (1) managerial accounting in the sense that its purpose can be to provide internal reports for use in planning and control and in making nonroutine decisions, and (2) financial accounting because its product costing function satisfies requirements for reporting externally to shareholders, government, and various outside parties.

Cost allocation is the process of assigning and reassigning costs to cost objects. It may also be defined as a distribution of costs that cannot be directly assigned to the cost objects that are assumed to have caused them. In this sense, allocation involves choosing a cost object, determining the direct and indirect costs traceable thereto, deciding how costs are to be accumulated in cost pools before allocation, and selecting the allocation base. Allocation is necessary for product costing, pricing, investment decisions, managerial performance evaluation, profitability analysis, make-or-buy decisions, etc.

Cost center is a responsibility center that is accountable for costs only.

Cost driver "is a measure of activity, such as direct labor hours, machine hours, beds occupied, computer time used, flight hours, miles driven, or contracts, that is a causal factor in the incurrence of cost to an entity" (SMA 2A).

Cost objects are the intermediate and final dispositions of cost pools. Intermediate cost objects receive temporary accumulations of costs as the cost pools move from their originating points to the final cost objects. Final cost objects, such as a job, product, or process, should be logically linked with the cost pool based on a cause and effect relationship.

Cost pools are accounts in which a variety of similar cost elements with a common cause are accumulated prior to allocation to cost objects on some common basis. The overhead account is a cost pool into which various types of overhead are accumulated prior to their allocation. In activity-based accounting, a cost pool is established for each activity.

Cost of goods manufactured is equivalent to a retailer's purchases. It equals all manufacturing costs incurred during the period, plus beginning work-in-process, minus ending work-in-process.

Cost of goods sold equals beginning finished goods inventory, plus cost of goods manufactured (or purchases), minus ending finished goods inventory.

Cost-volume-profit (See breakeven analysis.)

Differential (incremental) cost is the difference in total cost between two decisions.

Direct cost is one that can be specifically associated with a single cost object in an economically feasible way.

Direct (variable) costing (See variable costing.)

Direct labor costs are wages paid to labor that can feasibly be specifically identified with the production of finished goods.

Direct materials costs are the costs of raw materials included in finished goods that can feasibly be traced to those goods.

Direct method of service cost allocation apportions service department costs directly to production departments. It makes no allocation of services rendered to other service departments.

Discretionary costs are characterized by uncertainty about the relationship between input (the costs) and the value of the related output. They also tend to be the subject of a periodic (e.g., annual) outlay decision. Advertising and research costs are examples.

Efficiency variances (e.g., for direct materials or labor) compare the actual use of inputs with the budgeted quantity of inputs allowed for the activity level achieved. When the difference is multiplied by the budgeted unit price, the resulting variance isolates the cost effect of using more or fewer units of input than budgeted. An efficiency variance is the sum of a mix variance and a yield variance.

Engineered costs are costs having a clear relationship to output. Direct materials cost is an example.

Equivalent unit of production is a set of inputs required to manufacture one physical unit. Calculating equivalent units for each factor of production facilitates measurement of output and cost allocation when work-in-process exists.

Factory (manufacturing) overhead consists of all costs other than direct materials and direct labor that are associated with the manufacturing process. It includes both fixed and variable costs.

Fixed costs remain unchanged within the relevant range for a given period despite fluctuations in activity. Per unit fixed costs do change as the level of activity changes.

Full cost is the absorption cost plus a share of selling and administrative costs.

Gross margin (profit) is the difference between sales and the full absorption (inventory) cost of goods sold. It should be contrasted with contribution margin (sales – variable costs).

Imputed costs require no dollar outlay but should be considered in decision making. An example of an imputed cost is the profit lost as a result of being unable to fill orders because the inventory level is too low.

Indirect costs cannot be specifically associated with a given cost object in an economically feasible way. They are also defined as costs that are not directly identified with one final cost object but that are identified with two or more final cost objects or with at least one intermediate cost object.

Investment center is a responsibility center that is accountable for revenues (markets), costs (sources of supply), and invested capital.

Job-order cost system of accounting is appropriate when producing products with individual characteristics and/or when identifiable groupings are possible, e.g., batches of certain styles or types of furniture. The unique aspect of job-order costing is the identification of costs to specific units or a particular job.

Joint products are two or more separate products produced by a common manufacturing process from a common input. The common (joint) costs of two or more joint products with significant values are allocated to the joint products based upon their net realizable values at the point they become separate.

Managerial accounting primarily concerns the planning and control of organizational operations, considers nonquantitative information, and is usually less precise than cost accounting.

Margin of safety is the excess of budgeted revenues over the breakeven point.

Marginal cost is the sum of the costs necessary to effect a one-unit increase in the activity level.

Mix variances measure the effects of changes in the proportions of various inputs, e.g., different mixes of direct materials or labor. (See also sales mix variance.)

Mixed (semivariable) costs combine fixed and variable elements.

Net realizable value is an alternative to the relative sales value method.

Normal capacity is the long-term average level of activity that will approximate demand over a period that includes seasonal, cyclical, and trend variations. Deviations in 1 year will be offset in subsequent years.

Normal costing (vs. actual costing) charges product costs based on actual direct labor and materials but applies overhead on the basis of budgeted (normalized) rates.

Normal spoilage is the spoilage that occurs under normal operating conditions. It is essentially uncontrollable in the short run. Normal spoilage arises under efficient operations and is treated as a product cost.

Operation costing is a hybrid of job-order and process costing systems. It is used by companies that manufacture goods that undergo some similar and some dissimilar processes. Operation costing accumulates total conversion costs and determines a unit conversion cost for each operation. However, direct materials costs are charged specifically to products as in job order systems.

Opportunity cost is the maximum benefit forgone by using a scarce resource for a given purpose. It is the benefit provided by the next best use of that resource.

Period costs are expensed when incurred. They are not inventoriable because they are not sufficiently identifiable with specific production.

Practical capacity is the maximum level at which output is produced efficiently. It usually results in underapplied overhead.

Price variance equals the difference between the actual and standard price of an input, multiplied by the actual quantity.

Prime costs are the costs of direct materials and labor.

Process costing should be used to assign costs to similar products that are mass produced on a continuous basis. Costs are accumulated by departments or cost centers rather than by jobs, work-in-process is stated in terms of equivalent units, and unit costs are established on a departmental basis. Process costing is an averaging process that calculates the average cost of all units.

Product (inventoriable) costs are directly or indirectly incurred to produce units of output and are deferred to future periods to the extent output is not sold.

Profit center is a segment of a company responsible for both revenues and costs. A profit center has the authority to make decisions concerning markets (revenues) and sources of supply (costs).

Quantity (usage) variance is an efficiency variance for direct materials.

Rate variance is a price variance for direct labor.

Reciprocal method uses simultaneous equations to allocate each service department's costs among the departments providing mutual services before reallocation to other users.

Relative sales value method is used to allocate joint costs at split-off to joint products based upon their relative proportions of total sales revenue ultimately attributable to the period's production. An alternative is to use estimated final net realizable value (final sales value – costs of completion and costs of sale) to allocate joint cost.

Relevant costs are those expected future costs that vary with the action taken. All other costs are assumed to be constant and thus have no effect on (are irrelevant to) the decision.

Relevant range is the range of activity (production volume) within which variable unit costs are constant and fixed costs are constant in total. In this range, the incremental cost of one additional unit of production is the same.

Residual income is the excess of the return on an investment over a targeted amount equal to an imputed interest charge on invested capital. The rate used is ordinarily the weighted-average cost of capital. Some enterprises prefer to measure managerial performance in terms of the amount of residual income rather than the percentage ROI. The principle is that the enterprise is expected to benefit from expansion as long as residual income is earned. Using a percentage ROI approach, expansion might be rejected if it lowered ROI even though residual income would increase.

Responsibility accounting stresses that managers should be held responsible only for factors under their control. To achieve this purpose, the operations of the business are organized into responsibility centers. Costs are classified as controllable and noncontrollable to assign responsibility, which implies that some revenues and costs can be changed through effective management. A responsibility accounting system should have certain controls to provide feedback reports indicating deviations from expectations. Management may then focus on those deviations for either reinforcement or correction.

Revenue center in a responsibility accounting system is accountable for revenues only.

Sales mix variance measures the effect on the contribution margin of a change in the projected proportions of the different products composing an entity's total sales.

Sales quantity variance is the product of the difference between actual and budgeted units sold and the budgeted average contribution margin for the budgeted sales mix.

Sales volume variance is the sum of the sales mix and sales quantity variances. It is the difference in the contribution margin attributable to the difference between actual sales and budgeted sales.

Scrap consists of raw materials left over from the production cycle but still usable for purposes other than those for which it was originally intended. Scrap may be sold to outside customers, usually for a nominal amount, or may be used for a different production process.

Separable costs are those incurred beyond the split-off point and identifiable with specific products.

Spending variance is an overhead variance. For variable overhead, it is the difference between actual costs and the product of the actual activity times the budgeted application rate. For fixed overhead, the spending (also known as the budget or flexible budget) variance is the difference between actual and budgeted fixed costs. In three-way analysis, the two spending variances isolated in four-way analysis are combined. In two-way analysis, the two spending variances and the variable overhead efficiency variance are combined.

Split-off point is the stage of production at which joint products and by-products are separable.

Spoilage (See abnormal spoilage and normal spoilage.)

Standard cost is a predetermined, attainable unit cost. Standard cost systems isolate deviations (variances) of actual from expected costs. Standard costs can be used with job-order and process costing systems.

Step-cost functions are nonlinear cost functions. These costs are constant over small ranges of output but increase by steps (discrete amounts) as levels of activity increase. They may be fixed or variable. If the steps are relatively narrow, these costs are usually treated as variable. If the steps are wide, they are more akin to fixed costs.

Step-down method of service department cost allocation is a sequential (but not a reciprocal) process. These costs are allocated to other service departments as well as to users. The process usually starts with the service department that renders the greatest percentage of its services to other service departments.

Sunk cost is a past cost or a cost that the entity has irrevocably committed to incur. Because it is unavoidable and will therefore not vary with the option chosen, it is not relevant to future decisions.

Theoretical (ideal) capacity is the maximum capacity assuming continuous operations with no holidays, downtime, etc.

Transfer price is the price charged in an intracompany transaction.

Transferred-in costs are those incurred in a preceding department and received in a subsequent department in a multi-department production setting.

Treasurer has the responsibility for safeguarding financial assets (including the management of cash) and arranging financing.

Variable cost is an operating expense that varies directly and proportionately with activity. (See fixed costs.)

Variable (direct) costing considers only variable manufacturing costs to be product costs, i.e., inventoriable. Fixed manufacturing costs are considered period costs and are expensed as incurred.

Variance analysis concerns deviations of actual costs from budgeted amounts. (See entries for specific variances.)

Volume (idle capacity or production volume) variance is the amount of under- or overapplied fixed factory overhead. It is the difference between budgeted overhead and the amount applied based on a predetermined rate and the standard input allowed for actual output. It measures the use of capacity rather than specific cost outlays.

Waste is the amount of raw materials left over from a production process or production cycle for which there is no further use. Waste is usually not salable at any price and must be discarded.

Work-in-process (manufacturing) account is used to accumulate the costs of goods that have been placed in production but have not yet been completed.

Yield variances determine the effect of varying the total input of a factor of production (e.g., direct materials or labor) while holding constant the input mix (the proportions of the types of materials or labor used) and the weighted-average unit price of the factor of production.

PROCESS COSTING

A. Process costing is accounting for the costs of manufacturing. It is peculiar to inventoriable goods or services. The objective is to determine

   1. The portion of manufacturing cost that is to be expensed (because the goods or services were sold)
   2. The portion of manufacturing cost to be deferred (because the goods and services are still on hand)

B. Process costing can be distinguished from job-order costing in that it is used for continuous process manufacturing of units that are relatively homogeneous (e.g., oil refining and automobile production lines). Job-order costing is used when the production output is heterogeneous. It is discussed later in this study unit.

   1. Job-order costing is used to account for the cost of specific jobs or projects.
   2. The differentiation between process and job-order costing is often over-emphasized. Actually, job-order costing only requires subsidiary ledgers (to keep track of the specific jobs) for the same work-in-process (manufacturing) account and finished goods inventory account that are basic to process costing.

C. In process costing, materials, labor, and overhead are debited to the manufacturing (work-in-process) account when they are committed to the manufacturing process.

   1. Materials are usually accounted for in a separate account.

Materials inventory	$XXX	
Accounts payable or cash		$XXX

   2. When materials are transferred to the manufacturing work-in-process (WIP), the inventory account is credited.

Manufacturing WIP	$XXX	
Materials inventory		$XXX

   3. Direct labor is usually debited directly to the manufacturing account when the payroll is recorded. Any wages not attributable directly to production, e.g., those for janitorial services, are considered indirect labor and debited to overhead.

Manufacturing WIP	$XXX	
Overhead	XXX	
Wages payable		$XXX
Payroll taxes payable		XXX

   4. Overhead is a separate account to which all indirect expenses are debited.

      a. For example, supplies, plant depreciation, etc.

Overhead	$XXX	
Insurance expense		$XXX
Supplies expense		XXX
Depreciation expense (or accumulated depreciation)		XXX

      b. Overhead is credited and the manufacturing account is debited on some systematic basis.

Manufacturing WIP	$XXX	
Overhead		$XXX

         1) The objective is to charge all overhead incurred over a period of time, such as a year, to manufacturing work-in-process.

D. As goods are completed, their cost is credited to manufacturing and debited to finished goods inventory.

Finished goods inventory	$XXX	
Manufacturing WIP		$XXX

1. As the finished goods are sold, their cost is debited to cost of goods sold.

Cost of goods sold	$XXX	
Finished goods inventory		$XXX

2. The deferred manufacturing costs are accumulated in
   a. EWIP (ending manufacturing work-in-process)
   b. Ending inventory (EI) of finished goods
   c. EI of materials

   NOTE: Beginning and ending refer to the beginning and end of the time period under study, e.g., 1 day, 1 week, or 1 month.

3. The following T-account diagram illustrates the process:
   a. Each arrow represents a journal entry.
      1) Each transfer (arrow) indicates a credit to the original account and a debit to the next account in the sequence.

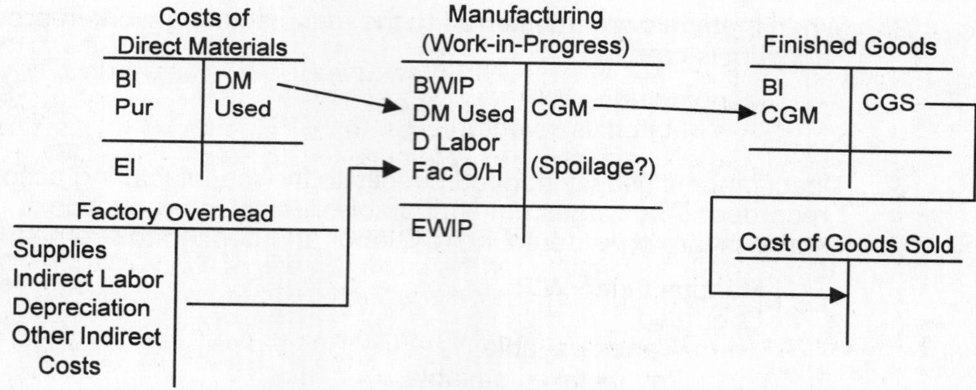

   b. Direct labor is debited to manufacturing directly from the payroll entry.
   c. For simplicity, a single overhead control account is shown. However, many accountants prefer to accumulate actual costs (debits) in the overhead control account and the amounts charged to work-in-process in a separate overhead applied account. This account will have a credit balance. Overhead applied is based on a predetermined rate (see Overhead Allocation on page 485).

4. All the debits to the manufacturing account are the total costs incurred and must equal (because debits equal credits) the sum of the following:
   a. Cost of goods manufactured
   b. EWIP (ending work-in-process)
   c. Spoilage
      1) If spoilage is abnormal (not inherent in the particular process), it can be charged off as a loss.
      2) If spoilage is normal, it should be included as part of the cost of goods manufactured.
5. Also, the number of units in BWIP plus those units added during the period can be accounted for in the same way; i.e., they are either completed and transferred to finished goods or spoiled goods, or incomplete (EWIP).
6. In each real account, the ending debit balance of the current period becomes the BI or BWIP for the next period.
7. The major problems are computing the cost of goods manufactured (CGM) and the cost of EWIP.
   a. This is an allocation
      1) **Of** total manufacturing costs (total debits in the manufacturing account) incurred each period
      2) **To** cost of goods manufactured (CGM), EWIP, and possibly spoilage
   b. The allocation is facilitated by computing equivalent units of production (EUP).

EQUIVALENT UNITS OF PRODUCTION (EUP)

A. Equivalent units of production (EUP) measure the amount of work performed in each production phase in terms of fully processed units during a given period. An equivalent unit of production is a set of inputs required to manufacture one physical unit. Calculating equivalent units for each factor of production facilitates measurement of output and cost allocation when work-in-process exists.
   1. Incomplete units are restated as the equivalent amount of completed units. The calculation is made separately for materials (transferred-in costs are treated as materials for this purpose) and conversion cost (direct labor and overhead).

B. **FIFO versus Weighted-Average Assumptions for EUP Calculations**
   1. One equivalent unit is the amount of conversion cost (direct labor and overhead) or direct materials cost required to produce one unit of finished goods.
      a. EUP are computed for both processing and direct materials.
      b. EXAMPLE: If 10,000 units in EWIP are 25% complete, they equal 2,500 (10,000 x 25%) equivalent units.
      c. Some units may be more advanced in the production process with respect to one factor than another; e.g., a unit may be 75% complete as to direct materials but only 15% complete as to direct labor.
         1) EXAMPLE: If EWIP is 25% complete, it is presumably 25% complete as to conversion costs. If material B is added at the 30% point, no equivalent units of B are in EWIP. Furthermore, EWIP is included in the computation of EUP for conversion costs, and material B is not.
   2. EUP cost allocation
      a. The objective is to allocate materials costs and processing (labor and overhead) costs to finished goods, EWIP, and, possibly, spoilage.
      b. Costs are allocated based on relative EUP.

3. Under the FIFO assumption, only the costs incurred this period are allocated between finished goods and EWIP. Beginning inventory costs are maintained separately from current period costs.
   a. Goods finished this period are costed separately as either started last period and completed this period or started this period and completed this period.
   b. The FIFO method determines equivalent units by subtracting the work done on the BWIP in the prior period from the weighted-average total.
4. The weighted-average assumption averages all materials and all processing (conversion) costs (both those incurred this period and those in BWIP).
   a. Thus, no differentiation is made between goods started in the preceding and the current periods.
   b. The result is that weighted-average EUP differs from FIFO EUP by the amount of EUP in beginning work-in-process.
      1) EUP under weighted average is equal to the EUP transferred to finished goods plus the EUP in ending work-in-process.
         a) Total EUP completed in beginning work-in-process are not deducted.
5. Example of the weighted-average assumption
   a. Roy Company manufactures Product X in a two-stage production cycle in Departments A and B. Direct materials are added at the beginning of the process in Department B. Roy uses the weighted-average method. BWIP (6,000 units) for Department B was 50% complete as to conversion costs. EWIP (8,000 units) was 75% complete. During February, 12,000 units were completed and transferred out of Department B. An analysis of the costs relating to WIP and production activity in Department B for February follows:

	Transferred-In Costs	Materials Costs	Conversion Costs
BWIP	$12,000	$2,500	$1,000
Costs added	29,000	5,500	5,000

The total cost per equivalent unit transferred out is equal to the unit cost for transferred-in costs, materials costs, and conversion costs. Transferred-in costs are by definition 100% complete. Given that materials are added at the beginning of the process in Department B, all units are complete as to materials. Conversion costs are assumed to be uniformly incurred.

	Units	%	T-I	%	DM	%	CC
Completed	12	100	12	100	12	100	12
EWIP	8	100	8	100	8	75	6
Equivalent units			20		20		18

Transferred-in: $\frac{(\$12{,}000 + \$29{,}000)}{20{,}000 \text{ EUP}} = \$2.05$

Materials cost: $\frac{(\$2{,}500 + \$5{,}500)}{20{,}000 \text{ EUP}} = .40$

Conversion cost: $\frac{(\$1{,}000 + \$5{,}000)}{18{,}000 \text{ EUP}} = .33$

Total unit cost = $2.78

6. Example of the FIFO assumption

   a. The Cutting Department is the first stage of Mark Company's production cycle. BWIP for this department was 80% complete as to conversion costs and EWIP was 50% complete. Information as to conversion costs in the Cutting Department for January is given below.

	Units	CC
WIP at January 1	25,000	$ 22,000
Units started and costs incurred during January	135,000	143,000
Units completed and transferred to next department during January	100,000	

   When using the FIFO method of process costing, EUP for a period include only the work done that period and exclude any work done in a prior period. The total of conversion cost EUP for the period is calculated below.

	Units	Work Done in Current Period	CC (EUP)
BWIP	25,000	20%	5,000
Started & completed	75,000	100%	75,000
EWIP	60,000	50%	30,000
Total EUP			110,000

   The total of the conversion costs for the period is given as $143,000. Dividing by total EUP of 110,000 gives a unit cost of $1.30. The conversion cost of the EWIP inventory is equal to the EUP in EWIP (30,000) times the unit cost ($1.30) for the current period, or $39,000.

OVERHEAD ALLOCATION

A. Factory or manufacturing overhead is usually assigned to products based on a predetermined rate (e.g., $5 per direct labor hour or 75% of direct labor cost). The rate is determined by dividing budgeted overhead by budgeted volume (in hours or labor cost). This method of allocating overhead has several advantages.

   1. It smooths cost fluctuations that would otherwise occur as a result of fluctuations in production from period to period. Thus, higher overhead costs are not assigned to units produced in low production periods and vice versa.

   2. It is a simple method of charging overhead costs to units for inventory purposes because the quantity of the allocation base (e.g., direct labor hours) is ordinarily known for a batch of product.

B. The activity base for overhead allocation should have a high correlation with the incurrence of overhead. For example, as people work, overhead for general support services (such as janitorial costs) is incurred.

   1. Direct labor is often used, but machine hours could be more appropriate in a highly automated environment (but see the next sideheading, Activity-Based Costing).

   2. Other activity bases are units of output, value of output, units of direct materials, and cost of direct materials.

C. Actual production overhead costs are accumulated on the debit side of an account called manufacturing overhead. Overhead applied (allocated to product) is credited to this account. But a separate overhead applied account is often used.
   1. The overhead applied is debited to work-in-process.
   2. The journal entries are illustrated at C.4. under Process Costing on page 481.

D. Rarely will the overhead incurred equal the overhead applied at the end of the period.
   1. **Overapplied** overhead (a credit balance in manufacturing overhead) results when product costs are overstated because the
      a. Activity level was higher than expected, or
      b. Actual overhead costs were lower than expected.
   2. **Underapplied** overhead (a debit balance in manufacturing overhead) results when product costs are understated because the
      a. Activity level was lower than expected, or
      b. Actual overhead costs were higher than expected.
   3. The treatment of the balance in the manufacturing overhead account (over- or underapplied overhead) depends on the materiality of the amount.
      a. If the amount is immaterial, it is usually debited to cost of goods sold.

	Debit	Credit
Cost of goods sold	$XXX	
Manufacturing overhead		$XXX

      b. If the amount is material, it should theoretically be allocated to work-in-process, finished goods, and cost of goods sold on the basis of the currently applied overhead in each of the accounts. This procedure will restate inventory costs and cost of goods sold to the amounts actually incurred.
         1) EXAMPLE: If actual overhead equals $231,000 and applied overhead equals $220,000, allocate $11,000 of underapplied overhead (debit balance in manufacturing overhead) according to the applied overhead in cost of goods sold, work-in-process, and finished goods of $140,000, $50,000, and $30,000, respectively.

a) Cost of goods sold $\$11{,}000 \times \frac{\$140{,}000}{\$220{,}000} = \$7{,}000$

b) Work-in-process $\$11{,}000 \times \frac{\$50{,}000}{\$220{,}000} = \$2{,}500$

c) Finished goods $\$11{,}000 \times \frac{\$30{,}000}{\$220{,}000} = \$1{,}500$

         2) To record the allocation

	Debit	Credit
Cost of goods sold	$7,000	
Work-in-process	2,500	
Finished goods	1,500	
Manufacturing overhead		$11,000

ACTIVITY-BASED COSTING

A. SMA 2A, *Management Accounting Glossary*, defines an ABC system as one that "Identifies the causal relationship between the incurrence of cost and activities, determines the underlying driver of the activities, establishes cost pools related to individual drivers, develops costing rates, and applies cost to product on the basis of resources consumed (drivers)."

B. Thus, ABC determines the activities that will serve as cost objects and then accumulates a cost pool for each activity using the appropriate activity base (cost driver). It is a system that may be employed with job-order or process costing methods.

   1. For example, a traditional system might use a single indirect cost pool for the assembly department of a manufacturing operation, but ABC would designate multiple activities within that department (materials handling, testing, packaging, etc.) for the accumulation of costs, each based on the cost driver specific to that activity. Even throughput (the rate of production over a given time) is beginning to be used more often as an application base.

      a. The result is a more accurate application of costs because of the more detailed and focused methodology.

C. To create an ABC system to allocate indirect costs such as those traditionally included in factory overhead, the flow of the production processes must be analyzed and the activities within each must be defined. The cost driver for each activity is then determined.

   1. Direct labor (hours or dollars) has long been the most common base for allocating overhead, but it is not always relevant. Companies now use dozens of different allocation bases depending upon how activity affects overhead costs. The result is multiple cost pools.

      a. Other allocation bases include machine hours, raw materials costs, setup time, waiting time, number of engineering hours, number of requisitions or purchase orders, and number of units produced.

         1) One company recently reported that it used 37 different bases to allocate overhead, some of which were averages of several activities.

   2. Historically, direct labor was a larger component of total production cost than overhead and was usually the activity that drove (caused) overhead costs. Today, overhead is more likely to be a large component of total production cost, with direct labor often representing a small percentage. Indeed, direct labor itself may be treated as an indirect factory overhead cost in an automated factory.

      a. This development resulted from the increased use of computers and robotics. In many companies, direct labor is less than 10% of production cost.

      b. Allocating a very large cost (overhead) using a very small cost (direct labor) as a base is irrational. A small change in direct labor on a product can make a significant difference in total production cost, an effect that may rest on an invalid assumption about the relationship of the cost and the allocation base.

      c. Most overhead costs today vary in proportion to product diversity and the complexity of an operation. Direct labor is not a cost driver for most overhead costs.

      d. ABC is not new; it was suggested at least as early as 1908. However, ABC was not cost beneficial until the advent of widespread computer use because allocating overhead over several different bases is time-consuming if done manually.

      e. Moreover, ABC was not needed when overhead was low relative to direct labor. For example, assume that, in a traditional system, direct labor totaled $100 and factory overhead $10. If $60 of direct labor were incurred for Product A and $40 for Product B, the overhead allocation would be $6 to A and $4 to B. The total conversion costs for A and B would be $66 and $44, respectively.

1) But if the $10 of overhead represented setup costs, an ABC system would allocate the $10 on the basis of setup time, not direct labor. If equal amounts of setup time were required for A and B, total conversion cost would be $65 ($60 + $5) for A and $45 ($40 + $5) for B. These results differ very little from those obtained under the traditional direct labor system. When overhead is low in relation to direct labor cost, the gain in accuracy is minimal.

f. If the manufacturer in the example on the previous page replaces its direct laborers with robots and computers, overhead will be a greater proportion of production cost. If overhead is $100 and direct labor is $10 ($6 for A and $4 for B), the traditional overhead allocation would be $60 to A and $40 to B. The total conversion cost would be $66 ($60 + $6) and $44 ($40 + $4) for A and B, respectively.

1) The ABC allocation would be significantly different. If the $100 constituted setup cost, and again A and B required equal amounts of setup time, ABC would allocate $50 to each product, resulting in total conversion cost of $56 ($50 + $6) for A and $54 ($50 + $4) for B. The latter costs represent a 23% difference between direct-labor-based costing and reality.

3. ABC is ordinarily more useful when overhead costs are relatively high. Also, the more diverse a factory's product line, the more beneficial ABC will be.

a. Simple averaging procedures such as direct-labor-based costing are valid only when all products are absolutely uniform. Hence, a simple allocation basis in a factory with large and small machines and high-priced and low-cost labor that work together would not be very exact.

4. An ABC costing system will also be beneficial when a company's products have significant volume differences.

a. Comprehensive example. Assume that a company produces two similar products. Raw materials costs are $20 per unit, direct labor is $70 per unit, and factory overhead totals $20,000. The company produces 1,000 units of Product 1 and 100 units of Product 2. Using direct labor as the allocation base, costs are as follows:

	Product 1	Product 2
Raw materials	$ 20,000	$ 2,000
Direct labor	70,000	7,000
Overhead	18,182*	1,818**
Total cost	$108,182	$10,818
Cost per unit	$ 108.18	$108.18

* {[$70,000 ÷ ($70,000 + $7,000)] x $20,000}
** {[$7,000 ÷ ($70,000 + $7,000)] x $20,000}

Alternatively, assume that the overhead represents setup costs, with equal setup times required for the products. Thus, the $20,000 would be allocated equally under an ABC system. The ABC costs would be

	Product 1	Product 2
Raw materials	$ 20,000	$ 2,000
Direct labor	70,000	7,000
Overhead	10,000	10,000
Total cost	$100,000	$19,000
Cost per unit	$ 100.00	$190.00

Because of the low volume of Product 2, the difference between the traditional allocation base and ABC is significant. If the company were selling Product 2 at $150 each (resulting in an apparent unit profit of $41.82 based on the $108.18 direct-labor-based cost), it would be losing money on every sale.

b. As the previous example illustrates, differences in volume can distort cost allocations even when overhead is relatively low. The distortion is worse when overhead is a higher proportion of total costs. Assume that direct labor costs are only $10 per unit and that overhead totals $140,000. The traditional allocation basis would result in the following costs:

	Product 1	Product 2
Raw materials	$ 20,000	$ 2,000
Direct labor	10,000	1,000
Overhead	127,273*	12,727**
Total cost	$157,273	$15,727
Cost per unit	$ 157.27	$157.27

* {[$10,000 ÷ ($10,000 + $1,000)] x $140,000}
** {[$1,000 ÷ ($10,000 + $1,000)] x $140,000}

When the ABC system is used, the allocation of overhead setup costs based on equal setup times results in the following production costs:

	Product 1	Product 2
Raw materials	$ 20,000	$ 2,000
Direct labor	10,000	1,000
Overhead	70,000	70,000
Total cost	$100,000	$73,000
Cost per unit	$ 100.00	$730.00

Thus, the combination of relatively high overhead and a substantial difference in product volume results in unit costs for Product 1 and Product 2 that are 36.4% lower and 464% higher, respectively, than those computed using the traditional method.

1) The practical effect of this difference can be illustrated in a competitive bid situation for Product 1. A manager using direct-labor-based cost would bid some amount slightly greater than $157.27, and, after losing, would then wonder how a competitor could make a profit with a bid just over $100. The ABC system provides more relevant costing figures.

5. Allocating overhead using a direct labor base has the virtue of simplicity. Also, the cost of the information needed to use more than one activity base has been high relative to the benefits. Because of the advent of computers and related technology such as bar codes, however, the cost of processing cost information has decreased, and a system based upon multiple cost pools and cost drivers can now be profitably used. Companies have begun adopting ABC because of its ability to solve costing problems that conventional cost accounting either creates or fails to address.

a. These problems include suboptimal pricing, poor allocation of costs, and incorrect direction by management. For example, if overhead is allocated at 700% of direct labor, managers may try to reduce direct labor costs by $1 to reduce the amount of overhead allocated by $7. But the better decision is to ignore direct labor and concentrate on such cost-cutting efforts as eliminating setups, engineering changes, and movement of materials.

SERVICE DEPARTMENT COST ALLOCATION

A. Service department costs are considered part of overhead (indirect costs) and should be allocated to the production departments that use the service.

1. EXAMPLE: A hospital operates its own electricity generating plant. The cost of operating the plant should be assigned to the producing departments (e.g., radiology and obstetrics).
2. When service departments also render services to each other, their costs are usually allocated to each other before allocation to producing departments.
3. The entry to record such allocation would be

Radiology overhead	$XXX	
Obstetrics overhead	XXX	
Other	XXX	
Electrical generation cost		$XXX

B. A basis reflecting cause and effect should be used to allocate service department costs.

1. The number of kilowatt hours used by each producing department is probably the best allocation base for the hospital's electricity costs in the previous example.
2. If exact criteria are not available (departments often do not have their own electric meters), some other reasonable base should be used, e.g., electric capacity of each department.
3. Other examples of allocation bases
   a. Number of employees in the producing department, for allocation of personnel department costs
   b. Square footage, for building maintenance costs
   c. Passenger miles, for company airplane
   d. Machine time, for data processing service
4. Sometimes variable costs of service departments are allocated based on actual usage, and fixed costs are allocated with regard to peak requirements, maximum level of usage, etc.

C. The most widely used methods of service department allocation are (in increasing order of sophistication) the direct method, the step method, and the reciprocal method.

1. The **direct method** allocates service department costs directly to the producing departments without recognition of services provided among the service departments.
   a. EXAMPLE: Departments Y and Z were the only production departments using service department B, and on a relative basis used 60% and 40% of B's services. Department B had costs of $82,000. Y and Z would be allocated $49,200 and $32,800 of the costs, respectively, even though B provided services to other service departments (or received services from other service departments).
   b. Under the direct method, no attempt is made to allocate the costs incurred by one service department in providing services to other service departments.
   c. Allocations of service department costs are made only to production departments based on their relative use of services.

2. The **step method** (also called the step-down method) allocates service department costs to other service departments in addition to the producing departments. It involves a sequence of steps.

   a. The process begins with the service department that provides services to the greatest number of other service departments, that provides the greatest percentage of its services to other service departments, or that incurs the greatest costs in serving other service departments.

   b. The costs of the remaining service departments are allocated in the same manner, but no cost is assigned to service departments whose costs have already been allocated.

   c. The process continues until all service department costs are allocated.

   d. EXAMPLE: Departments K, L, and M provide services to each other and to producing departments Y and Z.

Total Cost		Percent of Services				
		K	L	M	Y	Z
$100,000	K	---	15%	5%	55%	25%
70,000	L	10%	---	9%	18%	63%
50,000	M	---	---	---	20%	80%
$220,000						

Department K's costs are allocated first because it provides service to two other service departments, provides the greatest percentage of its service to other service departments, and has incurred the greatest costs. L's costs are then allocated, followed by M's.

	K	L	M	Y	Z
Costs prior to allocation	$100,000	$70,000	$50,000	---	---
Allocation of K	(100,000)	15,000	5,000	$55,000	$ 25,000
Allocation of L		(85,000)	8,500	17,000	59,500
Allocation of M			(63,500)	12,700	50,800
	-0-	-0-	-0-	$84,700	$135,300

All $220,000 is allocated to producing departments Y and Z. Also, when L's costs were allocated, no costs were allocated back to K. L's total cost of $85,000 was allocated 9/90, 18/90, and 63/90.

3. The **reciprocal method** uses simultaneous equations to allocate costs of all reciprocal services among service departments.

   a. The step method considers only services rendered in one direction. In the previous example, the services provided by K to L were considered in the allocation, but not the services provided by L to K.

   b. The reciprocal method considers services from K to L and from L to K.

   c. If the information given in 2.d. above is used, and if all reciprocal services are recognized, the following equations result:

$$K \text{ (costs)} = \$100{,}000 + .10L$$
$$L \text{ (costs)} = \$\ 70{,}000 + .15K$$
$$M \text{ (costs)} = \$\ 50{,}000 + .05K + .09L$$

1) These algebraic equations can be solved simultaneously.

a) Substituting the equation for K into the L equation gives the value of L.

$$L = \$70,000 + .15(100,000 + .10L)$$
$$L = \$70,000 + \$15,000 + .015L$$
$$.985L = \$85,000$$
$$L = \$86,294$$

b) Substituting the value of L into the K equation gives the value of K.

$$K = \$100,000 + .10(\$86,294)$$
$$K = \$108,629$$

c) The M equation can then be solved by substituting the foregoing values of K and L.

$$M = \$50,000 + .05(\$108,629) + .09(\$86,294)$$
$$M = \$50,000 + \$5,431 + \$7,766$$
$$M = \$63,197$$

d) The allocation of the costs of K, L, and M is as follows:

	K	L	M	Y	Z
Costs prior to allocation	$100,000	$70,000	$50,000	---	---
Allocation of K	(108,629)	16,294	5,431	$59,746	$ 27,158
Allocation of L	8,629	(86,294)	7,766	15,533	54,366
Allocation of M			(63,197)	12,640	50,557
	-0-	-0-	-0-	$87,919	$132,081

d. For example, the $59,746 allocated to Y from K was 55% of K's total cost of $108,629.

JOINT PRODUCTS AND BY-PRODUCTS

A. Joint products are separate products created from processing a single set of inputs.

1. EXAMPLE: The processing of crude oil yields gasoline, fuel oil, diesel fuel, naphtha, and other residuals. These are the joint products.
2. Joint products (as well as by-products, discussed on page 494) are common to many industries, including beef processing, mining, lumber milling, tobacco, and chemicals.
3. Key terms in the discussion of joint products
   a. **Common costs** cannot be identified with a particular joint product. By definition, joint products have common costs until the split-off point.
      1) EXAMPLE: The cost of harvesting an oak tree for a lumber mill is a common cost. Thus, the various types and qualities of final wood product have this cost in common at this stage of production.
   b. **Split-off point** is the stage at which the joint products acquire separate identities. Costs incurred prior to this point are common costs; costs incurred after split-off are separable costs.

c. **Separable costs** can be identified with a particular joint product and allocated to a specific unit of output. They are the costs incurred for a specific product after the split-off point.

1) EXAMPLE: The cost of aging strip steaks is a separable cost for a meat packer.

B. For inventory costing purposes, common costs are often allocated to joint products based on the relative sales values at the split-off point of the production for the period.

1. Common costs are allocated as follows:

$$\frac{\textit{Relative sales value of product P}}{\textit{Relative sales value of all products}} \times \textit{Total common costs}$$

a. Estimated final sales values minus completion and selling costs (net realizable values) are an alternative to relative sales values.

b. A third possibility is to assign common costs on the basis of the number of units of each product at the split-off point. However, basing allocations on physical quantities (pounds, gallons, etc.) of joint products is usually not desirable because costs assigned may have no relationship to value. This method can be used when NRV is unavailable.

2. EXAMPLE: Products X and Y are joint products. Common costs are \$40,000, separable costs are \$20,000 for X and \$30,000 for Y, and 10,000 pounds of each product results. Final selling prices are \$6(X) and \$4(Y). Selling costs are negligible. Inventory costs are assigned as follows:

Net realizable value

$$X = (10{,}000 \textit{ units} \times \$6) - \$20{,}000 = \$40{,}000 \textit{ NRV}$$
$$Y = (10{,}000 \textit{ units} \times \$4) - \$30{,}000 = \$10{,}000 \textit{ NRV}$$

Common cost allocation

$$X = \frac{\$40{,}000}{\$50{,}000} \times \$40{,}000 = \$32{,}000 \text{ *}$$

$$Y = \frac{\$10{,}000}{\$50{,}000} \times \$40{,}000 = \$8{,}000 \text{ **}$$

Inventory costs

	X	Y
Common costs	\$32,000*	\$ 8,000**
Separable costs	20,000	30,000
	\$52,000	\$38,000

C. The decision to begin production must be made for joint products as a whole. Once the decision has been made to start production, the decision to continue processing beyond split-off is made separately for each product; i.e., common costs are ignored.

1. EXAMPLE: Management is considering selling product Y (in B.2. above) at the split-off point at a price of \$2 per pound.

a. The only costs relevant to this decision are the separable costs because they can be avoided by selling Y at the split-off point.

b. Total common costs are not affected by the decision to sell at split-off or process further.

D. **By-products** are joint products that are relatively insignificant in value in relation to overall production. One method for the initial recognition of by-products is to account for their sales value at the time of sale as a reduction in the cost of goods sold of the main products or as a separate revenue item. Thus, cost of sales does not exist for by-products. An alternative is to recognize the net realizable value at the time of production, a method that results in the recording of by-product inventory. Under this method, by-product revenue may also be recognized either as a reduction of cost of goods sold or as a separate revenue item.

1. Regardless of the timing of their recognition in the accounts, by-products usually do not receive an allocation of joint costs. The cost of this accounting treatment would ordinarily exceed the benefit.
2. It is acceptable to allocate joint costs to by-products as well as to joint products. In that case, they are treated as joint products despite their small relative values.
3. Although scrap is similar to a by-product, joint costs are almost never allocated to scrap.

JOB-ORDER COSTING

A. Job-order costing, in contrast to process costing, is concerned with accumulating costs by specific job. For example, determining the cost of a custom printing job requires job-order costing.

1. Units (jobs) should be dissimilar enough to warrant the special record keeping required by job-order costing.

B. Costs are recorded by classification (direct materials, direct labor, and manufacturing overhead) on a job-cost sheet specifically prepared for each job.

1. Job-cost sheets serve as a subsidiary ledger; i.e., the total of all job-cost sheets should equal the balance in the general ledger manufacturing (work-in-process) account. Under process costing, costs are kept in a single inventory account.
2. Source documents for costs incurred include stores' requisitions for direct materials and work (or time) tickets for direct labor.
3. Overhead is usually assigned to each job through a predetermined overhead rate, e.g., $3 of overhead for every direct labor hour.

C. Journal entries record direct materials, direct labor, and manufacturing overhead used for a specific job, (e.g., job number 32). The entries to transfer the cost of a completed job to finished goods are as follows:

1. They are similar to the entries used in process costing.

Work-in-process (Job 32)	$XXX	
Materials inventory		$XXX
Accrued payroll		XXX
Applied overhead		XXX

2. Costs are also recorded on a job-cost sheet for Job 32. The amount transferred to finished goods is the total cost of Job 32, as shown on the Job 32 cost sheet.

Finished goods (Job 32)	$XXX	
Work-in-process (Job 32)		$XXX

D. Evaluating the efficiency of the production process under a job-order system can be accomplished

1. Through the use of a standard cost system (see Study Unit 24), or
2. By budgeting costs for each job individually, based on expected materials and labor usage

E. **Summary of Accounting Process for a Job-Order System**

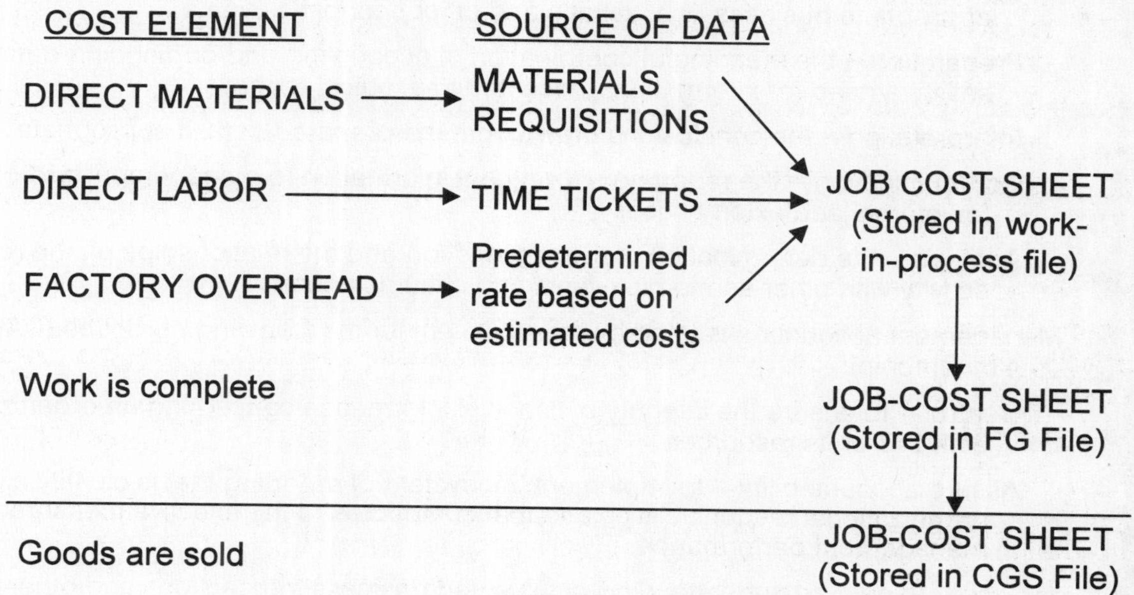

STATEMENTS ON MANAGEMENT ACCOUNTING

A. The Management Accounting Practices (MAP) Committee was created in 1969 by the National Association of Accountants (now the Institute of Management Accountants or IMA) to provide a means of developing and communicating the organization's positions on management accounting practices.

1. The stated committee objectives were to

   a. Express official positions on relevant accounting matters to other professional groups, government bodies, the financial community, and the general public

   b. Provide guidelines for the membership of the association and to business management on management accounting concepts, policies, and practices

2. The MAP Committee pronouncements (Statements on Management Accounting) that are currently in print are summarized in the following sections.

B. **SMA 1A**, *Objectives: Definition of Management Accounting* (March 1981).

1. "Management accounting is the process of identification, measurement, accumulation, analysis, preparation, interpretation, and communication of financial information used by management to plan, evaluate, and control within an organization and to assure appropriate use of and accountability for its resources. Management accounting also comprises the preparation of financial reports for nonmanagement groups such as shareholders, creditors, regulatory agencies, and tax authorities."

2. Management accounting processes include the following (MIA-PICA is a helpful mnemonic):

   Measurement -- the quantification, including estimates, of business transactions or other economic events that have occurred or may occur

   Identification -- the recognition and evaluation of business transactions and other economic events for appropriate accounting action

   Accumulation -- the disciplined and consistent approach to recording and classifying appropriate business transactions and other economic events

   Preparation -- the meaningful coordination of accounting and/or planning data to satisfy a need for information, presented in a logical format

   Interpretation -- the conclusions drawn from the prepared data, if appropriate

   Communication -- the reporting of pertinent information to management and others for internal and external uses

   Analysis -- the determination of the reasons for, and the relationships of, the reported activity with other economic events and circumstances

3. Management accounting is used by management for the following purposes (CAPER is the mnemonic):

   Control -- to ensure the integrity of financial information concerning an organization's activities or its resources

   Assure accountability -- to implement the system of reporting that is closely aligned to organizational responsibilities and that contributes to the effective measurement of management performance

   Plan -- to gain an understanding of expected business transactions and other economic events and their impact on the organization

   Evaluate -- to judge the implications of various past and/or future events

   Report -- to prepare external reports in conformity with GAAP and disseminate them to stockholders, creditors, and regulators

4. The order of these lists was rearranged to facilitate the use of the mnemonics. The definitions (copyright 1980) are reproduced with permission by the IMA.

C. **SMA 1B**, *Objectives: Objectives of Management Accounting* (June 1982)

   1. In 1982, the MAP Committee issued a pronouncement outlining two objectives of management accounting.

      a. Providing information. Management accountants select and provide, to all levels of management, information needed for

         1) Planning, evaluating, and controlling operations

         2) Safeguarding the organization's assets

         3) Communicating with interested parties outside the organization, such as shareholders and regulatory bodies

      b. Participating in the management process. Management accountants at appropriate levels are involved actively in the process of managing the entity. This process includes making strategic, tactical, and operating decisions and helping to coordinate the efforts of the entire organization. The management accountant participates, as part of management, in assuring that the organization operates as a unified whole in its long-run, intermediate, and short-run best interests.

D. **SMA 1C**, *Objectives: Standards of Ethical Conduct for Management Accountants* (June 1983), is presented in Study Unit 10, pages 259-260.

E. **SMA 1D**, *Objectives: The Common Body of Knowledge for Management Accountants* (June 1986). The common body of knowledge "identifies the composite subject matter that constitutes the body of knowledge common to management accounting at the professional level of competency." Understanding and use of the core of professional management accounting knowledge depend on general education, continuing education, the ability to adapt to new conditions and to acquire ancillary knowledge, leadership, and interpersonal abilities. Moreover, the common body of knowledge must be considered not as discrete topics but as "an integrated educational program." The following are the areas into which the common body of knowledge is divided:

1. Information and decision processes
    a. Management decision processes
        1) Repetitive
        2) Nonprogrammed
        3) Strategic
    b. Internal reporting
        1) Generating data
        2) Organizing and analyzing information
        3) Presenting and communicating information
    c. Financial planning and performance evaluation
        1) Forecasting and budgeting
        2) Analysis and evaluation
2. Accounting principles and functions
    a. Organizational structure and management
        1) Structure and management of the accounting function
        2) Internal control
        3) Internal auditing
3. Entity operations
    a. Principal entity operations
        1) Finance and investments
        2) Engineering and R&D
        3) Production and operations
        4) Sales and marketing
        5) Human resources
    b. Operating environment
        1) Legal environment
        2) Economic environment
        3) Ethical and social environment
    c. Taxation
        1) Taxation policies
        2) Structure and types of taxes
        3) Tax planning
    d. External reporting
        1) Reporting standards
        2) Information needs of user groups
    e. Information systems
        1) Systems analysis and design
        2) Database management
        3) Software applications
        4) Technological literacy
        5) Systems evaluation

F. **SMA 1E**, *Objectives: Education for Careers in Management Accounting* (February 1988). The common body of knowledge is the basis for the IMA's suggested curricula for students of management accounting. They are divided into three topics: general, business, and accounting education. The curricula are for 120 and 150 semester hours, but the IMA encourages completion of the program leading to a master's degree.

G. **SMA 2A**, *Practices and Techniques: Management Accounting Glossary* (November 1990), provides 84 pages of definitions drawn from textbooks, authoritative accounting literature (e.g., FASB and CASB pronouncements), and suggestions of committee members. It does not cover all areas of accounting.

1. The opening section of this study unit gives definitions for a variety of managerial accounting terms, but some candidates may also be interested in SMA 2A, which can be obtained from the IMA. See the Special Order Department address in Chapter 1 under the sideheading IMA Publications. CMA candidates will find that SMA 2A is an excellent study aid.

H. The MAP Committee has issued a number of SMAs dealing with specific areas of accounting and financial management.

1. **SMA 4A**, *Practices and Techniques: Cost of Capital* (November 1984). The statement is intended to be a practical guide to understanding and computing the cost of capital.

   a. The statement does not provide a standard formula that applies in all situations. Instead, several alternatives are discussed and their differences are described.

   b. Cost of capital is defined as the composite of the cost of various sources of funds included in a firm's capital structure. It is the minimum rate of return that must be earned on new investments that will not dilute the interests of the shareholder.

   c. A knowledge of the cost of capital is useful for

      1) Making capital investment decisions
      2) Managing working capital
      3) Evaluating performance

   d. For capital investment decisions, the cost of capital is used as the discount rate of return in evaluating the present value of a project's cash flows or as the hurdle or threshold rate when evaluating the internal rate of return.

   e. The cost of capital may also be useful in acquisition analysis, liquidation studies, R&D decisions, and source-of-financing decisions. In regulated industries, the cost of capital is used to set rates.

   f. Each source of capital (loans, notes, bonds, preferred stock, common stock, retained earnings) has its own cost, and the cost of each component may change as the mix of components changes.

   g. The cost of capital is found by first determining the costs of the individual types of capital and then multiplying the cost of each type by its proportion in the firm's total capital structure. Cost of capital is therefore a weighted-average figure.

   h. EXAMPLE: Firm A has three types of capital -- common equity, preferred stock, and debt. Common equity (cost = 20%) is 50% of the firm's total capital structure, preferred stock (cost = 16%) is 30%, and debt (cost = 12%) accounts for the balance. The cost of capital for Firm A is .5(20%) + .3(16%) + .2(12%) = 17.2%.

   i. Cost of capital calculations should be based on the current cost of the various sources of capital, not historical cost.

j. The cost of debt capital is the after-tax cost; i.e., interest rate x (1 - the firm's tax rate).

   1) Amortization of premium or discount and the need to maintain compensating balances should be considered.

k. Convertible debt should be treated as equity for cost of capital purposes unless the conversion price is close to the market value of the firm's common stock.

   1) Otherwise, it should be treated as debt, and a premium may be added to the interest rate to reflect the value of the conversion right.

l. The cost of preferred stock is the annual dividend requirement divided by the proceeds from issuance or the current price per share.

m. Deferred items such as deferred taxes payable are often classified as a part of common shareholders' equity. Alternatively, they may be considered to have a zero cost.

n. The cost of common equity is the most difficult to determine because no fixed payments are involved. Options for estimating the cost of equity include

   1) Historical rate of return
   2) Earnings/price ratio (the inverse of the P-E ratio)
   3) Dividend growth model (dividend yield + expected dividend growth rate)
   4) Capital asset pricing model
   5) Addition of a risk premium to the firm's pretax bond yield

      a) This method is rather judgmental.

2. **SMA 4B**, *Practices and Techniques: Allocation of Service and Administrative Costs* (June 1985). This statement deals only with indirect costs (costs that cannot be directly associated with a given cost object).

   a. There are two types of cost allocations -- the allocation of costs to time periods and the allocation of the costs of a time period to the cost object (product, contract, project, division, etc.) whose costs are measured during that time period. This statement deals only with the latter type of allocation.

   b. When the objective is to measure full costs, the preferable method of allocating service and administrative costs is based on a hierarchy of options, arranged in the order of how closely they are related to the cause of the cost's incurrence.

      1) Allocate by the amount of resources consumed by the cost center receiving the service (e.g., hours of legal staff used).

      2) Allocate on the basis of a presumed causal connection (e.g., personnel-related costs can be allocated on the basis of number of personnel in a department).

      3) If no causal connection can be found, costs should be allocated on the basis of relative overall activity of the cost center (such as total costs incurred or an average of several types of activity).

         a) A commonly used measure of average activity is the Massachusetts Formula, a simple average of the cost center's payroll, revenue, and assets as a proportion of the company's total payroll, revenue, and assets.

c. Responsibility costs are cost constructions designed to motivate the managers of responsibility centers to act in the best interests of the company.

   1) These costs should be allocated only if they

      a) Can be influenced by actions of the center's manager
      b) Are helpful in measuring support given to the responsibility center
      c) Improve comparability
      d) Are used in product pricing

   2) To encourage the use of such staff services as consulting or internal audit, their costs are often not charged to responsibility centers.

d. The four criteria used in selecting a specific allocation base are benefit, cause, fairness, and ability to bear. Benefit and cause are the most used. Fairness is difficult to measure. Ability to bear (based on profits) is usually not an acceptable method because it has a dysfunctional effect on management behavior.

3. **SMA 4C**, *Practices and Techniques: Definition and Measurement of Direct Labor Cost* (June 1985)

   a. Direct labor cost consists of labor quantities that can be specifically identified with a cost object in an economically feasible manner, priced at the unit price of direct labor.

   b. The following cost elements should be included in the unit price of direct labor because they can be specifically identified with a quantity of labor and measured accurately for the quantity used on a cost object: basic compensation, production efficiency bonuses, employer's portion of FICA taxes, and cost-of-living allowances.

   c. Several other costs should be included in the unit price of direct labor although the relationship between direct labor quantities and these cost elements is less certain than for those listed above. These costs include health insurance, group life insurance, holiday pay, vacation pay, sick leave, pension costs, workers' compensation insurance expense, and unemployment compensation tax expense.

   d. Premium pay for holidays, overtime, or undesirable shifts will normally be considered an indirect cost unless incurred because of a particular product or cost object.

   e. The following costs are excluded from the unit price of direct labor: wage continuation plans, contributions to Supplemental Unemployment Benefit (SUB) plans, membership dues, safety items, company-sponsored cafeteria, profit-sharing plans, and recreational facilities.

4. **SMA 4D**, *Practices and Techniques: Measuring Entity Performance* (January 1986)

   a. Net income and EPS are traditional measures with many limitations, e.g., failure to measure value-creating activities that do not meet the criteria of certainty and ability to be estimated.

   b. Cash flows may be useful in assessing entity performance as well as in evaluating the entity's capacity to service debt and pay dividends.

   c. Other measures of entity performance include return on investment, residual income, market value of the entity's securities, economic income (change in present value of future cash flows expected to accrue to owners from one period to the next less net investments by the owners of the entity), and inflation-adjusted performance measures.

d. The measures of financial performance tend to exhibit specific patterns depending upon the stages of an entity's growth.

  1) In the start-up stage, the entity usually experiences revenue growth, negligible profits, negative cash flows, and negligible or negative return on assets.

  2) In the growth stage, growth is rapid, and net income and cash from operations are positive. Investment requirements later slacken, and positive operating cash flows result. ROI improves.

  3) In the maturity stage, revenues slow, net income remains positive, investment in capital equipment is low, and a high return is earned on assets employed.

  4) In the decline stage, revenues decline, operations remain profitable, but cash flows increase because of a reduction in working capital.

e. A manager should be aware of the growth stage of the entity before evaluating the results of performance. Different measures of performance take on different degrees of importance depending upon the growth stage in the entity's life cycle.

f. Although financial measures of performance are generally more important, nonfinancial measures also require management's understanding, particularly as the environment becomes more competitive. Measures such as market share, innovation, quality of product, service, productivity, and employee development are all important.

g. The IMA suggests that

  1) Many measurement practices are currently too narrow in that they focus on one or a few measures rather than on a more comprehensive set of measures. Comprehensive measures are preferred.

  2) Some measures rely too heavily on historical-cost-based figures rather than on real economic changes.

  3) Performance measures that use only financial measures may emphasize the short term at the expense of the long term; thus, nonfinancial measures provide a more complete picture of entity performance.

5. **SMA 4E**, *Practices and Techniques: Definition and Measurement of Direct Material Cost* (June 1986)

a. Direct material cost consists of quantities of material that can be specifically identified with a cost object in an economically feasible manner, priced at the unit price of direct material.

b. Direct material cost should include the material cost of scrap, waste, and normally anticipated defective units. Also included are samples destroyed during quality assurance testing. However, materials used in marketing samples and prototypes are excluded.

c. The unit cost of direct materials includes the invoice price and other costs paid to vendors to deliver the materials to the production facility, including sales taxes, customs duties, and the cost of delivery containers and pallets (net of return refunds).

d. Trade discounts, refunds, and rebates should be deducted when calculating material costs.

e. Cash discounts should be deducted from the unit cost of direct materials if the rate of the discount exceeds reasonable interest rates.

f. Estimates may be used in the calculation of direct material costs if sufficiently accurate.

g. Costs that cannot be specifically identified as direct material costs but are closely related include the costs of purchasing, receiving, receiving inspection, storage, and material issuance. These costs are not to be treated as direct material costs. However, they should be allocated to cost objects on the basis of some measure of direct material quantity or cost rather than direct labor hours or cost.

6. **SMA 4F**, *Practices and Techniques: Allocation of Information Systems Costs* (February 1987)

   a. The elements of information systems costs include systems development costs, operating costs, and software maintenance costs.

   b. Responsibility accounting considerations

      1) Some advantages of allocating costs to users are increased user involvement and encouragement of efficient operation and allocation of resources.

      2) The arguments for not charging users for information services include

         a) Discouragement of innovation and conflict between users and the system department

         b) Its cost and use of resources

         c) Difficulty of determining the allocation and explaining its basis

         d) Addition of administrative detail

   c. Allocation methods may be based on full cost or less than full cost. They may also be based on cost plus an allowance for profit or on market price.

   d. Allocation bases may be labor (or machine) based (e.g., CPU time). A multiple-base charge is also possible.

      1) The allocation may be based on a single rate for all services or multiple prices. The latter is more appropriate in more sophisticated environments, especially those involving a significant amount of communications.

7. **SMA 4G**, *Practices and Techniques: Accounting for Indirect Production Costs* (June 1987)

   a. The purpose of allocating indirect production costs is to assign an appropriate share of total costs for a given period to each cost object.

      1) An indirect cost is common to two or more cost objects and cannot be identified specifically with a single cost object in an economically feasible way.

   b. The cost accounting system collects costs and assigns them to cost objects. It should be useful not only for management decision making but also for financial accounting purposes. It should identify responsibility costs, full costs, and differential costs, including separating variable from fixed costs.

c. Responsibility costs are usually identified with a specific manager for control purposes. Indirect costs may be difficult to control because some are variable, some are discretionary, and some are fixed.

1) The flexible budget is the best device for measuring a manager's control of indirect costs.

2) Service cost and production cost centers should be separately identified because of the dual responsibility for service costs. The service center manager and the production center manager are both responsible; hence, the latter should be charged and the former credited for actual services used.

d. Full production cost is the inventory (or unbilled services) cost. It should be used in calculating cost of sales and includes direct production costs and a share of indirect production costs.

1) Indirect production cost

a) Is assigned to a production or service cost center

b) If included in total service center cost, will be reassigned to a production cost center

c) If included in total indirect costs of a production cost center, will be assigned to products

2) Service costs are allocated on the basis of direct identification or a causal relationship.

a) Service center costs are allocated to other service centers by the step-down or algebraic method.

3) Costs that cannot be directly assigned to a cost object must be allocated based upon a causal relationship between the center and the cost. Indirect costs are allocated according to the following categories of allocation bases: people, payroll, equipment, materials, space, transactions, and total activity.

4) The basic technique for allocating indirect costs is the use of annual predetermined overhead rates for each equivalent unit of production, such as direct labor hours or dollars, machine hours, production orders, or a product-related physical measure.

a) Annual rates are preferable to avoid seasonal fluctuation and facilitate accounting. They require estimates of activity in each responsibility center and of average production volume in each production cost center.

b) Under- or over-absorbed overhead should be adjustments to earnings for management accounting but should be allocated to inventory and cost of sales for financial accounting.

5) Standard costing identifies spending variances as adjustments of periodic earnings for management purposes and states units produced at standard rather than actual cost.

a) Thus, over- or under-absorbed overhead in a standard cost system is treated as a volume variance since spending variances have been separately accounted for.

8. **SMA 4H**, *Practices and Techniques: Uses of the Cost of Capital* (January 1988). SMA 4H expands upon SMA 4A (see H.1. on page 498). It treats the cost of capital as a cost of doing business for purposes of internal reporting and financial analysis. Because this treatment is inconsistent with GAAP, it is not recommended for general purpose reporting. The following are the IMA's recommendations:
   a. Debt and equity capital must be allocated to cost objects for full cost performance, measurement, product costing, and pricing decisions.
   b. Responsibility costing requires allocation to cost objects of the cost of capital to encourage efficient asset use and to avoid inappropriate asset growth. This allocation should be consistent with overall company objectives.
   c. Differential costs may be considered for both short- and long-term decisions. The cost of capital is "associated with the alternatives to determine cost differences for short-term decisions and incorporated into the discounted-cash-flow model for longer-term decisions."
   d. The investment (whether to invest) and financing (how to fund a project) decisions are distinct. The former decision includes an allocation of the cost of capital. The cost of financing chosen should be consistent with the cost of capital assumption.
9. **SMA 4I**, *Practices and Techniques: Cost Management for Freight Transportation* (June 1989), provides guidelines for the identification, measurement, and control of material freight costs.
   a. The increased concern about the costs of transporting goods, materials, and finished products arises from the greater costs incurred in the expansion of markets, especially international suppliers and customers; from diversification of channels of distribution; and from deregulation, which broadens the opportunities for cost control or reduction.
   b. One intention of the Statement is to establish a framework for a database that will help to meet the need for comprehensive transportation information.
      1) An effective information system provides support for such functions as transportation analysis, traffic scheduling and routing, freight rate maintenance and audit, carrier cost comparisons, least-cost freight consolidations, cost allocations, budgeting, transporting performance, and management reporting.
   c. The emphasis is on "costs as financial measures of performance in transportation."
   d. SMA 4I applies to the total costs of company-operated as well as outside transportation services, including inbound freight, interfacility shipments, and transportation to customers, but not to materials flow costs in production or in warehouses or to passenger transportation.
   e. Transportation cost management is applicable to support costs, including those associated with people and information, as well as to the costs of modes of transport (truck, rail, ocean, barge, air, pipeline, etc.).
   f. The Statement concerns not only direct transportation costs but also costs included in the cost of materials or cost of goods sold.
   g. The key objective of transportation cost management is direct assignment and allocation of costs to the business elements that consume the costs. The assignment or allocation should be based on causal factors because effective decisions require an understanding of actual causes of costs.

10. **SMA 4J**, *Practices and Techniques: Accounting for Property, Plant, and Equipment* (July 1989), is largely a restatement of GAAP promulgated in authoritative financial accounting literature (see Study Unit 12, Financial Statement Presentation).
11. **SMA 4K**, *Practices and Techniques: Cost Management for Warehousing* (September 1989), closely parallels the SMA on management of freight costs. Freight and warehousing are the largest components of logistics and distribution costs. The Statement addresses
    a. An information model for managing warehousing costs
    b. The drivers of warehousing costs
    c. Planning and budgeting for warehousing
    d. An activity-based approach to direct assignments and allocations of warehousing costs
12. **SMA 4L**, *Practices and Techniques: Control of Property, Plant, and Equipment* (February 1990), applies to both owned and leased operating assets that have an economic life greater than 1 year. These fixed assets have physical substance in contrast with intangibles.
    a. Asset control extends to planning and budgeting the authorized acquisition of assets.
        1) The capital expenditures budget is a key control document.
    b. It also extends to methods that evaluate acquisition programs; verify ending asset balances and depreciation; confirm the existence of assets; detect unused, underused, and improperly maintained assets; provide for risk control; and plan for asset maintenance and replacement.
13. **SMA 4M**, *Practices and Techniques: Understanding Financial Instruments* (September 1990), is primarily concerned with economic analysis of the most commonly used financial instruments. The background information provided includes
    a. Reasons for new financial instruments
    b. The general uses of financial instruments
    c. Particular features and risks of specific instruments
    d. An introduction to hedging
    e. Internal control issues
    f. The economic, general, and market risks of owning or issuing financial instruments
14. **SMA 4N**, *Practices and Techniques: Management of Working Capital: Cash Resources* (September 1990), applies to management of financial working capital, not to receivables, inventories, or payables.
    a. This process entails managing cash payments, cash receipts, and the short-term investment and borrowing portfolios.
    b. Management of financial working capital requires an understanding of the cash management system, an ability to estimate costs and benefits of strategies, and reliance upon an appropriate evaluation method (especially one based on discounting).
    c. The understanding of the central issues involved in a cash management system is the crux of SMA 4N. The elements of the system discussed are
        1) Collection of cash
        2) Disbursement of cash
        3) Movement of cash to the concentration bank from deposit banks
        4) Funding of disbursements
        5) Banking relations and compensation issues
        6) Cash forecasting

15. **SMA 4O**, *Practices and Techniques: The Accounting Classification of Real Estate Occupancy Costs* (January 1991), makes recommendations concerning the identification, classification, and treatment of the costs incurred by companies to provide space for the operation of their business units, whether such space is owned or leased.
    a. SMA 4O lists suggested categories of occupancy costs and the types of costs that should be included in each but does not address the determination of these costs. However, it assumes that full costing (as opposed to responsibility or differential costing) is the most appropriate method for determining occupancy costs.
    b. SMA 4O also discusses the uses and limitations of the measurement of the costs of occupancy and provides suggested tests for identification of these costs and an illustrative chart of accounts.
16. **SMA 4P**, *Practices and Techniques: Cost Management for Logistics* (June 1992), is intended to improve the identification, measurement, and management of logistics costs. It concerns integrated logistics, supply chain management, and activity-based costing.
    a. "Logistics is the process of planning, implementing, and controlling the efficient, cost-effective flow and storage of raw materials, in-process inventory, finished goods, and related information from point of origin to point of consumption for the purpose of conforming to customer requirements" (Council of Logistics Management).
        1) Logistics includes the functions of purchasing, transportation, warehousing, materials and inventory management, customer service and order processing, forecasting and production planning, related information systems, and support activities.
            a) It excludes costs of raw materials, production costs, selling expenses, and other unrelated support costs.
    b. This pronouncement uses historical costs as the key measure of logistics performance, although nonfinancial performance and productivity measures are relevant.
    c. A key issue is reduction in the time needed to cycle orders (procurement, production, and distribution) consistent with effective cost management.
        1) A JIT philosophy involves minimizing times needed for logistics activities.
        2) A fully integrated logistics function not only minimizes costs but also contributes to profitability.
            a) Trade-offs must be understood (e.g., cost of holding versus cost of ordering inventory), and an integration of functions is emphasized (i.e., consideration of how an action regarding one function affects another.
    d. The supply chain management approach advocated by SMA 4P uses new performance measures in lieu of traditional functional measures, emphasizes customer requirements, and moves logistics decisions to a lower management level.

e. The scope of SMA 4P extends to the direct assignment and allocation of logistics costs through activity-based costing (see page 487). Activities, their frequencies, cycle times, and costs for the logistics functions should be determined. Moreover, cost drivers should be identified for the various activities.

1) The following are the steps in development of a cost flow model based on activity-based costing:

a) Collect financial data.
b) Identify activities.
c) Develop preliminary model.
d) Identify cost drivers.
e) Collect cost driver data.
f) Calculate activity costs.
g) Determine time cost of money.
h) Calculate product costs.

f. Logistics performance management considers responsibility and accountability from the lowest (activity) level up to top management and includes measures for all levels.

1) Critical success factors should be determined for every level, and their relative importance assigned.

2) For each activity, the current state of performance and appropriate goals can be established.

3) Performance measures should be related to overall entity goals. Furthermore, they must be continuously improved.

g. An integrated information management approach operating from a common database is necessary because logistics activities occur across the entity's supply chain and therefore transcend the traditional business functions.

1) Applications of information and telecommunications are expanding rapidly, for example, to expedite delivery of materials for manufacture and, for outbound logistics, to reduce order cycle time.

17. **SMA 4Q**, *Practices and Techniques: Use and Control of Financial Instruments by Multinational Companies* (June 1992), describes how multinationals use financial instruments and methods of controlling their use. Financial instruments may be issued to raise capital, purchased as investments, and purchased or issued to reduce risk. SMA 4Q provides information on using and controlling financial instruments and assistance in reviewing the relevant control procedures. Tax issues, financial reporting requirements in detail, and mathematical analysis of complex instruments are not addressed.

a. Part I of SMA 4Q concerns short-term investments in the U.S.

1) It considers the types of short-term investments, including complex short-term investments. It also considers

a) Administration of short-term instruments

b) Internal control, including separation of duties, operating policies and procedures, and internal auditing

b. Part II covers long-term investments, including fixed investments purchased to hedge foreign-exchange-rate risk.

c. Part III discusses short-term and long-term borrowings.

   1) Short-term borrowings include bank borrowings, such as lines of credit; commercial paper; asset-backed financing, e.g., factoring or mortgaging property; and bankers' acceptances.

   2) Nonfinance companies often limit issuances of long-term instruments to traditional securities.

      a) The concern is that complex instruments may be hard to value.

      b) Shelf registration and hedging to lock in interest rates are other matters of concern.

d. Part IV discusses use of financial instruments in foreign operations. Some companies allow the local operating units to purchase short-term investments, but others prefer to make and control these investments at the corporate level. Reasons are

   1) Local restrictions on transfer prices, investments, and fund transfers
   2) The need to transfer funds from positive to negative cash flow units
   3) Local tax regulations
   4) Temporarily high local interest rates
   5) Use of local borrowings or investments as hedges of company-wide risk

e. Part V relates to hedges of foreign currency risk.

   1) The risks include exchange-rate risk and translation risk.

   2) See SFAS 52, *Foreign Currency Translation*.

      a) Certain consensus opinions of the Emerging Issues Task Force are also relevant.

   3) Exposures commonly hedged include large specific transactions, the entire net transaction exposure in a foreign currency, and the expected future net income of a foreign subsidiary.

   4) Instruments used as hedges include options, futures contracts, forward contracts, foreign-currency swaps, and local-currency borrowings.

   5) Instruments used as hedges are typically evaluated based on the Block-Scholes options pricing model; financial theory related to futures, forwards, and swaps; online systems using software to compute theoretical values given current prices; and competitive bidding.

   6) The choice of hedging policies depends on whether the policy hedges corporate accounting income and whether the hedge is worth the cost.

   7) Internal control of foreign-exchange operations should be designed to prevent errors and unauthorized trading.

f. Part VI covers the use of commodity options, futures, and forwards by commodity dealers, producers, and purchasers.

18. **SMA 4R**, *Practices and Techniques: Managing Quality Improvements* (June 1993), provides guidelines for implementing total quality management (TQM).

    a. Quality is difficult to define, and any single definition will have weaknesses. Consequently, multiple perspectives should be maintained: attributes of the product (performance, serviceability, durability, etc.), customer satisfaction, conformity with manufacturing specifications and value (relation of quality and price).

    b. TQM emphasizes the supplier's relationship with the customer, identifies customer needs, and recognizes that everyone in a process is at some time a customer or supplier of someone else, either within or without the organization.

        1) Thus, TQM begins with external customer requirements, identifies internal customer-supplier relationships and requirements, and establishes requirements for external suppliers.

        2) Companies tend to be vertically organized, but TQM requires strong horizontal linkages.

    c. The management of quality is not limited to quality management staff, engineers, production personnel, etc.

        1) The role of management accountants includes assisting in designing and operating quality information, measurement, and reporting systems.

            a) In particular, they can contribute to problem solutions through measuring and reporting quality costs.

    d. Implementation of TQM cannot be accomplished by application of a formula, and the process is lengthy and difficult. The following phases are typical:

        1) Establishment of an executive-level quality council of the top managers with strong involvement by the CEO

        2) Providing quality training programs for senior managers

        3) Conducting a quality audit to identify improvement opportunities and identify strengths and weaknesses compared with competitors

        4) Preparation of a gap analysis to ascertain what is necessary to bridge the gap between the company and its competitors and to establish a database for the development of the strategic quality improvement plan

        5) Development of strategic quality improvement plans for the short and long term

        6) Conducting employee communication and training programs

        7) Establishment of quality teams

        8) Creation of a measurement system and setting of goals

        9) Revision of compensation, appraisal, and recognition systems

        10) Review and revision of the entire effort periodically

e. Various management processes, tools, and measures should be adopted. They include

1) Policy deployment
2) Quality function deployment
3) Kaizen
4) Employee involvement
5) Suppliers' management
6) Competitive benchmarking
7) Quality training
8) Reward and recognition
9) Customer retention
10) Statistical methods

f. The cost of quality includes

1) Cost of conformance

a) Cost of prevention
b) Cost of appraisal

2) Cost of nonconformance

a) Cost of internal failure
b) Cost of external failure (lost opportunity)

g. Management accounting should

1) Determine which accounts are relevant to TQM
2) Restructure the accounting system to provide accurate quality cost data
3) Apply activity-based costing to TQM to relate quality costs to activities
4) Standardize cost of quality reports

19. **SMA 4S**, *Practices and Techniques: Internal Accounting and Classification of Risk Management Costs* (June 1993), defines the process of managing exposures to loss as including risk assessment, risk control, risk finance, and risk administration.

a. The objectives of SMA 4S are to

1) Provide a methodology for classifying and accounting for risk management costs
2) Identify those costs
3) Promote consistency in accounting
4) Promote comparability

b. This pronouncement applies to the following principal exposures and any related cash inflows:

1) Property damage
2) Tort liability
3) Workers' compensation

c. The types of costs to which SMA 4S applies are

1) Insurance premiums
2) Retained losses
3) Internal administration
4) Outside services
5) Financial guarantees
6) Imposed expenses (fees, taxes, etc.)

d. The recognition and measurement requirements are consistent with GAAP.

20. **SMA 4T**, *Practices and Techniques: Implementing Activity-Based Costing* (September 1993), describes the design and implementation of an activity-based costing (ABC) system (see page 487 for the basic concepts of ABC).
    a. This pronouncement is intended to provide
        1) An understanding of the role of management accounting
        2) Assistance in convincing the organization to revise the cost system
        3) An overview of the implementation process
        4) A design method
        5) Alternatives for actual implementation
        6) A way of insuring that planned benefits are achieved
21. **SMA 4U**, *Practices and Techniques: Developing Comprehensive Performance Indicators* (March 1995), addresses the need in a customer-oriented, rapidly changing, increasingly global competitive environment to develop new performance measures. In accordance with TQM, the focus should be on leading indicators, not on the traditional, historical, internal financial measures. Emphasis on such measures as market penetration, customer satisfaction, quality, speed, worker competence, and morale permits a firm to take corrective action before realization of actual financial results.
    a. This guideline provides a framework for **performance indicators** intended to respond to needs at all levels of a firm and describes the steps in the implementation of such a system.
    b. Development of new performance indicators requires consideration of such objectives as
        1) Clarifying strategic objectives
        2) Focusing on core processes
        3) Focusing on critical variables
        4) Signaling the trend in performance
        5) Identifying the critical variables that do not meet expectations
        6) Using performance indicators as a basis for rewarding key contributors
        7) Aligning top management's goals, strategies, and objectives with fundamental processes of the firm
    c. A broad-based performance indicator system must be forward-looking, focus on significant external as well as internal relationships, and track nonfinancial as well as financial indicators.
        1) Key external relationships and internal processes drive performance; management must make certain decisions well, and those drivers and decisions affect measures of performance.
            a) A firm is in a set of relationships with its external environment, customers, competitors, and suppliers.
            b) A firm's internal business processes include market development, product development, operations, distribution, sales, and service, supported by administrative processes.
            c) Management decisions about revenues, costs, investments, and financing influence results measured in terms of market share, growth, profitability, return on capital and equity, cash flow, and shareholder value.

2) Performance indicators must provide different kinds of feedback at different levels of management and will also vary with the needs of the individual firm. However, for many firms, the core performance indicators would be included in the following categories:
   a) Environmental indicators
   b) Market/customer indicators
   c) Competitor indicators
   d) Internal business process indicators
   e) Human resource indicators
   f) Financial indicators

d. The sequence of steps needed to implement new performance indicators includes
   1) Recognizing the need for better performance indicators
   2) Ensuring top management commitment
   3) Creating a cross-functional implementation team
   4) Developing a business performance model
   5) Understanding the firm's goals and strategies
   6) Defining critical success factors
   7) Assessing the current performance measurement system
   8) Determining the measures to eliminate
   9) Developing the information needed to manage the business, the method used to generate it, and the rules for its flow and use
   10) Establishing the underlying technology
   11) Reevaluating performance evaluation and the reward system
   12) Ensuring continual improvement

22. **SMA 4V**, *Practices and Techniques: Effective Benchmarking* (July 1995), describes techniques for improving the effectiveness of benchmarking, which is a means of helping companies with productivity management and business process reengineering.

   a. "Benchmarking involves continuously evaluating the practices of best-in-class organizations and adopting company processes to incorporate the best of these practices." It "analyzes and measures the key outputs of a business process or function against the best and also identifies the underlying key actions and root causes that contribute to the performance difference."

      1) Benchmarking is an ongoing process that entails quantitative and qualitative measurement of the difference between the company's performance of an activity and the performance by the best in the world. The benchmark organization need not be a competitor.

b. The first phase in the benchmarking process is to select and prioritize benchmarking projects.

   1) An organization must understand its critical success factors and business environment to identify key business processes and drivers and to develop parameters defining what processes to benchmark. The criteria for selecting what to benchmark relate to the reasons for the existence of a process and its importance to the entity's mission, values, and strategy. These reasons relate in large part to satisfaction of end users or customer needs.

c. The next phase is to organize benchmarking teams. A team organization is appropriate because it permits an equitable division of labor, participation by those responsible for implementing changes, and inclusion of a variety of functional expertise and work experience. Team members should have knowledge of the function to be benchmarked, respected positions in the company, good communication skills, teaming skills, motivation to innovate and to support cross-functional problem solving, and project management skills.

d. The benchmarking team must thoroughly investigate and document the company's internal processes. The organization should be seen as a series of processes, not as a fixed structure. A process is "a network of related and independent activities linked by the outputs they exchange." One way to determine the primary characteristics of a process is to trace the path a request for a product or service takes through the organization.

   1) The benchmarking team must also develop a family of measures that are true indicators of process performance and a process taxonomy, that is, a set of process elements, measures, and phrases that describes the process to be benchmarked.

e. Researching and identifying best-in-class performance is often the most difficult phase. The critical steps are setting up databases, choosing information-gathering methods (internal sources, external public domain sources, and original research are the possible approaches), formatting questionnaires (lists of questions prepared in advance), and selecting benchmarking partners.

f. The data analysis phase entails identifying performance gaps, understanding the reasons they exist, and prioritizing the key activities that will facilitate the behavioral and process changes needed to implement the benchmarking study's recommendations. Sophisticated statistical and other methods may be needed when the study involves many variables, testing of assumptions, or presentation of quantified results.

g. Leadership is most important in the implementation phase of the benchmarking process because the team must be able to justify its recommendations. Moreover, the process improvement teams must manage the implementation of approved changes.

23. **SMA 4W**, *Practices and Techniques: Implementing Corporate Environmental Strategies* (July 1995), suggests principles and approaches to help organizations to determine the need for or to implement environmental strategies. These approaches should improve environmental performance and aid in integrating environmental considerations into management decisions.

a. Other objectives are to recognize global environmental trends early; to increase stakeholder satisfaction; to improve profitability; to seek competitive advantages by minimizing environmental impact; to adopt a creative approach to environmental challenges; to reduce costs through conservation and eco-friendly technology; to minimize risk from product liability, changes in laws, or increases in consumer demands; and to meet compliance and due diligence requirements.

b. SMA 4W groups the elements of an effective corporate environmental strategy into three stages.

   1) The first stage of implementing a strategy includes

      a) Ensuring top management commitment and support
      b) Developing an environmental policy statement
      c) Creating an environmental management system
      d) Preparing an environmental action program
      e) Establishing an environmental audit program

   2) The second stage includes

      a) Developing a strategy for external environmental reporting
      b) Designing products and processes that consider environmental impact
      c) Integrating environmental impact information into decision making

   3) The third stage includes

      a) Integrating environmental impact into performance evaluation
      b) Generating revenue through waste management and recycling
      c) Marketing eco-efficient products and services
      d) Integrating the principles of sustainable development

24. **SMA 5A**, *Evaluating Controllership Effectiveness* (January 1990), provides assistance to controllers in measuring and evaluating their performance. The Statement defines controllership functions (transaction processing, internal control, and decision support), specifies the key areas to be evaluated, and provides checklists of service attributes and quantitative performance indicators. Moreover, the self-assessment extends not only to specific controllership responsibilities but also to the organization's control framework (policies, organizational structure, and procedures), including the internal audit function.

25. **SMA 5B**, *Fundamentals of Reporting Information to Managers* (June 1992), presents internal management reporting guidelines that are primarily concerned with periodic reporting of financial information. Its rationale is that the means of communication can have a material effect on the usefulness of the information.

   a. This pronouncement concerns the following aspects of communication of management information:

      1) Media used

         a) Print
         b) Oral presentation
         c) Tele- and/or videoconferencing
         d) Videotape
         e) Computer-generated video display
         f) Combinations of the above

2) Timeliness of the information

   a) Frequency
   b) Length of delay

3) Report format, which is a function of the

   a) Information communicated
   b) Preferences of recipients
   c) Costs and benefits of alternatives

4) Report design. Reports should be

   a) Readable
   b) Appropriately detailed
   c) The proper size
   d) Designed to place data in context
   e) Standardized
   f) Prepared with a responsibility orientation

5) Content of reports

   a) Actual performance reports (comprehensive reports and key indicator reports)
   b) Analytical reports
   c) Strategic reports

6) Distribution of reports

26. **SMA 5C**, *Managing Cross-Functional Teams* (June 1994), postulates that traditional organizational structures are unable to cope with the new competitive order, which demands rapid response, an understanding of the interdependencies among processes, and the need for multiple, simultaneous changes. Continuous creation of value for the firm's stakeholders requires crossing traditional boundaries and effective use of resources, including people. Thus, teams are increasingly used to conduct research, design products, reengineer processes, improve operations, market products, etc. A cross-functional team is defined as a small group of individuals that cross formal departmental boundaries and hierarchies, that are committed to a common purpose of improvement, and that act as a unit.

   a. This pronouncement is intended to help organizations to understand the following matters about cross-functional teams:

      1) Their benefits
      2) Prerequisites for high performance
      3) Guidelines for planning, organizing, building, maintaining, and evaluating them
      4) Group problem-solving tools
      5) Requirements for effective group processes and decision making
      6) The need for balancing individual, team, and organizational needs
      7) Reasons for failure

STUDY UNIT 20
VARIABLE AND ABSORPTION COSTING

The choice between absorption and variable costing is of special concern in textbooks and on professional exams. Absorption costing is primarily used for inventory valuation and external reporting. Variable costing is used solely for internal decision making. Some firms use variable costing throughout the year but make a year-end adjustment to inventory to convert it to absorption costing.

VARIABLE AND ABSORPTION COSTING

A. Accountants have two different views about whether fixed factory overhead (manufacturing) costs should be assigned to products.

1. The prevailing view for external reporting purposes is that product cost should include all manufacturing costs: direct labor, direct materials, and factory overhead. This method is commonly known as full costing or **absorption costing**.

   a. Absorption costing is currently required for external reporting under GAAP and for tax purposes.

B. However, **variable (direct) costing** has won increasing support.

1. This method assigns only variable manufacturing costs to products.

2. The term direct costing may be misleading because it suggests traceability, which is not what cost accountants mean when they speak of the direct costing method.

   a. Many accountants believe that **variable costing** is a more suitable term, and some even call the method **contribution margin reporting**.

C. Under variable costing, all direct labor, direct materials, variable factory overhead costs, and selling and administrative costs are handled in precisely the same manner as under absorption costing. Only fixed factory overhead costs are treated differently.

1. Absorption costing includes a provision for fixed factory overhead in the total cost of each product manufactured.

2. In variable costing, the inventoriable or product cost includes only the variable costs. Variable factory overhead is part of product cost, but fixed factory overhead is treated as an expense of the accounting period (as are selling and administrative expenses).

   a. EXAMPLE: Assume that a firm, during its first month in business, produced 100 units of product X and sold 80 units while incurring the following costs:

Direct materials	$100
Direct labor	200
Variable overhead	150
Fixed overhead	300
Total costs	$750

      1) Given total costs of $750, the absorption cost per unit is $7.50 ($750 ÷ 100 units). Thus, total ending inventory is valued at $150 (20 x $7.50).

      2) Using variable costing, the cost per unit is $4.50 ($450 ÷ 100 units), and the total value of the remaining 20 units is $90.

3) Assume also that the 80 units were sold at a price of $10 each, and the company incurred $20 of variable selling expenses and $60 of fixed selling expenses. The income statements prepared using the two methods follow.

Variable Cost			Absorption Cost		
Sales		$800	Sales		$800
Beginning inventory	$ 0		Beginning inventory	$ 0	
Variable cost of manufacturing	450		Cost of goods manufactured	750	
	$450		Cost of goods available for sale	$750	
Ending inventory	(90)		Ending inventory	(150)	
Variable cost of goods sold		(360)	Cost of goods sold		(600)
Manufacturing contribution margin		$440	Gross profit		$200
Variable selling expenses		(20)	Selling expenses		(80)
Contribution margin		$420	Net income		$120
Fixed overhead		(300)			
Fixed selling expenses		(60)			
Net income		$ 60			

a) The $60 difference in net income ($120 – $60) is the difference between the two ending inventory figures ($150 – $90). In essence, the absorption method treats 20% of the fixed overhead costs (20% x $300 = $60) as an asset (inventory) because 20% of the month's production (100 – 80 sold = 20) is still on hand.

i) The variable costing method assumes that the fixed costs are not related to production because they would have been incurred even if there had been no production.

b) The contribution margin is an important element in the variable costing income statement.

i) The contribution margin is the difference between sales and total variable costs.

ii) It indicates how much sales contribute toward paying the fixed costs and providing a profit.

COMPARISON OF VARIABLE AND ABSORPTION COSTING

A. Absorption and variable costing differ in two respects; one is significant for external reporting and the other for internal reporting.

1. The manufacturing costs included when determining inventory values
2. The classification and order of presentation of costs in the income statement

B. Both methods treat selling and administrative expenses, whether fixed or variable, as period costs and variable manufacturing costs as product costs.

C. They differ only as to the classification of fixed factory overhead costs, but the result is different inventory values and incomes.

D. With fixed costs excluded, inventory costs computed under variable costing are lower than under absorption costing; income may be higher or lower, depending upon whether inventories are increased or liquidated.

E. Under absorption costing, recurring costs are classified into three broad categories: manufacturing, selling, and administrative. In the income statement, the cost of goods sold is subtracted from sales revenue to give the gross margin on sales. Selling and administrative expenses are deducted from the gross margin to arrive at net operating income.

1. If operations are above or below some capacity set as normal or standard, adjustments are made for volume variances (see Study Unit 24 for discussion of variances).

F. Under variable costing, sales minus variable costs equals contribution margin.

1. *Net income = Sales - VC - FC*
2. Because fixed factory overhead is not applied to products under variable costing, no volume variance occurs.
3. The contribution margin under variable costing is considerably different from the gross margin under absorption costing.

G. **The Comparative Results of Using Variable and Absorption Costing**

1. When production and sales are equal for a period, they report the same net income. Total fixed costs budgeted for the period are charged to sales revenue in the period under both methods.
   a. When sales = production, variable income = absorption income.
2. When production exceeds sales and ending inventories are increased, the net income reported under absorption costing is higher than under variable costing. Under absorption costing, a portion of the fixed costs budgeted for the period is deferred to the following period via the ending inventories. Under variable costing, the total fixed costs are charged to profit and loss.
   a. When production exceeds sales, absorption income exceeds variable income.
3. When sales exceed production and ending inventories are decreased, variable costing shows the higher profit. Under absorption costing, a portion of the fixed costs brought forward from the preceding period in beginning inventory is charged to cost of sales. These fixed costs would already have been absorbed by operations of the previous period if variable costing had been used.
   a. When sales exceed production, variable income exceeds absorption income.
4. Under variable costing, profits always move in the same direction as sales volume. Profits reported under absorption costing behave erratically, and sometimes move in the opposite direction from sales.
5. Profit differences tend to be larger when calculations are made for short periods. In the long run, the two methods will report the same total profits if sales equal production.
   a. The inequalities between production and sales are usually minor over an extended period.
   b. Production cannot continually exceed sales because an enterprise will not produce more than it can sell in the long run.

H. Differences in net income reported under absorption and variable costing are also reflected in inventory values.

1. The principal issue is the timing of charging fixed overhead costs to operations in the process of matching costs with revenues.
2. A more fundamental issue is the relation of fixed overhead to assets: ending inventories of finished goods and work-in-process.

I. EXAMPLE: The following information was used to prepare the income statements shown on the following page to illustrate the differences between the two methods:

Unit sales price: $1.00
Unit variable cost: $.50
Production in units: 1995 - 40,000; 1996 - 50,000; 1997 - 0
Sales: 30,000 units each year
Ending FIFO inventories in units: 1995 - 10,000; 1996 - 30,000; 1997 - 0
Fixed costs: Manufacturing - $4,000 per year
General expenses - $2,000 per year

1. Assuming zero inventory at the beginning of 1995 and at the end of 1997, the total income for the 3-year period is the same under either costing method.

2. In 1996, despite the same cash flow, there is a $1,400 difference between the final net income figures, with an even greater difference in 1997. Absorption costing shows a higher income than variable costing in 1995 and 1996 because the cost of fixed overhead is capitalized as an asset under the absorption method.

3. If fixed costs increase relative to variable costs, the differences become more dramatic (here 50% of the selling price is variable manufacturing cost, and fixed manufacturing cost is no more than 20% of the variable manufacturing cost).

4. Variable costing treats fixed factory overhead as an expense of the period in which the cost is incurred, but in 1997, the absorption income statement must reflect not only the costs incurred in 1997 but also those capitalized as inventory in preceding years.

Variable Costing Income Statement	1995	1996	1997
Sales	$30,000	$30,000	$30,000
Beginning inventory	$ 0	$ 5,000	$15,000
Variable manufacturing costs	20,000	25,000	0
Goods available for sale	$20,000	$30,000	$15,000
Minus ending inventory	(5,000)	(15,000)	(0)
Variable cost of goods sold	$15,000	$15,000	$15,000
Contribution margin	$15,000	$15,000	$15,000
Fixed manufacturing overhead	(4,000)	(4,000)	(4,000)
Fixed general expenses	(2,000)	(2,000)	(2,000)
Net income	$ 9,000	$ 9,000	$ 9,000

Absorption Costing Income Statement	1995	1996	1997
Sales	$30,000	$30,000	$30,000
Beginning inventory	$ 0	$ 6,000	$17,400
Mfg. costs (variable & fixed)	24,000	29,000	4,000
Total in production	$24,000	$35,000	$21,400
Minus ending inventory	(6,000)	(17,400)	(0)
Cost of goods sold	$18,000	$17,600	$21,400
Gross profit	$12,000	$12,400	$ 8,600
General expenses	(2,000)	(2,000)	(2,000)
Net income	$10,000	$10,400	$ 6,600

BENEFITS OF VARIABLE COSTING FOR INTERNAL PURPOSES

A. Although the use of variable costing for financial statements is controversial, most agree about its superiority for internal reporting. It is far better suited than absorption costing to the needs of management. Management requires a knowledge of cost behavior under various operating conditions. For planning and control, management is more concerned with treating fixed and variable costs separately than with calculating full costs. Full costs are usually of dubious value because they contain arbitrary allocations of fixed cost.

1. Under variable costing, the cost data for profit planning and decision making are readily available from accounting records and statements. Reference to auxiliary records and supplementary analyses is not necessary.

2. For example, cost-volume-profit relationships and the effects of changes in sales volume on net income can easily be computed from the income statement prepared under the variable costing concept, but not from the conventional absorption cost income statement based on the same data.

3. Profits and losses reported under variable costing have a relationship to sales revenue and are not affected by inventory or production variations.

4. Absorption cost income statements may show decreases in profits when sales are rising and increases in profits when sales are decreasing, which may be confusing to management. Attempts at explanation by means of volume variances often compound rather than clarify the confusion.

5. Production volume variances not only are unnecessary but also are frustrating and confusing to management.

6. If variable costing is used, the favorable margin between selling prices and variable cost should provide a constant reminder of profits forgone because of lack of sales volume. A favorable margin justifies a higher production level.
7. The full impact of fixed costs on net income, partially hidden in inventory values under absorption costing, is emphasized by the presentation of costs on an income statement prepared under variable costing.
8. Proponents of variable costing maintain that fixed factory overhead is more closely correlated to capacity to produce than to the production of individual units.
9. Production managers cannot manipulate income by producing more or fewer products than needed during a period. Under absorption costing, a production manager could increase income simply by producing more units than are currently needed for sales.

B. Variable costing is also preferred over absorption costing for studies of relative profitability of products, territories, and other segments of a business. It concentrates on the contribution that each segment makes to the recovery of fixed costs that will not be altered by decisions to make and sell. Under variable costing procedures,
   1. The marginal income concept leads to better pricing decisions, which are the principal advantage of variable costing.
   2. The impact of fixed costs on net income is emphasized by showing the total amount of such costs separately in financial reports.
   3. Out-of-pocket expenditures required to manufacture products conform closely with the valuation of inventory.
   4. The relationship between profit and the major factors of selling price, sales mix, sales volume, and variable manufacturing and nonmanufacturing costs is measured in terms of a single index of profitability.
   5. This profitability index, expressed as a positive amount or as a ratio, facilitates the analysis of cost-volume-profit relationships, compares the effects of two or more contemplated courses of action, and aids in answering many questions that arise in profit planning. See also Study Unit 27 on CVP analysis.
   6. Inventory changes have no effect on the breakeven computations.
   7. Marginal income figures facilitate appraisal of products, territories, and other business segments without having the results hidden or obscured by allocated joint fixed costs.
   8. Questions regarding whether a particular part should be made or bought can be more effectively answered if only variable costs are used.
      a. Management must consider whether to charge the product being made with variable costs only or to charge a percentage of fixed costs as well.
      b. Management must also consider whether the making of the part will require additional fixed costs and a decrease in normal production.
   9. Disinvestment decisions are facilitated because whether a product or department is recouping its variable costs can be determined.
      a. If the variable costs are being covered, operating a department at an apparent loss may be profitable.
   10. Management is better able to judge the differences between departments if certain fixed costs are omitted from the statements instead of being allocated arbitrarily.
   11. Cost figures are guided by the sales figures.
      a. Under variable costing, the cost of goods sold will vary directly with the sales volume, and the influence of production on gross profit is avoided.
      b. Variable costing also eliminates the possible difficulties of having to explain over- or underapplied factory overhead to higher management.

STUDY UNIT 21
PLANNING

This is one of two study units in Part 3 covering Planning (20% to 30% of Part 3). The two study units are

Study Unit 21: Planning
Study Unit 22: Budgeting

NATURE OF THE PLANNING PROCESS

A. Planning is the determination of **what** is to be done, and of **how**, **when**, **where**, and **by whom** it is to be done. Plans serve to direct the activities that all organizational members must undertake and successfully perform to move the organization from where it is to where it wants to be (i.e., toward its goals).

1. Planning must be completed before undertaking any other managerial function.
2. Planning establishes the means to reach organizational ends or goals.
   a. This means-end relationship extends throughout the organizational hierarchy and ties together the parts of the organization so that the various means all focus on the same end.
   b. One organizational level's ends provide the next higher level's means, and so on.
      1) EXAMPLE: Management by objectives (MBO) is partially designed to show relationships between an individual's job objectives (ends) and the immediate superior's objectives (ends) so an individual can see how his/her job is the means by which the superior's job is accomplished (see the discussion of MBO in Study Unit 8, Motivation and the Directing Process).
   c. Because plans are the means to organizational ends, the means-end chains extending down the organization can create semantic confusion between plans and goals.
      1) EXAMPLE: The ends of the maintenance manager's job (properly running machines) are a means by which the plant manager reaches production goals or ends.

B. **The Planning Process**

1. Long-range (strategic) planning is from 1 to 10 years or more. It embodies the concerns of top management and is based on
   a. Identifying and specifying organizational goals and objectives, i.e., the future course of the organization consistent with its mission statement

b. Evaluating the strengths and weaknesses of the organization (e.g., what it does well and/or poorly)

c. Assessing risk levels

d. Forecasting the effects of environmental factors relevant to the organization (e.g., market trends, changes in technology, international competition, and social change)

e. Deriving the best strategy for reaching the objectives, given the organization's strengths and weaknesses and the relevant future trends

2. Strategic plans are translated into measurable and achievable intermediate and operational plans.

   a. Intermediate plans (6 months to 2 years) are developed by middle management.

   b. Operational plans (1 week to 1 year) are developed by lower level managers.

3. Intermediate and operational plans must be retranslated into policies, procedures, and rules.

PLANNING PREMISES

A. Premises are the underlying assumptions about the expected environment in which plans will operate. Thus, the next step in planning is **premising**, or the generation of planning assumptions.

1. Premises should be limited to those crucial to the success of the plans.

2. Managers should ask, "What internal and external factors would influence the actions planned for this organization (division, department, program)?" Premises must be considered at all levels of the organization.

   a. Thus, capital budgeting plans should be premised on assumptions (forecasts) about economic cycles, price movements, etc.

   b. The stores department's plans might be premised on stability of parts prices or on forecasts that prices will rise.

3. EXAMPLES:

   a. The general economy will suffer an 11% decline next year.

   b. Our closest competitor's new model will provide greater competition for potential sales.

   c. Union negotiations will result in a general wage increase of 8%.

   d. Over the next 5 years, the cost of our raw materials will increase by 30%.

   e. The elasticity of demand for the company's products is 1.2.

OBJECTIVES AND GOALS

A. The terms **objectives** and **goals** are most often used interchangeably. However, some writers distinguish between overall organizational objectives and individual, departmental, or subunit goals.

B. The determination of organizational objectives is the first step in planning.

C. Organizations usually have multiple objectives, which are often contradictory.

1. The objective of maximizing profit and the objective of growth could be mutually exclusive within a given year. Maximizing short-term profit might hamper or preclude future growth.
2. Conflict among an organization's objectives is common.

D. Objectives vary with the organization's type and stage of development.

E. **Management Objectives**

1. The primary task of management is to reach organizational goals and objectives effectively and efficiently.
   a. **Efficiency** refers to maximizing the output for a given quantity of input.
   b. **Effectiveness** refers to the degree to which the goal or objective is accomplished.
   c. In practice, effectiveness is of prime importance, and efficiency may be secondary because trade-offs are frequently made between efficiency and effectiveness.
      1) EXAMPLE: In a hospital, efficiency is much less important than effectiveness. Reducing the night nursing staff to the theoretical minimum might increase efficiency by reducing payroll, but if even one patient dies because of inadequate care, the hospital has failed to effectively carry out its mission.
   d. Effectiveness is doing the right things. Efficiency is doing things right.
2. Subordinate goals of management may include
   a. Survival
   b. Growth of market influence
   c. Employee development
   d. Social responsibility
   e. Creativity
   f. Personal need satisfaction

F. Each subunit of an organization may have its own goals.

1. Subunit goals may conflict with overall organizational objectives.
2. Subunit goals are formed to unite the efforts of the people in the subunit and consequently
   a. The people in each subunit are bound by their collective wisdom, training, and experiences into a tunnel vision of the organization's purpose.
      1) EXAMPLE: "Why doesn't anybody take the time to see our problems in production? After all, if it weren't for us they wouldn't have anything to sell!"
   b. Subunits tend to be designed to make decisions that optimize the results of each subunit, to the possible detriment of the overall organization.
      1) Decentralized profit centers are the classic illustration.
         a) EXAMPLE: A profit center that buys raw materials from another profit center in the same organization will seek to maximize its own welfare regardless of the consequences for corporate objectives.
3. Subunit goals must be established to translate broad overall corporate objectives into meaningful and measurable terms for the subunit members.

G. Objectives and goals should be
   1. Clearly stated in specific terms. General or poorly defined objectives are not useful for guiding the actions of managers or measuring their performance.
   2. Easily communicated to all concerned. The executives who determine objectives cannot have the desired impact on the organization until they successfully communicate the objectives to all from whom action is required.
   3. Accepted by the individuals concerned. An objective is unlikely to be attained if it is thought to be unachievable by those affected.

H. Broad objectives should be established at the top and retranslated in more specific terms as they are communicated downward in a means-end hierarchy.
   1. EXAMPLE:
      a. A firm has a socioeconomic purpose, such as providing food.
      b. The firm's mission is the accomplishment of its socioeconomic purpose through the production of breakfast cereal.
      c. The firm develops long-range or strategic objectives with regard to profitability, growth, and/or survival.
      d. A more specific overall objective might be to provide investors with an adequate return on their investment.
      e. Divisional goals can be developed, e.g., to increase the sales of a certain kind of cereal.
      f. Departmental goals are developed, e.g., to reduce waste in the packaging department.
      g. Low-level managers and supervisors then develop personal performance and development goals.

I. A divergence of opinions exists regarding the determination of organizational objectives.
   1. One view is that **service** (need satisfaction for the consumer) is primary and that profit results from service.
   2. The other view is that **profit** or **return on investment (ROI)** is primary and that service results from profit.
   3. The most relevant view for a given organization is contingent upon its particular situation or environment.
      a. EXAMPLE: A fast-food company has customer service as its primary objective and would expect profits to result from the successful satisfaction of consumer needs. On the other hand, a private utility can provide service only if a reasonable return on investment attracts the capital needed for system maintenance and expansion. For a utility, service results from profit.

J. Objectives and goals change over time.
   1. EXAMPLE: The 19th-century industrialist's main goals were to make money and increase personal power. In the latter part of the 20th century, social responsibility has become a significant force that must be accommodated. This change is evidenced by, for example, the expanding pressures for information disclosures to outside parties, for environmental-impact studies, and for training the hard-core unemployed.

POLICIES, PROCEDURES, AND RULES

A. After objectives, goals, and premises are formulated, the next step in the planning process is the development of policies, procedures, and rules. These elements are necessary at all levels of the organization and overlap both in definition and in practice.

B. Policies, procedures, and rules are standing plans for repetitive situations.

C. **Policies** -- general statements that guide thinking and action in decision making

   1. Policies may be explicitly published by management.
   2. Policies may be implied by the actions of management.
      a. Managers should be certain that their subordinates do not misinterpret minor or unrelated decisions as precedents for policy.
   3. Policies indicate a preferred method for achieving objectives.
   4. Policies define a general area within which a manager may exercise discretion.
   5. Policies should
      a. Involve known principles
      b. Be in keeping with higher-level policies
      c. Be consistent with the policies of parallel units in the organization
      d. Be clear and comprehensive
      e. Be workable
      f. Be published
   6. Difficulties arise in the administration of policies that are not properly
      a. Formulated
      b. Understood
      c. Flexible
      d. Communicated
      e. Updated
      f. Accepted

D. **Procedures** -- specific directives that define how work is to be done

   1. Procedures may be described as follows:
      a. Usually consist of a set of specific steps in chronological order
      b. Are found at every level of the organization
      c. Reduce the need for managerial direction of subordinates in the accomplishment of routine matters
      d. Improve efficiency through standardization of actions
      e. Facilitate the training of personnel
      f. Provide coordination among different departments of the organization
   2. Procedures should be
      a. Balanced
      b. Efficient in use of resources
      c. Subject to organized control
      d. Flexible enough to handle most normal situations
      e. Clearly defined and easily accessible, as in procedures manuals

E. **Rules** -- specific, detailed guides that restrict behavior

   1. Rules are the simplest plans.
   2. A rule requires a specific action to be taken with regard to a given situation.
   3. Rules allow no discretion or flexibility.
   4. A procedure may contain a sequence of rules, or a rule may stand alone.
   5. For example, “No smoking in the paint shop. Violators will be dismissed without exception.”

PROGRAMS AND BUDGETS

A. **Program** -- an organized set of goals, policies, procedures, and rules designed to carry out a given course of action

1. A major program may call for many derivative programs (subprograms).
2. Most significant programs depend upon or affect other programs within an enterprise.

B. **Budget** -- a plan that contains a quantitative statement of expected results. A budget may be defined as a quantified program.

1. Budgets are very useful control devices, but their formulation is a planning function.
   a. See Study Unit 23, The Controlling Process, for more on budgeting as a control tool. Also see Study Unit 22, Budgeting.
2. Budgets are developed for, among other things,
   a. Cash flows
   b. Expenses and revenues
   c. Capital outlays
   d. Labor usage
   e. Machine-hour usage
   f. Advertising
3. Budgets may be written based on a single, unknown, central variable, such as sales volume or production quantity. These budgets are **flexible** or **variable**.
4. **Zero-base budgeting** is an effective means of bringing objective thinking to the budgeting process and avoiding a tendency to add to the preceding year's budget.
   a. The programs of the organization are divided into **packages** that include goals, activities, and resources.
   b. The cost of each package for the coming period is calculated, starting from zero.
   c. The principal advantage of this approach is that managers are forced to review each program in its entirety (justify all expenditures) at the beginning of every budget period, rather than merely extrapolate the historical figures (costs).

C. Budgets serve to

1. Present organizational plans in a formal, logical, integrated manner
2. Quantify objectives and the means selected for achieving them by relating expected occurrences to the resources available
3. Force consideration of all the events needed to meet the goals of each organizational function and thus serve as a motivational tool
4. Provide a basis for coordinating the plans of all the subunits of the organization into an integrated whole, thereby promoting goal congruence
5. Provide a means for communicating detailed plans to all concerned
6. Provide a basis for control of performance through comparisons of actual with budgeted data. They permit analysis of variations from plans and signal the need for corrective managerial action.

D. **Program budgets** are formulated by objective rather than function and can cut across functional lines.

E. The budget for an operating unit should include as much specific information from that unit's management as possible, but

1. Budgets must be in line with the strategic plans of corporate management.

   a. Top management provides a context within which operational managers can prepare their budgets.

   b. Corporate support might include economic forecasts, overall market sales forecasts, capital budgets, etc.

2. Input from the lowest relevant unit must be included because managers at this level have knowledge of actual production needs, etc., without which overall planning may be ineffective or inaccurate.

3. Successful budgets represent a compromise between top-level and operating management.

F. A fundamentally different use of the word budget is common in governmental organizations.

1. Because governmental endeavor is difficult to measure (there is usually no revenue function), the use of budgets in the appropriation process is extremely important.

2. Also, the stewardship function is emphasized; thus, spending limits are important. Governmental units are encouraged to expend all of their appropriated funds.

G. Budgets have a significant behavioral impact. The setting of realistic and attainable goals has been shown to have a positive effect on performance.

1. Unrealistically high or low goals have a negative effect on performance.

2. Participation in the budgeting process by the individuals affected usually improves performance by fostering a sense of involvement. Also, participants better understand what is expected of them.

TYPES OF PLANS

A. Planning can be either formal or informal.

1. Formal plans are written in a stylized format for distribution to those concerned with carrying them out.

   a. EXAMPLES:

      1) Budgets
      2) Schedules
      3) Business plans in the form of pro forma income statements
      4) Statements of specific objectives or goals

2. Informal plans are made by an individual to guide his/her activities. They may consist of lists or notes on what (s)he plans to accomplish during a day or they may cover a longer period of time.

B. Plans are made for different periods of time.

1. Short-range or operational planning is usually considered to be for 1 year or less. All organizations create short-range plans.

   a. Short-range plans concern such matters as

      1) Production
      2) Materials procurement
      3) Expenses and revenues
      4) Cash flows

2. Long-range or strategic planning is for periods from 1 to as many as 20 years. These plans are sometimes divided into intermediate (6 months to 2 years) and long range (1 to 10 years or more).
   a. Planning for very long periods is a relatively new idea.
   b. Long-range plans are difficult to make because of uncertainty about future conditions. Thus, long-range plans are more general and exclude operational detail.
   c. Long-range plans concern such matters as
      1) New product development
      2) Capital budgeting
      3) Major financing
      4) Mergers, acquisitions, or divestitures
3. The expansion of computer capacity and the decrease in cost of computer acquisition and operation have increased the use of quantitative models for long-range as well as short-range planning purposes.
   a. This effect is particularly evident in large organizations, in which quantitative models may be used with greater statistical reliability.

C. Both single-purpose and standing-purpose plans exist.

1. Single-purpose plans are for objectives of known duration.
   a. EXAMPLES:
      1) The construction of a plant
      2) The installation of a new accounting system
      3) The introductory phase of a marketing program
2. Standing-purpose plans are for objectives that will continue to exist for the foreseeable future.
   a. EXAMPLES:
      1) Maintenance of market share
      2) Operation of an existing production facility
      3) Administration of a pension plan

GENERAL PRINCIPLES IN THE PROCESS OF PLANNING

A. The lowest possible relevant units in management should be involved in the planning process. This form of upward communication is important for several reasons.

1. Lower-level managers are aware of operational details and limitations. Thus, they can contribute to the feasibility and precision of the plan with regard to their individual areas of responsibility.
2. Plans prepared at higher levels, without the participation of the managers who will be involved in their execution, appear to be dictated to the lower-level managers, with a consequent reduction in performance.

B. **Additional General Planning Principles**

1. Plans should not allocate more than the known available resources.
2. Planning must precede action.
3. Plans must be coordinated among related functions.
4. Plans must be flexible and recognized as subject to change.
5. Plans should be limited to only highly probable future events; it is impossible to include every possible action and consequence.

THE DECISION-MAKING PROCESS FOR PLANNING

A. The decision-making process is an integral part of the planning process. The consideration of choices and the selection of the choice expected to give the best results are a key part of the planner's job. Rational decision making involves

   1. Defining of the problem
   2. Identifying choices
   3. Evaluating choices
   4. Making the choice
   5. Following up

B. Awareness of the existence of a problem, i.e., realization that a gap exists between planned results and reality (between where the enterprise is and where it wants to be), precedes defining the problem.

   1. **Bounded rationality** (the inability to see all aspects of the situation) may prevent accurate problem definition.
   2. Perception may preclude seeing the correct problem.
      a. We see what we **expect** to see.
      b. We see what we are **trained** to see.
      c. Our **needs** influence what we observe.
      d. **Group pressure** may influence what problems we perceive or how we define them.

C. **Searching for Solutions**. The search

   1. Can be primary (e.g., surveys, samples, attitude questionnaires)
   2. Can be secondary (e.g., reading scholarly papers)
   3. Can be creative
      a. **Brainstorming** is an example.
   4. In open systems, cannot feasibly consider all possibilities
   5. Ordinarily ends for most people when they find a solution they consider good enough (satisficing)

D. **Evaluation of Solutions**. The analysis of facts and the development of solutions have been improved in recent years through the adoption of mathematical techniques. These techniques are not a panacea -- they will not provide useful solutions for poorly formulated problems -- but they will provide valuable results for well-defined quantitative problems. Some of these quantitative tools or approaches are defined below and on the following page. Also see Study Unit 29, Decision Making under Uncertainty, and Study Unit 31, Quantitative Methods.

   1. **Operations research** is really an overall approach, which involves the
      a. Recognition of the complete system, including interrelationships, in which the problem operates
      b. Formulation of a mathematical model
      c. Testing of the model
      d. Implementation of the optimal solution as produced by the model

2. **Simulation** is an approach that has only recently become possible because of the economic availability of high-speed computers.
   a. Simulation is used when an optimization model is not possible.
      1) For example, the number of variables may exceed the number of equations describing the variables.
   b. Simulation requires the construction of a quantitative model that incorporates most of the features of the problem situation.
   c. The model is then tested in a variety of hypothetical situations.
      1) For example, if certain conditions hold true, what performance can be expected from the system being modeled?
   d. The modeled response to the situations can then be measured.
3. **Linear programming** is a tool for allocating scarce resources in the presence of constraints.
   a. The problem must be described by a system of linear equations. An objective function (usually cost or revenue) is maximized or minimized subject to constraint equations. This description is seldom strictly accurate, but provides useful approximations.
   b. The simultaneous solution to the system of equations maximizes profit (or minimizes cost).
4. **Cost-benefit analysis** is a simple test for possible solutions. Cost should be less than the benefits realized.
5. **Queuing theory** is a technique to analyze waiting-line problems through the use of probability theory. It minimizes the sum of the cost of waiting lines and the cost of reducing or eliminating queues.
6. **Decision trees (decision theory)** map out possible actions given probabilistic events. Probabilities are assigned, and the expected value (payoff or loss) for each decision choice and the events that might follow from that choice is calculated.
   a. A current decision may entail a choice among multiple options, each of which may lead to different future events (states of nature).
      1) EXAMPLE: If one invests in a fast-food franchise and the economy improves, investing in the franchise is the action, and the improvement in the economy is the future event.
7. **Monte Carlo method**. Random behavior may be added to otherwise deterministic models to simulate the uncertainty inherent in real-world situations. The model is then run a large number of times, and the variance of the probability distribution of the results and the average performance are determined.
8. However, it is not always possible to account for uncertainty by assigning probabilities or to assume away uncertainty with precise mathematical formulas.

E. **Making the Choice**. The selection of the best available solution is the objective of the decision-making process.

1. The optimal solution is selected.
   a. If the complete decision-making process has been followed, the result will be profit-maximizing behavior rather than satisficing behavior.
      1) This result should be attained if cost-benefit analysis is applied to the overall decision-making process as well as to its individual steps.
2. Human aspects of the choice must be considered. A decision is only useful if it can be sold to those responsible for its implementation.
   a. Decisions are made in a multi-dimensional environment and therefore have many, sometimes unexpected, effects.
   b. An otherwise optimal solution may fail if the opinion and attitudes of the people involved are not considered in the decision-making process.
   c. The multi-step process of decision making must be followed when making organizational changes.
      1) Implementing change is a critical part of the decision-making process because people are crucial to the effectiveness of the choice.

F. **Following Up on the Effects of the Action**. The proper delegation of authority is made to the individual responsible for implementing the action to be taken. Performance measurement is then provided for.

1. This process puts the solution into a feasible framework, which assures it will be carried out.
2. The failure to provide for practical implementation causes many otherwise correct decisions to fail to produce the desired results.
3. Decisions cannot be fully implemented until they are effectively communicated. See Study Unit 9, Communication.

PLANNING AIDS AND PITFALLS

A. **Aids to Planning**

1. **Gantt charts** -- bar charts with time (in days, months, years, or any time unit) on the horizontal axis and the duration of a task represented as a bar running from the starting date to the ending date of the task. By moving vertically up the chart on a given date, it is easy to see
   a. How expected performance compares with actual performance for a given task
   b. Which tasks should be in progress on a given date
   c. How close to completion a task should be on a given date

2. **PERT (Program Evaluation and Review Technique)** -- a type of network analysis. A network is constructed of tasks, including a probabilistic estimate of the time required for completion of each task in the network. The network establishes a strict priority relationship among tasks. The **critical path** is the string of tasks with the longest total completion time.
   a. Three times are usually estimated for each task
      1) Best
      2) Worst
      3) Average
   b. The critical path identifies those tasks that have a direct effect on the completion date of the entire project.
   c. PERT forces planning by all levels of management.
   d. PERT provides information on the effect of a delay in one task on the project as a whole.
   e. PERT shows where excess (slack) time and resources are available to help reduce the critical path.
   f. PERT gives continuing objective feedback as to whether the planned completion date is attainable.
3. **PERT-cost**. Costs are applied to all activities in the network so that the effect of a change in any given task on cost as well as on time may be projected.
4. **CPM (Critical Path Method)** is essentially a subset of PERT, but it uses a deterministic rather than a probabilistic estimate of the time required for task completion.
5. **PPBS (Planning-Programming-Budgeting System)**. The objectives are identified and various methods of meeting the objectives are subjected to systematic analysis comparing projected costs with benefits. The key decision variable is program output value in comparison with program cost, i.e., cost effectiveness.
6. **Delphi Technique** is a group approach to forecasting or decision making that attempts to avoid **groupthink** (the tendency of individuals to conform to what they perceive to be the consensus).
   a. The technique allows only written, anonymous communication among group members.
   b. Each member takes a position on the problem at hand.
   c. The central thrust of these positions is communicated to each member.
   d. The process is repeated for several iterations as the members move toward a central common position.
7. **Contingency planning** is based on different sets of premises. It stipulates different sets of actions for management based on these premises.
   a. Contingency planning allows for forecasting error.
   b. Contingency planning is more expensive than formulating a single plan, so this additional cost must be more than balanced by improved performance.

B. **Causes of Failure in Planning**

1. A lack of commitment to planning. For the planning process to be successful, there must be a genuine commitment to planning on the part of each manager in the enterprise.
2. Failure to put in the necessary time. People are usually unwilling to put in the time required because the benefits of planning are hard to measure, but the time and costs of planning are not.
3. Failure to develop and implement sound overall strategies. A clear definition of what the organization, as a whole, wishes to accomplish and a feasible strategy to achieve organizational objectives are the bases of successful planning.
4. Lack of meaningful objectives and goals for organizational subunits. Effective planning requires that goals be
   a. Clear; i.e., people can understand them
   b. Attainable; i.e., they can be accomplished, and the people involved believe they can be accomplished
   c. Verifiable; i.e., progress toward the goals is measurable and accomplishment of goals is obvious
5. Inconsistency in planning premises (assumptions about future conditions)
6. Excessive reliance on past experience. A failure to appreciate the nature of future situations will result in basing plans on inappropriate premises.
7. Failure to use the principle of the limiting factor. A successful plan must concentrate on the few most critical variables in a problem situation, rather than attempting to describe all variables.
8. Lack of support for a plan by top management
9. Lack of adequate control techniques and information. A successful plan requires control and follow-up during implementation.
10. Lack of participation in planning. In any type of plan, especially one involving organizational change or the budget process, the involvement of the people affected will help assure understanding of and commitment to the plan.
11. Resistance to change. Planning for future events requires change, and people tend to resist change.
    a. Resistance may be overcome by the participation of those affected in planning for the change, by full and accurate communication by management, by timely notice, and by other steps taken by management to reduce unfounded fears of the personal, social, and economic adjustments that may occur.

HUMAN RESOURCE PLANNING

A. A human resource audit is a thorough analysis of the strengths and weaknesses of the human assets in and available to an organization. Advantages include
   1. Training programs can be scheduled to provide experienced staff when needed.
   2. Promotion decisions can be improved.
   3. Hiring decisions can be based on future requirements.

B. The audit should compile information such as employees' education, experience, work histories, and salary histories.

C. See also the discussion of Human Resource Accounting in Study Unit 23, The Controlling Process.

STUDY UNIT 22
BUDGETING

The ICMA devotes 20% to 30% of Part 3 to planning. We cover this topic in two study units:

Study Unit 21: Planning
Study Unit 22: Budgeting

Although the underlying budgetary concepts are simple, the computations, amount of data, and detail are often complex. Thus, you must emphasize preparation of complete solutions to the essay questions/computational problems for this study unit in Volume II. Because budgeting also entails use of such techniques as regression analysis, learning curves, and other forecasting methods, Study Units 30 and 31 should be read in conjunction with Study Unit 22.

BUDGETS

A. A **budget (profit plan)** is a realistic plan for the future expressed in quantitative terms.
   1. The budget is a **planning** tool.
      a. A budget is a written plan for the future.
      b. Companies that prepare budgets anticipate problems before they occur.
         1) EXAMPLE: If a company runs out of a critical raw material, it may have to shut down. At best, it will incur extremely high freight costs to have the needed materials rushed in. The company with a budget will have anticipated the shortage and planned around it.
      c. A firm that has no goals may not always make the best decisions. A firm with a goal, in the form of a budget, will be able to plan.
   2. The budget is a **control** tool.
      a. A budget helps a firm control costs by setting cost guidelines.
      b. Guidelines reveal the efficient or inefficient use of company resources.
      c. A manager is less apt to spend money for things that are not needed if (s)he knows that all costs will be compared with the budget.
         1) (S)he will be accountable for controllable costs exceeding budgeted amounts.
      d. Budgets can also reveal the progress of highly effective managers. Consequently, employees should not view budgets negatively. A budget is just as likely to provide a boost to a manager's career as it is to be detrimental.

e. Managers can also use budgets as a personal self-evaluation tool.

f. Budgetary slack (overestimation of expenses) must be avoided, however, if a budget is to have its desired effects. The natural tendency of a manager is to negotiate for a less stringent measure of performance so as to avoid unfavorable variances from expectations.

g. For the budgetary process to serve effectively as a control function, it must be integrated with the accounting system and the organizational structure. Such integration enhances control by transmitting data and assigning variances to the proper organizational subunits.

3. The budget is a **motivational** tool.

   a. A budget helps to motivate employees to do a good job.

      1) Employees are particularly motivated if they help prepare the budget.

      2) A manager who is asked to prepare a budget for his/her department will work hard to keep costs within the budget.

   b. A budget must be seen as realistic by employees before it can become a good motivational tool.

   c. Unfortunately, the budget is not always viewed in a positive manner. Some managers view a budget as a restriction.

   d. Employees are more apt to have a positive feeling toward a budget if some degree of flexibility is allowed. See Flexible vs. Fixed Budgets on page 539.

4. The budget is a means of **communication**.

   a. A budget can help tell employees what goals the firm is attempting to accomplish.

   b. If the firm does not have an overall budget, each department might think the firm has different goals.

   c. For example, the sales department may want to keep as much inventory as possible so that no sales will be lost, and the company treasurer may want to keep the inventory as low as possible so that cash need not be spent any sooner than necessary. If the budget specifies the amount of inventory, all employees can work toward the same objectives.

5. A discussion of budgets also appears in Study Unit 6, Capital Structure Finance.
6. Study Unit 27, Cost-Volume-Profit (CVP) Analysis, concerns a related subject.
7. Capital Budgeting is in Study Unit 28.

B. Budgets coordinate the various activities of a firm. A company's overall budget, often called the **master** or **comprehensive budget**, consists of many smaller budgets.

   1. Sales budget (projected sales)
   2. Production budget (manufacturing firms)
   3. Purchases budget
   4. Individual departmental expense budgets
   5. Equipment purchases budget
   6. Cash budget

C. **Budget Manuals**

   1. A budget manual describes how a budget is to be prepared. Items usually appearing in a budget manual include a budget planning calendar and distribution instructions for all budget schedules. Distribution instructions are quite important because, once a schedule is prepared, other departments within the organization use the schedule to prepare their own budgets. Without distribution instructions, someone who needs a particular schedule might be overlooked.

TYPES OF BUDGETS

A. **Sales budget** is usually the first budget prepared.

1. Once a firm can estimate sales, the next step is to decide how much to produce or purchase.
2. Sales are usually budgeted by product or department.
3. The sales budget establishes targets for sales personnel.
4. Sales volume affects production and purchasing levels, operating expenses, and cash flow.

B. **Production budgets** (manufacturing firms) are based on sales in units plus or minus desired inventory buildup or reduction.

1. They are prepared for each department.
2. They are used to plan when items will be produced.
3. They are usually stated in units instead of dollars.
4. When the production budget has been completed, it is used to prepare three additional budgets.
   a. Raw materials purchases, which is similar to the purchases budget of a merchandising firm
   b. Direct labor budget, which includes hours, wage rates, and total dollars
   c. Factory overhead budget, which is similar to a department expense budget

C. **Purchases budget** can follow after projected sales have been set.

1. It is prepared on a monthly or even a weekly basis.
2. Purchases can be planned so that stockouts are avoided.
3. Inventory should be at an appropriate level to avoid unnecessary carrying costs.
4. See Study Unit 30, Inventory Models, for discussion of inventory economic order quantities and stockout models.

D. **Expense Budgets**. Department heads prepare departmental expense budgets using the sales budget as a basis.

1. Expense budgets are based on prior year's costs and adjusted for changes in prices, wages, and sales volume estimates.
2. See also Zero-Base Budgeting (ZBB) on page 540.

E. **Equipment purchases** (or **capital expenditures**) **budgets** may be prepared more than a year in advance to allow sufficient time to

1. Plan financing of major expenditures for equipment or buildings
2. Receive custom orders of specialized equipment, buildings, etc.
   a. Note that the capital expenditures budget is technically not part of the operating budget, but it must be incorporated into the preparation of the cash budget and pro forma financial statements.

F. **Cash budget** is probably the most important part of a company's budget program. An organization must have adequate cash at all times. Even with plenty of other assets, an organization with a temporary shortage of cash can be driven into bankruptcy. Proper planning can keep an entity from financial embarrassment.

1. A cash budget details projected cash receipts and disbursements.

2. It cannot be prepared until the other budgets have been completed.
3. Almost all organizations, regardless of size, prepare a cash budget.
4. It is particularly important for organizations operating in seasonal industries.
5. Cash budgeting facilitates loans and other financing.
   a. A bank is more likely to lend money to a firm if the money will not be needed immediately.
6. For example, assume that a company had budgeted sales of $9,000 for January, $9,700 for February, and $13,950 for March. Its cash budget might appear as follows:

Sample Company
CASH BUDGET
For Quarter Ending March 31, 199X

	January	February	March	Total
Beginning cash balance	$ 80	$ 20	$ 1,957	$ 80
Receipts:				
Collection from sales*	6,800	9,350	11,825	27,975
TOTAL CASH AVAILABLE	$6,880	$9,370	$13,782	$28,055
Payments:				
Purchases**	$3,150	$2,760	$ 3,960	$ 9,870
Sales salaries	1,350	1,455	2,093	4,898
Supplies	360	388	588	1,306
Utilities	120	110	100	330
Administrative salaries	1,800	1,800	1,800	5,400
Advertising	80	80	80	240
Equipment purchases	0	820	3,000	3,820
TOTAL PAYMENTS	6,860	7,413	11,591	25,864
ENDING BALANCE	$ 20	$1,957	$ 2,191	$ 2,191

* Sales are 50% cash sales and 50% on credit (net 30 days). Thus, 50% of each month's sales are collected in the month of the sale and 50% are collected in the following month. For example, the February collections ($9,350) were calculated as follows:

50% of January sales	$4,500
50% of February sales	4,850
	$9,350

** Purchases are on terms of net 30 days. Thus, purchases are paid for in the month following the purchase. The amount paid in February ($2,760) was the total purchases for January.

G. The **budget planning calendar** is the schedule of activities for the development and adoption of the budget.

1. It should include a list of dates indicating when specific information is to be provided to others by each information source.
2. The preparation of a master budget usually takes several months. For instance, many firms start the budget for the next calendar year sometime in September anticipating its completion by the first of December. Because all of the individual departmental budgets are based on forecasts prepared by others and the budgets of other departments, it is essential to have a planning calendar to integrate the entire process.

H. The following is a partial summary of the budget sequence for a manufacturing firm (costs of marketing, distribution, and administration are omitted).

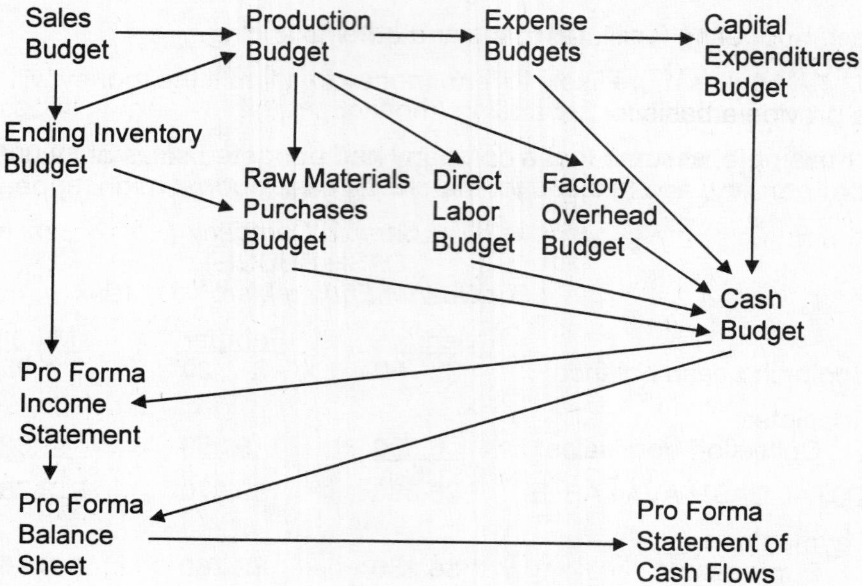

ESTIMATED FINANCIAL STATEMENTS

A. Once the individual budgets are complete, budgeted financial statements can be prepared. They are often called **pro forma** statements because they are prepared before actual activities commence.

1. The **pro forma income statement** is based on the sales, production, and expense budgets.
   a. It is used to decide whether the budgeted activities will result in an acceptable level of income.
   b. If it shows an unacceptable level of income, the whole budgeting process must begin again.
2. The **pro forma balance sheet** is the beginning of the period balance sheet updated for projected changes in cash, receivables, payables, inventory, etc., as determined in the cash budget.
   a. If the balance sheet indicates that a contractual agreement may be violated, the budgeting process must be repeated.
      1) For example, some loan agreements require that owners' equity be maintained at some percentage of total debt or that current assets be maintained at a given multiple of current liabilities.
3. The **pro forma statement of cash flows** classifies cash receipts and disbursements depending on whether they are from operating, investing, or financing activities.
   a. The direct presentation reports the major classes of gross cash operating receipts and payments and the difference between them.
   b. The indirect presentation reconciles net income with net operating cash flow.
      1) The reconciliation requires balance sheet data, such as the changes in accounts receivable, accounts payable, and inventory, as well as net income.

4. All the pro forma statements are interrelated.
   a. EXAMPLE: The pro forma cash flow statement will include anticipated borrowing. The interest on this borrowing will appear in the pro forma income statement.

BUDGET REPORTS

A. Budgets provide a basis for controlling (monitoring and revising) activities of an organization.
   1. **A budget report** compares actual performance (actual costs incurred) with budgeted performance (budgeted costs).
   2. A budget report has columns for budgeted costs and actual costs incurred.
      a. The difference between the two is the **variance**.
         1) If actual costs are higher than budgeted, the variance is **unfavorable**.
         2) If actual costs are lower than budgeted, the variance is **favorable**.

	Budget	Actual	Variance	
Variable expenses	$175,000	$178,000	$3,000	unfavorable
Selling and administration	85,000	83,000	2,000	favorable
	$260,000	$261,000	$1,000	unfavorable

Upon receiving this performance report, management may want to review variable expenses to determine the source and cause of the variance(s).

B. Differences between budgeted and actual revenues are analyzed in Study Unit 24, Standard Costs and Variance Analysis, especially under the sideheading Sales and Product Mix Variances.

C. The initial budget is a planning tool, and the budget report is a control tool. Both are steps in the **control loop**.
   1. Establishing standards of performance (the budget)
   2. Measuring actual performance
   3. Analyzing and comparing performance to standards (budget report)
   4. Constructing and implementing corrective actions
   5. Reviewing and revising the standards

D. A **continuous (rolling) budget** is one that is revised on a regular (continuous) basis. Typically, a company extends such a budget for another month or quarter in accordance with new data as the current month or quarter ends. For example, if the budget is for 12 months, a budget for the next 12 months will be available continuously as each month ends.

FLEXIBLE vs. FIXED BUDGETS

A. A **fixed budget** is based on only one level of sales or production.
   1. It is not very useful if the expected level is not reached or is exceeded.
   2. EXAMPLE: Assume that a company budgeted sales at $80,000 and supplies expense at $6,000. What can be said about the efficiency of management if supplies expense is actually $480 when sales are only $40,000? Management cannot evaluate the variance because it does not have a budget for a sales level of $40,000.

B. A **flexible budget** is actually a series of several budgets prepared for many levels of sales.

1. At the end of the period, management can compare actual costs or performance to the appropriate budgeted level in the flexible budget.
2. New columns can quickly be made by interpolation or extrapolation, if necessary.
3. A flexible budget is designed to allow adjustment of the budget to the actual level of activity before comparing the budgeted activity with actual results.
   a. In the example on variable expenses in Budget Reports, A.2.a.2) on page 539, assume that the $175,000 estimate of manufacturing costs was based on expected production of 25,000 units at $7 per unit, but actual production was 25,500 units. Production cost should have been $178,500 ($7 x 25,500).

	Budget	Flexible Budget	Actual	Variance	
Var. mfg. costs	$175,000	$178,500	$178,000	$ 500	favorable
Selling & admin.	85,000	85,000	83,000	2,000	favorable
	$260,000	$263,500	$261,000	$2,500	favorable

   b. The report now reflects the actual level of activity. The variance is known as the flexible budget variance.

ZERO-BASE BUDGETING (ZBB)

A. The concept of zero-base budgeting originated in the U.S. Department of Agriculture in the early 1960s but was then abandoned. Texas Instruments Corporation began using the concept in the late 1960s and early 1970s, as did the state of Georgia under Governor Jimmy Carter. Carter also tried to introduce the concept into the federal budget system when he became President.

B. Zero-base budgeting is a budget and planning process in which each manager must justify a department's entire budget every year (or period).

1. ZBB differs from the traditional concept of budgeting in which next year's budget is largely based on the expenditures of the previous year.
2. Under ZBB, a manager must build the budget every year from a base of zero. All expenditures must be justified regardless of variance from previous years.
3. The objective is to encourage periodic reexamination of all costs in the hope that some can be reduced or eliminated.
4. ZBB begins with the lowest budgetary units of the entity. It requires determination of objectives, operations, and costs for each activity and the alternative means of carrying out that activity.
5. Different levels of service (work effort) are evaluated for each activity, measures of work and performance are established, and activities are ranked according to their importance to the entity.
6. For each budgetary unit, a decision package is prepared that describes various levels of service that may be provided, including at least one level lower than the current one. Accordingly, ZBB requires managers to justify each expenditure for each budget period and to review each cost component from a cost-benefit perspective.

STUDY UNIT 23
THE CONTROLLING PROCESS

Control and performance evaluation accounts for 20% to 30% of Part 3. We cover this topic in three study units:

Study Unit 23: The Controlling Process
Study Unit 24: Standard Costs and Variance Analysis
Study Unit 25: Responsibility Accounting

THE NATURE AND TYPES OF CONTROL

A. Control is the process of assuring that plans are achieving the desired objectives.

   1. The essence of control is feedback information on the results of actions taken by the enterprise for the purposes of

      a. Measurement
      b. Regulation

   2. Control can be precise, imprecise, formal, informal, good, or bad.

   3. Control has two aspects.

      a. Performance is measured against a standard.

      b. Performance is corrected (if necessary) in light of that measurement (thus, timeliness of feedback is important).

B. A typical control process functions by

   1. Selecting strategic control points at which to gather information about the activities being performed

   2. Observing the work, or collecting samples or other significant data

   3. Accumulating, classifying, and recording this information

   4. Comparing it with predetermined quality, schedule, and cost standards

   5. Determining whether performance is satisfactory

   6. Reporting significant deviations to managers concerned

   7. Determining, by repeating the steps, whether action taken is effective in correcting reported deviations (follow-up)

   8. Reviewing and revising standards

C. A successful control process is one that institutes corrections before the deviations become serious.

D. Planning and control overlap to some extent, and some common managerial tools apply to both.

   1. Budgets and breakeven charts are used as both planning and control devices.
   2. Comprehensive planning includes creation of control mechanisms, i.e., measurement and follow-up.
   3. Program Evaluation and Review Technique (PERT) systematically combines planning with control.

E. Control devices may be either quantitative or qualitative.

   1. Budgets, schedules, quotas, charts, etc., are quantitative.
   2. Job instructions, quality-control standards, and employment criteria are qualitative.

F. The total control process is a closed system consisting of a series of control elements or functions.

   1. As the final managerial function, control also closes the total managerial system by leading back to revised plans and corrective action when necessary to accomplish objectives.

G. A control system operates through the repetition of five sequential steps.

   1. Establishing standards of performance
   2. Measuring actual performance
   3. Analyzing performance and comparing it with standards
   4. Constructing and implementing a program of corrective actions
   5. Reviewing and revising the standards

H. Effective control systems should display the following characteristics:

   1. Economical: Excessive controls are costly in time as well as money.
   2. Meaningful: They must measure performance in important areas.
   3. Appropriate: They must fairly reflect the events they are designed to measure.
   4. Congruent: They must be consistent with the need for and ability to obtain precision in measurement (e.g., morale is good, not morale is 6.381).
   5. Timely: Outdated information is inappropriate.
   6. Simple: Control should be understandable to people using it.
   7. Operational: Controls should be relevant to a planned result and not just interesting.

I. Control has been facilitated by the recent improvements in computer capabilities, which have made real-time information common. Examples are airline reservation systems, retail point-of-sale systems, and production-line status systems.

SETTING STANDARDS

A. Standards are specific goals or objectives with which performance is compared.

B. Standards are commonly classified in terms of

   1. **Quantity** -- how many units to be produced
   2. **Quality** -- rejects, rework costs
   3. **Time** -- schedules, promised deliveries
   4. **Cost** -- how many dollars to produce the required number of units

C. Selection of points at which performance will be measured is critical.

1. It is not possible to oversee or measure the performance of every aspect of a business organization's activity.
   a. The cost would be prohibitive.
   b. The information system generating such data would overload the manager's capacity for review.
   c. Too much control is demoralizing.
   d. Measuring the wrong performance is unproductive.
   e. Developing surrogate quantitative measures for many qualitative issues may focus attention on the wrong issues (an example is teaching students how to maximize test scores instead of teaching concepts).
   f. The choices of control points and standards will affect behavior. Standards and control points must be selected so they are congruent with organizational goals.
      1) EXAMPLE: One study of the management of a police force revealed a dysfunctional result of a poor choice of a control point. An administrator, who had noticed that those units with the most miles logged on their patrol car odometers also had the most arrests, began rewarding those units with the most miles driven. This choice of control point did not increase the number of arrests, but it did increase mileage greatly.
2. Key questions in the selection of control points
   a. What will best reflect the goals of the department?
   b. What will best indicate when these goals are not being met?
   c. What will best measure critical deviations, i.e., those with the greatest impact on departmental goals?
   d. Which standards will cost the least?
3. Examples of good control points are
   a. Inspecting a motor **before** its cover is attached
   b. Balancing columns of figures **before** entering the answers into a ledger
   c. Inspecting components **before** assembly
   d. Reviewing progress reports **at** intermediate points
   e. Inspecting materials **before** approving payment

D. **Additional Guides for Standards**

1. Standards should assist in implementing plans.
2. Standards should be applied at those points that significantly influence subsequent progress.
3. Standards must be accepted by those who will carry them out if they are to have maximum effectiveness.
   a. Subordinates should believe that standards are both fair and achievable, or they will tend to sabotage, ignore, or circumvent them.
   b. Participation in the standard-setting process will encourage acceptance of standards and increase understanding of their meanings, measures, and purposes by those affected.

4. Standards should be reviewed periodically for adjustment or elimination because of changed circumstances.
5. Standards may need to be flexible in the same way budgets are flexible. The appropriate standard might be a ratio between cost and service produced rather than an absolute dollar amount of cost.
   a. EXAMPLES:
      1) Labor hours per unit rather than total labor hours
      2) Pounds of material consumed per customer, not total pounds consumed
6. Standards take different forms, depending on organizational function and level.
   a. Production standards
   b. Sales standards
      1) Percentage margin on sales
   c. Finance standards
      1) Return on investment at various levels
      2) Return on investment for decentralized divisions
      3) Budgets
   d. Personnel standards
      1) Turnover rates
      2) New hire rates
      3) Voluntary termination rates
      4) Absentee rates
      5) Sales per employee
      6) Return on investment per employee
      7) Affirmative action programs
      8) Human asset accounting
      9) Training needs, costs
   e. Management standards
      1) Management audits (operational audits of all activities of a particular function or department)
      2) Audits based on performance standards in social areas (social responsibility audits)

E. **Setting Tight Standards**
1. The degree of difficulty in meeting a standard is known as tightness. The more difficult a standard is to achieve, the tighter it is said to be.
2. Tight standards can have positive behavioral implications if they motivate employees to strive for excellence.
3. They can have negative effects if they are difficult or impossible to attain.

MEASURING PERFORMANCE

A. Every product, output, or action can be measured in some way.
1. The difficulty is in selecting appropriate measures for the performance activity being monitored.

2. EXAMPLES:

   a. A decentralized structure in which the manager is evaluated on a return on investment (ROI) basis forces the manager to seek short-run profit-maximizing solutions to the detriment of long-run survival factors such as

      1) Social responsibility and ethics
      2) Research and development
      3) Capital purchase decisions

   b. The budgeting process may send unintended messages to managers who play the budget game instead of accomplishing objectives.

3. The measurement must be carefully chosen because it is the message to the controlled activity's personnel and directs their behavior.

B. Complete measurement is often not possible (e.g., because of destructive tests) or not desirable (possibly because it is too costly) or inappropriate (the measure may be irrelevant to actual performance).

   1. Statistical sampling is useful for some quantitative measures (e.g., quality control).

   2. Sampling of the work process may be better than observing work output (e.g., behavior control).

C. The people doing the measuring may or may not be involved in the performance.

D. Behavioral considerations are important factors in selecting who does the measuring, as well as what is measured and what standards are used.

   1. Self-measurement may create confidence and trust. Moreover, feedback, correction, and learning may occur more quickly.

      a. It may also lead to distortion, concealment, and delay in reporting when goals and measurement criteria are unclear.

      b. It forces clear definition and open communication of organizational goals because employees must know the standards and measures.

   2. Second-party measurement may create hostility, concern, rebellion, and other negative reactions.

      a. It may also minimize bias, influence, and suspicion.

COMPARISON OF PERFORMANCE WITH STANDARDS

A. Care must be taken to compare like items. Thus, any alteration in the production process may make previously used or company-wide standards inapplicable to the case at hand.

B. The determination of variation from standards opens up the critical areas of evaluation and correction. A thorough understanding of applicable standards is required if appropriate corrective action is to result.

EVALUATION AND CORRECTION

A. Some control situations require little evaluation and lead to immediate corrective action.

   1. In situations for which the number of possible future states is limited, a precise (usually quantitative) decision rule may be adopted.

   2. EXAMPLE: A cash budget may call for a certain minimum balance in a given account. The automatic correction for this deviation from plan merely calls for transferring into the account an amount of cash equal to the deficiency.

B. If subjective factors are important (e.g., employee evaluation), correction may need to be more gradual. Because the decision maker must rely on a number of less precise measures, the formulation of appropriate corrective action is more complex.

1. One of the major disadvantages of trait-type performance appraisals is their inability to measure performance accurately, which makes corrective action difficult.
2. One of the major advantages of management by objectives is that it closely ties job performance to a standard that can be used as a guide to corrective action.
3. Participation by affected employees in all control systems (especially the judgmental areas) permits all concerned to understand both the performance levels desired and the measurement criteria being applied. Some benefits of participation are that it
   a. Develops a perception by those being evaluated that the process is fair
   b. Communicates to everyone the need for control
   c. Enhances acceptance of the need for control standards
   d. Indicates the direction of the desired behavior, which permits self-control and self-correction

CONTROL TECHNIQUES

A. Control includes such planning devices as PERT, Gantt charts, and budgets. (Turn to Study Unit 29, Decision Making under Uncertainty, and Study Unit 31, Quantitative Methods, for descriptions of these tools. Budgets are further discussed in Study Unit 22, Budgeting.) All these tools are considered here for their contribution to the control process. Study Unit 24, Standard Costs and Variance Analysis, is also applicable to this section.

1. **Budget** -- the traditional control device. The word budget has developed some negative connotations, and more positive phrases (**profit plan** or **business plan**) are sometimes used.
   a. A budget is a formal statement, usually in financial terms, of the goals and plans of an organization.
   b. A budget may also be stated in terms other than financial (e.g., budgets of direct labor hours, materials, or unit sales).
   c. The budget of an organization has the same structure as the organization itself; i.e., the total organizational budget is made up of a hierarchy of smaller budgets, each representing the plan of a division, department, or other unit in the organizational structure.
   d. Successful budgeting requires completion of a plan that states organizational goals before the budgeting process. Budgeting without a plan leads to political jockeying for favor (so familiar to those in universities or government).
   e. Prevention and detection of deviations from budget are the control purposes of budgets. Such deviations have obvious implications for the success of planning.
      1) The amount of deviation and the portion of the budget affected are the starting points for corrective action.
      2) **Management by exception** is often used to foster cost control. Deviations from budget are the exceptions that attract the attention of management and consume the majority of management time and effort. However, management by exception has the disadvantages of not spotting trends at an early stage and not reinforcing employees for work well done.
      3) If deviations from the budget become more common than conformity to the budget, management by exception degenerates into putting out fires, and a serious reappraisal of either the budget or the managers is necessary.

2. **PERT** is a control technique that breaks down a project into a set of events, arranges the events into a strict priority network, and establishes a completion time for each event.
   a. With PERT it is possible to find a **critical path**, i.e., the order of events that determines the time required for completion of the project. For an example and further discussion turn to Study Unit 31, Quantitative Methods.
   b. The critical path is important for control purposes because
      1) Management can concentrate its efforts on the most important activities and not waste time controlling noncritical activities.
      2) As the plan is executed and variations change the critical path, PERT provides a means of identifying the new critical path and applying the appropriate management effort.
3. **Gantt charts** compare scheduled production with actual production. Their control use comes from the ability to identify variations and thus stimulate corrective action. Gantt charts are not as effective as PERT because interactions between various steps in a project are not identified. For further discussion, turn to Study Unit 31, Quantitative Methods.
4. **Statistical quality control techniques** are used when measurement of 100% of the output is impossible because
   a. The cost of measurement would exceed the benefit gained by physically identifying all errors, or
   b. Testing destroys the product. Thus, a fuse factory would have to ruin all of its products to measure their quality.

B. Special control programs have been effective in educating employees about control requirements. In these programs, the problem (the deviation from the plan) is defined, and the employees are given feedback about the effect of their actions on the problem.
   1. A program of **zero defects** sets a goal for employees that may seem unreasonable but is surprisingly approachable. Employees' awareness of the results of their actions is heightened by
      a. Education about the program
      b. Periodic notification of the results
      c. An emphasis on the desirability of high quality
      d. An emphasis on the minimization of defects through individual and group efforts **before** errors occur
         1) EXAMPLE: Ongoing safety programs emphasizing zero defects help to reduce accidents.
   2. A short-run effect is often observed, however. Zero-defect programs require continuous implementation to be effective.

C. Management control processes can take two approaches.
   1. **Imposed control** is the traditional, mechanical approach, consisting of measuring performance against standards and then taking corrective action through the individual responsible for the function or area being evaluated.
      a. Though common in organizations, it has one striking drawback: Corrective action tends to come **after** the performance has taken place (often resulting in negative disciplinary action).
   2. **Self-control** is an emerging and increasingly important approach. It evaluates the entire process of management and the functions performed, as well as attempts to improve the managerial process (in contrast to correcting specific output performance of the manager). Management by objectives (MBO) is a good example of this approach. See Study Unit 8, Motivation and the Directing Process.

HUMAN FACTORS IN CONTROL SYSTEMS

A. The success of a control system is determined by its effectiveness in getting people to modify their performance.

B. The classical approach assumes people will act to correct their behavior when ordered to do so, but in practice individuals may resist formal controls for many reasons:

1. Control procedures highlight the things people do poorly, thus damaging their self-esteem.
2. People tend to avoid unpleasant situations.
3. The goals of a control system may not be accepted as worthwhile by an employee.
   a. The employee may believe that the stated standard of performance is too high.
   b. Established standards of performance may be considered irrelevant to accomplishment of what an individual regards as the primary job objective.
4. An individual may resent the assignment of control authority to another individual or group. The assignment of responsibility for failure to achieve objectives may be dysfunctional for the organization.
   a. The pressure to conform to plans, when exerted by management accountants, may have a negative effect on performance.
   b. But the same feedback from someone inside the operational unit may be a motivator for higher performance.
5. When informal group norms differ from control objectives, members of the group may resist the controls.

C. Human reactions to feedback should be considered in setting performance standards and designing control systems.

1. The nature of the feedback should motivate employees to improve their performance and reach the planned objectives, rather than offend or intimidate them.
2. The timing, form, and content of the information on deviations should be considered in order to obtain maximum compliance by those affected.

D. Modern behavioral theory provides for some measure of self-control at the lowest possible level (i.e., increased participation by the employees).

1. Self-control appears to be more effective than the traditional approach, which emphasizes centralized flow of control information toward top management and the use of outside staff control groups.
2. A participative approach to standard setting is more apt to obtain acceptance of the standards by the employees whose performance will be measured.

SURVEILLANCE OF CONTROL SYSTEMS

A. The control process must itself be controlled. No control system is so perfect that it can function without outside review of its effectiveness or ability to provide adequate results.

1. The control system should evolve continuously because of changes in
   a. The nature of the firm's business
   b. The managers who are available to implement the plans
   c. The nature of the plans themselves
2. Overreliance on a control system merely because it seemed adequate in the past can be disastrous to a business.
   a. No control system can anticipate all possible events.
   b. There may be deliberate or unintentional omissions or distortions by employees in providing feedback information.
   c. Resistance to a control system that employees do not believe in or understand may lead to attempts to subvert the system.

B. Unreliable feedback is a significant problem for any control system. Managers must observe the control process critically and imaginatively to uncover difficulties in the generation of feedback that could lead to erroneous information. Sources of problems include

1. Technical difficulties in measurement because of
   a. Mechanical problems
   b. Poor statistical design
   c. Delays in transmission of data
2. Behavioral problems because of
   a. Failure to observe employee morale
   b. Training inadequacies
   c. Fraud
   d. Malicious behavior
3. Failure to use appropriate internal audits periodically to measure the effectiveness of control systems
4. Inappropriate measurement criteria leading to unintended or undesired behavior
5. Inappropriate standards

HUMAN RESOURCE ACCOUNTING

A. A cost-based human resource accounting (HRA) system views employee recruiting and training costs as having long-term benefits to the company. Therefore, these costs are capitalized as assets. The costs are then amortized over the expected useful lives of the employees.

1. Because these are sunk costs, they should play no role in deciding whether to terminate the employees, assuming that the employees are not going to be needed again at some future time.
2. If employees are apt to be needed again in the near future, the HRA system provides management with some idea of the amount of future training costs that could be avoided by keeping the present employees on the payroll when they are not needed.
3. See also the discussion of Human Resource Planning in Study Unit 21, Planning.

PRODUCT QUALITY COSTS

A. Cost accounting systems can contribute to improved product quality programs by accumulating and reporting their costs. The IMA issued Statement on Management Accounting (SMA) No. 4-R in 1993. It is entitled *Practices and Techniques: Managing Quality Improvements*. SMA 4-R discusses the implementation of a Total Quality Management (TQM) system and the role of the management accountant in developing a cost system that incorporates all costs of poor quality. See page 509 for a summary of SMA 4-R.

1. The costs of external failure, e.g., warranty, product liability, and customer ill will costs, arise when problems occur after shipment.
2. Internal failure costs are incurred when detection of defective products occurs before shipment. Examples are scrap, rework, tooling changes, and downtime.
3. Prevention attempts to avoid defective output. These costs include preventive maintenance, employee training, review of equipment design, and evaluation of suppliers.
4. Appraisal embraces such activities as statistical quality control programs, inspection, and testing.

B. **ISO 9000 Standards**

1. In 1987, the International Standards Organization (ISO) introduced ISO 9000, a series of international standards designed for quality assurance. These standards, which have been adopted by the European Community (EC), provide a uniform set of rules for evaluating the quality of a company's operations.
   a. Though they do not have the force of law, these standards do carry weight in that, if a company fails to gain ISO 9000 registration, it risks not being able to find customers for its products. Some people fear that the EC will use the standards as a way of reducing imports. This is particularly true with regulated products for which health and safety are concerns.
   b. The intent of the standards is not to ensure product quality -- the marketplace determines whether a product is good or bad. The intent is to ensure that quality is consistent and that the product is the same from batch to batch.
2. The standards are rather broad in nature; they specify what is required without specifying how to do it. The 9000 series contains five standards:
   a. Standard 9000 is an overview and introduction to other standards in the series, including definitions of terms and concepts related to quality.
   b. Standard 9001 is a comprehensive general standard for quality assurance in design, development, manufacturing, installation, and servicing of products.
   c. Standard 9002 is a more detailed standard focusing specifically on manufacturing and installation of products.
   d. Standard 9003 is a detailed standard covering final inspection and testing of finished products.
   e. Standard 9004 provides guidelines for managing a quality control system. This standard is intended for use in auditing quality systems.
3. The ISO Standards have given birth to a new industry of consultants who advise companies on how to meet the standards and obtain registration.

C. **Malcom Baldrige National Quality Awards**

1. The U.S. Congress created the Malcom Baldrige National Quality Award in 1987 to encourage quality among American companies. The award was named for President Reagan's Secretary of Commerce who was killed in a rodeo accident.
   a. Companies must audit their operations using the Baldrige standards to measure their quality and productivity.
   b. The award promotes an awareness of quality as a vital competitive element.
2. Applicants for the Baldrige Award are grouped into three categories: the manufacturing group, the service group, and the small business group (firms which employ fewer than 500 people; may be either manufacturing or service). Officials say that a category for schools, hospitals, and possibly medical practices may be added soon.
   a. Very few awards are given -- sometimes only one per year in each category. The law allows two awards annually in each category.
   b. Winners typically use the award as a centerpiece of their advertising campaigns. Winners have included Federal Express Corporation and the Cadillac Division of General Motors.
3. Judges look to seven performance areas in selecting winners. These areas are
   a. Senior executive leadership and dedication to quality
   b. Information and analysis demonstrating that the firm has measured its quality performance
   c. Strategic quality planning, including goal setting and how goals have been achieved
   d. Human resource development and management, including the authority of employees to deviate from established procedures if it will improve quality or customer service
   e. Management of process quality, with emphasis on procedures to look across departmental lines to improve quality
   f. Quality and operational results focusing on objective data, including customer reports, that show that a company is achieving continuous improvement
   g. Customer satisfaction, the most heavily weighted of the criteria. Knowledge of the customer and responsiveness to customer needs are particularly important.

STUDY UNIT 24
STANDARD COSTS AND VARIANCE ANALYSIS

One topic that the candidate is almost certain to find on every CMA exam is standard cost variance analysis. Most previous exams have had at least one problem or question that required the candidates to compute or explain certain variances. A prerequisite to understanding variance analysis is the study of standard costing.

Control and performance evaluation accounts for 20% to 30% of Part 3. We cover this topic in three study units:

Study Unit 23: The Controlling Process
Study Unit 24: Standard Costs and Variance Analysis
Study Unit 25: Responsibility Accounting

A standard cost is an estimate of what a cost should be under normal operating conditions based on accounting and engineering studies. These standard costs are used to control the actual costs incurred. Comparing actual and standard costs permits an evaluation of the effectiveness of managerial performance.

STANDARD COSTS

A. Standard costs are budgeted unit costs established to motivate optimum productivity and efficiency. They are an excellent example of the control loop, as discussed in Study Unit 23, The Controlling Process.

1. The control loop consists of
    a. Establishing standards
    b. Measuring actual performance
    c. Comparing actual performance with standards
    d. Taking corrective action when needed
    e. Revising standards
    f. Taking other appropriate steps that are added, e.g., feedback and investigation of variances
2. A standard cost system is designed to alert management when the actual costs of production differ significantly from target or standard costs.
    a. A standard cost, as used in cost accounting, is similar to par on a golf course.
    b. It is a monetary measure to which actual costs are compared.
    c. A standard cost is not just an average of past costs but a scientifically determined estimate of what costs should be in the future. Standard costs are often the result of time and motion studies.
    d. A standard costing system facilitates the preparation of a flexible budget.

B. When actual costs and standard costs differ, the difference is a **variance**. A variance can be either favorable or unfavorable.

1. A favorable variance arises when actual costs are less than standard costs.
2. An unfavorable variance occurs when the actual costs are greater than standard.
   a. EXAMPLE: Management has calculated that, under efficient conditions, a worker should be able to complete one unit of product per hour. If workers are normally paid $6 per hour, the standard labor cost per unit is 1 hour x $6/hour = $6 per unit.
      1) If the actual labor costs per unit for a 1-week period were 1.1 hours x $6.25 = $6.88 per unit, the variance is $.88 per unit.
      2) The variance is unfavorable because actual cost exceeded standard cost.
      3) Management is signaled that costs have exceeded the norm and that corrective action may be needed.
3. Management will usually set standards so that they are currently attainable.
   a. If standards are set too high (or tight), they might be ignored by workers, and morale may suffer.
   b. Standards are designed to alert management when a process is out of control.
4. Standard costs must be kept current. If prices have changed considerably for a particular raw material, there will always be a variance if the standard cost is not changed. Much of the usefulness of standard costs is lost if a large variance is always expected. The primary reason for computing variances is to let management know whenever an unusual event has occurred.

C. Standard costs are usually established for materials, labor, and factory overhead. These standards can then be used to compute

1. Direct materials variances
   a. Price variance
   b. Quantity variance
   c. EXAMPLE: A local widget-producing company has determined that 3 pounds of raw materials are required to produce one widget. The standard cost is $2 per pound. Thus, the standard direct materials cost of producing one widget is $6. During the past month, 1,000 widgets were produced. The actual cost incurred for raw materials used was $2.10 per pound for 3,100 pounds, so that materials costing $6,510 were placed into production. The total materials variance was thus $510.

Standard cost for month (3,000 lb. x $2.00)	$ 6,000
Actual cost for month (3,100 lb. x $2.10)	(6,510)
Total materials variance--unfavorable	$ (510)

2. Direct labor variances
   a. Rate variance
   b. Efficiency variance
3. Manufacturing overhead variances (four-way analysis)
   a. Variable overhead variances
      1) Spending variance
      2) Efficiency variance
   b. Fixed overhead variances
      1) Budget (or fixed overhead spending) variance
      2) Volume (idle capacity or production volume) variance

MATERIALS VARIANCES

In reference to the example on page 553, knowing that the materials variance in the widget department was $510 is not sufficient to determine what, if any, corrective action should be taken. The cause of the variance must be known before the decision can be made. Variances are usually divided into price and quantity components. In the example, part of the total variance can be attributed to using more raw materials than the standard quantity and part to a cost that was higher than standard. These two sources of the total variance can be isolated.

A. **Materials quantity variance** is the actual quantity minus standard quantity times standard price: (AQ – SQ)SP.

   1. EXAMPLE: Excess quantity (100 lb.) x standard cost ($2.00) = $200 unfavorable. Thus, $200 of the total variance is attributable to using an excessive amount of raw materials. This is the materials quantity variance.
   2. When determining the materials quantity variance, the actual cost of the materials is ignored because the only concern is the amount of variance that would have occurred if there had been no price variance. Standard cost is multiplied times the excess quantity used in arriving at the quantity variance.
   3. An unfavorable materials quantity variance is usually caused by waste, shrinkage, or theft. As a result, an unfavorable quantity variance may be the responsibility of the department foreman or supervisor of the production department because the excess usage occurred while the materials were under that person's supervision.
   4. A favorable materials quantity variance indicates that the workers either have been unusually efficient or are producing lower quality products with less than the standard quantity of materials. Hence, a favorable variance is not always desirable. A favorable variance may be as bad as or worse than an unfavorable variance. It may suggest that costs have been reduced at the expense of product quality.

B. **Materials price variance** is the actual price minus the standard price times the actual quantity: (AP – SP)AQ.

   1. The actual quantity of raw materials consumed during the period is used in computing the price variance.
   2. An unfavorable materials price variance results when the actual price was greater than the standard price.
   3. EXAMPLE: Excess material cost ($.10) x actual quantity (3,100 lb.) = $310 unfavorable. Of the total variance, $310 is attributable to the increase in the cost of the materials since the standard costs were established.

C. The materials quantity variance plus the materials price variance equals the **total materials variance**.

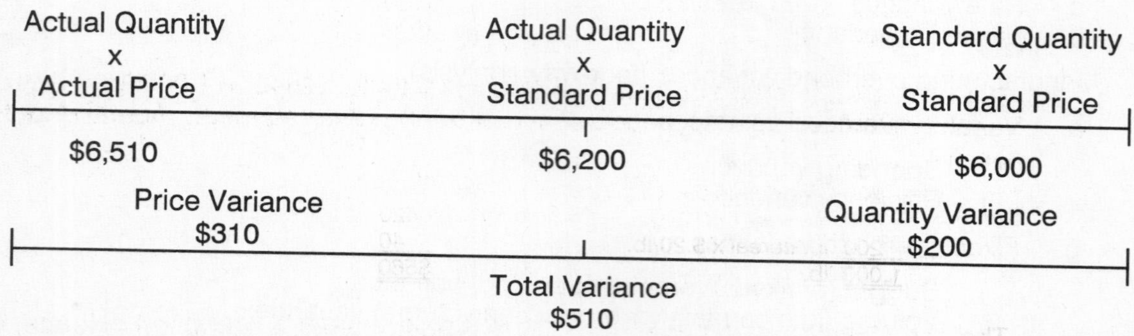

1. Interaction effects. The isolation of variances as illustrated in this study unit causes a slight problem as shown in the following diagram:

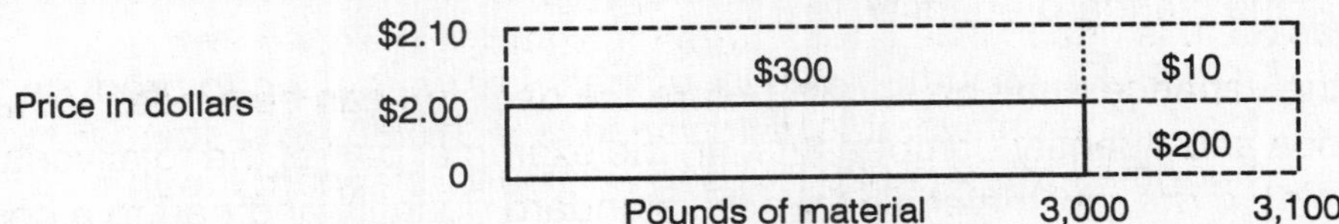

   a. The area enclosed by the solid lines is the standard cost area. The dotted line area represents the actual costs incurred. The differences are the variances. The variance analysis performed in the previous example did not recognize separately the small rectangle at the upper right-hand corner of the illustration.

   b. An alternative is to say that the firm had an unfavorable quantity variance of $200, an unfavorable price variance of $300, and a $10 unfavorable variance attributable to the combination of excess price and excess quantity.

   c. This three-way analysis is usually not undertaken because the price variance occurred on all materials used and a price variance is involved; i.e., the excessive usage should be charged only at standard cost.

   d. The following diagram depicts traditional analysis of unfavorable variances:

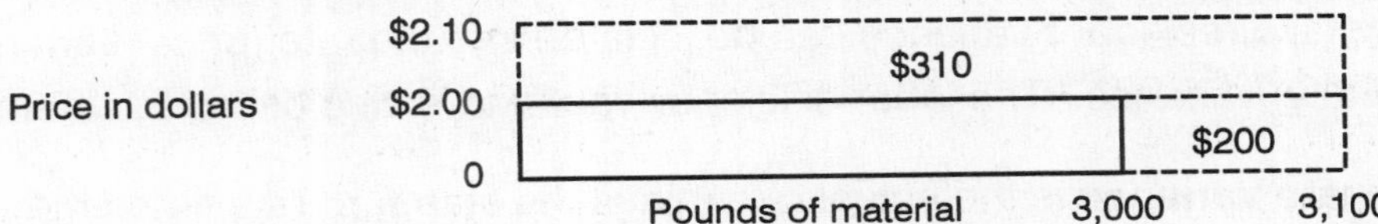

D. The materials quantity (usage) variance is sometimes supplemented by the materials mix variance and the materials yield variance.

1. These variances are calculated only when the production process involves combining several materials in varying proportions (substitutions are allowable in combining materials).

   a. EXAMPLE: The production of dog food might involve combining ingredients such as horse meat, beef byproducts, and cereal. Within certain limits, any of the raw materials can be substituted for one of the other ingredients.

2. The **materials mix variance** equals total actual quantity times the difference between the average unit standard cost of the planned mix of ingredients and the average unit standard cost of the actual mix.

   a. EXAMPLE: Assume that a company wants to produce 1,000 pounds of dog food with the following ingredients and standard costs:

300	lb. horse meat x $.50/lb.	$150
500	lb. beef x $.70/lb.	350
200	lb. cereal x $.20/lb.	40
1,000	lb.	$540

   The budgeted average unit standard cost is $.54/lb. ($540 ÷ 1,000 lb.). Actual results differed, however, because of a shortage of horse meat. Actual quantities were

200	lb. horse meat x $.50/lb.	$100
600	lb. beef x $.70/lb.	420
200	lb. cereal x $.20/lb.	40
1,000	lb.	$560

   The actual average unit standard cost is $.56/lb. ($560 ÷ 1,000 lb.). Hence, the materials mix variance is $20 [($.56 – $.54) x 1,000 lb.].

3. The **materials yield variance** is the budgeted average unit standard cost at the budgeted mix multiplied by the difference between the actual quantity of materials used and the standard quantity.

   a. EXAMPLE: Assume 1,020 lb. of materials were used to produce 1,000 lb. of dog food. The unfavorable yield variance is $10.80 [$.54 standard unit cost at the budgeted mix x (1,020 lb. used – 1,000 lb. standard input)].

4. Certain relationships may exist among the various materials variances. For instance, an unfavorable price variance may be offset by a favorable mix or yield variance because materials of better quality and higher price are used. Also, a favorable mix variance may result in an unfavorable yield variance, or vice versa.

5. Care must be used in assigning responsibility for materials mix and yield variances (and all other variances as well). The assignment depends upon the level of management at which the substitution decision is made. Only the manager who has control over the composition of a mix should be held responsible for a variance.

DIRECT LABOR VARIANCES

The direct labor variance is similar to the materials variance in that it arises from two different sources. The total direct labor variance can be isolated into the rate (price) variance and the efficiency (quantity) variance. The labor efficiency variance is also called the labor time variance.

A. The **labor rate variance** is the actual rate minus the standard rate times the actual quantity: (AR – SR)AQ.

B. The **labor quantity variance** is the actual quantity minus the standard quantity times the standard rate: (AQ – SQ)SR.

C. Except for terminology, there is no difference between the labor and materials variances. The objective of both is to divide the total variance into a price (rate) component and a quantity (efficiency) component.

D. EXAMPLE: A widget manufacturer has established a standard of 3 hours of direct labor per widget produced, and the standard cost of labor is $5 per hour. The standard cost of direct labor included in each widget is $15. During a month when 1,000 widgets were produced, the company incurred direct labor costs of $16,000. The total direct labor variance for the period was $1,000 unfavorable [$16,000 – ($15 x 1,000 units)]. To be meaningful, the variance should be divided into its components.

   1. If only 2,800 hours of direct labor was used instead of the standard 3,000 (3 hours x 1,000 units) and actual labor rates varied from $4 to $6 per hour, the efficiency (quantity of labor used) variance is $1,000 favorable (200 difference in hours x $5 standard rate). The $1,000 favorable efficiency variance suggests that the workers in the department were extremely efficient during the period and probably should be commended for their efforts.

      a. Alternatively, a favorable efficiency variance might indicate that the workers did not give enough attention to some products and quality may have deteriorated. The reasons should be determined.

      b. Sometimes an unfavorable efficiency variance may be caused by workers' taking unauthorized coffee or lunch breaks.

2. The labor rate (price) variance for the period is

Standard cost at actual hours ($5 x 2,800 hours)	$ 14,000
Actual labor cost for the period	(16,000)
Labor rate variance--unfavorable	$ (2,000)

The unfavorable rate variance more than offsets the favorable efficiency variance.

a. Often, an unfavorable rate variance is the result of a renegotiated labor contract and thus is outside the control of management. In that case, the cost standards should be revised.

b. An unfavorable rate variance might also indicate that a foreman is using the wrong workers for a particular job. Perhaps the job could have been performed by an unskilled worker at $4 per hour, but for some reason the foreman may have assigned a more skilled worker at $6 per hour. The foreman and supervisor of a department should always examine an unfavorable rate variance to be sure that workers are being allocated most efficiently.

OVERHEAD VARIANCES

The total overhead variance is divided into variable overhead and fixed overhead variances, each of which may be further subdivided.

A. In four-way analysis of overhead variances, the **variable overhead variance** consists of the **spending variance** and **efficiency variance**. Variable overhead is usually assigned to the product, and its variances are analyzed in terms of an activity base.

1. Variable overhead spending and efficiency variances can be diagrammed.

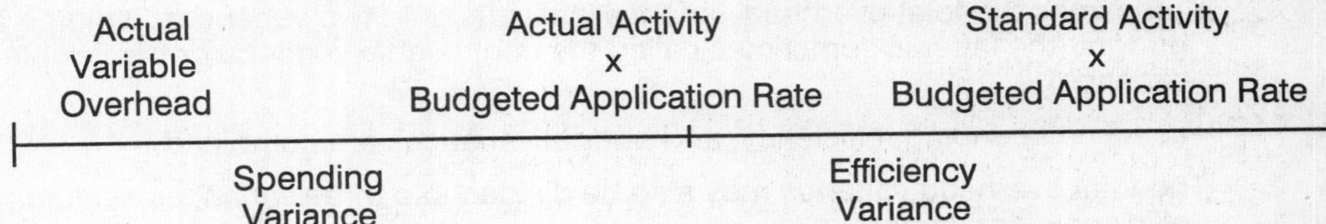

a. The spending variance
Actual variable overhead – (*Actual activity* x *Budgeted application rate*)

b. The efficiency variance
Budgeted application rate x (*Actual activity* – *Standard activity*)

B. The total **fixed overhead variance** is the difference between actual fixed costs and the product of standard fixed overhead per unit (standard cost per unit of input x standard units of input allowed per unit of output) times actual units of output.

1. The overall fixed overhead variance includes the
    a. **Budget variance** (sometimes called the fixed overhead spending variance), which is the difference between actual fixed costs and budgeted costs
    b. **Volume variance** (idle capacity variance or production volume variance), which is the difference between budgeted fixed costs and the product of the standard cost per unit of input times the standard units of input allowed for the actual output
2. Diagram of fixed overhead variances

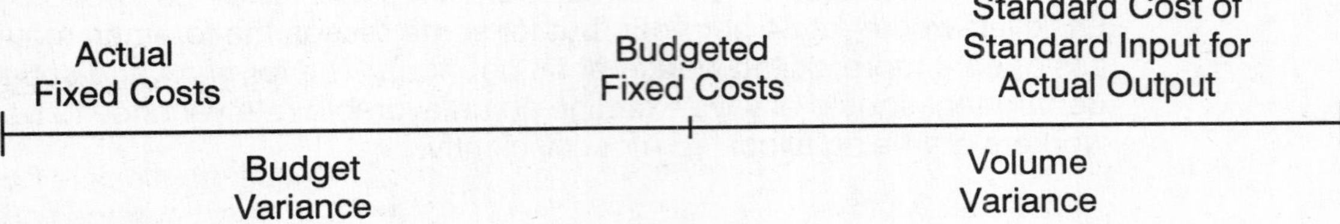

C. One of the prerequisites for computing fixed overhead variances is a flexible budget. A flexible budget can be adapted to any level of production.

1. The volume variance is similar to over- or underapplied overhead in a system without standard costs.
    a. Thus, fixed costs applied equal the standard cost of the standard input allowed for the actual output.

D. **Two-Way and Three-way Analysis of the Overhead Variance**

1. Sometimes the total overhead variance is divided into two variances: volume and budget (the latter is sometimes called the controllable variance or the flexible-budget variance).
    a. The spending, efficiency, and budget variances are combined.
2. The total overhead variance may also be divided into three variances: volume, efficiency, and spending.
    a. The spending variance combines the fixed overhead budget and variable overhead spending variances.
        1) The variable overhead efficiency and fixed overhead volume variances are the same as in four-way analysis.
3. EXAMPLE: Assume that a firm's standard cost system is based on a normal production level of 8,000 units per month at a budgeted overhead cost of $16,000, or $2 per unit. Half of this cost is fixed and half variable. The firm actually produced 6,000 units last month at an overhead cost of $14,300.
    a. Budgeted fixed cost is $8,000 (50% x $16,000), and budgeted unit variable cost is $1 [(50% x $16,000) ÷ 8,000 units]. Thus, according to the flexible budget, costs should have been $14,000 at this activity level. However, the finished goods account would have been debited for only $12,000 during the month ($2 standard cost x 6,000 units produced).
    b. It actually cost $2,300 more to produce the finished goods. This $2,300 is the total overhead variance. It can be divided into the portion attributable to not producing at the normal level (volume variance) and the portion controllable by first-line management (controllable variance).

c. The volume variance is

Budgeted overhead at 6,000 units	$ 14,000
Standard cost charged to product	(12,000)
Volume variance	$ 2,000 unfavorable

1) The $2,000 volume variance is solely attributable to the firm's not producing at the previously selected normal level of production.

2) An unfavorable volume variance is caused by not producing enough goods. It is often the result of labor strikes, major machine breakdowns, or lack of sales orders. The unfavorable volume variance is also known as the idle capacity variance.

3) The volume variance is the least important of all variances for cost control purposes because it usually cannot be controlled by the manufacturing departments.

d. The budget variance in two-way analysis (sometimes called a flexible budget or controllable variance -- a combination of two variable cost variances and one fixed cost variance) is the difference between the overhead that is budgeted at the actual level of production and the actual costs incurred. In the previous example, the controllable variance is

Budgeted overhead at 6,000 units	$ 14,000
Actual overhead costs incurred	(14,300)
Controllable variance	$ (300) unfavorable

e. The total overhead variance may be divided into two, three, or four components. No matter how many components are isolated, one is always the volume variance. The more sophisticated analysis techniques merely divide the controllable variance into smaller units.

1) Assume that, of the $14,300 in overhead costs that were incurred in the above example, $8,050 was for fixed costs. Assume also that $6,250 of variable overhead was incurred based on 6,100 activity units, e.g., labor hours. The standard number of activity units of input allowed for the actual output of 6,000 units of product was 6,000.

2) For two-way analysis of variance, there were a $300 unfavorable controllable variance and a $2,000 unfavorable volume variance as computed above.

3) For three-way analysis of variance, volume, efficiency, and spending variances are isolated.

   a) The fixed overhead volume variance remains $2,000 unfavorable.

   b) The variable overhead efficiency variance is $100 unfavorable [(6,100 actual – 6,000 standard activity units) x $1 per activity unit (see D.3.a)].

   c) The spending variance is $200 unfavorable [($8,050 actual FOH – $8,000 budgeted) + ($6,250 actual VOH – 6,100 actual activity units x $1)].

4) Four-way analysis of variance divides the spending variance into variable ($150 unfavorable) and fixed ($50 unfavorable). See d.3)c) just above.

E. Another Example of Variance Analysis

	STANDARD COSTS	ACTUAL COSTS
DIRECT MATERIALS	600,000 units of materials at $2.00 each	700,000 units at $1.90
DIRECT LABOR	60,000 hours allowed for actual output at $7/hour	65,000 hours at $7.20
FACTORY OVERHEAD	$8.00/direct labor hour on normal capacity of 50,000 direct labor hours:	
	$6.00 for variable overhead	$396,000 variable
	$2.00 for fixed overhead	$130,000 fixed

MATERIALS VARIANCES		
Price		
Price variance x actual quantity $0.10 F x 700,000 =	$ 70,000	favorable
Quantity		
Standard price x quantity variance $2.00 x 100,000 U =	$200,000	unfavorable
LABOR VARIANCES		
Rate		
Price variance x actual quantity $0.20 U x 65,000 hours =	$ 13,000	unfavorable
Efficiency		
Standard price (rate) x quantity variance $7.00 x 5,000 U =	$ 35,000	unfavorable
VARIABLE OVERHEAD VARIANCES		
Spending		
Actual – actual hours at standard rate $396,000 - (65,000 hrs x $6) =	$ 6,000	unfavorable
Efficiency		
Standard rate (actual – standard hours) $6(65,000 - 60,000) =	$ 30,000	unfavorable
FIXED OVERHEAD VARIANCES		
Budget		
Actual – budget $130,000 - $100,000 =	$ 30,000	unfavorable
Volume		
Budget – standard hours allowed for actual output at standard rate $100,000 - (60,000 hrs x $2) =	$ 20,000	favorable
NET UNFAVORABLE VARIANCE	$224,000	

	Actual Output at Actual Input and Cost	Actual Output at Standard Input and Cost
Material	$1,330,000	$1,200,000
Labor	468,000	420,000
Variable overhead	396,000	360,000
Fixed overhead	130,000	120,000
Net unfavorable variance		224,000
	$2,324,000	$2,324,000

VARIANCES IN THE LEDGER ACCOUNTS

A. Variances usually do not appear on the financial statements of a firm. They are used for managerial control and are recorded in the ledger accounts.

B. When standard costs are recorded in inventory accounts, direct labor and materials variances are also recorded.

1. Direct labor is recorded as a liability at actual cost, but it is charged to work-in-process control at its standard cost for the standard quantity used. The direct labor rate and efficiency variances are recognized at that time.

2. Direct materials, however, should be debited to materials control at standard prices at the time of purchase. The purpose is to isolate the direct materials price variance as soon as possible. When direct materials are used, they are debited to work-in-process at the standard cost for the standard quantity, and the materials quantity variance is then recognized.

C. Actual overhead costs are debited to overhead control and credited to accounts payable, wages payable, etc. Applied overhead is credited to overhead control or to an overhead applied account and debited to work-in-process control.

1. The simplest method of recording the overhead variances is to wait until year-end. The variances can then be recognized separately when the overhead control and overhead applied accounts are closed (by a credit and a debit, respectively). The balancing debits or credits are to the variance accounts.

D. The following are the entries to record the variances described above (favorable variances are credits and unfavorable variances are debits):

		Dr	Cr
1.	Materials control (AQ x SP)	$XXX	
	Direct materials price variance (dr or cr)	XXX	
	Accounts payable (AQ x AP)		$XXX
2.	Work-in-process control (SQ x SP)	XXX	
	Direct materials quantity variance (dr or cr)	XXX	
	Direct labor rate variance (dr or cr)	XXX	
	Direct labor efficiency variance (dr or cr)	XXX	
	Materials control (AQ x SP)		XXX
	Wages payable (AQ x AP)		XXX
3.	Overhead control (actual)	XXX	
	Wages payable (actual)		XXX
	Accounts payable (actual)		XXX
a.	Work-in-process control (standard)	XXX	
	Overhead applied (standard)		XXX
b.	Overhead applied (standard)	XXX	
	Variable overhead spending variance (dr or cr)	XXX	
	Variable overhead efficiency variance (dr or cr)	XXX	
	Fixed overhead budget variance (dr or cr)	XXX	
	Fixed overhead volume variance (dr or cr)	XXX	
	Overhead control (actual)		XXX

4. The result of the foregoing entries is that work-in-process contains standard costs only.

E. **Disposition of Variances**

1. Immaterial variances are customarily closed to cost of goods sold or income summary.
2. Variances that are material may be prorated. A simple approach to proration is to allocate the total net variance to work-in-process, finished goods, and cost of goods sold based on the balances in those accounts. However, more complex methods of allocation are possible.

F. **Alternative Approaches**

1. Direct materials and labor might be transferred to work-in-process at their actual quantities. In that case, the direct materials quantity and direct labor efficiency variances might be recognized when goods are transferred from work-in-process to finished goods.
2. The direct materials price variance might be isolated at the time of transfer to work-in-process.
3. The difficulty with these methods is that they delay the recognition of variances. Early recognition is desirable for control purposes.

SALES VARIANCES

A. Variance analysis not only is a tool of the manufacturing divisions but also is a method used to judge the effectiveness of the selling departments. If a firm's sales differ from the amount budgeted, the difference could be attributable to either the sales price variance or the **sales volume variance** (sum of the sales quantity and mix variances).

1. EXAMPLE: Assume that a firm has budgeted sales of 10,000 units at $17 per unit. Variable costs are expected to be $10 per unit and fixed costs are budgeted at $50,000. Thus, the company anticipates a contribution margin of $70,000 and a net income of $20,000. However, the actual results are

Units sold	11,000
Sales	$ 176,000
Variable costs	(110,000)
Contribution margin	$ 66,000
Fixed costs	(50,000)
Net income	$ 16,000

a. Because sales were greater than predicted, it may be surprising that the contribution margin is less than expected. The $4,000 discrepancy can be divided into the sales price variance and the sales volume variance.

b. The **sales price variance** is the reduction in the contribution margin because of the change in selling price. In the example, the actual selling price of $16 per unit is $1 less than expected. Thus, the sales price variance is $1 times 11,000 units actually sold, or $11,000 unfavorable.

c. The **sales quantity variance** is the change in contribution margin caused by the difference between the actual and budgeted volume.

Expected unit CM × *Change in volume* =
$7 × 1,000 *units* = $7,000 *favorable*

d. The sales mix variance is zero because the firm sells one product only. Hence, the sales volume variance equals the sales quantity variance.

2. The sales price variance ($11,000 unfavorable) combined with the sales volume variance ($7,000 favorable) equals the total change in the contribution margin.
   a. In the previous example, the contribution margin in terms of dollars was used to compute the volume variance. However, contribution margin percentage figures must be used when multiple products are sold at varying prices.
   b. A similar analysis may be done for cost of goods sold. The average production cost per unit is used instead of the average unit selling price, but the quantities for production volume are the same. Finally, the overall variation in gross profit is the sum of the variation in revenue plus the variation in CGS.

B. **Sales mix variances** are also calculated in multi-product situations to explain why the contribution margin is not as predicted.

1. EXAMPLE: Assume that a company sells three products with the following estimates of sales and contribution margins:

	A	B	C	Total
Sales	$10,000	$20,000	$30,000	$60,000
Variable costs	6,000	14,000	24,000	44,000
Contribution margin	$ 4,000	$ 6,000	$ 6,000	$16,000
Contribution margin %	40%	30%	20%	26.67%

Actual sales and costs were as follows:

	A	B	C	Total
Sales	$5,000	$15,000	$40,000	$60,000
Variable costs	3,000	10,500	32,000	45,500
Contribution margin	$2,000	$ 4,500	$ 8,000	$14,500
Contribution margin %	40%	30%	20%	24.17%

2. What happened to profitability? Actual total sales met expectations. All products produced the desired contribution margin percentage, but total contribution margin was less than expected. The answer is that more low-profit products (product C) were sold than anticipated, whereas sales of high-profit products (A and B) were lower. This reduction in profitability is called the **sales mix variance**. It arises when the actual sales mix is different from that budgeted.

3. The sales mix variance for each product is calculated by taking the difference between its budgeted contribution margin and the actual contribution margin.

	A	B	C	Total
Expected CM	$4,000	$6,000	$6,000	$16,000
Actual CM	2,000	4,500	8,000	14,500
Variance	$2,000 U	$1,500 U	$2,000 F	$ 1,500 U

4. *Sales mix variance (AQ - SQ) x contribution margin %*

A($10,000 – $5,000) x 40%	=	$2,000 U
B($20,000 – $15,000) x 30%	=	1,500 U
C($30,000 – $40,000) x 20%	=	2,000 F
		$1,500 U

C. The CMA candidate must be able not only to calculate the sales price, quantity, and mix variances but also to explain their implications. The 1975 examination asked the candidate to calculate each of the three variances. The following is the second part of the question:

> *Explain the significance of quantity and mix variances and the conditions that must exist for this type of variance analysis to be meaningful.*

The unofficial answer was

> *Computation of quantity and mix variances provides management with additional information for analyzing why actual sales differed from budgeted sales. The quantity variances measure a change in volume (while holding the mix constant), and the mix variance measures the effect of a change in the product mix (while holding the volume constant). This type of variance analysis is useful when the products are substitutes for each other or when products, not necessarily substitutes for each other, are marketed through the same channels.*

1. Relevant data for calculating the variances are

	Plastic	Metal	Total
Budgeted selling price per unit	$6.00	$10.00	NA
Cost of sales at standard per unit	3.00	7.50	NA
Budgeted gross margin per unit	$3.00	$ 2.50	NA
Budgeted product	300	200	500
Budgeted mix percentage	60%	40%	100%
Actual units sold	260	260	520
Actual selling price per unit	$6.00	$ 9.50	NA

2. The total unfavorable gross margin variance was $100,000, explained as follows (000 omitted):

Price variance:			
Plastic	260 x ($6.00 – $6.00)	$ 0	
Metal	260 x ($10.00 – $9.50)	(130)	$130 unfavorable
Quantity variance:			
Plastic	[(520 x .6) – 300] x $3.00	$ 36	
Metal	[(520 x .4) – 200] x $2.50	20	$ 56 favorable
Mix variance:			
Plastic	[260 – (520 x .6)] x $3.00	$(156)	
Metal	[260 – (520 x .4)] x $2.50	130	$ 26 unfavorable
Total gross margin variance			$100 unfavorable

D. **Management by Exception.** Variance analysis is an important tool of the management accountant in that it enables responsibility to be assigned. It also permits management by exception. Management by exception is the practice of giving attention only to those situations in which large variances occur, thus allowing upper-level management to devote its time to problems of the business, not just routine supervision of subordinates. Variance analysis is an important tool that will become familiar to anyone working in industry, whether as an accountant, manager, department foreman, or marketing person. Variances affect everyone.

STUDY UNIT 25
RESPONSIBILITY ACCOUNTING

Control and performance evaluation accounts for 20% to 30% of Part 3. We cover this topic in three study units:

Study Unit 23: The Controlling Process
Study Unit 24: Standard Costs and Variance Analysis
Study Unit 25: Responsibility Accounting

RESPONSIBILITY CENTERS

A. Managerial performance should be evaluated only on the basis of those factors controllable by the manager. Managers may control revenues, costs, and/or investments in resources. A well-designed responsibility accounting system establishes responsibility centers within the organization.

1. Responsibility centers can be classified as

   a. **Cost center** -- responsible for costs only, e.g., a production department

   b. **Revenue center** -- responsible for revenues but not costs (other than those attributable to marketing)

   c. **Profit center** -- responsible for revenues and expenses, e.g., appliance department in a retail store

   d. **Investment center** -- responsible for revenues, expenses, and invested capital. A branch office is an example of an investment center.

      1) **Return on investment** (income ÷ invested capital) is the key performance measure of an investment center. Invested capital may be defined in various ways, for example, as

         a) Total assets available

         b) Total assets employed, which excludes assets that are idle

         c) Working capital plus other assets. Current liabilities are deducted from current assets to exclude the assets provided by short-term creditors. This investment base assumes that the manager controls short-term credit.

         d) Stockholders' equity. A portion of long-term liabilities must be allocated to the investment center to determine the manager's resource base. One problem with this definition of the resource base is that, although it has the advantage of emphasizing return to owners, it reflects decisions at different levels of the entity: short-term liabilities incurred by the responsibility center and long-term liabilities controlled at the corporate level.

2) **Residual income** is the excess of the amount of the ROI over a targeted amount equal to an imputed interest charge on invested capital. The rate used is ordinarily the weighted-average cost of capital.

a) The advantage of using residual income rather than percentage ROI is that it emphasizes maximizing an amount instead of a percentage. Managers are encouraged to accept projects with returns exceeding the cost of capital even if they reduce the percentage ROI.

e. **Service centers** -- primarily and sometimes solely responsible for providing specialized support to other organizational subunits. They are usually operated as cost centers, e.g., a maintenance department.

2. The responsibility system should induce management performance that adheres to overall company objectives (**goal congruence**).

a. **Suboptimization** occurs when one segment of a company takes action that is in its own best interests but is detrimental to the firm as a whole.

CONTRIBUTION APPROACH

A. The **contribution margin** equals revenue minus all variable costs. The contribution approach to performance evaluation is emphasized in responsibility accounting because it focuses on levels of controllability; that is, fixed costs are much less controllable than variable costs, and the contribution margin may therefore be a fairer basis for evaluation than the gross margin.

1. Manufacturing contribution margin -- sales minus variable manufacturing costs
2. Contribution margin -- manufacturing contribution minus nonmanufacturing variable costs
3. Short-run performance margin -- contribution margin minus controllable (discretionary) fixed costs
4. Segment margin -- short-run performance margin minus traceable (committed) fixed costs
5. Net income -- segment margin minus allocated common costs

Contribution Approach Income Statement

Sales			$150,000
Variable manufacturing costs			(40,000)
Manufacturing contribution margin			$110,000
Variable selling and administrative costs			(20,000)
Contribution margin			$ 90,000
Controllable fixed costs			
Manufacturing	$30,000		
Selling and administrative		25,000	(55,000)
Short-run performance margin			$ 35,000
Traceable fixed costs			
Depreciation		$10,000	
Insurance		5,000	(15,000)
Segment margin		$ 20,000	
Allocated common costs			(10,000)
Net income			$ 10,000

NOTE: All costs in the report are controllable by someone at some time. For evaluation of a **manager's** performance, consider only items (s)he controls.

TRANSFER PRICING

A. Transfer prices are the amounts charged by one segment of an organization for goods and services it provides to another segment of the same organization.

1. Transfer prices are used by profit and investment centers.
   a. A cost center's costs are allocated to producing departments according to methods described in Study Unit 19.
   b. The problem most companies typically face is the determination of exactly what transfer price should be used when one division purchases from another division.
   c. In a decentralized system, each division is theoretically a completely separate entity. Thus, Division A should charge the same price to Division B as would be charged to an outside buyer.
   d. The reason for decentralization is to motivate managers to achieve the best results. Thus, it would not be in the best interests of Division A to give a special discount to Division B if the goods can be sold at the regular price to outside buyers. However, it may be to the overall company's advantage to have A sell at a special price to B.
2. A transfer price should permit Division A to operate as an independent entity and achieve its goals while functioning in the best interest of the company.
3. Transfer prices can be determined in a number of ways. They may be based on
   a. Normal market price
   b. Negotiated price
   c. Variable costs
   d. Full costs (variable costs plus an allocation of fixed costs)
4. The choice of a transfer pricing policy (which type of transfer price to use) is normally decided by top management at the corporate level. The decision will typically include consideration of the following:
   a. Goal congruence factors. Will the transfer price promote the goals of the company as a whole?
   b. Divisional performance factors. The segment making the transfer should be allowed to recover its incremental cost plus the opportunity cost of the transfer. What could it have made by selling to an outsider?
      1) For this purpose, the transfer should be at market price.
      2) The selling manager should not lose income by selling within the company.
   c. Negotiation factors. If the purchasing segment could purchase the product or service outside the company, it should be permitted to negotiate the transfer price.
      1) The purchasing manager should not have to suffer increased costs by purchasing within the company.
   d. Capacity factors. Does the selling division have excess capacity?
      1) If Division A has excess capacity, it should be used for producing products for Division B.
      2) If Division A is operating at full capacity and selling its products at the full market price, profitable work should not be abandoned to produce for Division B.

e. Cost structure factors. What portions of production costs are variable and fixed?

1) If Division A has excess capacity and an opportunity arises to sell to Division B at a price in excess of the variable cost, the work should be performed for Division B because a contribution to cover the fixed costs will result.

5. EXAMPLE: Division A produces a small part at a cost of $6 per unit. The regular selling price is $10 per unit. If Division B can use the part in its production, the cost to the company (as a whole) will be $6. Division B has another supplier who will sell the item to B at $9.50 per part. Division B wants to buy the $9.50 part from the outside supplier instead of the $10 part from Division A, but making the part for $6 is in the company's best interest. What amount should Division A charge Division B?

a. The answer is complicated by many factors. For example, if Division A has excess capacity, B should be charged a lower price. If it is operating at full capacity, B should be charged $10.

b. Another question to consider is what portion of Division A's costs is fixed. For example, if a competitor offered to sell the part to B at $5 each, can Division A advantageously sell to B at a price lower than $5? If Division A's $6 total cost is composed of $4 of variable costs and $2 of fixed costs, it is beneficial for all concerned for A to sell to B at a price less than $5. Even at a price of $4.01, the parts would be providing a contribution margin to cover some of A's fixed costs.

6. Dual pricing is another internal price-setting alternative. For example, the selling division could record the transfer to another division at the usual market price that would be paid by an outsider. The buying division, however, would record a purchase at the variable cost of production.

a. Each division's performance would be improved by the use of a dual-pricing scheme.

b. The company would benefit because variable costs would be used for decision-making purposes. In a sense, variable costs would be the relevant price for decision-making purposes, but the regular market price would be used for evaluation of production divisions.

c. Under a dual-pricing system, the profit for the company will be less than the sum of the profits of the individual divisions.

d. In effect, the selling division is given a corporate subsidy under the dual-pricing system.

e. The dual-pricing system is rarely used because the incentive to control costs is reduced. The selling division is assured of a high price, and the buying division is assured of an artificially low price. Thus, neither manager must exert much effort to show a profit on divisional performance reports.

CHAPTER EIGHT
EXAM PART 4
DECISION ANALYSIS AND INFORMATION SYSTEMS

The ICMA Content Description of Part 4 follows:

A. **Decision Theory and Operational Decision Analysis (20% - 30%)**
Logical steps to reach a decision; relevant data concepts; cost/volume/profit analysis; marginal analysis; cost-based pricing; financial statement modeling; inventory models and systems. Income tax implications for operational decision analysis.

B. **Investment Decision Analysis (20% - 30%)**
Cash flow estimates; time value of money; discounted cash flow concepts; net present value; internal rate of return; and non-discounting analysis techniques. Income tax implications for investment decision analysis.

C. **Quantitative Methods for Decision Analysis (10% - 15%)**
Quantitative methods and techniques including regression analysis, learning curves, linear programming, sensitivity analysis, network analysis, probability concepts and expected values, decision trees, simulation, expert systems and artificial intelligence, and other appropriate aids to decision making.

D. **Information Systems (20% - 30%)**
Nature of management and accounting information systems; systems development and design; techniques and terminology applicable to the development of computer-based accounting information systems; systems controls and security measures in an accounting information system.

E. **Internal Auditing (10% - 15%)**
Objectives and scope of internal auditing; fundamentals of internal organizational control; professional standards and procedures for administering operational and financial internal audits; internal audit reports; assessing the adequacy of internal controls, particularly in an accounting information system; auditing in an EDP environment.

With the 1990 revision of the CMA exam (effective as of the December 1990 exam), the ICMA published a content specification outline for Part 4 that expanded the above Content Description for Part 4.

A. ***Decision Theory and Operational Decision Analysis (20% - 30%)***

1. *Logical steps to reach a decision*
2. *Relevant data concepts in the decision process*
   a. *Future oriented revenues and costs*
   b. *Sunk costs*
   c. *Opportunity costs*
   d. *Importance of cash flows*
3. *Cost/profit/volume analysis for decision making*
   a. *Profit performance and alternative operating levels*
   b. *Setting prices*
4. *Marginal analysis*
   a. *Special orders and pricing*
   b. *Make vs. buy*
   c. *Sell or process further*
   d. *Add or drop a segment*
   e. *Select marketing channels*
5. *Cost-based pricing*
   a. *Comparing to market-based prices*
   b. *Submitting bids*
   c. *Setting prices*
   d. *Government contract pricing and the Cost Accounting Standards Board*
6. *Financial statement modeling*
7. *Inventory models and systems*
   a. *Models*
   b. *Systems*

In conjunction with the decision subject areas in this topic, the impact of income taxes on operational decisions

-- *Operating income subject to income taxes*
-- *Gains and losses subject to taxes*
-- *Tax credits*

B. ***Investment Decision Analysis (20% - 30%)***

1. *Cash flows*
2. *Time value of money*
   a. *Present values*
   b. *Future values*
3. *Discounted cash flow*
4. *Net present value*
5. *Internal rate of return*
6. *Non-discounting methods*
   a. *Payback*
   b. *Accounting rate of return*

In conjunction with the decision subject areas in this topic, the impact of income taxes on investment decisions

-- *Tax shields from sunk costs*
-- *Transaction timing for favorable tax consequences*
-- *Property transactions*
-- *Tax elections*

C. **Quantitative Methods for Decision Analysis (10% - 15%)**

1. Regression analysis
2. Learning curve
3. Linear programming and transportation models
   a. Resource considerations
4. Sensitivity analysis
5. Network analysis
   a. Program Evaluation Review Technique (PERT)
   b. Critical Path Method (CPM)
6. Probability concepts and expected value
7. Decision tree analysis
8. Simulation
9. Artificial intelligence and expert system models
10. Other quantitative methods
    a. Queuing theory
    b. Markov analysis
    c. Game theory

D. **Information Systems (20% - 30%)**

1. Nature of management information systems (MIS)
   a. Purposes and objectives
   b. Components of a management information system
   c. Decision support systems
2. Nature of the accounting information system (AIS)
   a. Purposes, activities, benefits of an accounting information system
   b. Information economics of accounting information systems (cost/benefit)
   c. Environment of the accounting information system
   d. Components of the accounting information system
   e. Types of accounting information systems
   f. Terminology related to computer-based accounting information systems
3. Systems development and design
   a. Systems development life cycle
   b. Role of the management accountant in systems development
4. Techniques and terminology applicable to the development of computer-based accounting information systems
   a. Coding systems
   b. Flow charting techniques
   c. Forms and report design, screen layouts
   d. File design
   e. Work measurement
5. Systems controls and security measures in an accounting information system
   a. General accounting system controls
   b. Application accounting or transaction controls

E. ***Internal Auditing (10% - 15%)***

1. *Objectives and scope of internal auditing*
   a. *Responsibility and authority of the internal audit function*
   b. *Type of audits conducted by internal auditors*
   c. *Types of assistance provided to management*
2. *Fundamentals of internal organizational control*
   a. *Control environment*
   b. *Control procedures*
   c. *Foreign Corrupt Practices Act of 1977*
3. *Professional standards and procedures for internal auditing*
   a. *Role of Institute of Internal Auditors (IIA) in setting standards for internal auditors*
   b. *Standards for practicing internal auditing*
   c. *Steps in the audit process*
4. *Internal audit reports*
   a. *Types of reports*
   b. *Format of formal reports*
   c. *Standards for internal audit reports*
5. *Assessing the adequacy of the accounting information system*
   a. *Evaluation of internal accounting controls in AIS*
   b. *Evaluation of procedures in an AIS*
6. *Auditing in an EDP environment*
   a. *Audit of computer-based AIS*
   b. *Computer audit software to gather audit evidence*

The topics and subject areas above may include ethical considerations in decision analysis and information systems of concern to management accountants.

Statement on Management Accounting No. 1C, Standards of Ethical Conduct for Management Accountants

-- Competence
-- Confidentiality
-- Integrity
-- Objectivity

Manipulation of decision factors
Fraud prevention and internal controls

The ICMA lists five topics (A-E) in Part 4, and we have eight study units. We cover ICMA's topics A-C with six study units:

Study Unit 26: Incremental Costing
Study Unit 27: Cost-Volume-Profit Analysis
Study Unit 28: Capital Budgeting
Study Unit 29: Decision Making under Uncertainty
Study Unit 30: Inventory Models
Study Unit 31: Quantitative Methods

Ethics will be covered on at least two parts of the examination and will have between 30 and 60 total minutes of coverage (out of 16 hours of testing), i.e., 3% to 6% of the total exam.

STUDY UNIT 26
INCREMENTAL COSTING

INTRODUCTION

Questions involving incremental costing (sometimes called differential costing) decisions are based upon a variable costing analysis (see Study Unit 20 in Part 3). Incremental costs are the additional costs incurred by making one decision rather than another. Part 4 also includes questions on the related subject of cost-volume-profit (CVP) analysis (see Study Unit 27).

The tax consequences of business decision making are highly relevant. Thus, the outlines in Study Unit 18, Income Taxes, should be reviewed.

APPLICATIONS

A. The typical problem for which incremental cost analysis can be used involves two or more choices.

1. EXAMPLE: Assume that a firm produces a product for which it incurs the following unit costs:

Raw materials	$2.00
Direct labor	3.00
Variable overhead	.50
Fixed overhead	2.50
Total cost	$8.00

The product normally sells for $10 per unit. An application of incremental cost analysis is necessary if a foreign buyer, who has never before been a customer, offers to pay $5.75 per unit for a single order of the firm's product. The immediate reaction might be to refuse the offer because the selling price is less than the average cost of production by a considerable amount. However, incremental cost analysis results in a different decision.

2. Under incremental cost analysis, only the additional costs should be considered. In the above example, the only incremental costs are for raw materials, direct labor, and variable overhead. No additional fixed overhead costs would be incurred. Because the $5.75 selling price (incremental revenue) exceeds the $5.50 of incremental costs ($2 materials + $3 labor + $.50 variable OH), accepting the special order will be profitable.

B. In addition to special order situations, incremental costing can be used in other cases.

1. Make-or-buy decisions
2. Adding or dropping product lines
3. Sell-or-process-further decisions

C. Caution must always be used in applying incremental cost analysis because of the many nonquantitative factors that must be considered, including

1. Will special price concessions place the firm in violation of the price discrimination provisions of the Robinson-Patman Act of 1936?
2. What is the effect of government contract pricing regulations (see E. below)?
3. Will sales to the special customer affect sales in the firm's regular market?
4. Will regular customers find out about the special price and demand equal terms?
5. In the case of dropping a product line, will sales be hurt in the other product lines (e.g., the dropped product may have been an unintended loss leader)?

D. Additional cost terms may appear in decision analysis situations.

1. **Avoidable cost** -- a cost that can be saved by not adopting a particular option
2. **Imputed cost** -- a cost that exists but is not specifically stated. It pertains to a particular situation or choice. It is the result of a process designed to give recognition to economic reality and is often a part of an investment decision.
3. **Opportunity cost** -- the profit forgone by selecting one choice instead of another
4. **Postponable cost** -- a cost that may be shifted to the future with little effect on the efficiency of current operations, e.g., routine maintenance
5. **Sunk cost** -- a cost that cannot be avoided because the expenditure has occurred or an irrevocable decision to incur the cost has been made. Sunk costs are irrelevant to management decision making because they cannot vary with the option selected.

E. **Government Contracts and the CASB**

1. The Cost Accounting Standards Board was created in 1970 to promulgate cost accounting standards to achieve uniformity and consistency in cost accounting principles followed by defense contractors. The CASB was abolished as a result of a sunset review in 1980 because it was deemed to have accomplished its goals. However, all CASB standards are still effective. In 1988, Congress reestablished the CASB, granting it "exclusive authority to make, promulgate, amend, and rescind cost accounting standards and interpretations thereof" for negotiated contracts and subcontracts over $500,000.
   a. The CASB was originally established because of tremendous cost overruns on negotiated defense contracts and an inability to evaluate competing bids for government contracts resulting from inconsistent and noncomparable cost accounting practices.
   b. The new CASB is an independent entity within the Office of Federal Procurement Policy.
   c. CASB standards apply to all kinds of government contracts, not just those related to defense procurement.
2. CASB standards incorporated into the Federal Acquisition Regulations
   a. Standard 402 -- Costs incurred for the same purpose and in like circumstances shall be allocated as either direct costs or indirect costs, but not both.
      1) Each type of cost is to be allocated only once.

b. Standard 403 -- Home office expenses shall be allocated on the basis of the relationship between supporting and receiving activities. Expenses not directly allocable shall be grouped into homogeneous pools and indirectly allocated.

c. Standard 404 -- Acquisition costs of tangible capital assets shall be capitalized. Contractors shall provide written policies that are reasonable and consistently applied.

   1) Minimum life for capitalization shall not exceed 2 years.
   2) Minimum cost for capitalization shall not exceed $1,000.
   3) Acquisition cost equals

      a) Purchase price and preparation costs

      b) Fair market value of donated assets

      c) Direct and indirect costs, including general and administrative expenses, of self-constructed assets

d. Standard 405 -- Costs determined to be unallowable by agreement shall be identified and excluded from billings, claims, and proposals.

   1) If the contracting officer determines that a cost is unallowable, it shall be identified if used in a billing, claim, or proposal.

e. Standard 406 -- A contractor shall use the fiscal year as the cost accounting period unless another cost accounting period is an established practice of the contractor.

f. Standard 409 -- Depreciation shall be computed and allocated as follows:

   1) Depreciable basis is cost minus salvage value.

   2) Method of depreciation is to be based on the pattern of consumption of services.

      a) Method used for financial accounting may be used if it is accepted for income tax purposes.

   3) Gain or loss on disposition is allocated to period of disposition.

g. Standard 410 -- General and administrative expenses shall be grouped in a separate indirect cost pool and allocated only to final cost objectives.

h. Standards 412 and 413 -- Pension costs shall be assigned to the period for which computed.

i. Standard 414 -- Amortization of intangible assets shall be allocated to periods based on the cost of money (interest rates) of the period; i.e., if the cost of money is 12%, amortization shall be 12% of the cost of the amortizable assets.

j. Standard 415 -- Deferred compensation shall be allocated to periods in which obligation to pay arises (earned) and computed as the present value of future benefits.

k. Standard 416 -- Insurance costs shall be allocated to periods based on projected average loss for the period plus administration expenses for the period.

l. Standard 417 -- The imputed cost of money is an element of the cost of capital assets under construction and is recovered as depreciation.

m. Standard 418 -- Indirect costs must be accumulated in homogeneous pools and allocated to cost objectives based on some reasonable relationship of the costs and the objectives.

n. Standard 420 -- Independent research and development costs, and bid and proposal costs

   1) Shall be aggregated to the project for which they are incurred
   2) Consist of all allocable costs except general and administrative costs
   3) Shall be allocated to the period incurred

MAKE-OR-BUY DECISIONS

A. The concept behind a make-or-buy decision is to use available equipment as efficiently as possible before buying from an outside supplier. Often, an array of products can be produced efficiently if production capacity is available. If not enough capacity is available to produce them all, only the products that are produced most efficiently should be manufactured in-house (or capacity should be expanded).

B. In a make-or-buy decision, the manager considers only the costs relevant to the investment decision. If the total relevant costs of production are less than the cost to buy the item, it should be produced in-house. The key variable is relevant costs, not total costs.

   1. Past (sunk) costs are irrelevant. Hence, a production plant's $100,000 of repairs last year is irrelevant to this year's make-or-buy decision.
   2. Book value of old equipment is also irrelevant because it is a past (sunk) cost.
   3. Opportunity costs are of primary importance because they represent all of the forgone opportunities of the firm.
      a. For example, if the firm chooses not to produce the most profitable item, the opportunity cost is the difference between the profit on that item and the actual profit.
   4. When excess capacity is available, allocated fixed factory overhead is an irrelevant cost. This cost will be incurred whether the product is made or bought.
      a. However, at full capacity, the allocation of fixed factory overhead must be considered.

C. EXAMPLE: Should a company make or buy an item?

	Make	Buy
Total VC	$10	
Allocation of FC	5	
Total unit costs	$15	$13

   1. At excess capacity, the decision should be to produce the item. Total variable cost ($10) is less than the purchase price. However, if the plant is already running at 100% capacity, the fixed cost allocation becomes a relevant cost that would alter the decision in favor of purchasing the item from a supplier (with a $2 per unit savings).

DISINVESTMENT

A. Disinvestment decisions are the opposite of capital budgeting decisions, i.e., to terminate rather than start an operation. Four steps should be taken in making a disinvestment decision:

1. Identify fixed expenses that would be curtailed by the disinvestment decision, e.g., depreciation and insurance on equipment used.
2. Determine the revenue needed to justify continuing operations (variable cost of production).
3. Establish the opportunity cost of funds that will be received upon disinvestment (e.g., salvage value).
4. Determine if the book value of the assets is equal to the economic value of the capital. If not, reevaluate the decision using current fair value rather than the book value.

B. When a firm disinvests in a project, excess capacity exists unless another project uses this capacity immediately. The cost of idle capacity should be treated as a relevant cost.

C. In general, if the marginal cost of a project is greater than the marginal revenue, the firm should disinvest.

STUDY UNIT 27
COST-VOLUME-PROFIT ANALYSIS

Cost-volume-profit (CVP) analysis, also known as breakeven analysis, is tested in Part 4. It is a methodology useful in operational decision analysis, a topic that has a coverage percentage of 20% to 30%.

The tax consequences of business decisions are considered briefly in Study Unit 18, Income Taxes. Operating income subject to income taxes, gains and losses subject to taxes, tax credits, tax shields from sunk costs, transaction timing, tax elections, etc., are among the relevant issues.

BREAKEVEN ANALYSIS

A. CVP analysis describes the relationship of profit to sales volume.

1. Variables include
   a. Revenue
      1) Price per unit
      2) Quantity produced
   b. Fixed costs
   c. Variable cost as cost per unit or as percentage of sales
   d. Profit
2. Breakeven analysis assumes the linearity of costs and revenues.
   a. Costs can be classified as fixed or variable.
   b. Variable costs change at a linear rate.
   c. Fixed costs remain unchanged over a relevant range.
   d. Selling prices and the unit costs of inputs do not change as the physical sales volume changes.
   e. There is a single product, or the sales mix of multiple products remains constant.
   f. Productive efficiency does not change.
   g. Inventories are kept constant or at zero.
   h. Volume is the only factor affecting costs.
3. Definitions
   a. **Fixed costs (FC)** remain unchanged over short periods of time regardless of changes in volume.
   b. **Variable costs (VC)** vary proportionately with changes in volume.
   c. **Relevant range** is the limits within which the cost and revenue relationships remain linear and fixed costs are fixed.

d. **Breakeven point** is the sales volume in units or dollars at which total revenues equal total expenses.

e. **Margin of safety** is the excess of sales over the breakeven point.

f. **Sales mix** is the composition of total sales in terms of various products, i.e., the percentages of each product included in total sales.

g. **Unit contribution margin** is the unit selling price minus the unit variable cost, i.e., the contribution to cover fixed costs from the sale of one unit.

   1) It is expressed as either a percentage of sales or a dollar amount.

h. **Contribution margin ratio** is the difference between the unit selling price and the unit variable cost, divided by the unit selling price.

4. CVP analysis is used to examine the effects of changes in

   a. Volume
   b. Fixed costs
   c. Variable costs
   d. Product selling price

B. **Breakeven Formula**

1. $P = S - FC - VC$
   $S = XY$

If: P = profit. At breakeven, the profit is zero.
S = sales
FC = fixed costs, in dollars
VC = variable costs, as a percentage of sales or dollars per unit
X = quantity of units sold
Y = sales price of units

2. EXAMPLE: Widgets are sold at $.60 per unit and variable costs are $.20 per unit. If fixed costs are $10,000, what is the breakeven point?

$$X = \textit{units of production and sales}$$
$$\$.60X\ (\textit{sales}) = \$10{,}000\ (\textit{FC}) + \$.20X\ (\textit{VC})$$
$$\$.40X = \$10{,}000$$
$$X = 25{,}000\ \textit{units}$$

3. In other words, each unit has a contribution margin of $.40 ($.60 sales price – $.20 variable cost).

4. To cover $10,000 of fixed costs, 25,000 units must be sold to break even.

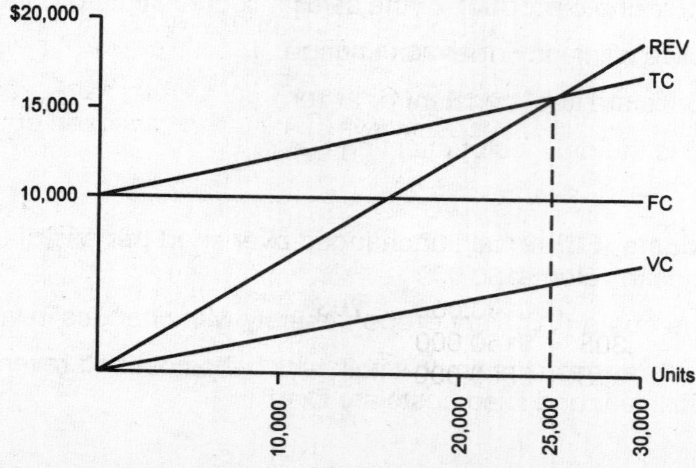

ALTERNATIVE APPLICATIONS

A. The standard, straightforward breakeven problem requires equating sales with fixed costs plus variable costs.

1. EXAMPLE: Given a unit selling price of $2.00 and unit variable cost of $.80, what is the breakeven point in units if fixed costs are $6,000?

$$\begin{aligned} S &= FC + VC \\ \$2.00X &= \$6{,}000 + \$.80X \\ \$1.20X &= \$6{,}000 \\ X &= 5{,}000 \textit{ units} \end{aligned}$$

a. The same result can be obtained by dividing the fixed costs by the unit contribution margin.

$$\begin{aligned} S &= FC \div UCM \\ S &= \$6{,}000 \div (\$2.00 - \$.80) \\ S &= 5{,}000 \textit{ units} \end{aligned}$$

2. The breakeven point in sales dollars equals fixed costs divided by the contribution margin ratio.

$$\begin{aligned} S &= FC \div CMR \\ S &= \$6{,}000 \div [(\$2.00 - \$.80) \div \$2.00] \\ S &= \$10{,}000 \end{aligned}$$

B. An amount of profit, either in dollars or as a percentage of sales, is frequently included.

1. EXAMPLE: If units are sold at $6.00 and variable costs are $2.00, how many units must be sold to realize a profit of 15% ($6.00 x .15 = $.90 per unit) before taxes, given fixed costs of $37,500.

$$\begin{aligned} S &= FC + VC + P \\ \$6.00X &= \$37{,}500 + \$2.00X + \$.90X \\ \$3.10X &= \$37{,}500 \\ X &= 12{,}097 \textit{ units at breakeven} + 15\% \textit{ profit} \end{aligned}$$

a. The desired profit of $.90 per unit is treated as a variable cost. If the desired profit were stated in total dollars rather than as a percentage, it would be treated as a fixed cost.

b. Selling 12,097 units results in $72,582 of sales. Variable costs are $24,194 and profit is $10,888 ($72,582 x 15% of the $6.00 selling price). The proof is that fixed costs of $37,500 plus variable costs of $24,194 plus profit of $10,888 equals $72,582 of sales.

C. Occasionally, two products are involved in calculating a breakeven point.

1. EXAMPLE: If A and B account for 60% and 40% of total sales, respectively, and variable costs are 60% and 85%, respectively, what is the breakeven point, given fixed costs of $150,000?

$$\begin{aligned} S &= FC + VC \\ S &= \$150{,}000 + [.60S\,(.60)] + [.40S\,(.85)] \\ S &= \$150{,}000 + .36S + .34S \\ S &= \$150{,}000 + .70S \\ .30S &= \$150{,}000 \\ S &= \$500{,}000 \end{aligned}$$

D. Sometimes breakeven analysis is applied to special orders to determine the effect of the order. This application is essentially contribution-margin analysis.

1. EXAMPLE: What is the effect of accepting a special order for 10,000 units at $8.00, given the following operating data:

	Per Unit	Total
Sales	$12.50	$1,250,000
Mfg. costs -- variable	$ 6.25	$ 625,000
Mfg. costs -- fixed	1.75	175,000
Mfg. costs -- total	$ 8.00	$ 800,000
Gross profit	$ 4.50	$ 450,000
Selling expenses -- variable	$ 1.80	$ 180,000
Selling expenses -- fixed	1.45	145,000
Selling expenses -- total	$ 3.25	$ 325,000
Operating income	$ 1.25	$ 125,000

a. Because the variable cost of manufacturing is $6.25, the unit contribution margin is $1.75, and the increase in operating income is $17,500 ($1.75 x 10,000 units).

b. This calculation assumes that the idle capacity is sufficient to manufacture the 10,000 extra units and that the sale at $8.00 per unit will not affect the price or quantity of other units sold. It also assumes no additional selling expenses for the special order.

OPERATING LEVERAGE

A. Operating leverage is the change in operating income resulting from a percentage change in sales.

1. It measures how a change in volume affects profits.

2. $$\textit{Operating leverage} = \frac{\textit{Percentage change in operating income}}{\textit{Percentage change in sales}}$$

3. The assumption is that companies with larger investments (and greater fixed costs) will have higher contribution margins and more operating leverage.

a. Thus, as companies invest in better and more expensive equipment, their variable production costs should decrease.

b. EXAMPLE: If sales increase by 40% and profit increases by 50%, the operating leverage is 1.25 (50% ÷ 40%).

4. Given that Q equals the number of units sold, P is unit price, V is unit variable cost, and F is fixed cost, the degree of operating leverage can also be calculated from the following formula:

$$\frac{Q(P - V)}{Q(P - V) - F}$$

STUDY UNIT 28
CAPITAL BUDGETING

INTRODUCTION

Because the subject is well-defined, preparing for capital budgeting (CB) questions is straightforward. This study unit provides definitions and outlines (with examples) of the most important techniques. Risk analysis is also discussed.

Remember to consider the tax consequences of business decision making by reviewing the outlines in Study Unit 18, Income Taxes.

DEFINITIONS

A. Capital budgeting is the process of planning expenditures for assets, the returns on which are expected to continue beyond 1 year.

1. Capital budgeting decisions are long-term.

   a. Once made, they tend to be relatively inflexible because the commitments extend well into the future.

2. Without proper timing, additional capacity generated by the acquisition of capital assets may not coincide with changes in demand for output, resulting in capacity excess or shortage.

   a. Accurate forecasting is needed to anticipate changes in product demand so that full economic benefits flow to the firm when the capital asset is available for use.

3. A capital budget usually involves substantial expenditures. The sources of these funds are critical.

   a. Planning is important because of possible changes in capital markets, inflation, interest rates, and the money supply.

B. **Types of Costs Relevant to Capital Budgeting Analysis**

1. **Incremental cost** -- the difference in cost resulting from selecting one option instead of another
2. **Sunk cost** -- a cost that cannot be avoided because an expenditure has been made or an irrevocable decision to incur the cost has been made
3. **Opportunity cost** -- the profit forgone by selecting one option instead of another
4. **Avoidable cost** -- a cost that may be saved by not adopting an option
5. **Imputed cost** -- a cost that may not entail a specified dollar outlay formally recognized by the accounting system but that is relevant to establishing the economic reality analyzed in the decision-making process
6. **Fixed cost** -- a cost that does not vary with the level of activity within the relevant range
7. **Cost of capital** -- the interest cost of debt proceeds (net of tax) or the cost of obtaining equity capital to be invested in long-term plant and equipment
8. **Common cost** -- a cost common to all possibilities in question and not clearly allocable to any one of them
9. **Deferrable cost** -- a cost that may be shifted to the future with little or no effect on current operations

C. Capital budgeting requires choosing among investment proposals. Thus, a ranking procedure for such decisions is needed. The following are steps in the ranking procedure:

1. Determine the asset cost or net investment.
   a. The net investment is the net outlay, or gross cash requirement, minus cash recovered from the trade or sale of existing assets, with any necessary adjustments for applicable tax consequences.
   b. The investment required also includes funds to provide for increases in working capital, for example, the additional receivables and inventories resulting from the acquisition of a new manufacturing plant. This investment in working capital is treated as an initial cost of the investment (a cash outflow) that will be recovered at the end of the project.
2. Calculate estimated cash flow, period by period, using the acquired assets.
   a. Reliable estimates of cost savings or revenues are necessary.
   b. Net cash flow is the economic benefit, period by period, resulting from the investment.
   c. **Economic life** is the time period over which the benefits of the investment proposal are expected to be obtained, as distinguished from the physical or technical life of the asset involved.
   d. **Depreciable life** is the period used for accounting and tax purposes over which cost is to be systematically and rationally allocated. It is based upon permissible or standard guidelines and may have no particular relevance to economic life.
3. Relate the cash-flow benefits to their cost by using a method to evaluate the advantage of purchasing the asset. See Capital Budgeting Methods on page 586.
4. Rank the investments.

D. The rating methods can sometimes yield different solutions to an investment problem. Managers should thus use all the methods and then apply judgment in making the final decision. All of these techniques consider only the economic factors in a decision, but sometimes noneconomic factors can take precedence.

PRESENT VALUE AND FUTURE VALUE

The basic **time value of money** concept is that a quantity of money sometime in the future is worth less than the same amount of money today. The difference is measured in terms of interest calculated according to the appropriate discount rate. Interest is the payment received by holders of money to forgo current consumption. Conversely, the current consumer of money pays interest for its use.

A. Standard tables have been developed to facilitate the calculation of present and future values. Each entry in one of these tables represents the result of substituting in the pertinent present value or future value equation a payment of $1, the number of periods, and an interest rate.

B. The **present value (PV)** of an amount is the value today of some future payment.

   1. It equals the present value of $1 (a factor found in a standard table) for the given number of periods and interest rate times the future payment.

C. The **future value (FV)** of an amount is the amount available at a specified time in the future based on a single investment (deposit) today. The FV is the amount to be computed if one knows the present value and the appropriate discount rate.

   1. It equals the future value of $1 (a factor found in a standard table) for the given number of periods and interest rate times the current payment.

D. **Annuities**. An annuity is usually a series of equal payments at equal intervals of time, e.g., $1,000 at the end of every year for 10 years.

   1. An ordinary annuity (annuity in arrears) is a series of payments occurring at the end of the periods involved. An annuity due (annuity in advance) is an annuity in which the payments are made (or received) at the beginning of the periods.

      a. The difference for PV calculations is that no interest is computed on the first payment of an annuity due.

   2. The **PV of an annuity**. The same present value tables may be used for both kinds of annuities. Most tables are for ordinary annuities. The factor for an ordinary annuity of one less period (n – 1), increased by 1.0 to include the initial payment (for which no interest is computed), is the factor for an annuity due.

   3. The **FV of an annuity** is the value that a series of equal payments will have at a certain moment in the future if interest is earned at a given rate.

      a. In an ordinary annuity, the payments are made (or received) at the end of the periods, and the future value is determined at the date of the last payment. Hence, no interest is earned during the first period or on the last payment.

      b. In an annuity due, the payments occur at the beginning of the periods. The difference for FV calculations is that interest is computed on the first payment of an annuity due, and the future value is determined one period after the last payment. Hence, the same future value tables may be used for both kinds of annuities. The factor for the FV of an ordinary annuity of one more period (n + 1), decreased by 1.0 to exclude the last payment (for which no interest is computed), is the factor for an annuity due.

CAPITAL BUDGETING METHODS

A. Techniques for Ranking Investment Proposals

1. **Payback** is the number of years required to complete the return of the original investment, i.e., the time it takes for a new asset to pay for itself. This measure is computed by dividing the net investment required by the periodic constant expected cash flow to be generated, resulting in the number of years required to recover the original investment.

   a. $$\frac{\textit{Net investment}}{\textit{Periodic constant expected cash flow}}$$

   b. Payback is easy to calculate but has two principal problems:

      1) No consideration for the time value of money
      2) No estimate or consideration of returns after the payback period

   c. Its strength is its simplicity.

   d. It is sometimes used for foreign investments if foreign expropriation of company assets is feared.

   e. Even in these circumstances, the payback method is most often used in addition to another, more sophisticated, method.

   f. It does measure risk. The longer the payback period, the more risky the investment.

   g. The payback reciprocal (1 ÷ payback) is sometimes used as an estimate of the internal rate of return.

   h. The **bail-out payback** incorporates the salvage value of the asset into the calculation. It measures the length of the payback period when the periodic cash inflows are combined with the salvage value.

   i. If periodic cash flows are not constant, the calculation must be in cumulative form.

   j. **Breakeven time** is a more sophisticated version of the payback method that is growing in popularity. Breakeven time is defined as the period required for the discounted cumulative cash inflows on a project to equal the discounted cash outflows (usually the initial cost). This period begins at the outset of a project, not when the initial cash outflow occurs.

2. **Net present value (NPV)** is broadly defined as the excess of the present values of the estimated net cash inflows over the net cost of the investment (discounted net cash outflows).

   a. The NPV method is used when the discount rate (the cost of capital, required rate of return, hurdle rate) is specified.

   b. $$NPV = \left[\sum_{t=1}^{n} \frac{\textit{Annual net cash inflows}}{(1 + k)^t}\right] - \textit{net cash investment}$$

   If: n = number of years of future cash flows
   k = discount rate

c. The reinvestment rate often becomes critical when choosing between the NPV and IRR methods. NPV assumes the cash flows from the investment can be reinvested at the particular project's cost of capital.

d. Present value tables are used to reduce the future cash flows to current dollars.

e. If the NPV is positive, the project should be accepted. If NPV is negative, the project should be rejected.

3. **Internal rate of return (IRR)** is an interest rate (r) computed such that the present value of the expected future cash flows is equal to the cost of the investment.

   a. The IRR method specifies the NPV as zero. The computation finds the value of r such that the present value of future net cash inflows is equal to the cost of the investment.

      1) The IRR can be found by trial and error using arbitrarily selected interest rates. One may go from column to column on a present value table until an NPV of zero is obtained.

      2) As long as r is greater than k, NPV must be greater than zero.

      3) The IRR and NPV methods rank projects differently if

         a) The cost of one project is greater than the cost of another.
         b) The timing of cash flows differs among projects.

   b. The IRR method assumes that the cash flows will be reinvested at the internal rate of return (r).

      1) If the project's funds are not reinvested at the IRR, the ranking calculations obtained may be in error.

      2) The NPV method gives a better grasp of the problem in many decision situations because the reinvestment is assumed to be the cost of capital (k).

4. **Profitability or excess present value index** is the ratio of the present value of future net cash inflows to the discounted initial net investment.

   a. $$\frac{\textit{PV of future net cash inflows}}{\textit{Discounted initial net investment}}$$

   b. This variation of the net present value method facilitates comparison of different-sized investments.

5. **Accounting rate of return** (also called unadjusted rate of return or book value rate of return) is the increase in accounting net income divided by the required investment.

   a. Sometimes the denominator is the average investment rather than the initial investment.

   b. The accounting rate of return ignores the time value of money.

B. EXAMPLE: Hazman Company plans to replace an old piece of equipment that is obsolete and expected to be unreliable under the stress of daily operations. The equipment is fully depreciated, and no salvage value can be realized upon its disposal. One piece of equipment being considered as a replacement would provide an annual cash savings of $7,000 before income taxes and without regard to the effect of depreciation. The equipment would cost $18,000 and has an estimated useful life of 5 years. No salvage value would be used for depreciation purposes because the equipment is expected to have no value at the end of 5 years.

Hazman uses the straight-line depreciation method on all equipment for both book and tax purposes. Hence, annual depreciation is $3,600. The company is subject to a 40% tax rate. Hazman has an aftertax cost of capital of 14%, so it would use the 14% column from a present value table.

Analysis of cash flows

		Annual Before-Tax Cash Flow	Annual Tax Savings (Tax)	Annual Aftertax Cash Flow	Annual Aftertax Net Income
Investment	Year 0	$(18,000)	-0-	$(18,000)	-0-
Annual cash savings	Years 1-5	$ 7,000	$(2,800)	$ 4,200	$ 4,200
	Years 1-5		1,440	1,440	(2,160)
Totals				$ 5,640	$ 2,040

1. Payback period $= \dfrac{\textit{Investment}}{\textit{Aftertax cash flow}}$

$= \dfrac{\$18,000}{\$5,640}$

$= 3.19$ *years*

2. Net present value = *(Aftertax cash flows × Present value of annuity) - Initial investment*

= ($5,640 × 3.43) - $18,000

= $1,345.20

3. Internal rate of return

Net present value at 16%	$5,640 x 3.27	=	$18,443
Net present value at 18%	$5,640 x 3.13	=	17,653
Difference			$ 790

Net present value at 16%	$18,443
Initial investment	18,000
Difference	$ 443

Estimated increment	($443 ÷ $790) x 2% =	1.1%
Rate used		16.0
Internal rate of return		17.1%

4. Profitability index (PI) $= \dfrac{\textit{Present value of aftertax cash flows}}{\textit{Initial investment}}$

$$= \frac{\$5,640 \times 3.43}{\$18,000}$$

$$= 1.07$$

5. Accounting rate of return $= \dfrac{\textit{Annual aftertax net income}}{\textit{Investment (initial or average)}}$

Initial investment	Average investment
$\dfrac{\$2,040}{\$18,000} = 11.3\%$	$\dfrac{\$2,040}{\$9,000} = 22.7\%$

C. EXAMPLE: The management of Flesher Farms is trying to decide whether to buy a new team of mules at a cost of $1,000 or a new tractor at a cost of $10,000. They will perform the same job. But because the mules require more laborers, the annual return is only $250 of net cash inflows. The tractor will return $2,000 of net cash inflows per year. The mules have a working life of 8 years and the tractor 10 years. Neither investment is expected to have a salvage value at the end of its useful life.

1. Payback period

Mules: $\dfrac{\$1,000}{\$250} = 4$ years

Tractor: $\dfrac{\$10,000}{\$2,000} = 5$ years

2. Accounting rate of return

Mules: $\dfrac{\$250 - \$125 \textit{ depreciation}}{\$1,000} = 12.5\%$

Tractor: $\dfrac{\$2,000 - \$1,000 \textit{ depreciation}}{\$10,000} = 10\%$

3. Net present value assuming that the company's cost of capital is 6%

Mules:	$250 x 6.209 =	$1,552
		(1,000)
	Net present value	$ 552
Tractor:	$2,000 x 7.360 =	$14,720
		(10,000)
	Net present value	$ 4,720

4. Profitability index

$$\text{Mules: } \frac{\$1,552}{\$1,000} = 1.552$$

$$\text{Tractor: } \frac{\$14,720}{\$10,000} = 1.472$$

5. Internal rate of return

Mules: *\$250 × Factor = \$1,000*
Factor = 4

On the 8-year line, the factor of 4 results in a rate of return of approximately 18.72%.

Tractor: *\$2,000 × Factor = \$10,000*
Factor = 5

On the 10-year line, the factor of 5 results in a rate of return of approximately 15.2%.

6. The mule investment has the better payback and the higher IRR and accounting rate of return. Also, the mules have the better profitability index. The tractor has a better net present value, however. The various methods thus give different answers to the investment question. Either investment would be profitable for the company. Management may decide to let noneconomic factors influence the decision. For example, the mules would require the use of more laborers. If unemployment in the community is high, management might wish to achieve a social goal of providing more jobs. Alternatively, a labor shortage might convince management to buy the tractor to reduce labor worries.

D. NPV and IRR are the soundest investment rules from a shareholder wealth maximization perspective.

1. In some cases, NPV and IRR will rank projects differently.

a. EXAMPLE:

Project	Initial Cost	Year-End Cash Flow	IRR	NPV (k=10%)
A	\$1,000	\$1,200	20%	\$91
B	\$ 50	\$ 100	100%	\$41

IRR preference ordering: B,A
NPV preference ordering: A,B

2. If one of two or more mutually exclusive projects is accepted, the others must be rejected.

a. EXAMPLE: The decision to build a shopping mall on a piece of land eliminates placing an office building on the same land.

b. When choosing between mutually exclusive projects, the ranking differences between NPV and IRR become very important. In the example D.1.a., a firm using IRR would accept B and reject A. A firm using NPV would make exactly the opposite choice.

3. The problem can be seen more clearly using a net present value (NPV) profile. The NPV profile is a plot of a project's net present value at different discount rates. The NPV is plotted on the vertical axis and the rate of return (k) on the horizontal axis.

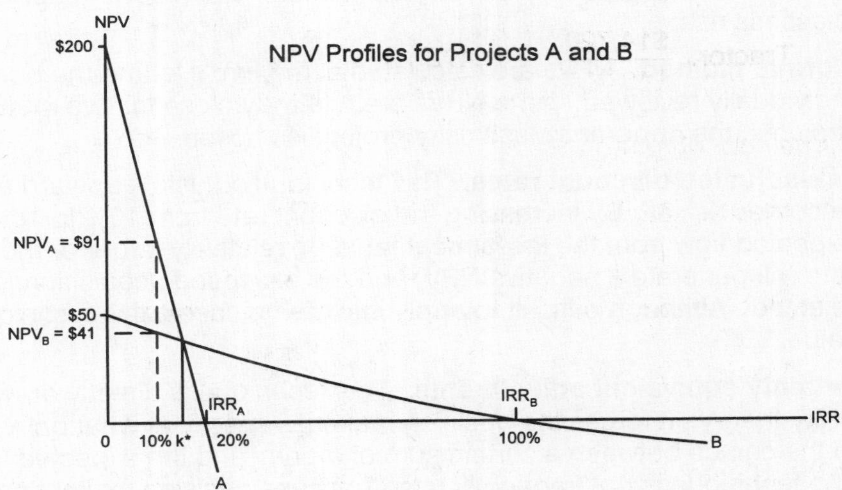

These profiles are downward sloping because a higher discount rate implies a lower NPV.

a. The graph shows that, for all discount rates higher than k*, the firm should select project B over A because NPV_B is greater than NPV_A. This preference ordering also results from applying the IRR criterion. Below k*, however, NPV_A is greater than NPV_B, so A should be selected, even though IRR_B is greater than IRR_A.

4. These profiles show that IRR will always prefer B to A. NPV will prefer B to A only past some critical discount rate k*.

5. The manager concerned with shareholder wealth maximization should choose the project with the greatest NPV, not the largest IRR. IRR is a percentage measure of wealth, but NPV is an absolute measure. Shareholder well-being is also measured in absolute amounts.

a. The choice of NPV over IRR is easy to see with a simple example. Assume that you must choose between investing $1 and getting back $2 or investing $100,000 and getting back $150,000. The IRR of the projects are 100% and 50%, respectively, which gives support to choosing the first project. But assume instead that the interest rate is 10%. The NPV of the projects are $.81 and $36,363, respectively. To select the first project because of the IRR criterion would lead to a return of $.81 instead of $36,363. Thus, the NPV is the better criterion when choosing between mutually exclusive projects.

6. The NPV profile can be of great practical use to managers trying to make investment decisions. It gives the manager a clear insight into the following questions:

a. At what interest rates is an investment project still a profitable opportunity?
b. How sensitive is a project's profitability to changes in the discount rate?

RISK ANALYSIS

A. Risk analysis attempts to measure the likelihood of the variability of future returns from the proposed investment. Risk cannot be ignored entirely, but mathematical approaches can be impossible because of a lack of critical information. The following approaches are frequently used to assess risk:

1. **Informal method.** NPVs are calculated at the firm's k, and the possible projects are individually reviewed. If the NPVs are relatively close for two mutually exclusive projects, the apparently less risky project is chosen.
2. **Risk-adjusted discount rates.** This technique adjusts k upward as the investment becomes riskier. By increasing the discount rate from 10% to 15%, for example, the expected flow from the investment must be relatively larger or the increased discount rate will generate a negative NPV, and the proposed acquisition/investment would be rejected. Although difficult to apply in extreme cases, this technique has much intuitive value.
3. **Certainty equivalent adjustments.** This technique is directly drawn from the concept of utility theory. It forces the decision maker to specify at what point the firm is indifferent to the choice between a certain sum of money and the expected value of a risky sum. The technique is not frequently used because decision makers are not familiar with the concept.
4. **Sensitivity analysis.** Forecasts of many calculated NPVs under various assumptions are compared to see how sensitive NPV is to changing conditions. Changing or relaxing the assumptions about a certain variable or group of variables may drastically alter the NPV. Thus, the asset may appear to be much riskier than was originally predicted.
5. **Simulation analysis.** This method represents a refinement of standard profitability theory. The computer is used to generate many examples of results based upon various assumptions. Project simulation is frequently expensive. Unless a project is exceptionally large and expensive, full-scale simulation is generally not worthwhile.
6. **The Capital Asset Pricing Model.** This method is derived from the use of portfolio theory. It assumes that all assets are held in a portfolio. Each asset has variability in its returns. Some of this variability is caused by movements in the market as a whole, and some is specific to each firm. In a portfolio, the firm's specific variability is eliminated through diversification, and the only relevant risk is the market component. The more sensitive an asset's rate of return is to changes in the market's rate of return, the riskier the asset.
7. See also the section on Forecasting in Study Unit 31, Quantitative Methods.

STUDY UNIT 29
DECISION MAKING UNDER UNCERTAINTY

INTRODUCTION

This study unit has been developed separately to make the quantitative methods material on the CMA examination more manageable for CMA candidates. The next two study units, Inventory Models and Quantitative Methods, explain various managerial optimization and planning techniques. This study unit outlines the probability and statistical material that underlies many optimization models and explains regression (least squares) analysis, which has had considerable coverage on past CMA exams. The additional importance of this study unit is that it supports the next two study units.

Remember to consider the tax consequences of business decision making by reviewing the outlines in Study Unit 18, Income Taxes.

PROBABILITY

A. Probability is important to management decision making because of the uncertainty of future events. Probability estimation techniques assist in making the best decisions in the face of uncertainty.

B. Probability provides a method for mathematically expressing doubt or assurance about the occurrence of a chance event. The probability of an event varies from 0 to 1.

   1. A probability of 0 means the event cannot occur, whereas a probability of 1 means the event is certain to occur.

   2. Values between 0 and 1 indicate the likelihood of the event's occurrence; e.g., the probability that a fair coin will yield heads is 0.5 on any single toss.

C. There are two types of probability -- objective and subjective. They differ in how they are calculated.

   1. **Objective probabilities** are calculated from either logic or actual experience. For example, in rolling dice one would logically expect each face on a single die to be equally likely to turn up at a probability of 1/6. Alternatively, the die could be rolled a great many times, and the fraction of times each face turned up could then be used as the frequency or probability of occurrence.

   2. **Subjective probabilities** are estimates, based on judgment and past experience, of the likelihood of future events. Weather forecasts often include the subjective probability of rain. In business, subjective probability can indicate the degree of confidence a person has that a certain outcome will occur, e.g., future performance of a new employee.

D. **Basic Terms Used with Probability**

1. Two events are **mutually exclusive** if they cannot occur simultaneously (e.g., heads and tails cannot both occur on a single toss of a coin).
2. The **joint probability** for two events is the probability that **both** will occur.
3. The **conditional probability** of two events is the probability that one will occur given that the other has already occurred.
4. Two events are **independent** if the occurrence of one has no effect on the probability of the other (e.g., rolling two dice).
   a. If one event has an effect on the other event, they are **dependent**.
   b. Two events are **independent** if their joint probability equals the product of their individual probabilities.
   c. Two events are **independent** if the conditional probability of each event equals its unconditional probability.

E. Probabilities can be combined using these rules.

1. The joint probability for two events equals the probability (Pr) of the first event multiplied by the conditional probability of the second event, given that the first has already occurred.
   a. EXAMPLE: If 60% of the students at a university are male, Pr(male) is 6/10. If 1/6 of the male students have a B average, Pr(B average given male) is 1/6. Therefore, the probability that any given student (male or female) selected at random, **both** is male **and** has a B average is

$$\begin{array}{ccccc} Pr(male) & \times & Pr(B|male) & = & Pr(male \cap B) \\ 6/10 & \times & 1/6 & = & 1/10 \end{array}$$

   Pr(male ∩ B) is .10; that is, the probability that the students are males **and** have B averages is 10%.

2. The probability that either one or both of two events will occur equals the sum of their separate probabilities minus their joint probability.
   a. EXAMPLE: If two fair coins are thrown, the probability that at least one will come up heads is Pr(coin #1 is heads) plus Pr(coin #2 is heads) minus Pr(coin #1 and coin #2 are both heads), or

$$(.5) + (.5) - (.5 \times .5) = .75$$

   b. EXAMPLE: If in the earlier example 1/3 of all students, male or female, have a B average [Pr(B average) is 1/3], the probability that any given student either is male or has a B average is

$$\begin{array}{ccccccc} Pr(male) & + & Pr(B\ avg.) & - & Pr(B \cap male) & = & Pr(male\ or\ has\ B\ avg.) \\ 6/10 & + & 1/3 & - & 1/10 & = & 25/30 \end{array}$$

   The term Pr(B ∩ male) must be subtracted to avoid double counting those students who belong to both groups.

3. The probabilities for all possible mutually exclusive outcomes of a single experiment must add up to one.

   a. EXAMPLE: Flipping two coins (H = heads, T = tails)

If Coin #1 is	If Coin #2 is	Probability of This Combination
H	H	.25
H	T	.25
T	H	.25
T	T	.25
Probability that one of the four possible combinations will occur		1.00 (certainty)

F. A probability distribution specifies the values of the variables and their respective probabilities. Certain standard distributions seem to occur frequently in nature and have proven useful in business.

1. Discrete distributions include

   a. **Uniform distribution**. All outcomes are equally likely, such as the flipping of one coin, or even of two coins, as in the example above.

   b. **Binomial distribution**. Each trial has only two possible outcomes, e.g., accept or reject, heads or tails. This distribution shows the likelihood of each of the possible combinations of trial results. It is used in quality control.

      1) EXAMPLE: The social director of a cruise ship is concerned that the occupants at each dining room table be balanced evenly between men and women. The tables have only 6, 10, or 16 seats. If the population of the ship is exactly 50% male and 50% female [Pr(male) = .5 and Pr(female) = .5], what is the random chance for an equal balance of males and females at each table?

      The binomial formula is

$$\frac{n!}{r!(n - r)!} \times p^r(1 - p)^{n-r}$$

      If: p is the probability of the given condition.
      n is the sample size.
      r is the number of occurrences of the condition within the sample.
      ! is factorial, i.e., 1 x 2 x 3 x ... n, or 1 x 2 x 3 x ... r.

      Given a .5 probability that any person in the population is male, the probability that exactly three males (and therefore three females) will be seated randomly at a table for six persons is

$$\frac{6!}{3!(6 - 3)!} \times .5^3(1 - .5)^{6-3} = .3125$$

      The probability is only 31% that an equally balanced group of males and females will be randomly chosen. For the tables with 10 and 16 seats, the probabilities are .2461 and .1964, respectively. The social director will have to assign seats.

c. **Bernoulli distribution** deals with only one trial, whereas the binomial distribution deals with as many as necessary. Thus, the binomial distribution reduces to the Bernoulli distribution when n is 1.

d. **Hypergeometric distribution**. Similar to the binomial distribution, the hypergeometric is used for sampling without replacement.

1) For finite populations, sampling without replacement removes each item sampled from the population, thus changing the composition of the population from trial to trial.

a) EXAMPLE: For a standard, well-shuffled deck of cards, the probability of picking the 2 of spades on the first draw is 1/52. If the card drawn is not replaced, the probability is 1/51 on the second draw, 1/50 on the third draw, etc. (unless, of course, the 2 of spades is drawn, in which case subsequent trial probabilities are 0). Sampling with replacement returns the card to the deck. The probability that any given card will be drawn is then 1/52 on every trial when sampling with replacement.

2) For large populations and small samples, the binomial distribution approximates the hypergeometric distribution and is computationally more convenient.

e. **Poisson distribution**. The Poisson distribution is useful when the event being studied may happen more than once with random frequency during a given period of time.

1) The Poisson distribution is defined as

$$f(k) = \frac{\lambda^k e^{-\lambda}}{k!} \qquad \textit{mean and variance} = \lambda$$

If: k is the number of occurrences.
e is the natural logarithm (2.71828...).

2) When sample size is large and λ is small (preferably less than 7), the Poisson distribution approaches the binomial distribution.

$$\lambda \ (\textit{lambda}) = np$$

If: n = number of items sampled and
p = probability of a binomial event's occurrence.

3) EXAMPLE: A trucking company has established that, on average, two of its trucks are involved in an accident each month. It wishes to calculate the probability of a month with no (0) crashes and the probability of a month with four crashes. The mean of the Poisson distribution is λ, and the average monthly crash rate is two, so λ = 2. The probability of zero crashes in a given month is

$$f(0) = \frac{\lambda^0 e^{-\lambda}}{0!} = \frac{1e^{-2}}{1} = e^{-2} = .135 \qquad (\textit{Note}: \ 0! = 1)$$

The probability of four crashes in a given month is

$$f(4) = \frac{\lambda^4 e^{-\lambda}}{4!} = \frac{2^4 e^{-2}}{4!} = .09$$

2. Continuous distributions include

   a. **Normal distribution**. The most important and useful of all probability distributions, it describes many physical phenomena. In sampling, it describes the distribution of the sample mean regardless of the distribution of the population. It has a symmetrical, bell-shaped curve centered about the mean (see the diagram below). For the normal distribution, about 68% of the area (or probability) lies within plus or minus 1 standard deviation of the mean, 95.5% lies within 2 standard deviations, and 99% lies within 3 standard deviations of the mean.

      1) A special type of normal distribution is called the standard normal distribution. It has a mean of 0 and variance of 1. All normal distribution problems are first converted to the standard normal distribution to permit use of standard normal distribution tables.

      2) Normal distributions have the following fixed relationships concerning the area under the curve and the distance from the mean.

Distance in Standard Deviation (confidence coefficient)	Area under the Curve (confidence level)
1.0	68%
1.64	90%
1.96	95%
2.0	95.5%
2.57	99%

EXAMPLE: If standard deviation (σ) = 10

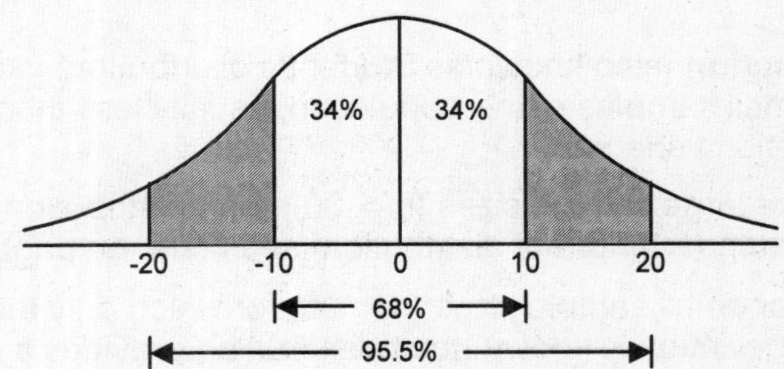

      3) The standard deviation (sigma) is explained under the Statistics sideheading on page 601.

   b. **Exponential distribution.** Related to the Poisson distribution, the exponential distribution is the probability of zero occurrences in a time period T.

      1) The Poisson distribution has just been defined as

$$f(k) = \frac{\lambda^k e^{-\lambda}}{k!}$$

Moreover, based on the example in e.3) on page 596,

$$f(0) = e^{-\lambda}$$

If: k = 0 (no occurrences in the time period)

2) For the exponential distribution, M is used instead of λ.

$P = e^{-M}$
M = LT = frequency of the event's occurrence in this period
L = frequency or rate of the event's occurrence per unit of time
T = number of time units in this period
P = probability under exponential distribution

3) EXAMPLE: The trucking company mentioned in e.3) on page 596 may wish to calculate the probability that a month will elapse without a single crash (the probability of a 1-month period between crashes).

L = 2 crashes per month
T = 1 month
∴ M = 2 x 1 = 2

The probability of a 1-month interval between crashes is then

$$P = e^{-M} = 2.71828^{-2} = .135$$

The probability of a 2-month period between crashes is

L = 2
T = 2
M = 2 x 2 = 4
$P = e^{-M} = 2.71828^{-4} = .0183$, or much less likely

c. **t-distribution** (also known as Student's distribution) is a special distribution used with small samples of the population, usually less than 30, with unknown population variance.

1) For large sample sizes ($n > 30$), the t-distribution is almost identical to the standard normal distribution (see F.2.a. on page 597).

2) For small sample sizes ($n < 30$) for which only the sample standard deviation is known, the t-distribution provides a reasonable estimate for tests of the population mean if the population is normally distributed.

3) The t-distribution is useful in business because large samples are often too expensive. For a small sample, the t-statistic (from a t-table) provides a better estimate of the variance than that from a table for the normal distribution.

4) See also section E. under Hypothesis Testing on page 610.

d. **Chi-square distribution**. Another special distribution, it is used in testing the goodness of fit between actual data and the theoretical distribution. In other words, it tests whether the sample is likely to be from the population, based on a comparison of the sample variance and the population variance.

1) The Chi-square statistic (χ^2) is the sample variance (s^2), multiplied by its degree of freedom ($n - 1$), and divided by the hypothesized population variance (σ^2), if n is the number of items sampled.

2) A calculated value of the Chi-square statistic greater than the critical value in the χ^2 table indicates that the sample chosen comes from a population with greater variance than the hypothesized population variance.

3) The Chi-square test is useful in business for testing hypotheses concerning populations. If the variance of a process is known and a sample is tested to determine if it has the same variance, the Chi-square statistic may be calculated.

4) EXAMPLE: A canning machine fills cans with a product and has exhibited a long-term standard deviation of .4 ounces, ($\sigma = .4$). A new machine is tested, but because the tests are expensive, only 15 cans are examined. The following is the result:

Sample standard deviation (s) = .311

The Chi-square statistic is calculated as follows:

$$\chi^2 = \frac{(n-1)s^2}{\sigma^2} = \frac{(15-1).311^2}{.4^2} = 8.463$$

Assume the null hypothesis (H_o) is that the new machine has a variance lower than or equal to the variance of the old machine, and that a probability of error (α) of .05 is acceptable. The χ^2 statistic for an α of .05 and 14 degrees of freedom is 23.68 in the χ^2 table. This critical value is much greater than the sample statistic of 8.463, so the null hypothesis cannot be rejected. Alpha (α) error is the error of incorrectly rejecting the true hypothesis. (See Hypothesis Testing on page 607.)

EXPECTED VALUE

A. For decisions involving risk, the concept of expected value provides a rational means for selecting the best alternative. The expected value of an alternative is found by multiplying the probability of each outcome by its payoff and summing the products. It represents the long-term average payoff for repeated trials. The best alternative is the one having the highest expected value.

1. EXAMPLE: An investor is considering the purchase of two different pieces of property. The value of the property will change if a road, currently planned by the state, is built. The following are estimates that road construction will occur:

Future State of Nature (SN)	Probability
SN 1: No road is ever built.	.1
SN 2: A road is built this year.	.2
SN 3: A road is built more than 1 year from now.	.7

Next, estimate the value of each property under each of the three possible future states of nature.

Property	Value if SN 1	Value if SN 2	Value if SN 3
Property 1	\$10,000	\$40,000	\$35,000
Property 2	\$20,000	\$50,000	\$30,000

Then calculate the expected value of each property by multiplying the probability of each state of nature by the value under that state of nature and adding all of the partial results together.

P1: (.1 x \$10,000) + (.2 x \$40,000) + (.7 x \$35,000) = \$33,500 expected value
P2: (.1 x \$20,000) + (.2 x \$50,000) + (.7 x \$30,000) = \$33,000 expected value

Thus, Property 1 is the better investment if the two properties cost the same.

B. Some managers are reluctant to use subjectively derived numbers, arguing that they are not measurable. Certainly, there is no way to prove the accuracy of the estimates. Their use, however, makes explicit what would otherwise be decided subconsciously or intuitively. Once stated, the reasonableness of subjectively derived numbers can be examined.

1. Another criticism of expected value is that it is based on repetitive trials, whereas many business decisions involve only one trial.

   a. EXAMPLE: A company wishes to launch a communications satellite. The probability of launch failure is .2, and the value of the satellite if the launch fails is $0. The probability of a successful launch is .8, and the value of the satellite would then be $25,000,000. The expected value is thus

      (.2 x $0) + (.8 x $25,000,000) = $20,000,000

      But $20,000,000 is not a possible value for a single satellite; either it flies for $25,000,000 or it crashes for $0.

C. **Decision trees** and **payoff tables** may be used to describe decision situations.

1. EXAMPLE: A dealer in luxury yachts may order 0, 1, or 2 yachts for this season's inventory, but no more or less. There is a $50,000 cost for carrying each excess yacht, and a $200,000 gain for each yacht sold. The situation may be described by a payoff table as

Season's Actual Demand	Order 0	Order 1	Order 2
0 yachts	0	$ (50,000)	$(100,000)
1 yacht	0	200,000	150,000
2 yachts	0	200,000	400,000

Given the probabilities of the season's demand,

Pr	Demand
.10	0
.50	1
.40	2

the dealer may calculate the expected value of each course of action as follows:

Order 0	Order 1	Order 2
.1 x 0	.1 x $ (50,000)	.1 x $(100,000)
.5 x 0	+ .5 x 200,000	+ .5 x 150,000
.4 x 0	+ .4 x 200,000	+ .4 x 400,000
EV(0) = 0	EV(1) = $175,000	EV(2) = $ 225,000

The decision with the greatest expected value is to order two yachts, so, in the absence of additional information, the dealer should order two. The decision tree representation of this situation is

Action	State of Nature	Payoff
Order 0	Demand = 0	$ 0
	Demand = 1	0
	Demand = 2	0
Order 1	Demand = 0	(50,000)
	Demand = 1	200,000
	Demand = 2	200,000
Order 2	Demand = 0	(100,000)
	Demand = 1	150,000
	Demand = 2	400,000

D. Value of Perfect Information

1. **Perfect information** is the knowledge that a future state of nature will occur with certainty, i.e., being sure of what will occur in the future.

   a. The expected value of perfect information (EVPI) is the difference between the expected value without perfect information and the return if the best action is taken given perfect information.

   b. EXAMPLE (from the yacht dealer problem on page 600): If the yacht dealer were able to poll all potential customers and they truthfully stated whether they would purchase a yacht this year (i.e., if perfect information about this year's yacht sales could be purchased), what is the greatest amount of money the dealer should pay for this information? What is EVPI?

   If the dealer had perfect knowledge of demand, (s)he would make the best decision for each state of nature. The cost of the other decisions is the conditional cost of making other than the best choice. This cost may be calculated by subtracting the expected value from the expected value given perfect information. This difference measures how much better off the decision maker would be with perfect information. From the payoff table on page 600, we find the expected value of the best choice under each state of nature.

Pr	State of Nature	Best Action	Best Action Payoff	Expected Value (Pr x Payoff)
.1	Demand = 0	Buy 0	$ 0	$ 0
.5	Demand = 1	Buy 1	200,000	100,000
.4	Demand = 2	Buy 2	400,000	160,000
				$260,000

   The dealer expects to make $260,000 with perfect information about future demand, and $225,000 if the choice with the best expected value is made. The expected value of perfect information (EVPI) is then

Expected value with perfect information	$260,000
Expected value of the best choice	(225,000)
EVPI =	$ 35,000

   The dealer will not pay more than $35,000 for information about future demand, because it would then be more profitable to make the expected value choice than to pay more for information.

STATISTICS

A. The field of statistics concerns information calculated from sample data. The field is divided into two categories: descriptive statistics and inferential statistics. Both are widely used in business.

   1. Descriptive statistics includes ways to summarize large amounts of raw data.

   2. Inferential statistics draws conclusions about a population based on a sample of the population.

   3. A **parameter** is a characteristic of a population.

      a. A parameter is a numerical value computed using every element in the population.

         1) For example, the mean and the mode are parameters of a population.

4. A **statistic** is a characteristic of a sample (taken from a population).
   a. A statistic is a numerical value computed using only the elements of a sample of the population.
      1) For example, the mean and the mode are statistics of the sample.
5. Nonparametric, or distribution-free, statistics is applied to problems for which rank order is known, but the specific distribution is not. Thus, various metals may be ranked in order of hardness without having any measure of hardness.

B. **Descriptive statistics** summarizes large amounts of data. Measures of central tendency (e.g., average) and measures of dispersion (e.g., variance) are such summaries.
1. **Measure of central tendency** indicates the middle of a set of numbers.
   a. **Mean** -- the arithmetic average of a set of numbers or, simply, the average
      1) The mean of a sample is often represented with a bar over the letter for the variable ($\overline{x}$).
      2) The mean of a population is often represented by the Greek letter μ (mu).
   b. **Median** -- the halfway value if raw data are arranged in numerical order from lowest to highest. Thus, half the values are smaller than the median and half are larger. It is the 50th percentile.
   c. **Mode** -- the most frequent value. If all values are unique, there is no mode.
   d. **Asymmetrical distributions**
      1) Some frequency distributions are asymmetrical to the right (positively skewed); that is, the mean is greater than the mode.

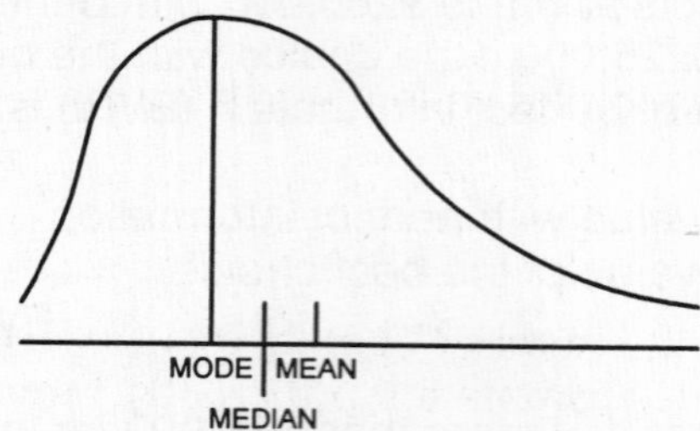

      2) Accounting distributions tend to be asymmetrical to the right. Recorded amounts are zero or greater, many low-value items are included, but a few high-value items may also be recognized in the accounts.
      3) The following is a distribution that is asymmetrical to the left; that is, the mode is greater than the mean.

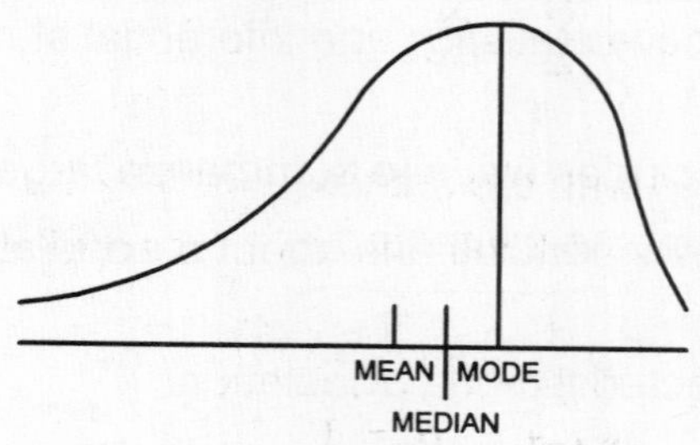

e. For symmetrical distributions, the mean, median, and mode are the same, and the tails are identical. Hence, there is no skew. The normal and t-distributions are symmetrical distributions.

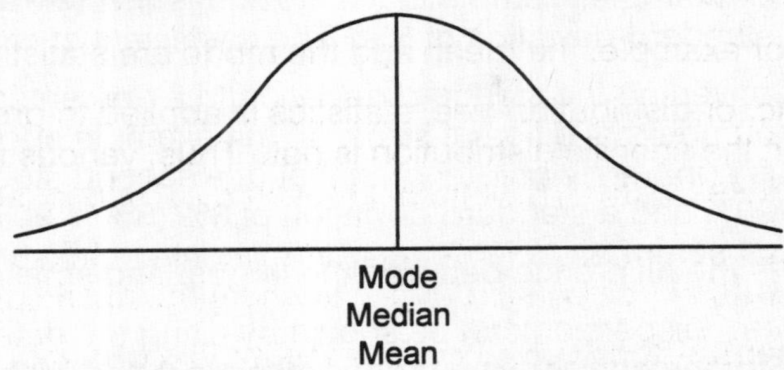

f. EXAMPLE: Given items of $300, $800, $1,100, $300, and $1,000, what are the mode, median, and mean?

1) The mode (the most frequently occurring value) is $300.
2) The median is $800 (two values lie above and two below $800).
3) The mean is $700 [($300 + $800 + $1,100 + $300 + $1,000) ÷ 5].

2. **Measures of dispersion** indicate the variation within a set of numbers.

a. An important operation involved is summation, represented by the capital Greek letter Σ (sigma). The summation sign means to perform the required procedure on every member of the set (every item of the sample) and then add all the results together.

b. **Variance** is the average of the squared deviations from the mean. It is found by subtracting the mean from each value, squaring each difference, adding the squared differences (summing them), and then dividing the sum by the number of data points.

1) The formula for the variance of a set is

$$\sigma^2 = \sum_{i=1}^{N} \frac{(x_i - \mu)^2}{N}$$

If: N = the number of elements in the population (If a sample is used to estimate the population variance, use n – 1 instead of N.)

μ = the population mean

x_i = the ith element of the set

c. The **standard deviation** is the square root of the variance.

1) The formula is the square root of the one just above.

$$\sigma = \sqrt{\sum_{i=1}^{N} \frac{(x_i - \mu)^2}{N}}$$

2) For a sample with the sample mean $\bar{x}$, the population standard deviation (sigma) may be estimated from the **sample standard deviation**, s.

$$s = \sqrt{\sum_{i=1}^{n} \frac{(x_i - \bar{x})^2}{n - 1}}$$

3) The standard deviation and the sample standard deviation are always expressed in the same units as the data.

d. The **coefficient of variation** equals the standard deviation divided by the expected value of the dependent variable.

1) For example, assume that a stock has a 10% expected rate of return with a standard deviation of 5%. The coefficient of variation is .5 (5% ÷ 10%).

2) Converting the standard deviation to a percentage permits comparison of numbers of different sizes. In the example above, the riskiness of the stock is apparently greater than that of a second stock with an expected return of 20% and a standard deviation of 8% (8% ÷ 20% = .4).

e. **Range** is the difference between the largest and smallest values of any group.

f. **Quartiles**. Dispersion can be shown by citing the data values for the 25th, 50th, and 75th percentiles. The range limits are 0 and 100. The 50th quartile is the median.

3. A **frequency distribution** is used to summarize raw data by segmenting the range of possible values into equal intervals and showing the number of data points within each interval.

a. EXAMPLE: A **histogram** is a bar graph of a frequency distribution with a vertical bar to represent the count of each interval. A histogram of the number of occurrences of various net cash flows looks like the following diagram:

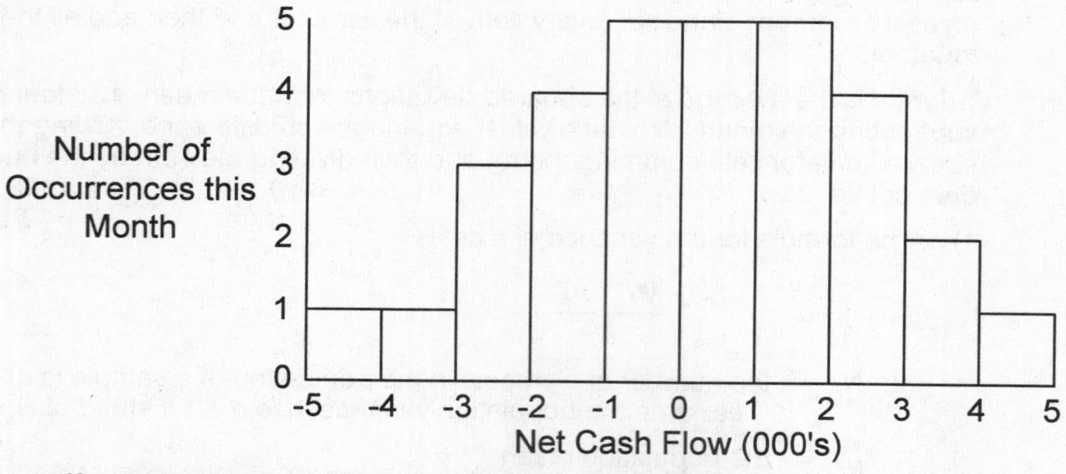

If: 5 days had cash flows between 0 and $1,000.
5 days had cash flows between $1,000 and $2,000.
3 days had cash flows between –$2,000 and –$3,000, etc.

C. **Inferential statistics** provides methods for drawing conclusions about populations based on sample information, including

- Estimating the population parameters
- Testing hypotheses
- Examining the degree of relationship between two or more random variables

1. **Sampling** is important in business because a complete census, i.e., measuring the entire population, is usually too costly, too time-consuming, impossible (as in the case of destructive testing), and error-prone. Sampling is used extensively in auditing, quality control, market research, and analytical studies of business operations.

2. The **central limit theorem** states that, regardless of the distribution of the population from which random samples are drawn, the shape of the sampling distribution of $\bar{x}$ (the average) approaches the normal distribution as the sample size is increased. Given simple random samples of size n, the mean of the sampling distribution of $\bar{x}$ will be μ (the population mean), and its variance will be $\sigma^2 \div n$ when the sample is large. Therefore, whenever a process includes the average of independent samples of the same sample size from the same distribution, the normal distribution can be used as an approximation of that process even if the underlying population is not normally distributed. The central limit theorem explains why the normal distribution is so useful.

3. Population parameters may be estimated from sample statistics.

   a. Every statistic has a sampling distribution that gives every possible value of the statistic and the probability of each of those values.

   b. Hence, the point estimate calculated for a population parameter (such as the sample mean, $\bar{x}$) may take on a range of values.

   c. EXAMPLE: From the following population of 10 elements, samples of three elements may be chosen in several ways. Assume that the population is normally distributed.

Population		Sample 1		Sample 2		Sample 3
4		4		7		6
7		5		6		9
9		3		5		5
5	$\Sigma x_i =$	12	$\Sigma x_i =$	18	$\Sigma x_i =$	20
6	n =	3	n =	3	n =	3
5						
3		$\bar{x} = 12 \div 3$		$\bar{x} = 18 \div 3$		$\bar{x} = 20 \div 3$
5		= 4		= 6		= 6 2/3
6						
6						
$\Sigma x_i =$ 56		$\mu = 56 \div 10 = 5.6$				
N = 10						

σ *(standard deviation)* = 1.562 *based on* $\sqrt{\Sigma(x_i - \mu)^2 \div N}$

NOTE: This sample population was chosen for computational convenience only. The population in this example is so small that inference is not required, and the samples are so small that the t-distribution would be more appropriate than the normal distribution. A different estimate of the population mean is obtained depending upon the exact sample selected. Moreover, the central limit theorem indicates that these sample means are normally distributed around the actual population mean.

4. The quality of the estimates of population parameters depends on two things.

   a. The sample size
   b. The variance of the population

5. The **interval estimator (confidence interval** or **precision or prediction interval)** incorporates both the sample size and the population standard deviation along with a probability that the interval includes the true population parameter.
   a. For the population mean, this interval is

$$\bar{x} \pm z\,(\sigma \div \sqrt{n})$$

If: $\bar{x}$ = the sample mean, which is a point estimate of the population mean

z = the number of standard deviations needed to ensure a specified level of confidence

σ = the standard deviation of the population

n = the sample size

$\sigma \div \sqrt{n}$ = the standard error of the mean (square root of the variance of the sampling distribution of $\bar{x}$)

1) This representation of the confidence interval assumes that the variance (σ^2) of the population is known, the sample means are normally distributed with a mean equal to the true population mean (μ), and the variance of the sampling distribution is $\sigma^2 \div n$.

2) In the more realistic case in which the population variance is not known, and a sample is being evaluated, the distribution is described as a Student's t-distribution with mean equal to μ and variance equal to $s^2 \div n$, when s^2 is the sample variance.

3) To compute a confidence interval for the mean of the population given in 3.c. based on a sample, the mean of the sample must be determined. For example, the mean of Sample 2 is 6. Thus, the sample standard deviation is

$$s = \sqrt{\frac{(7-6)^2 + (6-6)^2 + (5-6)^2}{3-1}} = 1.0$$

4) To compute the confidence interval at the 95% confidence level, the z-value is found in a table for the standard normal distribution. For example, a confidence level of 95% corresponds to a z-value of 1.96. This means that 95% of the area under the standard normal distribution lies within 1.96 standard deviations of the mean. Hence, the 95% confidence interval is $6 \pm 1.96(\sigma \div \sqrt{n})$. Because the population standard deviation is not known, the sample standard deviation ($s = 1.0$) is used (see B.2.c.2) on page 603). The confidence interval then becomes

$$6 \pm 1.96\,(1.0 \div \sqrt{3}) = 6 \pm 1.13 = 4.87 \text{ to } 7.13$$

Consequently, the probability is 95% that this interval contains the population mean.

HYPOTHESIS TESTING

A. A hypothesis is a supposition about the true state of nature. Hypothesis testing calculates the conditional probability that both the hypothesis is true **and** the sample results observed have occurred. There are four steps.

1. A hypothesis is formulated to be tested for truth or falsity.
2. Sample evidence is obtained.
3. The probability that the hypothesis is true, given the observed evidence, is computed.
4. If that probability is too low, we reject the hypothesis. Too low is a subjective measure dependent on the situation. A probability of .6 that your favorite team will win may be sufficient to place a small bet on their next game. A probability of .95 that a parachute will open may be too low to allow you to take up skydiving.

B. The hypothesis to be tested is known as the **null hypothesis** or H_o; the alternative hypothesis is denoted H_a.

1. The null hypothesis, H_o, may state an equality (=) or that the parameter is equal to or greater (less) than (≥ or ≤) some value.
2. The alternative hypothesis, H_a, contains every other possibility.
   a. It may be stated as not equal to (≠), greater than (>), or less than (<) some value, depending on the null hypothesis.
3. The probability of error in hypothesis testing is usually labeled as

	Decision	
State of Nature	Do not reject H_o	Reject H_o
H_o is true	Correct	Type I Error $P(I) = \alpha$
H_o is false	Type II Error $P(II) = \beta$	Correct

   These are the same α (alpha) and β (beta) errors that auditors have always been concerned with.

4. EXAMPLE: The hypothesis is that a component fails at a pressure of 80 or more lb. on the average; i.e., the average component will not fail at a pressure below 80 lb. For a group of 36 components, the average failure pressure was found to be 77.48 lb. Given that n is 36, $\bar{x}$ is 77.48 lb., and σ is 13.32 lb., the following are the hypotheses:

   H_o: The average failure pressure of the population of components is ≥ 80 lb.

   H_a: The average failure pressure is < 80 lb.

a. If a 5% chance of being wrong is acceptable, α (Type I error or the chance of incorrect rejection of the null hypothesis) is set equal to .05 and the confidence level at .95. In effect, 5% of the area under the curve of the standard normal distribution will constitute a rejection region. For this one-tailed test, the 5% rejection region will fall entirely in the left-hand tail of the distribution because the null hypothesis will not be rejected for any values of the test statistic that fall in the right-hand tail. According to standard tables, 5% of the area under the standard normal curve lies to the left of the z-value of –1.645.

The following is the formula for the z-statistic:

$$z = \frac{\bar{x} - \mu_o}{\sigma \div \sqrt{n}}$$

If: σ = given population standard deviation
μ_o = hypothesized true population average
n = sample size
z = number of standard deviations needed to ensure the specified level of confidence

Substituting the hypothesized value of the population average failure pressure (μ_o = 80 lb.) determines the z-statistic.

$$z = \frac{77.48 - 80}{13.32 \div \sqrt{36}} = -1.135$$

Because the calculated z-value corresponding to the sample mean of 77.48 is greater than the critical value of –1.645, the null hypothesis cannot be rejected.

We may graph the situation as follows:

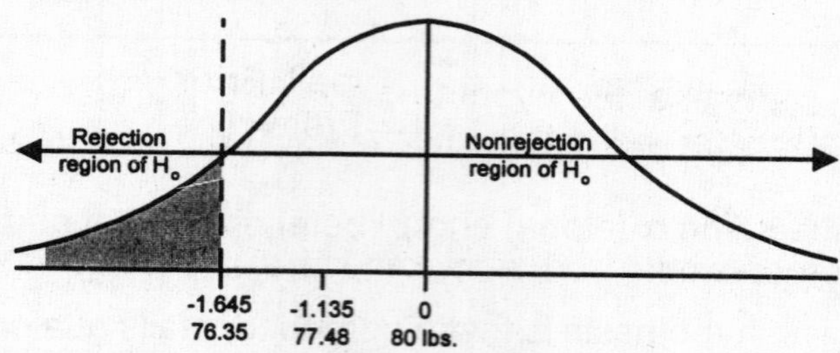

The lower limit of the 95% nonrejection area under the curve is

$80 \text{ lb.} - 1.645 (\sigma/\sqrt{n}) =$
$80 \text{ lb.} - 1.645 (13.32 \div \sqrt{36}) =$
76.35 lb.

Because a sample average of 77.48 lb. (a z of –1.135) falls within the nonrejection region (i.e., > 76.35 lb.), the null hypothesis that the average failure pressure of the population is ≥ 80 lb. cannot be rejected. The null hypothesis is rejected only if the sample size is equal to or less than the critical value (76.35 lb.).

C. Hypothesis tests may be one-tailed or two-tailed.

1. A one-tailed test results from a hypothesis of the following form:

H_o: parameter ≤ or ≥ the hypothesized value
H_a: parameter > or < the hypothesized value

a. One-tailed test, upper tail

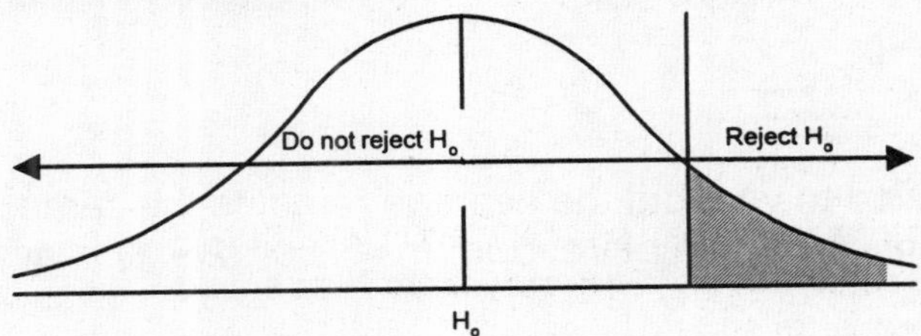

H_o: parameter ≤ the hypothesized value
H_a: parameter > the hypothesized value

b. One-tailed test, lower tail

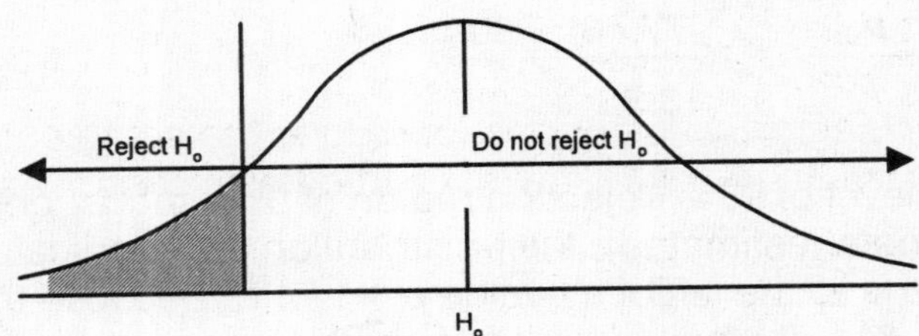

H_o: parameter ≥ the hypothesized value
H_a: parameter < the hypothesized value

2. A two-tailed test results from a hypothesis of the following form:

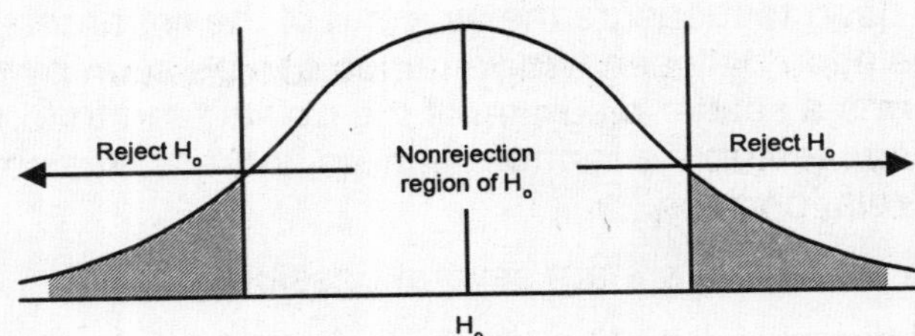

H_o: parameter = the hypothesized value
H_a: parameter ≠ the hypothesized value

D. A failure to prove H_o is false does not prove that it is true. This failure simply means that H_o is not a rejectable hypothesis. In practice, however, auditors often use acceptance as a synonym for nonrejection.

E. Given a small sample (less than 30), the t-statistic (t-distribution) must be used.

1. The t-distribution requires a number called **the degrees of freedom**, which is (n – k) for k parameters. When one parameter (such as the mean) is estimated, the number of degrees of freedom is (n – 1). The degrees of freedom is a correction factor that is necessary because, given k parameters and n elements, only (n – k) elements are free to vary. After (n – k) elements are chosen, the remaining k elements' values are already determined.

   a. EXAMPLE: Two numbers have an average of 5.

$$\bar{x} = \frac{(x_1 + x_2)}{2} = 5$$

   If x_1 is allowed to vary but the average remains the same, x_1 determines x_2 because only 1 degree of freedom (n – 1) or (2 – 1) is available.

   If: $x_1 = 2, x_2 = 8$
   $x_1 = 3, x_2 = 7$

2. The t-distribution is used in the same way as the z or normal distribution. Standard texts have t-distribution tables. In the example in B.4. on page 607, if the sample size had been 25 and the sample standard deviation had been given instead of the population value, the t-statistic would have been

$$t = \frac{\bar{x} - \mu_o}{s \div \sqrt{25}} = \frac{77.48 - 80}{13.32 \div \sqrt{25}} = -.946$$

   At a confidence level of 95% (rejection region of 5%) and 24 degrees of freedom (sample of 25 – 1 parameter estimated), the t-distribution table indicates that 5% of the area under the curve is to the left of a t-value of –1.711. Because the computed value is greater than –1.711, the null hypothesis cannot be rejected in this one-tailed test.

   As the number of degrees of freedom increases, the t-distribution approximates the z-distribution. For degrees of freedom > 30, the z-distribution may be used.

CORRELATION ANALYSIS

A. Correlation analysis is used to measure the strength of the linear relationship between two or more variables. Correlation between two variables can be seen by plotting their values on a single graph. This forms a scatter diagram. If the points tend to form a straight line, there is high correlation. If they resemble a random pattern, there is little correlation. Correlation measures only linear relationships.

1. If the points form a curve, there are several possibilities.

   a. A linear relationship (i.e., straight line) may be used to approximate a portion of the curve.

   b. A linear relationship exists between some other function of the independent variable x (e.g., log x) and the dependent variable y.

   c. No relationship exists.

2. In standard notation, the coefficient of correlation is r.

   a. The coefficient of determination is r^2.

3. The **coefficient of correlation** measures the strength of the linear relationship. It has the following properties:
   a. The magnitude of r is independent of the scales of measurement of x and y.
   b. $-1.0 \leq r \leq 1.0$
      1) A value of –1.0 indicates a perfectly inverse linear relationship between x and y.
      2) A value of zero indicates no linear relationship between x and y.
      3) A value of +1.0 indicates a perfectly direct relationship between x and y.
4. Scatter diagrams may be used to demonstrate correlations. Each observation creates a dot that pairs the x and y values. The collinearity and slope of these observations are related to the coefficient of correlation by the above-stated rules.

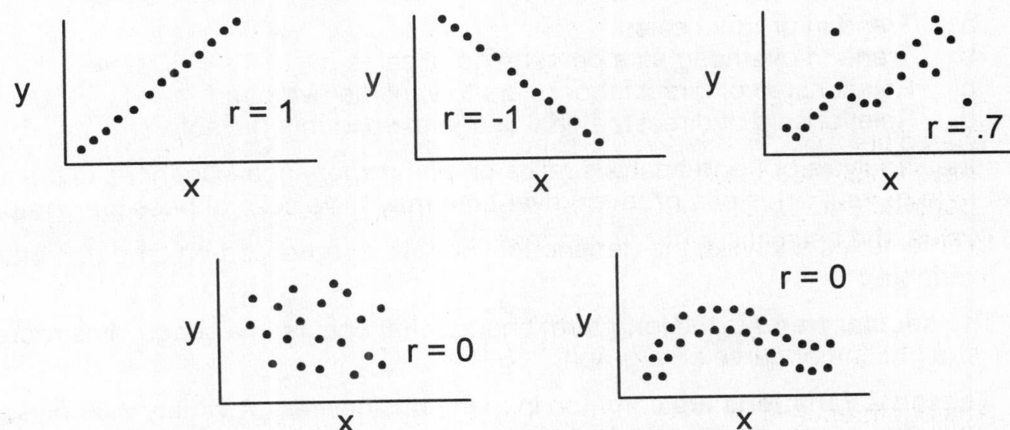

5. The **coefficient of determination**, or the coefficient of correlation squared, may be interpreted as the proportion of the total variation in y that is explained or accounted for by the regression equation.
   a. EXAMPLE: The statement, "new car sales are a function of disposable income with a coefficient of correlation of .8," can be interpreted as

      $(r^2) = (.8^2) = .64$ *or* 64%

      Thus, the same statement can be expressed as "64% of the variation of new car sales (from average new car sales) can be explained by the variation in disposable income (from average disposable income)."
6. Other measures and terms of correlation
   a. **Autocorrelation (serial correlation)**. The observations are not independent; e.g., certain costs rise with a volume increase but do not decline with a volume decrease.
   b. **Rank-correlation coefficient** -- a statistical measure of association based on the rank of each variable in the absence of normal data
   c. **Multicorrelation** -- a statistical measure of association between more than two variables
   d. **Spearman rank correlation** -- a statistical, asymmetrical measure of association for two ranked (orderable and discrete) variables
   e. **Multicollinearity** -- a dependence between different independent variables

REGRESSION (LEAST SQUARES) ANALYSIS

A. Regression analysis extends correlation to find an equation for the linear relationship among variables. The behavior of the dependent variable is explained in terms of one or more independent variables. Thus, regression analysis determines functional relationships between quantitative variables.

1. Simple regression has one independent variable, and multiple regression has more than one independent variable.

   a. EXAMPLE: A dependent variable such as sales is dependent on advertising, consumer income, availability of substitutes, and other independent variables.

2. Regression analysis is used to find trend lines in business data such as sales or costs (time series analysis or trend analysis) and to develop models based on the association of variables (cross-sectional analysis, i.e., not time related, as is trend analysis). Examples are

   a. Trend in product sales
   b. Trend in overhead as a percentage of sales
   c. Relationship of direct labor hours to variable overhead
   d. Relationship of direct material usage to accounts payable

B. Time series analysis or trend analysis relies on past experience. Changes in the value of a variable (e.g., unit sales of a product) over time may have several possible components.

1. In time series analysis, the dependent variable is regressed on time (the independent variable).

2. The **secular trend** is the long-term change that occurs in a series. It is represented by a straight line or curve on a graph.

3. **Seasonal variations** are common in many businesses. A variety of analysis methods includes seasonal variations in a forecasting model, but most methods make use of a seasonal index.

4. **Cyclical fluctuations** are variations in the level of activity in business periods. Although some of these fluctuations are beyond the control of the firm, they need to be considered in forecasting. They are usually incorporated as index numbers.

5. **Irregular or random variables** are any variations not included in the categories above. Business can be affected by random happenings (e.g., weather, strikes, fires, etc.).

C. **Qualifications**

1. There should be some reasonable basis for expecting the variables to be related.

   a. If they are obviously independent, any association found by regression is mere coincidence.

   b. Regression does not determine causality, however. We may conclude that x and y move together, but the apparent relationship may be caused by some other factor.

      1) EXAMPLE: A strong correlation exists between car-wash sales volume and sunny weather, **but** sales volume does not cause sunny weather.

   c. The statistical relationships revealed by regression and correlation analysis are valid **only** for the range of the data in the sample.

2. Mathematically, the regression equation is

$$y = a + bx + e$$

If: y is the dependent variable.
a is the y-axis intercept (the fixed cost in cost functions).
b is the slope of the regression line (the variable portion of the total cost in cost functions).
x is the independent variable.
e is the error term.

a. Assumptions of the model are that

1) x and y are linearly related.

2) The error term is normally distributed with mean = 0.

3) Errors in successive observations are statistically independent.

a) That is, the estimators are unbiased.

4) The distribution of y around the regression line is constant for different values of x.

b. Graphically, the model is represented by a series of distributions around the regression line.

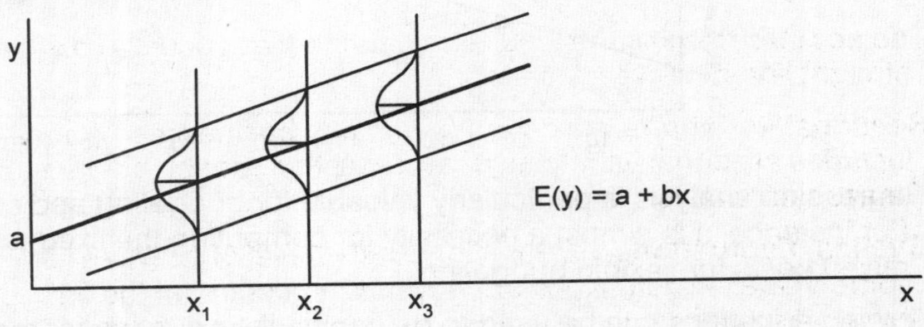

3. From linear algebra, the equation for a straight line may be stated as

$$y = a + bx$$

If: a is the y-axis intercept.
b is the slope of the line (rise over run).

a. Regression analysis uses the method of least squares, which minimizes the sum of the squares of the vertical distance between each observation point and the regression line.

b. EXAMPLE: Observations are collected on advertising expenditures and annual sales for a firm.

Sales ($000,000s)	Advertising ($000s)
28	71
14	31
19	50
21	60
16	35

1) According to the regression equation that results from using least squares computations, expected sales equal 4.2 plus .31 times the advertising expenditure.

$$y = 4.2 + .31(x)$$

2) The observations are graphed as follows:

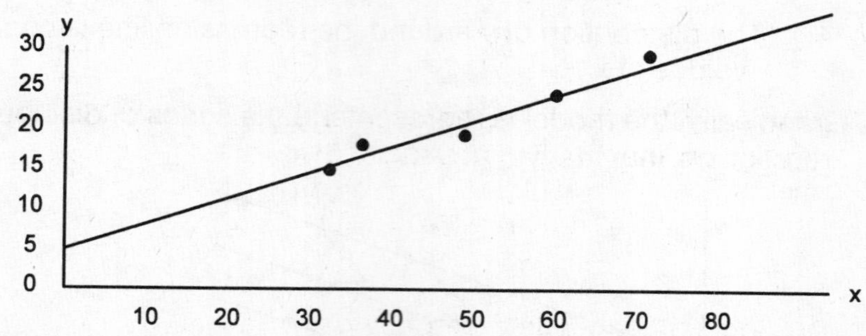

4. Regression analysis is particularly valuable for budgeting and cost accounting purposes. For instance, it is almost a necessity for computing the fixed and variable portions of mixed costs for flexible budgeting.

D. The following equations can be used to determine the equation for the least squares regression line (remember, the equation for the line is in the form of y = a + bx):

$$\Sigma y = na + b(\Sigma x)$$
$$\Sigma xy = a(\Sigma x) + b(\Sigma x^2)$$

1. EXAMPLE: The use of the two equations can be illustrated with the following data based on a set of six paired observations (n = 6):

y	x
$ 6	2
7	3
5	2
4	1
8	3
6	2
Σy = $36	Σx = 13

Σxy	Σx^2
6 x 2 = 12	4
7 x 3 = 21	9
5 x 2 = 10	4
4 x 1 = 4	1
8 x 3 = 24	9
6 x 2 = 12	4
83	31

a. Substituting into the two equations gives

$$36 = 6a + 13b$$
$$83 = 13a + 31b$$

b. Solving simultaneously for the two unknowns,

$$1116 = 186a + 403b$$
$$\underline{1079} = \underline{169a} + \underline{403b}$$
$$\underline{37} = \underline{17a}$$

c. Thus, a = 2.176. Solving for b in the second original equation gives

$$83 = 13(2.176) + 31b$$
$$83 = 28.288 + 31b$$
$$31b = 54.712$$
$$b = 1.765$$

d. Hence, future costs can be predicted using the following equation:

$$y = \$2.176 + \$1.765x$$

e. Alternative formulas that are ordinarily simpler to use are given below:

1) The slope may be expressed as

$$b = \frac{n\Sigma xy - \Sigma x\Sigma y}{n\Sigma x^2 - (\Sigma x)^2}$$

2) The value of the y-intercept may be expressed as

$$a = \bar{y} - b(\bar{x})$$

E. **Discriminant analysis** is a variation of regression analysis in which independent variables are categorical; i.e., each observation is assigned a category.

1. EXAMPLES:

   a. High, medium, low
   b. Good, bad
   c. Male, female

F. **Less Sophisticated Methods**

1. **Scattergraph** involves visually observing the diagram of a series of cause-and-effect relationships and then roughly drawing a line that depicts the relationship.

   a. The scattergraph method suffers from being reliant on the judgment of the person visualizing the line.

   b. Once the line has been drawn, the equation of the line can be determined from any two points on the line.

   c. See also the scatter diagrams under Correlation Analysis on page 611.

2. **High-low method** is used to generate a regression line by basing the equation on only the highest and lowest of a series of observations

   a. EXAMPLE: A regression equation covering electricity costs could be developed by using only the high-cost month and the low-cost month. If costs were $400 in April when production was 800 machine hours and $600 in September when production was 1,300 hours, the equation would be determined as follows:

High month	$600	for	1,300 hours
Low month	400	for	800 hours
Increase	$200		500 hours

   Because costs increased $200 for 500 additional hours, the variable cost is $.40 per machine hour. For the low month, the total variable portion of that monthly cost is $320 ($.40 x 800 hours). Given that the total cost is $400 and $320 is variable, the remaining $80 must be a fixed cost. The regression equation is $y = 80 + .4x$.

   b. The major criticism of the high-low method is that the high and low points may be abnormalities not representative of normal events.

STUDY UNIT 30
INVENTORY MODELS

INTRODUCTION

Inventory problems ask for a decision concerning how much of some item to order (or produce) and when to place the order (or commence production). The concepts most frequently tested are the economic order (production) quantity (EOQ) and its attendant costs, the reorder level, and safety stocks.

The objective of inventory management is to maintain an adequate amount of product on hand to meet demand but at the same time to minimize the costs of keeping inventories. Too little inventory can result in lost sales, a reduction of customer goodwill, production delays, incremental shipping costs, etc. In a production setting, an inventory shortage can result in shutting down an entire factory because sufficient components are not available. Alternatively, too much inventory can tie up funds that could be invested elsewhere or cause such storage problems as obsolescence and high carrying costs.

Remember to consider the tax consequences of business decision making by reviewing the outlines in Study Unit 18, Income Taxes.

INVENTORY CONTROL MODELS

A. Inventories provide a buffer to smooth the differences between the time and location of demand and supply of product. The purpose of inventory control is to determine the optimal level of inventory necessary to minimize costs.

B. Although the traditional approach to inventory management has been to minimize inventory and the related carrying costs, many companies find inventory a good hedge against inflation.

   1. Stockpiles also guarantee future availability of inventory.
   2. Also, note the applicability of the EOQ model to cash management.

C. Inventory carrying costs can sometimes be transferred to either suppliers or customers.

   1. If a manufacturer has good enough control of production schedules to know exactly when materials are needed, orders can be placed so that materials arrive no earlier than when actually needed.

      a. This practice relies on a supplier who is willing to take the responsibility for storing the needed inventory and shipping it to arrive on time.

      b. Suppliers are more willing to provide this service when they have many competitors.

   2. Customers can sometimes be persuaded to carry large quantities of inventory by allowing them special quantity discounts or extended credit terms.

   3. If customers are willing to accept long lead times, inventory can be manufactured to order to avoid storing large quantities.

4. Although these measures can reduce inventory carrying costs, additional costs might be incurred by adopting them.

   a. Stockout costs may increase because customers may not always be willing to wait for goods to be produced.

   b. Production shutdowns and additional shipping costs may also prevent minimization of carrying costs from being cost effective.

D. Inventory costs fall into three categories.

1. Order costs include all costs associated with preparing a purchase order.

2. Carrying costs include storage costs for inventory items plus opportunity cost (i.e., the cost incurred by investing in inventory rather than the next best use of the funds). Carrying costs may also include a charge for spoilage of perishable items or for obsolescence.

3. Stockout costs are the costs incurred when an item is out of stock. These include the lost contribution margin on sales plus lost customer goodwill.

E. Inventory models are quantitative models designed to control inventory costs by determining the optimal time to place an order and the optimal order quantity.

1. The timing of an order can be periodic (placing an order every X days) or perpetual (placing an order whenever the inventory declines to X units).

F. The basic EOQ model minimizes the sum of ordering and carrying costs. Demand is assumed to be known and constant throughout the period. Order cost is assumed to be constant per order, and unit carrying costs are also assumed to be constant. Because demand is assumed to be deterministic, there are no stockout costs.

1. The EOQ is the square root of the quotient of twice the periodic demand multiplied by the order cost, divided by the periodic unit carrying cost.

$$X = \sqrt{\frac{2aD}{k}}$$

If: X = EOQ
a = Variable cost per purchase order
D = Periodic demand in units
k = Unit periodic carrying cost

2. EXAMPLE: Assume the periodic demand is uniform at 1,000 units. If the cost to place an order is \$4 and the cost to carry one unit in inventory for the period is \$2, then:

$$EOQ = \sqrt{\frac{2(\$4)(1{,}000)}{\$2}}$$

$$= \sqrt{4{,}000}$$

$$= 63.25 \textit{ units}$$

3. The average level of inventory for this model will be one-half of the EOQ. The formula shows that the EOQ varies directly with demand and order costs but inversely with holding costs. Thus, if demand quadruples, the EOQ will only double.

4. The EOQ is a periodic model. The number of orders per period equals the periodic demand divided by the EOQ.

5. The EOQ results from differentiating the total cost with regard to order quantity. The model is based on variable costs. The fixed costs of ordering are eliminated when the total cost equation is differentiated. The cost per order and the unit carrying cost are variable; that is, they are constant per order and per unit, respectively, and vary only with the number of orders or units.

$$c = \left(\frac{D}{x}\right)a + \frac{xk}{2} + F$$

$$dc/dx = \frac{-Da}{x^2} + \frac{k}{2}$$

If: c = Total cost
x = EOQ
a = Variable cost per purchase order
D = Periodic demand in units
k = Unit periodic carrying cost
F = Fixed costs of ordering

Setting dc/dx = 0 at minimum total cost,

$$\frac{-Da}{x^2} + \frac{k}{2} = 0$$

$$\frac{k}{2} = \frac{Da}{x^2}$$

$$x^2 = \frac{2Da}{k}$$

$$x = \sqrt{\frac{2aD}{k}}$$

G. Variations of the EOQ model are numerous.

1. The effects of quantity discounts can be considered by using trial and error. The EOQ is found as above and, if it is below the discount level, the total cost equals the sum of the purchase cost plus annual carrying and ordering costs. Next, the minimum order quantity needed to obtain the discount is considered, and total cost is found for this level. This process is repeated for multiple levels of discount. The optimal order quantity is the one giving the lowest periodic total cost.
2. Uniform rates of supply can also be included in the EOQ model. The denominator of the EOQ formula is multiplied by 1 minus the ratio of demand to supply rates. The effect is to decrease the denominator and increase the EOQ.
3. Lead time is accounted for by simply placing orders in advance. If back ordering is acceptable to customers, it can also be incorporated into the model.
4. The limitations of the EOQ model are its restrictive assumptions, especially that of constant demand. But it can be combined with probability concepts to form an effective perpetual system.
5. For manufacturers, production setup cost is substituted for ordering cost in the EOQ model to calculate the optimal production run.

H. Probabilistic models have been developed for the situation in which demand is random yet has a known distribution. In a perpetual system, the possibility of running out of stock exists only during the reorder period, the time between placing and receiving the order. The reorder point is found by using the probability distribution for demand during the period. The order quantity is found by using the basic EOQ model and average demand. If stockout costs are known, an optimal reorder point can be found. If these costs are unknown, management can select a service level or probability of being in stock that can be used to find the reorder point.

I. Inventory policies should consider the three types of costs and any limitations the firm may have, such as storage space. Constraints may also be imposed by suppliers. The cost of maintaining inventory records should also be considered.

1. Periodic order systems place minimal emphasis on record keeping. However, there is a risk of substantial overstock or understock unless inventories are checked for assurance that the model is still appropriate.
2. Perpetual systems require the ability to detect inventory's decline to the reorder point. This can be done by entering every withdrawal on a perpetual record that shows the balance. An alternative is to use the two-bin method for physical storage. In this system, the reorder level amount is stored separately from the balance of the items. When the stock clerk removes the last item from the balance bin, it is time to place an order. The reorder level bin is then used until the order is received.
3. Physical inventories should be taken to reconcile records and verify models in either a periodic or a perpetual system.

J. The limitations of inventory models for control include that they are restricted to one item at a time and that they consider each item of equal importance. If a firm has 10,000 line items, 10,000 calculations would have to be made. Computer programs are available to perform the computations, but they still need periodic review. The importance of items can vary from essential to immaterial. The priority of an item needs to be considered in establishing controls. A third limitation is that demand is often more variable than expected. Seasonal variations, as well as unexpected changes, can be provided for by including a forecasting model to estimate the demand to be used in the inventory model.

K. **Reordering and Stockouts**

1. It is desirable to minimize both the cost of carrying safety stock and the cost of running out of an item, i.e., stockouts.
   a. Safety stock is the amount of extra stock that is kept to guard against stockouts. It is the inventory level at the time of reordering minus the expected usage while the new goods are in transit.
   b. Stockout costs are lost sales, lost production, customer dissatisfaction, etc.
2. The problem may be diagrammed as follows:

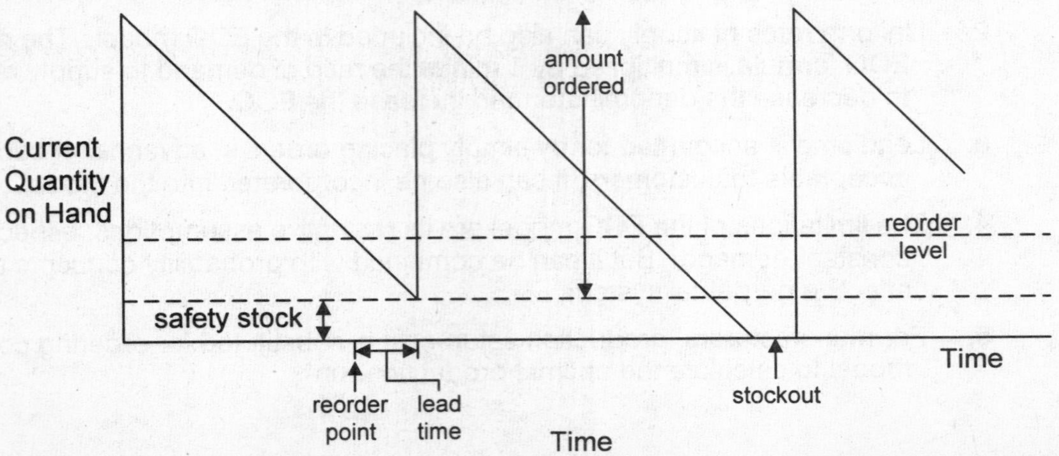

3. The EOQ determines order size. The reorder point is the intersection of the reorder level and the downward-sloping total inventory line that allows sufficient lead time for an order to be placed and received.

4. Safety stocks decrease stockout costs and increase carrying costs. The minimum total cost occurs at the intersection of the stockout cost curve and the carrying cost curve.

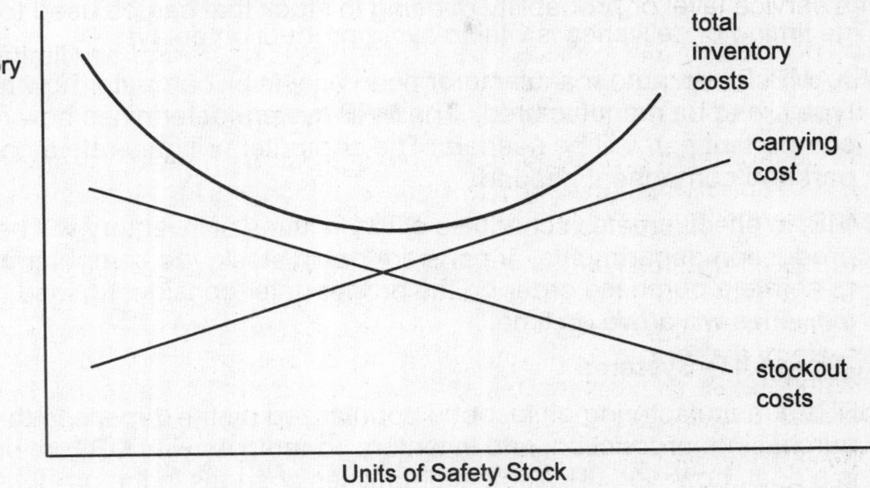

OTHER INVENTORY CONTROL TECHNIQUES

A. **The ABC System**

1. This method controls inventories by dividing items into three groups.
   a. Group A -- high-dollar value items, which account for a small portion (perhaps 10%) of the total inventory usage
   b. Group B -- medium-dollar value items, which may account for about 20% of the total inventory items
   c. Group C -- low-dollar value items, which account for the remaining 70% of sales or usage
2. The ABC system permits the proper degree of managerial control to be exercised over each group. The level of control reflects cost-benefit concerns.
   a. Group A items are reviewed on a regular basis.
   b. Group B items may not have to be reviewed as often as group A items, but more often than group C items.
   c. For group C, extensive use of models and records is not cost effective. It is cheaper to order large quantities infrequently.

B. **Materials Requirements Planning (MRP)**

1. MRP is a computer-based information system designed to plan and control raw materials used in a production setting.
2. It assumes that the demand for materials is typically dependent upon some other factor, which can be programmed into the computer.
3. The timing of deliveries is vital to avoid production delays.
4. EXAMPLE: An auto manufacturer need only tell a computer how many autos of each type are to be manufactured. The MRP system determines how many of every component part will be needed. The computer will generate a complete list of every part and component needed.
5. MRP, in effect, creates schedules of when items of inventory will be needed in the production departments. If parts are not in stock, the computer will automatically generate a purchase order on the proper date (considering lead times) so that deliveries will arrive on time.

C. **Just-in-Time (JIT) Systems**

1. JIT is a manufacturing philosophy popularized by the Japanese that combines purchasing, production, and inventory control. As with MRP, minimization of inventory is a goal; however, JIT also encompasses changes in the production process itself.
2. An emphasis on quality and a pull of materials related to demand are key differences between JIT and MRP.
3. The factory is organized so as to bring materials and tools close to the point of use rather than keeping them in storage areas.
4. A key element of the JIT system is reduction or elimination of waste of materials, labor, factory space, and machine usage. Minimizing inventory is the key to reducing waste. When a part is needed on the production line, it arrives just in time, not before. Daily deliveries from suppliers are the ultimate objective, and some Japanese users have been able to get twice-daily deliveries.
5. The Japanese term **kanban** and JIT have often been confused. JIT is a broader concept that encompasses the total system of purchasing and production. Kanban is one of the many elements in the JIT system as it is used in Japan. The word kanban means ticket. Tickets control the flow of materials through the system in Japanese companies.
6. U.S. companies have not been comfortable with the idea of controlling production with tickets on the production floor. Computerized information systems have been used for many years, and U.S. companies have been reluctant to give up their computers in favor of the essentially manual kanban system.
   a. Instead, U.S. companies have integrated their existing MRP systems, which are complex computerized planning systems, with the JIT system.
7. U.S. companies have traditionally built parts and components for subsequent operations on a preset schedule. Such a schedule provides a cushion of inventory so that the next operation will always have parts to work with -- a just-in-case method. In contrast, JIT limits output to the demand of the subsequent operation.
8. Reductions in inventory levels result in less money invested in idle assets; reduction of storage space requirements; and lower inventory taxes, pilferage, and obsolescence risks. Less inventory means less need for a sophisticated inventory control system, and fewer control people are needed.

9. High inventory levels often mask production problems because defective parts can be overlooked when plenty of good parts are available. If only enough parts are made for the subsequent operation, however, any defects will immediately halt production.

10. The focus of quality control under JIT shifts from the discovery of defective parts to the prevention of quality problems. Zero defects is the ultimate goal. Higher quality and lower inventory go together.

11. The lower inventory levels eliminate the need for several traditional internal controls.

    a. Frequent receipt of raw materials often means the elimination of central receiving areas, hard copy receiving reports, and storage areas. A central warehouse is not needed because deliveries are made by suppliers directly to the area of production.

    b. The quality of parts provided by suppliers is verified by use of statistical controls rather than inspection of incoming goods. Storage, counting, and inspecting are eliminated in an effort to perform only work that adds to the product's value.

    c. Thus, the supplier's dependability is crucial.

D. Computer-Aided Design and Manufacturing (CAD/CAM)

1. CAD/CAM models and predicts the outcomes of alternative product decisions.

    a. CAD/CAM is essentially a system that combines

        1) Database management for storing and retrieving drawings and parts attributes

        2) Computer graphics for drawing and display

        3) Data acquisition and control

        4) Mathematical modeling and control

    b. Alternatively, an MRP system can be based primarily on database management and exclude the other components.

    c. The database created in the design phase (CAD) can be used to produce a bill of materials for the manufacturing phase (CAM). CAM can use CAD drawings and information to give specific instructions to individual machines.

    d. CAD/CAM helps engineers examine more options, conduct sophisticated simulations and tests, and make themselves more effective.

        1) The key contribution is effectiveness, not efficiency or economy.
        2) Product value and quality are improved.
        3) The need for physical prototypes is reduced.

    e. CAD/CAM systems are usually expensive, high-risk, high-payback investments.

E. Computer-Integrated Manufacturing (CIM)

1. CIM entails a holistic approach to manufacturing in which design is translated into product by centralized processing and robotics. The concept also includes materials handling.

    a. The advantages of CIM include

        1) Flexibility
        2) Integration
        3) Synergism

b. Flexibility is a key advantage. A traditional manufacturing system might become disrupted from an emergency change, but CIM will reschedule everything in the plant when a priority requirement is inserted into the system. The areas of flexibility include

1) Varying production volumes during a period
2) Handling new parts added to a product
3) Changing the proportion of parts being produced
4) Adjusting to engineering changes to a product
5) Adapting the sequence in which parts come to the machinery
6) Adapting to changes in materials
7) Rerouting parts as needed because of machine breakdowns or other production delays
8) Allowing for defects in materials

c. CIM integrates all production machinery using one computer system.

d. Benefits of CIM include improved product quality (less rework), better customer service, faster response to demand, greater product variety, and lower production costs.

e. JIT is sometimes adopted prior to CIM because JIT simplifies production processes and provides a better understanding of actual production flow, which are essential factors for CIM success.

f. The flexibility offered by CIM is almost a necessity for JIT suppliers. For example, a company that provides JIT deliveries to automobile plants cannot adapt to changing customer production schedules with a manual system unless a high inventory level is maintained.

g. The emphasis is on materials control rather than the direct labor control that is dominant in most cost systems.

h. CIM is an addition to, not a substitute for, other types of manufacturing concepts such as JIT. In other words, JIT should already be in place for CIM to work most effectively.

F. **Manufacturing Resource Planning (MRP-II)**

1. MRP-II is a closed-loop manufacturing system that integrates all facets of a manufacturing business, including production, sales, inventories, schedules, and cash flows. The same system is used for both the financial reporting and managing operations (both use the same transactions and numbers).

   a. MRP-II uses an MPS (master production schedule), which is a statement of the anticipated manufacturing schedule for selected items for selected periods.

   b. MRP also uses the MPS. Thus, MRP is a component of an MRP-II system.

JOINT COSTS

A. Joint-cost problems may appear in Part 3 of the new CMA format. However, the December 1993 exam had such a problem in Part 4. See Joint Products and By-Products in Study Unit 19, Process and Job-Order Costing.

STUDY UNIT 31
QUANTITATIVE METHODS

INTRODUCTION

Most quantitative methods questions relate to the objectives, the relevant variables, and the general approach of various optimization techniques (models). When calculations are required, formulas are usually provided. Thus, you should emphasize a conceptual overview of the following outline, followed by answering the multiple-choice questions and problems in Volume II. Study Unit 29, Decision Making under Uncertainty, includes probability, statistics, least squares, etc. Statistics has been separated from Quantitative Methods because of the extensive coverage of statistics and probability in Part 4.

Remember to consider the tax consequences of business decision making by reviewing the outlines in Study Unit 18, Income Taxes.

DEFINITION AND OVERVIEW

A. **Quantitative methods**, also referred to as **operations research**, is a broad term used to describe various applications of mathematics in business or any complex system. They are used to find the best estimates of expected results. **Management science** is a broader term that includes information systems (including EDP). All three terms refer to the scientific approach to problem solving for managers. The construction of mathematical, econometric, or statistical models of business situations allows the rational treatment of complex business problems that often include uncertainty.

1. Operations research is, more specifically, the discipline of applying quantitative methods oriented to planning.

B. Typical quantitative method applications include

1. Inventory control -- to determine how much and when to order
2. Forecasting -- to project future sales, costs, etc.
3. Statistical control -- to aid in the detection of variances in production quality, costs, etc.
4. Allocating resources -- to find the most economical production plan, assignment of sales territories, locations of warehouses, etc.
5. Corporate planning models -- to help managers explore the consequences of alternative policies

C. Quantitative methods are important to the management accountant because

1. Familiarity with these methods and their uses permits the management accountant to recognize possible applications within the firm and to seek the assistance of an expert.
2. Quantitative methods often make use of accounting data. Knowledge of quantitative methods permits the management accountant to judge whether the accounting data are being used correctly.
3. Quantitative methods can significantly reduce the cost of obtaining information concerning the operation of a business.

D. **Advantages of Using Mathematics**

1. To make explicit (i.e., to quantify) most of the decision-making factors
2. To make rational decisions that can be repeated, possibly using a computer
3. To uncover solutions that might appear contrary to intuition, or to support intuitive conclusions
4. To provide better insight into complex problems that could not otherwise be understood

E. **Limitations of Quantitative Methods**

1. It is seldom possible to include all relevant variables in a mathematical model. Thus, managers should not rely solely on a model. They should review the model's results in light of other considerations.
2. Mathematical models are supposed to be representations of the real world. But errors in the data used, the variables, or their relationships may never be eliminated. Also, models are usually oversimplifications.
3. The techniques used can become complex, cumbersome, and costly. Their use should be justified on a cost-benefit basis.

F. Computers have allowed rapid advances in the use of quantitative methods.

1. Computers have led to the widespread use of techniques such as linear programming.
2. Managerial decision making in many fields, e.g., inventory control, can be automated by incorporating mathematical models into the data-processing programs.
3. Although the first applications of computers merely replaced human clerical effort, most modern applications involve the use of methods impossible to implement in manual form.
4. Study Unit 32 outlines computer systems and controls.

GRAPHS

A. Graphs ordinarily depict functional relationships.

1. Independent variables are shown on the horizontal or x-axis.
2. Dependent variables are shown on the vertical or y-axis.
3. EXAMPLE: Overhead cost (dependent variable) applied on the basis of labor hours is graphed on the vertical axis, with labor cost (independent variable) plotted on the horizontal axis.

B. Natural numbers, e.g., 1, 2, 3, 4, 5, usually calibrate both horizontal and vertical axes.

1. If the vertical axis is calibrated in logarithms, the growth rate of the independent variable is expressed, and the graph is a semilog graph.
2. If both axes are calibrated in logarithms, the rate of growth of the dependent variable is expressed in terms of the rate of growth of the independent variable (a log-log graph).

C. **Types of Graphs**

1. **Bar chart** -- a chart that shows direct comparison of magnitudes. One variable, e.g., years, is plotted on one axis, and another, e.g., sales or growth data, is on the other axis.
2. **Subdivided bar chart** -- a more complex bar chart that shows variation in both total and component parts
3. **Line chart** -- a chart used in conjunction with a bar chart to show changes and trends over a time period
4. **Component part line** -- a line chart that breaks down a whole subject into its component parts
5. **Pie diagram** -- a diagram that shows changes in totals and in component parts. A circle is divided into percentage parts of a whole (such as total labor force).
6. **Pictogram** -- a diagram that depicts a variable and its trends by use of descriptive pictures (e.g., 3½ tractors to show farm output in billions of bushels)
7. **Gantt chart** -- a bar chart used mainly in industry as a method of recording progress toward goals for employees and machinery
8. **Statistical map** -- a breakdown of a map in order to show changes, trends, and concentrations among the states or other geographical subdivisions

D. Graphs may also diagram other processes with uncalibrated time flows on the horizontal axis.

1. Network analysis
2. Decision trees
3. Internal control flowcharts
4. Systems flowcharts
5. Program flowcharts

ALGEBRA

A. Algebra is a means of expressing relationships between variables (e.g., 2X = 4Y). Through basic mathematical operations (addition, subtraction, multiplication, and division) on both sides of an equation, solutions are obtainable (e.g., X = 2Y). Given the value of one variable, the value of the other can be obtained (e.g., if Y = 4, X = 8).

B. Linear equations are those with variables only to the first order (not squared, cubed, etc.). For example, X = 10 or X + Y + 2 = 77.7. These equations, when graphed, are depicted by straight lines (linear relationships).

1. Many economic relationships are expressed in linear terms to facilitate analysis.
   a. Cost-volume-profit analysis
   b. Linear programming
   c. Method of least squares
2. Procedures for implementing curvilinear analysis by adapting these and similar methodologies either are not known or are more cumbersome.

C. Nonlinear (curvilinear) functions are higher order functions; their variables are squared, cubed, or of a higher order. Their graphs depict curves or other shapes, but not a straight line.

1. Cost and revenue functions, such as the EOQ model, are frequently nonlinear.
2. Managers are interested in the point at which revenue is maximized or cost minimized.
3. Differential calculus is used to calculate the maxima or minima of curvilinear functions.

D. Multiple unknowns (variables) require as many equations as there are unknowns for a finite solution. Thus, for two variables (i.e., a two-dimensional space) two lines and two equations are needed to define a point. In a three-dimensional space, three lines (three variables and three equations) are necessary to define a point.

1. The number of equations must be equal to the number of variables.
2. EXAMPLE: Three service departments (K, L, and M) provide some services to each other as well as to user departments. The relationships among the departments and the total costs incurred by each can be expressed in the following set of three equations:

$$K = \$100{,}000 + .10L$$
$$L = \$\ 70{,}000 + .15K$$
$$M = \$\ 50{,}000 + .05K + .09L$$

3. These simultaneous equations can be solved algebraically by using substitution.

Substitute K into the L equation, and solve for L.

$$L = \$70{,}000 + .15(\$100{,}000 + .10L)$$
$$L = \$70{,}000 + \$15{,}000 + .015L$$
$$.985L = \$85{,}000$$
$$L = \$86{,}294$$

Substitute this value for L into the K equation, and solve for K.

$$K = \$100{,}000 + .10(\$86{,}294)$$
$$K = \$108{,}629$$

Finally, solve the M equation by plugging in these values for K and L.

$$M = \$50{,}000 + .05(\$108{,}629) + .09(\$86{,}294)$$
$$M = \$50{,}000 + \$5{,}431 + \$7{,}766$$
$$M = \$63{,}197$$

LINEAR, MATRIX, AND BOOLEAN ALGEBRA

A. **Linear algebra** uses the mathematical theory of straight lines and vectors.

1. It is not used to solve managerial problems directly.
2. It is the basis for more applied mathematical techniques such as matrix algebra.

B. **Matrix algebra** is an efficient method of manipulating multiple linear equations.

1. A matrix is a group of numbers ordered into rows and columns.

$$\begin{bmatrix} 6 & 4 \\ 3 & 7 \end{bmatrix}$$

6 4 is the first row.

3 7 is the second row.

6 is the first column. 4 is the second column.
3 7

2. Each number in a matrix is called an element. Elements are numbered by row and column.

$$\begin{bmatrix} X_{11} & X_{12} \\ X_{21} & X_{22} \end{bmatrix}$$

X_{11} is in the first row and first column.
X_{12} is in the first row and second column.
X_{21} is in the second row and first column.
X_{22} is in the second row and second column.

3. Matrices can be added, subtracted, and multiplied in a fashion very similar to that of variables in single equations. Matrices must be of compatible sizes before they can be manipulated, however.
   a. Addition and subtraction require matrices of the same dimensions.
      1) That is, a matrix of 2 rows and 2 columns can only be added to or subtracted from another 2-row-2-column matrix.
   b. Adding and subtracting matrices is accomplished by adding (subtracting) each element in the first matrix to (from) its corresponding element in the second matrix.
      1) EXAMPLE:

$$\begin{bmatrix} 2 & 6 \\ 4 & 7 \end{bmatrix} + \begin{bmatrix} 3 & 9 \\ 2 & 3 \end{bmatrix} = \begin{bmatrix} 5 & 15 \\ 6 & 10 \end{bmatrix}$$

$$\begin{bmatrix} 2 & 6 \\ 4 & 7 \end{bmatrix} - \begin{bmatrix} 3 & 9 \\ 2 & 3 \end{bmatrix} = \begin{bmatrix} -1 & -3 \\ 2 & 4 \end{bmatrix}$$

c. Multiplication of matrices requires that the matrices to be multiplied conform.

1) If matrices are identified as

A (m x n) and B (n x p)

the two can be multiplied; thus, if the number of columns in the first equals the rows in the second, the matrices conform.

$$\underset{A}{\begin{bmatrix} x & x & x \\ x & x & x \end{bmatrix}} \quad \underset{B}{\begin{bmatrix} x & x \\ x & x \\ x & x \end{bmatrix}}$$

2) Furthermore, the resulting matrix will have the number of rows of the first and columns of the second.

3) In other words,

A (m x n) B (n x p)

A can be multiplied by B, and AB = (m x p).

d. Matrices are actually large groups of numbers that are being manipulated.

4. Matrix division is accomplished by multiplying by an inverse matrix.

a. Multiplying an inverse matrix by its original matrix yields an identity matrix.

b. An identity matrix is a matrix in which all elements are zeros except the primary diagonal elements, which are ones. The primary diagonal consists of the elements that make up the line from the top left corner to the bottom right corner of the matrix.

5. Matrix algebra is the basis for solving complicated linear problems.

a. These are problems with a large number of variables (which require a large number of equations).

b. A good example is the simplex tableau. See Linear Programming on page 637.

C. **Boolean algebra** is the algebra of logic. It is sometimes called symbolic logic.

1. Boolean algebra is a method of expressing logic in a mathematical context.

a. It is primarily concerned with binary operations.

b. Boolean algebra is based on the commutative, associative, and distributive laws of binary operations.

2. Boolean algebra provides the theoretical concepts for computer design.

a. It is not used to solve managerial problems directly.

CALCULUS

A. The primary business application of **differential calculus** is to identify the maxima or minima of curvilinear functions.

1. In business and economics, these are the points of revenue or profit maximization (maximum) and cost minimization (minimum).
2. Maxima or minima occur if the slope is 0. When a line becomes horizontal, it has no slope. Thus, the first step is to find the slope of the equation. Slope is the change in y over the change in x.

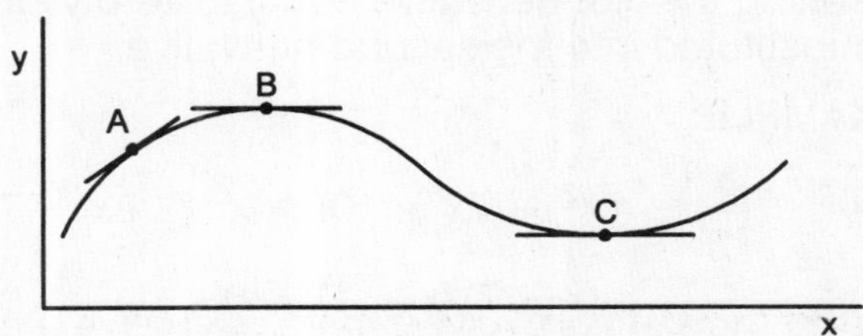

The straight lines tangent to the curve at points B and C have a slope of 0. Point B is a maximum; point C is a minimum.

3. The derivative of a function (equation) is its slope.
4. Derivatives are frequently expressed as f' or $\frac{df(y)}{dx}$, which means differentiate the function (equation) of y in terms of x.
   a. The function of y in terms of x might be an expression such as $y = x^2 + 12x + 7$, if x is an independent variable determining the value of y.
   b. The derivative $= f' = \frac{df(y)}{dx} = \frac{d(x^2 + 12x + 7)}{dx}$
   c. Alternatively, it can be expressed $f'(x^2 + 12x + 7)$.
5. The basic formula for finding the derivative is

   $f'(Ax^n) = nAx^{n-1}$

   If: A = the constant, i.e., the number of independent variables or x's
   x = the variable being differentiated
   n = the exponent of the independent variable
6. The derivative formula is applied to each term in the equation. The sum of the results is the derivative of the original equation.
7. EXAMPLE: $f'(x^2 + 12x + 7) = ?$
   $f'(x^2) = 2x$, $f'(12x) = 12$, $f'(7) = 0$
   Therefore, $f'(x^2 + 12x + 7) = 2x + 12$
8. EXAMPLES: $f'(12) = 0$
   $f'(12x) = 12$
   $f'(12x^2) = 24x$
   $f'(12x^3) = 36x^2$
   $f'(12x^4) = 48x^3$
   $f'(12x^{-2}) = -24x^{-3}$
9. The point(s) with zero slope on the graph of a function can be determined by
   a. First, computing the first derivative
   b. Second, setting the first derivative equal to zero and solving the equation

c. Third, computing the second derivative and determining whether it is positive or negative

1) The second derivative of a function is the derivative of the first derivative.

2) If the second derivative is positive, a point found by solving the first derivative for zero is a minimum; if it is negative, the point is a maximum.

a) In 7. on the previous page, the second derivative is positive $[f'(2x+12) = 2]$. Thus, the point is a minimum.

3) If setting the first derivative equal to zero yielded two solutions, each is substituted into the second derivative.

4) EXAMPLE:

a) $f'(\frac{x^3}{3} - 4x^2 + 7x + 10) = x^2 - 8x + 7$

$$(x - 7)(x - 1) = 0$$
$$x = 7$$
$$x = 1$$

b) $f'(x^2 - 8x + 7) = 2x - 8$

$$2(7) - 8 = 6$$
$$2(1) - 8 = -6$$

c) Thus, x=7 is a minimum, x=1 is a maximum.

10. EXAMPLE: The formula for the economic order quantity (EOQ) (see Study Unit 30) results from differentiating the total cost with regard to the order quantity (x) and solving for x. This expression must be a minimum because the second derivative must be positive.

$$c = \frac{Da}{x} + \frac{xk}{2} + F$$

$$df(c)/dx = \frac{-Da}{x^2} + \frac{k}{2}$$

$$\frac{-Da}{x^2} + \frac{k}{2} = 0$$

$$\frac{k}{2} = \frac{Da}{x^2}$$

$$x^2 = \frac{2Da}{k}$$

$$x = \sqrt{\frac{2Da}{k}}$$

If:
c = total cost
x = EOQ
a = cost per purchase order
D = annual demand in units
k = unit annual carrying cost
F = fixed cost of ordering

The derivative of $\frac{-Da}{x^2} + \frac{k}{2}$ *is* $\frac{2Da}{x^3}$

B. **Integral calculus** also has a very important business application. It permits computation of the area under a curve.

1. The area under a probability curve equals the probability. Thus, integral calculus is used to evaluate the probability that events will occur.

2. Integral calculus finds an antiderivative, i.e., the function that, if differentiated, would result in the function being integrated.

3. The general form of the integral is $\int f(x)dx$, which is the integral of f(x) with respect to x.

4. Some formulas for integration are

   a. $\int [kf(x)]dx = k \int f(x)dx$

      1) This formula indicates that constants (k) can be brought out of the integral.

   b. $\int x^n \, dx = \frac{x^{n+1}}{n+1}$

      1) The integral of x^n is x^{n+1} divided by n + 1. The degenerate case is n = 1, which is the same as x^1, i.e., $x = x^1$.

   c. EXAMPLE: For the function y = 4x,

$$\int ydx = \int (4x)dx = 4 \int (x)dx = 4(x^2/2) = 2x^2$$

FORECASTING

A. Forecasts are the basis for business plans. In addition to intuition, many quantitative methods are useful in projecting the future from past experience.

   1. Examples of forecasts

      a. Sales forecasts
      b. Inventory demand
      c. Cash flow
      d. Future capital needs
      e. Budgets

B. Most models are used in the forecasting process, i.e., to make decisions that optimize future results. Virtually all topics in this study unit involve or are concerned with forecasting.

C. The reliability of the forecast should be determined before using it. No objective method can determine the reliability of judgmental forecasts. When quantitative methods are used, however, it is usually possible to measure reliability, e.g., by calculating the standard error of the estimate.

D. **Exponential smoothing** is a technique used to level or smooth variations encountered in a forecast. This technique also adapts the forecast to changes as they occur. The simplest form of smoothing is the moving average, in which each forecast is based on a fixed number of prior observations. Exponential smoothing is similar to the moving average. Exponential means that greater weight is placed on the most recent data, with the weights of all data falling off exponentially as the data age. The selection of alpha (α), the smoothing factor, is important because a high alpha places more weight on recent data. The equation for the forecast (F) for period t+1 is

$$F_{t+1} = \alpha(x_t) + (1 - \alpha)F_t$$

If: x_t = the observation for period t
t = the most recent period
α = the smoothing factor $0 \leq \alpha \leq 1$
F_t = the forecast for period t

This method weights the observation for period t by α and the forecast for period t by (1 – α).

PROBABILITY AND STATISTICS

A. Statistics is covered in Study Unit 29, Decision Making under Uncertainty. It contains the following sideheadings. Review that study unit in conjunction with your study of this study unit.

1. Probability
2. Expected Value
3. Statistics
4. Hypothesis Testing
5. Correlation Analysis
6. Regression (Least Squares) Analysis

B. Probability is important to management decision making because of the uncertainty of future events. Probability assists in making the best decision in face of uncertainty.

C. Statistics is a methodology for describing an abundance of data with a few statistics, i.e., descriptive statistics.

1. Inferential statistics is the methodology for inferring population characteristics from population samples.

D. Regression analysis determines the relationship between one dependent variable and one or more independent variables.

1. It is also known as the least squares method. See Study Unit 29.

E. Time series analysis or trend analysis relies on past experience. Changes in the value of a variable (e.g., unit sales of a product) may have several possible components.

1. In time series analysis, the dependent variable is regressed on time (the independent variable).
2. The secular trend is the long-term change that occurs in a series. It is represented by a straight line or curve on a graph.
3. Seasonal variations are common in many businesses. A variety of methods include seasonal variations in a forecasting model, but most methods use a seasonal index.
4. Cyclical fluctuations are variations in the level of activity in business periods. Whereas some of these fluctuations are beyond the control of the firm, they need to be considered in forecasting. They are usually incorporated as index numbers.
5. Irregular or random variations are any variations not included in the three categories above. Business can be affected by random happenings -- weather, strikes, fires, etc.

F. Discriminant analysis is a variation of regression analysis in which independent variables are categorical; i.e., each observation is assigned a category.

1. EXAMPLES:

   a. High, medium, low
   b. Good, bad
   c. Male, female

STATISTICAL QUALITY CONTROL

A. Statistical quality control is a method of determining whether the shipment or production run of units lies within acceptable limits. It is also used to determine whether production processes are out of control.

1. Items are either good or bad, i.e., inside or outside of control limits.
2. Statistical quality control is based on the binomial distribution.

B. Acceptance sampling is a method of determining the probability that the defective rate in a batch is less than a certain level.

1. EXAMPLE: Assume a sample is taken and the probability that the sample was from a population of 500 with a specified error rate is calculated. According to standard acceptance sampling tables, if the sample consists of 25 items and none is defective, there is a 93% probability that the population error rate is less than 10%. If 60 items are examined and no defectives are found, the probability is 99% that the error rate is less than 10%. If two defectives in 60 units are observed, there is a 96% probability that the error rate is less than 10%.

C. Statistical control charts are graphic aids for monitoring the status of any process subject to random variations. Originally developed to control the quality of production processes, they also have applications of direct interest to the management accountant.

- Unit cost of production
- Direct labor hours used
- Ratio of actual expenses to budgeted expenses
- Number of calls by sales personnel
- Total accounts receivable

1. The chart consists of three horizontal lines plotted on a horizontal time scale. The center line represents the average or mean value for the process being controlled. The other two lines are the upper control limit (UCL) and the lower control limit (LCL). The processes are measured periodically, and the values are plotted on the chart (X). If the value falls within the control limits, no action is taken. If the value falls outside the limits, the process is considered out of control, and an investigation is made for possible corrective action. Another advantage of the chart is that it makes trends visible.

   a. P charts are based on an attribute (acceptable/not acceptable) rather than a measure of a variable. Specifically, it shows the percentage of defects in a sample.

   b. C charts are also attribute control charts. They show defects per item.

   c. An R chart shows the range of dispersion of a variable, such as size or weight.

   d. An X-bar chart shows the sample mean for a variable.

2. EXAMPLE:

```
Unit Cost ($)                    X Out of control
1.05 ---------------------------------------------UCL
1.00 _______________X_____________________________
0.95 -----X---------------------------------------LCL

     _____________________________________________
       March      April      May
```

D. Variations in the value of some process parameter may have several causes.

1. Random variations occur by chance. Present in virtually all processes, they are not correctable because they will not repeat themselves in the same manner. Excessively narrow control limits will result in many investigations of what are simply random fluctuations.
2. Implementation deviations occur because of human or mechanical failure to achieve target results.
3. Measurement variations result from errors in the measurements of actual results.
4. Model fluctuations can be caused by errors in the formulation of a decision model.
5. Prediction variances result from errors in forecasting data used in a decision model.

E. Establishing control limits based on benchmarks is a common method. A more objective method is to use the concept of expected value. The limits are important because they are the decision criteria for determining whether a deviation will be investigated.

F. Cost-benefit analysis using expected value provides a more objective basis for setting control limits. Basically, the limits of controls should be set so that the cost of an investigation is less than or equal to the benefits derived.

1. The expected costs include investigation cost and the cost of corrective action.

   (Probability of being out of control x Cost of corrective action)
   \+ (Probability of being in control x Investigation cost)
   Total expected cost

2. The benefit of an investigation is the avoidance of the costs of continuing to operate an out-of-control process. The expected value of benefits is the probability of being out of control multiplied by the cost of not being corrected.

CAPITAL BUDGETING AND CVP ANALYSIS

A. Study Unit 28, Capital Budgeting, concerns methods for maximizing the return on long-term investment. Thus, capital budgeting is part of the planning function of management. The general discussion of the time value of money (including present value and future value) is therefore presented in Study Unit 28. Decision-making techniques that are also discussed in Study Unit 28 include

1. Payback method
2. Net present value method
3. Internal rate of return method
4. Profitability index method
5. Accounting rate of return method

B. **Cost-volume-profit (CVP) analysis** facilitates the setting of marketing and production goals (see Study Unit 27). CVP analysis studies the relationships among

1. Revenues
2. Fixed costs
3. Variable costs
4. Contribution margins (revenue minus variable cost)
5. Profit levels
6. Levels of volume

C. **Replacement analysis** is used to determine the optimal time to purchase a new asset to replace an existing asset.

1. As equipment ages, operating and maintenance costs tend to rise. Obsolescence also can become a factor.
2. Replacement decisions must be based on a comparison of the cost of a new item and the consequent reduction in operating, maintenance, and obsolescence costs. Replacement analysis answers questions such as
   a. When should a fleet of cars be replaced?
   b. How long should a truck be kept before trading it in?
   c. When should truck tires be changed?
   d. Should all light bulbs be replaced periodically or only those that burn out?

LINEAR PROGRAMMING

A. Linear programming is a technique used to maximize a revenue or profit function, or minimize a cost function, subject to constraints, e.g., limited (scarce) resources or minimum/maximum levels of production, performance, etc. In business, linear programming is used for planning resource allocations. Managers are often faced with problems of selecting the most profitable or least costly way to use available resources.

1. EXAMPLE: A manufacturer should minimize production costs while satisfying production requirements, maintaining required inventory levels, staying within production capacities, and using available employees. The objective function is the production cost to be minimized; the constraints are production requirements, inventory levels, production capacity, and available employees.
2. Other business applications include
   a. Selecting a product mix
   b. Blending chemical products
   c. Scheduling flight crews
   d. Assigning jobs to machines
   e. Determining transportation routes
3. The conditions that restrict the optimal value of the **objective function** are the **constraints.**
   a. A **shadow price** is the amount by which the value of the optimal solution of the objective function in a linear programming problem will change if a one-unit change is made in a binding constraint.
      1) A nonbinding constraint is one that has excess capacity; i.e., the optimal solution does not use all of the given resource. The shadow price for a nonbinding constraint is zero because a one-unit change will not affect the optimal solution when excess capacity exists.
      2) The calculation of shadow prices is a simple example of sensitivity analysis, which is any procedure to test the responsiveness of the solution indicated by a model to changes in variables, alternative decisions, or errors.
4. The values used to construct the objective function and the constraints are the decision variables. They are usually the amounts of each scarce resource used.
5. Values that are fixed for purposes of solving the model (but are not fixed forever) are cost/profit coefficients for the objective function, technical coefficients for the constraints, and the constants on the right-hand side of the constraints.

6. When the number of constraint equations equals the number of variables, there is a unique solution. When the number of variables exceeds the number of constraint equations, there is usually an infinite number of possible solutions.
   a. The variables are the outputs from the process.
   b. The constraint equations usually concern the types of input or types of resources being allocated, e.g., available machine hours, raw materials, etc.
   c. The objective of linear programming is to choose the best solution (production alternative) from a potentially infinite number of possibilities.

B. Management accountants should recognize situations in which linear programming may be applicable. When an application is attempted, qualified operations research experts should assist in providing guidance in formulating and solving the problem. Linear programming is a powerful planning tool for management, but it is complex and usually requires a computer for solution.

C. Several solution methods are available to solve linear programming problems.
1. The graphical method, although the easiest technique, is limited to problems with two variables.
2. The algebraic method is a trial-and-error technique. Pairs of constraints are solved algebraically to find their intersection. The values of the decision variables are then substituted into the objective function and compared to find the best combination.
   a. The basic rule is that the optimal solution will be at the intersection of two or more constraint equations.
   b. Thus, all intersections can be computed and each solution evaluated in the objective function to determine which solution is optimal. See the graphical example in E. on page 639.
3. The simplex method is the technique most commonly used to solve linear programming problems. It is an algorithm to move from one corner solution to a better corner solution. When a better solution cannot be found, the optimal solution has been reached.
   a. The simplex method relies on an area of mathematics called matrix algebra. The equations that form the constraints are arranged in a matrix of coefficients and manipulated as a group with matrix algebra.
   b. Almost all practical applications of linear programming require the use of computers. Most computer facilities have a linear programming package that uses the simplex algorithm to find the optimal solutions.

D. EXAMPLE: A company produces products G and J. Product G contributes $5,000 per unit sold, and product J contributes $4,000 per unit. The company seeks to maximize profits, so the objective function is

Maximize $5G + 4J$ (which will be the maximum profit in thousands of dollars)

The objective function is subject to the following constraints:

1. $G + J \geq 5$ (minimal production requirement)
2. $G \leq 3J$ (market balance requirement)
3. $10G + 15J \leq 150$ (production capacity constraint)
4. $G, J \geq 0$ (nonnegativity constraint)

E. **Graphical Solution**. In order to plot this set of constraints,

1. Change inequalities to equalities.
2. Plot the equalities.
3. Identify the correct side of the line for the original inequalities.

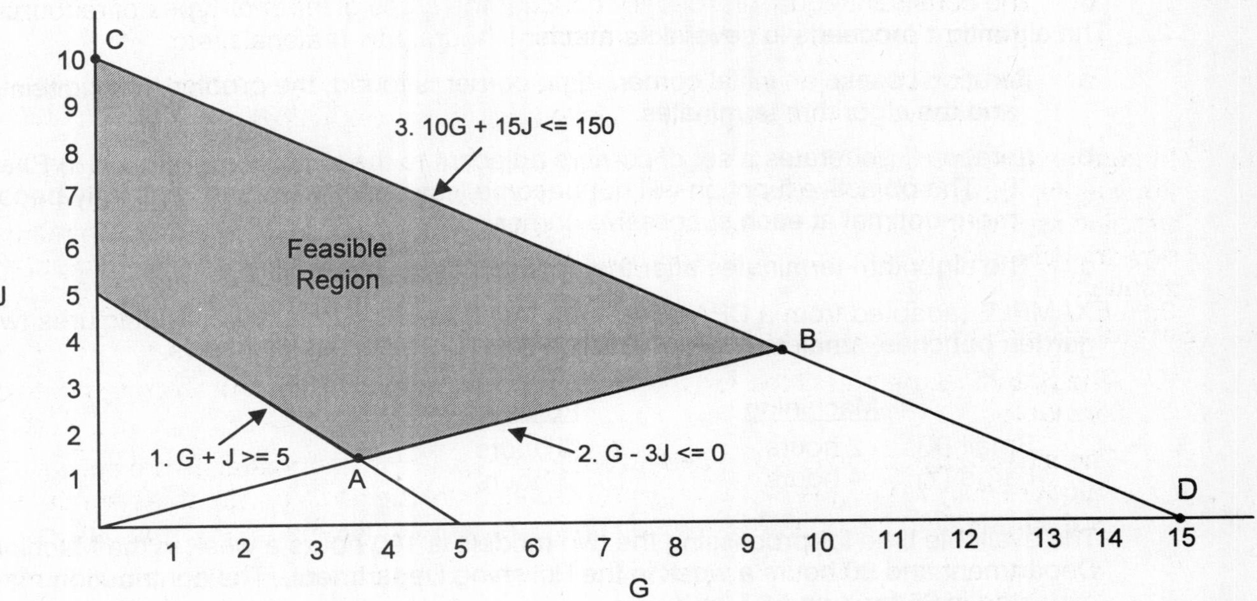

F. **Algebraic Solution**. The combination of G and J that maximizes the objective function will occur at one of the extreme points, i.e., corners, of the feasible region. Simultaneously solving the constraints intersecting at those corners and substituting into the objective function,

At point A:

$$\begin{array}{r} G + J = 5 \\ \underline{-G + 3J = 0} \\ 4J = 5 \end{array}$$

$J = 5/4,\ G = 15/4$

Profit $= \$5{,}000(15/4) + \$4{,}000(5/4) = \underline{\$23{,}750}$

At point B:

$$\begin{array}{r} G - 3J = 0 \\ \underline{10G + 15J = 150} \end{array} \longrightarrow \begin{array}{r} 5G - 15J = 0 \\ + \underline{10G + 15J = 150} \\ 15G = 150 \end{array}$$

$G = 10,\ J = 50/15$

Profit $= \$5{,}000(10) + \$4{,}000(50/15) = \underline{\$63{,}333}$

At point C:

$$\begin{array}{r} \underline{G \qquad = 0} \\ 10G + 15J = 150 \end{array}$$ (from nonnegativity constraint)

$J = 10,\ G = 0$

Profit $= \$5{,}000(0) + \$4{,}000(10) = \underline{\$40{,}000}$

Note that point D does not lie in the feasible region.

The firm would choose to produce at point B, i.e., 10 of product G and (50/15) of product J. (This assumes that partial units of J may be produced. If product J is produced in single units, e.g., steamships, the answer may be interpreted to be to produce 3⅓ ships per month, i.e., as a rate of production.)

G. Simplex Algorithm

1. A simplex algorithm is a systematic method of examining the corners (also called vertices or extreme points) of the feasible region while in search of the optimal solution. The algorithm always moves in the direction of improving the solution and terminates at the optimal solution.
2. The algorithm proceeds in several iterations.
   a. Iteration I seeks an initial corner. If no corner is found, the problem is inconsistent, and the algorithm terminates.
   b. Iteration II generates a set of corners adjacent to the initial corner (found in Phase I). The objective function will not become less optimal and will ordinarily become more optimal at each successive corner.
   c. The algorithm terminates after the optimal corner is reached.
3. EXAMPLE (adapted from a CPA question): The Wineroot Company manufactures two garden benches, small and large. Each model is processed as follows.

	Machining	Polishing
Small (X)	2 hours	3 hours
Large (Y)	4 hours	3 hours

The available time for processing the two models is 100 hours a week in the Machining Department and 90 hours a week in the Polishing Department. The contribution margin expected is $5 for X and $7 for Y.

   a. The objective function is the formula for the maximum total contribution margin. Because each X produces a $5 CM and each Y produces a $7 CM, the total CM will be 5X + 7Y. This is what Wineroot wants to maximize.
   b. A constraint equation can be set up for the Machining Department, which has a total of 100 hours available each week. Each X requires 2 hours of time from that department, and each Y requires 4 hours. Accordingly, the total Machining Department time taken by production is 2X + 4Y, which must be equal to or less than the 100 hours available.

$$2X + 4Y \leq 100$$

   c. The constraint equation for the Polishing Department is found in a similar manner. The Polishing Department has a total of 90 hours available each week. Each unit of X or Y requires 3 hours. Thus, the constraint for this department is that 3X + 3Y must be equal to or less than 90.

$$3X + 3Y \leq 90$$

   d. Both constraints are inequality expressions of the form less than or equal. To transform them to an equality form, a positive variable called the slack variable must be added to the left-hand side of each constraint.

$$2X + 4Y \leq 100$$
$$2X + 4Y + S_1 = 100$$

$$3X + 3Y \leq 90$$
$$3X + 3Y + S_2 = 90$$

In general, each slack variable makes zero contribution to the value of the solution.

Before we construct the tableau, let us restate the linear programming problem thus far:

$$\text{Maximize } 5X + 7Y + 0S_1 + 0S_2 \text{ subject to}$$

$$2X + 4Y + 1S_1 + 0S_2 = 100$$
$$3X + 3Y + 0S_1 + 1S_2 = 90$$

and given that $X \geq 0$

$Y \geq 0$

$S_1, S_2 \geq 0$

4. The initial simplex tableau (in its most common format) can be constructed from the Wineroot Company's LP problem. Remember that rows run horizontally and columns run vertically.

C_j	5	7	0	0	RHS
Variables	X	Y	S_1	S_2	
CB					
0	2	4	1	0	100
0	3	3	0	1	90
Z_j	0	0	0	0	0
C_j-Z_j	5	7	0	0	

a. After converting the constraint equations to equalities, build the tableau by beginning with the variables row, which consists first of the constraint variables (X and Y) and then the slack variables (S_1 and S_2). It is essentially a row of labels.

b. The C_j row lists the payoff coefficients for a profit-maximizing problem (or the cost coefficients for a cost-minimizing problem) given by the coefficients of the objective function.

   1) Remember that the slack variables have payoff/cost coefficients of 0.

   2) Thus, in constructing this tableau, the C_j row consists of the coefficients from the objective function (which was $5X + 7Y + 0S_1 + 0S_2$).

   3) The C_j row is 5, 7, 0, 0.

c. The machining and polishing constraint rows in the simplex tableau are formed from the constraint equalities, which were

$$2X + 4Y + 1S_1 + 0S_2 = 100$$
$$3X + 3Y + 0S_1 + 1S_2 = 90$$

Using these coefficients, the constraint rows (resource coefficient rows) are

2 4 1 0 100
3 3 0 1 90

   1) There must be as many resource coefficient rows in the tableau as constraints.

d. There are as many basic variables as there are constraints.

   1) Basic variables exist in the current tableau as a possible solution (not necessarily optimal).

   2) For our example, "S_1 equals 100, and S_2 equals 90" is the initial basic solution.

   3) Nonbasic variables are the variables that are equal to zero in the current solution, e.g., X and Y.

e. The basic variables are those that form an identity matrix. That is, they have one entry of 1 and the others of 0 in their corresponding variable columns. The variable columns are those beneath each variable, i.e., beneath X, Y, S_1, and S_2.

   1) Referring to the sample tableau, S_1 has 1, 0 in its column, and S_2 has 0, 1; that is, they form an identity matrix.

   2) In this tableau, the basic variables happen also to be the slack variables.

      a) But they may not necessarily be next to each other in other problems.

f. The values for the basic variables are given in the right-hand side (RHS) column of the tableau.

   1) Because the entry 1 for the S_1 variable is on the first row of the identity matrix, the value of S is given in the first row of the RHS column as 100.

   2) The entry of 1 for S_2 is in the second row, and its value is found in the second row under RHS to be 90.

   3) The values 100 and 90 come from the right-hand side of the constraint equations. Thus, the RHS values are also the amounts of available resources.

g. The CB column consists of payoff (cost) coefficients of the basic variables in profit-maximization (cost-minimization) problems.

   1) Hence, the column consists of as many numbers as there are basic variables (i.e., two for this tableau).

   2) The numbers entered are the same as for the basic variables found in the C_j row (0 and 0).

   3) Z_j and $C_j - Z_j$ are not part of the CB column.

h. The first element of the Z_j row is the sum of the products of multiplying each element in the CB column by each element in the first column, $(0 \times 2) + (0 \times 3) = 0$.

   1) The subsequent elements are obtained by multiplying each element in the CB column by each element in the next column and adding the products.

   2) For example, the third element in the Z_j row is $(0 \times 1) + (0 \times 0) = 0$.

i. The index row is the last (bottom) row. It provides a measure of the direction of improvement of the objective function value for a corresponding change in the tableau.

   1) It is obtained by subtracting each element in the Z_j row from each element in the C_j row.

   $$C_j - Z_j = 5 \ 7 \ 0 \ 0$$

   2) Positive elements in the index row for a maximization problem indicate that the solution could be improved.

j. The current (but not the optimal) solution to this simplex problem is obtained by multiplying the CB column times the RHS column and adding the products.

   1) The result is found in the far right column (RHS) in the Z_j row, which here is zero.

   2) The current solution does not always equal zero, although it does in this case because CB = 0.

k.

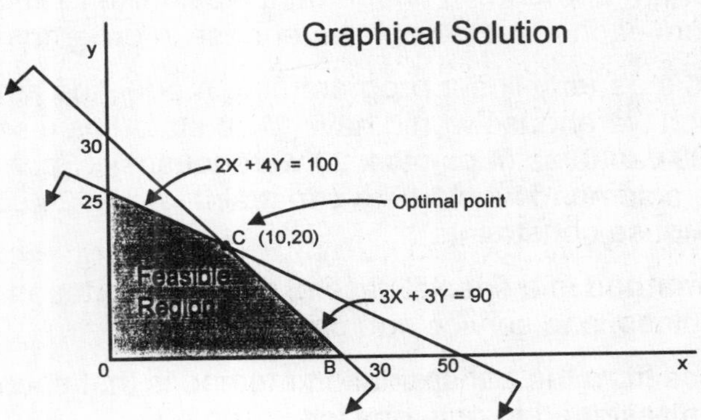

l. Given the objective function (OF) 5X + 7Y, the extreme points of the feasible region yield the following values:

At point	OF
(0, 0)	0
(0, 25)	(0 x 5) + (25 x 7) = 175
(30, 0)	(30 x 5) + (0 x 7) = 150
(10, 20)	(10 x 5) + (20 x 7) = 190

m. The CMA exam tests familiarity with the simplex tableau format, but it has not tested further manipulation of the tableau to achieve an optimal solution.

n. Computer software packages have been developed to manipulate linear programming problems with many more constraints. It is usually sufficient for the management accountant to recognize the basic method and its implications.

TRANSPORTATION MODEL

A. The transportation model is a special type of LP problem. It involves physical movement (transportation) of goods from sources of supply (such as factories) to destinations (warehouses).

1. EXAMPLE: A fleet of trucks may be available for daily deliveries in a city. Each day the transportation manager must determine the best route for each truck. Many possible combinations of trucks and destinations satisfy the constraints of meeting all deliveries with the available trucks, but the manager would like to have the minimum cost combination. In effect, the manager must allocate the available trucks (scarce resources) to the required destinations in a way that minimizes costs.

B. The objective function includes the transportation cost of each item from each source to each destination.

1. The constraints are the output for each supply point and the demand of each destination.
2. EXAMPLE: A manufacturer has four plants. Assume that each plant could ship products to any of 20 warehouses. Each plant has a maximum capacity, and each warehouse has a minimum demand. Management would like to know how much should be shipped from each plant to each warehouse in order to minimize transportation cost.
3. To formulate a general linear programming model, the amount to be shipped from each plant to each warehouse would have to be stated as a separate variable. The result would be 80 variables (4 plants x 20 warehouses). Each plant's capacity and each warehouse's demand would be a constraint, giving 24 constraints (4 plant constraints + 20 warehouse constraints).

C. The **assignment method** is a special case of the transportation method. It is used to assign employees, machines, and service equipment to jobs.

1. The difference from the transportation method is that each source (person, machine, etc.) can be assigned to only one job.

D. **Vogel's Approximation**, or the **penalty method**, solves transportation problems easily. The name penalty method comes from the amount that must be paid if the lowest cost alternative is not selected in each row and each column.

1. EXAMPLE: Assume that a company has two factories that produce 18 and 14 units of product, respectively, during a period of time. Three distribution warehouses demand 15, 10, and 7 units, respectively, during the same period. The table below depicts this information along with the shipping costs per unit (e.g., $4 to ship one unit from factory 1 to warehouse C). The objective is to minimize total shipping costs. The penalties (in dollars) are shown in parentheses to the right of, and below, the table.

from \ to	A	B	C	Supply	
Row 1	$8	$5	$4	18	(1)
Row 2	$5	$6	$7	14	(1)
Demand	15	10	7	32 / 32	
	(3)	(1)	(3)		

For row 1: If the lowest cost alternative is not used ($4 for C), then the shipment must go to B, whose cost of shipping is $1 higher than shipping to C. The firm would suffer a $1 penalty for not selecting the lowest cost box. For column A, the penalty would be $3 ($8 – $5) if the lowest cost box is not used.

The objective under the penalty method is to avoid the highest penalties; those columns or rows where the highest penalties might occur are filled first. Since columns A and C have the highest penalties, one of these (it does not matter which) should be filled first. Choose column C. The lowest cost box in the selected column should be filled with the maximum possible number of units. The maximum that can be placed into box 1C is 7 units because warehouse C only needs 7 units; this step eliminates column C from further consideration. Draw a line through column C and recompute the penalties for the remaining columns and rows (if necessary) as shown below.

from \ to	A	B	C	Supply		
1	$8	$5	$4 / 7	18	~~(1)~~	(3)
2	$5	$6	$7	14	(1)	
Demand	15	10	~~7~~	32 / 32		
	(3)	(1)	~~(3)~~			

Since column A still shares the highest penalty, fill its lowest cost box to the maximum extent possible; i.e., assign 14 units to box 2A. The row 2 total supply is 14, thus limiting the number of units that can be assigned to box 2A. This assignment of 14 units equals the row 2 constraint, so row 2 is crossed out (it no longer needs to be considered).

The final units are then assigned to row 1, columns A and B, as shown in the following table.

from \ to	A	B	C	Supply		
1	$8 1	$5 10	$4 7	18	~~(1)~~	(3)
~~2~~	$5 ~~14~~	$6	$7	~~14~~	~~(1)~~	
Demand	15	10	7	32 / 32		
	(3)	(1)	(3)			

The total shipping costs based on the assignments can be calculated by multiplying the number of units shipped times the shipping cost per unit, as follows:

$$1(\$8) + 10(\$5) + 7(\$4) + 14(\$5) = \$156$$

The use of the penalty method resulted in the optimal solution in this example, which is not always the case. The penalty method will occasionally result in a very good solution, but not the optimum. There is a quantitative technique to test for the optimality of a solution, but it is quite complicated and beyond the scope of this discussion.

GOAL PROGRAMMING

A. Goal programming was first introduced as a specialized type of linear programming to solve problems that had no feasible solution under regular linear programming.

B. Goal programming permits an ordinal specification (ranking) and solution to problems with multiple goals.

   1. With its ability to incorporate multiple goals, the method has the potential for solving problems with both financial and nonfinancial goals.

INTEGER PROGRAMMING

A. Integer programming (IP) deals with problems in which some variables are not continuous. Linear programming, on the other hand, assumes that all variables are continuous and all functions are linear (i.e., graphed with straight lines). Variables are thus allowed to take fractional values; 9, 9.367, and 10 are all possible values. In integer programming, fractions are not possible.

   1. EXAMPLE: It might be possible for an oil company to build 12 or 13 gas stations on a stretch of highway, but it is not clear what an optimal solution of 12.72 gas stations means.

   2. Integer programming problems are also known as **discrete** models because the variables take on discrete, noncontinuous values.

B. One way to solve IP problems is to solve them as LP problems and round to satisfy the integrality condition.

1. In the example, we would decide to build 13 gas stations by rounding 12.72 to 13.0.
2. Rounding raises several problems.

    a. The rounded solution may violate constraints.

    b. The rounded solution may be farther from the optimal solution than some other integer combination.

C. There is a class of IP problems in which the variables are constrained to take on values of 1 or 0, and no other values. These are yes and no or go, no-go decisions. This class of problems may be solved only with algorithms designed to handle these constraints. Rounding is never acceptable because the error induced would be too great.

DYNAMIC PROGRAMMING

A. This type of model is useful for problems that involve time-staged decisions, i.e., decisions affected by previous decisions.

1. Typically, they are applied to much smaller problems than LP, in terms of number of variables and constraints.

2. Dynamic programming is useful for problems like

    a. Inventory reordering rules
    b. Production scheduling in the face of fluctuating demand
    c. Spare parts level determination
    d. Capital budgeting for new ventures
    e. Systematic search for scarce resources

B. The key features of dynamic programming problems are

1. The probabilistic or stochastic nature of the variables

    a. However, deterministic variations exist.

2. The iterative formulation of the problems. The optimal solution is reached by a repetitive process.

C. A decision tree with probabilities of occurrence for each branch is a good example of a time-staged decision process that could be evaluated with dynamic programming.

PROJECT SCHEDULING AND NETWORK MODELS

A. Project scheduling techniques are designed to aid the planning and control of large-scale projects having many interrelated activities. Three of the more common techniques are Gantt or bar charts, PERT, and CPM. These techniques are suitable for any project having a target completion date and single start.

1. Example applications

    a. Building construction
    b. Research and development projects
    c. New product planning
    d. Feasibility studies
    e. Audit studies
    f. Book publishing

B. Gantt charts or bar charts are simple to construct and use. To develop a Gantt chart, divide the project into logical subprojects called activities or tasks. Estimate the start and completion times for each activity. Prepare a bar chart showing each activity as a horizontal bar along a time scale.

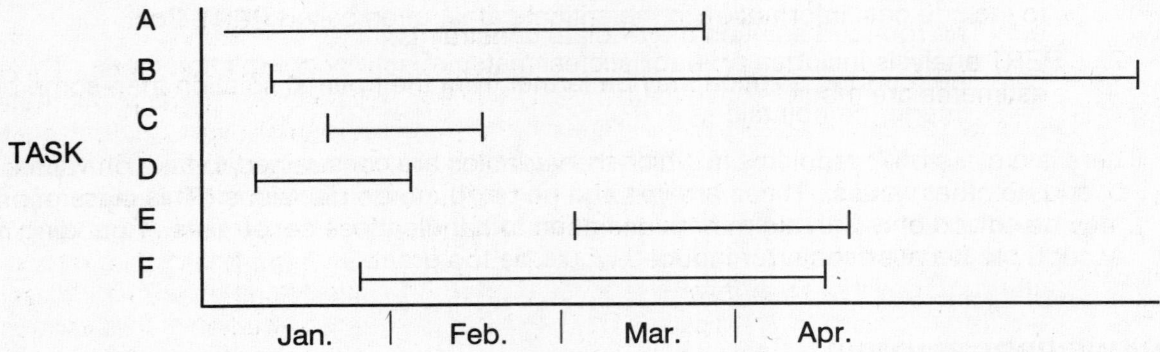

1. The major advantage of the Gantt chart is its simplicity. It forces the planner to think ahead and define logical activities. As the project progresses, actual completion times can be compared to planned times. Yet the technique requires no special tools or mathematics and can be used on small projects as well as large ones.

2. The major disadvantage is that interrelationships among activities are not shown. Several special methods have been developed to show these on a Gantt chart, but they are feasible only for simple relationships.

C. Program Evaluation and Review Technique (PERT) was developed to aid managers in controlling large-scale, complex projects. PERT diagrams are free-form networks showing each activity as a line between events. A sequence of lines shows interrelationships among activities. PERT is more complex than Gantt charts, but it has the advantages of incorporating probabilistic time estimates and identifying the critical path.

1. Events are discrete moments in time representing the start or finish of an activity. They consume no resources.

2. Activities are tasks to be accomplished. They consume resources (including time) and have a duration over time.

3. The network diagram is formed by

   a. The lines (activities) connected from left to right in the necessary sequence of their accomplishment. They can be marked with time lengths.

   b. Events are shown as circles and numbered for identification.

4. The critical path is the longest path in time through the network. It is critical in that if any activity on the critical path takes longer than expected, the entire project will be delayed. Every network has at least one critical path. Some have more than one.

   a. The mean completion time for the critical path is the sum of the means of the activity times.

   b. The standard deviation of the completion time for the critical path is the square root of the sum of the variances (squares of the standard deviations) of the activity times.

      1) EXAMPLE: If the critical path has two activities, and the standard deviations of the completion times are 3 and 4, the standard deviation for the critical path is

$$\sqrt{3^2 + 4^2} = 5$$

5. Paths that are not critical have slack time. One advantage of PERT is that it identifies this slack time, which represents unused resources that can be diverted to the critical path.

6. Activity times can be expressed probabilistically. Computer programs are available to make the calculations and find critical paths. Several techniques have been developed to include cost information in the critical paths, often called PERT-Cost.

7. PERT analysis includes probabilistic estimates of activity completion times. Three time estimates are made -- optimistic, most likely, and pessimistic. The time estimates for an activity are assumed to approximate a beta probability distribution. In contrast to the normal distribution, this distribution has finite endpoints (the optimistic and pessimistic estimates) and is unimodal; that is, it has only one mode (the most likely time). PERT approximates the mean of the beta distribution by dividing the sum of the optimistic time, the pessimistic time, and four times the most likely time (the mode) by six. The standard deviation is approximated by dividing the difference between the pessimistic and optimistic times by six. The basis for the latter approximation is that various probability distributions have tails that lie about plus or minus three standard deviations from the mean. For example, 99.9% of observations in the normal distribution are expected to lie within this range.

8. EXAMPLE: The usual formula for time estimation is

   1/6 [optimistic time + 4(most likely time) + pessimistic time]

   If an activity can be completed in the times indicated below,

   6 days = optimistic time
   10 days = most likely time
   20 days = pessimistic time

   the expected time for that leg would be

   $1/6\ [6 + 4(10) + 20] = 11$ days

   Thus, the most likely time is weighted the most heavily.
   The standard deviation is 2.33 $[(20 - 6) \div 6]$.

9. EXAMPLE:

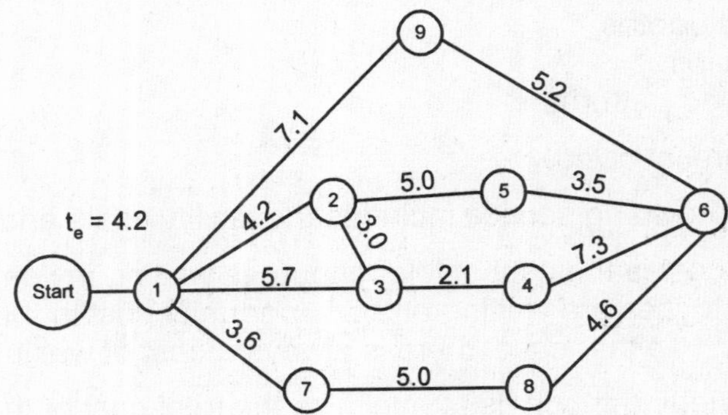

For the network above, we have the following paths and path times:

Path	Time
Start-1-9-6	16.5
Start-1-2-5-6	16.9
Start-1-2-3-4-6	20.8
Start-1-3-4-6	19.3
Start-1-7-8-6	17.4

Path Start-1-2-3-4-6 is the critical path because it has the longest time.

10. In the second example on page 649, the path of the task from 1 to 3 takes only 5.7, while the critical path events (1-2-3) take 7.2. The slack time represented by path 1-to-3 is thus 7.2 – 5.7, or 1.5. People assigned to path 1-to-3 have an extra hour and a half to help out elsewhere.

D. The Critical Path Method (CPM) was developed independently of PERT and is widely used in the construction industry. CPM may be thought of as a subset of PERT. Like PERT, it is a network technique, but, unlike PERT, it uses deterministic time and cost estimates. Its advantages include cost estimates plus the concept of "crash" efforts and costs.

1. Activity times are estimated for normal effort and crash effort. Crash time is the time to complete an activity assuming that all available resources were devoted to the task (overtime, extra crew, etc.).
2. Activity costs are also estimated for normal and crash efforts.
3. These estimates allow the project manager to estimate the costs of completing the project if some of the activities are completed on a crash basis.
4. The network diagram is constructed in the same manner as PERT diagrams. Once the diagram is constructed, the critical paths are found for normal and crash times. Remember that more than one critical path may exist for each diagram.
5. Crashing the network means finding the minimum cost for completing the project in minimum time.
6. CPM computer programs allow updating of the solution as work proceeds.

QUEUING THEORY

A. Queuing (waiting line) theory is a group of mathematical models for systems involving waiting lines. In general, a queuing system consists of a queue, or waiting line, and a service facility.

1. Examples of queuing systems
    a. Bank teller windows
    b. Grocery checkout counters
    c. Highway toll booths
    d. Docks for ships
    e. Airport holding patterns
2. Two basic costs are involved.
    a. The cost of providing service includes the facility costs and the operating costs.
    b. The waiting cost is the cost of idle resources waiting in line. It may be a direct cost if paid employees are waiting or an opportunity cost in the case of waiting customers. In either case, there is always a cost of waiting.
3. The objective of queuing theory is to minimize the total cost of the system, including both service and waiting costs, for a given rate of arrivals.
4. The structure of queuing systems depends on the number of lines and service facilities and how they are coupled. Grocery stores usually have multiple-line, multiple-server systems. Some banks have single-line, multiple-teller systems. Job shops can be conceived of as multistage systems in which each machine is a server with its own queue.

5. Mathematical solutions are available for simple systems having unscheduled random arrivals. For other systems, simulation must be used to find a solution.

6. The arrivals and services in a queuing model occur in accordance with a Poisson process; i.e., the probability of occurrence of an event is constant, the occurrence of an event is independent of any other, the probability of an occurrence is proportional to the length of the interval, and, if the interval is small enough, the probability of more than one occurrence approaches zero.

   a. The Poisson probability distribution is used to predict the probability of a specified number of occurrences of an event in a specified time interval, given the expected number of occurrences per time unit.

B. Formulas for a Single Service Facility and Random Arrivals of Work Units

If: B = average number of work units arriving in one unit of time
T = average number of work units serviced in one unit of time (if no shortage of work units), and

Given that $\frac{B}{T} < 1$ (otherwise the queue will grow to infinite length), then ...

1. The average number of work units waiting in line or being serviced is $N = \frac{B}{(T - B)}$

2. The average number in the waiting line (Nq) is $Nq = \frac{B^2}{T(T - B)}$

3. The average waiting time before service is $W = \frac{Nq}{B}$

4. CMA questions usually provide any necessary formulas, but it is important to be familiar with them because thoughtful interpretation is often required. Also, multiple-choice questions may consist of four wrong equations and the right one. Therefore, candidates should not neglect the formulas.

5. EXAMPLE: Cars arrive at a toll booth at the average rate of 3 cars per minute. The toll booth can serve (collect tolls from) 6 cars per minute on the average. In the formulas, B = 3, and T = 6

   a. The average number of cars waiting in line or paying tolls at any time is

$$N = \frac{B}{T - B} = \frac{3}{6 - 3} = 1 \text{ car}$$

   b. The average number in the waiting line, not being serviced, is

$$Nq = \frac{B^2}{T(T - B)} = \frac{9}{6(6 - 3)} = 1/2 \text{ car, or one car is waiting half the time}$$

   c. The average waiting time is

$$W = \frac{Nq}{B} = \frac{(1/2)}{3} = 1/6 \text{ minute, or 10 seconds}$$

LEARNING CURVES

A. Learning curves reflect the increased rate at which people perform tasks as they gain experience.

1. The time required to perform a given task becomes progressively shorter.
2. This technique is only applicable to the early stages of production or of any new task.
3. Ordinarily, the curve is expressed in a percentage of reduced time to complete a task for each doubling of cumulative production.

B. Case studies have shown learning curves to be between 60% and 80%. In other words, the time required is reduced by 20% to 40% each time cumulative production is doubled, with 20% being common.

1. One common assumption made in a learning curve model is that the **cumulative average time per unit** is reduced by a certain percentage each time production doubles.
   a. The alternative assumption is that **incremental unit time** (time to produce the last unit) is reduced when production doubles.
2. EXAMPLE: An 80% learning curve would result in the following performance for the lots shown, when run in sequence (top to bottom).

Cumulative Number of Tasks	Average Time/Unit
100	3.0
200	2.4 (3.0 X 80%)
400	1.92 (2.4 X 80%)
800	1.536 (1.92 X 80%)
1,600	1.228 (1.536 X 80%)

C. **Graphical Presentation**

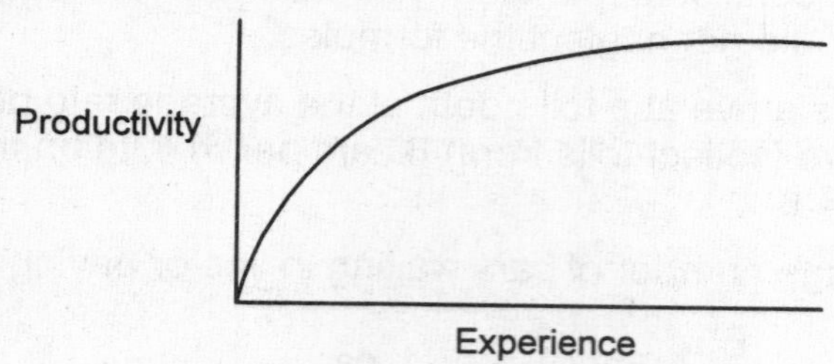

D. If the average time for 100 units in the example above were 3 minutes per unit, the total time would be 300 minutes. At an average time of 2.4 minutes for 200 units, the total time would be 480 minutes. In other words, the additional 100 units required only 180 minutes (480 – 300), or 1.8 minutes per unit.

GAME THEORY

A. Game (or decision) theory is a mathematical approach to decision making when confronted with an "enemy" or competitor.

B. Games are classified according to the number of players and the algebraic sum of the payoffs.

1. In a two-person game, if the payoff is given by the loser to the winner, the algebraic sum is zero and the game is called a zero-sum game.
2. If it is possible for both players to profit, however, it is called a positive-sum game.

C. Mathematical models have been developed to select optimal strategies for certain simple games.

1. Few applications of the mathematics of game theory have been made in business. The concepts can be useful, however.
2. For example, labor negotiations can be viewed as a two-person, nonzero-sum game.

D. Game theorists have developed various decision rules.

1. The **maximax criterion** is a decision rule adopted by risk-seeking, optimistic players who desire the largest possible payoff and are willing to accept high risk. The player determines the payoff for each state of nature expected to arise after each possible decision, ascertains the maximum payoff for each decision, and then chooses the decision with the maximum payoff.
2. A player who uses the **minimax decision criterion** determines the maximum loss for each decision possibility and then chooses the decision with the minimum maximum loss. This rule produces the same result as the maximin technique, which determines the minimum payoff for each decision and then chooses the decision with the maximum minimum payoff. Minimax and maximin are conservative criteria.
3. The **minimax regret criterion** is used by a player who wishes to minimize the effect of a bad decision in either direction. It chooses the decision that has the lowest maximum opportunity cost (profit forgone).
4. The **insufficient reason (Laplace) criterion** may be used when the decision maker cannot assign probabilities to the states of nature arising after a decision. The reasoning is that, if no probability distribution can be assigned, the probabilities must be equal, and the expected value is calculated accordingly; i.e., for each decision, the payoffs for the various states of nature are simply added, and the decision with the highest total is chosen. This criterion is risk-neutral.
5. An **expected value criterion** might be used by a risk-neutral player, that is, one for whom the utility of a gain is the same as the disutility of an equal loss.

MARKOV ANALYSIS

A. Markov processes are useful in decision problems in which the probability of the occurrence of a future state depends only on the current state.

1. A characteristic of the Markov process is that the initial state matters less and less as time goes on, because the process will eventually reach its steady state.
2. EXAMPLE: A machine tool may be in one of two states, in adjustment or out of adjustment. The machine moves from one state to the other in one day with the following probabilities:

From \ To	In adjustment	Out of adjustment
In adjustment	.8	.2
Out of adjustment	.6	.4

If the machine is in adjustment on day 1, the probabilities of its being in or out of adjustment are as follows:

			IN	OUT		Pr
On day 2	(1.0) x (.8)	=	.8	(1 – .8)	=	.2
On day 3	(.8) x (.8) + (.2) x (.6)	=	.76	(1 – .76)	=	.24
On day 4	(.76) x (.8) + (.24) x (.6)	=	.752	(1 – .752)	=	.248
On day 5	(.752) x (.8) + (.248) x (.6)	=	.7504	(1 – .7504)	=	.2496

The process approaches a probability of .75 on day n of being in adjustment.

SIMULATION

A. Simulation is a technique for experimenting with logical/mathematical models using a computer. Despite the power of mathematics, many problems cannot be solved by known analytical methods because of the behavior of the variables and the complexity of their interactions, e.g.,

1. Corporate planning models
2. Financial planning models
3. New product marketing models
4. Queuing system simulations
5. Inventory control simulations

B. Experimentation is neither new nor uncommon in business. Building a mockup of a new automobile, having one department try out new accounting procedures, and test-marketing a new product are all forms of experimentation. In effect, experimentation is organized trial-and-error using a model of the real world to obtain information prior to full implementation.

C. Models can be classified as either physical or abstract.

1. Physical models include automobile mockups, airplane models used for windtunnel tests, and breadboard models of electronic circuits.
2. Abstract models may be pictorial (architectural plans), verbal (a proposed procedure), or logical/mathematical. Experimentation with logical/mathematical models can involve many time-consuming calculations. Computers have alleviated much of this costly drudgery and have led to the growing interest in simulation for management.

D. The simulation procedure has five steps.

1. Define the objectives. The objectives serve as guidelines for all that follows. The objectives may be to aid in the understanding of an existing system (e.g., an inventory system with rising costs) or to explore alternatives (e.g., the effect of investments on the firm's financial structure). A third type of objective is estimating the behavior of some new system such as a production line.
2. Formulate the model. The variables to be included, their individual behavior, and their interrelationships must be spelled out in precise logical/mathematical terms. The objectives of the simulation serve as guidelines in deciding which factors are relevant.
3. Validate the model. Some assurance is needed that the results of the experiment will be realistic. This assurance requires validation of the model -- often using historical data. If the model gives results equivalent to what actually happened, the model is historically valid. There is still some risk, however, that changes could make the model invalid for the future.
4. Design the experiment. Experimentation is sampling the operation of a system. For example, if a particular policy is simulated on an inventory model for two years, the results are a single sample. With replication, the sample size can be increased and the confidence level raised. The number of runs to be made, length of each run, measurements to be made, and methods for analyzing the results are all part of the design of the experiment.
5. Conduct the simulation -- evaluate results. The simulation should be conducted with care. The results are analyzed using appropriate statistical methods.

E. The **Monte Carlo technique** is often used in simulation to generate the individual values for a random variable.

1. The performance of a quantitative model under uncertainty may be investigated by randomly selecting values for each of the variables in the model (based on the probability distribution of each variable) and then calculating the value of the solution. If this process is performed a large number of times, the distribution of results from the model will be obtained.
2. EXAMPLE: Suppose a new marketing model includes a factor for a competitor's introduction of a similar product within one year. Management estimates there is a 50% chance that this will happen. For each simulation, this factor must be determined, perhaps by flipping a coin, or by putting two numbers in a hat and selecting one number. Random numbers between 0 and 1 could be generated. Numbers under one-half reveal a similar product; numbers over one-half reveal no similar product.

F. The advantages of simulation are as follows:

1. Time can be compressed. A corporate planning model can show the results of a policy for 5 years into the future, using only minutes of computer time.
2. Alternative policies can be explored. With simulations, managers can ask "what if" questions to explore possible policies, providing management with a powerful new planning tool.
3. Complex systems can be analyzed. In many cases simulation is the only possible quantitative method for analyzing a complex system such as a production or inventory system, or the entire firm.

G. The limitations of simulation are as follows:

1. Cost. Simulation models can be costly to develop. They can be justified only if the information to be obtained is worth more than the costs to develop the model and carry out the experiment.
2. Risk of error. A simulation results in a prediction of how an actual system would behave. As in forecasting, there is always a chance that the prediction will be in error.

SENSITIVITY ANALYSIS

A. After a problem has been formulated into any mathematical model, it may be subjected to sensitivity analysis.

1. A trial-and-error method may be adopted in which the sensitivity of the solution to changes in any given variable or parameter is calculated.
   a. The risk of the project being simulated may also be estimated.
   b. The best project may be one that is least sensitive to changes in probabilistic (uncertain) inputs.

B. In linear programming problems, sensitivity is the range within which a constraint value, such as a cost coefficient or any other variable, may be changed without changing the optimal solution. Shadow price is the synonym for sensitivity in that context.

ARTIFICIAL INTELLIGENCE AND EXPERT SYSTEMS

A. Artificial intelligence (AI) is computer software designed to perceive, reason, and understand. In the business area, emphasis has been on the particular form of AI termed expert systems.

B. AI is largely based on powerful reasoning capabilities, but most human decision making hinges on knowledge (i.e., remembering relationships between variables based on experience).

   1. Human reasoning is based, for the most part, on IF-THEN processes (also known as production and situation-action rules), which are also being developed in AI software.

C. The advantage in a business environment is that, relative to human experts, AI systems

   1. Can work 24 hours a day
   2. Will not become ill, die, or be hired away
   3. Are extremely fast processors of data, especially if numerous rules (procedures) must be evaluated

D. The development of artificial intelligence and its subfield, expert systems, has been identified by the AICPA Future Issues Committee as one of the major concerns facing the accounting profession. Expert systems rely on a computer's ability to think and make decisions in a human way.

   1. An expert system is an interactive system that asks a series of questions and uses knowledge gained from a human expert to analyze answers and come to a decision.
   2. Expert systems were originally developed to make decisions in areas that did not have enough human experts to make decisions. Some of the earliest expert systems were used by doctors to diagnose diseases.
   3. Experimental work is being done with expert systems in taxation, financial accounting, managerial accounting, and auditing.

E. An expert system can be separated into six components -- knowledge database, domain database, database management system, inference engine, user interface, and knowledge acquisition facility. The knowledge database and domain database together are referred to as the knowledge domain.

   1. **Knowledge database** contains the rules used when making decisions on certain topics. The facts about certain topics are contained in the **domain database.** These facts are used as a basis for comparison when the system matches a pattern of events or facts with a decision situation.
   2. **Inference engine** is the heart of the expert system's processing. It performs the deductive thinking and logic portion of the processing.
   3. Rules from the knowledge database, facts from the domain database, and input from the system user are all used by the inference engine.

F. An expert system is developed using a continuous process of revision. As new knowledge or decision-making strategies become available, prior systems must be revised.

G. The most time-consuming and costly part of developing an expert system is gathering the knowledge of experts and decision makers.

H. By using expert systems, accountants can fulfill their duties in less time and with more uniformity. An expert system makes it more likely that different decision makers will come to the same conclusions given the same set of facts.

1. An expert system is useful in applying financial accounting standards in a consistent manner when preparing financial statements or performing audits.
2. Expert systems make compliance with tax laws much easier since all rules can be programmed into the computer. Tax planning has also benefited from the use of expert systems.
3. For management control, expert systems can be used to supplement management information systems by providing models of decisions used for planning and control.
4. For auditing, an expert system can be used to choose an audit program, select a test sample type and size, determine the level of error, perform analytical procedures, and then make a judgment decision based on the findings.

I. Expert systems are becoming so simple that virtually anyone can develop them, even without knowledge of computer programming. This result is accomplished through the use of programs known as **shells**. An expert system shell is a flexible system that provides the framework for developing a customized expert system. It is quite advantageous for a company that wishes to take its own expert knowledge and design an expert system to fit its needs.

J. The field of expert systems is an area of artificial intelligence that is open to development of new ideas and applications. These systems can provide accountants and auditors with a powerful tool for expanding and developing their activities. Even very small companies will be able to perform activities that only large firms could handle in the past.

K. **Neural networks** are another form of artificial intelligence. A neural network learns from its mistakes in that it changes its knowledge database when informed of the accuracy of its decisions.

STUDY UNIT 32
INFORMATION SYSTEMS

INTRODUCTION

Much business information is produced through the use of computer-based systems. The management accountant, as a provider of a portion of this information, is involved with these systems in the following three roles:

1. **Designer** -- a participant in the development of these systems
2. **Auditor** -- an evaluator of the quality of the system's output, the system's composition, and the administration of the system's function
3. **User** -- a recipient of the output of these systems; and a source of input for decision making

This study unit concentrates on systems concepts and the technical computer knowledge necessary to these functions of the management accountant. Study Unit 16, Internal Control, and Study Unit 17, External Auditing, in Part 2 are also relevant. In the current CMA examination format, 20% to 30% of the questions in Part 4 will be on information systems.

SYSTEMS OVERVIEW

A. A **system** is a regularly interacting or interdependent group of items (subsystems) forming a unified whole.
   1. Each system, e.g., a business, in turn is part of a larger system, such as the national economy.
   2. The **boundary** of a system defines its physical limits and segregates it from the **environment**.
   3. A system performs its processing functions within the boundary.
      a. **Inputs** flow into and **outputs** flow out of the system through the boundary.
      b. A boundary shared with another system is an **interface**.

4. To attain the objectives for which the system was established, it must have regulatory mechanisms (**controls**) to prevent, detect, and correct variances from standards.
   a. **Feedback loops** are essential to control.
   b. Another necessary aspect of control is stated by the **law of requisite variety**: Countermeasures must be available for the adjustment of out-of-control conditions; if the variety of countermeasures is not comparable to the variety of deviations, increased **entropy** (disorder in the system) will result.
5. The highest order systems (a large business organization is an example) have substantial memory (data storage), the ability to learn (to modify its decision rules), and the capacity to choose and achieve new objectives.
6. Feedback control systems are sometimes supplemented by **feedforward** control systems. The objective of a feedforward control system is to predict potential variations from plans so that adjustments can be made to prevent problems either before they occur or before they become too serious.

B. An **information system** transforms raw materials (**data**) into knowledge useful for decision making (**information**).

1. The following activities are involved in the transformation:
   a. The system must **acquire** (capture) data from sources within or outside the entity.
   b. Quantitative data must be **measured**.
   c. Data are **recorded** on source documents.
   d. The data are **checked** for accuracy.
   e. **Classification** of data is necessary to determine the appropriate treatment.
   f. **Aggregation** or summarization may occur before data are processed.
   g. **Transmission** of data from the point of acquisition to a processing location may be required.
   h. **Transcription** of data from source documents to another medium is often a step preliminary to processing.
   i. **Grouping** similar items may facilitate processing.
   j. Within a group of items, **sorting** on the basis of primary and/or secondary keys is another processing step.
   k. **Comparison and calculation** are logical and arithmetic steps, respectively, that transform quantitative data.
   l. Before, during, and after processing, data must be temporarily or permanently **stored**, for example, in files or databases.
   m. The system must be able to **retrieve** (obtain access to) stored data.
   n. **Updating** keeps stored data current.
   o. **Reports**, including replies to inquiries (whether or not interactive and/or unscheduled), contain the system's information output in a form understandable by users.
   p. **Communication** of output to internal or external users is the ultimate purpose of the system.
   q. At all stages, effective **control** should ensure the integrity of the data.

2. The following are the essential components of an information system model:
   a. The **input** component of the system consists of inflows from the environment necessary for maintenance (such as heat and light), data to be processed, and control information (for example, feedback and computer program instructions).
   b. **Output** includes outflows of information to users and waste; a reduction in the latter improves system efficiency.
   c. The **transformation** of inputs into outputs is accomplished by a processing component with three subsystems.
      1) **Storage** (memory) is necessary for retaining inputs (data and instructions), partial results, and finished output until processing is complete and transmittal is feasible.
      2) An **arithmetic-logic unit** manipulates the data in mathematical and logical ways (e.g., addition and comparison of numbers).
      3) The **control subsystem** manages the transformation process by overseeing the storage of data and instructions, their transfer to and from the arithmetic-logic unit, and the ultimate transmittal of the results to the output component of the system.

C. A **management information system (MIS)** provides information for management decisions.
1. A more complex definition is given by Gordon Davis and Margrethe Olson [*Management Information Systems* (2nd). McGraw-Hill, 1985. p. 6].

   An integrated, user-machine system for providing information to support operations, management, analysis, and decision-making functions in an organization. The system uses computer hardware and software; manual procedures; models for analysis, planning, control, and decision-making; and a database.

   a. An **integrated system** is planned as a group of subsystems within which applications are designed for compatibility and avoidance of redundancy.
      1) An overall plan for the MIS should be developed to ensure that it avoids duplicate or inconsistent applications, provides for common standards and procedures, allows many users to share applications and data, and is subject to effective control.
   b. An MIS segregates applications and their supporting data by creating a **database** to reduce data redundancy, exercise control, and improve data quality.
      1) A database management system is the software that integrates the data to achieve these purposes (see Databases on page 678).
   c. An MIS also includes embedded decision tables or **decision models** that permit processing of data to produce information directed toward particular decisions, such as those related to inventory control, budget analysis, or investment.
      1) Models may be generalized and useful for many decisions or highly specific, but they are often most useful when they permit a manager the flexibility to use the interactive capacity of the system to explore the ramifications of a problem.

a) **Decision support systems (DSSs)** are extensions of the MIS concept that are primarily useful for semistructured problems, that is, those requiring the decision maker to exercise judgment in controlling the process but allowing for certain aspects of the problem to be preprogrammed. A DSS does not automate a decision but rather provides tools for the user to employ in applying his/her own insight and judgment.

i) The system should be interactive to permit the user to explore the problem by using the computational capacities, models, and data resources (internal and external) of the DSS.

- The system needs flexible access through reliable communications, ready availability of terminals, and possibly stand-alone microcomputers.
- Models tend to be relatively simple, and system development requires substantial involvement by the user because of the need for it to evolve as the user gains experience and new conditions emerge.

d. The trend in the development of MISs is from data processing to **information resources management**, which encompasses at least the overlapping activities of data processing, telecommunications, and office automation.

2. An **executive information system** (EIS) focuses on strategic (long-range) objectives and gives immediate information about an organization's critical success factors. Information is traditionally supplied from nontraditional computer sources. An EIS can be used on computers of all sizes.

3. Davis and Olson (pp. 15-16) suggest that MISs can be classified by function or by activity.

a. **Functions** include

1) **Marketing** -- sales analysis, forecasting, and planning
2) **Manufacturing** -- production planning and cost control
3) **Logistics** -- planning and control of purchasing and inventory management
4) **Personnel** -- planning for the human resource function, evaluation of employees, and payroll
5) **Finance and accounting** -- capital budgeting, income measurement, and financial and cost analysis
6) **Information processing** -- planning systems development and cost-benefit analysis
7) **Top management** -- strategic planning and allocation of resources

b. **Activities** include

1) **Strategic planning** -- setting overall organizational objectives and drafting strategic plans
2) **Management control** -- budgeting and resource allocation
3) **Operational control** -- detailed scheduling of operations and performance supervision
4) **Transaction processing** -- receipts and disbursements, ordering and shipping

D. An **accounting information system (AIS)** is a subsystem of an MIS that processes financial and transactional data relevant to managerial as well as financial accounting.

1. An AIS is concerned not only with transactions with external parties (e.g., customers, suppliers, governments, owners, and creditors) reflected in financial statements prepared in conformity with GAAP, but also with the internal activities recorded in the cost accounting system and the preparation of related reports and analyses (e.g., production reports, pro forma financial statements, budgets, and cost-volume-profit analyses).

2. The major **components** of an AIS are the

   a. **General ledger systems**, including general ledger accounting, budgeting, responsibility accounting, cost allocation, and profitability determination

   b. **Cash receipts-disbursements systems**, including payroll, accounts receivable, and accounts payable

   c. **Production systems**, including materials inventory, work-in-process, cost estimation, and scheduling

   d. **Marketing**, including finished goods, order processing, and marketing (sales) analysis

E. **Computer System Evolution**

1. First generation computers became commercially available around 1950. They used vacuum tubes and were large and slow. Entry of data and programs was by punched cards.

2. Second generation computers used transistors, buffers, magnetic core storage, and tape drives. The result was greater speed and reliability, lower cost, and smaller size.

3. Third generation computers incorporated integrated circuits. This generation of systems also made substantial use of magnetic disks, terminals, and data communications hardware.

4. Fourth generation computers employ very large-scale integrated circuits, multiprogramming, vertical storage, and microprocessors.

5. Fifth generation. According to Davis and Olson (*Management Information Systems*, 2nd Ed., New York: McGraw Hill, 1985, p. 660), the next (fifth) generation of computer systems, as defined by the Japanese R&D project, has these functions:

   a. Increased intelligence and ease of use. The system will support human judgment and decision making.

   b. Input or output via voice, graphics, images, and documents

   c. Processing using natural language

   d. Specialized knowledge bases

   e. Learning, association, and inference capabilities

SYSTEMS DEVELOPMENT AND DESIGN

A. The **systems development life cycle** approach is the most common methodology applied to the development of large, highly structured application systems. The life cycle approach is based on the idea that an information system has a finite life span that is limited by the changing needs of the organization. This cycle is analytically divisible into stages. A new system life cycle begins when the inadequacy of the current system leads to a decision to develop a new or improved system. This method is a structured process for controlling the creative activity required to devise, develop, and implement an information system. The process is described in varying terms by different writers, but the nature and sequence of the steps are essentially the same.

1. Davis and Olson (p. 571) suggest that the cycle has the three steps given below.
   a. **Definition**. The following phases are involved in this stage:
      1) A **proposal** for a new or modified application should be prepared indicating the need, the support for it within the organization, and scheduling considerations (timing of the project, employee availability, etc.).
      2) **Feasibility studies** should be conducted to determine whether the system is technically, economically, and operationally feasible.
         a) Availability of required technology, cost-benefit considerations, motivation of interested parties, timing of the project, existence of necessary resources, and prospects of successful implementation are aspects of feasibility.
      3) **Information requirements** must be ascertained, including the inquiries to be made by users, reports generated, database needs, and operating characteristics.
      4) The **general (conceptual) design** contains the users' description of the application, required inputs and outputs, the functions to be carried out, an overview of the processing flow (relationship of the most important programs, files, inputs, and outputs) and control structure, and outlines of documentation.
   b. **Development**
      1) **Physical system design**
         a) This step involves work by specialists to develop specifications for
            i) Work flow and programs (but not coding)
            ii) Controls and points where they should be implemented
            iii) Hardware
            iv) Security measures, including backup
            v) Data communications
            vi) Quality assurance testing for the balance of the development process
         b) One approach to design of the physical system is **top-down design**, which is the practice of defining a system by its general purpose and then progressively refining the level of detail in the form of a hierarchy.
            i) The top-down method begins with analysis of broad organizational goals, objectives, and policies as the bases for the design process. This step requires an understanding of the entity's environment and significant activities.

ii) The next step is to determine the decisions to be made by managers and the information required to make those decisions. The necessary reports, databases, inputs, processing methods, and equipment specifications can then be defined.

iii) The weakness of the top-down approach is that it tends to concentrate on managers' information needs at the expense of the design of efficient transaction processing at the operational level.

c) **Structured design** of the physical system is a modular approach. Each module (subsystem) is functionally defined, and the degree of interdependence among the modules is minimized. This process simplifies development and enhances adaptability of the components of the system but requires careful definition of modules and the linkages (interfaces) between them.

d) **HIPO** (Hierarchy-Input-Process-Output) is a documentation technique developed by IBM that relies on stylized charts depicting increasingly more detailed levels of the system.

2) **Physical database design** depends on the existing system.

a) New files or a new database may have to be designed.

b) Modifying an existing database may be feasible.

c) If the existing database provides for the new application, modification may not be necessary.

3) **Program development** entails coding programs in accordance with the specifications in the physical design phase and then testing the results.

a) **Structured programming** is a method of developing computer programs that divides the system's set of programs into discrete modules by functional specifications.

i) The objective is to create modules that are independent logical units, each of which has one entry and one exit point. Data sharing among modules should also be minimized.

ii) This method reduces the complexity created when instructions jump back and forth among different sections of the program.

iii) Each module can be coded by a separate team, which facilitates security because no one group knows the complete set of programs.

iv) The development process is expedited because several programming teams can be working simultaneously.

v) Maintenance is facilitated because a change or patch would only need to be module-specific, a less complicated procedure than fitting a patch to a complex, multifunction program.

4) **Procedure development** includes writing technical manuals, forms, and other materials for all persons who will use, maintain, or otherwise work with the system.

a) A **printer layout chart** is a gridded spacing chart that is an aid to designing documents and reports generated as hardcopy paper output by a printer.

5) **Flowcharting** is an essential aid in the development process. For information on flowcharting, see Study Unit 16, Internal Control, in Part 2.

a) Other means of documenting the decision logic reflected in systems are matrices, decision tables, decision trees, and pseudocode.

c. **Installation and operation**

1) Training and educating system users is important not only for proper use of the system but also to offset the resistance of users whose jobs may have been substantially changed.

2) Acceptance testing by users of inputs, outputs, programs, and procedures is necessary to determine that the new system meets their needs.

3) Systems conversion is the final testing and switchover.

a) **Parallel operation** is the operation of the old and new systems simultaneously until satisfaction is obtained that the new system is operating as expected.

b) **Pilot operation** (modular or phase-in conversion) is the conversion to the new or modified system by module or segment, e.g., one division, department, function, or branch of the company at a time. One disadvantage is the extension of the conversion time.

4) Systems follow-up or post-audit evaluation is a subsequent review of the efficiency and effectiveness of the system after it has operated for a substantial time (e.g., 1 year).

2. Another paradigm for the life cycle approach is the following:

a. **Investigation**. The first step in systems development is identification and definition of a need relative to organizational objectives.

b. **Analysis**. The next step is to determine the scope of the required study and to proceed with a thorough analysis of the existing system.

c. **Systems design**. These steps lead to the general design of a new system. If the new system proves to be justified, the decision is then made to proceed with its implementation.

d. **Implementation**. Detailed systems design, including development and design of data files, is part of the implementation phase.

e. **Maintenance**. Following implementation, systems maintenance must be undertaken by systems analysts and applications programmers throughout the life of a system. Maintenance is the redesign of the system and programs to meet new needs or to correct design flaws. Ideally, these changes should be made as part of a regular program of preventive maintenance.

B. **Prototyping** (an experimental assurance process) is costly and time-consuming and thus is not currently the most common approach. It entails developing and putting into operation successively more refined versions of the system until sufficient information is obtained to produce a satisfactory design.

C. Systems development should be overseen by an **information systems steering committee**, which consists of top-level managers representing the functional areas of the organization, such as information systems, accounting, and marketing.

1. It provides overall guidance for information systems activities to assure that goals are consistent with those of the organization. Thus, the steering committee establishes priorities for implementing applications and either performs or approves high-level planning.

COMPUTER HARDWARE

A. **Hardware** is the configuration of electronic, magnetic, and mechanical devices that perform input, processing, output, storage, control, communications, and data preparation functions in a computer system.

B. **Central Processing Unit (CPU)**. All computers have a CPU that works in conjunction with peripheral devices.

1. The CPU is the main element of a computer system. The major function of the CPU is to fetch stored instructions and data, decode the instructions, and carry out the instructions in the arithmetic-logic unit (ALU). The principal components of the CPU are the arithmetic-logic unit and the control unit.

   a. The control unit directs and coordinates the entire computer system.

   b. Primary storage is closely connected to the CPU in the control processor. It consists of electronic components that store letters, numbers, and special characters used in processing.

      1) **Random-access memory (RAM)** -- a temporary storage area used to hold programs and data during processing. Data may be read from or written on RAM. A power interruption causes erasure of RAM.

      2) **Read-only memory (ROM)** -- a permanent storage area used to hold the basic low-level programs and data. A power interruption does not erase data written on ROM or on magnetic secondary storage devices.

      3) **Buffer memory (or buffer)** -- a temporary storage area within the CPU used to hold data during input and output operations. It compensates for the vast differences in speed between the CPU and the slower input and output units.

   c. The ALU is the circuitry in the CPU that performs the arithmetic and logic operations.

2. Computer systems are typically classified by computing power dictated by CPU speed, memory capacity, and hardware architecture (and thus cost).

   a. **Microcomputers (personal computers)** range in price and performance from low-end personal computers to powerful desktop models to high-performance workstations. Because of the large number of personal computers in use and aggressive pricing strategies, current personal computer prices have become very attractive. Personal computers have also crossed into the minicomputer arena by providing comparable power and multi-user capabilities previously unavailable until recent technological improvements. By adding a modem and communications software, the microcomputer can also serve as a smart terminal for interface with either mini or large general-purpose computers. Accordingly, many of the same control and security concerns that apply to larger computers also apply to a microcomputer environment.

   b. **Minicomputers** are typically used in multi-user or multi-terminal environments. The systems provide computing power and peripheral device access to a number of users and do not require a special environment for operation. Minicomputers have been used for industrial, general business, communications, and timesharing applications.

   c. **Large, general-purpose (mainframe) computers** are characterized by large memory sizes, large secondary storage capacity, tape drives, high-speed printers, and other peripheral equipment. They often provide data communications, support many terminal users, are capable of handling large databases, and can execute many millions of instructions per second (MIPS). They usually need an air-conditioned, dust-free, humidity-controlled environment. The cost of a large facility may approach $5 million.

C. **Peripheral devices** include equipment, other than the CPU, that provides for input, storage, output, outside communication, or additional facilities. They function much more slowly than the CPU, and a system is said to be input-output bound when the speed of peripheral devices determines the speed of an application's completion.

1. **Data entry devices**

   a. **Video display terminal (VDT)** with an **electronic keyboard** is online equipment that is the most common input device.

      1) A **dumb terminal** has no other functions.
      2) A **smart terminal** has processing capacity.
      3) An **intelligent terminal** has programming capacity.

         a) A microcomputer can serve as an intelligent terminal if it is connected to another computer.

      4) A **terminal emulator** permits a microcomputer to interface with a mainframe.

   b. **Magnetic ink character reader (MICR)** is used by a bank to read the magnetic ink on checks.

   c. **Optical character reader (OCR)** does not need special ink and can read bar codes and alphanumeric characters.

      1) **Turnaround document** is a computer output prepared in such a way that it can eventually be used as a source document for an input transaction. For example, an optical character recognition document might be used as a sales invoice to be mailed to a customer and returned with the payment. Thus, no new document would have to be prepared to record the payment.

   d. **Magnetic tape and disk drives** permit entry of data into primary storage from tapes and disks. These devices also serve an output function by transferring data from primary storage to tapes, disks, or output devices such as printers.

   e. Point-of-sale terminals, portable data entry terminals, scanners, and automated teller machines are other input devices.

   f. An alternative to keyboard and text-based input is the use of a **computer mouse**. Its point and click function controls a cursor on the video display screen. The user pushes a button on the mouse to choose the command indicated by the cursor.

   g. **Touch screen** technology provides another limited alternative to keyboard input.

   h. **Voice recognition** input devices are still another limited alternative to keyboard input. These systems can accept simple commands by comparing the speaker's voice patterns with prerecorded patterns.

2. **Output devices**

   a. A **VDT** (also known as a cathode ray tube or CRT) can be used to display output and thus is also the most common output device.

b. **Printers** are the most common devices used solely for output.

1) They include

a) **Impact printers**, e.g., a typewriter or dot matrix printer
b) **Nonimpact printers**, e.g., laser, inkjet, and thermal transfer printers

2) Printers may print one character, one line, or one page at a time at varying speeds and with varying quality.

3) Some newer printers have limited processing ability.

c. **COM (Computer Output to Microfilm)** is a device that records output directly on microfilm. It frequently takes the place of the printer or magnetic tape output.

3. **Storage devices**

a. **Floppy disk drives** serve as low capacity backup devices. The most common floppy disks are 3½" and 5¼" with capacities up to 1.44 MB and 1.2 MB, respectively.

b. **Hard disk drives** provide a permanent location for data and system files. Hard drives can be internal (i.e., fixed) or removable.

c. **Magnetic tape drives** are primarily used for system backup and data transfer (streaming tape, DAT tape, 1600 bytes per inch or 6250 bpi tape reels).

d. **CD-ROM (compact disk-read only memory) drives** are laser-optical disks that are almost identical to CD-audio disks. They contain prerecorded information and provide capacities of over 600 MB. Write once, read many (WORM) versions are also available.

e. **Floptical disks** provide the size advantage of 3½" floppy disks with the data capacity advantage of CD-ROM disks, providing capacities up to 20 MB.

4. **Other peripheral equipment**

a. **Controllers** are hardware units designed to operate (control) specific input or output units, e.g., card-reader controllers or magnetic-tape controllers. These devices eliminate the need for the CPU to operate such devices.

b. **Channels** are hardware units located within or outside the CPU that are designed to handle the transfer of data into or out of primary storage (memory). Thus, the CPU need not handle the transfer of data.

c. A **console** consists of a VDT, a keyboard, and a printer. It is used for communication between the operator or maintenance engineer and the computer.

1) It permits the computer to exchange instructions with the operator, logs jobs, and provides a printout of activity that can be reviewed by auditors and the control group.

d. A **node** is a hardware device in a network that can act as a message buffer (hold part of the message until the rest is received), switch messages, and serve as an error control. A node can be a computer, controller, or multiplexor.

e. An **emulator** is a hardware device that permits one system to imitate another, that is, to use the same data and programs and obtain the same results as the other system.

f. A performance **monitor** is hardware or software that observes and records system activities, e.g., electrical activity or data about program execution.

COMPUTER SOFTWARE

A. **Software** consists of computer programs, procedures, rules, and related documentation concerned with the operation of a computer system. It may be purchased from vendors or developed internally.

B. **Computer Languages**. Software is written in languages that are comprehensible by the computer either directly or after translation.

1. First generation. **Machine language** is written in a **binary code** (a combination of ones and zeros) unique to the type of computer. It requires no translation.
   a. Each instruction specifies the operation to be performed and the data to be manipulated.
2. Second generation. **Assembly (symbolic) languages** use mnemonic symbols to replace binary code.
   a. One assembly language instruction ordinarily corresponds to one machine language instruction.
   b. A program written in a language other than machine language is a source.
   c. A **language translator** must be used to convert a source program into an **object program** in machine language.
   d. An **assembler** translates assembly language source programs into machine language.
3. Third generation. **Procedural languages** consist of statements each of which corresponds to a group of machine language instructions. These languages are used to describe processing algorithms.
   a. Because each statement uses algebraic or English-like symbols to represent multiple machine language instructions, these languages are more readily learned, and coding is substantially simplified.
   b. Procedural languages also have the advantage of being adaptable to many different computers.
   c. The following are common procedural languages:
      1) **BASIC** is a widely used language for microcomputers but is not often used in large business application processing. BASIC stands for **B**eginner's **A**ll-Purpose **S**ymbolic **I**nstruction **C**ode.
      2) **COBOL** is a programming language consisting of a series of English-like statements. COBOL was designed to be easy to read and, when properly written, easy to maintain. COBOL stands for **CO**mmon **B**usiness **O**riented **L**anguage.
      3) **FORTRAN** is very effective for solving mathematical, engineering, and other types of problems, but not as useful for business applications. FORTRAN stands for **FOR**mula **TRAN**slation.
      4) **PL/1** is a cross between COBOL and FORTRAN, but it has not gained equal acceptance. PL/1 stands for **P**rogramming **L**anguage **1**.
      5) **RPG** stands for **R**eport **P**rogram **G**enerator. Its purpose is to produce business-related reports that do not require complex programming, such as for accounts that require substantial file updating (accounts receivable, accounts payable, and inventory are examples). RPG is not a standardized language.

6) **C** is a general-purpose programming language traditionally used for systems programming, but it has become increasingly popular for developing applications to be ported to different computers.

d. Procedural languages are often translated by a **compiler**. For example, COBOL and FORTRAN are always compiled.

1) After the source program has been translated (compiled) into object code, a computer program known as a **linkage editor** (or linker) must be used to process the object code modules into a single module that can be loaded (entered) into the computer. The linkage editor creates an executable module by resolving the cross-references among dependent modules.

e. Some procedural languages are translated by an **interpreter**, which is a program that translates source code into object code as it is needed during processing; thus, no separate compiling run is necessary because each statement is executed immediately after translation.

1) Greater efficiency in translation and the elimination of the linkage edit step are offset, however, by slower processing speeds and an inability to save the full translation for audit purposes.

2) BASIC may be compiled or interpreted, and most fourth-generation languages (see below) are interpreted.

4. Fourth generation. **Problem-oriented or nonprocedural languages** (i.e., those that are not intended to express a procedure as a specific algorithm) provide still further simplification of the programming task.

a. These interactive, English-like languages permit the unsophisticated user to describe the problem to, and receive guidance from, the computer instead of specifying a procedure.

1) **Query languages** are most often used with databases. They permit reading and reorganization of data but not its alteration.

2) **Program generators** allow the user to create an application program based on requirements entered in a specific format.

a) They differ from query languages because they permit data to be written or altered.

5. Specialized languages

a. Simulation and financial modeling languages have been created to support management decision making, e.g., for use in decision support systems.

b. Other languages have been developed for such purposes as database management and audits (generalized audit software permits an audit through the computer).

1) **Data-definition language** is used in database management systems (see Databases on page 678). It defines

a) The overall structure of a database (called its **schema**)

b) The structure of the portion of the database that each application program is authorized to access (called its **subschema** or external schema)

2) **Data-manipulation language** is also used in database management systems. It is for accessing and processing data from a database.

a) The best known data-manipulation language is Structured Query Language (SQL), which is used with relational database management systems.

3) **Generalized audit software** involves the use of computer software packages (programs) that may allow not only parallel simulation but also a variety of other processing functions, such as extracting sample items, verifying totals, developing file statistics, and retrieving specified data fields.

c. **Job control language (JCL)** is used in job control statements that accompany jobs submitted in a batch processing (delayed update) mode. These statements describe the files to be entered, input and output devices to be used, and the programs to be executed.

6. **Pseudocode** (structured English). In top-down coding, higher-level logic modules are coded in relatively broad form using an informal language (pseudocode). This procedure is necessary because the available programming languages are designed to represent more detailed forms of program design.

C. **Systems software** in machine or assembly language is necessary to facilitate the processing of applications programs by the computer. Systems software, which is ordinarily purchased from vendors, performs such fundamental tasks as language translation, monitoring of data communications, job instruction, control of input and output, file management, sorting data, and access control.

1. The **operating system** (also known as the executive or supervisor) mediates between the applications programs and the computer hardware. It

a. Communicates with the operator or user

1) For example, the operating system may include a graphical user interface with which users may interact. It employs graphic icons to represent activities, programs, and files. The computer mouse is used to make selections.

a) Windows is a graphical user interface shell initially developed by Microsoft to run in conjunction with DOS. Newer operating systems also have this feature.

b) Thus, windowing is the characteristic that allows a computer to display more than one program on the screen at the same time. Each program has its own section of the screen, but only one program is active.

b. Manages job scheduling and accounts for computer usage

c. Controls input and output

d. Assigns storage locations in main memory

e. Protects data in the event of a system malfunction

f. May permit a single configuration of hardware to function in several different modes

1) **Batch mode (single thread)**. Programs are processed from beginning to end without interruption in processing.

2) **Multiprogramming**. The operating system processes a program until an input or output operation is required. Because input or output can be handled by peripheral hardware (channels and controllers), the CPU can begin executing another program's instructions while output is in progress and therefore increase its throughput. Several programs are being processed concurrently, but only one is actually being executed in the CPU.

   a) **Throughput** is the quantity of work processed in a given period. It is used as a measuring tool to evaluate processors.

3) **Multiprocessing**. The operating system in conjunction with multiple CPUs actually executes instructions from more than one program simultaneously.

4) **Virtual storage**. The operating system automatically separates user programs into segments, allowing the user to have access to a memory virtually equivalent to the total of primary and secondary memories. To the user it appears as if unlimited memory is available for programs.

   a) **Paging**. A page is a fixed-length segment of a program. Paging is a memory-swapping technique. The major portion of a program or set of data may be kept in secondary storage while the remainder is held in main memory. This swapping means that the "virtual" capacity of primary storage is greatly expanded.

2. **Access control software** protects files, programs, data dictionaries, processing, etc., from unauthorized access, restricts use of certain devices (e.g., terminals), and may provide an audit trail for both successful and unsuccessful access attempts.
3. **File access managers** provide for organizing and controlling data in a logical manner and for different modes of access (e.g., sequential and/or direct).
4. **Database management systems**. See Databases on page 678.
5. **Library management software** stores, updates, and protects source programs, job command statements, and, in some cases, files and object programs.
   a. This software also logs program changes.
6. **Teleprocessing monitors** control execution of application programs in an interactive (online) system.
7. **Online editors** are useful to programmers for creating and maintaining source programs, files, and job command statements.
8. **Communications controllers** allocate network resources and functions, control the connections between programs and terminals, transfer data between control nodes and terminals, and permit monitoring of network operations and changes in the network's configuration.
9. **Utility programs** are service programs that perform certain standard tasks, such as sorting, merging, copying, and printing file dumps.
10. **Operations management software** provides for tape and disk management and for job scheduling in a batch processing environment.
11. **Software monitor** is a program or package that performs functions similar to those of hardware monitors; thus, it records signals emitted by the system's components (e.g., the number and length of accesses to a disk). It may also perform other tasks such as taking snapshots of internal conditions and indicators at predetermined times. This function is useful for reconstruction of records after a system failure.

12. **Firmware** is software wired permanently into the hardware. An example is read-only memory (ROM).

13. **Kernel program** is a short program that is run on different systems by a potential buyer to provide information about their processing characteristics.

D. **Application software** includes the programs that perform the tasks required by ultimate users, e.g., standard accounting operations.

1. Application programs may be developed internally or purchased from vendors.

   a. Vendor-produced software is in either source or object code, but vendors prefer to sell the latter.

   b. Application software production is obviously a vital aspect of system development, and control over its maintenance (changes to meet new user needs) after implementation is likewise crucial.

2. A **spreadsheet** is one type of application software. It displays a financial model in which the data are presented in a grid of columns and rows. An example is a financial statement spreadsheet.

   a. The model is based on a set of mathematical relationships defined by the user, with specified inputs and outputs. The effects of changes in assumptions can be seen instantly because a change in one value results in an immediate recomputation of related values.

   b. Thus, in designing a spreadsheet model, the first step is to define the problem. This is followed by an identification of relevant inputs and outputs, and the development of assumptions and decision criteria. Finally, formulas must be documented.

   c. Lotus 1-2-3 and VP-Planner are common spreadsheet programs.

BASIC DATA STRUCTURES

A. **Bit (binary digit)** is either 0 or 1 in the binary numbering system. The negative or positive polarity of an electrical charge on a magnetic medium is a means of representing a binary digit.

B. **Byte** is a group of bits (ordinarily six or eight) used to signify a character (a number, letter of the alphabet, or special character, such as a question mark or asterisk).

C. **Field** is an item in a record. It consists of a group of related characters (bytes) providing a unit of data about some entity (e.g., a customer or employee).

D. **Record** is a collection of related fields pertaining to some entity.

1. **Keys** are attributes of logical records that permit them to be sorted. A primary key is the data item(s) that is the principal identifier, e.g., a vendor number in a file of vendors' invoices. A secondary key is an alternative identifier used either for sorting or special processing, e.g., the payment date on a vendor's invoice.

2. **Logical records** are defined in terms of the information they contain. A logical record contains a number of fields relating to that record; e.g., a payroll record might include the Social Security number, the employee's name, the rate of pay, etc.

3. The attributes of the **physical record** vary according to the physical storage device. Thus, a logical record may be divided among a number of physical records either on a magnetic tape or on a disk. A physical record may also contain one logical record.

4. In addition, the various fields constituting a record may be distributed within a database and linked via pointers to maintain the relationship.

5. **Fixed-length computer records** facilitate the handling of data on both disk and tape. They allow data to be blocked, moved, and stored in a standard-size format, thus permitting simpler treatment in programs. To handle variable-sized records, the program would have to modify itself while data are being read and processed.

6. **Variable-length records** use space more efficiently because the storage size can vary with the record size. Data transmission is more efficient with variable-length records because they require less space.

7. **Blocking** means putting a number of logical records into a physical record, i.e., to place a block of logical records between two interblock gaps. This practice allows the computer to read more data at one time. Because reading data is much slower than processing it, blocking effectively increases the throughput of the computer.

8. A **record layout** is used to describe the fields in each logical record of each file used in input, output, and storage. Layout sheets are preprinted forms used as documentation for record layouts.

9. A **pointer** is an identifier that specifies the location of a data item. Pointers are used to connect logically related items, especially those stored in random (direct) access media in a database. A pointer usually consists of a storage address, but it may consist of a key value, not an address. In that case, a search must be made of an index of key values referenced to storage addresses.

10. An **index** is a list of contents of a file or document together with references to their locations, for example, an index of keys and their related addresses.

E. **File** is a logical collection of records, such as those for customer accounts.

1. A **master file** is relatively permanent.
   a. A **transaction file** contains relatively temporary records processed together with a master file for updating purposes.

2. File organization
   a. A **linked list** is a file organization in which each data record has a pointer field containing the address of the next record in the list.
   b. In a **direct file** organization, a randomizing formula or hashing scheme (a transform algorithm) converts a record key into a storage address. This method permits direct access without an index.
   c. The **indexed-sequential-access method (ISAM)** is a system in which records are stored sequentially in a direct access file and organized by a primary key stored in an index record. It does not use pointers. The virtue of an ISAM system is that it permits sequential processing of large numbers of records while providing for occasional direct access.

3. File management concerns creating, maintaining, retrieving information from, updating, and establishing control over data files. Updating totals, storing them in a record, comparing them periodically with record contents, and correcting discrepancies is an example of a file management control.

F. **Volatility** is a commonly used measure of the relative frequency of adds, deletes, and changes to a master file during a specified time period.

G. **Database**. See Databases on page 678.

DATA STORAGE

A. **Internal storage** in the main memory of the computer is made of integrated circuits to store binary representations of characters. Storage locations are measured in thousands of bytes (1 kilobyte = K) and millions of bytes (1 megabyte = M); thus, a 512K computer would have approximately 512,000 storage locations.

1. Early computers used core storage in which binary data were represented by positive or negative directions of magnetization on magnetic material in the shape of rings.
2. Today, **semiconductors** (on-off circuits on silicon chips) are used because of their smaller size and faster access time.

B. **Secondary Storage Media**

1. **Magnetic tape** is a magnetically coated plastic tape on which data can be recorded. A read/write head reads or writes on the tape sequentially as it passes the head. It is the most widely used data archival and backup medium.
   a. Retrieval of information on magnetic tape is limited to **sequential access**; each record on the tape must be read until the desired record is reached.
      1) **Access time** is the interval between the initiation of a call for data by an instruction control unit and the completion of the delivery of the data. For magnetic tape and a tape drive, tape speed, the size of the interblock gap, and tape density (data per inch of tape) determine access time.
2. **Magnetic disk** is a flat circular plate coated on both sides with a magnetic material. The surface of the metal or plastic disk is divided into concentric circles (tracks). Some disks also divide tracks into sectors. Addresses specify the disk, track, and sector. While the disk rotates, data are written or read by a read/write head. The time required for access equals the rotational delay (the time for the disk to revolve to the correct position under the read-write arm) and seek time (the time to position the read-write arm).
   a. Disks allow data to be retrieved through **direct access** without searching through other stored data; thus, random access is possible. They allow the transfer of data to the CPU at a faster rate. Disks also permit **indexed sequential** storage so that data may be accessed directly (e.g., for customer inquiries) or sequentially (e.g., for batch processing).
      1) **Floppy disks** are random access storage media for microcomputers. The most common disk sizes are 3½" and 5¼" with capacities of up to 1.44 MB and 1.2 MB, respectively. They should be distinguished from **hard disks**, which have higher capacity and are made of rigid material.
         a) Data stored on floppy disks only are more susceptible to loss or damage, making controls over physical use very important.
3. **Mass storage devices**. There are many devices that hold very large quantities of information. Although access is not direct and therefore not as fast as magnetic disk (but may be faster than mounting a magnetic tape), their relative slowness is offset by a much lower cost. These devices are typically used to store large amounts of data that are not frequently used (called archival storage).
   a. Microfilm is a popular storage medium because it is relatively inexpensive, is compact, and permits more rapid retrieval than paper documents.
   b. Laser-optical disks (CD-ROM) use the same technology as CD players. Information is recorded and read using light (laser beams). These disks now come in erasable versions, have a very large capacity, and are inexpensive. Their disadvantage is slow access time.

PROCESSING MODES

A. **Batch Mode**. Batch processing is the accumulation and grouping of transactions for processing on a delayed basis. The batch approach is suitable for applications that can be processed at intervals and involve large volumes of similar items, e.g., payroll, sales, inventory, and billing.

B. **Online Mode**. An online processing system is in direct communication with the computer, giving it the capability to handle transactions as they are entered. An online system permits both immediate posting (updating) and inquiry of master files as transactions occur.

   1. **Real-time processing** involves processing an input record and receiving the output soon enough to affect a current decision-making process. In a real-time system, the user interacts with the system to control an ongoing activity. The term online often used with real-time indicates that the decision maker is in direct communication with the computer. **Online, real-time systems** usually permit access to the main computer from multiple remote terminals.

   2. Firms may find it beneficial to incorporate both processing modes into one system. A database may be established for information that must be obtained quickly, for instance, a sales processing system in which credit information must be available to sales personnel on an ongoing basis. However, other processing requirements may take advantage of the speed and control provided in a batch processing system. For example, payroll transactions can be processed quickly and efficiently in a batch mode.

C. A **timesharing** system allows many users to have access through remote terminals to a CPU owned by a vendor of computing services. The CPU services them alternately.

   1. Timesharing is made possible by multiprogramming (see Computer Software on page 669).

D. **Service bureaus** perform batch processing for subscribers.

   1. This off-site mode of processing requires a user to prepare input and then transport it to the bureau, with attendant loss of time and increase in security problems.

E. **Totally Centralized Systems**. All data processing and systems development are done at one data processing center.

   1. All processing is done by one large computer.
   2. Remote users are serviced via data communications channels between themselves and the center.
   3. Terminals at the remote sites are usually dumb terminals (providing communications only, with no stand-alone processing capabilities).
   4. Requests for development of new systems are submitted for the consideration of the centralized systems development group.
   5. The centralized staff is large.
   6. Advantages of total centralization arise primarily from the economies of scale permitted and the strengthening of control.

F. **Totally Decentralized Systems**. Data processing functions are independently developed at each remote site. Each site has its own smaller computer and its own staff.

1. In a completely decentralized system, each computer stands alone, independent of any centralized or other computer.
2. The primary advantages of a decentralized system are that
   a. The individual units' personnel identify more closely with the system.
   b. Development projects are more easily accepted and meet local needs better.
3. Totally centralized and totally decentralized systems represent two ends of a continuum. The essential activities are the planning of data processing activities, systems development, programming, and operations. Any combination of these four is possible, ranging from complete centralization to total decentralization.

G. **Distributed Data Processing**. The advent of cheaper and smaller computers and intelligent or smart terminals (i.e., terminals with processing capabilities) has permitted the development of a somewhat different alternative to centralization or decentralization.

1. In a distributed data processing system, the organization's processing needs are examined in their totality.
2. The decision is not whether an application should be done centrally or locally but, rather, which parts of the application are better performed by small local computers as intelligent terminals and which parts are better performed at some other, possibly centralized, site.
3. In essence, the best distribution of processing tasks within application areas is sought.
4. The key distinction between decentralized and distributed systems is the interconnection among the nodes (sites) in the network.
5. EXAMPLE: In processing a sales order, order entry edit may be handled by an intelligent terminal. Upon the satisfactory completion of the sales order, the terminal will transmit it to a minicomputer located in a local warehouse. This computer will determine if the item is available by interrogating an inventory file maintained at the organization's manufacturing plant. If the item is available, the necessary paperwork is produced locally at the warehouse, and the clerk at the terminal is notified. If it is not available, the manufacturing plant's computer determines the probable time of delay before the item is available. This information is transmitted via the local warehouse computer to the terminal. If this delay is acceptable to the customer, the necessary production paperwork is performed at the manufacturing plant. Notice how the actual processing for the order entry is shared by the intelligent terminal warehouse minicomputer and the manufacturing plant computer.
6. The increased interdependence among processing sites allows greater flexibility in systems design and the possibility of an optimal distribution of processing tasks. The process of deciding on the best distribution of processing capabilities (hardware), safeguards (controls), information (files and databases), and personnel is not easy.
7. Under this form of in-house system, the firm may hire the services of an outside company, which employs the people to run the firm's computer-based system.
8. **Cooperative processing** is a system in which computers in a distributed processing network can share the use of application programs belonging to another end user. The system assigns different machines the functions they perform best in executing a transaction-based application program.
   a. For example, a microcomputer might be used to enter and validate data for the application, and a mainframe might handle file input and output.

DATABASES

A. A database is a series of related files combined to eliminate unnecessary redundancy of data items.

1. EXAMPLE: Consider the various files related to personnel in the conventional record systems of most organizations:

   a. Payroll
   b. Work history
   c. Permanent personnel data

2. The employee number may appear several times in these files. While this is necessary when each file is stored and processed separately, it does represent a great deal of redundancy.

3. When such data are stored in a database, these individual data items are usually stored only once.

   a. Physically, the data are stored on direct-access (e.g., magnetic disk) devices.
   b. Also, the data items are stored for efficient access.

      1) The most frequently accessed items are placed in the physical locations permitting the fastest access.

      2) However, when these items were stored in separate files (i.e., conventional systems), the physical location was usually similar to the logical structure of the data.

         a) Items that logically belonged together were stored in physical proximity to one another.

   c. The logical structure of a database may be of various kinds.

      1) A **tree** or **hierarchical structure** arranges data in a one-to-many relationship in which each record has one antecedent but may have an unlimited number of subsequent records.

      2) A **network structure** reduces redundancy by arranging data through development of many-to-many relationships; that is, each item may have multiple antecedent as well as successive relationships.

      3) A **relational structure** organizes data in conceptual tables. One relation (table or file) can be joined together or related to another by the DBMS (see the next page) without pointers or linked lists if each contains one or more of the same fields (also known as columns or attributes). The relational structure is expected to become the most popular structure because it is relatively easy to construct.

         a) Normalization is the term for determining how groups of data items in a relational structure are arranged in records in a database. This process relies on "normal forms," i.e., conceptual definitions of data records, and specified design rules. Normalization is intended to prevent inconsistent updating of data items.

4. The data in a database are subject to the constraint of referential integrity. Thus, if data are collected about something, e.g., a payment voucher, all reference conditions regarding it must be met; thus, for a voucher to exist, a vendor must also exist.

B. In a database, the logical relationship among items is achieved through the use of **pointers** (the disk address of a related item).

1. EXAMPLE: Consider the item EMPLOYEE #.

    a. For employee #123462, there are pointers stored with the employee # indicating the location on the disk of other items logically related to this employee.

2. The separation of the logical and physical structure of items in databases is a fundamental characteristic of databases.

C. **Database Management System (DBMS)** -- an integrated set of computer programs that create the database, maintain the elements, safeguard the data from loss or destruction, and make the data available to applications programs and inquiries

1. It allows programmers and designers to work independently of the physical and logical structure of the database.

2. If it were necessary for programmers and systems designers to know and consider the logical and physical structure of the database, creation of new applications and maintenance of existing applications would be extremely time consuming and therefore expensive.

3. The DBMS contains a description of the logical and physical structure of the database, which is called the **schema**. The schema uses **data definition language**.

    a. The **conceptual schema** is the overall logical model of the database.

    b. The **internal schema** is the physical data storage model for the database. It should be independent of the conceptual schema.

    c. The subschema or **external schema** describes the user's view of a part of the database.

4. A fundamental characteristic of databases is that applications are independent of the database structure; when writing programs or designing applications to use the database, only the name of the desired item is necessary.

5. Reference is made to the item(s) using the data manipulation language, after which the DBMS locates and retrieves the desired item(s).

6. The physical or logical structure of the database can be completely altered without having to change any of the programs using the data items; only the schema requires alteration.

7. Database management software for personal computers includes dBASE IV(R), dBASE III PLUS(R), Paradox, Rbase, and Foxbase. Mainframe DBMSs include DB2 and Oracle.

D. **Other Database Definitions**

1. **Database administrator (DBA)** -- the person who has overall responsibility for developing and maintaining the database

2. **Data dictionary** -- a file, either computer or manual, that describes the use of data from the database in applications. It provides a mapping from the database to applications and vice versa.

3. **Database mapping facility** -- software to evaluate and document the structure of the database

E. Storing all related data on one storage device creates security problems.

1. Should hardware or software malfunctions occur, or unauthorized access be achieved, the results could be disastrous.

2. Greater emphasis on security is required to provide backup and restrict access to the database.

3. The responsibility for creating, maintaining, securing, and restricting access to the database belongs to the database administrator.

F. Databases and the associated DBMS permit efficient storage and retrieval of data for formal system applications.

1. They also permit increased ad hoc accessing of data (e.g., to answer inquiries for data not contained in formal system outputs) as well as updating of files by transaction processing.

2. These increased abilities, however, require

a. The use of sophisticated hardware (direct access devices)
b. Sophisticated software (the DBMS)
c. Highly trained technical personnel (database administrator, staff)
d. Increased security controls

3. All of the abilities listed above result in increased cost.

DATA COMMUNICATIONS

A. The movement of data among CPUs and remote devices requires special hardware and software and telecommunications technology.

1. To connect computers and remote terminals, the following devices may be used:

a. **Communications processors** are minicomputers that are also called front-end processors. They perform message switching, move data to primary storage, translate coded data, and otherwise relieve the CPU of certain communications control functions.

1) They are located between the computer and the modem in the network.
2) Nonprogrammable units are known as communications controllers.

b. **Multiplexors** are switching devices that route or channel the flow of data. They intermix the two-way flow of data so that data may flow over one line. A multiplexor channel permits sending more than one message on a communication line (interleaving). Thus, several terminals may be able to share a communication line to a CPU.

1) A **concentrator** is a programmable, more expensive alternative to a multiplexor.

c. **Modem (modulator-demodulator)** is a hardware device to convert digital signals from terminals and the CPU into analog signals for transmission across data (usually telephone) lines. The receiving modem converts the analog signal back to digital form for use by the receiving terminal or CPU.

1) If digital transmission facilities are available, however, a modem is not required. Instead, the user must employ a digital interface or data service unit as a connection with the digital transmission service.

a) Digital transmission is less prone to error because it is less sensitive to electrical interference.

2) One way in which modems may differ is in their **bit rates**, not to be confused with **baud rates**. The bit rate, usually measured in bits per second, is a measurement of the transmission speed. The baud rate is the number of signal changes or cycles per period of time on the phone line and cannot exceed the bandwidth of the communication line.

a) At high speeds, more than one bit may be transmitted by a signal change. Hence, the bit rate may be greater than the baud rate.

b) A telecommunications medium's transmission capacity depends on its frequency, i.e., the number of signal changes or cycles per second that can be sent through the medium. The bandwidth is the range of frequencies that a given telecommunications channel can accommodate.

d. **Communications channels** differ from the data channels connecting the CPU and peripheral equipment.

1) They are the communications media for transmitting data and are classified according to their capacity.

a) Narrowband (baseband), e.g., telegraph lines
b) Voiceband, e.g., telephone lines
c) Broadband, e.g., microwave circuits and satellite channels

2. Transmission modes may be asynchronous or synchronous.

a. **Asynchronous** or **start-stop transmission** is used for slow, irregular transmissions, such as from a keyboard terminal. Each character is marked by a start and stop bit.

b. **Synchronous transmission** is used when rapid, continuous transmission is desired. It transfers blocks of characters without start and stop bits but requires that the sending and receiving modems be synchronized.

3. The following are the types of transmission circuits:

a. **Simplex** transmission is in one direction only, such as for display purposes.

b. **Half-duplex** transmission is in both directions but not at the same time. It is appropriate when processing is online but a response is not required.

c. **Duplex** transmission is in both directions at once, which is a necessity for real-time processing.

4. **Teleprocessing** is computer processing via remote terminals. Communications software for teleprocessing is necessarily complex because of the multiple tasks to be performed when many terminals are in simultaneous use.

a. The CPU, the front-end processor, and the concentrator may all have communications software.

b. Communications software performs, among other things, the following functions:

1) Receive input, locate the appropriate program, load it into memory, transmit the input to the program, and pass the output to the user

2) Identify and correct errors and provide for security

a) **Encryption** is a typical security measure. A program codes data prior to transmission. Another program decodes it after transmission.

3) Maintain a log of activity and a database or file of updated records

4) Manage buffers (special storage areas) that hold input before processing

5) Manage the sequencing and proper routing of messages

c. A **protocol** is a set of rules for message transmission among the devices in the network.

1) Each device should adhere to the same protocol.

5. Conducting an electronic meeting among several parties at remote sites is **teleconferencing**. It can be accomplished by telephone or electronic mail group communication software.

a. **Videoconferencing** permits the conferees to see each other on video screens.

b. These practices have grown in recent years as companies have attempted to cut their travel costs.

B. **Types of Networks**

1. **Private networks** are dedicated facilities, e.g., satellites, microwave transmitters, or telephone lines, leased from a common carrier. Hence, no dial-up access is required, and security is enhanced.

2. **Public switched networks** use public telephone lines. This arrangement may be the most economical, but data transmission may be of lower quality, no connection may be available, and security measures may be ineffective.

3. **Value-added networks (VANs)** lease the communications medium of a common carrier (such as telephone lines) but adds value by improving the efficiency of transmissions, for example, by repackaging transmissions to increase speed and by providing error detection and correction services.

4. **Local area network (LAN)** is a local distributed computer system, e.g., within a single office. Computers, communication devices, and other equipment are linked by cable. Special software facilitates efficient data communication among the hardware devices.

a. **Automated (electronic) office** is an extension of a local area network that provides an integrated system of multifunction workstations.

1) The workstation is usually said to be intelligent if it has data processing capacity and stored programs can be modified. Such a workstation usually includes a microcomputer, an output device, disk storage, and communications links. Intelligent workstations are often connected in a local area network and can therefore communicate with each other. Thus, they are not mere stand-alone microcomputers.

2) **Electronic mail** is an application of office automation. It is a computer-based message system (software) that permits transfer, receipt, and storage of messages within or between computer systems via telephone lines. The "mail" consists of electronically transmitted messages. A user's "mailbox" is the storage area allocated for messages. The advantages of electronic mail are high-speed transmission, reduction of message preparation costs, and the possibility of sending or reading messages at a convenient time. Moreover, electronic mail can be read wherever the recipient may be, provided (s)he has access to a terminal and a telephone link. Electronic mail can also be sent to remote offices via modem if the correct software has been configured.

a) A typical system permits a user to answer messages, compose or delete messages, edit, file, forward messages to other users, move items among files, read, retrieve from files, scan contents of files, send messages, and print.

3) An **electronic bulletin board** is a database into which computer users may dial to read or post messages.

5. **Wide area networks (WAN)** provide data communication and file sharing among remote offices.

C. **Network Configurations**

1. **Point-to-point** networks provide a separate, direct link between each remote terminal and the CPU.
2. **Multidrop** (or **BUS**) networks provide links for each terminal to a single communications line connected to the CPU. However, only one terminal may send or receive messages at one time.
    a. A superior but more costly alternative is to use a line-sharing device (a multiplexor or a concentrator) to connect the group of terminals to the CPU.
3. **Ring networks** have no central computer. Each node is a computer that is connected directly to only two other nodes.
4. **Completely connected networks** have direct links among all computer locations.
5. **Star networks** permit each remote computer a direct link to the central location but not to other remote computers.

INTERNAL CONTROL STRUCTURE FOR COMPUTER SYSTEMS

A. **Introduction**. The use of computers in information systems has fundamental effects on the internal control structure, but not on its objectives or basic philosophy. These effects flow from the characteristics that distinguish computer-based from manual processing.

1. **Transaction trails**. A complete trail useful for audit purposes might exist for only a short time or only in computer-readable form.
2. **Uniform processing of transactions.** Computer processing uniformly subjects like transactions to the same processing instructions and thus virtually eliminates clerical error. However, programming errors (or other similar systematic errors in either the hardware or software) will result in all like transactions being processed incorrectly when they are processed under the same conditions.
3. **Segregation of functions.** Many control procedures once performed by separate individuals may be concentrated in computer systems. Hence, an individual who has access to the computer may perform incompatible functions. As a result, other control procedures may be necessary to achieve the control objectives ordinarily accomplished by segregation of functions. Other controls may include, for example,
    a. Adequate segregation of functions within the computer processing activities
    b. Establishment of a control group to prevent or detect processing errors or irregularities
    c. Use of password control procedures to prevent incompatible functions from being performed by individuals with online access to assets and records
4. **Potential for errors and irregularities.** The potential for individuals, including those performing control procedures, to gain unauthorized access to data, to alter data without visible evidence, or to gain access (direct or indirect) to assets may be greater in computer systems. Decreased human involvement in handling transactions can reduce the potential for observing errors and irregularities. Errors or irregularities in the design or changing of application programs can remain undetected for a long time.

5. **Potential for increased management supervision.** Computer systems offer management many analytical tools for review and supervision of operations. These additional controls may enhance the internal control structure. For example, traditional comparisons of actual and budgeted operating ratios and reconciliations of accounts are often available for review on a more timely basis. Additionally, some programmed applications provide statistics regarding computer operations that may be used to monitor actual processing.
6. **Initiation or subsequent execution of transactions by computer.** Certain transactions may be automatically initiated or certain procedures required to execute a transaction may be automatically performed by a computer system. The authorization of these transactions or procedures may not be documented in the same way as those in a manual system, and management's authorization may be implicit in its acceptance of the design of the system.
7. **Dependence of other controls on controls over computer processing.** Computer processing may produce reports and other output that are used in performing manual control procedures. The effectiveness of these procedures can be dependent on the effectiveness of controls over the completeness and accuracy of computer processing. For example, the effectiveness of a manual review of a computer-produced exception listing is dependent on the controls over the production of the listing.

B. **Classification of Control Procedures**. The broad categories of controls are defined below.

1. **General controls** concern all computer activities. They relate to all or many computerized accounting activities and often include control over the development, modification, and maintenance of computer programs and control over the use of and changes to data maintained on computer files. General controls encompass
   a. The plan of organization and operation of the computer activity
      1) Organizational controls are concerned with the proper segregation of duties and responsibilities within the computer processing environment.
         a) The responsibilities of systems analysts, programmers, operators, file librarians, and the control group should be performed by different individuals, and proper supervision should be provided.
      2) Operating controls ensure efficient and effective operation within the computer department.
         a) These controls also assure proper procedures in case of data loss because of error or disaster.
         b) Typical operating controls include the proper labeling of all files both internally (machine-readable file header and trailer labels) and externally, halt and error procedures, duplicate files, and reconstruction procedures for files.
   b. The procedures for documenting, reviewing, testing, and approving systems or programs and changes thereto
      1) Program development and documentation controls are concerned with the proper planning, development, writing, and testing of computer application programs.
         a) These activities require proper documentation, including flowcharts, listings, and run manuals for programs already written.
         b) Controls over proper authorization of any changes in existing programs are also necessary.

c. Controls built into the equipment by the manufacturer (hardware controls)

1) Hardware controls assure the proper internal handling of data as they are moved and stored.

a) Hardware controls include parity checks, echo checks, read-after-write checks, and any other procedure built into the equipment to assure data integrity.

d. Controls over access to equipment and data files

1) Access controls provide assurance that only authorized individuals use the system and that usage is for authorized purposes.

a) Such controls include physical safeguards of equipment, proper library security, and passwords.

e. Other data and procedural controls affecting overall computer operations

2. **Application controls** relate to specific tasks performed by the system. They should provide reasonable assurance that the recording, processing, and reporting of data are properly performed. Application controls relate to individual computerized accounting applications, for example, programmed edit controls for verifying customers' account numbers and credit limits.

a. **Input controls** provide reasonable assurance that data received for processing have been properly authorized, converted into machine-sensible form, and identified, and that data (including data transmitted over communication lines) have not been lost, suppressed, added, duplicated, or otherwise improperly changed. Input controls also relate to rejections, correction, and resubmission of data that were initially incorrect.

b. **Processing controls** provide reasonable assurance that processing has been performed as intended for the particular application, i.e., that all transactions are processed as authorized, that no authorized transactions are omitted, and that no unauthorized transactions are added.

c. **Output controls** assure the accuracy of the processing result (such as account listings or displays, reports, magnetic files, invoices, or disbursement checks) and that only authorized personnel receive the output.

C. **Organizational and Operating Controls**

1. **Segregation of duties**. This general control is vital because a segregation of functions (authorization, recording, and access to assets) may not be feasible in a computer environment. For example, a computer may print checks, record disbursements, and generate information for reconciling the account balance, which are activities customarily segregated in a manual system. If the same person provides the input and receives the output for this process, a significant control weakness exists. Accordingly, certain tasks should not be combined.

a. **Systems analysts** are specifically qualified to analyze and design computer information systems. They survey the existing system, analyze the organization's information requirements, and design new systems to meet those needs. These design specifications will guide the preparation of specific programs by computer programmers.

1) Systems analysts should not perform programming tasks or have access to computer equipment, production programs, data files, and input-output controls.

b. **Programmers** design, write, test, and document the specific programs developed by the analyst.

1) Programmers as well as analysts may be able to modify programs, files, and controls and should therefore have no access to them and to the equipment

c. **Computer (console) operators** are responsible for the actual processing of data in accordance with the program run manual and messages received from the system (preferably in hardcopy form for review by the control group). They load data, mount storage devices, and operate the equipment.

   1) The console operator should not be assigned programming duties or responsibility for systems design, and should have no opportunity to make changes in programs and systems as (s)he operates the equipment. Ideally, a console or data conversion operator (see d.) should not have programming knowledge or access to documentation not strictly necessary for his/her work.

d. **Data conversion operators** perform the tasks of data preparation and transmission, for example, conversion of source data to magnetic disk or tape and entry of transactions from remote terminals.

e. **Librarians** should maintain control over and accountability for documentation, programs, and data files.

   1) Librarians should have no access to equipment or the skills to perpetrate fraud.

f. The **data control group** must be independent of systems development, programming, and operations. It receives user input, logs it, transfers it to the computer center, monitors processing, reviews error messages, compares control totals, distributes output, and determines whether error corrections have been made by users.

2. **Backup and recovery policies and procedures**. A computer center should have a reconstruction and recovery plan that will allow it to regenerate important programs and data files. The center should create backup (duplicate) copies of data files, databases, programs, and documentation, store backup copies off-site, and plan for auxiliary processing at another site.

   a. It is important in any information processing environment not to lose or otherwise destroy data. Not only is the loss of data a problem, but the organization may also require continuous processing without disruptions. For these reasons, it is imperative that any system have adequate backup and recovery procedures in the event of system failure, power loss, or other potential corruption of data. The procedures implemented will normally be a function of the specific computer environment, type of processing, or storage mode.

      1) **Sequential processing** -- magnetic tape, magnetic disks, and batch processing

         a) **Grandfather-father-son approach**. Over a 3-day period, three generations of master files are generated. These master files are retained during this period along with the transaction files. If the current (son) file is destroyed or damaged, the information can be reconstructed using the father and running the current transaction file against it. If both father and son are destroyed, the grandfather along with the previous and current transaction files can be used to reconstruct the information.

b) **Checkpoint procedures** involve capturing all the values of data and program indicators at specified points and storing these values in another file. If processing is interrupted, it can be resumed at the last checkpoint rather than at the beginning of the run.

2) **Random processing** -- magnetic disks, online processing

a) **Rollback and recovery** -- involves the dumping of the master file's contents and associated data structures onto a backup file. In the event of a faulty run, the dump is used together with the transaction log or file to reconstruct the file.

3) **Database management systems** -- magnetic disks, online processing

a) **Database systems** require a more elaborate backup procedure. Normally, recovery and restart procedures must provide for continued operations during reconstruction of lost information.

b) **Dual logging** involves the use of two transaction logs written simultaneously on two separate storage media.

c) **Before-image/after-image** captures the data values before and after transaction processing and stores them in files. These files can be used to recreate the database in the event of data loss or corruption.

4) **Fully protected systems** have generator or battery backup to prevent data destruction and downtime from electrical power disturbances. Loss of electrical power or voltage fluctuations need not disturb the vulnerable contents of main memory if a noninterruptible system is in place.

5) **Computer virus** is a software program that infects another program by altering its logic. Infection often results in destruction of data.

a) Once infected, a software program can spread the virus to another software program. To date, most viruses have been spread on college campuses where networking is common. Easy access makes a network susceptible to the rapid spread of computer viruses.

b) Ways to minimize computer virus risk in a networked system include

i) Formal security policy

ii) Restricted access

iii) Passwords (updated regularly)

iv) Formal backup-recovery plan

v) Periodic testing with virus detection software

vi) Using anti-virus software on all shareware prior to introducing it into the network

D. Program Development and Documentation Controls

1. **Documentation** is the collection of documents that support and explain data processing applications, including systems development. It is helpful to operators and other users, control personnel, new employees, and auditors as well as programmers and analysts who maintain the old or develop the new system.
   a. Documentation should be secured in a library and access carefully controlled.
   b. It should be subject to uniform standards regarding flowcharting techniques, coding, and modification procedures (including proper authorization).
   c. **System documentation** includes narrative descriptions, flowcharts, the system definition used for development, input and output forms, file and record layouts, controls, change authorizations, and backup procedures.
   d. **Program documentation** contains descriptions, program flowcharts and decision tables, program listings of source code, test data, input and output forms, detailed file and record layouts, change requests, operator instructions, and controls.
   e. **Operating documentation** (computer run manual) provides information about setup, necessary files and devices, input procedures, console messages and responsive operator actions, run times, recovery procedures, disposal of output, and controls.
   f. **Procedural documentation** includes the system's master plan and operations to be performed, documentation standards, procedures for labeling and handling files, and standards for systems analysis, programming, operations, security, and data definition.
   g. **User documentation** describes the system and procedures for data entry, error checking and correction, and formats and uses of reports.
2. Systems and program development controls
   a. Effective systems development requires participation by top management. This can be achieved through a steering committee composed of higher level representatives of system users. The committee approves or recommends projects and reviews their progress.
   b. Studies of the economic, operational, and technical feasibility of new applications will necessarily entail evaluations of existing as well as proposed systems.
   c. Another necessary control is the establishment of standards for system design and programming. These standards represent user needs and system requirements determined during the systems analysis.
   d. Changes in the computer system should be subject to strict control procedures. For example, a written request for an application program change should be made by a user department and authorized by a designated manager or committee.
      1) The program should then be redesigned using a working copy, not the version currently in use. Also, the systems documentation must be revised.
      2) Changes in the program will be tested by the user, the internal auditor, and a systems employee who was not involved in designing the change.
      3) Approval of the documented change and the results of testing should be given by a systems manager. The change and test results may then be accepted by the user.

e. Proposed programs should be tested with incorrect or incomplete data as well as typical data to determine if controls have been properly implemented in the program.

1) Test data should test all branches of the program, including the program's edit capabilities. The edit function includes sequence checks, valid field tests, reasonableness checks, and other tests of the input data.

2) Expected results should be calculated and compared with actual performance. These results should include both accurate output and error messages.

E. **Hardware Controls**

1. **Boundary (storage) protection** protects programs or data from interference (unauthorized reading and/or writing) caused by activity related to other programs or data stored on the same medium. Primary storage locations in the CPU may be protected by features built into the hardware, but boundary protection for disk storage is effected through programming.
2. **Diagnostic routines** check for hardware problems. If built into the equipment, they permit the system itself to give notice of imminent failure.
3. **Dual read**. An input device, such as a tape drive, may read an input twice for comparison.
4. **Dual read-write heads**. A dual head first writes on the storage medium and then reads what was written. If the comparison shows that the data written differ from the data at the source of the transfer, the device will back up and rewrite the data. This process provides a check on recorded information.
5. **Duplicate circuitry**. Dual circuits in the arithmetic-logic unit of the CPU permit calculations to be performed twice and compared.
6. An **echo check** provides for a peripheral device to return (echo) a signal sent by the CPU. For example, the CPU sends a signal to the printer, and the printer, just prior to printing, sends a signal back to the CPU verifying that the proper print position has been activated.
7. **File protection**. All data storage media, except hard disks, have a ring, tab, or notch that can be used to prevent or allow writing.
8. A **parity check** adds the bits in a character or message and checks the sum to determine if it is odd or even, depending on whether the computer has odd or even parity. This check verifies that all data have been transferred without loss. For example, if the computer has even parity, a bit will be added to a binary coded character or message that contains an odd number of bits. No bit is added if a character or message in binary form has an even number of bits.
9. **Preventive maintenance**. Regular servicing avoids equipment failure.
10. **Read-write suppression**. A control on a disk drive may prevent reading from or writing on a disk, e.g., one containing production programs.
11. **Validity checks**. Hardware that transmits or receives data compares the bits in each byte to the permissible combinations in order to determine whether they constitute a valid structure.

F. **Access Controls**. Access controls, such as passwords, ID numbers, access logs, and device authorization tables, prevent improper use or manipulation of data files and programs. They ensure that only those persons with a bona fide purpose and authorization have access to data processing.

1. **Passwords and ID numbers**. The use of passwords and identification numbers is an effective control in an online system to prevent unauthorized access to computer files. Lists of authorized persons are maintained in the computer. The entry of passwords or identification numbers, a prearranged set of personal questions, and the use of badges, magnetic cards, or optically scanned cards may be combined to avoid unauthorized access.
   a. A security card may be used with a microcomputer so that users must sign on with an ID and a password. The card controls the machine's operating system and records access data (date, time, duration, etc.).
2. A **device authorization table** may restrict file access to those physical devices that should logically need access. For example, because it is illogical for anyone to access the accounts receivable file from a manufacturing terminal, the device authorization table will deny access even when a valid password is used.
   a. Such tests are often called **compatibility tests** because they ascertain whether a code number is compatible with the use to be made of the information. Thus, a user may be authorized to enter only certain kinds of data, have access only to certain information, have access but not updating authority, or use the system only at certain times. The lists or tables of authorized users or devices are sometimes called **access control matrices**.
3. A **system access log** records all attempts to use the system. The date and time, codes used, mode of access, and data involved are recorded.
4. **Encrypting** the data before transmission over communications lines makes it more difficult for someone with access to the transmission to understand or modify its contents.
5. A **callback** feature requires the remote user to call the computer, give identification, hang up, and wait for the computer to call the user's authorized number. This control ensures acceptance of data transmissions only from authorized modems.
   a. However, call forwarding may thwart this control.
6. **Controlled disposal of documents**. One method of enforcing access restrictions is to destroy data when they are no longer in use. Thus, paper documents may be shredded and magnetic media may be erased.

G. **Application Controls**

1. **Input controls**
   a. **Edit checks** are programmed into the software. They include
      1) **Error listing**. Editing (validation) of data should produce a cumulative automated error listing that includes not only errors found in the current processing run but also uncorrected errors from earlier runs. Each error should be identified and described, and the date and time of detection should be given. Sometimes, the erroneous transactions may need to be recorded in a suspense file. This process is the basis for developing appropriate reports.
      2) **Field checks** are tests of the characters in a field to verify that they are of an appropriate type for that field. For example, the field for a Social Security number should not contain alphabetic characters.

3) **Financial totals** summarize dollar amounts in an information field in a group of records.

4) A **hash total** is a control total without a defined meaning, such as the total of employee numbers or invoice numbers, that is used to verify the completeness of data. Thus, the hash total for the employee listing by the personnel department could be compared with the total generated during the payroll run.

5) **Limit and range checks** are based on known limits for given information. For example, hours worked per week is not likely greater than 45.

6) **Preformatting**. To avoid data entry errors in online systems, a screen prompting approach may be used that is the equivalent of the preprinted forms routinely employed as source documents. The dialogue approach, for example, presents a series of questions to the operator. The preformatted screen approach involves the display of a set of boxes for entry of specified data items. The format may even be in the form of a copy of a transaction document.

7) **Reasonableness (relationship) tests** check the logical correctness of relationships among the values of data items on an input and the corresponding master file record. For example, it may be known that employee John Smith works only in departments A, C, or D; thus, a reasonableness test could be performed to determine that the payroll record contains one of the likely department numbers. In some texts, the term reasonableness test is defined to encompass limit checks.

8) **Record count** is a control total of the number of records processed during the operation of a program.

9) **Self-checking digits** may be used to detect incorrect identification numbers. The digit is generated by applying an algorithm to the ID number. During the input process, the check digit is recomputed by applying the same algorithm to the code actually entered.

10) **Sequence checks** determine that records are in proper order. For example, a payroll input file is likely to be sorted into Social Security number order. A sequence check can then be performed to verify record order.

11) **Sign checks** assure that data in a field have the appropriate arithmetic sign. For example, hours worked in a payroll record should always be a positive number.

12) **Validity checks** are tests of identification numbers or transaction codes for validity by comparison with items already known to be correct or authorized. For example, Social Security numbers on payroll input records can be compared with Social Security numbers authorized by the personnel department.

13) An **overflow test** is a programmed control that checks computational results and issues a warning if the result exceeds the capacity of the storage location, which would result in the loss of data. For example, if 5428 were stored as 542, the 8 lost on overflow would be discovered.

b. **Key verification** entails rekeying input and comparing the results.

c. A **redundancy check** requires sending additional data items to serve as a check on the other transmitted data; for example, part of a customer name could be matched against the name associated with the transmitted customer number.

d. An **echo check** is an input control over transmission along communications lines. Data are sent back to the user's terminal for comparison with the transmitted data.

e. **Completeness checks** of transmission of data determine whether all necessary information has been sent. The software notifies the sender if something is omitted.

1) A complementary transmission control numbers and dates each message sent from a given terminal. This procedure allows verification of the completeness of the sequence and establishment of control totals for each terminal.

H. **Processing Controls**

1. Some input controls are also processing controls, e.g., limit, reasonableness, and sign tests.
2. Other tests of the logic of processing are posting, cross-footing, and zero-balance checks.
   a. Comparing the contents of a record before and after updating is a posting check.
   b. Cross-footing compares an amount to the sum of its components.
   c. A zero-balance check adds the positive and negative amounts posted. The result should be zero.
3. **Run-to-run control totals** (e.g., record counts or certain critical amounts) should be generated and checked at designated points during processing.
   a. **Proof account activity listing**. In an online system, the change in a file for the day can be compared with source information.
4. **Internal header and trailer labels** ensure that incorrect files are not processed.
   a. A matching test should make certain an updating transaction is matched with the appropriate master file.
5. Programs used in processing should be tested, for example, by reprocessing actual data with a known result or by employing test data.
6. **End-of-file procedures** should be available to avoid errors such as prematurely closing the transaction file when the end of the current master file is reached. The transaction file may contain new records to be added to the master file.
7. **Concurrency controls** manage situations in which two or more programs attempt to use a file or database at the same time.
8. An **audit trail** should be created through the use of input-output control logs, error listings, transaction logs, and transaction listings.
9. **Key integrity checks** prevent the updating process from creating inaccuracies in keys. Keys are attributes of records that permit them to be sorted. A primary key is the data item(s) that is the principal identifier, e.g., the vendor number. A secondary key is an alternative used either for sorting or special processing, e.g., the payment date on the vendor's invoice.

I. **Output Controls**

1. The **data control group** supervises output control.
   a. The daily proof account activity listings (changes in master files) should be sent to users for review.
   b. **Error listings** should be received directly from the system by the control group, which should make any necessary inquiries and send the errors to users for correction and resubmission.
   c. The **console log** should be reviewed for unusual interruptions, interventions, or other activity.
   d. Output should be distributed in accordance with distribution registers that list authorized users.
   e. **End-of-job markers** on the last page of printed output permits verification that the entire report has been received.
   f. **Spooler controls** prevent access to spooled output, i.e., to the results of processing that are temporarily stored in an intermediate file rather than immediately printed.
2. An important detective control is user review of output. Users should be able to determine when output is incomplete or not reasonable, particularly when the user prepared the input. Thus, users as well as computer personnel have a quality assurance function.

J. **Additional Control Approach**. Another approach to classifying controls is applicable to computer environments and internal control structures in general.

1. Preventive controls prevent errors from occurring.
   a. For example, training, segregation of duties, prenumbered forms, documentation, passwords, compatibility tests, and turnaround documents
2. Detective controls detect the existence of errors or wrongdoing.
   a. For example, batch totals, hash totals, reasonableness tests, check digits, aging of receivables, reconciliations, and reviews of logs
3. Corrective controls aid in the correction of erroneous data entry or application, or correction of faulty application runs.
   a. For example, transaction trail, backup and recovery, error reports, and error source statistics

ELECTRONIC DATA INTERCHANGE (EDI)

A. EDI is the communication of electronic documents directly from a computer in one entity to a computer in another entity.

   1. EXAMPLE: Ordering goods from a supplier
   2. EDI was developed to enhance JIT (just-in-time) inventory management.
   3. Advantages

      a. Reduction of clerical errors
      b. Speed
      c. Elimination of repetitive clerical tasks
      d. Elimination of document preparing, processing, and mailing costs

         1) Both outbound and inbound documents

   4. An extension of EDI is computer-stored records, which can be less expensive than traditional physical file storage.

B. **EDI Terms/Components**

   1. Standards concern procedures to convert written documents into a standard electronic document-messaging format to facilitate EDI.

   2. Conventions are the procedures for arranging data elements in specified formats for various accounting transactions, e.g., invoices, materials releases, and advance shipment notices.

   3. A data dictionary prescribes the meaning of data elements, including specification of each transaction structure.

   4. Transmission protocols are rules on how each envelope is structured and processed by the communications devices.

      a. Normally, a group of accounting transactions is combined in an electronic envelope and transmitted into a communications network.

      b. Rules are required for transmission and the separation of envelopes.

C. **Methods of Communication between Computers**

   1. **Point to point** -- use of dedicated computers by both parties. Each must be designed to be compatible with the other(s). This is very similar to networks within one company. A dedicated line or modems are used.

   2. **Value-added networks** -- a mailbox service whereby dedicated computers waiting for incoming messages are unnecessary. By storing messages, companies can batch outgoing and incoming messages.

   3. **Third-party networks** -- a mailbox service plus translation of senders' protocol (data configuration) to receivers' protocol. Thus, the sender and receiver do not have to conform to the same standards, formats, etc.

STUDY UNIT 33
INTERNAL AND OPERATIONAL AUDITING

This study unit constitutes 10% to 15% of Part 4. Management accountants require an understanding of internal auditing because it performs an essential management control function. For a full treatment of this topic, see Gleim's *CIA Review*. Also, internal control concepts relevant to internal auditing are presented in Study Unit 16, Internal Control.

DEFINITION OF INTERNAL AUDITING

A. "Internal auditing is an independent appraisal function established within an organization to examine and evaluate its activities as a service to the organization. The objective of internal auditing is to assist members of the organization in the effective discharge of their responsibilities. To this end, internal auditing furnishes them with analyses, appraisals, recommendations, counsel, and information concerning the activities reviewed. The audit objective includes promoting effective control at reasonable cost. The members of the organization assisted by internal auditing include those in management and the board of directors" (SRIA).

B. **Three Methods of Categorizing Internal Auditing Services**

1. General character of the auditing activities
   a. Protecting existing operations (control)
   b. Finding better ways to meet operating objectives (efficiency)
2. Type of operational area to be reviewed
   a. Auditors go beyond traditional accounting and financial control areas.
3. Organizational level of review, e.g., function, department, division, etc.

C. Internal auditing should encompass every phase and sector of the organization.

1. It should not be restricted to or from any operational areas or other types of areas; i.e., it extends beyond accounting and financial control areas to operations.
2. It should have unlimited access to any documents, records, or properties of the organization relevant to the subject under review.

REASON FOR INTERNAL AUDITING

A. The growth of public and private organizations has made it difficult or impossible for middle and executive-level managements to have personal knowledge of

1. Current operations
2. Effectiveness with which
   a. Objectives are met
   b. Policies are followed
   c. Control systems are functioning

B. Thus, modern internal auditing evolved to assist management in discharging its responsibilities efficiently and effectively. Internal auditors assist management in regard to the following matters:

1. Adequacy of accounting, financial, and operating controls
2. Compliance with established procedures and laws
3. Risk assessment
4. Safeguarding of assets
5. The reliability of data generated for management
6. Accomplishment of business objectives
7. Efficient use of resources
8. Prevention and detection of fraud
9. Coordination with the external auditor

ORGANIZATIONAL STATUS OF THE INTERNAL AUDIT DEPARTMENT

A. Organizational status must be sufficient for internal auditing to accomplish its responsibilities. Proper organizational status enhances the independence and objectivity of internal auditing.

1. Without management and board of directors' support, cooperation of auditees may be lacking.
2. The director of internal auditing should be responsible to an officer with sufficient authority to promote and ensure
   a. Internal auditing independence
   b. Broad audit coverage
   c. Adequate consideration of audit reports
   d. Appropriate action on audit recommendations
3. The board should concur in appointment and removal of the director.
   a. The director should communicate regularly with the board, including annual activity reports.

B. A formal, written charter should define internal auditing's purpose, authority, and responsibilities.

1. The charter should
   a. Establish the department's position within the organization
   b. Define the scope of internal auditing activities
   c. Authorize access to records, personnel, and physical properties relevant to the performance of audits
2. Reasons for having a charter include
   a. Documenting a commitment by executive management to internal auditing
   b. Defining the organizational and reporting relationships between internal auditing and others within the organization
   c. Defining the authority or responsibilities of internal auditing
   d. Providing a basis for organizing and staffing the internal auditing function
   e. Providing an authoritative guide to audit planning, including the setting of goals and objectives
   f. Providing a basis for evaluating overall audit effectiveness
3. Topics to be included in the charter are the
   a. Primary goal, or objective, of internal auditing
   b. Approval of senior management or the audit committee
   c. Authority granted to internal auditing
   d. Basic responsibilities of internal auditing (scope of work)
   e. Organizational status
   f. Relationships, both internal and external, of internal auditing to others
   g. Reporting relationships
   h. Responsibility to follow up on audit findings and recommendations

C. The director of internal auditing is responsible for the entire internal audit function, including

1. Accomplishment of audit objectives set by management and the board
2. Development of a charter approved by the board and management
3. Development of plans to carry out internal auditing goals
4. Development of a program to select and develop audit personnel
5. Development of written policies and procedures to guide audit staff
6. Coordination of internal auditing with external auditors
7. Review and approval of all audit reports
8. Establishment and maintenance of a quality assurance program
9. Conformity of audit work with Standards for the Professional Practice of Internal Auditing

AUTHORITY AND RESPONSIBILITY OF INTERNAL AUDITORS

A. The internal auditor's responsibility is to review and appraise policies, procedures, plans, and records for the purpose of informing and advising management.

B. Internal auditors have neither authority nor responsibility for any operating activities.

   1. If they had either authority or responsibility, their objectivity would be impaired.
   2. Thus, it is only through their organizational status (defined in the charter) that internal auditors have the authority to conduct audits.
      a. They must have full access to all relevant records, properties, and personnel.
   3. Persons transferred or temporarily assigned to internal auditing should not audit functions they previously performed.

C. The auditor's findings, recommendations, etc., are only advisory to auditees.

   1. Auditors can only bring disputed or ignored findings to the attention of top management and the board of directors.
      a. The board has the authority to implement the recommendations if they desire.
   2. The correct procedure is to bring all recommendations to the appropriate level of management for review and implementation.

D. The auditor may, however, recommend control standards for systems.

   1. The auditor may also review procedures prior to their implementation.
   2. The auditor may not draft procedures.
   3. The auditor may not design, install, or operate systems.

TYPES OF INTERNAL AUDIT SERVICES

Internal auditors assist management in discharging its responsibilities by examining and evaluating controls and performance in regard to the following:

A. **Adequacy and Effectiveness of the Organization's System of Internal Control**

   1. For more about the internal auditors' services with respect to internal control, see Statement of Internal Auditing Standards (SIAS) 1, *Control: Concepts and Responsibilities*, issued by The IIA. An overview of this pronouncement can be found under Internal Control According to IIA Pronouncements in Study Unit 16. The balance of this study unit is also relevant.
   2. The IIA's internal control concepts and terminology currently differ from those in AICPA pronouncements.

B. **Reliability and Integrity of Information**

   1. Financial and operating data provided to management should be
      a. Accurate
      b. Reliable
      c. Timely
      d. Complete
      e. Useful
   2. Internal auditors evaluate the adequacy of controls over
      a. Financial and operating records
      b. Record keeping
      c. Reporting

3. Internal auditors' responsibility with respect to the reliability and integrity of information is more extensive than that of external auditors.
   a. External auditors are primarily concerned with the entity's ability to record, process, summarize, and report financial data consistent with the assertions embodied in the financial statements.
   b. Internal auditors are also concerned with matters that are not relevant to a financial statement audit, such as the policies and procedures concerning the effectiveness, economy, and efficiency of management decision making.

C. **Safeguarding Assets**

1. Auditors emphasize avoidance of losses due to theft, fire, improper or illegal activities, and exposure to the elements.
2. The primary control is accountability; i.e., assets are recorded when acquired and inventoried periodically.

D. **Compliance with Established Procedures**

1. Internal auditors determine if employees are doing what they are supposed to do, i.e., following specified policies, plans, and procedures.
2. In the absence of compliance, the internal auditor determines
   a. The reasons for noncompliance
      1) Procedures are faulty.
      2) Better procedures are available.
      3) Conditions have changed.
   b. The cost of noncompliance
   c. How to obtain compliance if desirable

E. **Accomplishment of Business Objectives**. Internal auditors

1. Ascertain whether goals, objectives, and control procedures developed by lower levels of management conform with the overall objectives of the organization
   a. As set forth by the board and top management
2. Ascertain whether operations are being carried out as planned
3. Are able to report to management on the success of operations, if operating standards
   a. Have been set
   b. Are understood
   c. Are reasonable
   d. Are consistent with overall organization objectives and goals
   e. Result in analysis of deviations from the standards

F. **Efficient Use of Resources**

1. Efficiency is evaluated in terms of operating standards.
2. Auditors should determine that standards have been set, are understood, and are being met.
3. Auditors should identify and report inefficiency, e.g., underused facilities, nonproductive work, over or understaffing, and uneconomical procedures.

G. **Identification of Risk Areas**

1. Internal auditors identify areas with high expected or suspected risk and notify management to determine if additional auditing procedures should be applied.
2. Risk areas are identified by
   a. Prior audits
   b. Indications from audits elsewhere in the organization
   c. Auditor's experience (educational and on-the-job)
   d. Problems in other companies and related industries
   e. Interaction with top management and the board of directors
   f. Other procedures as appropriate
3. Areas of risk are brought to the attention of top management and the board through the internal audit department's work schedule (particularly its operational audits) and changes in it.

H. **Detection and Prevention of Fraud**. See the next sideheading.

I. **Coordination with External Auditors**

1. The objective of coordination is to minimize duplicate efforts and encourage broad audit coverage.
2. To the extent that internal auditing of accounting control provides a basis for reliance thereon by external auditors, the cost of internal auditing is offset by the reduced cost of external auditing.
3. Because internal auditing has a broader scope, duplication of efforts is of concern only for areas addressed in a financial statement audit.
4. Coordination of audit effort includes
   a. Periodic meetings to discuss matters of mutual interest
   b. Access to each other's audit programs and working papers
   c. Exchange of audit reports and management letters
   d. Common understanding of audit techniques, methods, and terminology

J. Many of the above services (for example, D., E., and F.) are performed in operational audits rather than financial audits.

DETECTION AND PREVENTION OF FRAUD

A. **General Responsibilities**. The internal auditor

1. Should not be regarded as an insurer (guarantor) against the existence of fraud in an organization
2. Has a responsibility for ensuring the existence of control, with systems designed to prevent or deter the forms of fraud generally known to be possible
3. Is responsible for seeking to identify areas of risk where theft or manipulation may be likely to occur
4. Is responsible for the adequacy and effectiveness of controls in financial accounting and other areas subject to theft, fraud, or embezzlement, even if the internal auditor emphasizes operational audits
5. Is responsible in all these undertakings for ordinary prudence and professional care
   a. Must exercise the care and skill of a reasonably prudent and competent internal auditor

B. **Auditor Objectives Concerning Fraud**

1. Prevention through proper and sufficient controls is preferable to detection.
   a. Fraud should not occur with proper controls.
2. This is a change in emphasis from 50 years ago when 100% verification of transactions for the purpose of detection of fraud and other errors was emphasized.
   a. Use of internal controls and other control systems is more cost beneficial than 100% auditor verification.

C. When auditors suspect wrongdoing, the proper authorities within the organization should be informed.

1. The auditor may recommend the type of investigation.
   a. Ordinarily, specialists, e.g., security personnel, should conduct investigations (especially questioning of those suspected).
   b. Auditors should avoid personal contact with suspects to avoid
      1) Hindering further investigation
      2) Giving cause for legal action against the auditor for libel, slander, false imprisonment, etc.
2. The auditor's interest in fraud is to determine
   a. How fraud was possible, i.e., how it occurred
   b. How to correct it
   c. How to eliminate future occurrences

D. **Factors Contributing to and/or Permitting Fraud**

1. Insufficient internal controls, such as
   a. Insufficient separation of functional responsibilities of authorization, custodianship, and record keeping
   b. Not limiting access to assets
   c. Not recording transactions, i.e., insufficient accountability
   d. Not comparing asset existence with recorded accountability
   e. Not executing transactions in accordance with proper authorization
   f. Not implementing prescribed controls because of
      1) Lack of personnel
      2) Unqualified personnel
2. Other reasons
   a. Collusion among employees for whom there is little backup control
   b. Highly convertible assets
      1) Cash
      2) Securities payable to bearer
      3) Highly marketable merchandise

E. The IIA has issued a pronouncement on the internal auditor's responsibilities with regard to fraud. The summary of SIAS 3, *Deterrence, Detection, Investigation, and Reporting of Fraud*, is quoted below.

> *This statement interprets the Standards and establishes guidelines for internal auditors regarding their responsibility for deterring, detecting, investigating, and reporting of fraud. It does not provide guidance on specific audit procedures used in performing audits; rather, it establishes guidelines by which internal auditors conform their activities with the stated concepts of due professional care. As used in this statement, the term management includes anyone in an organization with responsibilities for setting and/or achieving objectives.*
>
> *Major conclusions of this statement are:*
>
> ***Deterrence of fraud.*** *This is the responsibility of management. Internal auditors are responsible for examining and evaluating the adequacy and the effectiveness of actions taken by management to fulfill this obligation.*
>
> ***Detection of fraud.*** *Internal auditors should have sufficient knowledge of fraud to be able to identify indicators that fraud might have been committed.*
>
> *If significant control weaknesses are detected, additional tests conducted by internal auditors should include tests directed toward identification of other indicators of fraud.*
>
> *Internal auditors are not expected to have knowledge equivalent to that of a person whose primary responsibility is to detect and investigate fraud. Also, audit procedures alone, even when carried out with due professional care, do not guarantee that fraud will be detected.*
>
> ***Investigation of fraud.*** *Fraud investigations may be conducted by or involve participation of internal auditors, lawyers, investigators, security personnel, and other specialists from inside or outside the organization.*
>
> *Internal auditing should assess the facts known relative to all fraud investigations in order to:*
>
> - *Determine if controls need to be implemented or strengthened.*
> - *Design audit tests to help disclose the existence of similar frauds in the future.*
> - *Help meet the internal auditor's responsibility to maintain sufficient knowledge of fraud.*
>
> ***Reporting of fraud.*** *A written report should be issued at the conclusion of the investigation phase. It should include all findings, conclusions, recommendations, and corrective action taken.*

FOREIGN CORRUPT PRACTICES ACT OF 1977 (FCPA)

A. The FCPA made it a criminal offense for any U.S. business (incorporated or unincorporated) to bribe any foreign official, political party, or candidate to obtain or direct business to any person.

B. The FCPA also amended the Securities Exchange Act of 1934 to require all **public** companies that must register under the act to

1. Establish and maintain reasonably complete and accurate accounting records
    a. The accuracy of the books and records must be adequate to reflect fairly the transactions and dispositions of assets in reasonable detail.
2. Devise a sufficient internal control structure to provide **reasonable assurance** that
    a. Transactions are executed in accordance with management's general or specific authorization.

b. Transactions are recorded as necessary

1) To permit preparation of financial statements in conformity with generally accepted accounting principles or any other criteria applicable to such statements

2) To maintain accountability for assets

c. Access to assets is permitted only in accordance with management's general or specific authorization.

d. The recorded accountability for assets is compared with the existing assets at reasonable intervals, and appropriate action is taken with respect to any differences.

NOTE: The four management objectives given in B.2. were originally stated in a now-superseded AICPA pronouncement.

C. The requirement of an accurate accounting record means that bribes to foreign and domestic officials, businesses, etc., cannot be buried in other accounts.

1. The law now requires public companies to devise and maintain sufficient internal controls regardless of whether the company has foreign operations. Furthermore, cost-benefit considerations are not a permissible basis for failing to implement a control structure that provides reasonable assurance of meeting the pronouncement's stated objectives.

2. The FCPA was definitely a boon to internal auditing.

AUDIT COMMITTEES OF BOARDS OF DIRECTORS

A. The audit committee of a company's board of directors is a subcommittee made up of outside directors, i.e. directors who are independent of corporate management. They help to

1. Keep external and internal auditors independent of management
2. Assure that the directors are exercising due care

B. **Audit Committee Functions**

1. Select an external auditor and review the audit fee and the engagement letter
2. Review the external auditor's overall audit plan
3. Review preliminary annual and interim financial statements
4. Review results of external and internal audits, e.g., restrictions, audit findings and recommendations
5. Review the internal audit work schedule, budget, reports, etc.
6. Meet regularly with the internal audit director
7. Review evaluations of internal control
8. Review the company's accounting, financial, and operating controls
9. Review policies on unethical and illegal procedures
10. Review financial statements for regulatory agencies
11. Review observations of company personnel
12. Participate in the selection of accounting policies
13. Review the impact of new or proposed legislation or governmental regulations
14. Review the company's insurance program
15. Review the external auditor's management letter

C. The AICPA has recognized the importance of internal reporting to audit committees in SAS 61 (AU 380), *Communication with Audit Committees*. See Study Unit 17.

THE IIA *CODE OF ETHICS*

The IIA *Code of Ethics* consists of introductory statements of purpose and applicability and 11 Standards of Conduct. It applies to members of the Institute and to CIAs. The *Code of Ethics* was formally adopted in July 1988 as an extensive revision and combination of the separate codes for Institute members and CIAs.

THE INSTITUTE OF INTERNAL AUDITORS CODE OF ETHICS

PURPOSE. *A distinguishing mark of a profession is acceptance by its members of responsibility to the interests of those it serves. Members of the Institute of Internal Auditors (Members) and Certified Internal Auditors (CIAs) must maintain high standards of conduct in order to effectively discharge this responsibility. The Institute of Internal Auditors (Institute) adopts this Code of Ethics for Members and CIAs.*

APPLICABILITY. *This Code of Ethics is applicable to all Members and CIAs. Membership in the Institute and acceptance of the Certified Internal Auditor designation are voluntary actions. By acceptance, Members and CIAs assume an obligation of self-discipline above and beyond the requirements of laws and regulations.*

The standards of conduct set forth in this Code of Ethics provide basic principles in the practice of internal auditing. Members and CIAs should realize that their individual judgment is required in the application of these principles.

CIAs shall use the Certified Internal Auditor designation with discretion and in a dignified manner, fully aware of what the designation denotes. The designation shall also be used in a manner consistent with all statutory requirements.

Members who are judged by the Board of Directors of the Institute to be in violation of the standards of conduct of the Code of Ethics shall be subject to forfeiture of their membership in the Institute. CIAs who are similarly judged also shall be subject to forfeiture of the Certified Internal Auditor designation.

STANDARDS OF CONDUCT

I. *Members and CIAs shall exercise honesty, objectivity, and diligence in the performance of their duties and responsibilities.*

II. *Members and CIAs shall exhibit loyalty in all matters pertaining to the affairs of their organization or to whomever they may be rendering a service. However, Members and CIAs shall not knowingly be a party to any illegal or improper activity.*

III. *Members and CIAs shall not knowingly engage in acts or activities which are discreditable to the profession of internal auditing or to their organization.*

IV. *Members and CIAs shall refrain from entering into any activity which may be in conflict with the interest of their organization or which would prejudice their ability to carry out objectively their duties and responsibilities.*

V. *Members and CIAs shall not accept anything of value from an employee, client, customer, supplier, or business associate of their organization which would impair or be presumed to impair their professional judgment.*

VI. *Members and CIAs shall undertake only those services which they can reasonably expect to complete with professional competence.*

VII. *Members and CIAs shall adopt suitable means to comply with the Standards for the Professional Practice of Internal Auditing.*

VIII. *Members and CIAs shall be prudent in the use of information acquired in the course of their duties. They shall not use confidential information for any personal gain nor in any manner which would be contrary to law or detrimental to the welfare of their organization.*

IX. *Members and CIAs, when reporting on the results of their work, shall reveal such material facts known to them which, if not revealed, could either distort reports of operations under review or conceal unlawful practices.*

X. *Members and CIAs shall continually strive for improvements in their proficiency, and in the effectiveness and quality of their service.*

XI. *Members and CIAs, in the practice of their profession, shall be ever mindful of their obligation to maintain the high standards of competence, morality and dignity promulgated by the Institute. Members shall abide by the Bylaws and uphold the objectives of the Institute.*

STATEMENT OF RESPONSIBILITIES OF INTERNAL AUDITING (SRIA)

A. The Statement of Responsibilities is a conceptual statement. In contrast, the five general standards and 25 specific standards are rule oriented.

   1. The content of the SRIA is already reflected in the previous outlines on internal audit definition, status, authority, services, detection of fraud, etc.

B. The sections of the SRIA are objective and scope, responsibility and authority, and independence.

C. A more detailed outline of the Statement of Responsibilities follows:

   1. Objective and scope

      a. Independent appraisal function

      b. Service to the organization

      c. Assisting members of the organization (including management and the board) by furnishing analyses, appraisals, recommendations, counsel, and information concerning activities reviewed

      d. Promotion of effective control at reasonable cost

      e. Examination and evaluation of the adequacy and effectiveness of internal control and of the quality of performance. The scope of internal auditing extends to

         1) Compliance with policies, plans, procedures, laws, and regulations
         2) Accomplishment of established objectives and goals
         3) Reliability and integrity of information
         4) Economy and efficiency of resource use
         5) Safeguarding of assets

   2. Responsibility and authority

      a. Responsibility and authority need to be clearly defined by management in a formal charter.

      b. The scope of work should be unrestricted.

      c. Internal auditors have neither authority nor responsibility for activities audited.

      d. The practice of internal auditing throughout the world is affected by the diversity of environments, organizations, laws, and customs.

      e. Internal auditors should ensure that there is compliance with the Standards.

   3. Independence

      a. Internal auditors are independent of the activities they audit when they can

         1) Work freely and objectively
         2) Render impartial and unbiased judgments

      b. Organizational status of internal auditing must be sufficient to assure

         1) A broad range of audit coverage
         2) Adequate consideration of reports
         3) Appropriate action on audit recommendations

      c. Objectivity means an independent mental attitude.

         1) Internal auditors may not subordinate their judgment to that of others.

         2) Designing, installing, and operating systems and the drafting of procedures for systems are not audit standards.

INTERNAL AUDITING STANDARDS FRAMEWORK

A. The Internal Auditing Standards Board (IASB) (formerly the Professional Standards Committee, or PSC) is the official IIA body charged with developing professional standards. According to an article by Marjo N. Miller in the *Internal Auditor*, June 1988,

> *The current objectives of the committee are to develop, recommend, and monitor approved programs that will enunciate professional standards. The primary responsibility of the PSC [now the IASB] is to maintain the Standards in a manner that provides useful guidance to all practitioners.*

The IASB also

1. Considers needed changes in the *Code of Ethics* and the SRIA
2. Approves Statements on Internal Auditing Standards (SIASs) and Practice Directives (PDs)
3. Recommends requirements for the CIA designation and continuing education for CIAs
4. Investigates complaints against IIA members and CIAs
5. Issues Professional Standards Bulletins (PSBs) in response to practitioners' questions

B. The following tabular presentation of the elements of the internal auditing standards is from the aforementioned article:

DOCUMENT	FINAL-APPROVAL AUTHORITY	DEFINITION
SRIA	IIA Board	Discusses the role and responsibilities of internal auditing.
Code of Ethics (approved July 1988)	IIA Board	Defines standards of professional behavior for IIA members and CIAs.
SPPIA		
• General Standards	IIA Board	States five general standards.
• Specific Standards	IASB	States 25 specific standards that must be complied with to follow the general standards.
• Guidelines	IASB	States the most generally accepted guidelines to meet the general and specific standards.
SIASs	IASB	SIASs are authoritative interpretations of the Standards. They may also add or change guidelines.
PDs	IASB	PD No. 1, *Standards Framework*, was approved in December 1987. PDs define IIA policy on various administrative matters.
PSBs	IASB Chair	PSBs are unofficial answers to questions about IIA pronouncements.

STANDARDS FOR THE PROFESSIONAL PRACTICE OF INTERNAL AUDITING

A. The five general and 25 specific standards are outlined below for your information. They probably will not be tested, as such, on the CMA exam. The standards describe the nature of internal auditing, and accordingly their outlines are presented here (as summaries of AICPA Statements on Auditing Standards were presented in Study Unit 17, External Auditing).

B. There are 25 specific standards. To comply with each general standard, the associated specific standards relating to it must be followed. When the general standards are arranged to create the mnemonic PP-MIS, the number of specific standards for each makes the easily memorized number 84,625. Professional Proficiency has twice as many specific standards as Performance.

1. **Professional Proficiency** has eight specific standards: three for the internal audit department and five for internal auditors themselves.
   a. Internal audit department -- The mnemonic is SKS.
      1) **S**taffing
      2) **K**nowledge, skills, and disciplines
      3) **S**upervision
   b. Internal auditors -- The mnemonic is CCCKP.
      1) **C**ompliance with standards
      2) **C**ommunication and human relations
      3) **C**ontinuing education
      4) **K**nowledge, skills, disciplines
      5) **P**rofessional (due) care
2. **Performance of Audit Work** has four specific standards.
   a. The mnemonic is PECF.
      1) **P**lanning
      2) **E**xamining and evaluating
      3) **C**ommunicating results
      4) **F**ollowing up
3. **Management of the Internal Audit Department** has six specific standards.
   a. The mnemonic is PPPP-EQ.
      1) **P**urpose, authority, and responsibility
      2) **P**lanning
      3) **P**olicies and procedures
      4) **P**ersonnel management and development
      5) **E**xternal auditors
      6) **Q**uality assurance
4. **Independence** has two specific standards.
   a. The mnemonic is OO.
      1) **O**rganizational status
      2) **O**bjectivity
5. **Scope of Work** has five specific standards.
   a. The mnemonic is CARES.
      1) **C**ompliance with policies, laws, etc.
      2) **A**ccomplishment of established goals of operations
      3) **R**eliability and integrity of data
      4) **E**conomical and efficient use of resources
      5) **S**afeguarding assets

C. In addition to general and specific standards, the SPPIA include guidelines that provide further clarification. A complete outline follows. You do not have to memorize or study this outline diligently for the CMA exam. It is presented to give you a better understanding of internal auditing.

1. **Professional Proficiency**. Internal audits should be performed with professional proficiency and due professional care. Professional proficiency is required of both the internal audit department and each internal auditor.

   a. **Internal audit department** (SKS)

      1) **Staffing** -- assures that internal auditors are technically proficient

         a) Establishes criteria for education and experience of internal auditors, given scope of work and level of responsibility

      2) **Knowledge, skills, and disciplines** -- as needed to carry out the audit responsibilities

         a) Should collectively possess knowledge and skills sufficient to apply internal auditing standards, procedures, and techniques

         b) Should have employees and consultants with collective qualifications in accounting, economics, finance, statistics, electronic data processing (EDP), engineering, taxation, and law as needed

      3) **Supervision** -- Internal audits should be properly supervised.

         a) The director of internal auditing is responsible for supervision.

         b) Supervision involves the following:

            i) Subordinates are instructed at the beginning of the audit.

            ii) The audit program is carried out.

            iii) Working papers are adequately supported.

            iv) Audit reports are accurate, clear, objective, concise, constructive, and timely.

            v) Audit objectives are being met.

         c) Documentation of appropriate supervision is required.

         d) Amount of supervision depends on auditor proficiency and assignment difficulty.

         e) All internal audit assignments are the director's responsibility.

   b. **The internal auditor** (CCCKP)

      1) **Compliance** -- maintained with standards of conduct

         a) The IIA *Code of Ethics* sets forth standards.

      2) **Communication** -- Internal auditors should

         a) Understand human relations and maintain good relationships with auditees

         b) Be skilled in oral and written communications for clear and effective communication

3) **Continuing education** -- necessary to maintain proficiency
   a) Participation in professional societies
   b) Attendance at conferences
   c) Seminars
   d) College courses
   e) In-house training programs
   f) Participation in research projects
4) **Knowledge, skills, and disciplines**
   a) Each internal auditor should possess
      i) Proficiency in internal audit standards, procedures, and techniques
      ii) Proficiency in accounting principles and techniques
      iii) Understanding of management principles
      iv) An appreciation of fundamentals of accounting, economics, law, taxation, finance, quantitative methods, and EDP
5) **Professional (due) care** must be exercised by internal auditors.
   a) Application of care and skill expected of a reasonably prudent and competent internal auditor
      i) Appropriate to the complexities of the audit
      ii) Alert to possibility of errors and wrongdoing
      iii) Alert to activities susceptible to irregularity
      iv) Able to identify inadequate controls and recommend improvements
   b) Reasonable care and competence, not infallibility or extraordinary performance
      i) No absolute assurance that irregularities do not exist
   c) Appropriate authorities informed when wrongdoing is suspected
      i) May recommend investigation
      ii) Should follow up to see that appropriate action has been taken
   d) Reasonable audit skill and judgment, i.e., auditor considers
      i) Extent of audit work required
      ii) Relative materiality or significance of audited matters
      iii) Adequacy and effectiveness of internal controls
      iv) Cost-benefit analysis
   e) Determining that operating standards are understandable and clear
      i) When vague, clarification should be sought.
      ii) Auditees should agree on standards as interpreted by the internal auditor.

2. **Performance of Audit Work** (PECF). An internal auditor is responsible for planning and conducting the audit, subject to supervisory review and approval.
   a. **Planning** the audit
      1) Planning should be documented and include
         a) Audit objectives and scope of work
         b) Background information about auditee activity
         c) Determining resources required for the audit
         d) Communicating with auditees
         e) On-site survey to identify areas of audit emphasis
         f) Writing the audit program
         g) Establishing the communication plan for audit results
         h) Obtaining approval of the audit work plan

b. **Examining and evaluating** the information

   1) Data should be collected on all matters related to audit objectives and scope.

   2) Information should be

      a) Sufficient, i.e., factual, adequate, and convincing
      b) Competent, i.e., reliable and the best obtainable
      c) Relevant, i.e., support audit findings and recommendations
      d) Useful, i.e., help the organization meet its goals

   3) Audit procedures should be selected in advance and altered as necessary.

   4) The collecting, analyzing, interpreting, and documenting of audit data should be supervised.

   5) Working papers should be prepared.

   6) Working papers should be reviewed by the supervisor.

c. **Communicating results**

   1) A signed, written report is issued at audit completion.

      a) Interim reports may be written or oral.

   2) Conclusions should be discussed at the appropriate levels of auditee management before issuing the written report.

   3) The report should be objective, clear, concise, constructive, correct, and timely.

   4) The report should present the purpose, scope, and results of an audit.

      a) May include recommendations for potential improvement and acknowledge satisfactory performance or corrective action

   5) Auditee views about audit conclusions may be included.

   6) Director of internal auditing should review and approve the final report before issuance and decide on distribution.

d. **Following up**

   1) The internal auditor must determine that

      a) Corrective action was taken and is achieving desired results, or
      b) Management has assumed the risk of not taking corrective action.

3. **Management of the Internal Audit Department** (PPPP-EQ). The director is responsible for ensuring that audit work fulfills its general purpose, internal audit resources are used efficiently and effectively, and audit work is in conformity with SPPIA.

   a. **Purpose, authority, and responsibility**

      1) Director should seek approval by management and acceptance by the board of a formal charter for the internal audit department.

   b. **Planning**

      1) Internal audit plans should be consistent with the charter and with the organization's goals.

2) Planning process involves
   a) Goals
   b) Audit work schedules
   c) Staffing plans and financial budgets
   d) Activity reports
3) Internal audit goals should be accomplishable and measurable with
   a) Measurement criteria (standards)
   b) Completion dates
4) Audit work schedules
   a) Should include
      i) Activities to be audited
      ii) When they will be audited
      iii) Estimated time required
      iv) Audit work schedule priorities
   b) Are based on
      i) Date and results of last audit
      ii) Financial exposure
      iii) Potential risk of loss
      iv) Requests by management
      v) Changes in operations, etc.
      vi) Operating benefit opportunities
      vii) Capabilities of the audit staff
5) Staffing plans and financial budgets should be based upon the number and abilities of internal auditors.
6) Periodic activity reports for the internal audit department should be submitted to management and the board. These reports should
   a) Compare department goals with internal audit activity
   b) Compare expenditures with budgets
   c) Explain the variances of each

c. **Policies and procedures**

1) Form and content of written policies and procedures are based on size and structure of internal audit department.
   a) A small department may be managed informally.
   b) In larger departments, more formal, comprehensive policies are necessary.

d. **Personnel management and development** for the internal audit personnel necessitate

1) Written job descriptions for each level of staff
2) Selection of qualified and competent individuals
3) Provision for continuing education opportunities
4) Evaluation of each auditor's performance at least annually
5) Counseling of auditors on performance and professional development

e. **External auditor coordination**

1) Coordination of internal and external audit work ensures broad audit coverage and minimizes duplication.

2) Coordination involves

a) Periodic meetings to discuss matters
b) Access to each other's audit programs and working papers
c) Exchange of audit reports and management letters
d) Common understanding of audit techniques, methods, etc.

f. **Quality assurance** program should be established.

1) Quality assurance program assures conformance with The IIA Standards.
2) Requires

a) Continual supervision to assure conformance with standards, departmental policies, and audit programs

b) Internal reviews to appraise quality of work being performed

c) External reviews independent of the organization

i) Performed at least once every 3 years

ii) Providing a required formal written report expressing an opinion on compliance with the Standards

4. **Independence** (OO). Internal auditors must carry out their work freely and objectively, rendering impartial and unbiased judgments.

a. **Organizational status**

1) Requires management and board support for cooperation of auditees

a) The internal audit director should be responsible to a high-level individual to promote independence.

b) Director should have direct communication with the board.

c) The board should concur in the appointment or removal of the director.

d) Purpose, authority, and responsibility of internal audit department should be defined in a charter, which

i) Defines the department's position within the organization

ii) Authorizes access to records, personnel, and physical properties

iii) Defines the scope of internal audit activities

e) The director should submit an audit work schedule, staffing plan, and financial budget annually to management and the board.

f) Activity reports should be submitted to management and the board annually, with interim notification of significant deviations from approved audit work schedules, budget, etc.

b. **Objectivity**

1) Objectivity is an independent mental attitude, i.e., no subordination of judgment to others.

2) It requires honest belief in work product and no significant quality compromises.

   a) Staff assignments must avoid potential and actual conflicts of interest.

   b) Staff assignments should be rotated as practicable.

   c) Internal auditors cannot assume operating responsibilities.

      i) Any nonaudit work should be recognized as such.

      ii) Internal auditors cannot audit areas where previous authority or responsibility existed.

   d) Temporary internal auditors should not audit activities with which they had previously been associated until a reasonable period of time passes.

   e) Results of internal audit work should be reviewed for objectivity.

3) Objectivity is not adversely affected when the auditor recommends standards of control for systems or review procedures before they are implemented.

   a) However, the designing, installing, and operating of systems are not audit functions.

   b) Drafting of systems procedures is not an audit function.

   c) These activities would impair audit objectivity.

5. **Scope of Work** (CARES)

- Scope includes the examination and evaluation of the adequacy and effectiveness of internal controls and the quality of performance of assigned responsibilities.
- Management and the board of directors provide general direction for the scope of work and activities to be audited.
- Purpose of internal control review is to determine whether the system provides reasonable assurance that objectives and goals will be met efficiently and economically.
- Review for effectiveness is to ascertain whether the system is functioning as intended.
- Review for quality of performance is to determine whether the organization's objectives and goals have been achieved.
- A control is a management action to enhance the likelihood of achieving objectives and goals.
- Management plans, organizes, and directs to provide reasonable assurance of achieving objectives and goals.
- Internal auditing examines and evaluates these processes to determine whether reasonable assurance exists. These evaluations provide information to appraise the system of control.

a. **Compliance** with policies, plans, procedures, laws, regulations, etc.
   1) Management is responsible for creating systems to ensure compliance with these requirements.
      a) Internal auditors determine whether systems are adequate and effective.
      b) Internal auditors decide whether the activities comply with the appropriate requirements.

b. **Accomplishment of established objectives and goals** for operations and programs
   1) Management is responsible for
      a) Establishing operating and program objectives and goals
      b) Developing and implementing control procedures
      c) Accomplishing desired operating and program results
   2) Internal auditors should ascertain conformity with organizational goals and objectives.
   3) Internal auditors can assist managers in developing and evaluating goals, objectives, and systems by determining whether
      a) Their underlying assumptions are appropriate.
      b) Accurate, current, and relevant information is being used.

c. **Reliability and integrity of information**
   1) Information systems provide data for decision making, control, and compliance with external requirements. Thus
      a) Financial and operating records must contain accurate, reliable, timely, complete, and useful information.
      b) Controls over record keeping and reporting must be adequate and effective.

d. **Economical and efficient use of resources**
   1) Management is responsible for setting operating standards to measure economical and efficient use of resources. Internal auditors are responsible for determining that
      a) These standards have been established.
      b) The standards are understood and being met.
      c) Deviations are being identified, analyzed, and communicated for corrective action.
      d) Corrective action has been taken.
   2) Audits should identify
      a) Underused facilities
      b) Nonproductive work
      c) Uneconomical procedures
      d) Overstaffing or understaffing

e. **Safeguarding assets**
   1) From losses such as fire, theft, improper or illegal activities, and exposure to the elements
   2) By using appropriate audit procedures

PURPOSE AND FUNCTIONS OF THE INTERNAL AUDIT PROGRAM

A. **Audit Programs**

1. Outline what is to be accomplished
2. Specify how it is to be done
3. Provide for a record of what has been done
4. Facilitate supervision and control of the audit

B. The emphasis and extent of the audit program depend on the nature (scope) of the review to be undertaken.

1. The review can be an all-inclusive, in-depth audit of controls throughout an entire department or activity.
2. The review can have a narrower scope and focus on one aspect of the internal audit objectives as applied to a department or activity. Thus, the mnemonic CARES can be used to list the various kinds of reviews. The audit program could be directed to a review of an activity's
   a. **C**ompliance with policies, plans, procedures, laws, and regulations
      1) Requires control systems based on
         a) Explicitly communicated policies, plans, and procedures
         b) A system to comply with the laws and regulations
      2) Transaction tests to determine compliance are important.
   b. **A**ccomplishment of established objectives and goals for operations or programs
      1) Program objectives and goals should conform to those of the organization as a whole.
         a) Goals should be reasonable.
      2) Control procedures are required, i.e., the control loop (system).
         a) Including evaluation and rewriting of standards, if appropriate
   c. **R**eliability and integrity of information
      1) Require internal control over financial data
   d. **E**conomical and efficient use of resources
      1) Requires standards by which to measure performance
         a) Standards should be set by appropriate levels of management.
         b) If standards have not been explicitly set, auditee and auditor must agree on appropriate measurement prior to audit. Without standards, audit has no basis for conclusions.
      2) Requires a control loop (system) to assure continuous striving toward standards
   e. **S**afeguarding of assets
      1) Involves protecting assets from fire, theft, improper activities, and the elements
      2) Requires an effective system of internal control
         a) Including periodic inventories of assets
      3) Physical inspection by the auditor is an important audit test.

C. The scope of the audit program was determined during the first step in the preliminary survey: establishing audit objectives and scope of work. See the SPPIA standards for the scope of work.

1. The director of internal auditing, with the guidance of the board and top management, must determine the relative emphasis of each of the above types of review for each audit project.

   a. The review emphasis depends on the type of operation being audited. The following should be considered:

      1) The operation's objectives
      2) Cost-benefit analysis

   b. The emphasis of the review depends on the available internal audit personnel.

D. The audit program is prepared after the preliminary survey and before the start of field work.

1. The audit program is usually a rewrite of programs used for previous or related audits, or a pro forma program.

   a. Pro forma audit programs are generalized audit programs that have been developed for both financial and operational audits.

   b. The audit program must then be custom-tailored to each specific client, engagement, situation, etc.

      1) A shift in audit emphasis from audit to audit may be the result of past audits, changed operations, etc.

         a) The board and top management may request a special emphasis to help in long- or short-range planning.

2. Substantial attention should always be directed to known and/or suspected areas of risk.

   a. SAS 47, *Audit Risk and Materiality in Conducting an Audit* (AU 312), defines audit risk broadly as "the risk that the auditor may unknowingly fail to appropriately modify the opinion on financial statements that are materially misstated." Its elements are control risk, inherent risk, and detection risk. Because the scope of internal auditing is greater than that of external auditing, the overall audit risk extends not only to financial statements but also to unwitting failure to uncover material errors, irregularities, or weaknesses in the operations audited. The following four definitions are from AU 312 (i.e., the AICPA), but they may be extended to the broader internal auditing environment.

      1) **Audit risk.** At the account-balance or class-of-transactions level, audit risk consists of the following:

         a) The risk (consisting of inherent risk and control risk) that the balance or class and related assertions contain misstatements that could be material to the financial statements when aggregated with misstatements in other balances or classes

         b) The risk (detection risk) that the auditor will not detect such misstatements

2) **Inherent risk** -- the susceptibility of an assertion to a material misstatement, assuming that there are no related internal control structure policies and procedures

3) **Control risk** -- the risk that a material misstatement that could occur in an assertion will not be prevented or detected on a timely basis by the entity's internal control structure policies or procedures

4) **Detection risk** -- the risk that the auditor will not detect a material misstatement that exists in an assertion

3. Audit programs are tentative because deviations from expected results discovered during performance of the audit should be pursued.

   a. Exceptions should be analyzed to determine the control weakness that

      1) Permitted the exception
      2) Allowed the exception to go undetected

   b. Then, cost-benefit analysis must be applied to

      1) Determine the materiality
      2) Evaluate the advisability of strengthened or new controls

E. The audit program should indicate the objectives of the operations being audited, as disclosed during the preliminary survey.

1. The audit program should also indicate the controls in effect or needed to carry out the objectives of the operation.

2. Matching the activity's objectives to its existing controls may reveal that

   a. One or more controls necessary to attain objectives are missing.

   b. One or more controls are unnecessary, redundant, inefficient (too expensive for the benefit gained).

3. The program should provide for tests of transactions to obtain evidence of whether the controls are functioning as intended and desired results (objectives) are being achieved.

F. IIA Standard 420 requires audit evidence to be sufficient, competent, relevant, and useful.

1. **Sufficient** information is factual, adequate, and convincing so that a prudent, informed person would reach the same conclusions as the auditor.

2. **Competent** information is reliable and the best obtainable through the use of appropriate audit techniques.

3. **Relevant** information supports audit findings and recommendations and is consistent with the objectives for the audit.

4. **Useful** information helps the organization meet its goals.

OPERATIONAL AUDITING

A. Sawyer and Summers, in *Sawyer's Internal Auditing* (Altamonte Springs, FL: The Institute of Internal Auditors, 1988), page 4, defines operational auditing as "the comprehensive review of unit activities, systems, and controls within an enterprise to reach economic, efficiency, effectiveness, or other objectives." An operational audit is thus a thorough examination of a department or division. Its purpose is to appraise managerial organization, performance, and techniques.

1. It attempts to determine the extent to which organizational objectives have been achieved.
2. It is a control technique that provides management with a method for evaluating the effectiveness of operating procedures and internal controls.
3. The focus is on efficiency, effectiveness, and economy.
4. The audit report resulting from an operational audit consists primarily of pointing out where problems exist or emphasizing the absence of problems.
5. The auditor compares a department's operations with company policies and procedures, industry averages, and departmental trends.
   a. Common business sense is an important aspect of the auditor's work.
6. The basic tools of the auditor include
   a. Financial analysis
   b. Observation of departmental activities
   c. Questionnaire interviews of departmental employees
7. The operational audit evolved as an extension of the typical financial audit in that it goes beyond what is generally considered to be the accounting function, e.g.,
   a. Reviewing purchasing policies
   b. Appraising compliance with company policies and procedures
   c. Appraising safety standards and maintenance of equipment
   d. Reviewing production controls and scrap reporting
   e. Reviewing adequacy of facilities

B. Some writers have contrasted financial (external) auditing and operational auditing. Based on the success of The Institute of Internal Auditors and their leadership in this area (including issuance of the Statement of Responsibilities and the Standards for the Professional Practice of Internal Auditing), your authors conclude that internal auditing includes, but is not limited to, operational auditing; i.e., internal auditing is the broader and preferable term.

C. Reviews for operating controls include audits of the control loops throughout the organization.

1. The controls relevant to a financial statement (external) audit concern the R and S of CARES.
2. Operating controls concern the C, A, and E of CARES.

   Compliance with policies, plans, etc.
   Accomplishment of established objectives
   Reliability and integrity of information
   Economical and efficient use of resources
   Safeguarding of assets

D. The control loop consists of

1. Establishing standards for the operation to be controlled
2. Measuring performance against the standards
3. Examining and analyzing deviations
4. Taking corrective action
5. Reappraising the standards, based on experience. Sometimes this step is not listed separately.

E. The control loop

1. Begins with planning
2. Requires organizing
3. Monitors directing and motivating
4. Is the essence of controlling

INTERNAL AUDIT REPORT FORMATS

A. **Types of Reports**

1. Formal -- with carefully structured formats
2. Informal -- in letters or memoranda to operating management
3. Progress -- with brief statements of conditions requiring immediate attention
4. Oral -- with formal audiovisual presentations or informal comments
5. Overall -- with an opinion on the entire operation reviewed
6. Deficiency -- including comments on only those matters calling for corrective action
7. Financial -- with statements of account balances and opinions on whether they fairly reflect results of operations
8. Operational -- with discussions of the adequacy and effectiveness of the operating controls in any sector of the enterprise

B. The report format depends on

1. The type of audit
2. The results of the audit
3. The needs of management
4. The nature of the company and its centralized or decentralized organization
5. The acceptance by managers, at various levels, of internal auditing's position in the company

C. **Formal Report Format Suggested by Lawrence B. Sawyer**

1. Summary
2. Introduction (foreword)
3. Statement of purpose
4. Statement of scope
5. Statement of opinion
6. Audit findings

PREPARATION OF INTERNAL AUDIT REPORTS

A. Except for particularly simple reports, the auditor should prepare an outline of the proposed audit report.

1. The outline should be brief.
2. The auditor should first divide the outline into the main headings, such as
    a. Capsule summary
        1) Provides an overview of the report
    b. Foreword
        1) Regular or special exam
        2) Organizations or functions reviewed
        3) Relevant prior examinations
        4) Size of auditee, e.g., volume of transactions
        5) Any other necessary explanation
    c. Purpose
        1) Audit objectives
    d. Scope
        1) Any limitation on the examination
        2) Any special audit procedures
    e. Opinion
        1) Constitutes an overall summary of the auditor's assessment of auditee operations
    f. Findings
        1) Favorable or unfavorable for each condition
        2) Unfavorable findings may require the following points of explanation:
            a) Capsule summary
            b) Criteria
            c) Condition (facts found)
            d) Cause
            e) Effect
            f) Recommendation
            g) Corrective action taken
3. Thereafter, the details under each major heading may be developed in capsule form.
4. Standards for internal audit reports
    a. Accurate
    b. Clear
    c. Concise
    d. Timely
    e. Courteous
    f. Simple style

EXAMPLE INTERNAL AUDIT REPORT

The following report, taken from Sawyer and Summers, *Sawyer's Internal Auditing* (Altamonte Springs, FL: The Institute of Internal Auditors, 1988), pages 666-671, concerns the highway transportation department of a large airplane manufacturing company. The department transports personnel and maintains company vehicles. The section entitled Audit Highlights is the capsule summary of the report, and the purpose and scope have been combined into one section.

Each section is written for use by a different level or levels of management. After reading the report, use the distribution sheet to decide which section(s) would be most useful for each person on the list.

This internal audit report is made up of four main sections, in addition to the distribution sheet.

1. Distribution sheet, listing all persons to receive the report
2. Highlights (capsule summary)
   a. Provides top management with a quick glimpse of audit results
3. Summary report, with several subsections
   a. Foreword
      1) Sets the report in perspective within the organization
   b. Purpose and scope of audit
   c. Overall opinion
   d. Summary of findings, both satisfactory and unsatisfactory
4. Details of deficiency findings
5. Summary of findings requiring corrective action
   a. Including action already taken

XYZ CORPORATION
INTERNAL AUDIT REPORT

Audit Project R7X-18 *Date: August 26, 19XX*

DISTRIBUTION	*TAKE ACTION*	*SECURE ACTION*	*INFORMATION*	*REVIEWED PRIOR TO RELEASE*
President			X	
Executive Vice President		X	X	
Vice President-Controller			X	
Director of Material		X		X
Manager, Procurement	X			X
Manager, Highway Transportation Dept.	X			X
Director of Industrial Relations				X
Chief, Security Division				X
Chief, Plant Protection				X

AUDIT HIGHLIGHTS

Highway Transportation Department
(A Regularly Scheduled Review)

Prior Audit: *No deficiency findings.*

Audit Coverage:
1. *Equipment maintenance and vehicle dispatching*
2. *Fuel, parts, and repair services*
3. *General administrative activities*

Overall Opinion: *In general, the operation was functioning in a reasonably satisfactory manner.*

We did find some control weaknesses. The most serious involved the lack of separation of duties in the procurement of parts and services. Steps are being taken to correct these weaknesses.

Despite the weaknesses, however, the department's activities were being performed satisfactorily.

Executive Action Required: *None.*

SUMMARY REPORT

Foreword

This report covers the results of our regularly scheduled review of the activities of the Highway Transportation Department. Our last review of the Department's activities disclosed no deficiencies.

The department's primary responsibilities are (1) to transport personnel and materials, and (2) to maintain and repair automotive equipment.

At the time of our review there were about 50 employees assigned to the department. Operating costs (not including labor) for equipment rental, repair parts and services, and fuel and oil are projected to reach about $900,000 for 19XX. Mileage for the year will total about 5 million miles.

During this review we issued one progress report to bring to management's attention certain matters requiring prompt corrective action.

Purpose and Scope

We have made an examination of the Highway Transportation Department's principal activities to determine whether they were being controlled adequately and effectively. In performing our review, we examined the system of controls concerned with the following activities:

1. *Equipment maintenance and vehicle dispatching, including (a) scheduling preventive maintenance inspections, (b) performing regular maintenance and repairs, and (c) dispatching cars and trucks.*
2. *Ordering, receiving, and disbursing fuel and parts and obtaining automotive repair services.*
3. *General administrative activities concerned with (a) property accountability, (b) plant protection, (c) accident reporting, (d) insurable value reporting, (e) gasoline credit cards, and (f) petty cash.*

Opinions and Findings

We formed the opinion that adequate controls had been provided over the activities we reviewed, except for a lack of separation of duties in the procurement of parts and services. Three other matters of lesser significance likewise involved control weaknesses.

We also formed the opinion that, despite the control weaknesses we had detected, the functions we reviewed were being performed in a generally satisfactory manner.

Our conclusions and findings on each of the three groups of activities covered in our examination are summarized in the following paragraphs.

Equipment Maintenance and Vehicle Dispatching

Adequate controls have been provided which were designed to make sure that (1) automotive equipment would receive inspection and preventive maintenance in accordance with the manufacturers' recommendations, and (2) truck and car dispatching would be accomplished in accordance with established procedures.

We examined preventive maintenance reports and related control records and satisfied ourselves that maintenance was being properly scheduled, monitored, and performed. We also examined documentation supporting vehicle dispatching and observed the dispatching operations; we concluded that dispatching was being adequately controlled and performed.

Ordering, Receiving, and Disbursing Fuel and Parts, and Obtaining Vehicle Repair Services

Controls had been provided which were designed to make sure that fuel, parts, and outside repair services were (1) ordered when needed, (2) recorded upon receipt, and (3) properly approved for payment; and that the disbursement of fuel and parts was adequately documented.

We did find, however, that there was (1) a lack of appropriate separation of duties in the procurement of parts and services, and (2) what we considered to be inadequate surveillance over the withdrawal of gasoline and oil by vehicle operators. These matters are discussed more fully in the Supplement to this Summary Report.

We examined representative samples of (1) reports, records, and blanket purchase orders covering the procurement and receipt of supplies and services; and (2) the logs and records covering fuel withdrawals. Despite the control weaknesses referred to, we concluded on the basis of our tests that the functions were being performed in a reasonably satisfactory manner. We made an analysis of the fuel pump meter records and compared them with the amounts of fuel recorded by vehicle operators. The results showed little variance between the two, indicating that fuel withdrawals were in the main being properly recorded.

General Administrative Activities

Controls had been devised to provide assurance that (1) property accountability records would be complete and accurate, (2) accidents to licensed vehicles would be reported promptly, (3) gasoline credit cards would be used for the purpose issued and only when vehicles were operated away from company-owned fuel supplies, and (4) petty cash would be properly safeguarded and used only for the purpose for which the petty cash fund was established.

It did seem to us that the area in which Highway Transportation was located was inadequately protected, and we did find that there was no provision for reporting the insurable values of repair parts and inventories. These matters are also discussed further in the Supplement.

We tested, among other things, (1) equipment information cards; (2) facilities location control cards; (3) acquisition and retirement fixed asset work orders; (4) the department's accident register; (5) the company insurance administrator's control number assignment log covering vehicle and other accidents; (6) a gasoline credit card assignment register; (7) credit card delivery tickets; (8) petty cash reimbursement requests; and (9) vouchers covering petty cash disbursements, making a petty cash count as well. Based on our tests, we concluded that, except for the lack of reports on insurable values, the activities we examined were carried out in a satisfactory manner.

* * *

The four deficiency findings previously mentioned are discussed in the Supplement which follows and are summarized at the end of the Supplement, along with the referrals for completion of corrective action.

Before we completed our review, provision was made to report insurable values, and steps were initiated to correct the remaining three control weaknesses.

________________________ *Auditor-in-Charge*

________________________ *Supervising Auditor*

________________________ *Manager of Internal Auditing*

Supplement to
Summary Report

DETAILS OF DEFICIENCY FINDINGS

1. There was no separation of functional authority in the procurement of parts and services, and effective administration of labor-hour agreements was beyond the Highway Transportation Department's resources.

Blanket Purchase Orders (BPOs) have been issued for the procurement of parts and services. The cognizant purchasing department has assigned to the Highway Transportation Department all authority and responsibility for controlling (a) releases of orders under the BPOs to suppliers; (b) receipt, inspection, and acceptance upon delivery; and (c) approvals of invoices for payment.

In practice, all of these functions are performed by the department manager or by one or two people under his direct control and supervision. Thus, there is none of the protection normally afforded by the separation of such functions among personnel of independent departments, such as establishing requirements, ordering, receiving, inspection, and approving for payment.

There are about 70 currently active BPOs which require suppliers to furnish automotive parts and/or services, as requested. Expenditures for the year are budgeted at about $230,000. Many of the BPOs specify labor-hour rates for the repair of automotive equipment. In effect, these BPOs are Time and Material (T and M) agreements since no fixed number of hours is established for the orders released. Thus, the scope of work is undefined. Yet, the BPOs do not include clauses providing the company with the right of audit, something normally included in T and M agreements.

In our opinion, these labor-hour BPOs do not appear to meet the intent of Procurement Instruction 501, in that they do not ensure the establishment of a fixed price for the order involved at the time of delivery. Furthermore, adequate and effective contract administration of these agreements is beyond the present resources of the Highway Transportation Department.

Because of the lack of separation of duties and the nature of the agreements, we made an extensive examination of the system and of transactions, but we found no basis for questioning any of the charges. Nevertheless, we recommend that Branch management review this condition with a view toward implementing some reasonable control through assignment of some of the key functions to other departments. Further, we recommend that management implement appropriate controls to preclude the use of T and M BPOs without an audit clause.

We discussed this matter with management personnel, and they informed us that they intended to review the methods used at other major divisions of the company to determine whether any of their practices may warrant adoption.

2. Gasoline and oil were being withdrawn by company employees without adequate surveillance.

Since our last examination, the department reassigned elsewhere the service station attendant who had recorded gasoline and oil disbursements on the form provided for that purpose. Under present practice, the vehicle operator serves himself and records his own withdrawals of gasoline and oil, without surveillance. There is no assurance, therefore, that the records are maintained accurately or that the information is always entered. Hence the dangers of misappropriation are increased. We estimate that the total yearly gasoline withdrawal will approximate 300,000 gallons at a cost of about $66,000.

We recognize that there must be a weighing of the benefits versus the costs of control. Nevertheless, we recommend that management consider some means of surveillance -- even on a spot check basis -- to provide minimum elements of control.

We discussed this matter with management personnel and they indicated that appropriate surveillance would be conducted over fuel pump operations.

3. The area in which the Highway Transportation Department is located was not adequately protected.

Area 10, the site of the Highway Transportation Department, is used to house vehicles, fuel pumps, oil, repair parts, and the garage. The area is completely fenced. But it has two large gates, one at the northwest corner and one at the southeast corner. At the time we began our review, both gates were kept open during the regular and swing shifts. A sign at the southeast gate warned that entrance is for company vehicles only. No such sign appeared at the other gate.

We observed that departmental employees, as well as other company employees, were allowed to park their private vehicles within the area. No guards were posted at the gates. Plant Protection personnel informed us that guards were not available for that purpose.

After we discussed this matter with the department manager, he closed the northwest gate to strengthen security somewhat. We believe that further action should be considered, however. While there are an adequate number of employees on hand during the day shift to provide some protection for property, it is doubtful that the reduced swing shift staff can do the same. Also, permitting private cars in the area violates the posted instructions and increases the danger of losses.

We recognize that the unavailability of Plant Protection guards creates some problems. But we believe that management should consider some substitute safeguards, particularly on swing shift.

During discussions with management personnel, they indicated that additional measures to strengthen plant protection would be considered.

4. The insurable value of repair parts on hand was not being reported.

We found that the value of the repair parts on hand in the Highway Transportation Department had not been reported for insurance purposes since the inventory records were decontrolled in 19XX. The value of these repair parts is about $4,500.

We called the matter to the attention of the Insurance Administrator, and he requested the Highway Transportation Department to report the estimated dollar value as of the end of June 19XX. He has also taken action to revise the Company Insurance Manual to show this requirement.

The Highway Transportation Department informed the Insurance Administrator of the insurable value on July 16, 19XX. Corrective action on this matter is considered complete.

SUMMARY OF FINDINGS REQUIRING CORRECTIVE ACTION

The four matters requiring corrective action are summarized as follows:

1. *There was no separation of functional authority in the procurement of parts and services, and effective administration of labor-hour agreements was beyond the Highway Transportation Department's resources.*
2. *Gasoline and oil were being withdrawn by company employees without adequate surveillance.*
3. *The area in which the Highway Transportation Department is located was not adequately protected.*
4. *The insurable value of repair parts on hand was not being reported.*

Finding 1 is referred jointly to the manager of the Procurement Department and the manager of the Highway Transportation Department for completion of corrective action. Findings 2 and 3 are referred to the manager of the Highway Transportation Department for completion of corrective action. Finding 4 has been corrected.

ORAL REPORTS AND PROGRESS REPORTS

A. Oral reports should be used to complement and support written audit reports.

1. Oral reports cannot substitute for written reports, but they do have the following purposes (advantages):

    a. They offer timeliness; i.e., they provide immediate feedback.

        1) Important for deficiencies needing immediate auditee action

        2) Auditor can provide instant response to auditee questions, positions, suggestions, etc.

    b. Oral reports support participative auditing and can improve auditor-auditee relationships.

        1) Auditor can become better known to auditee and reduce auditee tensions.
        2) Auditee can express views.
        3) Oral reports can reduce auditee resistance to auditor recommendations.

    c. Oral reports provide the auditor with additional information.

        1) Auditor can assess strength of auditee attitudes and convictions.
        2) Auditee can point out auditor misunderstandings and errors.

2. Although oral reports allow for flexibility, careful planning is necessary, which may include the following steps:

    a. Gain familiarity with the participants.
    b. Determine the objectives.
    c. List the materials, topics, etc., relevant to the objectives.
    d. Order the material.
    e. Prepare visual aids, handouts, etc.
    f. Practice the presentation.
    g. Anticipate and prepare for questions and arguments from the auditee.

B. Progress reports provide a prompt means of documenting a situation requiring immediate action.

1. Progress reports are preliminary reports and should indicate that

    a. Only current information, i.e., an incomplete study, is the basis for the report.
    b. The final report will follow up on the topics covered on the progress report.
    c. The final report will also cover the other topics on the audit program.

2. Progress reports prepared by audit staff should be reviewed by the director of internal auditing or other supervisory personnel.

3. Progress reports may also be used to report the status of long, sensitive, or otherwise special audits to the auditees and top management.

REPORT REVIEWS AND DISTRIBUTION

A. Reviews of report drafts with the auditee are a courtesy to the auditee and a form of insurance for the audit.

1. The auditee may have discussed all matters in the report during the review.

    a. As a matter of courtesy, however, the auditee should be given the opportunity to read what will be sent to his/her superior.

    b. The formal report may convey a different impression.

2. In complex operations, it is easy for the auditor to miss a point or report it incorrectly. Reviewing the report with the auditee can bring out any such inaccuracies before the final report is issued.
3. The auditor should carefully consider the following matters before scheduling the report review:
    a. Those with whom the draft report should be reviewed
    b. Whether each review should be handled separately or done partially on a group basis
    c. The timing of the reviews
    d. The order of the reviews
    e. Whether to try expediting reviews by sending out review copies in advance of the meeting
    f. Whether it is necessary to hold face-to-face discussions. Perhaps sending out copies and getting them back with comments will be sufficient.
4. The auditor should be in charge of the report review conference.
5. The auditor should be prepared for conflicts and questions.
    a. When the auditor has previously experienced difficulty with an individual, that individual's superior may be invited to attend.
    b. To be able to answer questions promptly, the auditor may wish to prepare notes, e.g., marginal references on a draft of the report and on pertinent working papers.
    c. The auditor should be flexible on matters that do not affect the substance of the report.
        1) But the auditor should never negotiate the audit opinion.
6. If the reviews result in significant changes in the report, the other people with whom the draft was reviewed should have an opportunity to see, or be told of, the revisions.
7. The auditor should maintain careful records of the review conferences, of any objections, and of the manner in which conflicts were resolved.
8. When drafts are to be mailed to the people who should review them, the auditor should
    a. Ask for the timely return of the drafts with any comments considered appropriate.
    b. Set a specific due date for the return of the draft.
    c. Offer to meet with those who wish to discuss the draft further.

B. Reports should be distributed to all those having a direct interest in the audit, including
1. The executive to whom the internal audit function reports
2. The person or persons to whom replies to the report will be addressed
3. Persons responsible for the activity or activities reviewed
4. Persons required to take corrective action

NOTE: Distribution sheets (like the one on page 721) can be devised that list the distributees and indicate with whom the report has been reviewed in draft.

AUDITOR FOLLOW-UP OF CORRECTIVE ACTIONS

A. IIA Standard 440 requires internal auditors to follow up to ascertain that appropriate action is taken on deficiency findings. The internal auditor should determine that

1. Corrective action being taken has the desired results, or
2. Management or the board has assumed the risk of not taking corrective action.

B. In following up, the auditor should

1. Receive all auditee replies to the audit report
2. Evaluate the adequacy of those replies
3. Be convinced that the action taken will cure the defects

C. The auditor is in the best position to carry out this responsibility, i.e., the auditor is

1. Better acquainted with the facts than higher management or other control agencies in the company
2. More objective than the operating manager who is called upon to take the corrective action

D. The responsibility for seeing that corrective action is adequate should be coupled with the authority to evaluate the adequacy of replies to audit reports. The internal auditor should

1. Report to management when corrective actions are not timely or effective.
2. Submit periodic reports to management on open audit findings.

E. The adequacy of a response depends on the circumstances in each case. In general, a satisfactory response

1. Addresses itself to the complete problem -- not only to those specific items included in the auditor's sample
2. Shows that action has also been taken to prevent a recurrence of the deficient condition

F. In evaluating the reply, the auditor should be satisfied that the action promised is actually taken. The auditor should

1. Obtain copies of revised procedures issued to correct conditions.
2. Make any field tests needed to provide assurance that the condition has been corrected.

G. A formal system should be designed to keep audit projects open until adequate corrective action is assured, e.g.,

1. Provisions for formal opening and closing of audit projects
2. Formal statement of closure, supported by copies of replies to audit reports and explanations of the action taken to ensure the adequacy and effectiveness of corrective measures
   a. Closure reports are directed to the director of internal auditing.
3. Audit projects should not be removed from the audit department's open project listing until all required corrective actions have been taken and evaluated.

COMPUTER AUDIT TOOL AND TECHNIQUE TABULATION

A. The basic processes underlying other audits are also applicable to audits of computer information systems. However, specific audit techniques and internal control structure policies and procedures must be considered. The controls in computer systems are discussed in Study Unit 32. The tools unique to these audits are presented in the tabulation on pages 730 through 732, which incorporates

1. Brief explanations
2. Advantages of the tool or technique
3. Disadvantages
4. The type of system or environment in which the tool or technique is used

USE OF MICROCOMPUTERS BY AUDITORS

A. Many auditors now use microcomputers to access the company's database directly. Ordinarily, the procedures outlined in the preceding sideheading can be performed directly by the auditor.

1. Advantages

    a. Auditor can work independently of the auditee.
    b. Auditee personnel are prevented from knowing auditor procedures.
    c. Auditor does not depend on availability of auditee personnel.
    d. Auditor has access to records at remote sites.

2. Disadvantages

    a. The auditor must have a working understanding of the EDP system, e.g., a complicated database system (may also be an advantage).

    b. Auditors may be exposed to accusations about altered data, programs, etc.

        1) Thus, they should retain complete documentation of their interactions with the database.

B. Audit procedures include

1. Scanning files for certain types of records, items, etc.
2. Building and using predictive models to identify high-risk areas
3. Applying statistical sampling item selection and analysis routines
4. Using input/output routines to provide hard copy and to reformat data to more usable formats
5. Preparing financial statements and other reports with spreadsheet routines
6. Illustrating analyses with graphs and other pictorial displays
7. Writing customized audit programs
8. Storing audit programs, routines, and results electronically
9. Implementing other types of audit procedures and analyses electronically

EDP AUDIT TOOL AND TECHNIQUE TABULATION

Tool/Technique	Explanation	Advantages	Disadvantages	Type of System or Environment Used In
Control Flowcharting (Analytic Audit Flowchart)	Consists of developing flowcharts of the overall system -- manual and computer processing	*Aids in consideration of the ICS *Familiarizes auditor with the system *Develops communication between auditor and auditee *No special training; normally used by auditors *Can use flowcharting software	*Costly to develop and maintain	*Any type of system
Test Data (Test Deck)	Involves the use of specifically prepared sets of input data that test application controls by running a variety of transactions to be compared with previously determined results. The ideal test deck includes every possible combination of transactions and master file situations.	*Can use test data generator software *Test data can be prepared by persons with little technical background.	*Difficult to anticipate all combinations of transactions *Must determine that routinely used edition of application program is used	*Batch processing
Integrated Test Facility (ITF or "Minicomputer" Approach)	Involves the use of a fictitious entity, such as a dummy customer in accounts receivable, against which data transactions are processed. Results are compared with previously determined results. This procedure is used within the framework of regular production, frequently without computer operator knowledge.	*Enables testing of the system as it routinely operates *Low processing costs *No special processing	*Effects of transactions on operations (books) must be nullified *Quantity of live data inputs may be limited when submitted with regular runs *Possibility of contamination of data base	*Online, real-time
Parallel Simulation	Involves the use of specially prepared application-type programs to process transactions that have also been run in routine processing. This in effect simulates routine processing in an effort to verify results.	*Testing can be done on a surprise basis. *Cost of preparing test data is eliminated. *Can process many of auditee's transactions, eliminating need for small samples. *More thorough than sampling	*Usually simulation is only for selected portions of a total application *Cost of developing program may be prohibitive *Auditor may need special skills *Does not have broad application	*Database Management System *Most effective when applied to calculations, decisions and large quantity of transactions

EDP AUDIT TOOL AND TECHNIQUE TABULATION (CONT'D)

Tool/Technique	Explanation	Advantages	Disadvantages	Type of System or Environment Used In
Generalized Audit Software Package (GASP)	Involves the use of computer software packages (programs) that may allow not only parallel simulation but also a variety of other processing functions, such as extracting sample items, verifying totals, developing file statistics, retrieving specified data fields.	*Can process several files (and file types) *Enables use with limited training *Packages interface with many types of hardware and software *Decreases auditor dependence on data processing personnel and time	*Limited application in online, real-time systems *Limited logical and mathematical capabilities	*Batch processing
Transaction Selection	Involves reprocessing transaction files with specialized computer programs that extract or select particular transactions. Transaction files are retained and given to the auditor.	*Programs are independent of application programs *Enables efficient selection of transactions for further review *Enables selection of targeted types of transactions	*May be costly to develop and execute	*All systems
Embedded Data Collection	A transaction selection approach incorporated within the regular production programs to routinely select/extract transactions meeting specified criteria for further testing.	*All system activity is subject to review *Can be used with online systems *Not limited to input transactions	*Additional processing cost of extra audit module program steps that must be executed *Difficult to implement unless it can be developed along with the system	*Online systems
Extended Records	Involves extending the record created using the snapshot technique (see below) to include data fields for all snapshots taken of a transaction.	*Reduces audit costs associated with tracing audit trails *Creates an audit trail that was previously nonexistent in hard copy	*May not be economical because of added storage costs *High cost of implementation	*Database Management Systems *Online systems *Systems that normally lack hardcopy of system input or other audit trail
Tracing	Involves the generation of a complete audit trail to trace transactions through processing. Normally provides a trail of the	*Aids in verifying application of internal controls *Allows tagging of certain live data	*Auditor must have significant knowledge of the program to follow logic *Can increase program	*Advanced

EDP AUDIT TOOL AND TECHNIQUE TABULATION (CONT'D)

Tool/Technique	Explanation	Advantages	Disadvantages	Type of System or Environment Used In
Snapshot	Involves capturing the content of primary storage before and after specific points in the stream of processing.	*No permanent effect on data *Can insert code quickly with minimum development time *Can help to generate hard copy transaction trail for a specified item *Can be used selectively to print out data that meet certain criteria, e.g., over limit *Can aid in debugging *Can aid in determining intermediate values of data in processing stream	*Code must be embedded in the application program *Code adds to the processing time *Requires skilled data processing personnel	*Effective in high-volume systems in which complete transaction trail would generate too much information
Mapping	Involves monitoring the execution of an application program to determine certain statistical information about the run, e.g., program lines not executed, CPU time for certain program lines, and the number of times certain lines were executed.	*Can aid in evaluating how well test data tested a run *Can indicate lines of code that are extraneous or not often used	*High cost	*Advanced
System Control Audit Review File (SCARF) (Specific Implementation of Embedded Data Collection)	Involves the incorporation of reasonableness tests into the normal processing of application programs, the results being reported to the auditor rather than to the user for the auditor's review and investigation.	*All system activity is subject to review *Can be used with online systems *Not limited to input transactions	*Additional processing cost of extra audit module program steps that must be executed *Difficult to implement unless it can be developed along with the system	*Advanced
Sample Audit Review File (SARF)	Similar to SCARF but random selection of transactions rather than special edit or reasonableness tests.	*All system activity is subject to review *Can be used with online systems *Not limited to input transactions	*Additional processing cost of extra audit module program steps that must be executed *Difficult to implement unless it can be developed along with the system	*Advanced

NOTES

CIA, CMA, CPA
TEST PREP Software --
Another Powerful Tool in the Gleim Knowledge Transfer System

Improve your study process and test yourself in an interactive environment with actual CIA, CMA, or CPA questions.

Four disks for each exam -- one for each exam section

stallation is very simple and takes only a few minutes. At your "c:" prompt, type a:install or b:install, depending on the drive into which you insert your Gleim **Test Prep** diskette. The step-by-step, on-screen nstructions are easy to follow.

o run **Test Prep** software, type CIATP, CMATP, or CPATP at your "c:" prompt and you will enter the program. The top line on your screen contains the main menu. Move your cursor from menu item to menu item and press "Enter" to access menu items and submenu items (or type the hotkeys, which are ndicated in bold typeface).

ur interactive system has two modes: "Study" and "Test." Study mode permits you to select questions rom specific sources, e.g., IIA, ICMA, AICPA Areas, Gleim Study Units, Questions Missed from Last Session, etc. You can also determine the order of the questions (Gleim or random), and you can andomize the order of the answer choices for each question, if you wish.

est mode randomly selects questions from the IIA, ICMA, or AICPA area or Gleim study unit you specify. You select the number of questions (up to 100) and determine the range of coverage. As in Study mode, you may randomize question and answer order.

ou can customize study and test sessions and receive diagnostic and performance analysis feedback.

our study and testing progress are reported to you by subject matter topic based on IIA, ICMA, or AICPA areas and Gleim study units. This will help you focus your study on the types of questions and subject matter that will improve your score the most.

he diskettes are organized into the same study units as the Gleim ***CIA Review, CMA Review, CPA Review*** books and contain over 3,500, 3,100, and 5,100 (respectively) questions.

ystem Requirements: IBM-compatible running DOS 3.2 or higher with 1.8 MB of hard disk space for one section or 5.2 MB for all four sections, and a 3½" floppy disk drive.

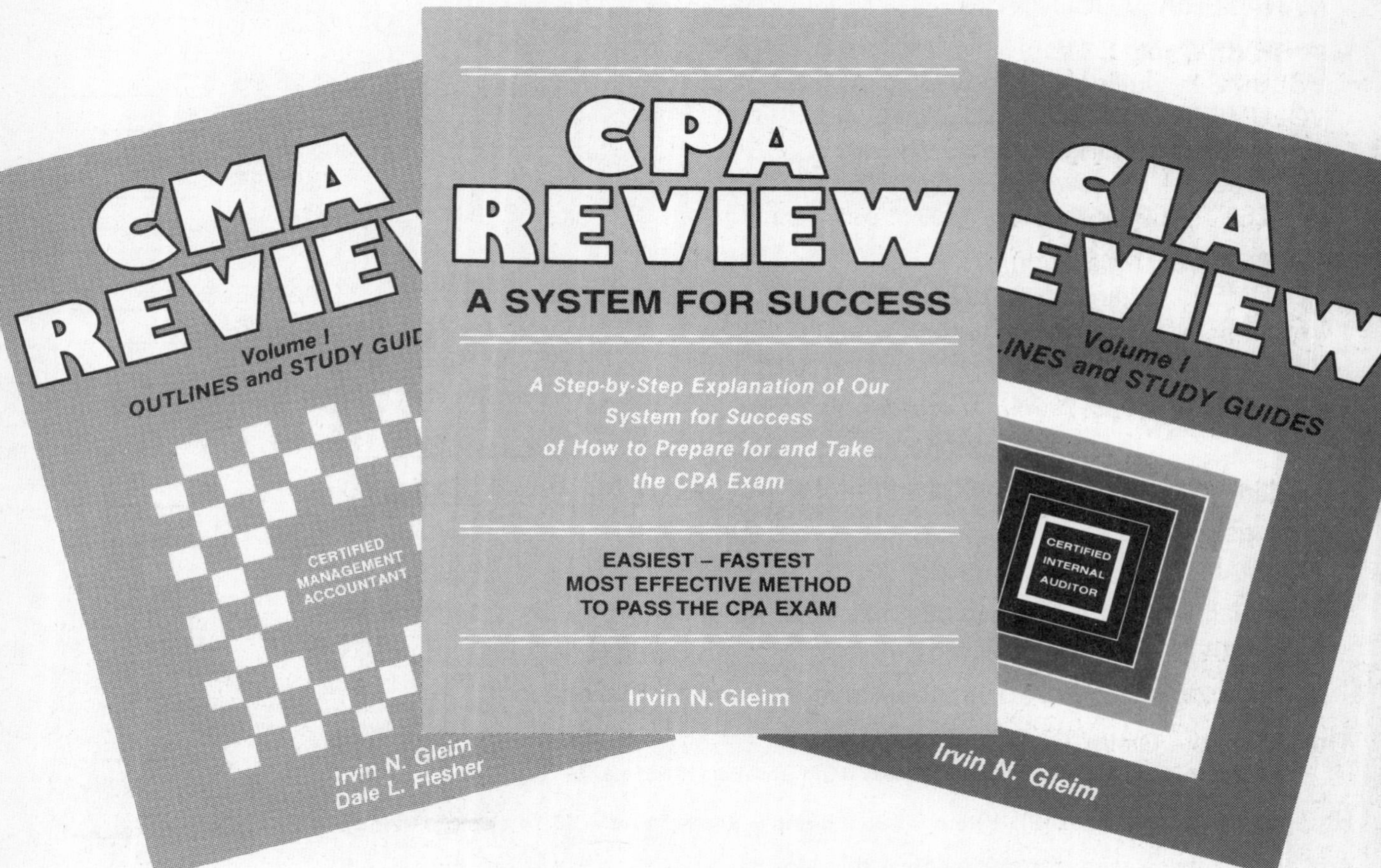

. . . AND ARE ACCELERATED WITH MULTIPLE CERTIFICATION PROGRAMS

Gleim Publications, Inc. • P.O. Box 12848 • Gainesville, FL 32604 • (800) 87-GLEIM
(352) 375-0772 FAX (352) 375-6940 E-mail: admin@gleim.com Internet: www.gleim.com
Telephone Hours: 8:00 a.m. - 7:00 p.m., Mon. - Fri. and 9:00 a.m. - 2:00 p.m., Sat. Eastern Time
Please have your VISA/MasterCard ready

"THE GLEIM SERIES" OBJECTIVE QUESTION AND EXPLANATION BOOKS

AUDITING & SYSTEMS .... *(704 pages • 1,784 questions)* .... $16.95 $________
BUSINESS LAW/LEGAL STUDIES ...... *(736 pages • 1,788 questions)* .... $16.95 ________
FEDERAL TAX .... *(800 pages • 2,524 questions)* .... $16.95 ________
FINANCIAL ACCOUNTING .... *(768 pages • 1,756 questions)* .... $16.95 ________
MANAGERIAL ACCOUNTING .... *(752 pages • 1,290 questions)* .... $16.95 ________

CIA REVIEW *(6th Edition)*

VOLUME I: Outlines & Study Guides .... $25.95 $________
VOLUME II: Problems & Solutions .... $25.95 ________
1995-1996 Updating Edition .... $18.95 ________
All Three CIA Review books (Save $5.00) .... $65.85 ________

CIA TEST PREP Software (@ $25.00 each part) ☐ Part I ☐ Part II ☐ Part III ☐ Part IV ________

CMA REVIEW *(7th Edition)*

VOLUME I: Outlines & Study Guides .... $27.95 $________
VOLUME II: Problems & Solutions .... $27.95 ________

CMA TEST PREP Software (@ $25.00 each part) ☐ Part 1 ☐ Part 2 ☐ Part 3 ☐ Part 4 ________

CPA REVIEW *(1995-1996 Edition)*

	Books*	Audiotapes	CPA Test Prep Software	
Auditing	☐ @ $24.50	☐ @ $75.00	☐ @ $35.00	$________
Business Law	☐ @ $24.50	☐ @ $75.00	☐ @ $35.00	________
TAX-MAN-GOV	☐ @ $24.50	☐ @ $75.00	☐ @ $35.00	________
Financial	☐ @ $24.50	☐ @ $75.00	☐ @ $35.00	________

A System for Success (free with the purchase of any *CPA Review* book)

*Contain outlines, examples, questions, and answer explanations.

The Complete Gleim System (Save 20%) .... ☐ @ $457.00 ________
(5 books, 4 audio cassette albums (41 tapes), 4 CPA Test Prep diskettes)

Shipping (nonrefundable): **1 item = $3; 2 items = $4; 3 items = $5; 4 or more items = $6** ... ________

Add applicable sales tax for shipments within Florida .... ________

Fax or write for prices/instructions for shipments outside the 48 contiguous states **TOTAL** $________

1. We process and ship orders daily, generally one day after receipt of your order.
2. Please PHOTOCOPY this order form for use by others.
3. No CODs. All orders from individuals must be prepaid. Library and company orders may be purchased on account. Shipping and a handling charge will be added to the invoice, and to telephone orders.
4. Gleim Publications, Inc. guarantees the immediate refund of all resalable texts if returned within 30 days. Applies only to books purchased direct from Gleim Publications, Inc. Refunds or credit are not offered on software and audiotapes. Our shipping charge is nonrefundable.

NAME (please print) ________________________________

ADDRESS ________________________________ Apt. ______
(street address required for UPS)

____

CITY ________________ STATE ____ ZIP ____________

____ MC/VISA ____ Check/M.O. Daytime Telephone (______)____________

MC/VISA ________-________-________-________

Exp. ___/___ Signature ________________________________
Mo. / Yr.

Printed 9/96. Prices subject to change without notice. 069D

FIVE CPE PROGRAMS USING OBJECTIVE QUESTION FORMAT

This is a totally different approach to CPE. Each program contains multiple individual courses based on self-diagnosing objective questions. They are designed to meet the needs of practitioners by providing low-cost, easy-to-use, effective CPE.

All of these programs provide you with an opportunity to review and study a wide range of topics.

- First, they provide a self-diagnosis of your knowledge.
- Second, they constitute a review and study of the professional and technical standards that are the basic proficiency package expected of professional accountants. As such, each individual course is a formal program of learning that contributes directly to your professional competence.
- Third, they are effective because you challenge yourself to do well by responding to multiple-choice questions. When you have difficulty, a thorough, easy-to-understand explanation is provided.
- Fourth, these courses are organized in a programmed learning format, i.e., from general to specific, easy to difficult, etc.
- Fifth, we keep these programs up-to-date with periodic revisions to comply with the currency standards of NASBA, AICPA, etc.

EASY TO USE

You are formally registered when we receive your order, which is shipped the next business day. With each program, you receive:

- Objective questions and explanations study book
- CPE final exam book and instructions
- One machine-readable final exam answer sheet (see note below), a course evaluation questionnaire, and a special protective return envelope

1. You study the questions and explanations in the objective questions and explanations study book when and where you want.
2. Then you take a final exam (open book) and record your answers on a machine-readable answer sheet.
3. Lastly, you return the answer sheet and evaluation form in the protective return envelope to us for grading. (We are currently able to grade final exams and then mail certificates of completion in one week.) If you score 70% or above, we will send you a certificate of completion (courses then become **nonrepeatable**). In the event of a failure, your answer sheet will be returned to you for correction after your additional study. Our charge for **regrading** is $15.

NOTE: In each program, you have the option of taking all of the courses, just one course, or any combination of individual courses. All of the courses in a single program can be completed at no additional charge by using the one answer sheet provided with each program. If you prefer to obtain CPE credit for a few courses at a time, there is a **$15 grading fee** (additional answer sheet) for each subsequent submission.

	Credit Hours
AUDITING & SYSTEMS CPE -- 6th Edition 8 separate courses with up to 49* CPE hours -- **all for $95**	
1. Audit Standards, Ethics, Planning, and Risk	7
2. Internal Control Structure	6
3. Audit Evidence and Procedures	8
4. Information Systems	9
5. Statistical Sampling	4
6. Audit Reports	6
7. Special Reports and Other Reporting Issues	4
8. Internal Auditing	5
BUSINESS LAW CPE -- 4th Edition 10 separate courses with up to 48* CPE hours -- **all for $95**	
1. The American Legal System	4
2. Criminal Law, Torts, and Insurance	4
3. Contracts	5
4. Sales, Consumer Protection, and Antitrust	5
5. Negotiable Instruments, Credit Law, and Liens and Mortgages	5
6. Secured Transactions, Suretyship, and Bankruptcy	5
7. Property Law and Environmental Regulations	5
8. Agency and Partnership	4
9. Corporations and Securities Regulation	5
10. Accountants' Legal Responsibilities, Estates and Trusts, and Employment Regulations	6
FEDERAL TAX CPE -- 6th Edition 12 separate courses with up to 51* CPE hours -- **all for $125**	
1. Gross Income and Exclusions	4
2. Business Expenses and Losses	3
3. Investment and Personal Deductions	5
4. Individual Loss Limits, Tax Calculations, and Credits	4
5. General Business Credit and Basic Property Transactions	5
6. Other Property Transactions	5
7. Partnerships	4
8. Corporate Formations and Operations	5
9. Advanced Corporate Topics	4
10. Accounting Methods and Employment Taxes	4
11. Estates, Trusts, Tax-Exempt Organizations, and Wealth Transfer Taxes	4
12. Tax Preparer Rules, Process, and Procedures	4
FINANCIAL ACCOUNTING CPE -- 6th Edition 13 separate courses with up to 46* CPE hours -- **all for $125**	
1. Basic Concepts and the Accounting Process	5
2. Current Assets	4
3. Noncurrent Assets	4
4. Current and Noncurrent Liabilities	3
5. Present Value, Pensions, and Leases	4
6. Shareholders' Equity and EPS	4
7. Income Tax Allocation, Accounting Changes, Error Corrections	2
8. Financial Statements and Disclosures	3
9. Statement Analysis, Interim Statements, and Segment Reporting	4
10. Investments and Business Combinations	4
11. Price-Level Changes and Foreign Exchange	2
12. Government and Nonprofit Accounting	4
13. Specialized Industry and Partnership Accounting	3
MANAGERIAL ACCOUNTING CPE -- 3rd Edition 11 separate courses with up to 43* CPE hours -- **all for $60**	
1. Cost Accounting Overview and Job Order Costing	4
2. Process Costing; Spoilage, Waste, & Scrap	4
3. Joint Products and By-Products	2
4. Service Cost Allocations and Direct Costing	3
5. Cost-Volume-Profit Analysis	5
6. Budgeting and Responsibility Accounting	4
7. Standard Costs	6
8. Nonroutine Decisions and Inventory Models	4
9. Capital Budgeting	4
10. Probability and Statistics; Regression Analysis	4
11. Linear Programming and Other Quantitative Approaches	3

* See the discussion of determining self-study CPE credit on page 739.

SAME-DAY grading service, available Mon.-Fri.: Send your materials and $50 prepayment for each answer sheet ($100 if out of the U.S.) via UPS Next Day Letter Service (if you use Federal Express, it must be priority so we receive it by noon) to 4201 N.W. 95th Blvd., Gainesville, FL 32606. We will hand-grade your answer sheet and send the results back to you the same day via UPS Next Day Letter Service.

Index

Please forward your suggestions, corrections, and comments concerning typographical errors, etc., to **Irvin N. Gleim • c/o Gleim Publications, Inc. • P.O. Box 12848 • University Station • Gainesville, Florida • 32604**. Please include your name and address so we can properly thank you for your interest.

1. ______________________________

2. ______________________________

3. ______________________________

4. ______________________________

5. ______________________________

6. ______________________________

7. ______________________________

8. ______________________________

9. ______________________________

10. ______________________________

11. ______________________________

12. ______________________________

13. ______________________________

14. ______________________________

15. ______________________________

16. ______________________________

17. ______________________________

18. ______________________________

19. ______________________________

20. ______________________________

21. ______________________________

22. ______________________________

Name: ______________________________

Company: ______________________________

Address: ______________________________

City/State/Zip: ______________________________

Phone: ( ) __________ FAX: ( ) __________ E-mail: __________